Danebury:
an Iron Age hillfort in Hampshire

Volume 2
The excavations, 1969–1978: the finds

Danebury:
an Iron Age hillfort in Hampshire

Volume 2
The excavations, 1969–1978:
           the finds

by Barry Cunliffe

with contributions from Tim Ambrose, Dennis Britton,
Lisa Brown, Jenny Coy, John Evans, Cyril Everard,
Annie Grant, Julian Henderson, Bari Hooper,
Hilary Howard, Martin Jones, Martyn Jope, Gary Lock,
Melinda Mays, Peter Northover, Brendan O'Connor,
Mark Pollard, Cynthia Poole, Chris Salter,
Lyn Sellwood, John Taylor, Lucy Walker,
Simuu Wandibba, and David Williams

1984

Council for British Archaeology

ISBN Volume 1: 0 906780 28 4
ISBN Volume 2: 0 906780 29 2
ISBN Volumes 1 and 2: 0 906780 27 6

Published 1984 by the Council for British Archaeology,
112 Kennington Road, London SE11 6RE

British Library Cataloguing in Publication data
Cunliffe, Barry
    Danebury.—(CBA research report;
    ISSN 0589–9036, v.52)
    1. Danebury Ring (England)
    I. Title II. Series
    936.2'2732   GN780.22.G7

ISBN 0–906780–27–6
ISBN 0–906780–28–4 v.1
ISBN 0–906780–29–2 v.2

The publishers wish to acknowledge with gratitude grants
from the Department of the Environment and Hampshire
County Council.

The A4 originals of the microfiche contained in this
publication (Volumes 1 and 2) are held by the National
Monuments Record (23 Savile Row, London W1X 2HE,
telephone 01-734 6010), from which copies can be purchased
on request.

PRINTED BY DERRY AND SONS LIMITED   CANAL STREET   NOTTINGHAM   ENGLAND

Contents of volume

Contents of microfiche

List of figures

6 The Iron Age pottery

6.1 Introduction
6.1.1 The size of the problem

The quantity of pottery from the excavation is considerable. From the 947 pits, 332 layers, and the 63 other features producing pottery, a total of some 103,417 sherds weighing 642 kg has been recovered. Pottery from the postholes has not been counted and weighed but is estimated to weigh an additional 33 kg (ie 5,300 sherds). Given that each pit contained, on average, three pottery-producing layers and at least half of the postholes had at least two layers distinguished in their filling, the number of separate stratigraphical units containing pottery is in the order of 4,000. It is clearly impracticable to attempt to publish in full all sherds from all stratified contexts. Whilst this might reasonably be done with a smaller collection, to follow such a procedure here would be excessive. A selective approach has therefore been adopted.

All pottery from the site has been kept, washed, marked, and stored according to its stratigraphical context. No sherds, even stray finds from superficial and disturbed situations, have been discarded. The pottery itself is a primary archive and will continue to serve as such (for a note on retrieval, see fiche 8, frame A2).

The three types of stratified context holding the pottery, pits, postholes, and layers, put different constraints upon the potential of the pottery itself for providing information relevant to the development of the community which used it. Pits, for example, since they are usually large, isolated, and filled over a short period of time, provide broadly contemporary assemblages often of reasonable size. Layers on the other hand usually contain little pottery but they provide a stratigraphical sequence which has the added advantage of allowing related pit groups to be placed in chronological order. Postholes were of less value as contexts for pottery. Of the 3,760 excavated only 13.4% produced pottery at all and even then the assemblages frequently amounted to only one or two abraded sherds. Moreover, the fillings of postholes were susceptible to disturbance by roots and animal burrows. Thus while pits and layers provided valuable, and complementary, contexts for study, the pottery recovered from postholes was of a totally different order of interest. This being so, the groups from layers and pits were subjected to a detailed analysis, the data being stored and sorted by computer, while the sherds from postholes were simply noted on a card index and excluded for further analysis at this stage except insofar as the evidence is relevant to the phasing of structures.

6.1.2 Approaches to analysis

Since the recordable variables inherent in each pot sherd are extremely numerous it is necessary to select what is recorded lest the data bank be bloated with minutiae. Some might argue that total characterization is a desirable end. Such a view is here totally rejected on the grounds that over-recording is grossly wasteful of scarce resources. Moreover it would be unbelievably arrogant of us to assume that we can anticipate what future generations may wish to ask of our material.

The guide lines adopted here have been to record and computerize only those aspects of the pottery which we may reasonably assume will be needed to enable us to approach a range of the more relevant questions. If more sophisticated questions are to be asked one must return once more to the pottery itself.

In brief, the procedure followed was to characterize the pottery in terms of form, fabric, and surface finish and to quantify it as number of sherds, number of rims, and total weight. Details of these six criteria (together with a seventh column for a unique number given to every sherd selected for drawing) were entered on record sheets and one record sheet was assigned to each stratigraphical unit. No attempt was made to assess the number of individual pots present. Thus two rim sherds of pot form X, fabric Y, and surface Z were recorded as two irrespective of whether they came from one or two pots, but if one differed in fabric or surface from the other then the two sherds appear on separate lines on the record sheet. The logic of this is that while fabric and surface finish can be objectively distinguished within certain defined limits it is often extremely difficult to be sure whether two apparently similar sherds belong to the same vessel. This is particularly true of the later Iron Age material where considerable standardization in form and fabric is apparent. Even diameter or angle of rim are uncertain guides when vessels may be irregular in profile and oval in plan! Since decisions on vessel numbers are therefore highly subjective the problems are best considered separately.

Body sherds or base fragments, unless they are diagnostic of form, were recorded on a line with no form attribution, even in those cases where it was probable that they belonged to the same vessel as a recognizable rim sherd.

The data, recorded on the completed record sheets for each context, were transferred to tape compatible with an ICL 2960 computer, operating under VME/K, upon which the information was stored and manipulated (fiche 8, frames A3–4). This was done in parallel with a formulation of the questions to be asked of the material.

Of prime concern was the establishment of a ceramic sequence since the pottery was the principal means of relative dating and a proportion of its contexts could be calibrated by radiocarbon dating. The procedures used and the results obtained are discussed in section 6.3. The next questions asked concern the origin of the pottery and the assessment of local fabrics in relation to imported wares (6.4). Then follows a brief consideration of technological change (6.5), the relationship between form and function (6.6), and aspects of the distribution of pottery within the fort (6.7). The regional implications of the Danebury assemblage are then outlined (6.8). Finally, since a data bank of the kind provided by the Danebury pottery can quite clearly be subjected to a wide range of analyses, some of the possibilities to be considered in the future are briefly mentioned (6.9).

6.2 The typological categories defined
6.2.1 Vessel forms

Considerable difficulty was experienced, while working on the pottery from the early seasons, in arriving at useful categories and arranging them in such a manner that the scheme could be expanded to contain new material as it became available. Indeed the scheme eventually adopted was not introduced until 1975 and involved two total reworkings of the pottery found in earlier years. The main problem to overcome was the degree of simplicity or complexity to be used. Increasing familiarity with the material suggested that over-elaborate schemes were to be avoided since they tended to impose a classificatory rigidity upon material the very quality of which was its shades of variety. Strict metrical parameters were also rejected for various reasons: seldom could diameter/height ratios be measured and diameter measurements were unreliable when dealing with hand-made pot sherds, while precise measurements of rim angle were in most cases impossible to obtain with any degree of assurance. In short, to use exact measurement as a criterion for classification when dealing with sherd material from a prehistoric site would impose a spurious pseudo-objectivity. Another problem to be faced was the degree of assurance with which a rim sherd could be assigned to a defined type. Sometimes precise attribution was possible but often a sherd could only be said to belong to one of a series of types without allowing specific identification. The scheme designed had therefore to allow a hierarchy of assessment. To force a vessel into one of a series of equal and fixed categories was clearly undesirable.

With these principal reservations in mind the method adopted here has been to recognize four levels of classification:

Basic class
Type
Form
Variety

There are four *basic classes*, broadly defined thus:

Jars (J)	heights usually in excess of maximum diameters; rim diameters usually less than maximum body diameters; bi- or tripartite division of profile
Bowls (B)	heights usually less than maximum diameters; rim diameters *may be* in excess of maximum body diameters; bi- or tripartite division of profile
Dishes (D)	heights always less than maximum diameters; maximum diameter usually at rim
Saucepan pots (P)	height approximately equal to diameter; rim diameter approximately equal to base diameters; profiles vertical or close to vertical

Within each of the basic classes a series of *types* has been defined. Jars, for example, are divided into five types, JA, JB, JC, JD, JE, the bowls are divided into four, and the dishes and saucepan pots are each divided into two. The types are further subdivided into *forms*. In the case of type JB, a shouldered 'situlate' vessel, four forms have been defined: JB1.O, JB2.O etc. These are further subdivided into *varieties* designated by a number following the decimal point: thus JB1.1, JB1.2 etc.

The system may at first sight appear to be unnecessarily unwieldly but it has the great advantage of allowing a degree of precision in classification, where sufficient of the vessel survives to be diagnostic, while at the same time providing the facility for a less distinctive sherd to be placed in a more generalized category. In other words it does not force the observer to be more dogmatic about classification than he feels justified in being. Another advantage is that, since all the pottery data are computerized, information can easily be retrieved or compared at any level within the hierarchy of classification.

The Danebury classification has been developed in such a way that it can easily be extended to incorporate material from other sites. The scheme was created in parallel with the classification of the pottery from the predominantly later site of Hengistbury Head. This has meant that a few categories, allowed for in the scheme, do not occur at Danebury. These include JD4, BD1, BD3, and BD5. The few sherds of wheel-made necked jars from Danebury (type JE) have not been classified in detail but are simply ascribed to the general type JE1/4. The Hengistbury collection has a rich variety of JE types and has also dominated the division of the BD type. The details of the classification are given in Appendix 1 (pp 259–307).

6.2.2 Fabrics

From the outset the fabrics were divided into eight categories based on the type and quantity of filler added to the clay. These were:

A Coarse flint-gritted
B Fine flint-gritted
C Shell-tempered
D Sandy
E Fine smooth clay with no aggregate
F Chaff-tempered (restricted to briquetage)
G Grog-tempered
H Oolitic limestone-tempered

In the early years of using the scheme it was expanded by subdivisions so that, for example, fourteen varieties of fabric D were recognized. But as familiarity with the pottery increased it became evident that the subdivisions were an unnecessary over-complication, difficult to apply with complete objectivity, and intensely time-consuming. For this reason the simpler system was returned to. It is not wholly satisfactory since there is a degree of overlap between the fabric types. For example, a vessel with coarse flint grits may have occasional flakes of shell mixed in with it. Such a sherd would be classified as fabric A. Similarly a sherd with predominant shell-tempering but occasional flint grits would be assigned to fabric group C, while one with significant quantities of both flint and shell would be called AC. Although it would be simple to devise a scheme to allow for the relative percentages of the fillers to be quantified and classified accordingly, such objectivity seems unnecessary particularly when one discovers that if such a scheme were applied rigidly different sherds from the same vessel would sometimes find themselves in different fabric categories. Thus attempts at superficial objectivity are here eschewed and we accept a degree of controlled subjectivity.

In reality the greatest percentage of the pottery belongs to fabrics A-E, E being confined to a particular class of fine haematite-coated bowls. Fabrics A and C are dominant in the early period while fabric B typifies the later. Sandy fabrics, D, appear throughout in varying percentages.

A number of samples have been examined in thin section and by heavy mineral analysis. In general the scientific characterization conforms closely to the fabric types adopted but these matters are discussed in detail in Appendix 2 (p 308) and fiche 8, frames D8–E3.

6.2.3 Surface treatment

Five types of surface treatment are recognized:

sA no special finish
sB rough burnishing or finger wiping
sC haematite coating
sD burnishing but streaky and discontinuous
sE fine overall burnishing

In addition, method of decoration is given a number:

1 geometric decoration scratched after firing
2 stamped or impressed decoration with a pre-made tool before firing
3 finger-tip or finger-nail impression before firing
4 applied or integral cordons
5 shallow tooled decoration

Thus the typical haematite-coated bowl of Meon Hill type would be assigned to category sC1.

In the case of shallow tooled decoration a bewildering variety of patterns was employed. These have been further categorized and the details given in Appendix 3 (pp 308–13). Other variations relevant only to the Hengistbury assemblage have been omitted from discussion. The classificatory system briefly stated here and given in more detail in the illustrated appendices 1–3 (pp 259–313) might sound over-elaborate particularly when it is realized that a single decorated saucepan pot might, for example, be the proud possessor of the code PA1.1/B/sE5.3af. In practice, however, the system is simple and quick to use and, with a little familiarity, the codes can easily be remembered. More important, the system neatly contains all the variables needed for the types of analysis here attempted.

6.3   The ceramic sequence

6.3.1   Current schemes

Let us begin with preconceptions. Sufficient is known of the Iron Age pottery of Wessex for the broad development of styles to be generally understood. Several schemes have been put forward to contain it. The present writer has suggested (Cunliffe 1978) that the local ceramic development can best be described in terms of a series of style zones, overlapping in time and space, and named after one or more type-sites. The earliest of these, the Early All Cannings Cross group, dating broadly to the 8th-7th centuries BC, is typified by large jars with outcurving rims and round shoulders, decorated with stamped and incised geometric designs, by tripartite jars with outflaring rims, and by small bipartite bowls with beaded rims and sharp shoulder angles. This style developed in the 7th-6th centuries into the Later All Cannings Cross group in which the large decorated jars became less common and the bowls were more frequently coated with haematite. The next development, called the All Cannings Cross-Meon Hill group, and tentatively assigned to the 5th-3rd centuries, was typified by the frequent occurrence of haematite-coated bowls, one type with flaring rims and horizontal furrowing on the shoulders, another with geometric designs scratched on the body often between horizontal cordons. The coarse ware component was represented by plain shouldered jars.

As envisaged, the three early style groups are essentially successive expressions of a single developing tradition, the significant threads of which are a gradual simplification of the coarse ware jar component and a series of innovations spawning a variety of fine bowls usually coated with highly-burnished haematite.

During the All Cannings Cross-Meon Hill phase it is possible to recognize the appearance of vessels made in burnished fabrics and fired in conditions giving rise to dark grey and black surfaces. These contrast with the predominantly oxidized fabrics of the early period but herald later developments in which reduced fabrics become the norm. In the same groups simple barrel-shaped vessels begin to become frequent. These too can be seen as the origin of a form which later becomes very common and is referred to as the saucepan pot.

In the Wessex area in the 3rd-1st centuries two distinct but contemporary style zones can be traced, one centred in Wiltshire and called the Yarnbury-Highfield style, the other in Hampshire and West Sussex called the St Catherine's Hill-Worthy Down style. Both are typified by saucepan pots, jars with simple incurving rims, and, less frequently, jars with evenly everted rims. Fabrics were usually reduced and the surfaces of the vessels sealed by burnishing. Shallow tooled decoration was common.

Sometime soon after 100 BC ceramic technology improved, largely as a result of increasing contact with the Continent through ports such as Hengistbury Head. Wheel-turning was introduced creating tighter and more precise profiles. The use of horizontal cordons to define zones on the vessel bodies also became popular. Assemblages of this type found in Wiltshire and Hampshire have been styled Atrebatic and are believed to continue to the Roman period.

This simple scheme, first put forward in 1966 and subsequently modified (Cunliffe 1966; 1973; 1974; 1978), was based upon an assessment of a large number of usually small and frequently unstratified groups of pottery most of which were recovered from pre-war excavations or as chance finds. The scheme was, therefore, necessarily crude but it had the advantage of allowing the available material to be arranged against a geographical and chronological network unrestricted by preconceived historical models. It is still a fair reflection of the situation but the enormous collection of closely-stratified pottery from Danebury, calibrated with a series of radiocarbon dates, has allowed a much clearer definition of style change and greater precision in dating. Its detailed study, hardly surprisingly, indicates significant modifications and improvements. The more general implications of this work in its regional context will be discussed below (section 6.8); here we must consider the internal evidence for sequence.

6.3.2   The hypothetical model of ceramic phases

Although it would be possible to design a series of procedures to work from the crude data towards a definition of sequential change it would be perverse to pretend that we do not already have some idea of ceramic development in the area. Moreover, as the excavation proceeded it was possible to recognize recurring assemblages and to observe their relative chronological positions in the sequence. Based on these observations a working hypothesis was evolved which recognized the possible existence of nine *ceramic phases*. Several of the ceramic phases were clear cut and were represented by a number of assemblages producing a consistently similar range of types. Other ceramic phases were hinted at in the material while others were allowed for, to contain external evidence, but were not demanded by the Danebury material itself. The hypothetical scheme is summarized in Table 28.

It must be readily admitted that the scheme is a hybrid of objective observation, based on the Danebury assemblages and other assemblages in the region, contained within a matrix of subjectivity. It has strengths and weaknesses; in parts it is clear cut, in others obscure. For example, ceramic phases 9, 8, and 7 are clear and unshakeable, but cp 6 is far less certain; stratified groups were found without the decorated vessels typical of cp 7

Table 28

ceramic phase (cp)	diagnostic characteristics	style zone equivalent
1	angular bipartite bowls stamped decoration	Early All Cannings Cross group
2	furrowed bowls	Later All Cannings Cross group
3	scratched-cordoned bowls	
4	plain round shouldered bowls	All Canning Cross-Meon Hill group
5	simple barrel and jar forms	
6	plain saucepan pots	Yarnbury-Highfield style and St
7	decorated saucepan pots	Catherine's Hill-Worthy Down style
8	early wheel-turned vessels and Dressel 1A amphorae	Atrebatic
9	developed wheel-turned	

but the absence of decorated types need not be of chronological significance. In other words cp 6 may not exist, but since it could theoretically exist it has to be allowed for. Cp 5 was represented by a distinctive and constantly recurring assemblage which typologically appeared to precede and anticipate the saucepan pot styles but had 'advanced' beyond early types contained within cps 1–4. On these grounds the assemblage was placed in the position which it occupies in the scheme. Whether or not cps 4 and 3 exist as separate chronological phases is debatable. Cp 3 with its haematite-coated scratched-cordoned bowls (SCBs) and associated coarse wares is highly distinctive and sufficiently different from cp 5 types to suggest either a chronological gap or the existence of an intermediate stage here called cp 4. There are indeed assemblages which could fit typologically between cps 3 and 5; thus the possibility of cp 4 must be allowed for. Beyond cp 3 the Danebury sequence is obscure. Cps 1 and 2 were designed to reflect the developments of central Wessex. No furrowed bowls were found at Danebury and only a few sherds which would be placed in the Early All Cannings Cross group. There are, however, coarse ware types similar to those in use throughout the Early and Later All Cannings Cross phase. Various explanations are possible: it might be that Danebury was too far from the centres producing the distinctive cps 1 and 2 fine wares for examples to reach the site; it could be that the centre of early occupation has not yet been reached within the fort; alternatively it is possible that the 'early' coarse wares are really contemporary with cp 3. These problems will be further examined but in the meantime it is advisable to allow the possible existence of cps 1 and 2 as distinct from cp 3.

Sufficient will have been said to expose some of the strengths and weaknesses of the hypothetical scheme. The problems are typical of those which emerge when one tried to impose a rigid sequence on something as fluid as style change in a plastic medium. Even if one accepts the reality of the ceramic phases their relationship one to another is uncertain. They are most unlikely to be 'end on'. The model that seems most likely can be expressed thus:

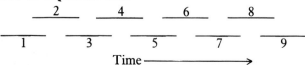

but other schemes are equally possible.

These problems have been explained here because they represent a stage in our developing understanding of the ceramic sequence, a stage beyond which, on very many sites, it is impossible to progress. However, as the excavation at Danebury advanced, the opportunity of further refinement presented itself. In the first place the sample of stratified assemblages increased to the point where statistical analysis became worthwhile, and in the second the deeply stratified layers from the quarry hollows behind the rampart, excavated in 1973–5 and 1977–8, provided sufficient material for a real sequence to be prepared based upon vertical stratigraphy. It is convenient to begin with the results of the study of the stratified material before considering the evidence of the isolated assemblages: this constitutes test 1.

Overall consideration of the fabrics suggested a well-defined change in relative proportion with time. This was examined first by reference to the stratified sequence (test 2) and further tested in a package of seriation experiments (tests 3 and 4). Evidence derived from a study of intercutting pits is presented in tests 5 and 6. A different approach, using radiocarbon dates obtained from more than 60 contexts, enabled the general validity of the ceramic phase sequence to be demonstrated (test 7) while suggesting absolute dates (bc) for the ceramic phases (test 8). Finally the possibility of subdividing cp 7 by seriation was examined in test 9.

6.3.3 Test 1: the sequence of ceramic phases in the quarry hollows

The stratified sequences explored in the quarry hollows excavated in 1973–5 and 1977–8 have been described above (Vol 1, pp 146–73). A matrix diagram was prepared for each allowing the sequence to be divided into phases each composed of a number of discrete archaeological contexts. The contexts, which included postholes, pits, and layers, produced varying amounts of pottery; some were devoid of finds, while others, such as pit fills, contained hundreds of sherds. For the purpose of analysis, however, all pottery-producing contexts were regarded as of equal value. The contexts were arranged in their stratigraphical phases and a ceramic phase (cp) was assigned to each context based on the latest distinctive sherds present. For each stratigraphical phase the number of contexts assigned to each ceramic phase was worked out and expressed as a percentage of the total number of pottery-producing contexts within the stratigraphical phase. The results are expressed graphically (Figs 6.1, 6.2).

Before commenting on the diagrams the significance of the ceramic phasing of the contexts must be made clear. A layer producing a few body sherds without characteristics distinctive of cps 4–7 would be assigned to cps 1–3 even though it was found stratigraphically above a context containing pottery of cp 6; to be assigned to cps 1–3 does not require sherds distinctive of cps 1–3 to be present — merely those distinctive of the later ceramic phases to be absent. For this reason one would expect the number of cp 1–3 contexts in the later phases to be inflated, as indeed is the case. Similarly, because a ceramic phase is assigned on presence of characteristics there will always be a tendency for some contexts, particularly those containing only a few sherds, to be assigned to an earlier ceramic phase than they deserve. This does not necessarily imply a high degree of rubbish survival since types characteristic of one ceramic phase may continue in contemporary use into the next. With these provisos in mind we can better understand the diagrams.

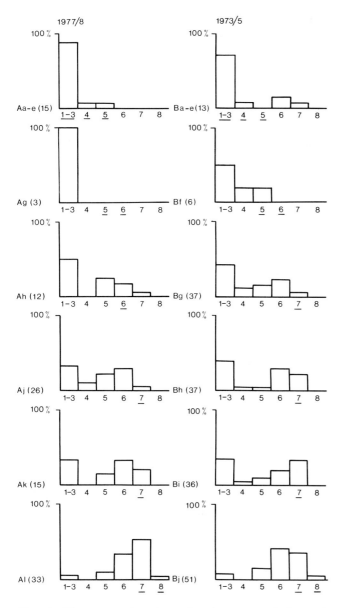

Fig 6.1 Histograms to show the number of contexts ascribed to each ceramic phase in the main stratigraphical levels defined in the stratified sequences of 1977–8 and 1973–5. Those underlined are the archaeologically preferred ceramic phases

demonstrated. Of particular interest is the position of cp 5. The diagram (Fig 6.1) would suggest that types characteristic of cp 5 may have continued in currency for some time although their apparent duration may well have been extended by rubbish survival.

The 1973–5 sequence

The picture is closely similar to that demonstrated for the 1977–8 sequence. Phase Bf, which represents occupation early in the quarry hollow, has produced a number of cp 5 contexts though whether occupation began during the currency of cp 5 or a little later remains uncertain. Thereafter (phases Bg-j), contexts containing cp 7 pottery increase in number while cp 6 contexts fluctuate. Cp 5 contexts are never numerous.

Taken together the two sequences confirm that the ceramic phase system is a valid scheme insofar as the stratigraphical sequence is able to offer a check.

From general observation it is evident that the proportions of the different pottery fabrics change with time. A simple test of the validity of the scheme of ceramic phases would therefore be to compare fabric changes expressed in terms of the ceramic phase system with that arrived at purely objectively by quantifying fabrics contained within the stratified sequences. If the ceramic phases are valid one would expect the pattern of fabric change arrived at by these two methods to be comparable.

In the test to follow the pottery from the two major stratified sequences, 1973–5 and 1977–8, was examined, independently of the original assessment, by Lisa Brown; her analysis is given below (test 2). Then follows a series of tests, based on seriation procedures, carried out by Gary Lock (tests 3–5). A brief comment is appended (p 237).

The 1977–8 sequence

The first diagram (Fig 6.1) shows that the earliest pottery, stratified beneath the rampart extension (phases Aa-Ae), contains a high percentage of cp 1–3 contexts together with a smaller number assignable to cps 4 and 5. This is exactly what would be expected since the layers span a considerable period of time. The latest contexts show that the rampart extension occurred after pottery of cp 5 had come into use. For phase Ag little can be said since only three contexts, all producing pottery of cps 1–3, have been found. The layers, however, were largely of material derived from the erosion of the sides of the quarry hollow and would therefore have contained redeposited earlier material.

The later phases (Ah-Al) clearly demonstrate the quantitative relationship of contexts producing cps 5, 6, and 7: cp 5 contexts decline steadily, cp 6 increases at first and remains steady, while cp 7 contexts are insignificant at the beginning but rapidly increase in number. The chronological relationship of all three is thus neatly

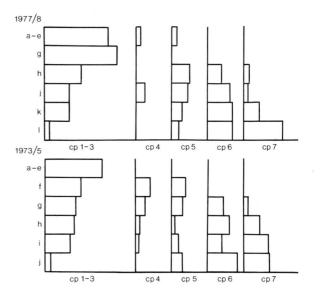

Fig 6.2 Histograms to show the relative number of contexts in each stratigraphical phase of the stratified sequences found in 1973–5 and 1977–8, containing pottery assigned to each of the ceramic phases

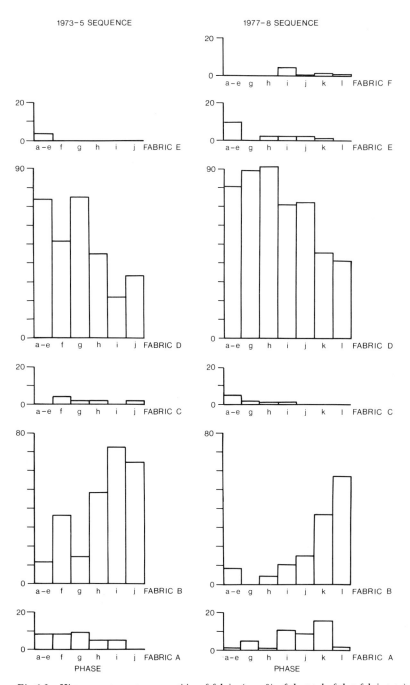

Fig 6.3 Histograms to compare quantities of fabrics (as a % of the total of that fabric type) in each of the stratigraphical phases defined in the stratified sequences found in 1973–5 and 1977–8

6.3.4 Test 2: fabric change within the stratified sequence
by Lisa Brown

All pottery from the stratified sequences within the quarry hollows excavated in 1973–5 and 1977–8 was reexamined in detail using subdivisions of the major fabric categories but otherwise maintaining the same recording procedure as that used for the rest of the pottery. A preliminary examination of the results showed that the minor fabric subdivisions were of little relevance adding nothing that was not already demonstrated by a comparison of the major fabric categories. For this reason the analysis to follow uses only the major divisions (fabrics A-H). The results are presented in two sets of histograms (Fig 6.3).

The pottery fabrics from the two sequences present closely comparable patterns. This is especially true of the relative percentages of the two commonest fabrics B and D but it is also reflected in the occurrence patterns of fabrics C and E. Fabrics F, G, and H are so rare as to be uninformative. The only significant difference between the two sequences is shown by the pattern of fabric A. The 1973–5 collection reflects a slow but unmistakable decline in the quantity of the fabric, whereas, in the 1977–8 group, there is a gradual increase followed by a sudden decline in the final phase. In view, however, of the comparatively small quantity of fabric A throughout the difference should not be given undue significance.

In more detail, taking the 1973–5 group first, fabric D predominates in the earliest phases (a-e) constituting 74%

of the pottery in comparison to only 11% of fabric B. Fabric E is here present in larger quantity than in any other phase of this sequence, standing at 5%. Fabric A represents 8% in this and the following phase (f).

In phase f, the amount of fabric B is uncharacteristically high for the early periods, representing 36% of the pottery, but fabric D is nevertheless higher at 52%. Fabric C is at its peak and E is absent altogether. This phase, however, is represented by only 156 sherds, so the proportions may be misleading.

Fabric D outnumbers both A and B in phase g at 75%, with B at only 14%. The transition of predominance from D to B comes in phase h where quantities of the two are similar (B 48%; D 45%) and A diminishes. Fabric B predominates noticeably in the last two phases (i and j) representing 72% in i and 63% in j, whilst D constitutes 22% and 33% respectively. Fabric C is present in small quantities throughout.

The pattern taken by fabric E in the 1973–5 sequence is certainly due to a degree of residuality in the later phases. It represents 5% of the pottery in the earliest phases (a-e), is absent in phases f, g, and h, and then constitutes a fraction of a percent in phases i and j.

For the 1977–8 group the examination demonstrated that in the earliest phases (a-e) the sandy fabric D predominates and fabric E, although representing only 9% of the pottery, is here present in larger quantity than in any other phase. Fabrics A and B are present in very small quantities (1% and 8% respectively). Phase g contained only nineteen sherds but was included in the test nonetheless. In that phase, B is absent, A and C together represent 10% of the pottery, and D is 90%. Fabric C is here seen in its largest quantity. As the phases ascend in time, D gradually diminishes at the expense of B, so that in phase k, D represents 45% and B 37%. By the latest phase (1) D is only 41% and B is 57%. At the same time, fabrics C and E diminish gradually. In phase 1 they each represent under 1% of the pottery. The pattern taken by fabric A, as already mentioned, is not as straightforward. It is present as a small percentage in every phase, but it starts out slowly (1% in phases a-e, 5% in g, 1% in h) and reaches its peak in phase k at 16%. It then drops dramatically in phase 1 to only 2%.

When the histograms for the two sequences are compared, the change in favoured fabrics can be seen to be generally consistent for both stratified groups. With the possible exception of fabric E there does not appear to have been a sudden abandonment of one fabric at the expense of another. Rather there is a gradual tendency, at least in the cases of B and D, for one to increase in popularity whilst the earlier favoured fabric continues to be used but in increasingly smaller quantities. At Danebury, the fine-tempered wares (especially flint-gritted) obviously became popular to the extent that, by the latest phases, they predominated over sandy wares.

6.3.5 Tests 3–5: fabric change according to ceramic phase
by Gary Lock

This test describes the seriation of the pottery from 947 pits. First, the technique of seriation is briefly outlined and the appropriateness of its application to the Danebury data discussed. Secondly, the two-stage, computer-assisted seriation technique that was used is described. This was applied initially to two data sets containing 50% samples drawn from the 947 pits. The pottery contained within them consisted of six fabric types which were used as the variables. A resulting seriated sequence is presented and compared with a three

period site-phasing which is based on the pottery typology (Early phase = cp 1–3, Middle phase = cp 4–5, Late phase = cp 6–8). The appropriateness of this three-phase model is considered and an alternative two-phase model suggested.

The results of three further seriations are then presented; firstly on all pits assigned to the Early phase, secondly on all pits assigned to the Middle-Late phase transition, and finally on all pits of the Late phase. These seriated sequences are then compared with the stratigraphic evidence of the intercutting pits. Finally the sequence of ceramic phases is examined in the light of these seriated sequences.

The technique of seriation

Seriation involves the comparison of frequencies of certain artefacts (*types*) contained within each context (*seriation unit*) and the assumption that contexts with similar proportions occupy a similar position in time. It is desirable that the types are approximately equivalent in chronological significance as it has been shown that unimportant types can obscure the significance of important ones (Hole & Shaw 1967, ch 1). Seriation, therefore, needs types that are defined by chronologically significant attributes. Variables other than time, for example social class or function, may be responsible for differences recognized within a seriated sequence. In an attempt to minimize this possibility three conditions have been suggested (Doran & Hodson 1975, 269) which, if met, increase the chances of the seriated sequence being chronologically significant. The three conditions are:

i that the seriation units all come from a single cultural tradition
ii that the seriation units (contexts) be drawn from a single locality to control for spatial variation
iii that attributes of the seriation units employed in the study (the types) are culturally, and therefore potentially chronologically, significant

In this exercise the seriation units are the pits and the types used for the seriation are the six recognized pottery fabrics described elsewhere (p 232). These satisfy all of the criteria mentioned above and the sequences generated, therefore, are likely to be chronologically significant. They are, however, orderings of pits and not linear sequences. This limitation applies to the results of all seriation exercises as there is no intrinsic way to scale the units within the sequence.

Establishing a seriated sequence

This procedure is in two stages, the first being the clustering of the pits into groups based on the similarity of the selected variables. Due to the large amount of numerical analysis required it would be impossible to perform this clustering by manual methods. It was therefore performed on the ICL 2960 at North Staffs Polytechnic using an available software package. The second stage, the ordering of these groups, was performed manually because the technique demands continual visual inspection and at the present time satisfactory computer software does not exist.

The cluster analyses were carried out using the **BMDP** package (University of California 1977) on a suitably formatted data file generated from the basic Danebury pottery file. The six recognized fabric types (A to F) were used as the variables for clustering rather than pot shape and/or decoration which are more difficult to quantify. The resulting data file consists of 947 cases with six variables per case, each case being labelled by a unique pit

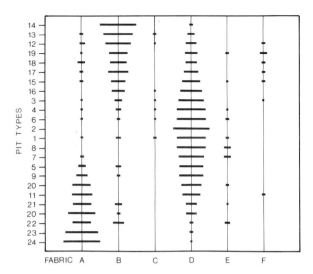

Fig 6.4 *The seriated sequence produced from the results of a cluster analysis carried out on a 50% sample of the 974 pits (amalgamation distance = 12.3, number of clusters = 24)*

number. A ceramic phase (cp) has already been assigned to each pit according to the pottery typology discussed elsewhere (pp 259–60).

Program P2M within the BMDP package imposes a limit of 500 cases. Therefore it was applied to every other case in the data file. This program performs average link cluster analysis using the sum of squares procedure giving graphical output as a horizontal tree as well as tabulated amalgamation sequences. Clusters were read at the amalgamation distance of 12.3. This was selected after experimentation since it produced intuitively sensible results—in this case, 24 clusters. Each was assigned a number which henceforth will be called a *pit type cluster*, being defined by the average of each variable for every pit within the group.

The second stage of the procedure was to order the pit type clusters manually using the standard seriation graph technique (Ford 1962). Since fabric D was present in every pit type it was treated as the key variable. Fig 6.4 shows the resulting seriated sequence for the 24 pit type clusters established from the 50% pit sample. As can be seen, fabric D produced the classic battleship curve and the sequence produced for fabrics A and B support the overall sequence. The whole procedure was repeated on another 50% sample drawn from the population in alternate blocks of seventeen pits. This produced a similar result.

Test 3: the relevance of the site phases

Three broad site phases have been suggested based on form and surface decoration. These were compared with the results of the seriation to assess whether they indicated a similar relative chronology. It should be noted that although the seriation has suggested a chronological sequence it could run in either direction along the vertical axis in Fig 6.4.

The percentages of pits falling into the Early (cp 1–3), Middle (cp 4, 5), and Late (cp 6, 7–8) site phases were calculated for each pit type cluster. The procedure for designating pits to these phases has been described elsewhere (p 237).

Fig 6.5 shows these percentages plotted against the seriated sequence of pit type clusters. It is immediately apparent that there is a broad agreement between the two relative chronologies with pit type cluster 24 being the earliest. The horizontal axis in Fig 6.5 can be considered as time. However, this scale is not linear as each pit type cluster may represent a different length of time.

The Early and Late phase curves appear to be in accord with the relative chronology produced by the pottery typology (Fig 6.5). The anomalous peak in pit type cluster 14 can be reasonably explained by residual material. The small amount of Late phase pottery present in pit type cluster 9 could be due to the pit type cluster being misplaced within the sequence as this is a small group (fourteen pits). If this is the case the Late phase pottery would not occur until pit type cluster 1.

The Middle phase curve has no obvious peak and shows Middle phase fabric profile being present intermittently through both the Early and Late phases. This suggests that a two-phase model in which the Early and Middle phases are amalgamated might be more appropriate; see Fig 6.6.

Additional seriations

Further seriations were performed to provide complete subsequences for comparison with stratigraphic evidence (see pp 239–40). Additionally these provided an opportunity for examination of the ceramic phases contained within the Middle and Late site phases (cp 4, 5 and cp 6, 7–8 respectively). Three new data files were generated: firstly all pits assigned to the Early site phase (cp 1–3), secondly all pits assigned to the Middle phase/Late phase

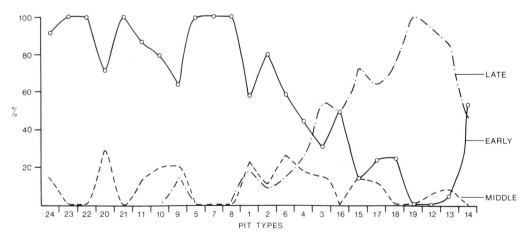

Fig 6.5 *Diagram showing fabric change against sequence of pit type clusters*

238

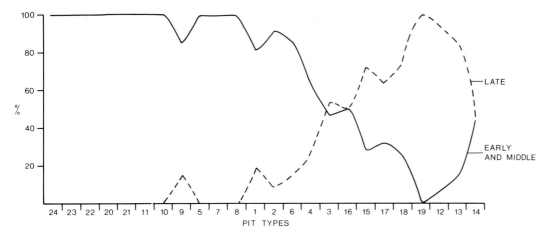

Fig 6.6 Diagram showing fabric change resolved into two phase groups against pit type clusters

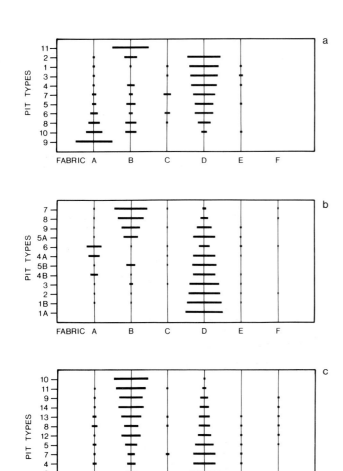

Fig 6.7 Seriated sequences produced for all pits in successive ceramic phases: (a) cp 1–3 pits (amalgamation distance = 12.1; no of clusters = 11 condensed from 28 for ease of display); (b) cp 4–6 pits (amalgamation distance = 13.6; no of clusters = 12); (c) cp 6–8 pits (amalgamation distance = 114; no of clusters = 14 condensed from 31 for ease of display)

transition (cp 4, 5, and 6), and finally all pits assigned to the Late phase (cp 6, 7–8). Each of these data files was seriated using the procedure outlined above and the three resultant sequences are presented in Fig 6.7.

Test 4: intercutting pits

Intercuts between pits of the same site phase were established by excavation (see pp 240–1). These provided an opportunity to corroborate sections of the seriated sequence. Additionally, if the relative chronology produced by the seriated sequence is accepted, then these pits will be relatively positioned within each site phase.

Thirty-four such intercuts exist for pits of the Early phase (cp 1–3) and six for the Late phase (cp 6, 7–8). Each of these pits can be positioned within the appropriate seriated sequence according to their pit type cluster established by the cluster analysis.

Figs 6.8 and 6.9 show the pairs of pits for the Early and Late phases. It can be seen that in 28 out of the 34 cases for the Early phase and all six cases from the Late phase, the earlier pit of the pair is contained in either the same pit type cluster as the later pit or an earlier one.

Five of the six anomalies (see right-hand side of Fig 6.8) could have occurred as a product of one of the following two types of error. Firstly individual pits could have been assigned incorrectly to a pit type cluster due to a small number of sherds being contained within the pit (anomalies 1, 2, and 3). Secondly a pit type cluster could be incorrectly positioned within the seriated sequence due to the small number of pits within the pit type cluster (anomalies 4, 5). The sixth anomaly cannot be easily explained. (Details of the anomalous pits are discussed in fiche 8, frames A5–7).

The detailed seriated sequences established for each of the Early and Late site phases are supported by the evidence of the intercutting pits. Additionally Figs 6.8 and 6.9 can provide a provisional relative chronology for these pits.

Test 5: the separation of the ceramic phases

The seriated sequences produced from all the pits assigned to cps 4, 5, and 6 and all the pits assigned to cps 6 and 7–8 provided an opportunity for a detailed examination of these ceramic phases. The percentages of pits of ceramic phases 4, 5, and 6 were calculated for each pit type cluster, and plotted against the appropriate seriated sequence (Fig 6.10). If the sequence of ceramic phases 4→ 5→ 6 is to be supported by the seriated

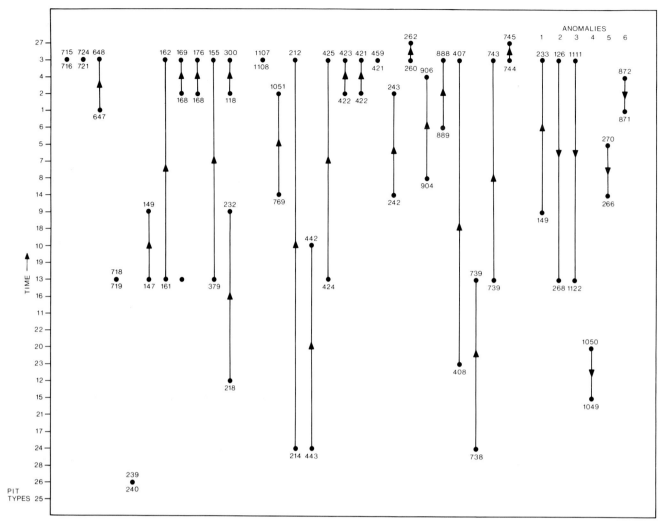

Fig 6.8 Intercutting pits of cp 1–3. Direction of arrow denotes 'cut by'

sequences produced on the basis of the fabric type then one would expect the three curves to peak sequentially. However, as can be seen, no clear pattern is discernible. In particular the sequence cp 4→ cp 5 is not supported by this analysis. A similar graph was produced for the sequence cp 6→ cp 7–8 (Fig 6.11). In this case the fabric analysis clearly supports the relative positions of these phases.

Conclusion

The proposed relative chronology based upon the seriated sequence presented here is in broad agreement with both the site phasing produced from the pottery typology (ie the scheme of ceramic phases) and the limited amount of available stratigraphic evidence. If, however, it is accepted that fabric type is chronologically significant, then the existence of the Middle phase defined by a distinctive fabric profile is in doubt. Additionally, it is clear from the more detailed analysis of ceramic phases 4 and 5 that fabric type has not been considered important in their construction.

The results of these two sets of experiments (tests 2–5) confirm that the supposed sequence of ceramic phases is in accord with overall fabric changes. The seriation

experiments, however, suggest that the fabric profile of the Middle phase pits (cps 4 and 5) is more akin to that of the Early period than the Late period and indicate that the significant divide, in fabric terms, comes between cp 5 and cp 6. Further it failed to support any distinction between cp 4 and cp 5 (for further comments see fiche 8, frame D5).

6.3.6 Test 6: intercutting pits
by Barry Cunliffe and Lisa Brown

A number of the pits were physically related to each other. In all there were 147 groups of intercut pits. The actual number of relationships between one pit and another was 568 but some of these represented pits which had simply eroded together at the top and evidence of relationship was lacking. However in 414 intersections it was possible to define the sequence of pit digging by archaeological observation. In all 327 pits were involved of which 285 produced pottery.

Within this body of relationships the potential exists for testing the validity of the ceramic phasing. We approach the problem in three ways:

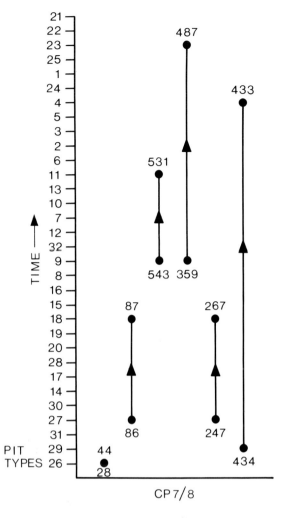

Fig 6.9   Intercutting pits cp 7/8. Direction of arrow denotes 'cut by'

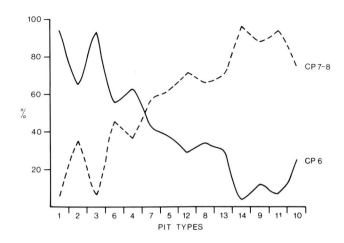

Fig 6.11   Plot of percentages of fabrics in cp 6 and 7/8 against sequence of pit type cluster

a   by considering anomalies
b   by discussing sequences
c   by attempting closer divisions within ceramic phases

Anomalies

An anomaly is defined as an intersection in which a pit containing pottery of a high number (later) ceramic phase is cut by one containing pottery of a lower number (earlier) ceramic phase. There are thirteen anomalies, the details of which are given in fiche 8, frames A5–7 where each is simply explained in terms of residuality or contamination.

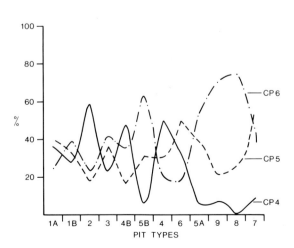

Fig 6.10   Plot of percentages of fabrics in cp 4, 5, and 6 against sequence of pit type cluster

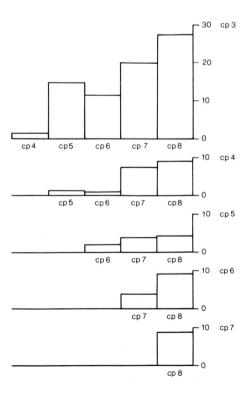

Fig 6.12   Histograms to show for each ceramic phase the relative proportions of the pits of different dates cutting pits of that ceramic phase (expressed as a %)

241

Sequences

Histograms showing how many pits of each phase cut those of an earlier phase are presented in Fig 6.12. The results conform to what would be expected, that the number of intercuts increases as time between the intercut pits increases. In other words it is less likely for a cp 4 pit to cut a cp 3 pit than it is for a cp 7 pit to cut a cp 3 pit, the reason presumably being that at the time that cp 4 pits were being dug cp 3 pits, though filled, could still be detected but they had passed from sight and memory when cp 7 pits were being dug.

Closer division within the phases

In theory where pits of the same ceramic phase intercut, the potential for a closer phasing of the pottery confined within them exists. The figures for intercut same-phase pits are as follows:

cp 1–3	41 (= 82 pits)
cp 4	1 (= 2 pits)
cp 5	0
cp 6	1 (= 2 pits)
cp 7	6 (= 12 pits)
cp 8	0

Only the cp 1–3 and cp 7 groups provided adequate samples for analysis. These were examined in relation to the pit type clusters produced by the seriation of the ceramic fabrics. Of the 34 well-defined intercuts between cp 1–3 pits, 28 conformed to the pit type cluster sequence (five of the six anomalies are easily explained) and of the six intercuts between cp 7 pits all were in accord with the pit type cluster sequence (for details see above, test 4).

6.3.7 Test 7: the ceramic phase sequence tested by radiocarbon dating

The programme of radiocarbon dating developed for the excavation and discussed in detail above (Vol 1, pp 190–8) allowed the possibility of testing the validity of the ceramic phase sequence. The results are given in full in the relevant section (pp 193–4). Here we need only say that the dates, considered statistically, confirmed the separate existence and sequential relationship of cp 1–3, cp 4–5, cp 6, and cp 7.

6.3.8 Test 8: the assignment of absolute dates

The sequence of radiocarbon dates, for contexts containing distinctive pottery, has allowed absolute dates (BC) to be assigned to the ceramic phases. The data are presented in detail above (Vol 1, pp 195–6) and may be summarized thus:

cp 1–3	550–450 BC
cp 4–5	450–400 BC
cp 6	400–300 BC
cp 7	300–100/50 BC

A statistical consideration of the dates further suggests that there is unlikely to be significant overlap of the ceramic phases as defined (pp 193–4).

6.3.9 Test 9: fine phasing by seriation within cps 7–8

by Gary Lock

All pits of cps 7–8 were seriated and subphases established. These were then analysed to investigate changes

Table 29   The seriated sequence for all cp 7-8 pits

Sub-phase	Fabric B	Fabric D	All other fabrics
7E	87	9	3
7D	75	23	2
7C	65	31	3
7B	52	42	6
7A	23	58	16

Figures are percentages

in the form, surface finish, and decoration of the pottery through the period which is estimated to have lasted for 200 years.

Establishing subphases within cps 7–8

A data file was generated from the basic Danebury pottery file consisting of all 148 pits of cps 7–8. The three variables computed for each case were percentages of fabric B, fabric D, and all other fabrics. It is evident from Fig 6.4 that fabrics B and D are the principal components in the fabric sequence for the later phases of the site. It was therefore decided to amalgamate the counts of the other four fabrics to reduce background noise.

Table 29 shows the seriated sequence established using the two-stage procedure described above (p 237). Clusters were read from the BMDP output at an amalgamation distance of 19.3. The resulting five clusters represent subphases cp 7A–cp 7E each being defined by its mean percentages for fabric types. Comparison of Table 29 and Fig 6.4 shows that cp 7A is the earliest subphase with a subsequent increase in fabric B and decrease in fabric D.

Analysis of the subphases

The five subphases were then used as the basis for a computer analysis of the pottery forms, surface finishes, and decoration through cps 7–8. A program written in COBOL and implemented on an ICL 2960 at North Staffs Polytechnic produced the descriptive statistics for each subphase presented in the four Tables (101–5) on fiche 8, frames B2–11. Percentage counts of forms, surface finishes, and decorative techniques characteristic of cps 7–8 were established along with actual counts of sherd numbers for each pit. The corresponding means for the five subphases were then calculated.

Table 30 shows the statistics describing the actual sherd counts per pit within each subphase.

Surface finish and decoration within cps 7–8

Surfaces D and E are indicative of cps 7–8 and were, therefore, counted separately from all other surfaces (see

Table 30   Sherd counts for each subphase

Number of pits	35	27	28	30	32
Mean number of sherds per pit	98	172	152	189	103
Total number of sherds	3448	4645	4268	5660	3285
Subphase	7A	7B	7C	7D	7E

Table 31 Surface and decoration counts for cp 7-8 subphases

	7A	7B	7C	7D	7E
All other surfaces	44.7	23.5	21.1	14.0	15.4
Surface E	33.2	58.4	58.1	66.3	68.3
Surface D	20.7	16.4	19.1	18.2	15.0
Decoration	4.0	4.7	7.6	7.8	14.1
Subphase	7A	7B	7C	7D	7E

Figures are percentages

Tables 101–5, fiche 8, frames B2–11). The means for each subphase are presented in Table 31. It can be seen by the decreasing total for all other surfaces (44.7% in cp 7A to 15.4% in cp 7E) that surfaces D and E together increase in importance through cps 7–8. The relationship between surfaces D and E is also of interest. Surface D increases in importance with time (from 33.2% to 68%) while surface E decreases from 20.7% in cp 7A to only 15% in cp 7E.

Table 31 also shows the means for each subphase of the percentage counts of decorated sherds from each pit. Decoration increases through cps 7–8, from 4% in cp 7A to 7.8% in cp 7D and then considerably in cp 7E to 14.1%.

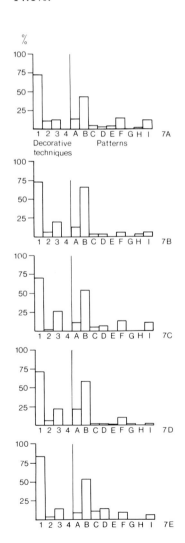

Fig 6.13 Data on which Table 32 is based

Table 32 Sherd counts of decorative techniques and patterns for each cp 7-8 subphase

		7A	7B	7C	7D	7E
Decorative techniques	1	74	73	71	72	84
	2	12	7	2	6	4
	3	13	20	26	22	14
	4		1			
Patterns	a	14	13	11	22	8
	b	43	66	54	59	54
	c	5	3	5	2	17
	d	3	3	6	2	14
	e	4			1	
	f	15	6	13	10	10
	g				1	
	h	1	3			
	i	15	6	11	2	7
Subphase		7A	7B	7C	7D	7E

Figures are percentages of total numbers of shallow-tooled decorated sherds

Another COBOL program was written to perform a more detailed analysis of shallow-tooled decorated pottery which is characteristic of cp 7. This produced sherd counts for all individual decorative techniques and patterns, the results of which are presented as percentages of the total number of shallow-tooled decorated sherds in Table 32 and graphically in Fig 6.13. The codification of the pottery is fully described elsewhere (pp 308–13) but can be summarized here as:

Decorative techniques
1 lines only
2 dots only
3 lines and dots
4 Glastonbury style deep tooling

Patterns
a horizontal
b diagonal
c cross-hatching
d zig-zag
e chevron
f arc
g swag
h wave
i dimple

It is apparent from Table 32 and Fig 6.13 that technique 1 and pattern B predominate in all subphases. Underlying this, however, are more subtle changes. The three important techniques (1–3) show differing trends. Technique 1 is constant for subphases 7A-7D with a large increase in cp 7E while 2 is highest in cp 7A and decreases thereafter and 3 reaches a peak in cp 7C with a subsequent decrease. In ceramic terms this shows that line only decoration was always by far the most important. Dots only decoration along with dots and lines are represented by equal amounts initially but the former soon falls out of favour while the latter doubles in quantity but then decreases towards the end of cps 7–8. Patterns a and b (horizontal and diagonal) are well represented throughout the sequence with the latter always being the more important. Table 31 shows a large increase in the amount of decorated pottery in cp 7E.

243

Table 33 Pot form counts for cp 7-8 subphases

All other forms	90.1	78.1	78.6	77.9	71.0
JC2	3.8	9.1	8.8	9.2	10.4
PB1	2.3	6.5	7.6	7.9	11.8
JD3	0.6	1.2	2.3	1.8	4.9
Other cp 7-8 forms	1.5	1.3	0.8	1.6	0.7
Subphase	7A	7B	7C	7D	7E

Figures are percentages

This correlates with the increases in this subphase of technique 1 and patterns c and d (cross-hatching and zig-zag). It seems, therefore, that in the last subphase a large increase in the use of pots decorated with cross-hatching and zig-zag lines occurred.

Pot forms within cp 7–8

The percentages of sherds for the fifteen pot forms characteristic of cps 7–8 (JC2) were counted together with the combined percentage for all the other pot forms (see Tables 101–5, fiche 8, frames B2–11). The means of these counts for each subphase are shown in Table 33. All cp 7–8 forms with subphase totals of less than 1% are combined for ease of presentation.

The occurrence of all cp 7–8 forms increases through time with a relative decrease in the amounts of pottery of all other forms. The two most important forms are JC2 and PB1 which show a parallel increase in importance through cps 7–8 (3.8% to 10.4% and 2.3% to 11.8% respectively). Form JD3 shows a sudden increase in the last subphase while the combined total of all other cp 7–8 forms remains at an insignificant level throughout.

Conclusion

The validity of the cp 7–8 subphases is supported by the detailed analyses of the form, surface finish, and decoration of the pottery. These show significant changes through time in all three pottery attributes. The percentage of sherds representing the characteristic cp 7–8 pot forms increases as does the relative use of surface E and decoration while the use of surface D decreases.

6.4 The fabrics and their origins

6.4.1 Resources

Danebury is comparatively well situated in relation to clay deposits (Fig 6.14). Although, with the exception of clay-with-flints which caps some of the neighbouring hills, there is little usable potting clay immediately to hand, fine deposits of Reading beds clay and London clay outcrop to the south in the Dean Hill syncline only 8-10 km away. Indeed, the nearest Reading beds deposit, at Bossington, is within 7 km of the hillfort. The Bagshot and Bracklesham deposits, which contain bands of adequate potting clay, outcrop to the south of the chalk downs on the fringe of the Hampshire basin in the vicinity of Timsbury and Romsey, about 14 km from the fort. A similar range of Tertiary clays is to be found to the north, in the region of Highclere, 24 km or more from Danebury. A selection of rather different clays, of Cretaceous and Jurassic origin, outcrops in the Nadder valley to the west of Salisbury from Barford St Martin westwards. Oolitic clays, together with Wealden and

Gault clays and glauconitic sands, are obtainable in this area between 27 and 34 km from the site. Finally, a fine-grained brickearth occurs on the fringes of the Nadder and Avon valleys immediately to the north of Salisbury, less than 20 km from Danebury. All of these materials were at one time or another exploited to make pottery or daub for use in the fort.

Evidence for clay storage is well attested at Danebury. In the 1969–78 excavation five pits of conical section were found containing carefully selected clays. They averaged 1.6 m in diameter and varied in depth from 0.7–1.0 m. The sides sloped steeply inwards to a flat bottom about 0.3 m across. In four cases flat flint nodules had been placed on the bottoms.

Three of the pits (P406, P571, P699) contained orange-brown coloured clay while the two others (P717, P754) were filled with red clay with grey-green streaks. The identification of the first clay is uncertain but it may be from the London clay beds; the red mottled clay is of Reading beds origin. Clay pits of this kind have been recorded in Iron Age contexts elsewhere. At Winklebury, eleven were excavated, all containing varicoloured clays largely derived from nearby outcrops of Reading beds. Analysis of the clay in comparison with ceramic fabrics suggested that the clay was probably used for functions other than pottery manufacture (Smith 1977, 48-50). Three pits of a similar kind were found at Hod Hill (Richmond 1968, 22–3). Although the clay was not analysed, the excavator suggested that it came from the nearby valley bottom where it had been washed before transport to the hillfort. Pottery manufacture was thought to be a likely reason for its storage. At Yarnbury (Cunnington 1933, 202) a single pit of this kind was recorded, but the nature of the clay was not specified.

The clays from the Danebury pits have been examined by Dr Williams (fiche 8, frames E2–3). The analyses allow that the clays may have been used for potting but do not prove that this was so. Nonetheless the careful mixing and puddling, which the existence of the pits implies was carried out, would suggest that the clay was being prepared for pottery manufacture rather than for making loom weights, ovens, or wall daub. The clay for these, more structural, purposes was usually ill sorted showing little sign of careful preparation.

Three of the pits (P699, P717, P754) were found close together in the centre of the fort in zone N3 alongside the main east-west road, one (P406) lay in the centre of zone N4, while the fifth (P571) was sited in the southern part of zone S3.

The dating evidence is slightly ambiguous since very little pottery was recorded and that which was found invariably came from the uppermost layer of soil filling the hollow in the pit top. P406 produced 27 sherds no later than cp 3 from the deliberate chalk packing in the pit top; it cut P407 (cp 3) and was cut by P404 (cp 7). P571 produced three sherds of cp 6/7 from the upper filling. P699 yielded two sherds assignable to cp 8 from the uppermost fill. P717 contained fourteen sherds no later than cp 3, while P745 produced a single sherd of cp 5; it was cut into P755 (cp 3) and cut by P753 (cp 7).

6.4.2 Ceramic phases 1–7; local fabrics

The great majority of vessels used at Danebury before c100 BC were made from locally available materials. Analysis shows that the clays could have come from sources within a 10 km radius of the site, while the fillers of crushed flint, sand, and crushed shell, used in different combinations and proportions, were readily

244

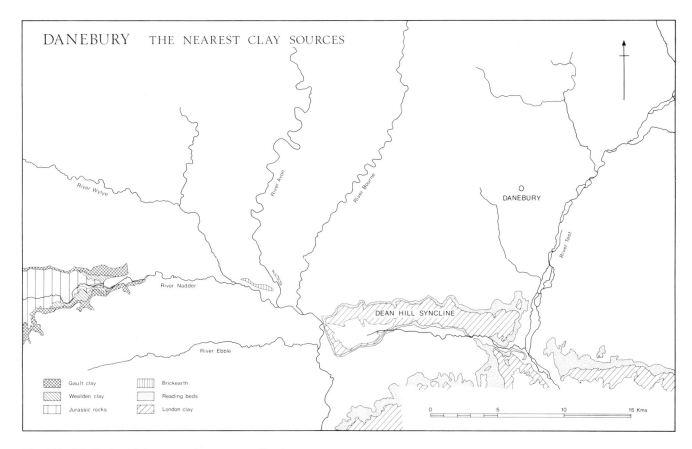

Gault clay
Wealden clay
Jurassic rocks
Brickearth
Reading beds
London clay

0   5   10   15 Kms

Fig 6.14 *Distribution of the nearest clay sources to Danebury*

available locally. Manufacture on site or in the vicinity is therefore likely.

Two distinctive fabrics, used for haematite-coated bowls and glauconitic sandy wares, which occur in some quantity at Danebury, did not come from the immediate neighbourhood.

Haematite-coated bowls

The distinctive haematite-coated bowls with scratched geometric decoration (our types BB1.1 and BB3.1) have long been considered to come from a single manufacturing centre (Liddell 1935, 27, 33) which, judging from the known distribution of the ware, was thought to lie somewhere in eastern Wiltshire. Recent analysis of the fabric (p 308: fabric 7c) has now shown that the clay used was a brickearth, the nearest local occurrences of which appear to be in the Salisbury region, in the centre of the distribution pattern (Fig 6.22), about 20 km from Danebury. If there was a single manufacturing centre near Salisbury, then the maximum distance over which the pottery is known to have been transported is about 40 km.

The quantity found at Danebury is large in comparison with other sites but this is only to be expected in view of the sample size. Nonetheless, the percentage of haematite-coated sherds in stratified groups at Danebury was comparatively high, averaging 16.0% for the 121 pit groups in which these forms were found, showing that considerable quantities of these bowls were reaching the site. At the two neighbouring hillforts of Quarley Hill and Figsbury, the percentage of haematite wares to other fabrics was equally high. While it would be tempting to argue that this reflected the enhanced status of hillforts,

the quantity of haematite ware found at the neighbouring site of Meon Hill shows that the farmsteads were also receiving fine wares in bulk.

Glauconitic sandy wares

A distinctive type of sandy fabric, containing well-rounded reddish-brown grains of limonite (altered glauconite), was identified by fabric analysis (p 308: fabric 6). Dr Williams points out that the presence of the glauconite suggests an origin in the Upper Greensand, the nearest deposits of which lie some 30 km south-west of Danebury at Compton Chamberlayne. This observation is of some interest when the forms are considered. These include flared dishes (DA1.1), saucepan pots (PB1.1), and everted rimmed jars (JD3.1, 3.2, 3.3). Moreover the range of decoration is restricted, frequently incorporating arcs with shallow impressions at the bases. Fig 6.15 illustrates a selection of these vessels. While the forms and decorative styles are not restricted to this fabric, but also occur on the common local flint-gritted fabrics, the combination of form, decoration, and glauconitic fabric serves to distinguish a well-defined component of the Danebury cp 7 assemblage. The distribution of vessels of this kind is shown on Fig 6.16; significantly the location of the supposed clay source is central. Excluding the outliers of Maiden Castle and Hengistbury, the other sites producing this assemblage all lie within a 30 km range of the source.

Although Danebury has produced a not inconsiderable number of vessels of this type, compared with contemporary local wares, the percentage is small, approximately 0.35% of the pottery found in pits of cp 7 (fiche 8, frames C1–2). This is not surprising when it is

245

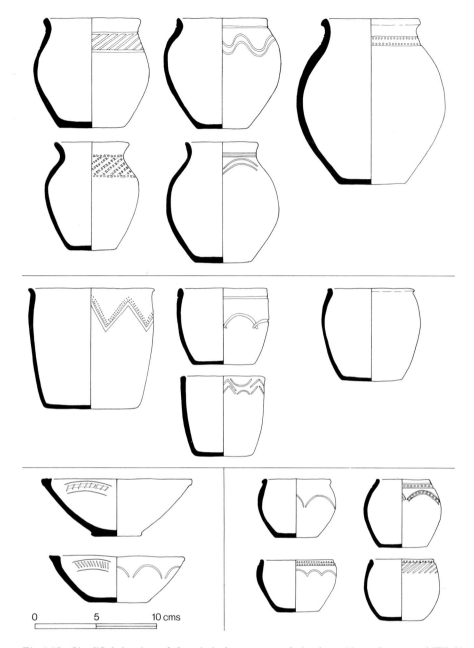

Fig 6.15 Simplified drawings of the principal pot types made in glauconitic sandy wares of Wiltshire origin

remembered that Danebury lies on the extremity of the distribution pattern.

6.4.3 Ceramic phases 1–7: imported fabrics
The pottery assemblages of ceramic phases 1–7 contain surprisingly little material imported from outside the Danebury territory. What there is may be briefly listed:

Oolitic limestone-tempered
Dr Williams has distinguished a fabric heavily tempered with ooliths derived from a Jurassic limestone source (fabric 1). The nearest outcrop to Danebury is at Teffont Evias 32 km to the south-west but there is no proof that this source was used; the vessels could have come from virtually anywhere along the Jurassic ridge.
Very few examples were found: in all there were only nine sherds, from pits P652 (cp 7), P582 (cp 7), P783 (cp 3).

Glastonbury wares
Five sherds of decorated Glastonbury ware (Form BD6) were found in the contexts of P507 (one sherd), P517 (one sherd), and layer 367 (three sherds).
One of the sherds from layer 367 belongs to Peacock group 1 (Gabbro:Lizard origin) while the other four are ungrouped (p 308: fabric 4).
Although it is possible that a few undecorated sherds may have been missed in the fabric sorting, the quantity of Glastonbury ware is minute compared to the total volume of contemporary pottery.
Layer 367 and P507 were of ceramic phase 7 while P517 produced only pottery of ceramic phase 6.

6.4.4 Ceramic phases 8-9: local fabrics
The fabrics of ceramic phases 8-9 reverted once more to a sandy type but it was invariably hard-fired and significantly stronger than the earlier sandy fabrics. Normally

246

the fabrics were without grit but occasionally sparse angular flint tempering had been added. The majority of the vessels were certainly or probably made, or at least finished, on a wheel, a technique which led to a tightening of the profile giving the vessels more precisely moulded rims and base angles. The influence of north-western French imported types is clearly seen in the pedestal bases, cordons, and rilling of some of the vessels.

Apart from the new technology involved and the copying of exotic forms there is nothing to suggest that the pottery was not made in the vicinity by potters local to the area.

6.4.5 Ceramic phases 8-9: imported fabrics
Coarse wares

Among the very small collection of pottery of ceramic phases 8-9 are a few vessels in a black sandy fabric made from clays found in the vicinity of Poole Harbour (p 308: fabric 7d). These were probably imports from the large pottery manufacturing industry which grew up in the 1st century BC and continued throughout the Roman period.

Amphorae

Seven body sherds of Mediterranean amphorae were

DISTRIBUTION OF GLAUCONITIC SANDY WARES

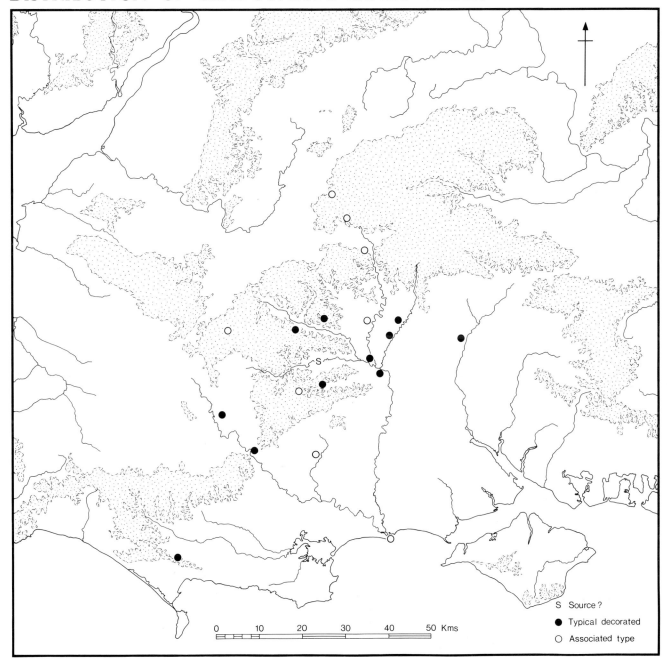

S Source?

● Typical decorated

○ Associated type

0 10 20 30 40 50 Kms

Fig 6.16 Distribution of glauconitic sandy wares in Wessex. No attempt has been made to distinguish quantities at each location

247

recovered from ceramic phase 8-9 contexts. Three were in a streaky fabric usually restricted to Dressel form 1A. Three were similar to the streaky fabric when seen in thin section, while one sherd conformed to Peacock's (1971) fabric 1 probably deriving from the Caecuban or Falernian regions of Italy. A detailed report by Dr Williams will be found in Appendix 2 (p 308).

The amphorae were probably imported through the Dorset harbours of Hengistbury or Poole. It may well be that the sandy coarse ware sherds, made in the Poole region, reached Danebury as the result of the same exchange mechanisms.

6.5   Technological change

Since the ceramic sequence at Danebury spans some 500 or 600 years it is only to be expected that certain technological changes will be distinguishable. The most dramatic appears at the moment when the site ceases to be densely occupied in about 100 BC; before that the ceramics are hand-made and clamp-fired, after that wheel-making and more controlled firing becomes apparent. It is convenient therefore to divide the discussion into two parts, the first dealing with ceramic phases 1–7, the second with ceramic phases 8–9.

6.5.1   Ceramic phases 1–7

The constitutents of the pottery in this early period are all locally derived (pp 244–5). Clay of various types was dug, weathered, and washed before being mixed with tempering material of which crushed flint and crushed shell were the most common. The possibility remains that at least some of these processes were undertaken within the fort.

In the early period (cps 1–3) a distinction between fine and coarse wares is evident. The coarse wares, functional cooking and storage vessels, were made in ill-sorted clays mixed with ungraded tempering materials. They appear to have been bonfire-fired to temperatures of 7–800°C and allowed to cool in oxidizing atmospheres so that the surfaces, especially the outer surface, were fired to a reddish or brownish colour. Technically the vessels were competently made by coiling, with the coils always well pulled together but with the surfaces only roughly hand-wiped. They would therefore have been porous but perfectly suitable for cooking or for the storage of solids.

The associated fine wares were of two types: haematite-coated scratched-cordoned bowls and other bowls. The haematite-coated vessels were highly competent examples of potting, demonstrating a total control of all the variables. The clay was carefully chosen for its fine-grained quality and was presumably cleaned of detritus before use. The manufacturing process would probably have involved a combination of coiling and slab working. When the form was complete it was carefully worked over with a fine burnishing tool inside and out to close the fabric and it may then have been further smoothed by wiping with a fine-textured material such as leather. After the pot had dried to leather-hardness it was dipped into a ferruginous slip or else painted externally with the slip. The inside was seldom coated but occasionally drips of slip trickled down the inner wall. The vessel would have been allowed to dry once more and may have been given an initial biscuit firing before being given a final burnish. It was probably at this stage that the decoration was scratched onto the surface with a fine point before the vessel was finally fired. The lack of distortion or disfigurement of the surface raises the question of whether the bowls were protected with saggars, but until

a production site is found the problem must remain open. What is clear is that the firing atmosphere was carefully controlled to provide a continuous supply of oxygen so that the haematite in the slip would oxidize to the desired bright red colour. Very occasionally, probably by accident, reducing conditions were created and black vessels resulted.

The other bowls and jars, though finely made, were of a coarser quality. The clay chosen was cleaned of rubbish but appears to have been mixed with a sand temper (unless a naturally sandy clay was selected). Vessels were coil-made, the coils and surfaces being sealed by burnishing. Firing conditions frequently resulted in the vessels being reduced.

Ceramic phases 4–5 saw a number of changes: the very coarse flint-tempered fabrics decreased, haematite-coated bowls ceased to be made, and sandy fabrics became common. A significant number of assemblages have been found in which heavily oxidized, very over-fired, and distorted sherds occur. These could well be wasters from on-site manufacturing, though the alternative view, that the distortions were not the result of poor firing but were caused by a single conflagration, should not be overlooked (fiche 8, frames D5–7).

The later period (ceramic phases 6–7) saw further changes. Two pottery components can be recognized: the local St Catherine's Hill-Worthy Down style assemblage and the Yarnbury-Highfield style deriving from the region south of Salisbury. The local fabrics were now completely uniform, consisting of a well-cleaned clay tempered with finely-crushed burnt flint graded for uniform grit size while the Wiltshire derived fabrics were of even sandy clays sometimes with occasional flint grits added. In both cases these uniform fabrics were used for the full range of ceramic forms.

Vessels were coil-made, the surfaces being extensively burnished inside and out and decorated with motifs lightly impressed with a blunt point of bone or wood when the vessel was leather-hard. Firing, presumably in clamps, aimed at retaining a reducing atmosphere until the pots had cooled. This could have been achieved by packing the clamp with wood chips and other organic material and ensuring that air vents were blocked after the initial stage of firing and before the clamp started to cool. The considerable uniformity in fabric and finish shows that the potters were able to control all the variables to produce the desired effect.

6.5.2   Ceramic phases 8-9

The sample of material from ceramic phases 8 and 9 is small (only 222 sherds) but even so, comparison with pottery of ceramic phase 7 shows a marked change in technology. Most evident is the use of the potter's wheel for forming or finishing the vessels. This has led to a tightening of the profiles, a general sharpening of rim and shoulder angles, and the appearance of horizontal grooves or cordons to zone the body. Many of the basic forms and decorative motifs clearly derive from preceding traditions but the shoulder cordon, upstanding necks, footring bases, and vertical zones of decoration are all techniques introduced into southern Britain from north-western France in the early 1st century BC at the moment when wheel-turning first became apparent in southern Britain. The ceramic revolution brought about by these long distance contacts had far-reaching effects (Cunliffe 1982, 49) but cannot be discussed in detail here.

In terms of the Danebury assemblages, some of the vessels may well be imports from the coastal regions

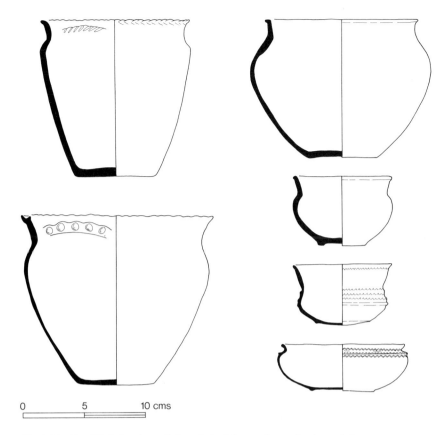

0   5   10 cms

Fig 6.17   Simplified drawings of the principal forms of ceramic phases 1–3

(p 259) but most are of local manufacture. Fabrics are now invariably sandy with little or no flint tempering except in the hand-made vessels which are still found alongside wheel-turned varieties. Decoration, where it occurs, is shallow-tooled as before. Firing procedures were aimed at producing a reducing atmosphere but the harder fabrics suggest that higher temperatures were attained.

Little change can be detected even two or three decades after the Roman conquest except for a general increase in factory-made products emanating from the specialized production centres which sprang up just before and in the wake of the invasion. Since little of this material is found at Danebury detailed discussion of these interesting factors should be reserved for a more appropriate site collection.

6.6   Forms and function

British archaeological literature is strangely reticent concerning the function of the pottery about which so much is otherwise written, largely one suspects because of the lack of tangible evidence. It is, nonetheless, a topic deserving consideration.

The most likely uses to which ceramic containers were put were for the storage, preparation, and serving of food. If we accept that function may be reflected in form, then some indication of use may be gleaned from a consideration of type. Figs 6.17–6.19 summarize the principal types in use respectively in ceramic phases 1–3, 4–5, 6–7, and 8. Viewed in this way perhaps the most striking point is the similarity of form range between each of the phases. The principal components are a variety of large jars of capacity ranging from 1.5 to 12.0 litres and a range of smaller vessels of bowl type usually

more finely finished and frequently decorated. Jars would have served for both storage and cooking. Some vessels show discolouration around the lower parts of the kind which might have been caused by heating over a fire, but since it is not always apparent whether this was caused in the manufacture, or subsequently, the observation cannot be too closely pursued. However, as a generalization, it may be said that the jars of ceramic phases 6–7 show far less discolouration than those of the earlier period and the possibility that cooking now took place more frequently in a metal cauldron should at least be entertained.

The jar forms are divisible into two basic types: those with outflaring rims and those with incurved tops and vestigial rims. The distinction holds good throughout. Vessels with incurved tops would have been suitable for heating liquids since the incurving of the upper part provided a cooler surface upon which condensation could have taken place during gentle simmering. The existence of lids, to prevent evaporation during more violent heating, is problematical; no obvious ceramic lid exists but a disc of wood would have been quite adequate and more durable. The flared-rim jars may possibly have been designed to allow coverings of fabric or skin to be securely attached. Such coverings can be imagined for a range of foods including milk products and meat as well as temporarily stored cereals. Far more rare are large storage jars, the largest with a capacity of *c* 70 litres, presumably designed for long term or bulk storage.

The bowls (including saucepan pots), produced in finer fabrics and often decorated, were probably used for serving food to the individual. Although the forms change with time volumes remain the same at approximately 1000–1300 cc. Vessels of this kind would have served well for fluid food stuffs or for drink; for solid

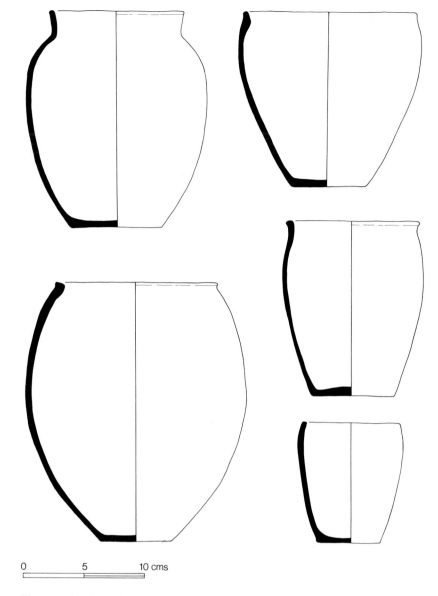

0   5   10 cms

Fig 6.18 Simplified drawings of the principal forms of ceramic phases 4 and 5

food requiring cutting, wooden platters would have been more serviceable.

Open dishes are not particularly common but in ceramic phases 6–7 a range of large shallow dishes makes its appearance. One possible function — as cream settling trays — may hint at an innovation in food preparation. The later pottery of ceramic phases 8 and 9 reflects a change of manners. While the traditional bowl and jar forms continue to be made in quantity a new range of exotic forms including amphorae, platters, and flagons denotes increasing contact with the more highly Romanized continental cultures.

6.7 The distribution of pottery within the fort

There are many questions which can be asked of the spatial distribution of pottery within the fort. Quantification may reflect the presence and absence of rubbish-producing activities and change in the location and intensity of these activities with time, while the percentages of different forms in assemblages may provide an insight into the activity or status differences within the fort. Questions of this type are best approached statisti-

cally and using as large a sample as possible. Detailed assessment will therefore be reserved for the end of the excavation programme when the results of the 1979–84 excavations are available for analysis; any statement made at this stage would be subject to considerable modification. For this reason we present here only a broad idea of the general patterns.

Four maps have been prepared showing, in diagrammatic form, the quantity of pottery found in each pit for ceramic phases 1–3, 4 and 5, 6, and 7–8 (fiche 8, frames C8–12), and in Fig 6.20 a summary of the data has been presented to show the quantity of pottery within each 5 m square based on the site grid system. It should be stressed that the patterns are, to some extent, controlled by the location of pits since all superficial layers within the fort, with the exception of those in the quarry hollows, have been removed by later activity. The pottery from the quarry hollow layers has been omitted because it would have distorted the patterns. Only where rubbish has been 'captured' in a pit is it mapped.

A number of general points emerge:
a There is a considerable increase in sherd loss between cp 1–3 and cp 7–8.

b In the early periods (cp 1–3, 4, and 5), in spite of the very uneven distribution of pits, there is a marked concentration of pottery in the southern part of the fort. Cp 7–8 shows a similar tendency but by this time a considerable quantity of pottery was finding its way into pits in certain parts of the northern zone.

c At no time was the area flanking the central roadway a focus for rubbish loss; in fact the reverse appears to be true.

d There is a progressive directional change in the pattern of rubbish loss with time, ie the cp 4 and 5 pattern is an intermediate stage between the cp 1–3 and cp 6 patterns. However the cp 6 pattern is to some extent complementary to the cp 4 and 5 pattern and appears to show different areas of concentration to the cp 7–8 pattern. These are matters which can be tested statistically. They suggest gradual change except possibly for the change between cp 4 and 5 and cp 6 which may be thought to indicate a possible dislocation.

No attempt has been made at this stage to examine the differential distribution of types or of concentrations of fine and decorated wares. These approaches will form part of the ancillary research carried out as the programme proceeds.

6.8 Regional implications

Although the general development of pottery styles in Wessex is comparatively well known, and our distribution maps of the different styles indicate an impressive number of sites, it is not widely realized how sparse the evidence really is. The majority of sites were either dug so long ago that they are lacking in any adequate stratigraphical control, or the quantity of pottery produced is so limited (less than 1000 sherds) that the sample is too small to warrant statistical treatment. Thus when a large excavation like Danebury produces over 100,000 closely stratified sherds, direct comparison

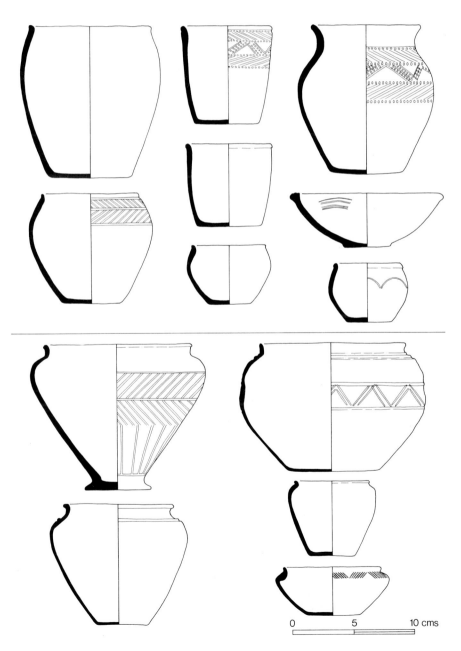

Fig 6.19 Simplified drawings of the principal forms of ceramic phase 7 (above) and ceramic phase 8 (below)

251

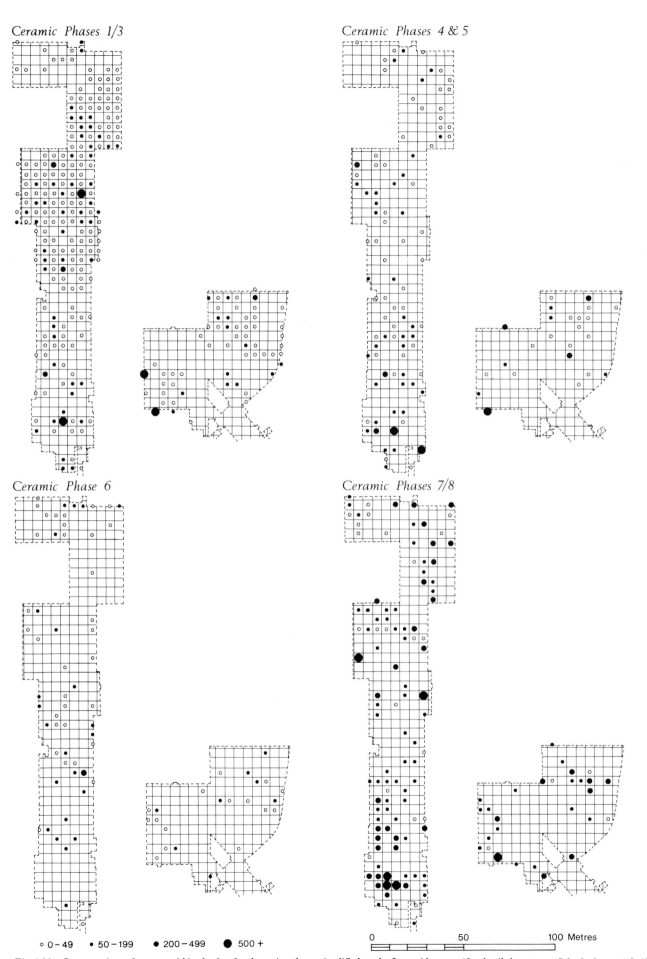

Ceramic Phases 1/3

Ceramic Phases 4 & 5

Ceramic Phase 6

Ceramic Phases 7/8

○ 0 – 49   • 50 – 199   ● 200 – 499   ⬤ 500 +

0   50   100 Metres

Fig 6.20   Concentrations of pottery within the fort for the major phases simplified to the 5 m grid square (for detailed maps see fiche 8, frames C8–12)

between sites becomes difficult and often irrelevant. Nonetheless, certain observations can be made at this stage and other comparisons will become worthwhile as new, or recent, excavations are published. For the purposes of this discussion we have selected four themes for consideration:

a   The earliest Wessex haematite-coated wares
b   The scratched-cordoned bowls and associated fabrics
c   The saucepan pot styles
d   The Atrebatic pottery

6.8.1   The earliest Wessex haematite-coated wares

Elsewhere the present writer has outlined, in general terms, the ceramic development of Wessex in the first half of the 1st millennium BC (Cunliffe 1978, 32–6). To summarize briefly, a distinctive group emerges in the 8th century or even a little earlier, which is characterized by bipartite haematite-coated bowls with furrowed decoration on the upper part of the body and large jars with everted rims decorated with geometric zones of stabbed

DISTRIBUTION OF ALL CANNINGS CROSS STYLE POTTERY

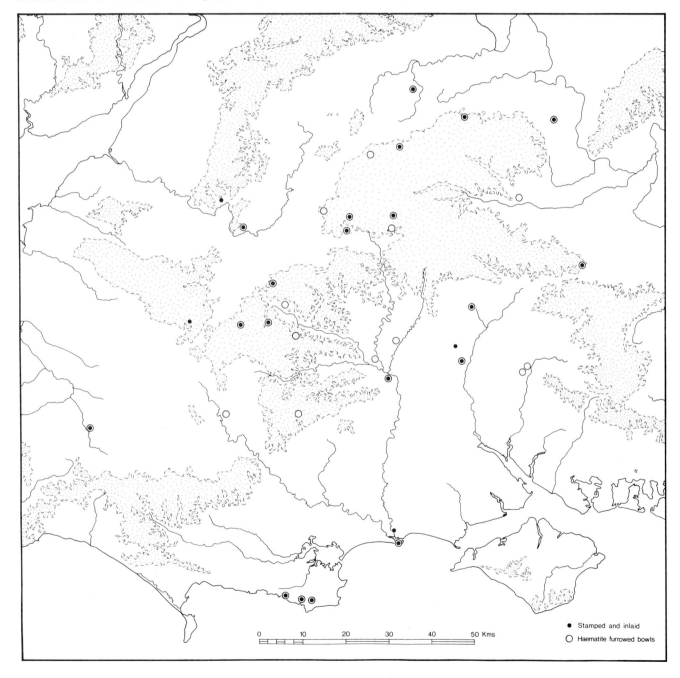

● Stamped and inlaid
○ Haematite furrowed bowls

Fig 6.21   Distribution of All Cannings Cross style pottery (for sites plotted with references see fiche 8, frames D2–3)

or deeply impressed motifs. These types are characteristic of the Early All Cannings Cross group which is thought to have evolved into the Later All Cannings Cross group, the only difference being that the large decorated jars became less common while the furrowed bowls developed flaring rims. The distinction between the two groups is not well defined stratigraphically but since several sites produce only the later styles the division is probably chronologically valid. It is not our purpose here to discuss the problems of this material in any detail but simply to draw attention to its existence as a significant component of the ceramic development of the area and to stress that the distribution spanned the Wessex chalkland as far east as the River Test (Fig 6.21). In other words, Danebury lies within the distribution pattern but towards the eastern limit. Sites in the vicinity of Danebury producing vessels typical of the All Cannings Cross styles include Winchester, Old Down Farm (Andover), and Meon Hill. In the limited excavation at Meon Hill, only 3 km south-east of Danebury, both furrowed bowls and stab decorated jars were found in reasonable quantity though not as a dominant element of the ceramic assemblage.

If Danebury had been occupied in this phase it is reasonable to suppose that some pottery might by now have been recovered from the site. In fact only two sherds of stab decorated jars are known and the furrowed bowls are entirely absent. While it is possible that the nucleus of the early settlement lies in a part of the site so far unexcavated, the present evidence would strongly argue that the hill was unoccupied, the two sherds perhaps being casual loss on an open hilltop. The total absence of the haematite-coated furrowed bowls further shows that there was no significant chronological overlap between them and the later haematite-coated scratched-cordoned bowls which were found in abundance at Danebury. This is a helpful observation when trying to establish chronologies. If, as the radiocarbon dates suggest, the scratched-cordoned bowls belong to the 6th-5th centuries then the All Cannings Cross styles must wholly pre-date them, lying within the 8th-7th century bracket and perhaps even beginning earlier.

A further observation of some potential interest is that vessels of the All Cannings Cross styles are absent from the small collections of material from the neighbouring hillforts of Figsbury, Quarley, and Bury Hill. Although the groups are far too small necessarily to reflect the occupation range of the sites, taken on face value they may suggest that these forts, like Danebury, were unoccupied in the 8th-7th centuries and were probably not built until the 6th.

The position of Balksbury in this pattern is not immediately clear. The large collection of pottery from the excavation of 1967 (Wainwright 1970) does not include the furrowed bowls of All Cannings Cross style nor the later scratched-cordoned bowls but nonetheless has an early appearance. It therefore remains a distinct possibility that it pre-dates the common occurrence of the All Cannings Cross groups.

6.8.2 The scratched-cordoned bowls and associated fabrics

Haematite-coated bowls with scratched decoration are comparatively common in the early phases of Danebury and a number of well-stratified groups allow the associated types to be readily defined. Elsewhere vessels of this type have been described as a late component of a style zone called the All Cannings Cross-Meon Hill style (Cunliffe 1978, 38-40).

Fig 6.22 gives a simple visual impression of the distribution of these characteristic bowls which, we have suggested, were probably made somewhere in the region of Salisbury. Although detailed arguments based on an assessment of absolute figures are meaningless when dealing with such a varied body of data, there is a marked fall off in quantity at the fringes of the distribution as might be expected. At the eastern extremity between the Test and the Itchen only two sherds are recorded, one from Winchester and one from Little Somborne. To the north All Cannings Cross has produced remains of at least twelve vessels, Oldbury two, Martinsell one, and Fyfield Down one. Given the small total sample of pottery from these last two sites the numbers themselves are not significant and it would be fair to assume that the Marlborough Downs was part of the primary receiving area. At the south-west extremity of the distribution the sites of Swallowcliffe, Fifield Bavant, and Winklebury have produced no more than four or five sherds each. Within the core of the distribution region the quantities of vessels recovered reflect the areas of each site excavated. By far the largest number come from Danebury (463); Meon Hill produced 35+, Quarley 20+. The other sites have produced fewer than ten sherds each.

Figures of this kind are not particularly informative. They could be rendered a little more comparable by presenting the numbers as a factor of the area excavated or as a percentage of the total number of sherds recovered but the labour involved in such calculations is hardly likely to justify the results. For this reason sophisticated numerical analyses have not been attempted. It is, however, self-evident that scratched-cordoned bowls were widely distributed over the Wessex chalkdowns from Cranbourne Chase in the south to the Marlborough Downs in the north and from Salisbury Plain to the Test — a distribution pattern which could appear to represent a well-defined social territory.

The impressive coincidence of this distribution with that of the Early and Later All Cannings Cross styles serves to demonstrate a social and economic unity in Wessex over a considerable period of time roughly from the 8th century until the 5th. Broadly defined, the maximum extent of the territory extends from the chalk scarp in the north and west southwards to the Tertiary sands and clays of the Hampshire Basin. The south-western limit would seem to lie in the vicinity of Stour with the River Test or the Test-Itchen zone forming an easterly limit. The implications of this assessment will be further considered below (p 259).

6.8.3 The saucepan pot styles

By the beginning of the 2nd century BC much of central southern Britain had developed assemblages of pottery so similar that we can refer to them as a saucepan pot continuum, after the commonly occurring straight-sided vessel found over a wide geographical area. Within this zone, which stretched across Sussex, Surrey, Hampshire, Wiltshire, Berkshire, and Somerset, regional variation in form and decoration can be detected allowing the definition of a number of distinctive style zones. These have been briefly described and plotted by the writer elsewhere (Cunliffe 1978, 45–7, summarized and modified after Cunliffe 1966). According to this scheme Danebury lies within the distribution pattern of the St Catherine's Hill-Worthy Down style close to the border with the Yarnbury-Highfield style. The detailed analysis of the Danebury assemblage has shown, as might be expected, that while the saucepan pot assemblages (cp 7) contain a majority of types assignable to the St Cather-

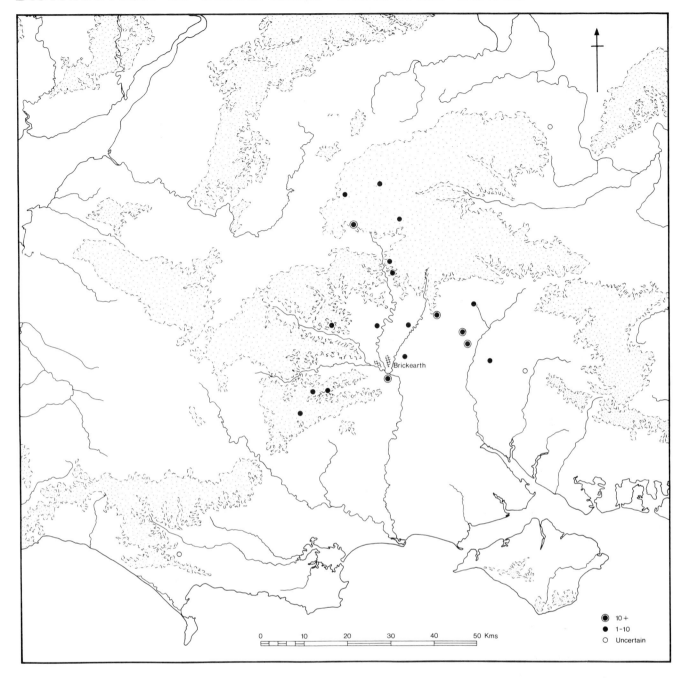

Fig 6.22   Distribution of scratched-cordoned bowls (for sites plotted with references see fiche, 8, frame D1)

ine's Hill-Worthy Down style a number of vessels of the Yarnbury-Highfield style also appear (p 256).

The newly excavated material from Danebury, together with a number of other sites producing smaller quantities of finds, provides the opportunity for a brief considera-tion of the present state of knowledge. Once more, however, we are faced with the disparity of the sample size. Taking the saucepan pot type alone, many of the locations on our distribution maps are represented by no more than five or ten sherds often without good stratigraphical associations; in contrast Danebury has produced 908 vessels from 267 groups sealed in pits and in total 2,510 vessels from 417 stratified contexts. Direct comparison is difficult and simple argument based on

presence and absence of a decorative style may be very misleading. All we can do at present is to offer certain generalizations and await the publication of more groups of comparable size.

If we plot the distribution of the most common and distinctive (even in small sherds) of the motifs of the St Catherine's Hill-Worthy Down style—a horizontal zone of oblique cross-hatching between horizontal rows of dots — a well-defined distribution pattern emerges covering the area from North Bersted in West Sussex to Danebury and from the Solent shore to Theale in the Thames Valley (Fig 6.23A). Although large parts of this region are without contemporary sites (eg the western Weald and most of Berkshire) the pattern is cohesive and

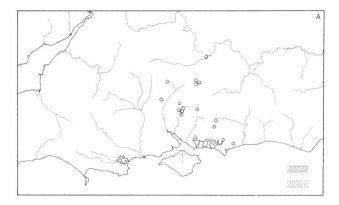

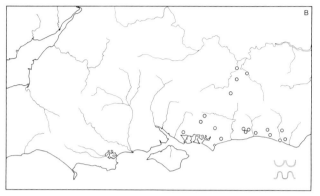

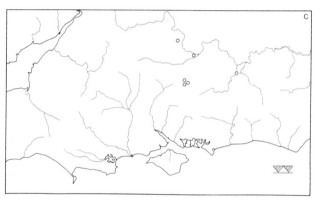

Fig 6.23 Distribution of three different linear tooled motifs on pottery equivalent to ceramic phase 7; sites taken from Fig 6.24 (see caption)

even the outlying sites have produced reasonable numbers of vessels decorated with the distinctive motifs.

The eastern part of this area shows some overlapping of decorative types. In Sussex east of the Adur a local style can be defined (the Caburn-Cissbury style), the characteristics of which are the frequent use of pendent swag motifs and of running curvilinear patterns. Motifs of this kind also recur in several of the assemblages extending for 20–30 km west of the Adur, among groups where the St Catherine's Hill-Worthy Down style is common, and occur on all of the contemporary Surrey sites (the Hawks Hill-West Clandon style) (Fig 6.23B). If we select, from among the running curvilinear patterns, the regular wave motif, it can be shown to be restricted to Surrey and West Sussex west of the Adur.

The northern part of the saucepan pot zone (the Southcot-Blewburton style) has produced comparatively little material but of the decorative motifs, the zone of pendent stroke-filled triangles is a recurring theme. Vessels decorated in this way are found mixed with St

Catherine's Hill-Worthy Down style wares in the Basingstoke region and with Hawks Hill-West Clandon style vessels in Surrey (Fig 6.23C).

Interlocking distribution patterns of distinctive motifs might be expected in a region in which communications were unhindered. What it means in social terms is less easy to determine. At the very least it must imply a degree of easy interchange of ideas, and presumably of goods. How extensive the actual movement of pottery was it is difficult to say; there has been too little petrological analysis (and in any event the fabrics are likely to be too similar for ready distinction into production zones). The impression given by the distribution pattern is of a gradation from one area to the next with no significant boundaries. Eventually it will be possible to quantify these impressions but such an exercise is not yet feasible and we must be content with the generalization. Even so the pattern of gradual change between one style zone and the next is sufficiently clear to suggest the absence of centralized ceramic production. It has been argued (Cunliffe 1983) that this region was divided into small socio-political territories based on hillforts. Such an organization is entirely consistent with the ceramic evidence.

To the west of Danebury another distinctive style zone, the Yarnbury-Highfield style, can be distinguished extending as far south-west as the River Stour but with a few vessels appearing in the large contemporary collection from Maiden Castle 30 km beyond the river (Fig 6.16). Danebury is the only site so far known at which pottery of the Yarnbury-Highfield style and of the St Catherine's Hill-Worthy Down style are found together. Whether this implies that there was little interchange between the two areas or whether it is simply the result of too few sites being found in the overlap zone it is impossible to be sure. The collection is, however, informative since it contains vessels imported from west of the Avon (p 245–6) together with what may well be copies in the local flint-gritted fabrics — a combination which emphasizes Danebury's complex relationship with the Wiltshire area. The cultural and structural similarities between the area of the Yarnbury-Highfield style and the more eastern areas of the saucepan pot continuum would suggest a similar socio-political organization, in which case considerable overlap in pottery styles might be anticipated. The point is emphasized here because in the period during which scratched-cordoned bowls were produced there did seem to be a boundary in the vicinity of the Test valley (p 254). What evidence there is for the later saucepan pot phase tends to suggest that no such boundary now survived. Instead it seems that there was a broad zone of convergent development, without major boundaries, stretching from Beachy Head westwards to the Bristol Channel and Cotswolds and northwards into the Welsh borderland (Fig 6.24).

6.8.4 The Atrebatic pottery

After the end of intensive occupation at Danebury two phases of limited reuse were distinguished on the basis of stratigraphy and of ceramic typology. Of these the earliest (cp 8) dates to the early 1st century BC. Although this assemblage shows a considerable improvement in ceramic technology (p 247) its basic forms and decorative motifs still owe much to the preceding local traditions. The style has been referred to as Atrebatic (Cunliffe 1978, 97–100) and several regional variations have been identified. The Danebury assemblage belongs to the hybrid group, most conveniently referred to as Northern and Southern Atrebatic ware, which is distri-

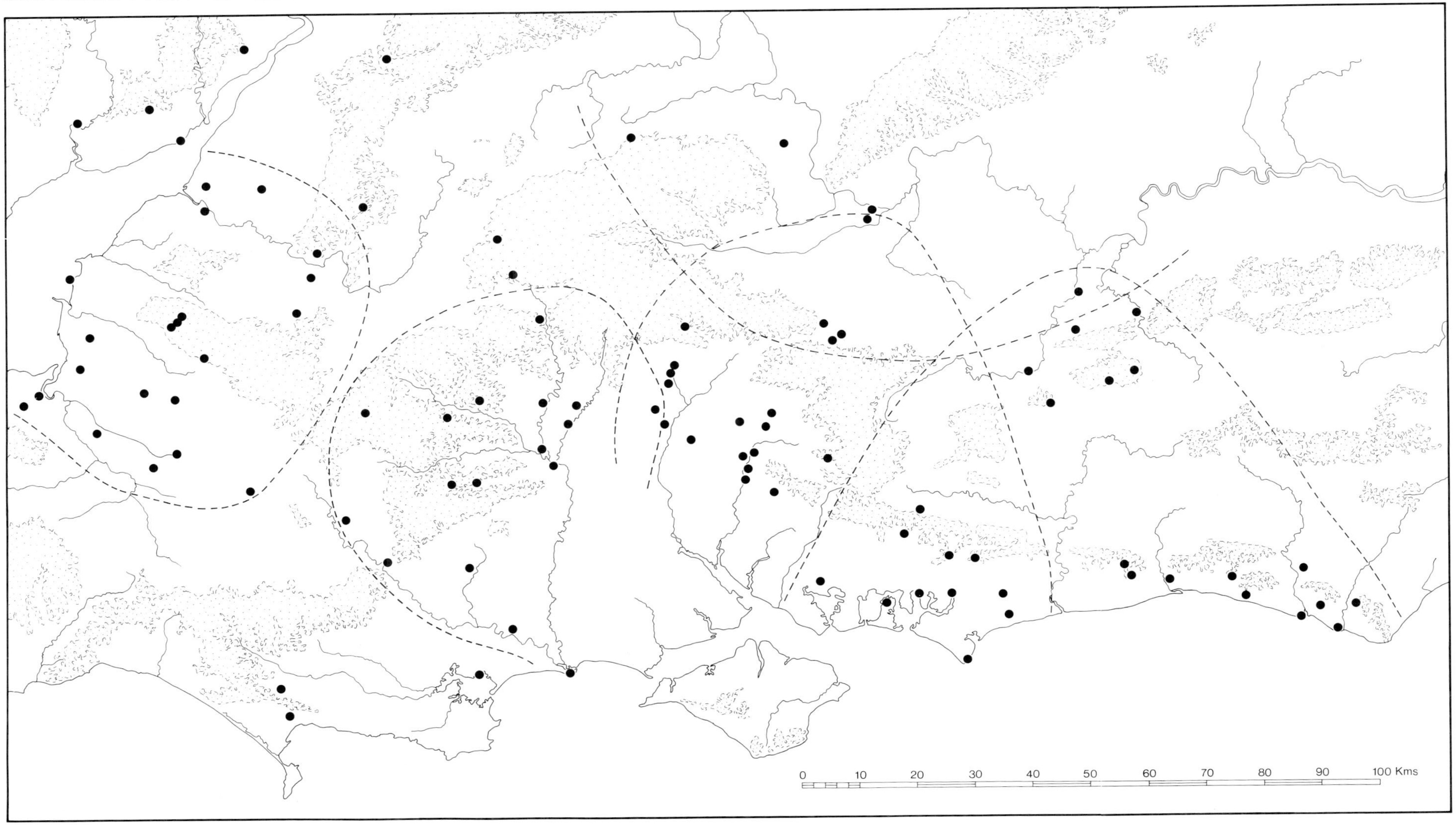

Fig 6.24 *Distribution of sites producing pottery of the 'saucepan pot continuum'. The broken lines indicate the approximate limits of distributions of distinctive decorative motifs (see Fig 6.23; for a list of the sites with references see fiche 8, frame D4)*

100 Kms

buted widely from the Salisbury Plain to the River Adur. The geographical extent is almost coincident with that of the earlier Yarnbury-Highfield, St Catherine's Hill-Worthy Down, and Hawks Hill-West Clandon styles with the significant exception that much of Cranborne Chase now seems to lie within the range of pottery of Durotrigan type produced in the region of Poole Harbour (Cunliffe 1978, fig 7:2). It is tempting to argue that this reorientation reflects changes consequent upon the establishment of long-distance trade among which the emergence of the Durotriges as a coin-using tribal entity is a significant factor. In all probability this is little more than the formalization of a cultural divide which existed in the vicinity of the Stour valley in the preceding saucepan pot phase (3rd-2nd century) and is possibly reflected in the even earlier distribution of the scratched-cordoned bowls. That the Cranborne Chase sites now produce pottery of Durotrigan type may hint that the boundary had shifted northwards to Ebble-Nadder ridge.

Although Danebury lies well within the Atrebatic style zone, links with the Durotrigan area are manifest in the Dressel 1 amphorae, imported from the coastal ports, a single Durotrigan coin, and a few vessels of fabrics similar to those from the manufacturing centres of the Poole Harbour region.

The Atrebatic forms continued to be made with increasing skill until several decades after the Roman conquest.

6.9 Other approaches to analysis

The large volume of stratified pottery from Danebury offers considerable scope for analysis. A number of approaches directly relevant to an understanding of the site and its socio-economic systems have been presented above. These, we believe, represent the minimum it is necessary to offer in the context of an excavation report; beyond this we are in the realms of pure research which could not be justified in a publication of this kind.

There are many studies which commend themselves. The sample is large enough to allow questions of the standardization of shape and volume to be approached; a sufficient number of decorated vessels now exists to make it possible to search for different techniques of applying decoration in the hope of being able to define the styles of individual craftsmen; while quantitative studies may well enable us to define rubbish assemblages of varying types reflecting on the function or status of different regions within the fort. These questions, and many others, are for the future; they form part of the continuing research programme which the ceramic data bank makes possible, and will be published in subsequent studies.

6.10 Summary

In the preceding pages we have explored a number of aspects of the ceramic assemblage from Danebury, in terms of the pottery itself, in relation to the site, and in a broader regional context. Here it only remains to offer a brief summary of the results obtained so far.

6.10.1 Sequence

Dividing the pottery into ceramic phases has proved to be a valid and useful procedure. It is an approach which has much to commend it when dealing with large quantities of well-stratified prehistoric material. At Danebury the analysis strongly supports the view that the major occupation of the site spanned the period 550–100 BC, during which time there were no recogniz-

able breaks in the ceramic sequence. In the following century and a half, occupation was much less intense and may well have been sporadic. The virtual absence of pottery of All Cannings Cross type (with the exception of two sherds), and its presence nearby at Old Down Farm and Meon Hill, is a strong indication that the hill was unoccupied at this time. Occupation began at Danebury towards the middle of the 6th century as indeed it appears to have done at the neighbouring forts of Figsbury and Quarley (though from both the evidence is far less sound).

The validity of the individual ceramic phases was examined in a variety of ways. The earliest phases have been treated together as a composite, ie cps 1–3. This is thought to be advisable because, although the characteristic pottery by which cps 1 and 2 is defined is absent from all groups, coarse wares, which *could* be early, occur. In all probability these coarse wares were made and used in cp 3 but the possibility that some of the pits without scratched-cordoned bowls could pre-date the appearance of these bowls must be allowed.

Ceramic phases 4 and 5 present problems. While they are clearly distinct from cps 3 and 6, the validity of the division between 3 and 4, and 4 and 5, is in doubt (for further comment see fiche 8, frame D5). The sample of material from the excavations of 1969–78 is too small to analyse in detail but the problem will be considered again in relation to the additional finds from the excavations of 1979 onwards. In reality what we are discussing are minor changes in assemblages over a period of a century or so. At present it would be advisable to consider cp 4 and 5 contexts together.

Fabric changes emphasize a major change between cp 4–5 and cp 6 but typological considerations offer no evidence of a significant dislocation. The problem is, however, of some interest and has been considered in final discussion (p 549).

Ceramic phases 6 and 7 were divided arbitrarily by the criterion of decoration (forms and fabrics are the same but decoration is characteristic of cp 7). Various analyses support the division but the radiocarbon series shows, what we may reasonably have guessed, that while the integrity of cp 6 is valid some assemblages assigned to cp 6 are likely to date to cp 7 but have no associated decorated sherds. The problem posed is insuperable — all we can do is to recognize its existence.

The change from cp 7 to 8, somewhere c 100–80 BC, raises questions of considerable interest. It is well defined typologically, technologically, and stratigraphically but the sample of cp 8 material is, so far, too small to allow the inherent possibilities to be pursued in detail. There is a strong element of continuity in form and decoration but links with the coastal contact zone have introduced new techniques of manufacture and alien ideas influencing form. It is at this stage that imported amphorae make their appearance.

Ceramic phase 9 is very poorly represented in the material recovered from the excavations of 1969–78 and is restricted to a few unstratified sherds in the topsoil and a small collection from the upper filling of the outer hornwork ditch. Given this evidence one might reasonably have suggested that the site was abandoned and only sporadically visited. However the excavation of 1979 produced several stratified assemblages of cp 9 types together with associated structural features, but so localized as to suggest occupation of limited spatial extent. These matters will be considered in subsequent volumes.

In summary therefore the pottery suggests continuous

occupation over half a millennium c 550–c 50 BC and may crudely be divided into early (cp 1–3), middle (cp 4–5), two late phases (cp 6 and cp 7), and latest (cp 8). What followed was subsequent reoccupation.

6.10.2   Sources of supply

The vast bulk of the pottery throughout the occupation was locally produced, but precisely where remains a problem. On-site manufacture cannot be ruled out; indeed, the presence of clay-mixing pits might be thought to strengthen the possibility. It is even possible that some of the over-fired vessels of cp 4–5 are wasters (but there are problems of interpretation: fiche 8, frames D5–7). There seems, however, to have been a steady supply of vessels from Wiltshire, first (in cp 1–3) haematite-coated scratched-cordoned bowls, probably from just north of Salisbury, and later (in cp 7) decorated vessels possibly from the Nadder valley. Some of the sandy fabrics of cp 4–6 may well have come from the same areas. Pottery from further afield is very restricted, the only distinctive types being a few scraps with oolitic limestone tempering and a few sherds of Glastonbury-style vessels. In cp 8 links with the coastal contact zone, centred on the Poole Harbour-Hengistbury region, became apparent in the form of imported coarse wares and amphorae. Related technological changes suggest that a major realignment was now forming, but the sample is too small to allow further examination of this interesting possibility.

6.10.3   Social implications

It would be tempting to suggest that the high percentage of haematite-coated fine wares in the early period and the equally high percentage of decorated wares in the later period are indicative of the high status of the site. This may be, but without formal comparison between Danebury and neighbouring settlements of smaller size the matter remains unproven. The ancillary research necessary to test the point is now in hand and the results will be published in a subsequent volume. Comparisons between zones within the fort have not been made at this stage but will form part of the analysis related to the publication of the excavations of 1979–1984.

6.10.4   Regional implications

From a general consideration of ceramic development in southern Britain, Danebury emerges as being on a border between the distribution patterns centring on central Wessex and those of Hampshire, the divide being the interfluve between the Rivers Bourne and Test. This is true of the distribution of All Cannings Cross styles, of scratched-cordoned bowls, and, later, of the various saucepan pot styles. In cp 1–3 the high percentage of scratched-cordoned bowls from Wiltshire at Danebury and Meon Hill strongly suggests that sites west of the Test were in the primary distribution area of these products, and hints that the Test may have been a significant divide. By the time of cp 7 the bulk of the Danebury decorated wares is of eastern type (St Catherine's Hill-Worthy Down style) as is that of neighbouring sites. Only a few of the contemporary Wiltshire types (Yarnbury-Highfield style) reach Danebury and are very rare on other sites nearby. It would be tempting to see this as a change in the fort's social territory, a change which may be linked to the rise in dominance of the fort from cp 6 onwards. These interesting questions are considered in a broader context below (p 562). The changes, reflected in the cp 8 assemblage, are part of a massive system of social and economic readjustment consequent upon the development of long-distance trade (Cunliffe 1982).

The 100,000 sherds of stratified pottery from the first ten years of excavation hold a considerable potential which we are just beginning to realize.

Appendix 1:   the ceramic forms described and illustrated

Some general remarks about the principles of classification adopted here have already been offered above (section 6.2). Simply stated, the assemblage has been divided into four basic *classes*: jars (J), bowls (B), dishes (D), and saucepan pots (P). Each class is divided into a number of *types*, each type into several *forms*, and each form into *varieties*. The full list is set out in Table 34. Thus from Danebury there are 4 classes, 13 types, 33 forms, and 49 varieties.

To present the material, each of the varieties is illustrated by at least one vessel but where a large body of material is available a number of vessels have been chosen in order to indicate the range of tolerance allowed within our definition. The accompanying text highlights the strengths and weaknesses of each classification and provides a range of basic statistical data. An indication is given where subdivision into further varieties seems possible. The scheme is capable of expansion in various directions.

The figures given for each form represent the total number of recognizable sherds in each fabric assignable to that form.

Jars

The height usually exceeds the maximum diameter (but see JA1.1); rim diameters are usually less than maximum body diameters. Precise adherence to these generalizations is not always possible when dealing with sherd material.

Four basic types are recognized:

JA Bipartite with maximum girth at the shoulder above which the upper part of the body slopes evenly inwards. The type is uncommon.

JB Tripartite with the profile divisible into three distinct zones, body, shoulder, and rim. The angle between body and shoulder may be rounded or sharp; the angle between the shoulder and rim may be rounded or sharp. The rim may be upstanding or flared outwards. Rim tops may sometimes be decorated with finger moulding.

JC Essentially bipartite but the body curves evenly through the shoulder to the rim. The rim diameter is always less than the shoulder diameter but the degree of curve on the shoulder varies. Rim tops are frequently beaded. In small sherds it is occasionally difficult to distinguish some JB forms from JA forms. Similarly with sherds it is not always possible to say whether a vessel is a JC type or a BC type; judgment has been used but when in real doubt the vessel has been assigned to JC.

JD Tripartite type with body and shoulder evenly curved and with the rim curved sharply outwards. The descriptive phrase 'S–profile' has sometimes been used for vessels of this type. Distinction between some JD and JB types may be uncertain in small sherds.

JE General category to include wheel-turned jars with necks or sharply moulded out-turned rims.

259

Table 34

Jars (class J)			Bowls (class B)			Dishes (class D)			Saucepan pots (class P)		
type	form	variety	type	form	variety	type	form	variety	type	form	variety
A	1	.1	A	1	.1	A	1	.1	A	1	.1
	2	.1			.2			.2			.2
B	1	.1		2	.1		2	.1		2	.1
		.2			.2	B	1	.1		3	.1
	2	.1			.3		2	.1	B	1	.1
		.2	B	1	.1		3	.1			.2
		.3			.2						
	3	.1		2	.1						
	4	.1		3	.1						
C	1	.1			.2						
	2	.1	C	1	.1						
		.2		2	.1						
	3	.1	D	[1	.1]						
		.2		2	.1						
D	1	.1		[3	.1]						
	2	.1		4	.1						
		.2		[5	.1]						
	3	.1		6	.1						
		.2									
		.3									
	[4]										
	5	.1									
E	1	.1									
	2	.1									
	3	.1	at Danebury E1/4 classification only used								
	4	.1									

Categories relevant only to Hengistbury are included in square brackets

JA I [·1]

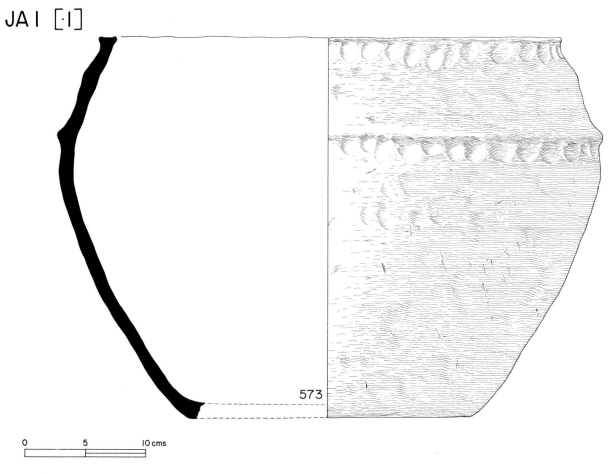

573

0   5   10 cms

Fig 6.25

Jar type JA

Form JA1 (one variety only) (Fig 6.25)
Large bipartite jar with evenly curved profile but with shoulder angle emphasized by finger impressions pushing up a rough cordon. Similar finger impressions below the rim give the rim top a slight outward projection.
Fabrics: A (34); D (43). Ceramic phases 1–3.

Form JA2 (one variety only) (Fig 6.25)
Exact body shape uncertain but possibly similar to JA1. Differs from JA1 in that the rim top is expanded inwards at right-angles in 'hammer-head' form.
Fabrics: A (6); C (16); D (4). Ceramic phases 1–3?

Jar type JB

Form JB1 (two varieties) (Figs 6.26, 6.27)
The basic form is a high shouldered jar with slightly flaring rim and with some form of moulding on the rim top, usually finger-tip or finger-nail decoration but occasionally shallow-tooled impressions (eg vessel 713). Division into two varieties is to some extent arbitrary but form JB1.1 is larger than JB1.2 and the finger impressions on the rim top are more pronounced causing the rim top to expand outwards. The surface often shows evidence of wiping.
Fabrics: A (399); B (433); C (35); D (1474); E (1). Ceramic phases 1–3.

Form JB2 (three varieties) (Figs 6.28-6.31)
Shouldered jars with upstanding or slightly everted rims. The rim tops are usually flattened but there is no finger-tip decoration. The form type encompasses a wide range of vessel shapes and finishes but these may be divided into three broad groupings. Form JB2.1 is squatter than the other varieties and therefore of more bulbous shape with height equal to or less than maximum diameter. Form JB2.2 is taller with height always greater than maximum diameter. The rim may be upright or flared. The distinction between these two varieties is to some extent arbitrary since one variety merges with another and in small sherds it is usually impossible to be sure which variety is represented. In this case the sherd will be categorized JB2.0. The range of profiles accepted can be judged from the illustrations; further subdivision while possible does not seem to be worthwhile. The variety JB2.3 is used to contain smaller, more thickly-made vessels, again showing a variety of profiles. Vessel 739 could well be put in one of the Bowl categories but its fabric and style of manufacture make it close to others in JB2.3. Fabrics: A (288); B (141); C (183); D (686); E (11). Ceramic phases 3–4.

Form JB3 (one variety) (Figs 6.32, 6.33)
Large jars with rounded profiles and upstanding or slightly everted necks. The rim tops are usually squared and sometimes hollowed slightly on the inside. The vessels are usually more carefully made than form JB2 and the surfaces are usually smoothed or burnished. There is a degree of gradation between JB2 and JB3 types but the quality of the finish is usually a distinguishing factor.
Fabrics: A (1); B (36); D (60). Ceramic phases 3–4.

Form JB4 (one variety) (Fig 6.34)
Large barrel-shaped jars without much emphasis on the shoulder. The fabrics are usually fairly coarse and sandy and the external surfaces are wiped or roughly burnished. Although the shapes grade between JB3 and JC3 the fabrics and surface finishes are usually decisive.

Fabrics: A (121); B (103); C (1); D (703). Ceramic phases 4–5.

Jar type JC

Form JC1 (one variety) (Figs 6.35, 6.36)
Large barrel-shaped storage jars with flattened rim tops, the rims being sometimes slightly upstanding. There is some variation in form particularly in the degree of roundness of the barrel shape and clearly subdivision is possible. Fabrics are usually sandy and the surfaces are usually smoothed or roughly burnished.
Fabrics: A (37); B (497); C (86); D (214). Ceramic phases 4–5.

Form JC2 (three varieties) (Figs 6.37–6.42)
Jars of varying sizes, with rounded profiles but distinct high shoulders. The mouth is slightly narrower than the shoulder diameter. The rims are usually slightly thickened and rolled outwards to form a proto-bead rim. There is a considerable variation within these limits but three basic varieties have been distinguished. Form JC2.1 is a large jar form of height greater than its maximum diameter and with base considerably less in diameter than the rim. Form JC2.2 is rather more barrel-shaped with base diameter less but not much less than rim diameter; in other words it is more open at the top than JC2.1. Form JC2.3 is a smaller jar than JC2.1 and JC2.2 but covers the shape range of both. There is overlap between all three varieties and when real doubt exists the JC2.0 grouping is used. There is also a gradation between JC2.3, BC1, BC2, and PB1 but JC2.3 tends to be more barrel-shaped. Strict metrical rules could be laid down to distinguish between the varieties but since, to be of value, complete profiles would be required, and these are seldom found, the more subjective sorting is the only practicable method. Surfaces are usually highly burnished and zones of shallow-tooled decoration are not uncommon around the upper part of the vessels.
Fabrics: A (57); B (1757); C (31); D (857); E (2); F (6); G (1). Ceramic phases 5–7.

Form JC3 (two varieties) (Figs 6.43, 6.44)
High-shouldered jars with short upstanding or beaded rims. The range of shapes is similar to JC2 but the JC3 forms are wheel-made or wheel-finished in a hard sandy fabric. Two varieties have been recognized here to distinguish between the deeper jars with beaded rims (JC3.1) and the wide high-shouldered type with a more upstanding rim (JC3.2). Form JC3.2 could have been classed as a bowl type but since the distinction between JC3.1 and JC3.2 is often difficult to make when dealing only with sherds it is preferable to keep them close together in the classificatory scheme. Some have zones of shallow-tooled decoration on the shoulder.
Fabrics: B (107); C (24); D (322). Ceramic phase 8.

Jar type JD

Form JD1 (one variety) (Fig 6.45)
Globular shaped jar with gently outcurving rim. Distinguished from JB3 which has a sharper demarcation between the rim and the rest of the body. JB4 is also similar but JD1 has a more gentle S–shaped profile. Smoothed or burnished surface in sandy fabrics.
Fabric: D (87). Ceramic phases 4–6.

Form JD2 (two varieties) (Fig 6.46)
Shouldered or globular jars with gently outcurving rims and pedestal or footring bases. It is virtually impossible

JBI [·1]

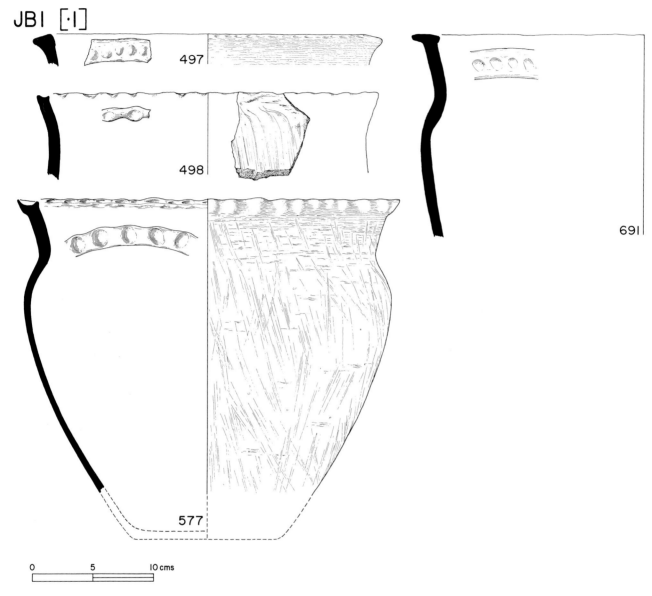

497

498

691

577

0   5   10 cms

Fig 6.26

JB1 [·2]

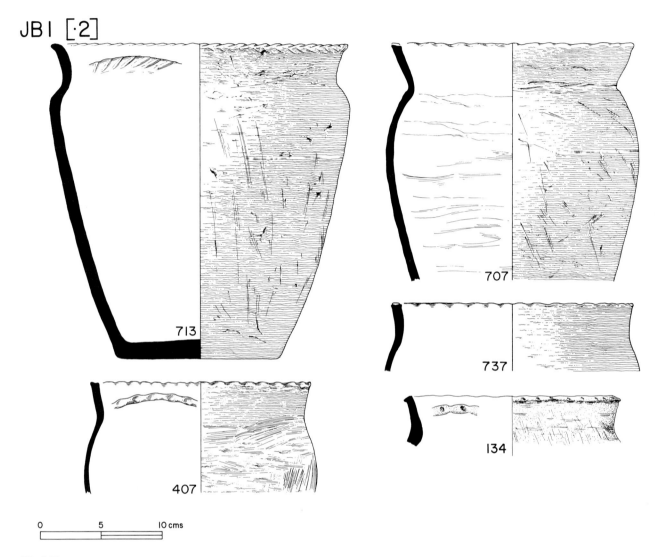

713

707

737

407

134

0   5   10 cms

Fig 6.27

JB 2 [·1]

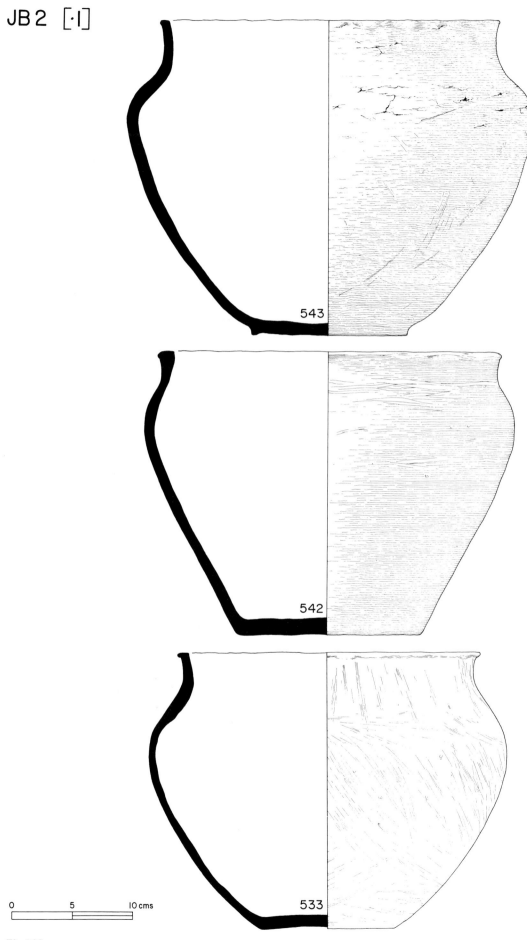

543

542

533

0   5   10 cms

Fig 6.28

264

JB2 [·2]

455

425

171

712

594

682

0   5   10 cms

Fig 6.29

265

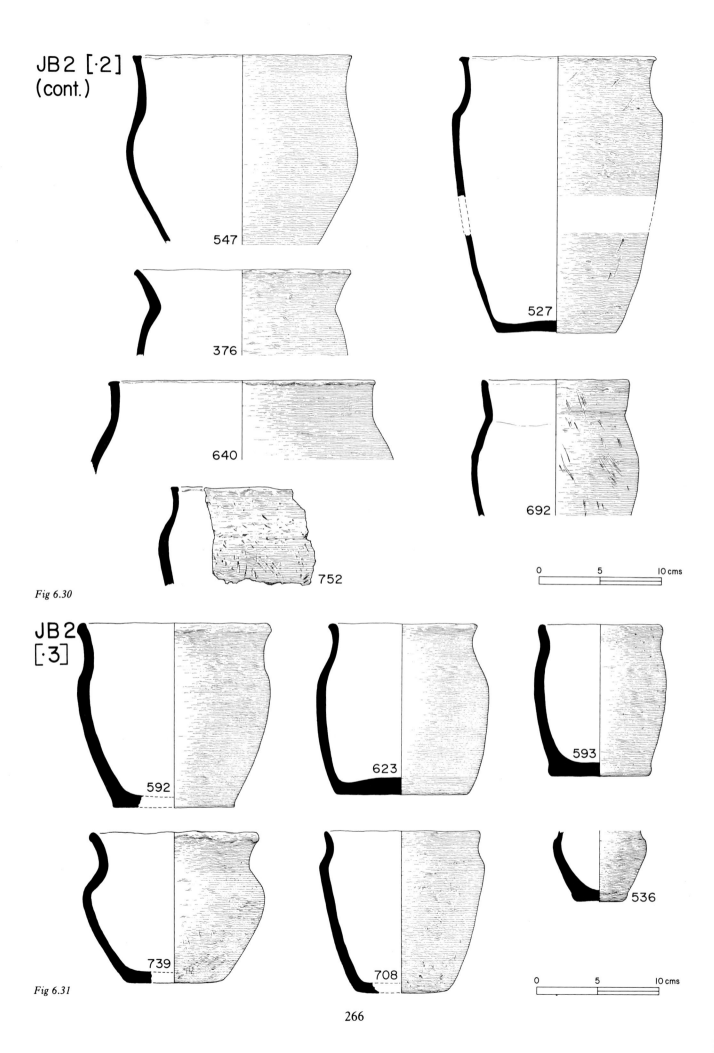

JB 2 [·2]
(cont.)

547

376

640

752

527

692

Fig 6.30

JB 2
[·3]

592

623

593

739

708

536

Fig 6.31

0   5   10 cms

JB3 [·1]

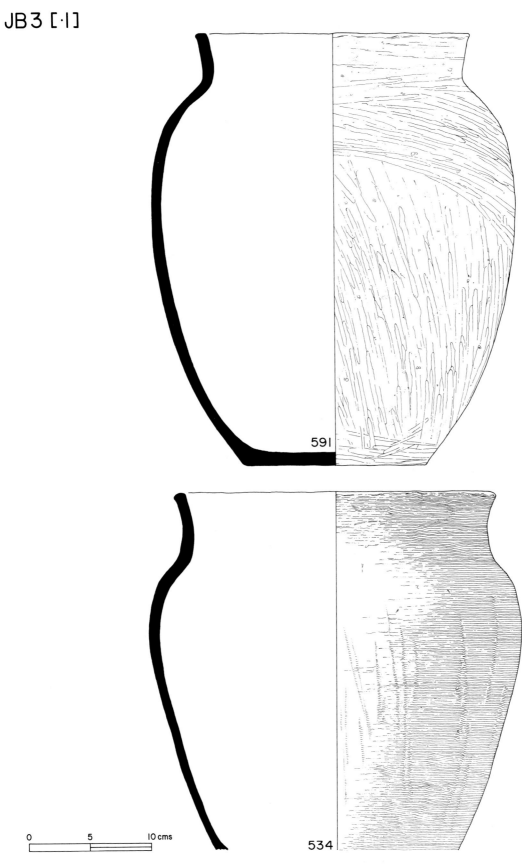

591

534

0   5   10 cms

Fig 6.32

267

JB3 [·1] (cont.)

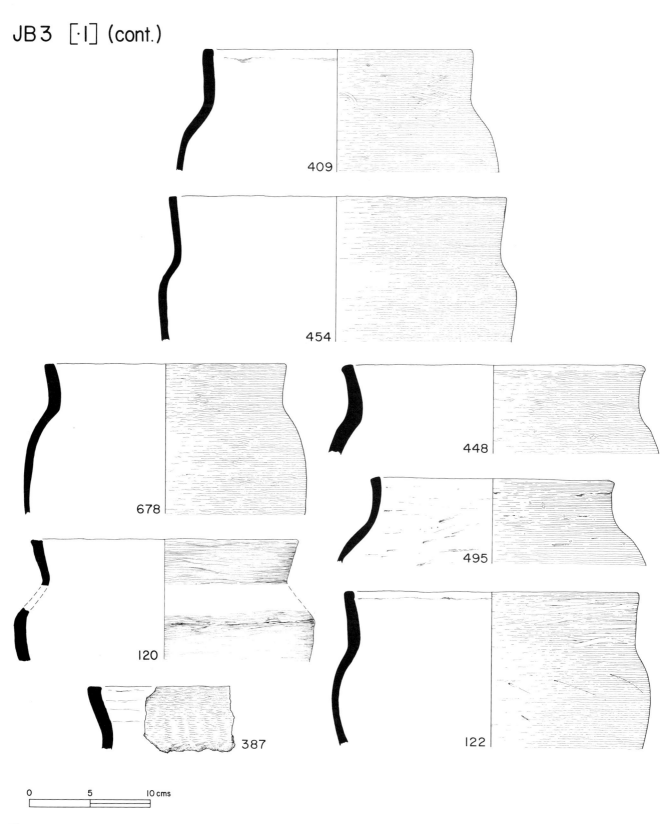

409

454

678

448

495

120

387

122

0   5   10 cms

Fig 6.33

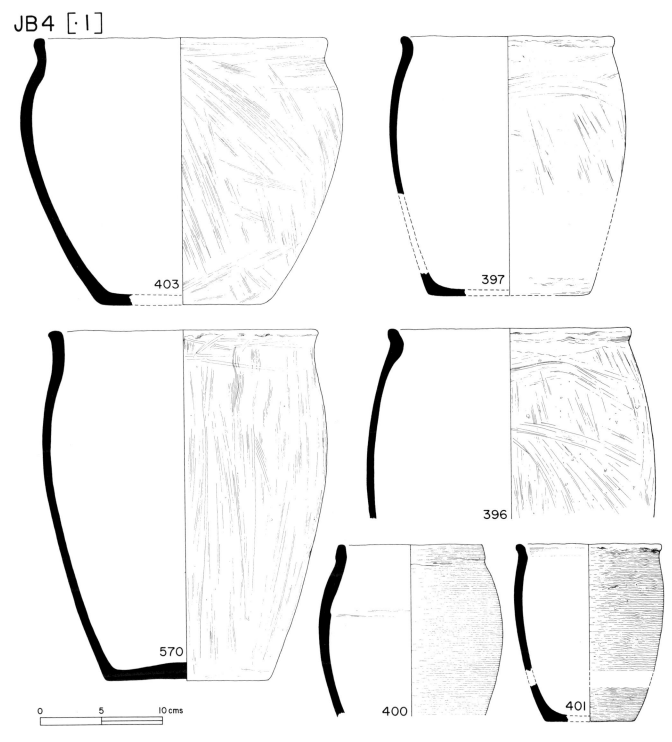

JB 4 [·1]

403

397

570

396

400

401

0   5   10 cms

Fig 6.34

JC 1 [·1]

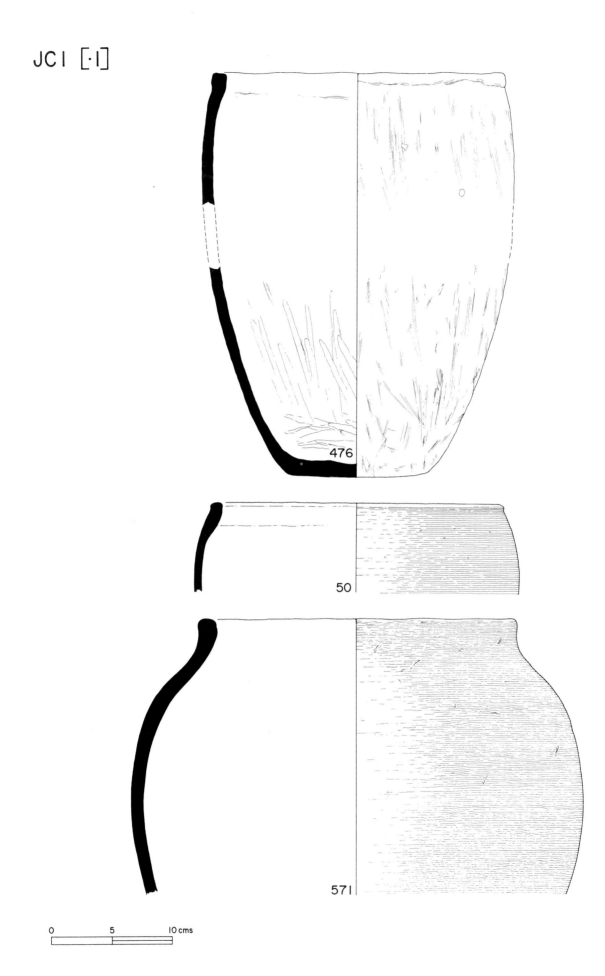

Fig 6.35

JC I [·I] (cont.)

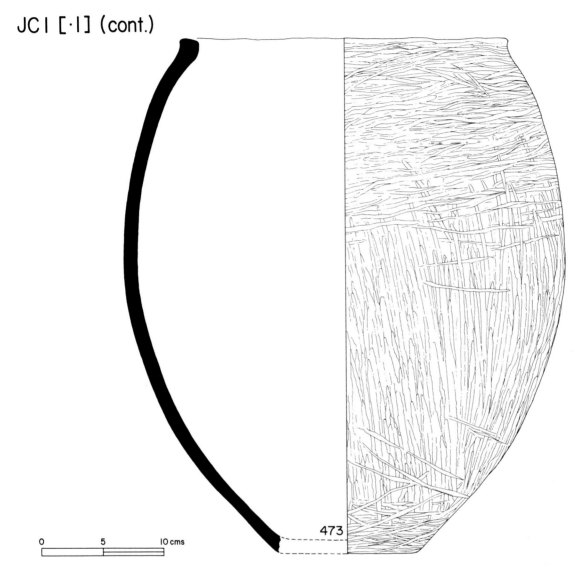

473

0   5   10 cms

Fig 6.36

271

JC 2 [·1]

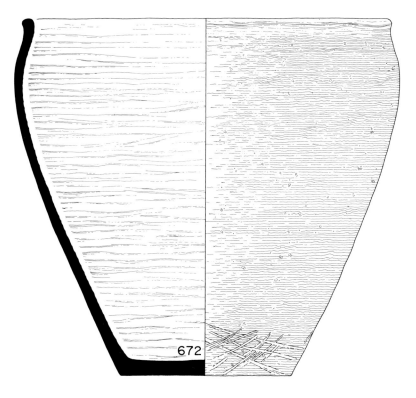

672

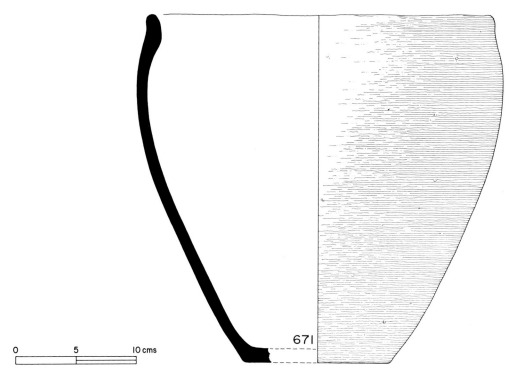

671

0   5   10 cms

Fig 6.37

272

JC 2 [·1] (cont.)

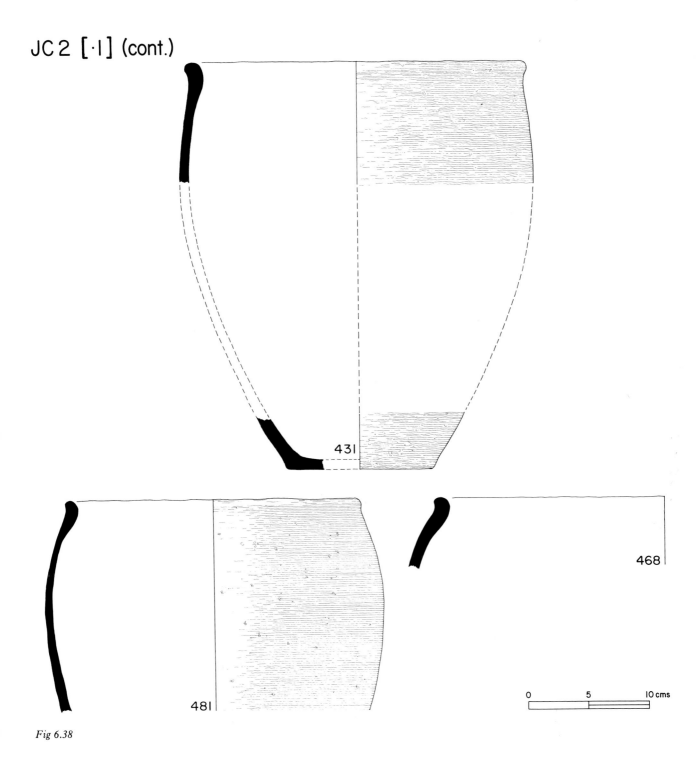

Fig 6.38

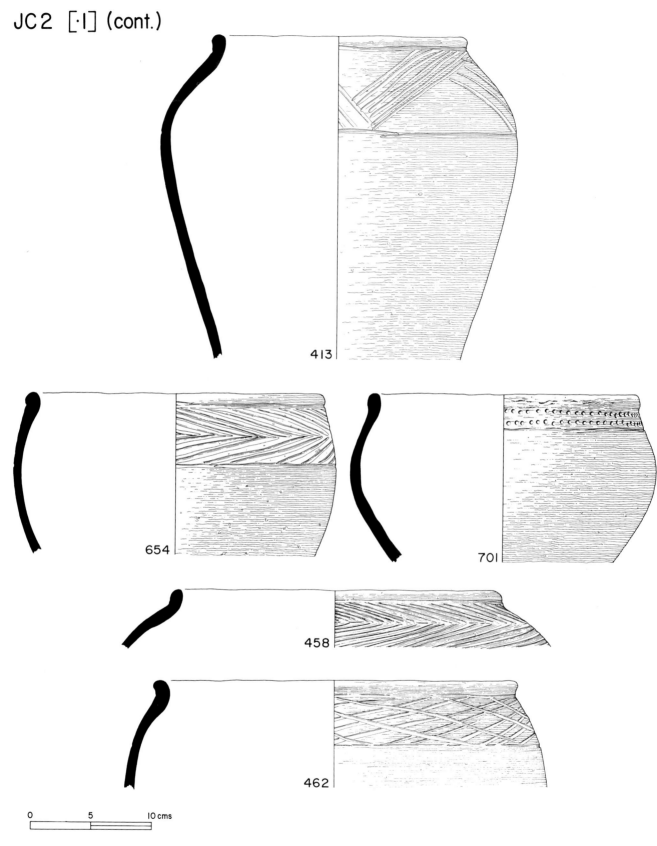

413

654

701

458

462

0   5   10 cms

Fig 6.39

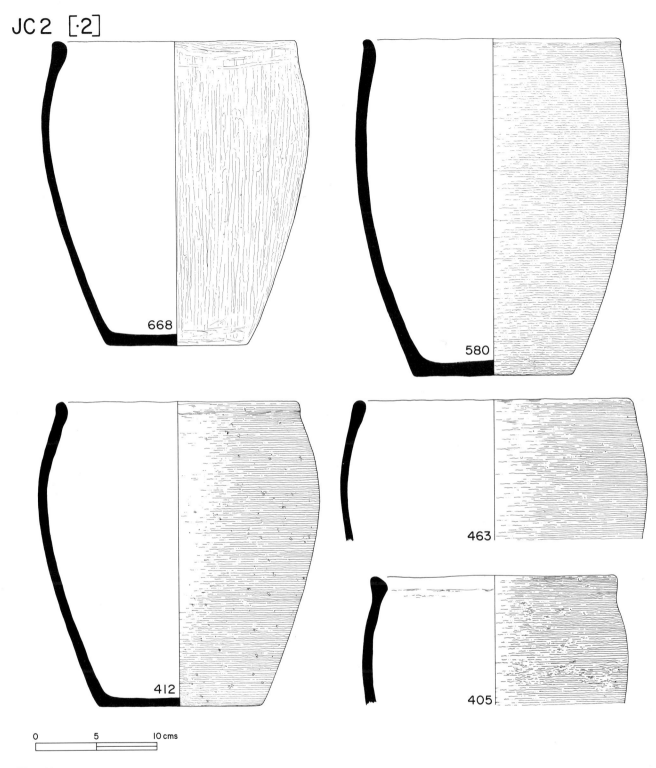

JC 2 [·2]

668

580

412

463

405

0   5   10 cms

Fig 6.40

275

JC 2 [·3]

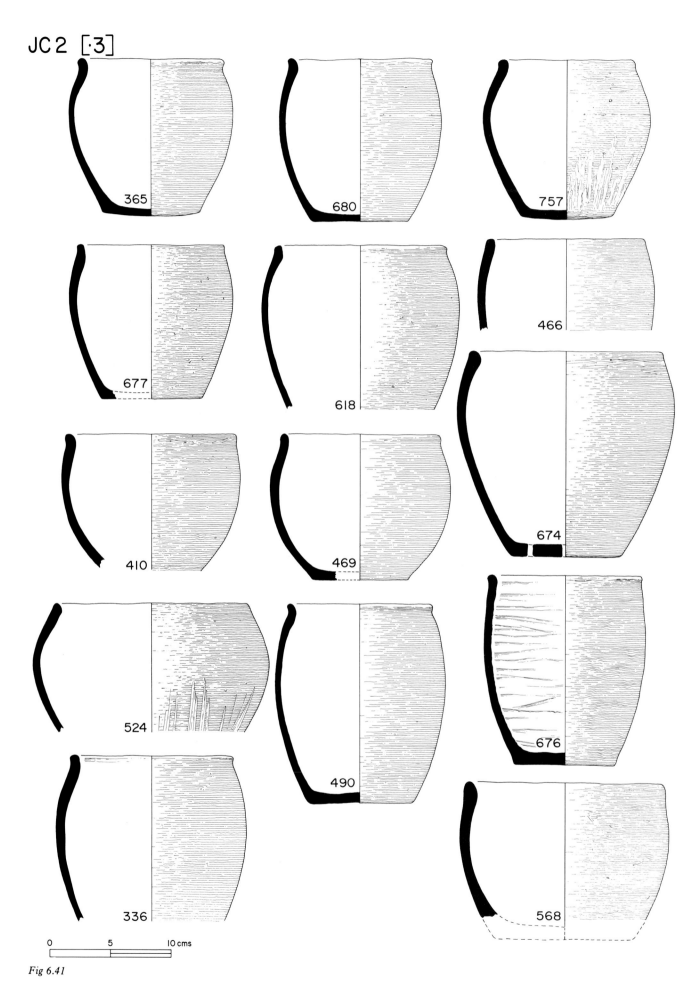

365

680

757

677

618

466

410

469

674

524

490

676

336

568

0   5   10 cms

Fig 6.41

276

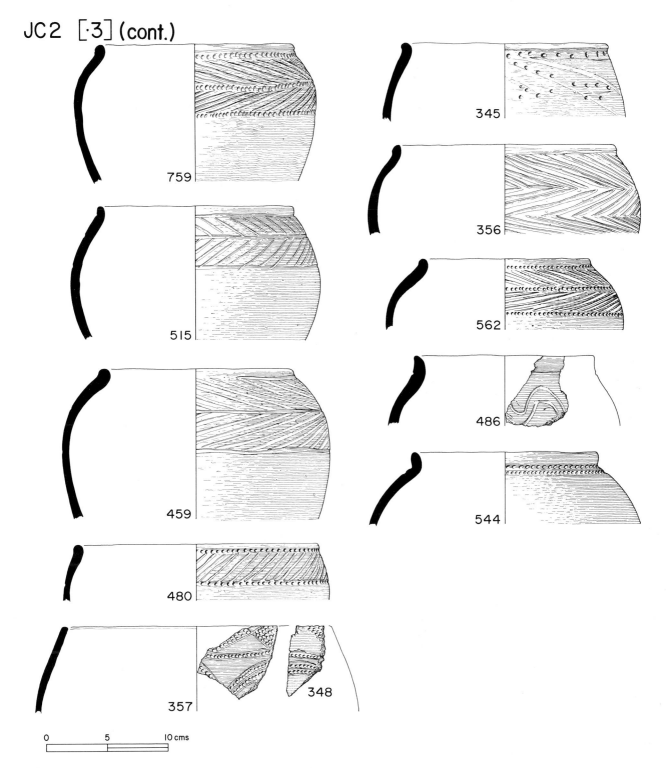

759

515

459

480

357 348

345

356

562

486

544

0 5 10 cms

Fig 6.42

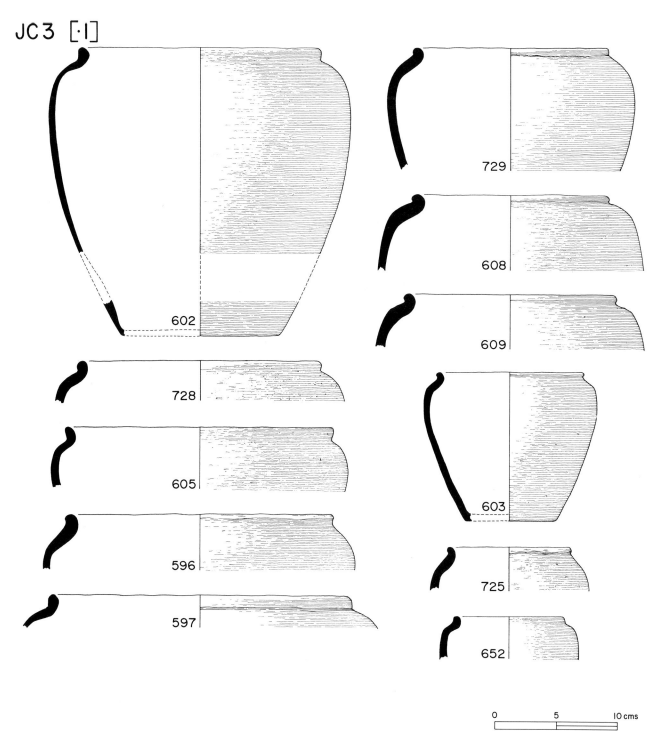

JC 3 [·1]

602

729

608

609

728

605

596

603

597

725

652

0   5   10 cms

Fig 6.43

278

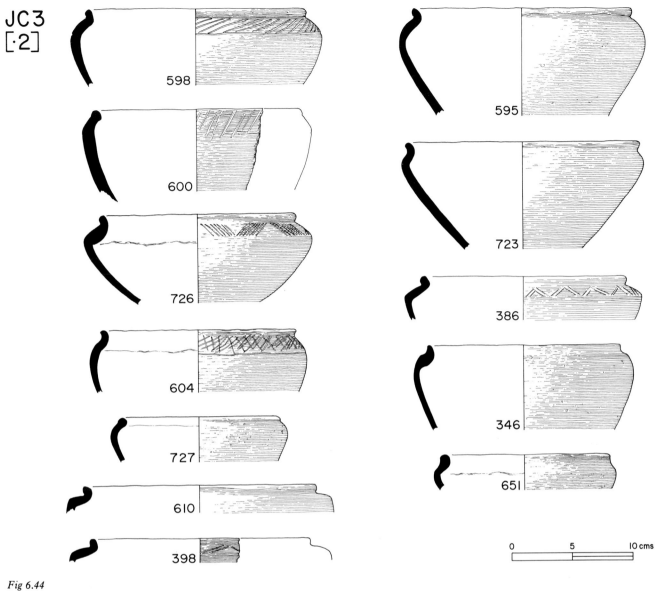

JC3
[·2]

598

600

726

604

727

610

398

595

723

386

346

651

0   5   10 cms

Fig 6.44

JD1 [·1]

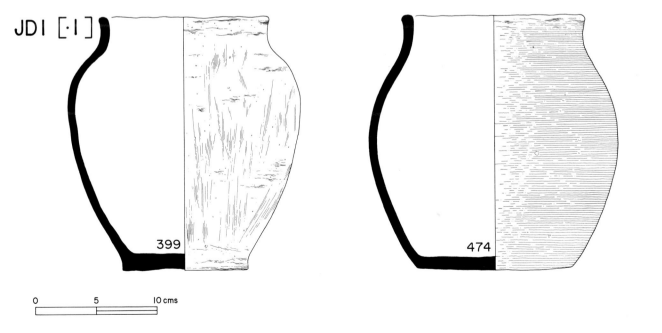

399

474

0   5   10 cms

Fig 6.45

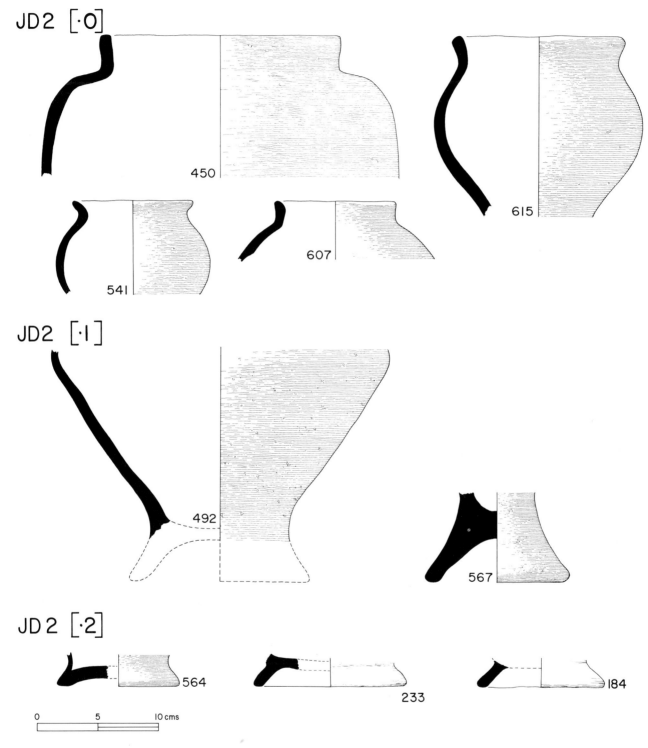

JD2 [·0]

450

615

541

607

JD2 [·1]

492

567

JD2 [·2]

564

233

184

0   5   10 cms

Fig 6.46

to tell from rim sherds alone whether a vessel should belong to this category or to JD3 since the only really distinguishing characteristic is the base. Where there has been doubt the JD3.0 grouping has been used. For this reason the quantity ascribed to JD2 may be depressed, but relative numbers are presumably fairly reflected in the number of bases. Base form allows two varieties to be distinguished, the high pedestal (JD2.1) and the low pedestal (JD2.2). Vessels are well made and the surface is usually burnished.
Fabrics: A (2); B (166); C (2); D (241). Ceramic phases 3–5.

Form JD3 (three varieties) (Figs 6.47–6.50)
Globular S–profiled jars with outcurving rims. The profiles vary but within the narrow limits demonstrated by the illustration. Three varieties have been distinguished. JD3.1 is a wide-bodied type. JD3.2 is a smaller and rather narrower-bodied type, while JD3.3 has rather sharper everted rims. They are also made in a distinctive highly burnished black sandy fabric with more deeply impressed shallow-tooled decoration. Shallow-tooled decoration in a zone around the upper part of the vessel is usual.
Fabrics: A (1); B (287); D (103). Ceramic phases 6–7.

Form JD4
Not present at Danebury

Form JD5 (one variety) (Fig 6.51)
Very large storage jar with outcurving rim.
Fabrics: B (34); C (2); D (59). Ceramic phases 5–7.

Jar type JE (Figs 6.52, 6.53)

The category JE is a catch-all for wheel-made jars of broadly globular or high-shouldered form and with upstanding or outcurving rims. Strictly the range warrants finer division but since the quantity of material is small and often in sherd form only no attempt at subdivision has been made, the general category JE1/4 being used. A finer subdivision has been adopted at Hengistbury. The Danebury sherds include the following varieties:
a   S–profile jar with outcurved rim
b   Globular jars with upstanding rims and with the body divided into horizontal zones by cordons or grooves
c   Jars of uncertain form but possibly globular decorated with close-set rilled grooves
d   Jar with high shoulder, upstanding rim, and projecting footring base
Fabrics: A (8); B (7); C (2); D (327); E (12). Ceramic phase 8.

Bowls

The height is less than the maximum diameter. The rim diameters may be in excess of maximum body diameters. Profiles vary between bi- and tripartite.
Four basic types are recognized:
BA   Simple form with well-defined but not accentuated shoulder and upstanding or flaring rim. Considerable variety of form makes classification difficult.
BB   Tripartite bowls with body angles emphasized with cordons. The type is characterized by its haematite-coated surface. Geometric decoration scratched after firing is common.
BC   Bowls with simple rounded profiles and gently incurving rims. The shoulder angles are neither sharp nor emphasized.

BD   Shouldered bowls with distinct upright necks with the distinction between neck and shoulder sharply defined. Wheel-turned or wheel-finished.

Bowl type BA

Form BA1 (two varieties) (Fig 6.54)
The type is not well represented but the category includes simple shouldered bowls with an inward sloping or upright side above the shoulder. Two varieties are allowed, a simple bipartite type (BA1.1) and one in which the upper part of the vessel is vertical (BA1.2).
Fabrics: A(35); B (39); C (7); D (42); E (1); F (1). Ceramic phases 1–4.

Form BA2 (three varieties) (Figs 6.55, 6.56)
A general category to contain all coarseware shouldered bowls of tripartite form including those with rounded shoulders. Of the three varieties allowed, BA2.1 has a sharp shoulder angle and a flaring rim. The variety may well have a footring base as well and is usually in a highly burnished black sandy fabric. BA2.2 is an amorphous group but each vessel has a distinct shoulder angle and flaring rim. BA2.3 is typified by more rounded profiles. The body and shoulder are continuously curved but a distinct change of angle usually marks the junction of the shoulder and rim. The three varieties merge one into another.
Fabrics: A (66); B (400); C (15); D (604); E (6). Ceramic phases 3–4.

Bowl type BB

Form BB1 (one variety) (Figs 6.57, 6.58)
Bowl of a very distinctive form, finely made and sharply moulded. The vessels have a flaring rim, a faceted shoulder, with facets frequently emphasized with cordons, and usually a simple footring base. Geometric decoration scratched after firing is frequently found on the rim and shoulder. Vessels are invariably coated with haematite.
In analysis sub-coding was used: BB1.0 referred to rim fragments only, 1.1 if cordons survived, and 1.2 if the fragments were of faceted shoulders. This is best abandoned and all vessels should be called BB1. Similarity is so great that subdivision seems unnecessary but it might eventually be worth distinguishing between those with flared rims and the few bowls with more upright rims.
Fabrics: A (29); B (81); C (131); D (584); E (306); F (1). Ceramic phases 3 and ?4.

Form BB2 (one variety) (Fig 6.59)
Bowl with flared rim and rounded shoulder decorated with cordons. Coarser and thicker than BB1 and without the sharpness of moulding. Haematite-coated surface.
Fabrics: B (2); D (1); E (1). Ceramic phases 3 and ?4.

Form BB3 (two varieties) (Fig 6.60)
Bowls with one or more cordons emphasizing a sharp shoulder angle above which the rim curves outwards. Two varieties are distinguished. BB3.1 is characterized by a sharply outcurved rim creating a deep concavity between cordon and rim top. They are coated with haematite and some have scratched geometric decoration. BB3.2 is similar but with a less concave neck and more upstanding rim. Many of the rim fragments classed as BB1 could belong to vessels of this form.
Fabric: D (5). Ceramic phases 3 and ?4.

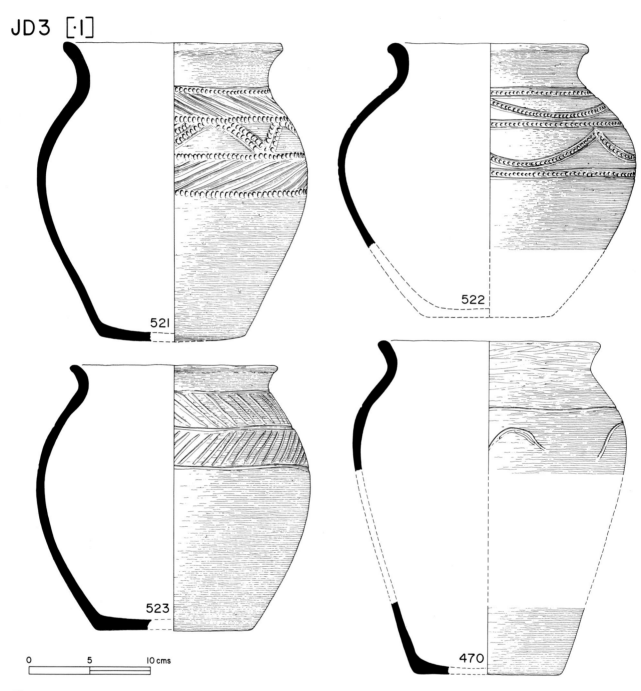

JD3 [·1]

521

522

523

470

0   5   10 cms

Fig 6.47

282

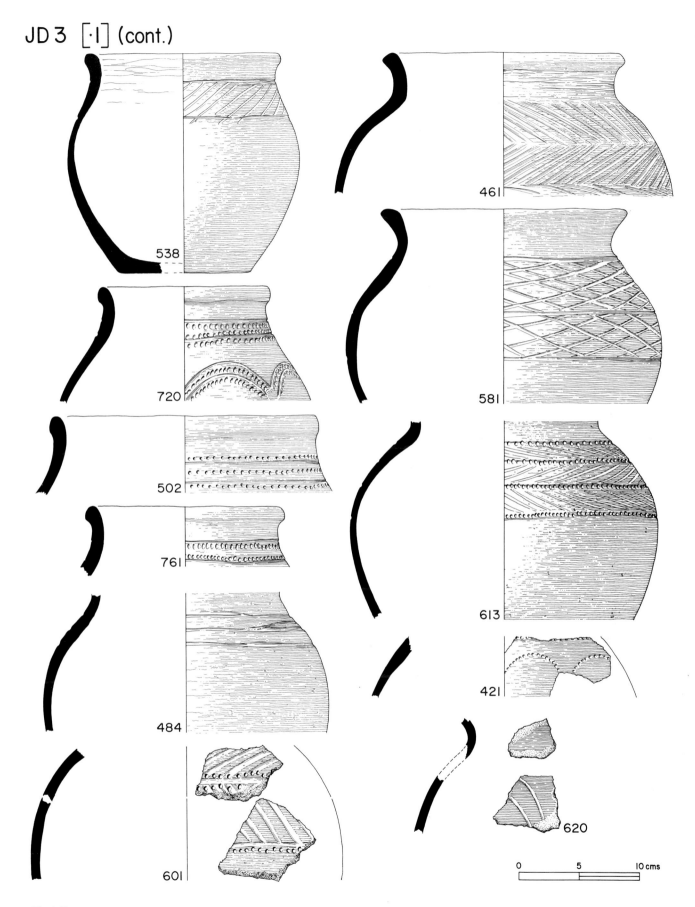

JD 3 [·1] (cont.)

538

461

720

581

502

761

613

484

421

601

620

0   5   10 cms

Fig 6.48

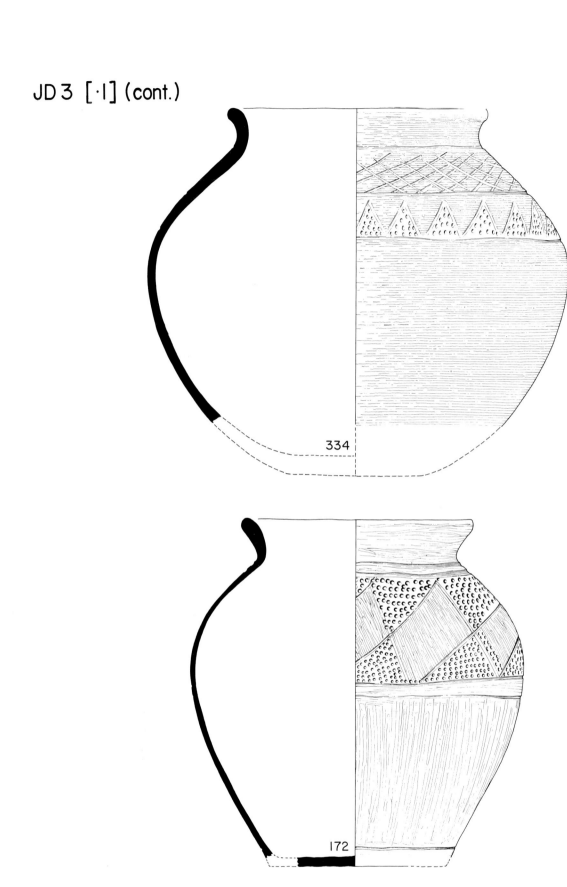

334

172

0   5   10 cms

Fig 6.49

284

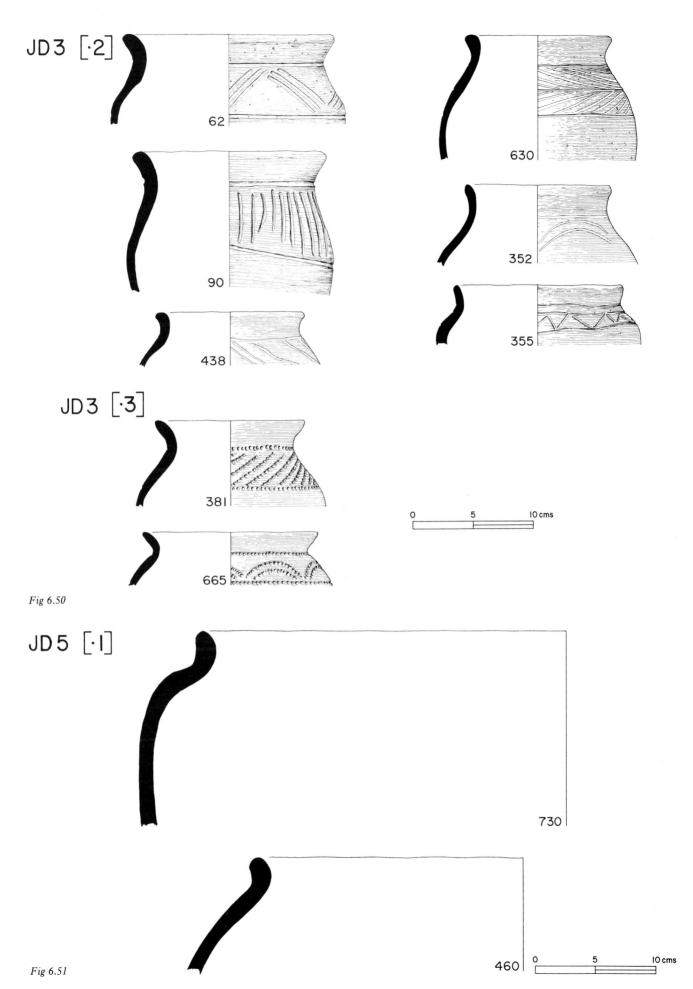

JD 3 [·2]

62

630

90

352

355

438

JD 3 [·3]

381

665

0   5   10 cms

Fig 6.50

JD 5 [·1]

730

460

0   5   10 cms

Fig 6.51

285

JE1/4

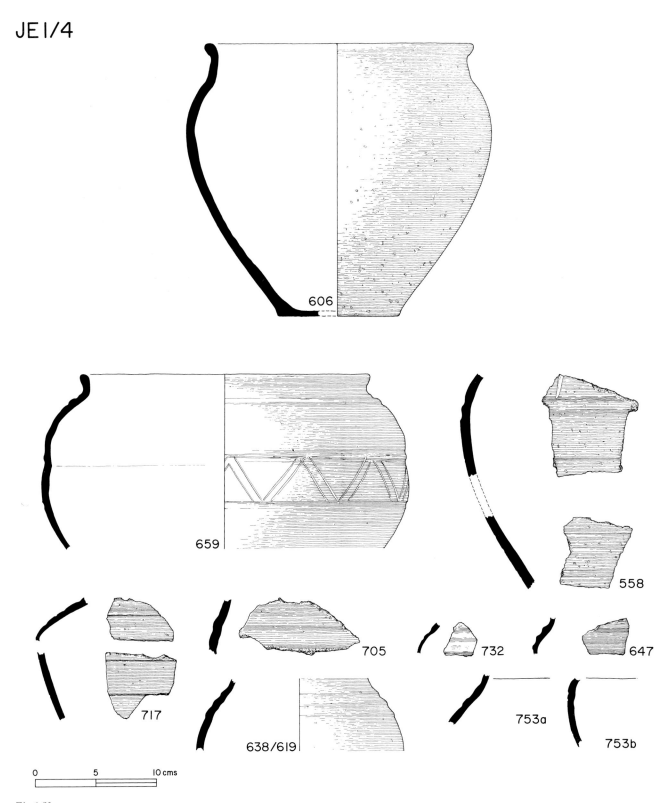

0   5   10 cms

Fig 6.52

JE1/4 (cont.)

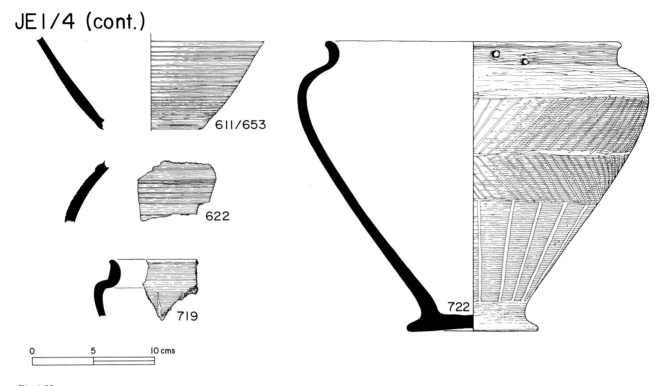

611/653

622

719

0   5   10 cms

Fig 6.53

BA1 [·1]

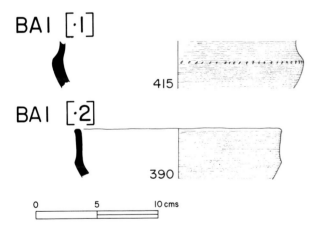

415

BA1 [·2]

390

0   5   10 cms

Fig 6.54

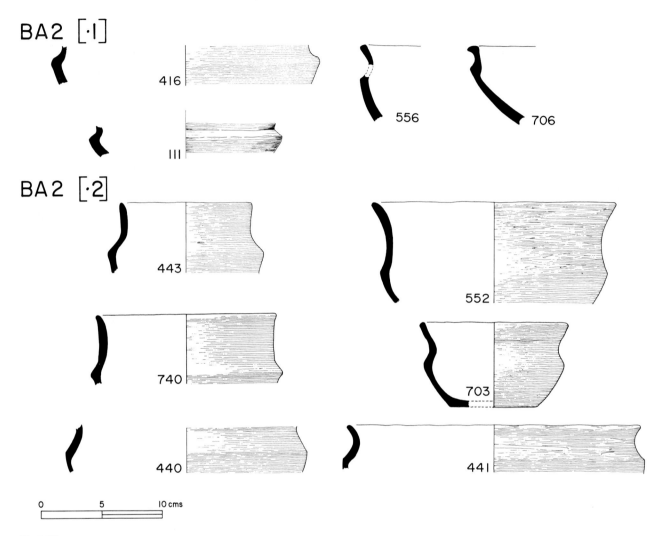

BA2 [·1]

416

111

556

706

BA2 [·2]

443

740

440

552

703

441

0   5   10 cms

Fig 6.55

BA 2 [·3]

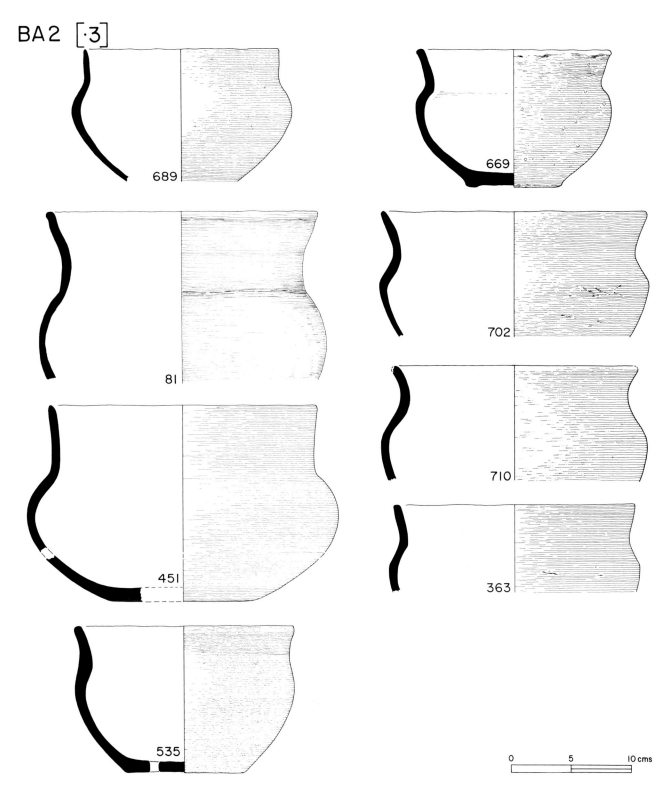

689

669

81

702

451

710

363

535

Fig 6.56

0   5   10 cms

BBI [·I]

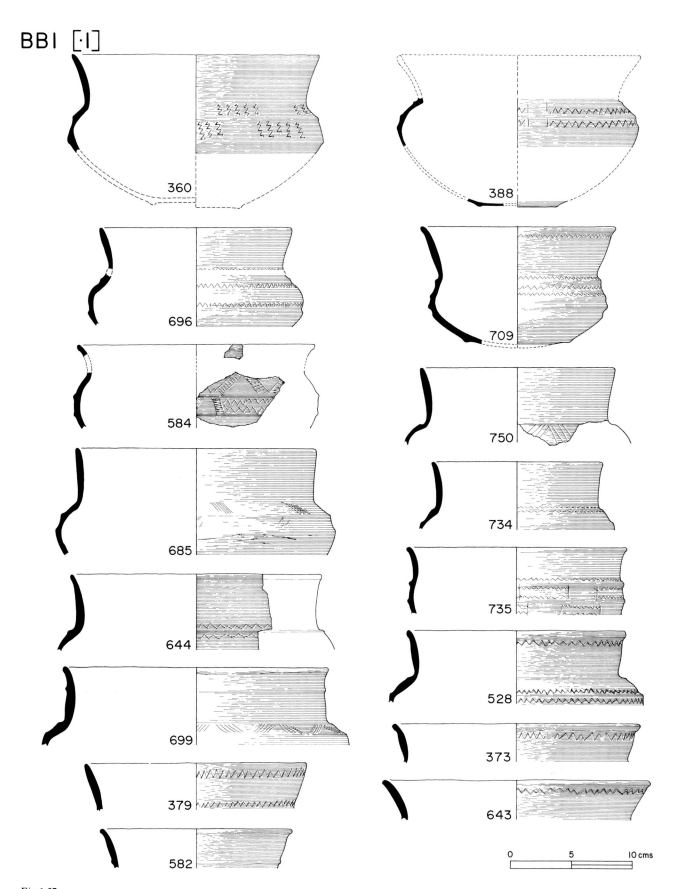

Fig 6.57

290

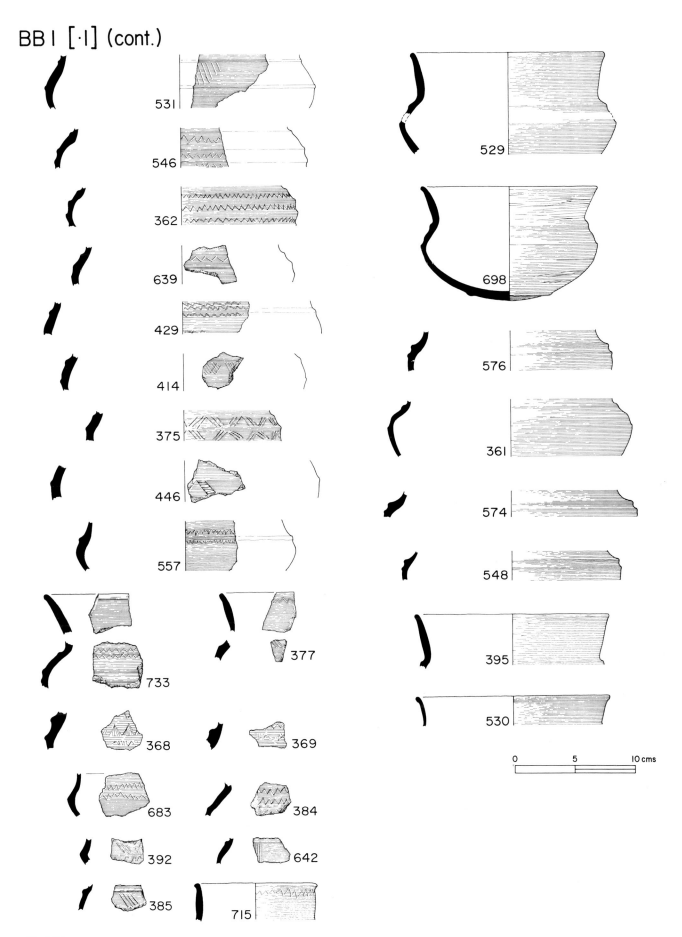

Fig 6.58

531

546

362

639

429

414

375

446

557

733

377

368

369

683

384

392

642

385

715

529

698

576

361

574

548

395

530

0   5   10 cms

BB2 [·1]

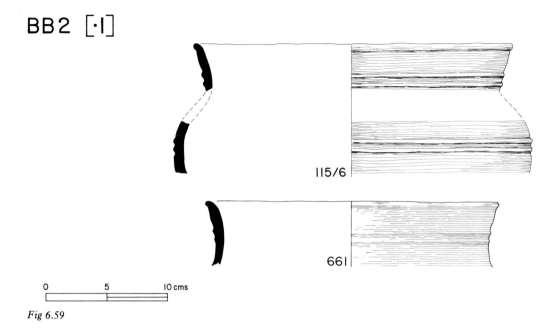

115/6

661

0 ___ 5 ___ 10 cms

Fig 6.59

BB3 [·1]

BB3 [·2]

BC1 [·1]

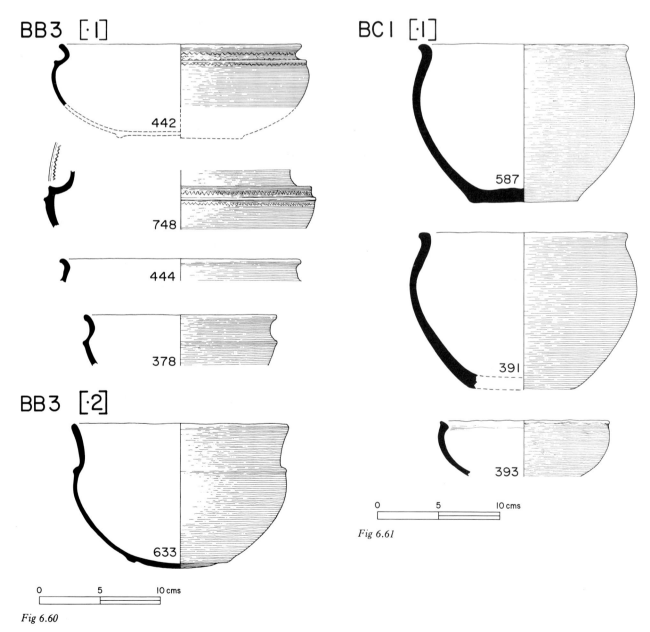

442

748

444

378

633

0 ___ 5 ___ 10 cms

Fig 6.60

587

391

393

0 ___ 5 ___ 10 cms

Fig 6.61

292

Bowl type BC

Form BC1 (one variety) (Fig 6.61)
Simple hemispherical bowls with thickened outcurved rim tops. The individual vessels vary in form but subdivision is difficult with so few adequate profiles. Usually well finished and with burnished surface. The form merges with JC2. When there is doubt sherds have been assigned to JC2.
Fabrics: B (34); D (39). Ceramic phases 4–7.

Form BC2 (one variety) (Fig 6.62)
Simple hemispherical bowls with largely undifferentiated rims. There is an area of overlap with form JC2 but when in doubt sherds have been assigned to JC2. A distinction between BC2 and BC1 could usually be made even though one form grades into the other. Vessels are burnished and often decorated with shallow-tooled motifs.
Fabrics: B (14); D (1). Ceramic phases 4–7.

Bowl type BD

Form BD1
Not present at Danebury

Form BD2 (one variety) (Fig 6.63)
Bowls with well-defined shoulder angles and upstanding or slightly flaring rims. The rim tops are sometimes beaded; there is a cordon between shoulder and rim. Wheel-made.
Fabric: D (30). Ceramic phases 8-9.

Form BD3
Not present at Danebury

Form BD4 (one variety) (Fig 6.63)
Bowls with well-defined shoulder and upstanding or flaring rim. The rim tops may be beaded. Wheel-made.
Fabric: D (10). Ceramic phases 8-9.

Form BD5
Not present at Danebury

Form BD6 (one variety) (Fig 6.64)
'Glastonbury ware' bowls. Shouldered bowls with upstanding necks. Only a few decorated sherds have been found but the general form is well known from other sites.
Fabric: unclassified. Ceramic phase 7.

Dishes

Vessels of height always less than maximum diameter. The maximum diameter is usually at the rim.
Two types have been recognized:
DA Wide-mouthed form generally with straight or only slightly curving flared sides.
DB Hemispherical in shape.

Dish type DA

Form DA1 (two varieties) (Fig 6.65)
Open wide-mouthed dish with straight or slightly curved sides. The rim is thickened and flattened. Of the two varieties DA1.1 has grooving or other forms of tooling on the rim top while DA1.2 has a plain flat rim top. Shallow-tooled decoration may occur on the body. The surfaces are usually well burnished.
Fabrics: B (24); D (74); H (15). Ceramic phases 5–7.

Form DA2 (one variety) (Fig 6.66)
Open-mouthed dish with straight or slightly curved sides and flattened, but not thickened, rim top. May be decorated with shallow tooling outside. Burnished surfaces.
Fabric: D (3). Ceramic phases 5–7.

Dish type DB

Form DB1 (one variety) (Fig 6.66)
Hemispherical dish with omphalos base and simple unthickened beaded rim. Burnished surfaces which may have shallow-tooled decoration.
Fabric: D (1). Ceramic phase 7.

Form DB2 (one variety) (Fig 6.66)
Hemispherical dish with thickened rim. Burnished surfaces which may have shallow-tooled decoration.
Fabric: B (2). Ceramic phases 6–7.

Form DB3 (one variety) (Fig 6.66)
Hemispherical dish with simple undifferentiated rim. This is a very generalized category.
Fabric: B (2). Ceramic phases 4–5.

Saucepan pots

Vessels with vertical or near vertical sides. Height is approximately equal to diameter; rim diameter is approximately equal to base diameter.
Two basic types have been recognized:
PA Slightly incurved sides with flattened or undifferentiated rims. Usually in sandy fabrics and never decorated.
PB Vessels with straight and more vertical sides and carefully rounded rim tops. In sandy and gritted fabrics frequently decorated.

Saucepan pot type PA

Form PA1 (two varieties) (Fig 6.67)
Vessels with sides incurving slightly towards the top and usually with undifferentiated rims. Fabrics are usually sandy and surfaces may be quite roughly finished. The distinction between the two varieties is made on the basis of size: PA1.1 are usually small vessels 150–200 mm high while PA1.2 are considerably higher. It is sometimes impossible to distinguish between varieties when dealing with sherds and there is a gradual gradation between PA1 types and JB4 and JC1.
Fabrics: A (143); B (519); C (49); D (828). Ceramic phases 3–5.

Form PA2 (one variety) (Fig 6.68)
Vessels with upright or slightly curving sides with rim tops flattened. Fabric with carefully burnished surfaces. The technique of flattening the rim top, in combination with the burnished fabric, is distinctive.
Fabrics: A (39); B (248); C (196); D (871); D (9); F (1). Ceramic phases 4–6.

Form PA3 (one variety) (Fig 6.69)
This is a general category to contain small and sometimes crudely-made vessels with straight sides. There is some uncertainty in distinguishing between sherds of PA1 and PA3. In such cases sherds are assigned to PA1.
Fabric: A (5). Ceramic phases 3–5.

Saucepan pot type PB

Form PB1 (two varieties) (Figs 6.70–6.77)
Vessels with straight or slightly curved sides and with rounded or slightly beaded rim tops. The range of shape is evident from the illustration. Subdivision, though possible, seems to be unnecessary at this stage except for

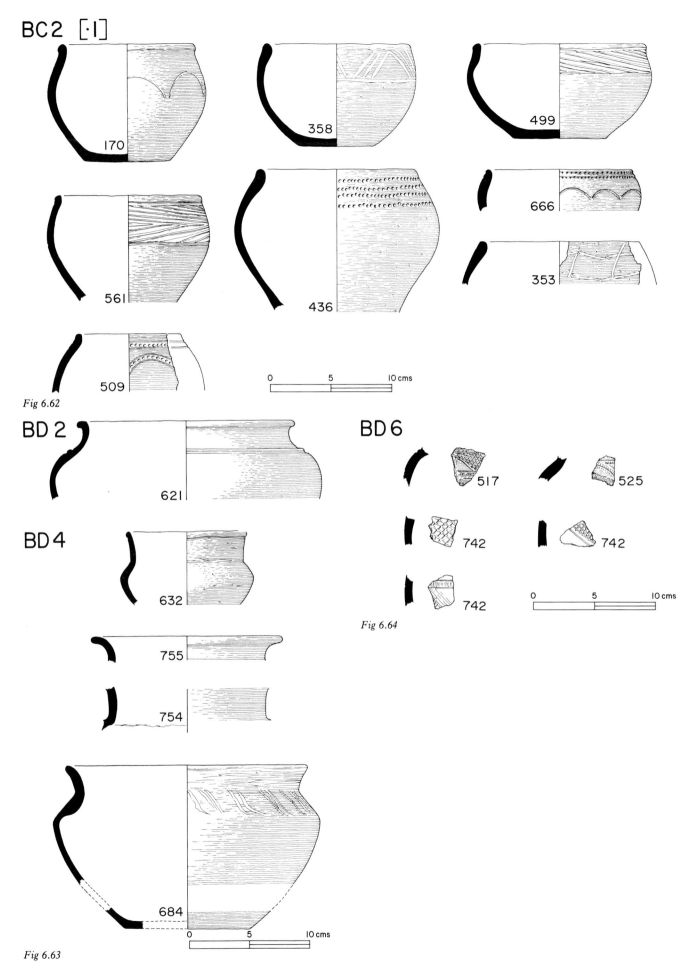

BC2 [·1]

170

358

499

561

436

666

353

509

Fig 6.62

0   5   10 cms

BD 2

621

BD 4

632

755

754

684

Fig 6.63

BD 6

517

525

742

742

742

Fig 6.64

0   5   10 cms

0   5   10 cms

DA I [·1]

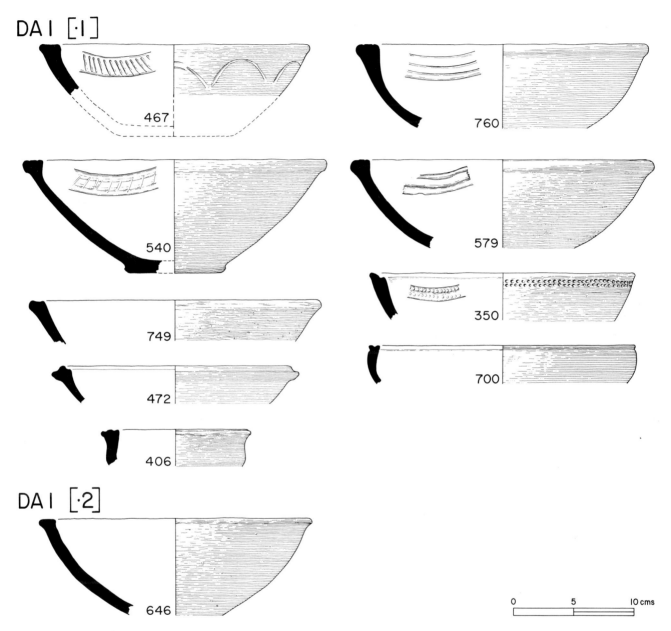

467

760

540

579

749

350

472

700

406

DA I [·2]

646

0 5 10 cms

Fig 6.65

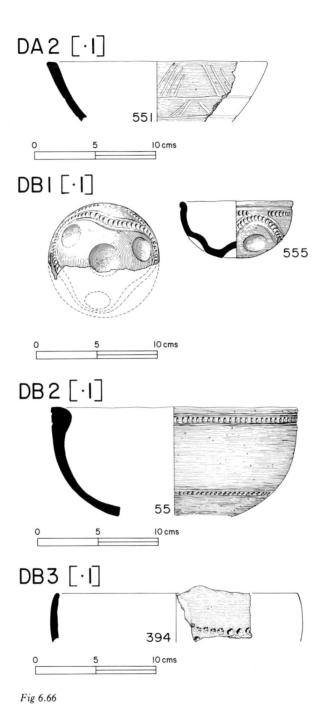

DA 2 [·1]

551

0   5   10 cms

DB1 [·1]

555

0   5   10 cms

DB 2 [·1]

55

0   5   10 cms

DB 3 [·1]

394

0   5   10 cms

Fig 6.66

PA1 [·1]

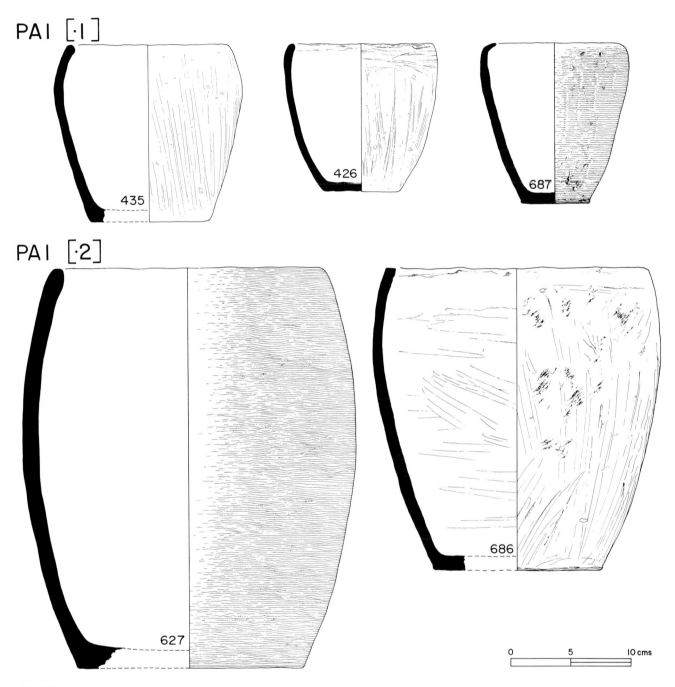

435

426

687

PA1 [·2]

627

686

0   5   10 cms

Fig 6.67

297

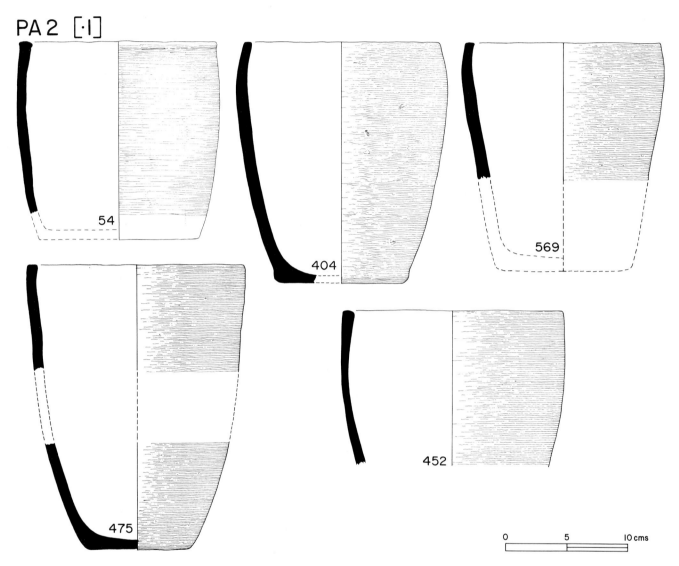

PA 2 [·1]

54

404

569

475

452

0   5   10 cms

Fig 6.68

298

PA3 [·1]

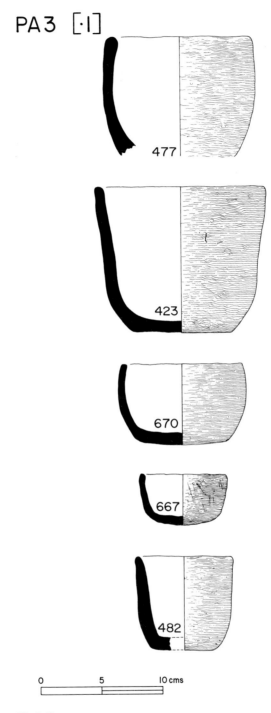

477

423

670

667

482

0   5   10 cms

Fig 6.69

PB1 [·1]

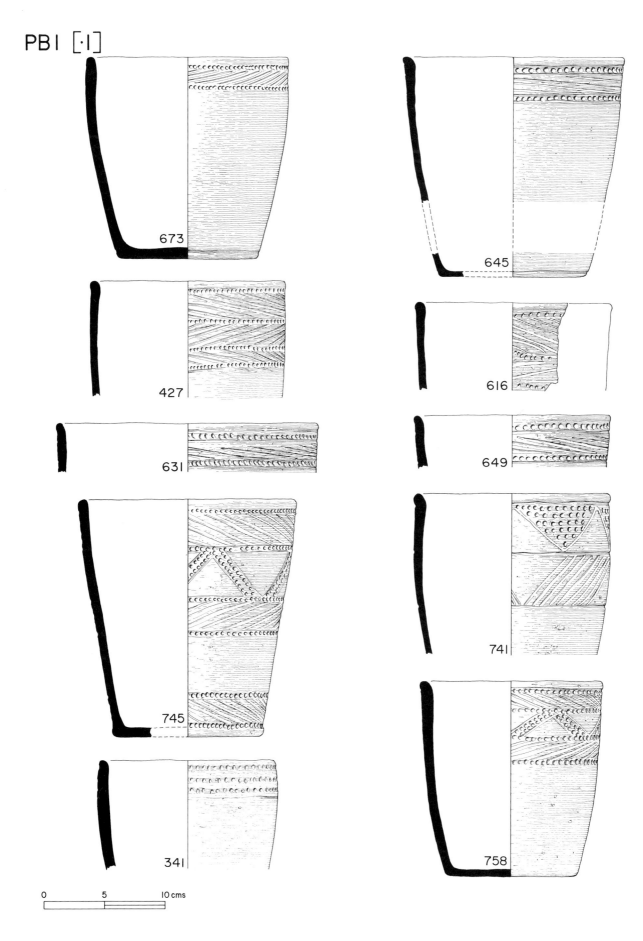

0   5   10 cms

Fig 6.70

300

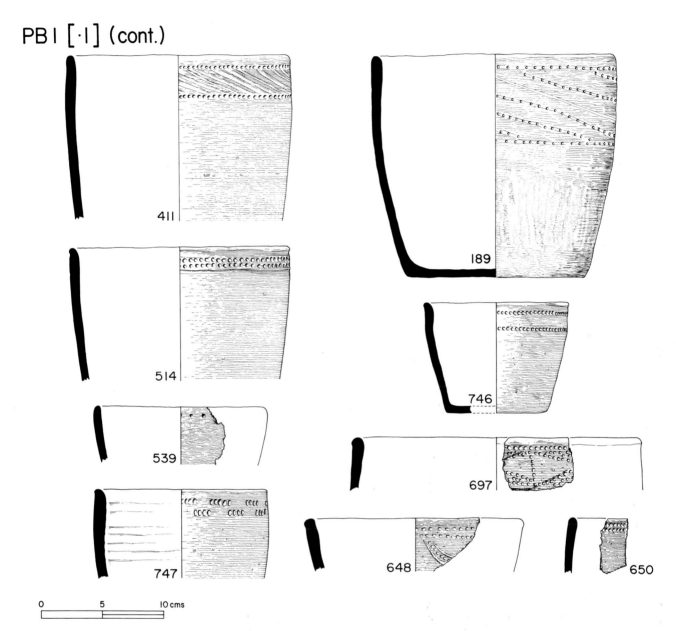

Fig 6.71

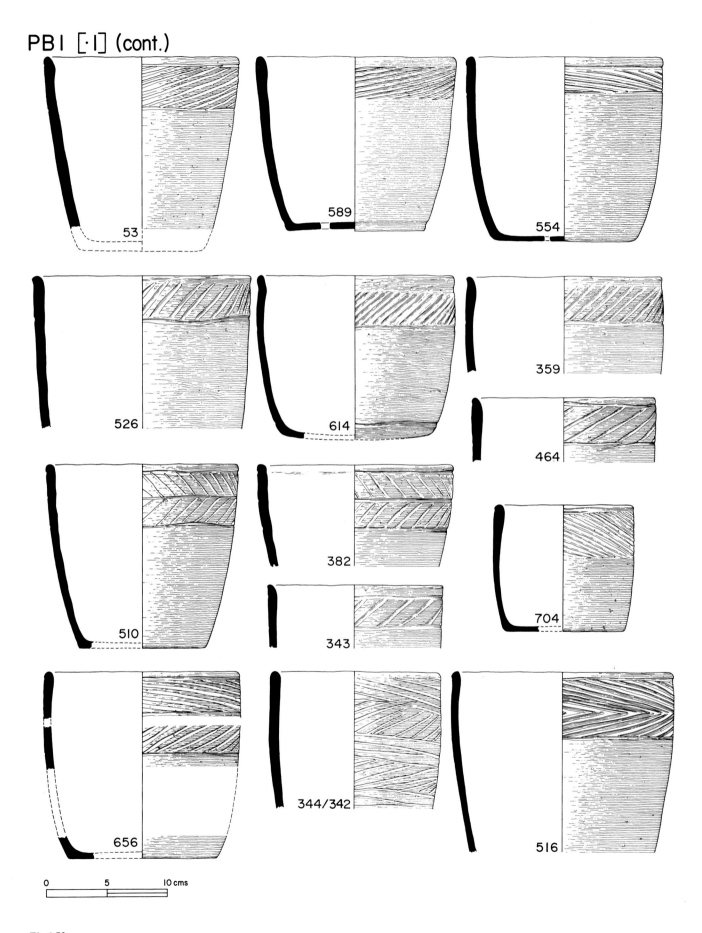

Fig 6.72

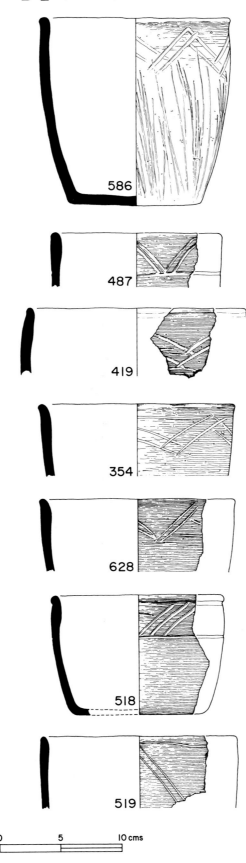

586

487

419

354

628

518

519

0   5   10 cms

Fig 6.73

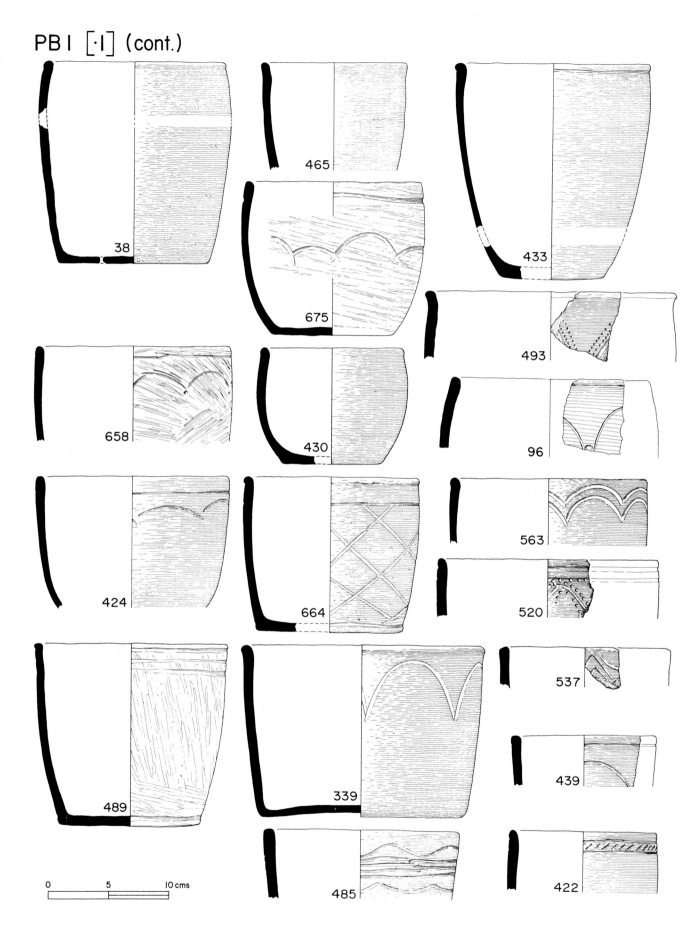

Fig 6.74

PB1 [·1] (cont.)

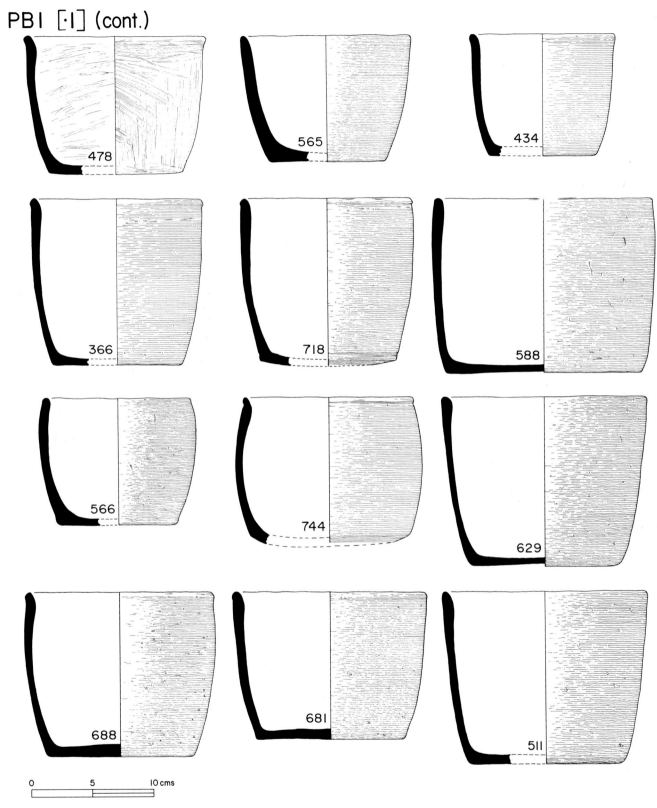

0   5   10 cms

Fig 6.75

PB1 [·1] (cont.)

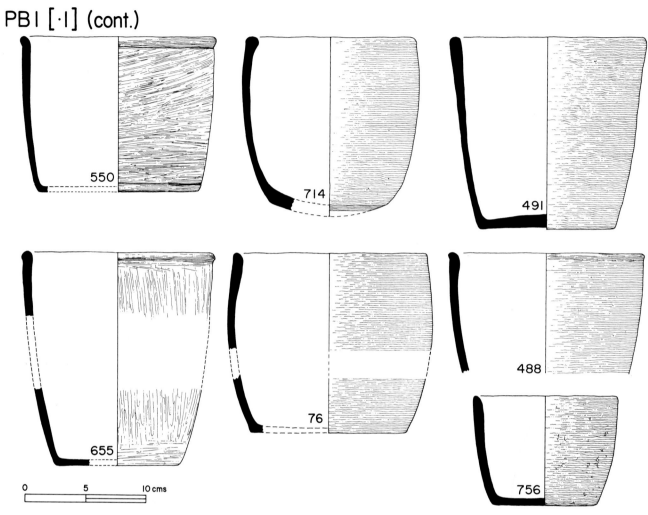

Fig 6.76

PB1 [·2]

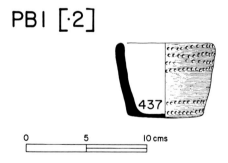

Fig 6.77

the distinction that can be made between the normal size saucepans (PB1.1) and the miniature vessels (PB1.2). Surfaces are burnished and shallow-tooled decoration is common.

Fabrics: A (156); B (5091); C (393); D (5175); E (11). Ceramic phases 6–7.

Miscellaneous

It is only to be expected that a collection of prehistoric pottery of the size of the Danebury collection contains a few sherds that cannot easily be fitted into a simple classificatory system. The individual examples are illustrated in full in Fig 6.78 and are briefly listed here.

Handles and lugs

Handles and lugs are rare. Three types can be recognized:

a   horizontally perforated (nos 721, 27, 370)
b   vertically perforated (no 338)

c   rim perforated lug (no 560)

The fabrics are sandy or coarsely flint-gritted; the forms of the vessels are uncertain.

Context: 721: P1089; 27: P7; 370: P241
        338: P3552
        560: P608

T-shaped rims

Rims of this kind are rare; only two are known both in sandy ware with some flint grit (512, 545).

Context: 512: P337; 545: P573

Vessel with heavy cordons

One vessel (in two sherds) is recorded (743). The fabric is DO.

Context: layer 367

Miniature 'closed' vessel

One example only (624) in sandy fabric (DO).

Context: P813

Miscellaneous

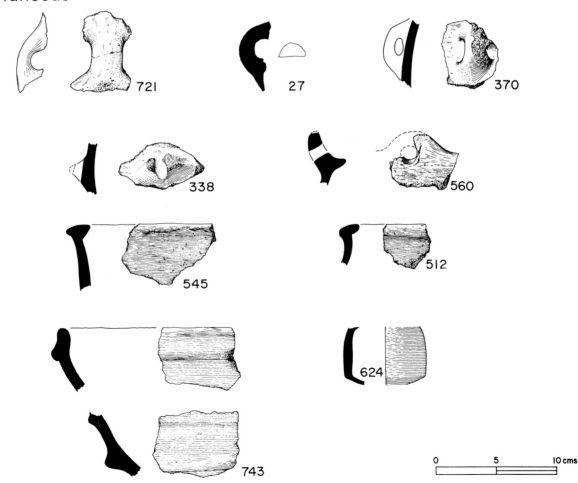

Fig 6.78

Appendix 2: the fabrics

Macroscopic classification

After a preliminary examination of the pottery from the first three years of excavation, eight fabric groups labelled A-H were defined. These were further subdivided and the scheme modified during use. Further experience, however, suggested that the subdivisions were too fine to be of much significance and accordingly the simplified eightfold division was returned to. However, in order to give a clear idea of the range within each of the fabric groups, full fabric descriptions of each of the subtypes are given in fiche 8, frames D8–12. The general characteristics of each of the main fabric categories are offered here.

A series: coarse grit-tempered

Medium hard sandy fabrics tempered with angular flint inclusions averaging 1–4 mm in size with occasional larger pieces. Other temperings of crushed chalk or shell may also occur. Firing was usually carried out in an oxidizing atmosphere giving rise to ochre or light red colours but the core is usually grey. The surfaces were left untooled or were roughly wiped.

B series: fine grit-tempered

Medium hard fabrics of differing degrees of sandiness tempered with well-sorted angular flint grits usually not exceeding 2 mm in length. The quantity of temper varies but is usually dense. Other occasional inclusions are grog and haematite. Usually fired to an even grey colour but sometimes with a red core. The surfaces are burnished.

C series: shell-tempered

Medium hard fabric of varying degrees of sandiness tempered with crushed shell usually added in large fragments up to 5 mm in length. In some varieties the shell is more finely crushed. Other inclusions may include quartz grits. Unevenly fired reddish-brown to black. The surface is usually untreated.

D series: sandy fabrics

Hard to medium sandy fabrics sometimes containing rare inclusions of chalk, crushed flint, haematite, or grog. Firing varies considerably as does surface treatment but smoothing or burnishing is common. There is a considerable variety within this series but clear cut subtypes are difficult to define macroscopically.

E series: fine smooth fabrics

Medium hard fine micaceous slightly sandy fabrics some with occasional inclusions of subangular flint. Usually fired black or dark grey. The fabric is commonly used for scratched-cordoned bowls which are finely finished and coated with an external haematite wash.

F series: chaff-tempered

Medium hard, friable fabric tempered with chaff. Other inclusions may include grog or shell. Fired red-brown with a grey core. Roughly wiped exterior.

G series: grog-tempered

Fine sandy fabric densely tempered with grog. Well-smoothed surfaces.

H series: limestone-tempered

Medium hard, fine sandy fabric tempered with crushed limestone and shell among which distinct ooliths can be made out. Fired brown to black. The outer surface is wiped.

Petrological analysis of the pottery fabrics

To test the petrological character of the Danebury fabrics a number of samples were taken by Drs Williams and Wandibba for macroscopic and thin-section analysis. On the basis of temper, eight major classes were recognized. These are described and discussed in the detailed report given in fiche 8, frames D13–E3.

The petrologically-defined fabrics may be correlated with those used in the visual characterization in the sherds in the following manner:

Petrological fabric

Fabric 1:
oolitic limestone tempering; equivalent to fabric H.
Fabric 2:
shell tempering; equivalent to fabric C.
Fabric 3:
chalk and sand tempering. Most of the sherds included in this group belong to a distinctive over-fired type, possibly wasters which are classed together with the other sandy fabrics as fabric D.
Fabric 4:
'Glastonbury wares'.
Fabrics 5a-c:
flint-gritted wares: equivalent to fabrics A and C the distinction between which was made on coarseness of fabric. Direct correlation to the petrologically-defined fabrics is not possible.
Fabric 6:
sandy with inclusions of limonite, classed with fabric D but recognized stylistically as a Wiltshire variant.
Fabrics 7a-d:
sandy fabrics. Fabrics 7a and 7b are equivalent to fabric D. Fabric 7c is equivalent to fabric E and fabric 7d though classed as fabric D was recognized stylistically as being represented only in ceramic phase 8.
Fabric 8:
equivalent to fabric G.
Refer to microfiche for details.

Appendix 3: surface treatment and decoration

The surface appearance of the individual vessels was classified according to three differently-coded sets of criteria:

the nature of the overall surface treatment
the method of applying decoration
the style of decoration

The overall surface treatment

Once constructed, vessels were variously treated to seal the surfaces and in some cases to enhance the appearance. Five types of surface finish were distinguished:

A No evident special treatment following the manufacturing process. Surfaces left rough. Usually fired in oxidizing conditions.
B Roughly smoothed with the fingers or with a fabric giving a coarsely wiped appearance. Sometimes rough finger groovings occur; sometimes there are vertical

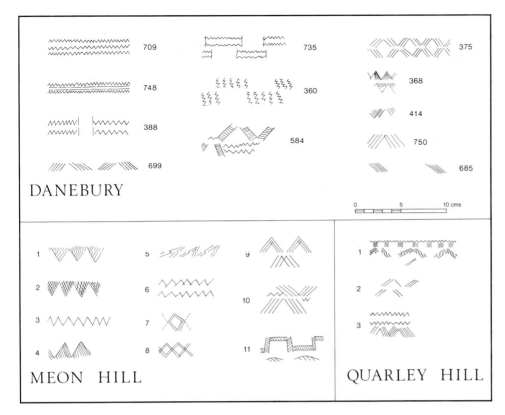

Fig 6.79 Motifs used to decorate scratched-cordoned bowls

striations caused either by the coarse fabric (or grass) wiping or by grits in the clay being dragged by the wiping process. Usually fired in oxidizing conditions.

C Haematite coating. Finely-burnished wares coated externally and sometimes internally with a thin slip containing haematite. The vessels were burnished again after coating and then fired in an oxidizing atmosphere to create a red shiny surface. Occasional examples with a black shiny slip may have resulted from the accidental creation of a reducing atmosphere during the firing process.

D Unevenly burnished surfaces produced by a burnishing tool of some kind. The burnishing is streaky and discontinuous. Usually fired in a reducing atmosphere.

E Overall burnishing and smoothing giving rise to an even smoothed surface. Usually fired in a reducing atmosphere. The distinction between D and E is sometimes arbitrary.

The method of applying decoration

Five methods of applying decoration were distinguished.

1 Geometric patterns scratched with a fine point after firing. This method is restricted to vessels with surface finish C (haematite-coated).

2 Stamped or impressed motifs applied with a pre-made tool before firing. Rare at Danebury.

3 'Pie-crust' or finger-tip decoration made with the finger-nail or finger-tip before firing. Restricted to rim tops and shoulders of jars.

4 Cordons applied as separate strips of clay or integral with the body of the vessel. Cordons may be slashed with finger-nails or impressed with finger-tips.

5 Linear decoration shallowly drawn on the leather-hard vessel with a rounded point. A common characteristic of ceramic phase 7.

Method 1: scratched decoration

Scratched decoration is restricted to haematite-coated bowls of type BB1. The motifs were inscribed on the vessel, after firing, using a sharp point. Decoration was usually restricted to the horizontal facets of the shoulder of the vessel but a simple zig-zag line was sometimes scored just below the rim top. The arrangement of the decorated zones on the body is best appreciated by reference to Figs 6.57 and 6.58.

Motifs are difficult to classify particularly since the sherds of bowls decorated in this way are usually small. For this reason no attempt at subdivision has been made. The full range of motifs is shown on Fig 6.79 together with motifs from comparable vessels found at the nearby sites of Meon Hill and Quarley Hill. Most common was the simple continuous zig-zag inscribed just below the rim or on the shoulder. Occasionally more complex zig-zags composed of multiple lines were employed. Another technique was to divide the shoulder facets into panels for decorative purposes. The infilling of the panels varied considerably but always emphasized simple geometric motifs.

Method 2: stamped or impressed motifs

This method of decoration is extremely rare at Danebury; only four examples have been found (Fig 6.80). Nos 716 and 751 together belong to a class of jars comparable in form to JD1 heavily decorated with panels of stabbing contained within deeply grooved lines. The style is well represented at All Cannings Cross and other Wessex sites of the 8th–6th centuries. The two Danebury sherds are

309

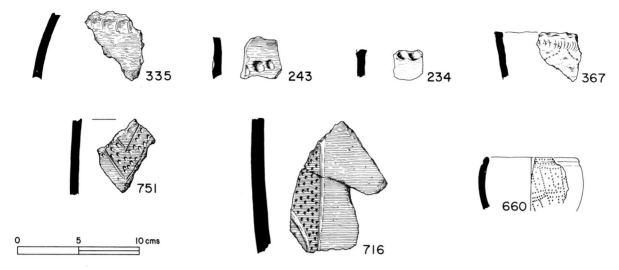

Fig 6.80 Sherds with various types of impressed decoration

likely to be strays from casual pre-hillfort use of the site but both were found in later contexts.

The other two vessels with stamped decoration are isolated examples. No 394 (Fig 6.66) was an open dish found in a cp 3 context decorated with a row of impressions made by the end of a stick or bone before firing. No 660 is a small bowl decorated by a deeply impressed point; it was found in a cp 8 context.

Method 3: finger-tip or finger-nail impressions

This style of decoration is rare at Danebury. It is usually found on rim tops giving a 'pie-crust' appearance to jars of JB1.1 and JB1.2 type. More rarely rows of finger impressions are found on the shoulders of jars (eg 234, 243, 335) (Fig 6.80). Sherds are too small to be certain of the type, but they are most likely to be jars of the JB1 category. Only one example of the use of the finger nail is known, used, in this case, in conjunction with scratched and stabbed decoration (no 367).

Method 4: applied cordons

Applied cordons occur at different stages in the Danebury sequence. Finger-impressed cordons (eg no 573, type JA1.1) are very rare. Plain cordons are, however, a characteristic of the BB1, 2, and 3 types and the technique is used again later on the vessels of ceramic phase 8 (BD1.2, JD4.2).

Method 5: shallow-tooled decoration

Shallow-tooled decoration, involving the use of a narrow blunt point to lightly draw patterns on vessels before firing, is a technique frequently used in ceramic phase 7 and, to a lesser extent, in ceramic phase 8. It has given rise to a wide variety of patterns incorporating a number of standardized motifs in different combinations. Any classificatory scheme which attempted to take cognizance of all the subtleties of combination would be cumbersome in the extreme. The simplest way to communicate something of the range is by illustration (Figs 6.39, 6.42, 6.44, 6.47–6.50, 6.62, 6.70–6.74) but in order to record and quantify the principal patterns a simplified scheme has been devised.

Decoration is usually in horizontal zones restricted to the upper part of the vessel beginning just below the rim and extending sometimes as far as the shoulder (in the case of jars) or as much as halfway down the wall (in the case of saucepan pots). A second band of decoration may sometimes be found just above the base.

Patterns are composed principally of shallow-tooled lines and/or shallow-tooled dots. This is used as the first part of the classification and is distinguished numerically while the nine principal motifs employed are denoted by letters thus:

1 lines only
2 dots only
3 lines and dots
4 Glastonbury style deep tooling
  a horizontal
  b diagonal
  c cross-hatching
  d zig-zag
  e chevron
  f arc
  g swag
  h wave
  i dimple

The definition of a decorative ensemble will therefore have one numeral and any number of letters. The full range of patterns is given in Figs 6.81–6.83 together with the codes appropriate to them and the sherd number from which they are drawn.

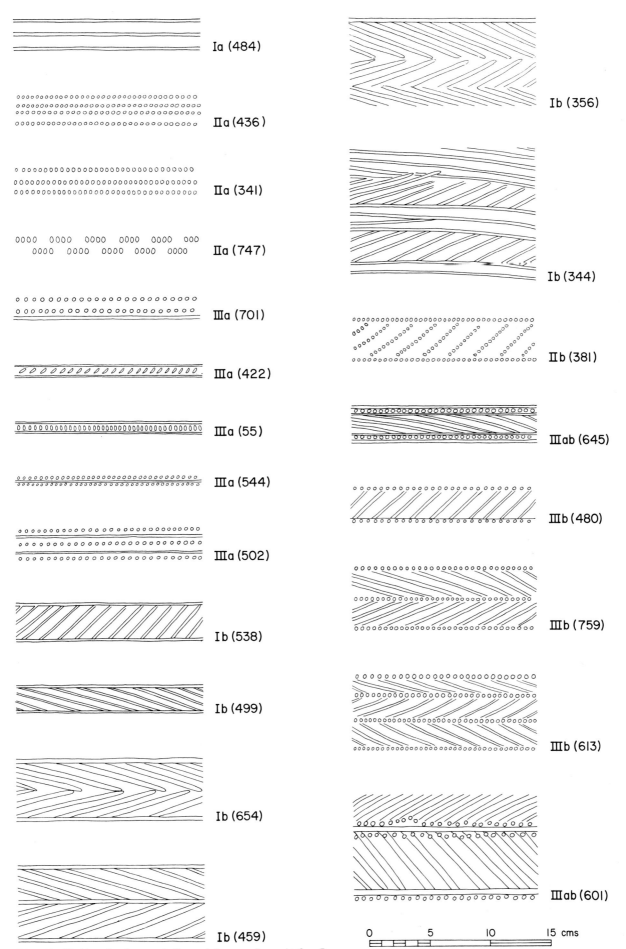

Ia (484)

IIa (436)

IIa (341)

IIa (747)

IIIa (701)

IIIa (422)

IIIa (55)

IIIa (544)

IIIa (502)

Ib (538)

Ib (499)

Ib (654)

Ib (459)

Ib (356)

Ib (344)

IIb (381)

IIIab (645)

IIIb (480)

IIIb (759)

IIIb (613)

IIIab (601)

0   5   10   15 cms

Fig 6.81   Motifs used to decorate shallow-tooled pottery of ceramic phase 7

311

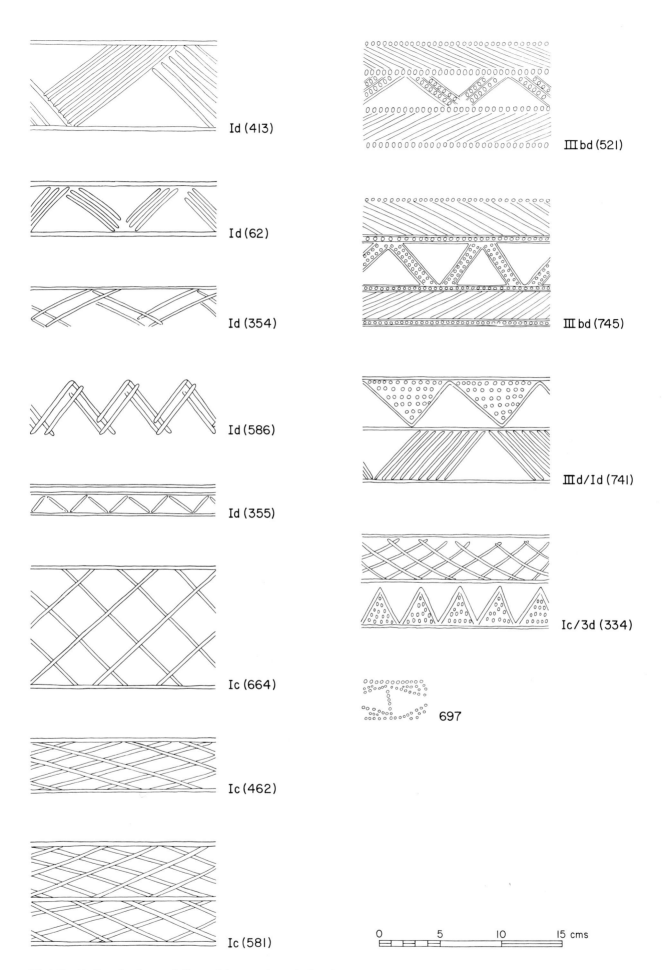

Id (413)

Id (62)

Id (354)

Id (586)

Id (355)

Ic (664)

Ic (462)

Ic (581)

IIIbd (521)

IIIbd (745)

IIId/Id (741)

Ic/3d (334)

697

0   5   10   15 cms

Fig 6.82   Motifs used to decorate shallow-tooled pottery of ceramic phase 7

312

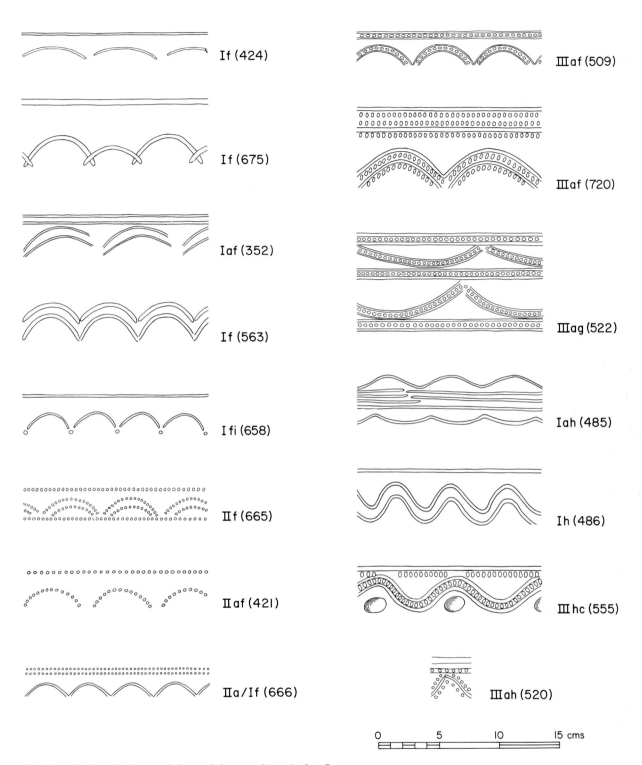

If (424)

If (675)

Iaf (352)

If (563)

I fi (658)

IIf (665)

IIaf (421)

IIa/If (666)

IIIaf (509)

IIIaf (720)

IIIag (522)

Iah (485)

Ih (486)

IIIhc (555)

IIIah (520)

0   5   10   15 cms

Fig 6.83   Motifs used to decorate shallow-tooled pottery of ceramic phase 7

313

Appendix 4: some typical stratified groups

As we have explained in the introduction, there are some 4,000 discrete pottery-containing contexts from the first ten years of excavation at Danebury; clearly to publish each group would be unnecessary and costly. However, a complete listing of the contents of every context, according to the classificatory system presented above, is available in the site archive in the form of a computer print-out.

To give some idea of the range of forms and fabrics found together and of the problems of residuality, a sample of 33 pits was selected for detailed presentation. The selection was made subjectively to display large, well-stratified groups and to represent the ceramic phases as evenly as possible bearing in mind the different sample sizes. By ceramic phase, the selection breaks down as follows:

	no of pits selected	*total no of pits excavated*
cp 3	9	535
cp 4 and cp 3/4	8	70
cp 5	1	73
cp 6	1	95
cp 7	11	145
cp 7/8	2	8
cp 8	1	9

For each pit all rims, bases, and decorated sherds are illustrated and for each illustrated sherd form, fabric, and decoration are listed. A brief preamble gives some basic statistics and a general comment.

The vessels are arranged roughly in their stratigraphical order in the pit starting from the top. The list is arranged in numerical order of sherd number for ease of reference. The data were compiled from the computer print-out and checked by Lisa Brown.

Of the 33 pits chosen for this treatment a representative eleven are presented here in the text; the remainder will be found in the fiche section (fiche 8, frames E6–G8).

Pit 906 cp 3 (Fig 6.84)

Radiocarbon date of 420 ± 80 bc (HAR 2032). Contains 248 sherds all of which are cps 1–3. Fabrics: A, 4 (1.6%); D, 244 (98.4%). Contains bowls and jars in more or less equal proportion but no definite haematite-coated sherds.

	Form	Fabric	Surface	Layer	
691	JB1.1	AO	B	5	
692	JB2.2	DO	B	3	
693	JB2.2	DO	D	3	
694	JB2.2	DO	D	3	
752	JB2.2	FO/DO	B	1	
983	base	A1	B	1	
984	JB3.0	DO	B	1	
985	JB2.2	DO	B	1	
986	JB3.0	DO	E	3	
987	BA2.3	DO	D	4	
988	BA2.3	DO	B	3	
989	JB1.1	DO	B	3	
990	BB1.1	EO	C	1	
991	BB1.1	EO	C?	1	over-fired
992	BA2.0	EO	E	1	

Pit 1133 cp 3 (Fig 6.85)

Contains 29 sherds all of which are cps 1–3. Fabrics: A, 7 (24.2%); B, 22 (75.8%). A typical early group with haematite-coated bowls and coarse jars.

	Form	Fabric	Surface	Layer
734	BB1.1	EO	C	2
735	BB1.1	EO	C	2
736	JB2.1	A2	A	2
737	JB1.2	DO	B	2
993	base	A1	D	2

Pit 325 cp 3 or 4 (Fig 6.86)

Contains 318 sherds all of which are cps 1–3 with the exception of 880 which is a PA2 type characteristic of cp 4. Fabrics: A, 75 (23.6%); B, 2 (0.6%); D, 123 (38.7%); E, 118 (37.1%). Contains a high percentage of bowl types most of which are haematite-coated. No 880 superficially looks like a PA2 type but the sherd is too small to allow one to be dogmatic; it comes from the top layer.

	Form	Fabric	Surface	Layer
527	JB1.2	A1	A	2
528	BB1.1	EO	C1	2
529	BB1.1	EO	C	2
530	BB1.1	EO	C	2
531	BB1.1	EO	C	1
878	BA2.3	EO	E	1
879	JB3.0	DO	D	1
880	PA2.1(?)	DO	D	1
881	JB2/3	DO	D	4

Pit 1033 cp 4 (Fig 6.87)

Contains 204 sherds all of which, with one exception, are cps 1–3. The exception is no 996 which is a PA2 type thought to be of cp 4. Fabrics: A, 4 (2.0%); C, 81 (39.7%); D, 119 (58.3%). There are no haematite-coated vessels in this pit. The presence of a PA2 type (no 996) would give the pit a cp 4 phasing.

	Form	Fabric	Surface	Layer
710	BA2.2	DO	E	4
711	JB2.2	DO	D	4
712	JB2.2	AO	D	3,4,6
713	JB1.2	A2	B	8
994	base	A1	B	3
995	BA2.3(?)	DO	D	2
996	PA2.1	DO	D	1
997	JB2.2	DO	B	3

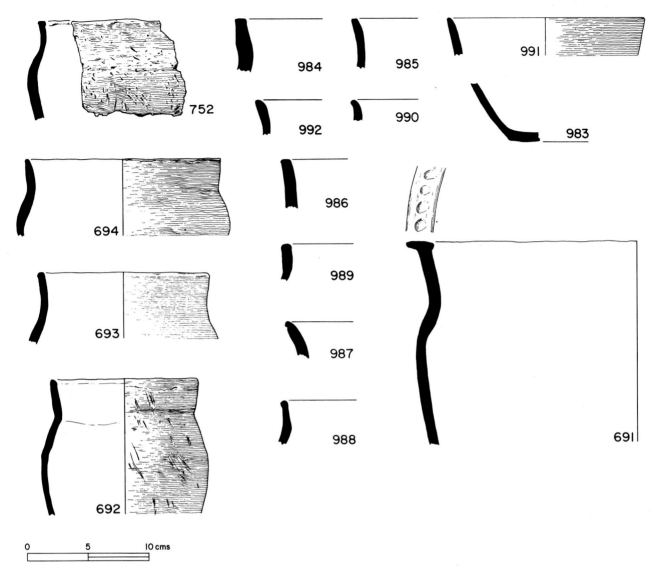

Fig 6.84   Key group: pit 906

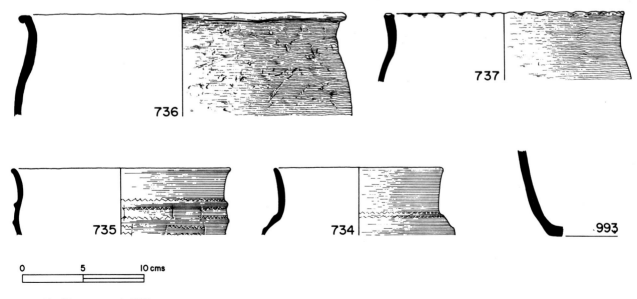

Fig 6.85   Key group: pit 1133

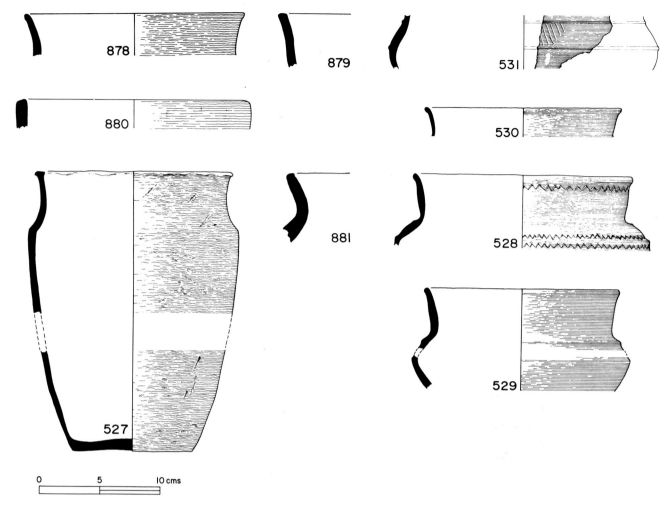

Fig 6.86 Key group: pit 325

Pit 117 cp 4 (or 5?) (Fig 6.88)

Contains 156 sherds, 27 of which (17%) are characteristic of cp 4. Fabrics: A, 17 (10.89%); D, 138 (88.47%); E, 1 (0.64%). An early-middle period pit typified by weak-shouldered jars and a saucepan pot of early (PA) type. A fragmentary rim of a haematite-coated bowl is also present. This pit could be as late as cp 5 but none of the distinctive cp 5 types is present.

	Form	Fabric	Surface	Layer
399	JD1.1	DO	B	3
400	JB4.1	DO	A	unstratified
401	JB4.1	DO	A	unstratified
402	PA2.1	DO	D	unstratified
403	JB4.1	DO	D	unstratified
842	BB1.1	E5	C	3

	Form	Fabric	Surface	Layer
295	JC1.1	CO	B	1
296	JC1.1	AO	B	1
297	JC2.2	DO	D	5
298	PA1.1	DO	D	6
299	JB4.1	A1	A	1
300	JB4.1	DO	D	1
301	JB4.1	DO	A	1
302	JC2.2/3	DO	E	4
303	JB2.1	A1	B	1
304	JC2.2	A2	B	6
305	JC2.3	DO	E	1
306	JC2.2/3	DO	D	6
307	JB4.0	A1	B	1
308	base	A1	B	5
615	JD2.0	DO	D	6

P657 cp 5 or 6 (Figs 6.90, 6.91)

Radiocarbon date of 280 ± 70 bc (HAR 964). Contains 362 sherds of which 13 (3%) are typical of cp 6. Fabrics: A, 6 (1.7%); D, 356 (98.3%). A typical middle period pit group with a few possibly residual sherds (567, 572, 1043, 1053, 1054). The group is composed almost entirely of jars with some saucepan pots of the early variety (PA). The bipartite jars (JC2) are all in sandy

Pit 19 cp 5 (Fig 6.89)

Radiocarbon date of 380 ± 90 bc (HAR 4328). Contains 241 sherds of which 4 (1%) are distinctive of cp 5. Fabrics: A, 82 (34%); C, 70 (29%); D, 89 (37%). The latest types are bipartite jars (JC2) but in sandy fabrics more characteristic of cp 5 than later.

316

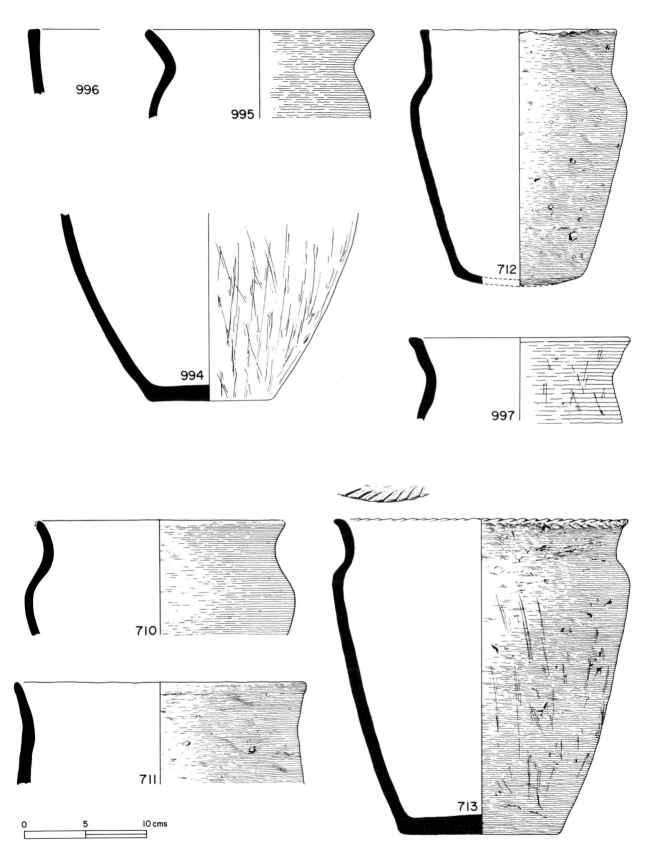

996

995

712

994

997

710

711

713

0   5   10 cms

Fig 6.87   Key group: pit 1033

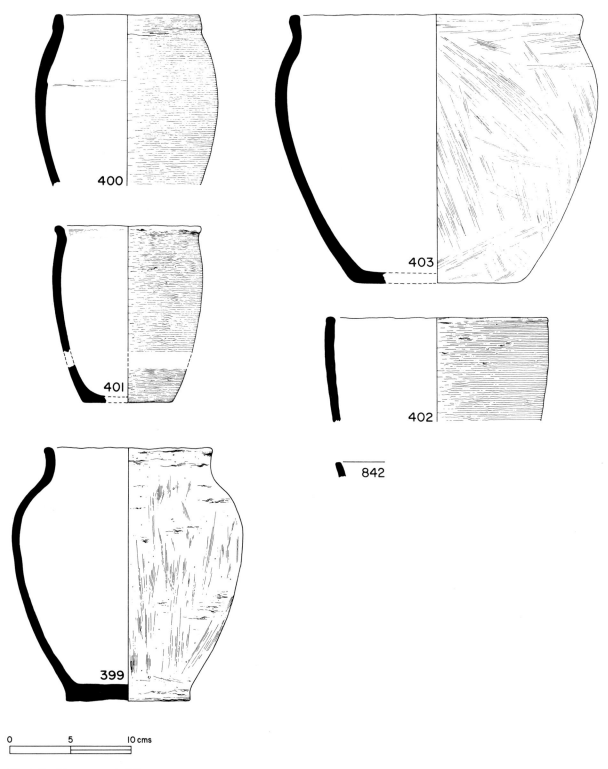

0   5   10 cms

Fig 6.88   Key group: pit 117

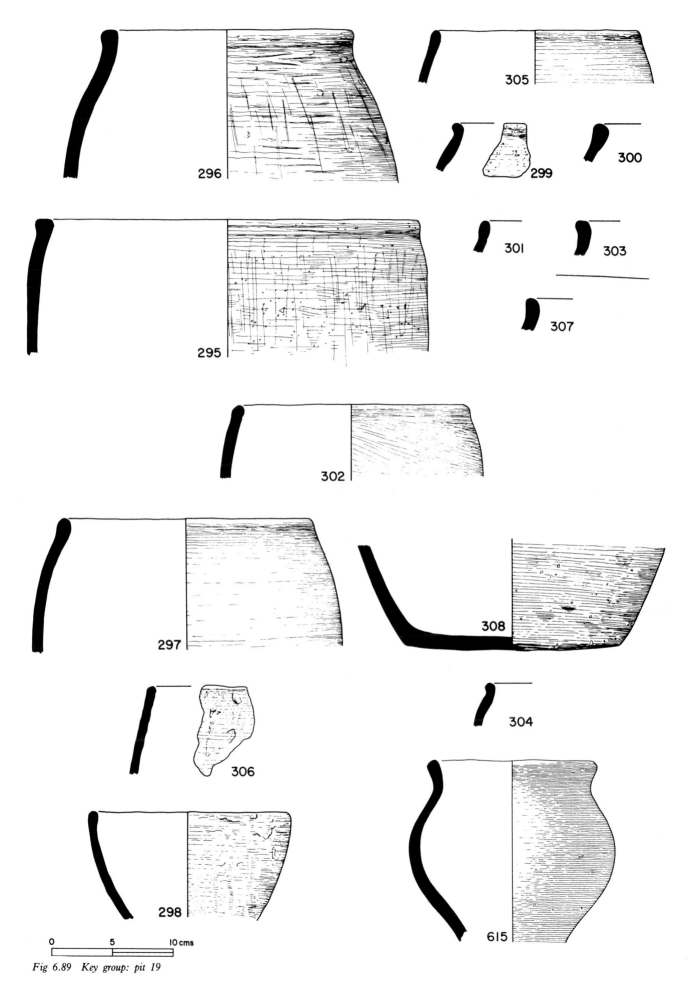

296

305

299

300

295

301

303

307

302

297

308

306

304

298

615

0   5   10 cms

Fig 6.89 Key group: pit 19

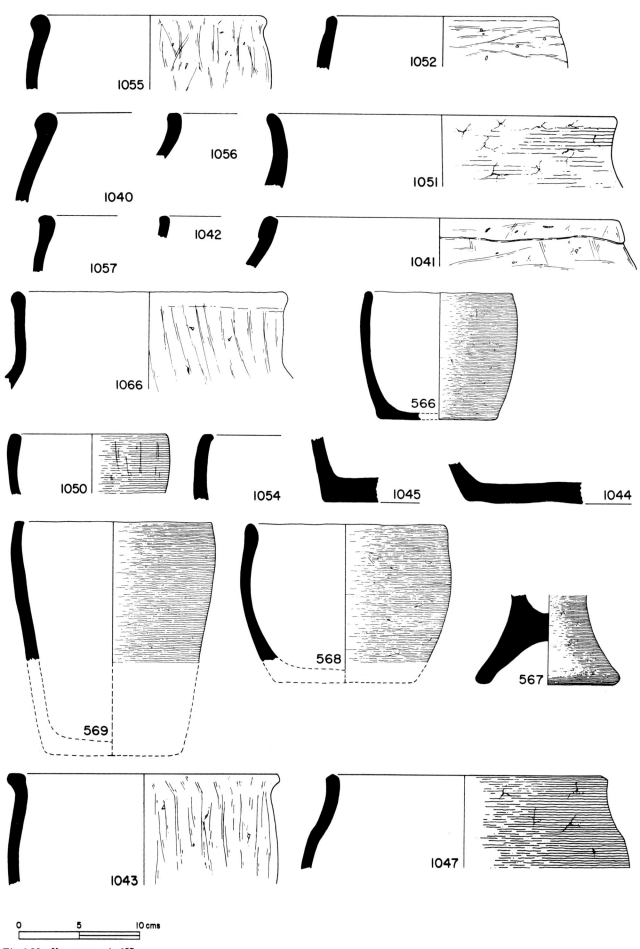

Fig 6.90   Key group: pit 657

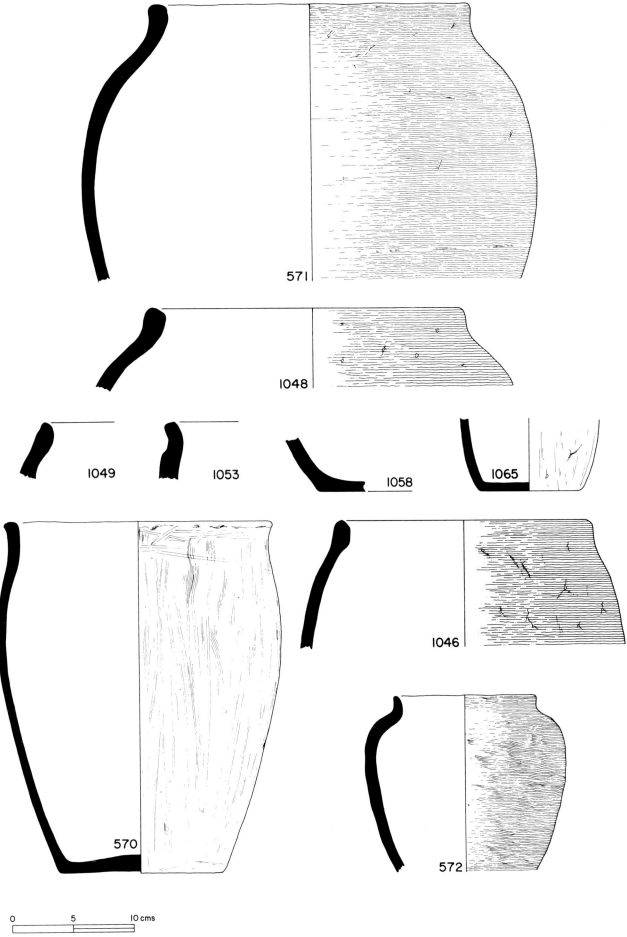

571

1048

1049

1053

1058

1065

1046

570

572

0   5   10 cms

Fig 6.91   Key group: pit 657

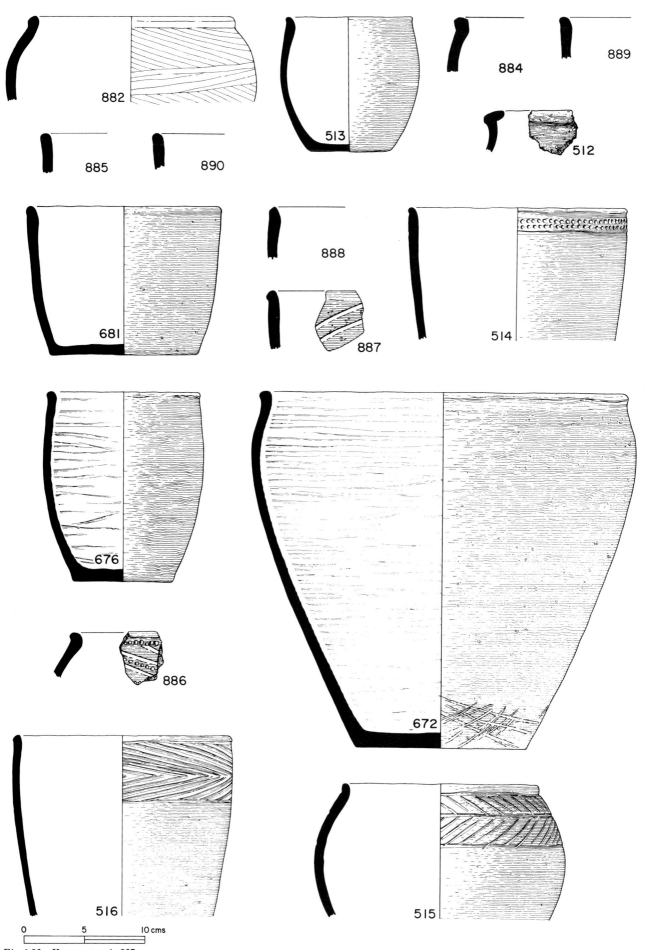

882

513

884

889

885   890

512

681

888

887

514

676

886

672

516

515

0   5   10 cms

Fig 6.92   Key group: pit 337

322

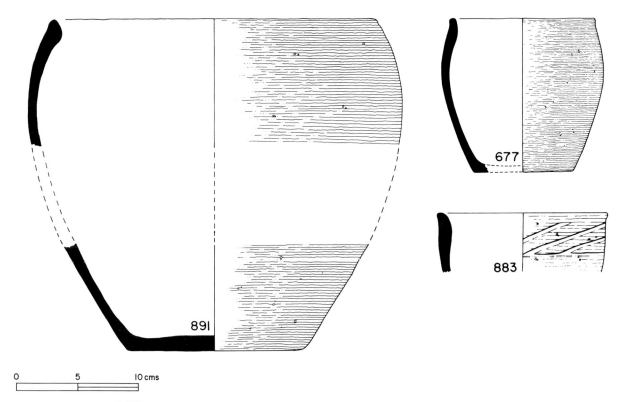

Fig 6.93   Key group: pit 337

fabrics and so would seem to be at the earlier end of the cp range (5–7) for this type. The pit contains a great many wasters.

The great majority of the pottery would be appropriate to cp 5; it is only the presence of a late type of saucepan pot (PB1) characteristic of cp 6 that indicates a later phasing. A transitional phasing would be acceptable.

	Form	Fabric	Surface	Layer	
566	PB1.1	DO	B	4	
567	JD2.1	D7	D	5	
568	JC2.3	DO	D	5	
569	PA2.1	A1-DO	D	5	
570	JB4.1	DO	B	7	
571	JC1.1	DO	D	7	
572	JD2.1	DO	B	8	over-fired
1040	JC2.1	DO	B	2	
1041	JB4.0	DO	B	3	
1042	JC2.2	DO	B	3	
1043	JB3.0	DO	A	7	
1044	base	DO	D	5	over-fired
1045	base	A1	A	5	
1946	JC2.1/2	DO	D	7	over-fired
1047	JB4.0	DO	E	7	over-fired
1048	JC1.1	AO	D	7	
1049	JC2.1	AO	A	7	over-fired
1050	PA2.1	DO	E	4,7	
1051	JB2.2	A1	B	3	
1052	JC2.2/3	DO	A	1	
1053	JB2.3	A2	B	7	
1054	PA1.1	DO	D	5	over-fired
1055	JB4.0	DO	B	1	
1056	JB3.0	DO	D	2	

	Form	Fabric	Surface	Layer
1057	JC2.1	DO	D	3
1058	base	DO	D	7
1065	base	DO	A	7
1066	JB2.2	DO	A	4,7

P337 cp 7 (Figs 6.92, 6.93)

Contains 240 sherds of which 23 (9.6%) are characteristic only of cp 7. Fabrics: A, 3 (1.25%); B, 209 (87.1%); C, 3 (1.25%); D, 23 (9.6%); F, 2 (0.8%). A typical late group of saucepan pots and jars mainly in fine flint-gritted fabrics. A relatively high percentage are shallow-tooled. No 512 is residual.

	Form	Fabric	Surface	Layer
512	JA2.1	CO:1	B	3
513	JC2.3	B3	E	3
514	PB1.1	B1	E5.2a	7,8,10
515	JC2.3	B3	E5.1b	10
516	PB1.1	B1	E5.1b	10
672	JC2.1	B3	E	8,10
676	JC2.3	DO	D	8,10
677	JC2.3	B3	E	10
681	PB1.1	B1	E	6,10
882	JC2.3	B1	E5.1b	2
883	PB1.1	B1	E5.1b	10
884	JC2.2/3	D8	D	3
885	PB1.1	CO:1	B	2
886	JC2.3	B1	E5.3b	9
887	PB1.1	B3	E5.1c	8
888	PB1.1	B1	E	4
889	PB1.1	B3	E	3
890	PB1.1	B3	D	3
891	JC2.1	B1	E	10

323

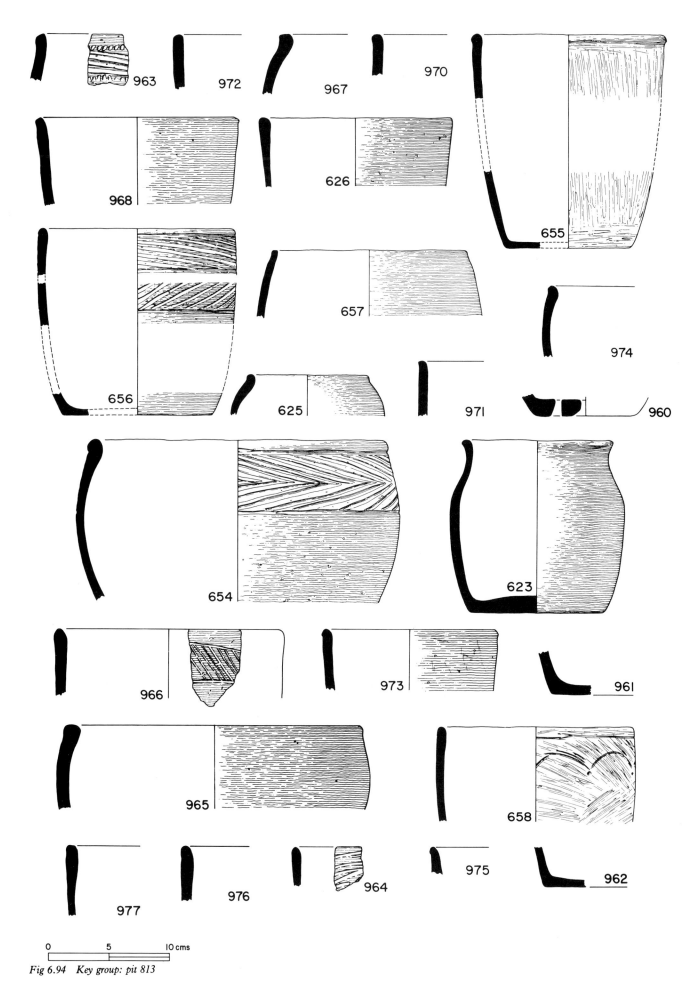

963
972
967
970
968
626
655
656
657
974
625
971
960
654
623
966
973
961
965
658
977
976
964
975
962

0   5   10 cms

Fig 6.94   Key group: pit 813

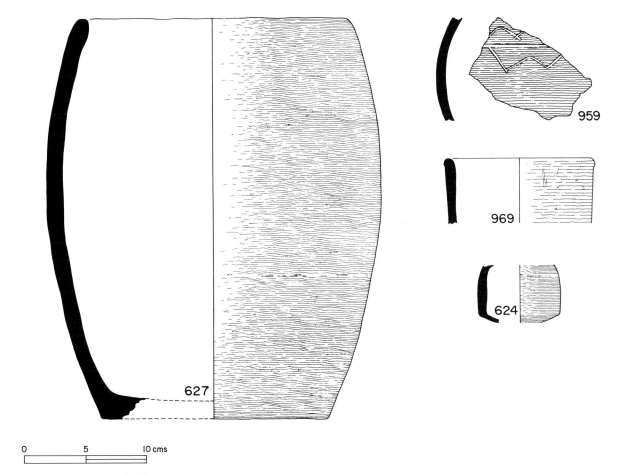

0   5   10 cms

Fig 6.95   Key group: pit 813

P813 cp 7 (Figs 6.94, 6.95)

Radiocarbon date of 210 ± 70 bc (HAR-1440). Contains 202 sherds of which 7 are characteristic only of cp 7. Fabrics: A, 9 (4.6%); B, 146 (72.3%); D, 47 (23.1%). A typical late group with a high percentage of fabric B and of shallow-tooled types. Residual sherds include 623 and 627. Vessel 624 is a unique type.

	Form	Fabric	Surface	Layer
623	JB2.3	DO	D	7,8
624	misc	DO	E	9
625	JC2.3	D11/D7	E	6
626	PB1.1	B3	E	5
627	PA1.2	DO	D	9,10
654	JC2.1	B1	E5.1b	7,8
655	PB1.1	D11	E	5,7,8,9,10
656	PB1.1	B3	E5.1b	6,7,8
657	JC2.3	DO	D	6,8
658	PB1.1	DO	E5.1fi	8

	Form	Fabric	Surface	Layer
959	body	B1	E5.1f	9,10
960	base	DO	B	6
961	base	B1	E	7
962	base	B1	E	8
963	PB1.1	B1	E5.3b	1,8
964	PB1.1	B1	E5.1b	8
965	JC2.2	B1	E	8
966	PB1.1	B1	E5.1b	7
967	JC2.2	B1	d	2
968	PB1.1	B1	E	5
969	PB1.1	b1	E	9 over-fired
970	PB1.1	B1	E	3,8
971	PB1.1	B1	E	6,7
972	PB1.1	B1	E	1,6,9
973	PB1.1	B1	E	7
974	JC2.3	B1	E	6,10
975	PB1.1	HO	B	8
976	PB1.1	B1	E	8
977	PB1.1	B1	E	8

325

P475 cp 7–8 (Fig 6.96)

Contains 286 sherds of which 3 (under 1%) are of cp 8. Fabrics: B, 209 (73%); D, 77 (27%). This is essentially a cp 7 pit in which only the top two layers (1 and 2) produced the sherds typical of cp 8 (611/653, 610, 612). The rest of the material from the lower layers is typical of a cp 7 assemblage with a high percentage of fabric B and a number of shallow-tooled sherds. A few scraps, eg 921, are residual.

	Form	Fabric	Surface	Layer
521	JD3.0	B1	E5.3b	6
524	JC2.3	B1	E	6
610	JC3.1	DO	E	2
611/653	JE1/4	DO	D	1 } cp 8
612	base	DO	E4	1
671	JC2.1	B1	E	6
902	base B1?	B1	E	5
903	base	B1	E	5
904	base	B1	E	6
905	base	B7	D	6
906	JC2.3	B1	E5.3b	4
907	JD1.1	DO	D	4
908	JC2.2	D8	E	6
909	JC1.1	B1	D	4
910	JC2.2	B1	D	3,4
911	PB1.1	B1	E	3,4
912	PB1.1	B3	E5.1c	3,4
913	PB1.1	B1	E	4
914	PB1.1	B1	E	4
915	JC2.3	B1	E5.3b	3
916	JC2.1	B1	E	4
917	PB1.1	B1	E5.3b	4
918	JC2.2	B1	E	3
919	JC2.3	B1	E5.1c	4
920	JC2.0	B1	E	3
921	JB2.2	DO	D	3
922	JB3.0	DO	E5.1b	3
923	JC2.2	DO	B	4
924	DA1.1	DO	E	4

P1089 cp 7–8 (Figs 6.97–6.99)

Contains 1,070 sherds of which 64 (5%) are of cp 8. Fabrics: B, 782 (73.1%); C, 2 (0.18%); D, 284 (26.54%); E, 2 (0.18%). This interesting assemblage is divisible into two stratified groups: the lower filling, layers 2–5, contained a typical cp 7 assemblage with a high percentage of fabric B and a number of typical shallow-tooled forms, while the uppermost layer produced vessels typical of cp 8 together with a few earlier residual sherds (eg 1014, 1031, 1032). Two body sherds of Dressel 1 amphorae were found in layer 1.

	Form	Fabric	Surface	Layer
721	handle	B3	B	2,5
722	JE1/4	D13	E5.1b	1
723	JC3.2	DO	E	1
724	BC1.1?	D13	E	1
725	JC3.1	B3	D	1
726	JC3.2	D13	E5.1d	1
727	JC3.1	B1	E	1

	Form	Fabric	Surface	Layer	
728	JC3.1	D13	E	1	
729	JC3.1	DO	E	1	
730	JD5.0	A1	A	1	
731	JC3.1	GO	E	1	
753	JE1/4	DO	E	1	
754	BD2.0	D13	E	1	
755	BD2.0	D13	E	1	
759	JC2.1	B1	E5.3b	5	
760	DA1.1	DO	E	5	
761	JD3.0	DO	E5.3a	4,5	
998	JC1.1	B7	D	4,5	
999	base	B1	E	4	
1000	JC2.2	B1	E	4,5	
1001	BC1.1	B1	E	4,5	
1002	JC2.1	B1	E	4	
1003	JC2.1	B7	D	3	over-fired
1004	JC2.1	B1	E5.1a	3,4	
1005	JD3.0	B1	E	3,4	over-fired
1006	JC2.1	B1	D	2	
1007	base	DO	B	3	
1008	base	DO	D	3	perforated
1009	base	B7	D	3	
1010	PB1.1	B1	E5.3b	2	
1011	JC2.3	B1	E5.1g/h	3	
1012	PB1.1	B1	E5.1b	3	
1013	base	D13	E	1	
1014	JB1.1	DO	B	1	
1015	JD3.0	B1	E	2	
1016	JD3.0	B1	E	2	
1017	PB1.1	B1	D	1	
1018	PB1.1	B1	E4	3	
1019	JC2.3	B1	E	2	
1020	JC2.2	B1	E	2	
1021	JC2.3	B1	E	2	
1022	PB1.1	B1	E	2	
1023	PB1.1	B1	E	2	over-fired
1024	JC2.2	DO	E	2	
1025	body	D2	E5.1f/h	2	
1026	body	B1	E5.1b	2	
1027	JC2.3	D8	D	2	
1028	PA2.0	DO	D	2	
1029	body	B1	E5.1b	2	
1030	PB1.1	B3	E	2	
1031	JC2.3	B1	E	1	
1032	JC2.2	B	E	1	
1033	PB1.1	DO	E5.1a	2	
1034	JC2.3	A1	B	2	
1035	PB1.1	B1	D	2	
1036	PB1.1	B1	E	2	
1037	JC2.3	D8	D	3	
1038	DA1.1	DO	D	2	
1039	JC2.2	B1	D	2	
1067	JD3.0	B1	E	3	

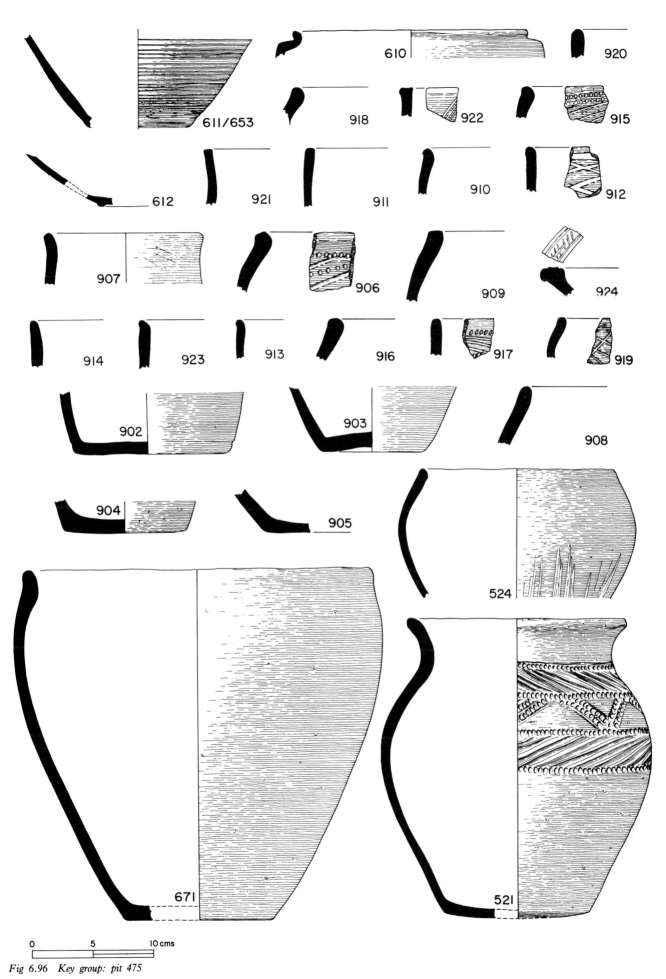

611/653

610

920

918

922

915

612

921

911

910

912

907

906

909

924

914

923

913

916

917

919

902

903

908

904

905

524

671

521

0 5 10 cms

Fig 6.96 Key group: pit 475

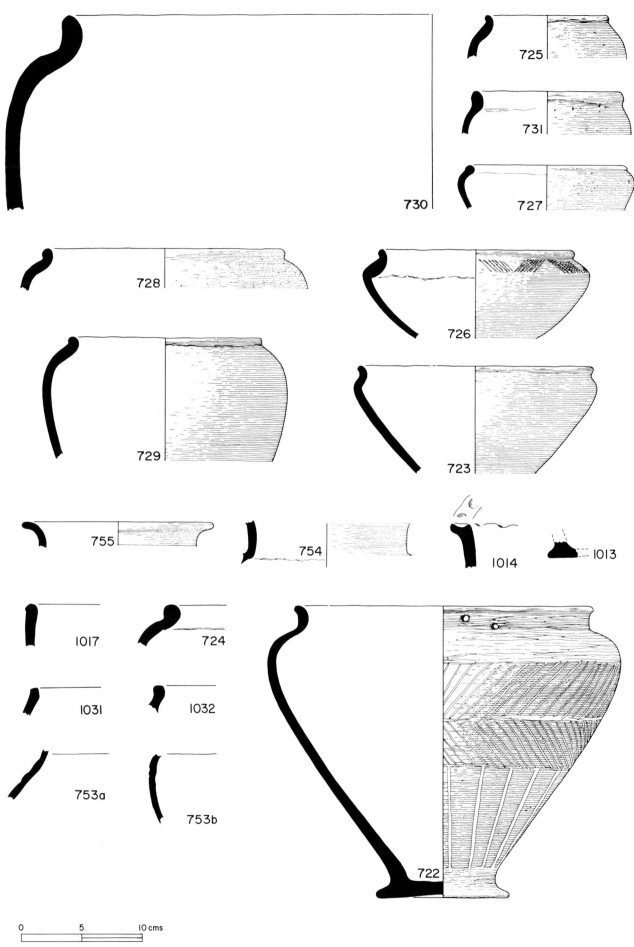

725

731

730

727

728

726

729

723

755

754

1014

1013

1017

724

1031

1032

753a

753b

722

0   5   10 cms

Fig 6.97   Key group: pit 1089

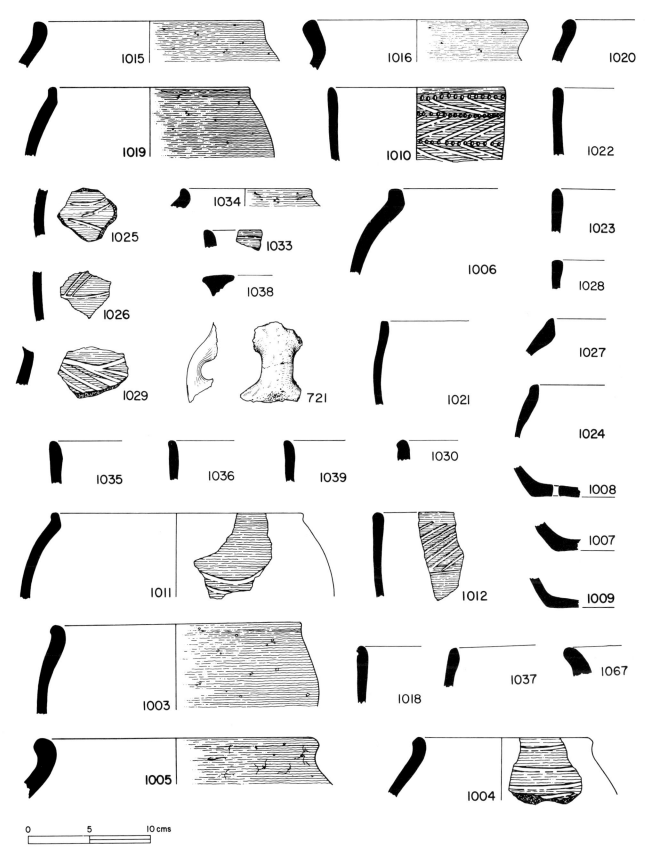

1015 1016 1020 1019 1010 1022 1025 1034 1033 1006 1023 1026 1038 1028 1029 721 1021 1027 1024 1035 1036 1039 1030 1008 1011 1012 1007 1009 1003 1018 1037 1067 1005 1004

0 5 10 cms

Fig 6.98   Key group: pit 1089

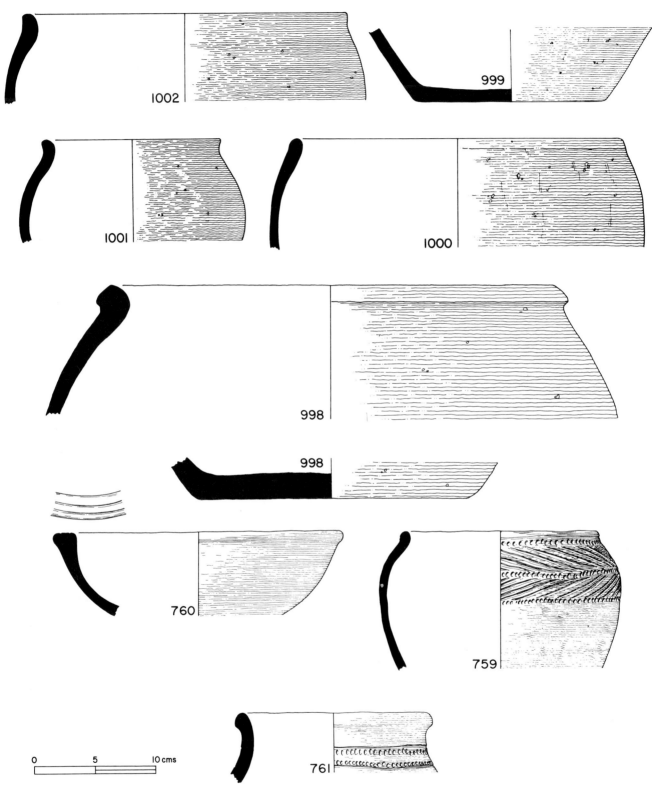

1002

999

1001

1000

998

998

760

759

761

0   5   10 cms

Fig 6.99   Key group: pit 1089

Appendix 5: the nature of the available archive

The primary archive is, of course, the pottery itself which at present is stored in the Institute of Archaeology at Oxford pending future study. It will eventually be transferred to the Hampshire County Museum Service to join the rest of the Danebury collection. The pottery is stored in context number order except for illustrated sherds which are arranged separately in the order of their unique number.

Four separate catalogues exist:

a *Context index*   A card index containing brief notes on the sherds from each context. The index was compiled on site during excavation and serves as a simple check list for pottery-containing contexts.

b *Sherd index*   A card index of all drawn sherds (whether published or not) listing context and fabric and with a reduced photograph of the sherd drawing attached. Arranged in unique sherd number order.

c *Context sheet*   An A4 sheet for each context recording form, fabric, surface treatment, number of sherds, number of rims, total weight, and unique sherd number if assigned. The context sheets represent the intermediate stage between the fine sorting of the sherds and the computer recording.

d *Computerized data bank*   The information recorded on the context sheet has been computerized (fiche 8, frames A3–4) from which source it can be listed in a variety of ways. Only pottery from postholes has not been computerized.

Bibliography

(includes bibliography for the relevant microfiche sections)

Bradford, J S P, 1942   An Early Iron Age site on Blewburton Hill, Berks, *Berkshire Archaeol J*, **46**, 97–104
Brailsford, J W, 1948   Excavations at Little Woodbury. Part II, *Proc Prehist Soc*, **14**, 1–23
Bushe-Fox, J P, 1915   *Excavations at Hengistbury Head, Hampshire in 1911–12*
Calkin, J B, 1949   The Isle of Purbeck in the Iron Age, *Proc Dorset Natur. Hist Archaeol Soc*, **70**, 29–59
————, 1951   Prehistoric Pokesdown, *Proc Bournemouth Natur Sci Soc*, **40**, 79–88
————, 1965   Some Early Iron Age sites in the Bournemouth area, *Proc Dorset Natur Hist Archaeol Soc*, **86**, 120–30
Calkin, J B, & Piggott, C M, 1939   Iron Age 'A' habitation sites at Langton Matravers, *ibid*, **60**, 66–72
Chadwick, S, & Thompson, M W, 1956   Note on an Iron Age habitation site near Battlesbury Camp, Warminster, *Wiltshire Archaeol Mag*, **56**, 262–4
Clay, R C C, 1924   An Early Iron Age site on Fifield Bavant Down, *ibid*, **42**, 457–96
————, 1925   An inhabited site of La Tène I date on Swallowcliffe Down, *ibid*, **43**, 59–93
————, 1927   Supplementary report on the Early Iron Age village on Swallowcliffe Down, *ibid*, **46**, 540–7
Collins, A E P, 1947   Excavations on Blewburton Hill, 1947, *Berkshire Archaeol J*, **50**, 4–29
————, 1953   Excavations on Blewburton Hill, 1948 and 1949, *ibid*, **53**, 21–64
Collins, A E P, & Collins, F J, 1959   Excavations on Blewburton Hill, 1953, *ibid*, **57**, 52–73
Cunliffe, B W, 1964   *Winchester excavations, 1949–1960*, 1
————, 1966   *Regional groupings within the Iron Age of southern Britain*, PhD thesis, Univ Cambridge
————, 1973   Chapter on Iron Age, in *VCH Wilts*, **1**.2 (ed E Crittal), 408–38
————, 1974   *Iron Age communities in Britain*, 1 edn
————, 1978   *Iron Age communities in Britain*, 2 edn
————, 1982   Britain, the Veneti and beyond, *Oxford J Archaeol*, **1**.1, 39–68
————, 1983   Settlement hierarchy and social change in southern Britain in the Iron Age, *Acta Archaeol Leidensia*, forthcoming
Cunliffe, B W, & Phillipson, D W, 1968   Excavations at Eldon's Seat, Encombe, Dorset, England, *Proc Prehist Soc*, **34**, 191–237
Cunnington, H, 1871   Oldbury Camp, Wilts, *Wiltshire Archaeol Mag*, **28**, 277

Cunnington, M E, 1908   Oliver's Camp, Devizes, *ibid*, **35**, 408-44
————, 1923   *An Early Iron Age inhabited site at All Cannings Cross*
————, 1925   Figsbury Rings: an account of excavations in 1924, *Wiltshire Archaeol Mag*, **43**, 48-58
————, 1932   Chisbury Camp, *ibid*, **46**, 4–7
————, 1933   Excavations in Yarnbury Castle Camp, 1932, *ibid*, **46**, 198-213
Cunnington, M E, & Cunnington, B H, 1913   Casterley Camp excavations, *ibid*, **38**, 53–105
————, & ————, 1917   Lidbury Camp, *ibid*, **40**, 12–36
Cunnington, M E, and Goddard, E H, 1934   *The Devizes Museum Catalogue*, Part 2
Davies, H, 1936   The shale industries at Kimmeridge, Dorset, *Archaeol J*, **93**, 200–19
Davies, S M, 1981   Excavations at Old Down Farm, Andover. Part 2: prehistoric and Roman, *Proc Hampshire Fld Club Archaeol Soc*, **37**, 81–163
Doran, J E, & Hodson, F R, 1975   *Mathematics and computers in archaeology*
Dowden, W A, 1957   Little Solsbury Hill Camp, *Proc Bristol Univ Spelaeol Soc*, **8**, 18-29
————, 1962   Little Solsbury Hill Camp, *ibid*, **9**, 177–82
Falconer, J P E, & Adams, S B, 1935   Recent finds at Solsbury Hill Camp near Bath, *ibid*, **4**, 133–222
Ford, J A, 1962   A quantitative method for deriving cultural chronology, *Technical Manual 1, Dept Social Affairs, Pan American Union*, Washington DC
Fowler, P J, Musty, J W G, & Taylor, C C, 1965   Some earthwork enclosures in Wiltshire, *Wiltshire Archaeol Mag*, **60**, 52–74
Hawkes, C F C, 1939   The excavations at Quarley Hill, 1938, *Proc Hampshire Fld Club Archaeol Soc*, **14**, 136–94
Hole, F, & Shaw, M, 1967   Computer analysis of chronological seriation, *Rice University Stud*, **53**(3), Houston
Hooley, W, 1927   Hallstatt pottery from Winchester, *Proc Hampshire Fld Club Archaeol Soc*, **10**, 63–8
Liddell, D M, 1933   Excavations at Meon Hill, *ibid*, **12**, 127–62
————, 1935   Report on the Hampshire Field Club's excavation at Meon Hill, *ibid*, **13**, 7–54
Meyrick, O, 1946   Notes on some Early Iron Age sites in the Marlborough district, *Wiltshire Archaeol Mag*, **51**, 256–63
Neal, D S, 1980   Bronze Age, Iron Age and Roman settlements at Little Somborne and Ashley, Hampshire, *Proc Hampshire Fld Club Archaeol Soc*, **36**, 91–144
Passmore, A D, 1914   Liddington Castle Camp, *Wiltshire Archaeol Mag*, **38**, 576–84
Peacock, D P S, 1971   Roman amphorae in pre-Roman Britain, in *The Iron Age and its hillforts* (eds M Jesson & D Hill), 161–88
Peake, H, Coghlan, H, & Hawkes, C F C, 1932   Early Iron Age remains in Boxford Common, Berks, *Trans Newbury Dist Fld Club*, **6**, 136–50
Piggott, S, & Piggott, C M, 1940   Excavations at Rams Hill, Uffington, Berks, *Antiq J*, **20**, 465–80
Pitt-Rivers, A H L F, 1887   *Excavations in Cranborne Chase*, 1
Richardson, K M, 1951   The excavation of Iron Age villages on Boscombe Down West, *Wiltshire Archaeol Mag*, **54**, 123–68
Richmond, I A, 1968   *Hod Hill, 2: Excavations carried out between 1951 and 1958*
Smith, K, 1977   The excavation of Winklebury camp, Basingstoke, Hampshire, *Proc Prehist Soc*, **43**, 31–129
Stevens, F, 1934   The Highfield pit dwellings, Fisherton, Salisbury, *Wiltshire Archaeol Mag*, **46**, 579–624
University of California 1977   *BMDP biomedical computer programs P-series*
Wainwright, G J, 1970   The excavation of Balksbury Camp, Andover, Hants, *Proc Hampshire Fld Club Archaeol Soc*, **26**, 21–55
————, 1979   *Gussage All Saints. An Iron Age settlement in Dorset*
Wheeler, R E M, 1943   *Maiden Castle, Dorset*
Williams, A, 1951   Excavations at Allard's Quarry, Marnhull, Dorset, *Proc Dorset Natur Hist Archaeol Soc*, **72**, 20–75

7 The material remains

7.1 Small finds
7.1.1 Introduction
In this section the small finds are arranged in categories based on the material of which they are made. Each group is given a prefix, thus:

1 bronze
2 iron
3 bone and antler
4 Kimmeridge shale
5 coral and amber
6 glass
7 baked clay
8 stone
9 wood

Within each group, the illustrated finds are numbered consecutively.

A high percentage of the total number of small objects is illustrated in this volume but in the case of repetitive items only a sample appears in the text while the rest are illustrated in the microfiche. Small amorphous fragments have generally not been drawn but all are fully listed in the fiche descriptions.

The general policy adopted is to discuss groups of objects in the text. The fiche lists all objects, giving for each basic measurements and details of stratigraphical context, but an item which receives extended treatment in the text (eg the objects comprising the bronze hoard) is given only summary listing in the fiche while objects discussed in groups in the text are more extensively described in the fiche. All objects have a unique small finds number; those illustrated in the text are also given a publication number.

To give some indication of the relative frequency of certain classes of finds a *frequency index* has been calculated. This is helpful because the number of pits in each phase varies considerably and therefore biases the number of objects recovered. The frequency index is calculated by dividing the total number of artefacts by the total number of pits from that phase. The smallest figure obtained is then divided into the other figures to give *relative frequency*, the original smallest figure becoming 1.

7.1.2 Coins (Fig 7.1)
Four coins have been found on Danebury:
1.1 Gallo-Belgic C stater; small find no 8; context: Trench 6, layer 21
1.2 Verica stater; small find no 43; context: Trench 14, layer 20
1.3 Durotrigan silver stater; found before 1858; now in British Museum
1.4 Dupondius of Vespasian; small find no 409; context: unstratified

1.1 Gallo-Belgic C stater
by Lyn Sellwood

Bronze core plated with gold. Weight: 4.24 gm. *Obverse:* Laureate head of Apollo towards the right. The face is visible in its entirety, but most of the flan is occupied by the lively pattern elements of the hair, and of the laurel wreath itself. *Reverse:* Disjointed horse facing right. Eight pellets and one crescent are visible above the horse, while a single pellet is visible below.

This coin is evidently an ancient forgery, and comprises a copper alloy core to which a skin of gold leaf has been applied. The bright green, heavily patinated core shows through clearly beneath the gilding particularly around the perimeter of the coin and on the high points of the relief design. The gold with which the coin was plated is very yellow in colour and corresponds exactly in appearance with the genuine gold stater coins of the series. X-ray fluorescence analysis was conducted on the Danebury coin and on three Gallo-Belgic C staters from the Heberden Coin Room, by Dr M Pollard (fiche 9, frames A4–5). The results are set out in Table 35.

Although it was not possible to measure the thin gilded layer of the coin with accuracy, the absence of silver in the alloy marks a significant departure from the normal composition. The XRF examination also revealed traces of mercury, which suggests that the mercury gilding process was used to apply the gold. This method was not common before the Later Roman Empire (Lins & Oddy 1975), and the Danebury coin is thus a very early example of the technique.

The phenomenon of false coins is generally quite commonplace among the Celts, although few examples are known amongst these very early Gaulish introductions to Britain. The Danebury coin, while not actually die-linked with any other example of Gallo-Belgic C in the Index of British Celtic Coin Finds (maintained in the Institute of Archaeology, Oxford), is very much akin to many of these in style. Both of the dies from which the coin has been struck are quite worn. This argues for considerable use, since 10,000 strikings to each die is a conservative estimate (Sellwood 1963). The implication is therefore that, while technically a forgery, the Danebury coin was probably minted from official dies, and indeed has the rather squared off flan shape common to this class of coin. The sole factor which would have led to the immediate detection of this coin as a forgery is its low weight. Simone Scheers has divided the Gallo-Belgic C series, which she refers to as *Ambiani bifaces*, into five classes. The Danebury example has been assigned to class II for which the likely weight, according to Scheers, is between 6.80 and 6.89 gm (Scheers 1977, 47).

The exact date of the Gallo-Belgic C series is far from certain. The chronological bracket proposed by Allen is derived by extrapolating backwards from the fixed point of the Le Câtillon hoard, in which a British B stater, a coin closely related to Gallo-Belgic was found. 'Gallo-Belgic C is two removes from British B, which we have now placed somewhere in the order of 70 or 80 BC. It is impossible yet to say by how many years Gallo-Belgic C preceded British B, but a date in the order of 100 BC

Table 35

Coin	Bequest	Weight	Cu	AV	Ag	Other
G-BC	Keble Coll	6.56	5.1	68.9	26.1	
G-BC	Willet	6.649	3.7	71.7	24.7	Fe, Sb?
G-BC	Vaux Cat 26	6.54	4.1	72.7	23.2	
G-BC	Danebury forgery (uncleaned surface)	4.24	35	65	—	Sn, Fe, Sb?

Weights expressed in gm and metals as percentages

Fig 7.1 Iron Age coins: 1 Gallo-Belgic C stater; 2 stater of Verica; 3 Durotrigan (scale 1:2; photo: Bob Wilkins)

would not be out of the question' (Allen 1961, 107). Since 1961 when Allen assessed these coinages, the date for the deposition of the hoard, and even the reliability of the associations within it, have been much questioned. Any attempt at estimating the time span of a Celtic coinage, let alone the chronological separation of a number of series, is a highly speculative pursuit. There is no reason to suppose that coinage was minted continuously once it had been introduced to any region or people. It is quite conceivable that it was struck sporadically, to meet particular internal or external needs, rather than being produced regularly as would suit a commodity utilized in everyday exchange. Scheers prefers a slightly later date for the coinage than that tendered by Allen, and suggests that it was struck during the first quarter or third of the 1st century BC (Scheers 1977, 48).

Archaeologists and numismatists have for a number of years considered the possibility that Gallo-Belgic C, which had a considerable influence on the style of subsequent British coinages, was the issue of King Diviciacus, the ruler of the Suessiones recorded by Caesar (*BG*, II,4) as having under his dominion part of Gaul and also Britain. Scheers, on the other hand, concludes from the Gaulish distribution of the coins — centred upon the départements of Somme, Pas-de-Calais, and Oise — that it is 'évident que le centre de la distribution est le pays ambien' (Scheers 1977, 46). The British distribution of Gallo-Belgic C has an apparent centre in north-west Kent, and the Danebury piece is situated on the western fringe of these widely scattered, somewhat sparse, coins.

1.2 Verica stater, Mack no 121

by Lyn Sellwood

Bronze core of gold-plated forgery. Weight: 3.037 gm. *Obverse*: The inscription COM. F, an abbreviation of *Commi Filius*, set within a sunken tablet. *Reverse*: Inscribed VIR RIX. Horse and naked rider facing right. The horseman's right arm is raised, and his hand in which he holds a dagger(?) is level with his head. The inscription VIR is located to the left of his lifted arm, and the final letter is partially obscured by it. Badly spaced lettering is a feature which occurs elsewhere in this series. Below the horse are found the letters RIX.

This latter feature is unique; on all other dies in this series the inscription in this position reads REX. Die wear does tend to obliterate the horizontal strokes of the E, but the example under discussion was evidently struck from a quite fresh die. The engraver of the dies from which the forged coin was minted may perhaps have copied the inscription from a worn official issue, although the interchangeable nature of the letters I and E is a feature encountered elsewhere on coins of this ruler whose name is sometimes abbreviated to VIR, as on this example, and on others recorded in full as VERICA. RIX could plausibly be seen as a deliberate Celticization of the Latin title. Some of the issues of Cunobelin display the epithet RIGONI, and the gold stater issues of the Dobunnic rulers Anted and Eisu include the inscription RIC after the name.

Neither the obverse nor the reverse die of this coin are encountered elsewhere, in what is otherwise a fairly closely die-linked series. One other forgery of the type is known, and this too is minted from a discrete set of dies. The obverse die of the Danebury coin, and both dies of the other forgery, display quite considerable wear.

The style of engraving on the reverse of the coin is very close indeed to that of one or two *bona fide* pieces within

the group, and these might reasonably be regarded as the work of a single engraver who had possibly received some provincial training. Many of the other extant dies do not betray such classical influence and are clearly the work of native craftsmen.

The coin is considerably patinated, although in a very good state of preservation. An examination with the naked eye reveals no sign of the gold with which it was presumably plated. Even allowing for such a covering, the weight of this stater would have been very much below the average for this series, which is 5.13 gm.

The dates of Verica's coinage can be determined with some precision. He was the last of the Atrebatic rulers who styled himself a son of Commius, and some of his later issues copy the portrait heads of Tiberius. Some of the coins of Tincommius, one of Verica's predecessors, may copy Augustan issues. The Mack 121 coins are stylistically very close to the horseman issues of Tincommius, and are thus likely to be early in Verica's reign. Their date can therefore be determined with some certainty as lying within the twenties and thirties of the 1st century AD (Allen 1944, 1–47).

Since two of the Celtic coins from the hillfort are forgeries, this note is concluded with a brief discussion of this phenomenon. 'Forgery' is perhaps an unfortunate, certainly an emotive term, which may in fact misrepresent the intended function of the coins. The precise usage of the false coin within the Celtic world remains the subject of considerable speculation. It has frequently been observed that they tend to occur at major centres or temple sites, or on the fringes of normal distribution patterns. These tendencies may be more apparent than real — the result, for example, of biases towards certain types of site or regions. In any case numbers are very small, and until the data base is improved, nothing can be said with certainty. Any patterns which emerge concerning the precise site location of coins will of course have bearings on their function. It has been suggested that the coins were utilized as tokens, equally valid in transactions of a specialized nature as were the full weight coins within their own particular sphere. It is also possible that the false coin was regarded as a perfectly acceptable offering to the gods. The proposal that the false coin did indeed function as a counterfeit, more easily passed in border areas where the population was less familiar with the official coinage, cannot be rejected on present evidence.

1.3 Durotrigan silver stater

by Melinda Mays

Durotrigan silver stater found at Danebury Hill before 1858; now in the British Museum (Cat 1147). Weight: 5.33 gm.

The stater is of Allen's type B, which is distinguished stylistically from the other types by the presence on the obverse of a 'forked branch' and on the reverse of ringed dots above the pellets over the horse's back, a little hook above the rear leg of the horse, and the lines leading down from the rear leg, which have dots in between them (Allen 1968, 47).

Other type B staters have been found in Dorset at Hod Hill (two coins), Langton (one and possibly two coins), Tarrant Hinton, Purbeck (vague find spot due to discovery by metal detector), and either Shroton or Mere (Wilts); in Hampshire at Tinker's Cross and Holdenhurst (the latter is a coin in a hoard deposited most probably in the first third of the 2nd century AD); and on the Isle of Wight and at Cambridge. A further five coins are recorded, but are without provenance (Macken-sen 1974, 60–1).

The Danebury coin is best seen against the background of the Durotrigan staters as a whole. Silver staters may be divided into two main phases, Phase I consisting of Allen's types A–C, and Phase II of types D–F (Mays forthcoming). Phase I staters stand out as being of fine metal and craftsmanship, higher weight, and of concave-convex shape, and therefore appear to be broadly contemporary.

Distribution of Phase I and II staters is distinct: Phase I coins are largely concentrated in a small area contained in the fork formed by the River Stour and its tributary the River Allen, while Phase II coins are more diffuse, spreading over most of the territory of the Durotriges.

The only fixed dating point for the earliest silver staters is found in the Le Câtillon hoard, which included six type A staters in fresh condition, suggesting that they had not long been in circulation. The hoard was dated to between 56 and 51 BC by Allen, who associated its depositing with Caesar's campaigns (Allen 1961, 297). It is possible, however, that the Le Câtillon hoard was deposited at a later date, in the 40s or even 30s BC, which would bring the introduction of the silver staters to a date around the 40s BC.

While the Le Câtillon hoard gives an indication of the date around which the Phase I silver staters first appeared, there is no secure evidence for the time at which they ceased to be struck. There may well have been a gap between the striking of Phase I and II staters, due to their great difference in style, metal content, weight, and distribution. It is not certain how long the gap would have been, but the date of the Phase II silver staters is likely to have been nearer to that of the struck bronze staters (to which they have a greater stylistic, metrological, and distributional affinity), which have been found in Claudian contexts. These matters are discussed in detail in Mays forthcoming.

1.4 Dupondius of Vespasian
by John W Taylor

R.I.C. 744 AE. AD 72–73. Lugdunum mint. Weight: 9.689 gm. *Obverse*: [IMP] CAES [AR] VESP [ASIAN AVG COS IIII.] Head of Vespasian facing right, radiate. *Reverse*: SECURITAS [AVGVSTI]. S.C. beneath ex-ergue, with dotted border. Securitas seated facing right; resting head on right hand; to right of figure an altar and torch.

This coin was found during the excavations of 1972. Its obverse is badly corroded, which obscures the portrait-ure and renders the legend largely illegible. Only a small area of patination survives on the obverse. In contrast, the reverse is quite well preserved, though the heavy green patina is slightly pitted, with some corrosion in evidence at the edges. Part of the legend and details of the relief are lost on the reverse due to wear which hints at some period of circulation prior to deposition.

7.1.3 The Late Bronze Age hoard (Figs 7.2–7.4)
by Dennis Britton, Brendan O'Connor, and Barry Cunliffe

The items classed together here form a coherent group but were found under conditions which seriously qualify the use of the word 'hoard'. The first item (no 1.11) was found in 1974 in the roots of a tree which had blown over. The find spot was noted and the object acquired by Dr N B Potter in whose collection it now resides. Subsequently, in 1977, the entire area was excavated

archaeologically. During this work a further eleven items were recovered in one group (nos 1.5–1.10; 1.12–1.16). They were found lying close together in soil which had been disturbed quite recently by tree roots and burrow-ing animals: ten of them lay in a cluster 2.5 m in diameter, the eleventh was a further 2 m from the main cluster. The most likely original location for the hoard seems to have been a small pit (P1007) c 1 m in diameter and 0.8 m deep. The pit was partially sealed by the rampart extension, dating approximately to the 4th century BC, and partly cut away by the deep quarry pit immediately behind the extended rampart. The bronzes therefore reached their final positions as the result of comparatively recent erosion of the pit sides, displace-ment by growing tree roots, subsequent disturbance by burrowing animals, and the movement of the roots by wind action.

There is, however, a second group of bronzes comprising seven items (1.17–1.23) which were recovered from a cp 7 occupation layer in the filling of the quarry hollow in the immediate vicinity of the pit. They stand out as quite distinct from other material in the layer and by virtue of their position are best regarded as part of the hoard, washed down from the face of the pit exposed in the quarry face in an earlier phase of erosion, to be incorporated in later occupation layers.

The objects are described individually below. Nos 1.5–1.16 are described by Brendan O'Connor and were first published in Cunliffe & O'Connor 1979, 236–9; nos 1.17–1.23 are described by Dennis Britton. Where the item has been analysed a note is appended by Peter Northover. Context data, small find numbers, and measurements are listed in the microfiche (fiche 9, frames A6–8).

1.5 Flat axe

The thin butt is irregularly curved. The sides diverge slightly to the central bevel, then more sharply to the edge, which has been expanded by resharpening. The sides are flat, the angles rounded.

This axe belongs to the form usually referred to as 'thin-butted', though Burgess prefers the term 'narrow-butted' (1974, 193, n 174). It is an example of Type B of Coles and Case (Coles 1968-9, 3–5; Case 1966, 150–2), Britton's Migdale type (1963, 270–1), and Harbison's Balleyvalley type (1969, 32–55, 78-9). The presence of the bevel indicates a certain typological development (Burgess 1974, 191). These axes are most common in Ireland; no comprehensive study of their distribution in England has been published. They belong to Stage III of Early Bronze Age metalworking as defined by Burgess (1964, 192–3), that is the early 2nd millennium BC. The Danebury axe is an unusually small example; the smallest in Harbison's corpus are both c 63 mm long (1969, 46, no 1290, pl 57, 2; 53, no 1954, pl 66, 18). Such examples were probably the blades of light woodworking tools (Britton 1963, 271).

1.6 Axe with cast flanges

The thin arched butt protrudes above the top of the flanges which are curved in profile and deepest above the transverse ridge across the blade. Below this ridge are five grooves, obscured by wear down the centre of the face. From the lowest groove the blade tapers in profile towards the edge which has been expanded by resharpen-ing; above the grooves the sides of the axe converge slightly towards the butt. The flanges are slightly convex in section. The blade is twisted out of alignment with the upper part of the axe. Modern damage has caused a notch

335

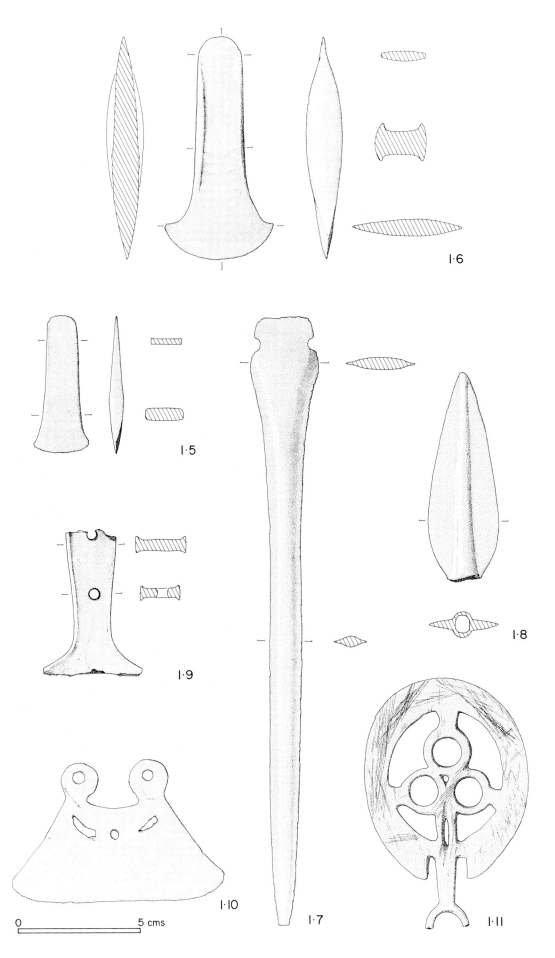

1·6

1·5

1·9

1·7

1·8

1·10

1·11

0   5 cms

Fig 7.2 Bronze hoard

in each flange on one side. This flanged axe belongs to the Arreton type (Britton 1963, 286, 305, fig 18, a-b, d, pl XXVII, first and second left), characteristic of the Arreton tradition of the end of the Early Bronze Age in southern Britain, the middle of the 2nd millennium BC (Britton 1963, 284–97; Burgess 1974, 193–4). The distribution of Arreton axes is largely confined to southern and eastern England, with concentrations on the south coast, in Wessex, the lower Thames valley, the northern part of East Anglia, and east Yorkshire (Burgess & Cowen 1972, fig 6,2), in contrast with the distribution of contemporary daggers and spearheads (*ibid*, figs 6,13–14). These areas were all to be centres of axe production during later phases of the Bronze Age. The Danebury axe is a small example (Britton 1963, 286).

1.7 Dirk or short rapier

The blade is slightly bent and the tip has been broken off recently. The trapezoidal hilt has two notches; a broad midrib extends from the base of the notches to the tip of the blade. The edges are irregularly serrated.

The form of the hilt and blade section of this dirk distinguishes it as a member of the Mildenhall variant of Burgess's Group IV of the Penard phase, the end of the 2nd millennium BC (1968b, 14–15; 1974, 206,n 275, fig 35, a1). The form of such weapons is consistent whatever their length (Rowlands 1976, fig 6), but longer examples are usually called 'rapiers' and shorter examples 'dirks'. In southern Britain, the distribution of Group IV weapons, Rowlands' Class 3, is concentrated in the Thames valley (Rowlands 1976, map 19).

1.8 Spearhead

Leaf-shaped spearhead with the socket broken off at the base of the blade. The socket is irregular in thickness and distorted at the break; it extends externally to the tip of the spearhead and internally for 32 mm. The wings are solid with bevelled edges which are worn, especially around the tip. This spearhead belongs to the plain type with peg holes in the socket. This type has a wide chronological range (Ehrenberg 1977, 13–15) but is most common in the Wilburton and Ewart Park phases of the Late Bronze Age, the early 1st millennium BC (Burgess 1968a, 36, 39).

1.9 The upper part of the hilt of a flange-hilted sword

The top of the pommel is straight; the scar of the casting-jet extends over the central 18 mm with casting seams on either side. There is one complete rivet hole and part of another. In section the flanges are straight and the rivet holes biconical. The form of the hilt and the size of the rivet holes suggest that it belongs to the Ewart Park type (Cowen 1933). This is Burgess's Group V, eponymous for the Ewart Park phase of the Late Bronze Age, centred on the 8th century BC (Burgess 1968a, 17, 39–40, fig 17,1).

Ewart Park swords are found over most of Britain and Ireland (*ibid*, fig 12) with the major British concentration in the lower Thames valley. There are three hilts in the Ashley Wood hoard, Hants, *c* 10 km south-east of Danebury (Burgess *et al* 1972, 237, figs 19–20) and a complete, though broken, example from the hillfort of Figsbury Rings, Wilts, *c* 14 km west of Danebury (Moore & Rowlands 1972, 61, no 72, pl XIV).

1.10 Razor

This razor is flat with a trapezoidal blade, tapering in profile towards the edge which is worn by resharpening. The two perforated ring-handles and the openwork ornament in the blade are irregular and asymmetrical; the openwork casting has not been trimmed or finished. The outer margins are rounded. This is an example of Jockenhövel's Endingen type of Ha C (1971, 238-9) found in western Germany, southern France, Belgium, and Britain. There are several other British examples including finds from hillforts at Ham Hill (Piggott 1946, 140, no 91) and South Cadbury, Somerset (Alcock 1971, 5, pl IV, c)

1.11 Razor

This razor has an annular blade with trefoil openwork ornament; the handle consists of a shaft with a ring terminal, now broken. There are extensive marks of sharpening on the blade.

The form of this razor cannot be matched precisely, but the annular blade, openwork ornament, and ring terminal can all be found on razors from a late Ha C group in Burgundy (Wamser 1975, 69, Taf 18,7; 19, 1–4).

1.12 Looped socketed axe (complete)

It has an irregular convex collar with an ill-defined moulding below; pendent from this are four thin ribs which end in small pellets. The blade is trapezoidal with straight sides; below the pellets it has been expanded by resharpening. There are transverse marks of grinding on the lower 15 mm of the blade. The broad loop springs from the moulding below the collar. There are distinct casting seams down the sides of the axe. The mouth is sub-rectangular and broader at right angles to the plane of the edge than in the plane of the edge. The axe is almost rectangular in section with slightly convex faces, straight sides, and well-defined angles.

1.13 The lower part of the blade of a socketed axe

Several pieces are broken off the edge. Decoration consists of three narrow vertical ribs ending in rings which contain pellets; these are slightly irregular. The blade is trapezoidal with straight sides. The edge bears marks of grinding on the faces and sides and the marks of the blows which removed the pieces from the edge; the ribs also bear marks of blows. The section is rectangular with well-defined angles; one face is thicker than the other. There are casting seams on both sides.

The complete socketed axe and this decorated fragment are shown by form and ornament to belong to the Sompting type (Burgess 1969). Associated finds indicate a date contemporary with Ha C and typological relationship with Armorican socketed axes, especially the 'back-to-front' mouth of the complete Danebury axe, confirms this dating. The distribution of Sompting axes in Britain is predominantly south-eastern, and there is a hoard of these axes from Figheldean Down, Wilts, *c* 17.5 km north-west of Danebury (see Coombs 1979).

1.14 The lower part of the blade of a socketed axe

This is very eroded and distorted. The edge is damaged. The section is rectangular.

This fragment cannot certainly be attributed to any particular type of socketed axe, though it could belong to one of the latest forms.

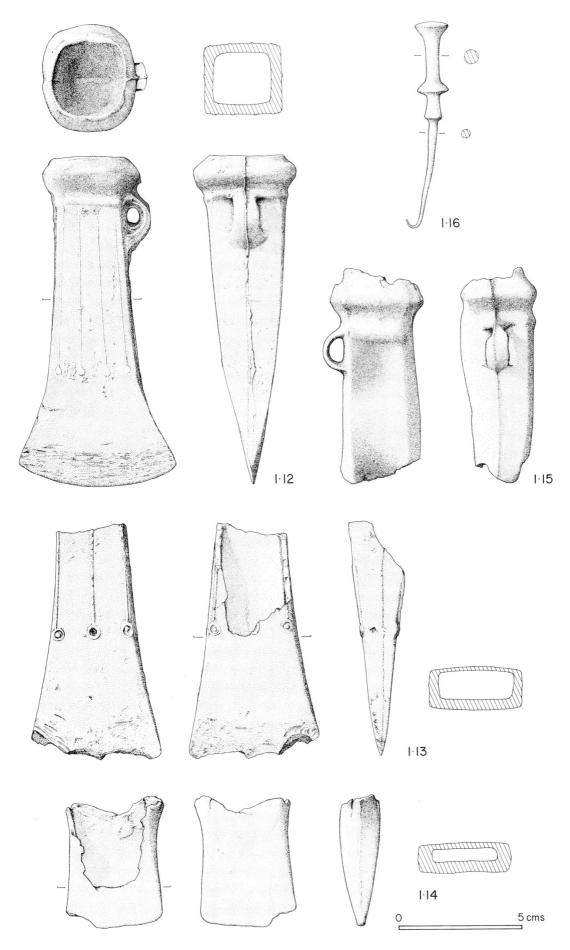

1·16

1·12

1·15

1·13

1·14

0   5 cms

Fig 7.3 Bronze hoard

338

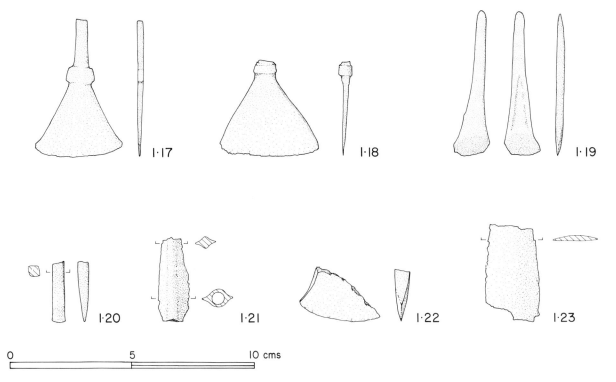

Fig 7.4 Bronze hoard

1.15 The upper part of a looped socketed axe

This is considerably distorted. The sub-biconical collar is untrimmed above and has an ill-defined moulding below. The sides diverge slightly from the base of the collar. The section appears to be rectangular with well-defined angles, the sides broader than the faces. The loop springs from the moulding.

The form of this fragment is clearly that of an Armorican socketed axe; distortion prevents confident identification of the sub-type but it appears to be closest to the Tréhou type, the common medium-sized axe (Briard & Verron 1976, 53–6). British writers have sometimes described these axes as 'Breton' but this is misleading, for their major area of distribution includes parts of Normandy as well as Brittany (Briard 1965, 241–2). Armorican socketed axes are rarely found together with other types, but associations and typology indicate that they stand at the end of the Bronze Age axe sequence in north-western France, broadly contemporary with the Hallstatt period (*ibid*, 271–5), and this is supported by the Danebury find. In Britain, hoards of Armorican socketed axes are concentrated in Wessex and one was found less than 2 km west of the Danebury bronzes, north of the village of Nether Wallop, the parish in which Danebury is situated (Moore & Lewis 1969).

1.16 Pin(?)

This object is possibly a pin; the shaft appears to be too fragile for use as an awl. Head and shaft appear to have been cast in one. The end of the shaft is bent and corroded, the tip broken off. The top of the head is trumpet-shaped, slightly convex, and irregular in diameter. Below, there is an inverted trumpet-shaped collar, also irregular, of slightly smaller diameter. The lower part of the head expands slightly to the junction with the shaft. The head is everywhere approximately circular in section but a little irregular.

The proportions are unusual for a pin, the head long in relation to the shaft, but there are no obvious signs that the shaft has been shortened and reworked. I can find no comparable pin. The Danebury 'pin' may be compared to Scandinavian Bronze Age 'awls', some of which have bronze handles (Broholm 1953, 64, nos 35–38, 74, no 145). Several burials contain such awls together with tweezers and razors (Broholm 1946, 14 Grav 15; 27 Grav 203; 31 Grav 248; 45 Grav 410; 51 Grav 485; 64 Grav 700; 76 Grav 908; 104 Grav 1255) and it has been suggested that the awls could have been employed as tattooing needles (Müller 1897, 261–4, Abb 127; Broholm 1953, 64). Tattoo marks have been found on Bronze Age bog bodies (Dieck 1976). While it appears too slender to have been used as an awl, it is possible that the Danebury 'pin' was used as a tattooing needle or toilet implement.

1.17 'Chisel'

The blade is approximately triangular; its sides are very slightly concave in outline and the cutting edge is expanded and convex. The faces of the blade continue without any thickening onto the tang. The tang is rectangular in cross-section and tapers slightly towards its tip; the tip itself is lost. On each side between the blade and the tang is a small projection, presumably a stop.

There is a somewhat similar object in the hoard from Brogyntyn, Shropshire. It resembles 1.17 in the general form of the blade, and in having a tang and side stops. The same hoard includes parts of a bronze sword with Hallstatt C affinities (Savory 1980, 123 and fig 44).

Analysed. The composition matches that of Hallstatt C material from south Wales. (PN)

1.18 'Chisel'

The blade is approximately triangular; one side is slightly convex in outline, the other somewhat ogival. The cutting edge is slightly convex; one corner is lost. Between the blade and the tang is a collar, with an indistinct moulding below it on each face. Above the collar, only a stump survives; it is presumably the base of a tang (or, less probably, of a socket).

A hoard found near Cardiff in 1928 contained four objects which are similar to 1.18 in the form of the blade and in the collar. These are complete and each has a socket for fixing on the handle. The same hoard includes other material which shows that it was not deposited before Hallstatt C bronzework was current in south Wales (Nash-Williams 1933, 299–300, pl 48; Grimes 1951, 189, fig 66).

Analysed. The composition matches that of Hallstatt C material from Danebury. (PN)

1.19 Chisel

The body is approximately an elongated triangle, with no distinction between blade and tang. The cutting edge seems to have been originally convex; it is now damaged and rather irregular. Each side of the body is slightly concave in outline and flat in cross-section. The blade expands slightly close to the cutting edge. The tang becomes thinner towards its tip, which is convex in outline. One face of the blade is flat, the other has a rather irregular hollow.

Simple chisel blades of this kind occur in Middle Bronze Age contexts in southern England, for example in the hoard from Sparkford, Somerset (Smith 1959, fig 1). The general group of such chisel blades is discussed by Rowlands (1976, 44), who gives references to other finds.

1.20 Chisel or punch

Only the lower part survives. The body is a bar with fairly flat faces and sides and rather a lozenge in cross-section. The cutting edge is not expanded; its original outline seems to have been convex.

It might be misleading to cite comparisons for a tool of such a simple form and of which only a part survives. The surviving fragment may, however, be compared with the two chisels or punches in the hoard from Glen Trool, Kirkcudbrightshire. The other material in this find shows it to be of Middle Bronze Age date (Callander 1921, 29–37, fig 1).

1.21 Fragment, probably from a socketed spearhead

The fragment comes from near the tip; the midrib and the cavity of the socket are rounded in cross-section. The surviving parts of the wings suggest a narrow blade, but they may have been altered by corrosion.

From this small and corroded fragment, it is not easy to determine the kind of spearhead from which it might derive, and spearheads of both the Middle and the Late Bronze Age might provide comparisons. The composition may perhaps point to a Middle Bronze Age date. Spearheads of this period are discussed and illustrated by Rowlands (1976, 49 ff).

Analysed. The composition may possibly indicate a Middle Bronze Age date. (PN)

1.22 Axe

Only a fragment of the cutting edge survives. The blade expands just above the cutting edge itself, the surviving part of which is convex in outline.

From the small fragment surviving, it is hardly possible to determine closely the kind of axe blade from which it comes. The composition may suggest a Middle Bronze Age date, and the surviving part is compatible with derivation from an axe blade of that date.

Analysed. The composition matches most closely material from the earlier part of the Middle Bronze Age. (PN)

1.23 Fragment, possibly from a knife

The blade is thin; one face is nearly flat, the other thicker towards the middle. Because of corrosion, and perhaps other damage, the original outline of the edges is uncertain; one is now roughly straight, the other slightly convex.

It is difficult to be sure what kind of object this corroded fragment comes from. The surviving features suggest a knife blade as a possibility. Knives with a blade of simple cross section (which is what 1.23 has) are known from the Early, Middle, and Late Bronze Age in southern Britain.

If, as seems reasonable, the nineteen bronzes discussed above constitute a hoard, it cannot have been deposited before the final phase of the Late Bronze Age in southern Britain which is contemporary with Ha C and should be dated to the 7th century BC. The flat axe, flanged axe, dirk, narrow chisels, and possibly the spear are all much older, but this need occasion no surprise for residual material is known from other Late Bronze Age hoards: there is a flat axe in the Yattendon hoard, Berks (Burgess et al 1972, 236, fig 17, 35) and a halberd in the Stoke Ferry, Norfolk hoard (*Inventaria Archaeol*, GB 8, 4). The Danebury hoard, however, contains more such material than most other Late Bronze Age hoards. The presence of old and broken objects suggests that the hoard was collected together by a bronzeworker.

Its relationship to the occupation of the hill is difficult to define. While it is possible that the hoard was the stock-in-trade of an itinerant bronze founder and was buried on a lonely, isolated hilltop, the possibility that the hill was in active use in the 7th century must be considered. Apart from evidence of Beaker period occupation, the earliest structures which may tentatively be dated to the Late Bronze Age are the 'ritual pits' which appear to lie across the neck of the promontory upon which the fort was built. The possibility that they, in some way, defined an area set aside for a communal activity has been suggested but it is difficult to test or to further examine this hypothesis; moreover, the pits themselves are impossible to date with any degree of accuracy.

7.1.4 Other objects of copper alloy (Figs 7.5–7.7)

Brooches (1.24–1.29)
by Martyn Jope
La Tène I fibula (1.24)
Small bronze brooch (45 mm long) of La Tène I type, with fairly high-arched bow swelling over the top. Its foot is returned parallel to the pin, and ends in a plain disc with a stumpy projection almost touching the bow. The mock spring/swivel mechanism simulates four turns

Fig 7.5 Bronze fibula no 1.24, and bronze strap junction no 1.35 (scale 1:2; photo: Bob Wilkins)

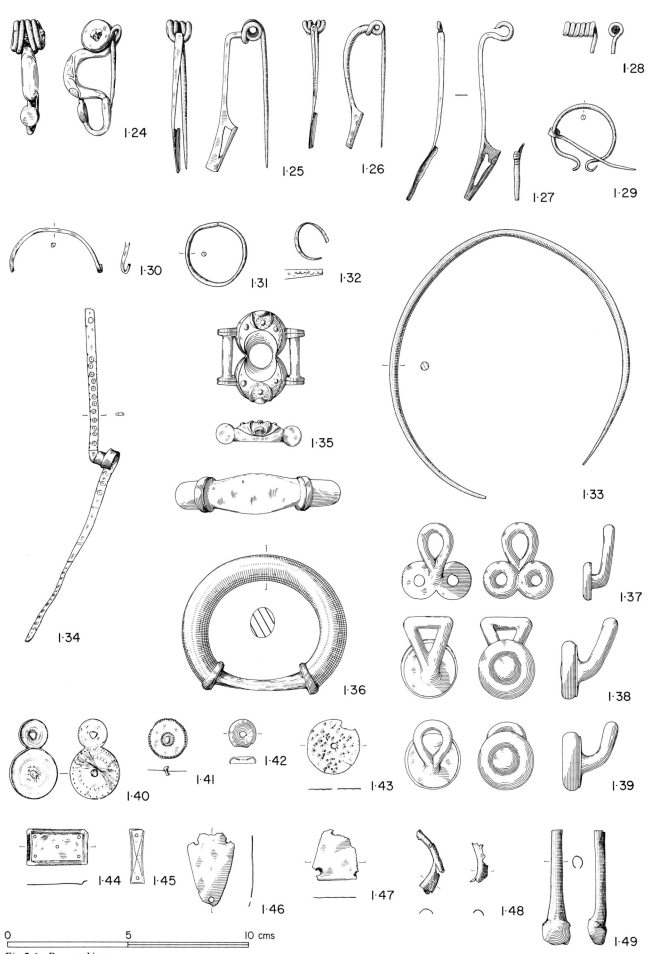

1·24
1·25
1·26
1·27
1·28
1·29
1·30
1·31
1·32
1·33
1·34
1·35
1·36
1·37
1·38
1·39
1·40
1·41
1·42
1·43
1·44
1·45
1·46
1·47
1·48
1·49

0   5   10 cms

Fig 7.6 Bronze objects

342

of moderate diameter (11 mm external) with external chord, and has a hardwood (?box) spindle with a thin (0.4 mm) bronze capping disc surviving on one side. This composite spring/swivel is of 2 mm gauge bronze and made up in several sections; a butt jointed discontinuity is well seen under the now missing capping disc, and nearby a long lapped joint is carried into the external chord.

This brooch design with mock-spring construction is a variant of the continental Marzabotto type current in some areas in the later 5th and into the 4th centuries BC (eg Fourdrignier 1876, pl VIII; Giessler & Kraft 1942, 38; Hodson 1968, 35). A few examples of this design (with true springs) were probably brought into Britain (eg Jope & Jacobsthal 1984, pls 34–5; Wainwright 1979, fig 84, 3031) and must have served as exemplars for the British development, where the frequent composite mock-spring seems to reveal an inherent technological difficulty in British workshops in making sufficiently springy long rod (or wire) projection to complete a pin and four-turn spring in one piece with the bow and foot. The Danebury example with characteristically British mock-spring/swivel mechanism (Stead 1979; Hodson 1971) is of a design which was probably under development among brooch-makers in Britain during the later half of the 4th century BC, for the prototype went out of fashion fairly quickly in at any rate some areas of Celtic Europe (Hodson 1968, pl 125, types 3–4). The swelling over the head of the bow is also seen on some continental brooches and became a notable feature of both European and British brooch design in the 3rd century BC (Jope & Jacobsthal 1984, pls 36–9).

The ornament over the swelling bow is a version of the widely used 8–figure with dot-and-circle end-rosettes each in a frame which is extended down the 8–body to touch and coalesce along a midway slanting line; this is one of a number of British variants on such a theme (eg the Box variety; Jope & Jacobsthal 1984, pls 34–5). The dots seem to be holes carefully drilled by twiddling a pointed tool, as is usual in the best work of the period from British workshops (Jope 1961, pl XXXI E).

In summary, this fine little brooch, intended by its shape to bunch up and show off a fairly ample fold of some reasonable quality fabric, was made by a craftsman working in Britain, very likely well before the end of the 4th century BC.

Later bronze fibulae (1.25, 1.26, 1.27)
These three bronze brooches are sub-variants of the simple one piece La Tène III design and construction developed in Celtic Europe during the later 2nd century BC (Werner 1955; Müller-Beck & Ettlinger 1962–3, 125, 137 ff; Planck 1980) and which led to the 'Nauheim' brooch family and its relatives and derivatives, one piece structures with four-coil spring and usually internal chord, and catch-plate, perforated or unperforated (the latter the abundant 'poor man's brooch').

The Danebury examples have individual features of some interest. All have long slender bows, suggesting that they were not really intended for gathering a coarse fabric. Two (1.25, 1.27) have an elegant concave curve in the bow as it sweeps down into the foot, a feature known but not particularly frequent in Britain, nor indeed in Europe (it is typified by Werner (1955, 187, fig 1.2) by a brooch from Warsingfehn, Kr Leer, near the Dutch border at the mouth of the Ems in north-west Germany). The third (1.26) has a sharp angle at the back of the bow just above the spring. This profile is more usual late in the series on the broad-bowed brooches of Langton Down and related

comparatively late types, but it can be early, as shown by one from Pommiers (Werner 1955, fig 1.8), and this was the original profile of the brooch from the burial on the Co Down coast at 'Loughey' near Donaghadee, which also had a purple glass armring, an infrequent material particularly associated with Manching (Jope & Wilson 1957; Jope 1960; Kunkel 1961) and with Hengistbury (Cunliffe 1978; Bushe-Fox 1915). Detailed analyses by Julian Henderson have now shown the Hengistbury and Loughey material to be closely similar to that from Manching.

Only one of these late Danebury brooches (1.26) has any ornament on the bow: a simple beaded channel running down to a stop of transverse grooves. These grooves probably represent a late reminder of the La Tène II bow/foot-return junction; such transverse features are often found much further back along the bow nearer to the spring, when they may equally be derived from a much earlier feature, the spring/bow sleeve junction of Italic tradition (cf the 'Certosa' type).

All three of these brooches have perforated catch-plates, two with triangular (or sub-triangular) open panels made apparently by widening with a small file from two (or more) round holes, as shown by the third brooch (1.26); indeed, the sub-triangular example (1.27) probably represents merely a less complete stage than 1.26.

The perforated catch-plate is to be found on many early examples of this general brooch type in Europe and also in Britain; but it evidently persisted well into the 1st century AD, though not perhaps significantly far into the second half, for perforated catch-plates are rarely to be found towards the outer northerly and westerly fringes of the distribution of this general brooch type in the British Isles (Jope & Wilson 1957, 78, fig 2, map).

Notwithstanding the individual features, there is no reason to suggest that these three Danebury brooches were not made locally in southern Britain.

Brooch spring? (1.28)
A spiral of 1 mm gauge bronze wound for 6 turns (or 7; diameter 4 mm) round an iron core. This looks like half a 6 + 6 (or 7 + 7) turn spring of a brooch. Brooches with 6 + 6 or 7 + 7 turn springs wound on an iron spindle are rare in pre-Roman Britain, but a group instructive in this respect were being produced locally in Somerset (Bulleid & Gray 1911, 195–7, pl XL, E22, E188, E244; Gray & Bulleid 1953, pl XLV, EE11, EE15). Note also Hunsbury (Fell 1936, 61, fig 2d) and Spettisbury, Dorset (Gresham 1939). The Glastonbury/Meare design of brooch noted above seems related to the involute design, and EE14 from Meare (Gray & Bulleid 1953, 207 and pl XLV) with its foot/bow riveted junction, a rare feature (cf Trevone, Cornwall: Dudley & Jope 1965) which could be as early as the early 2nd century BC.

Penannular brooches (1.29, 1.30)
No 1.29 is a penannular brooch of thin bronze (1 mm gauge) with curled ends tapering to a point (gilded?). The ring is surprisingly strong (though the pin less so) and presumably could have been used with a flimsy fabric. The pin has a flattened top folded round the ring. This type had been in use in Britain from the 3rd century BC (Fowler 1960). No 1.30 is a small fragment of another.

Finger rings and bracelets (1.31–1.34)
Finger rings and bracelets are rare at Danebury. Of the former there is only one certain example, probably a spiral type (no 1.32) from a cp 3 context. The plain ring

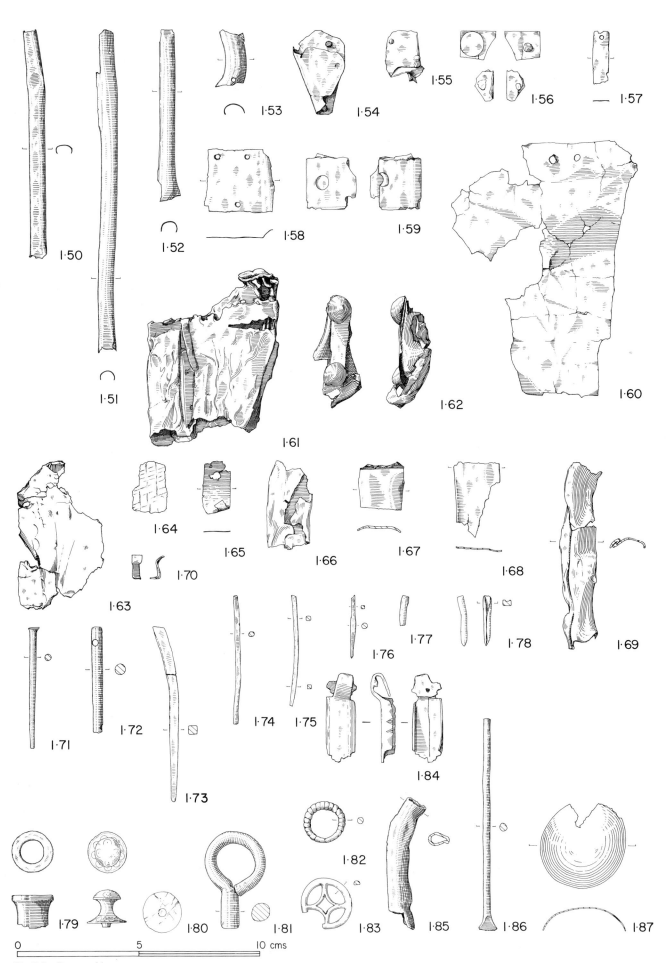

Fig 7.7 Bronze objects

0   5   10 cms

344

of circular section (no 1.31), from a cp 8 context, may have been intended for wearing but it could have served a more mundane function. One plain bracelet of circular section (1.33) comes from a cp 3 context, while the twisted decorated strip (1.34) which may once have been a bracelet is of cp 8 date or later.

Bronze fittings possibly for horse harness (1.35–1.39)

by Martyn Jope

Four items, the terret (1.36), the strap junction (1.35), and the two button-and-loop fasteners (1.38, 1.39) were found together on the floor of building CS7/8 securely stratified in a late cp 7 context for which a date of *c* 100 BC is suggested. Since they were found together they may be considered as part of the personal equipment of the resident(s). It is rare to find such items in a domestic context, suggesting here the house of a modest member of the knightly class, who was also a charioteer. The button-and-loop fasteners are most likely part of the horse gear, the strap junction more likely part of a man's accoutrement. Too little is known of the full horse rider's equipment of this age in Britain to be able to say how much more the complete gear would have needed, or whether the two button-and-loop fasteners were excessive; but this is most useful evidence for the data bank that will eventually lead to an understanding of early horsemanship in Britain.

The third button-and-loop fastener (1.37) was found in a cp 7 pit in the centre of the fort.

Button-and-loop fasteners (1.37–1.39)

The Danebury button-and-loop fasteners of bronze are of a general class studied by Gillam (1958), Wild (1970a), and MacGregor (1976). Cumulative evidence suggests that these devices were associated with horse gear rather than human accoutrements; they were probably used to insert the button through fabric rather than leather (Wild 1970, 146). The squared ending of the loop suggests a strap (though this may have been made of woven cloth), and the pear-shaped loop may even suggest a fairly thin leather thong. Straps to secure a horse-cloth are one possibility (Wild 1970a, 146).

Two of the Danebury examples (1.38, 1.39), each with a single button, have a heavy bronze ring filled by a low domed button, made in one casting, and are quite heavy pieces. The third is lighter, and has two buttons, with open circle centres. The example in the metalworker's hoard from Ringstead in Norfolk (Clarke 1951, 221–3, pl XIXc) is a fairly close parallel for 1.39 (though smaller) and shows that this design with central domed bun was in current use during the 1st century BC.

The terret ring (1.36)

Heavy bronze terret, of oval form and circular cross-section, with simple necking moulding at the junction with the flat slightly leaf-shaped emplacement bar. This is an entirely plain version of a type being made using clay moulds at Gussage All Saints in Dorset (Spratling in Wainwright 1979, 136, fig 102.1; cf also Glastonbury: Bulleid & Gray 1911, 230 and pl XLIII). This general type was widespread in Iron Age Britain, often with a midrib and a little chased ornament.

A little wear is detectable on the inner face at the widest point, on one side but not on the other, showing that it had been one of a pair, used in paired draught with a chariot or cart.

The strap junction (1.35)

A particularly fine strap junction of heavy cast bronze, perfectly preserved, a version of a general type (Jope & Jacobsthal 1984, pl 268). It is in the form of two bulbous swelling crescents set in opposition, with most delicately touching crescent tips. The solid crescents have their shape firmly outlined, to give a slightly set back panel over the swelling surface, with a stylized twin-petal flower in bold relief in the centre, flanked on either side by a knop free-standing in the recessed field; this gives a stiffish variant of the keeled roundel theme (Jope & Jacobsthal 1984, 267f), its open end closed off with a half-hemispherical slug. The two stylized flowers each have a central knop set in a small circle panel with fine radial lines (slightly encroached upon by the half-hemisphere slugs), giving a slightly Romanizing aspect. The strap attachments link the two crescent bodies on either side.

This object is here called a strap junction; it will take a strap of 15 mm width at the most, which is rather narrow for a real belt, and few other examples are significantly larger.

A few other strap junctions of this type (based on three intersecting circles) may be noted. One from Hunsbury (Fell 1936, pl II; Jope & Jacobsthal 1984, pl 268) is flat-surfaced, but the squashed-circle outline gives the crescent slugs some interest. The other is from Meare in Somerset (Gray & Bulleid 1953, pl XLVI, E103; Jope & Jacobsthal 1984, pl 263); it is a cruder version of the Danebury design, with filled central circle and its heavy roll border wholly obscuring the focal interest of the tip-touching crescents. A Sussex piece (Eustace 1923) and that from Bury Hill, Hants (Hawkes 1940) should also be noted. The simple one-ring or two-ring designs are widespread, and an ultimate continental origin for this device of strap junction is suggested by one from La Tène itself (Vouga 1925, pl VIII.49).

The whole object, with the delicate refinement of its fastidious tip-touching emphasized by the bulbous crescent bodies from which the claw- or beak-like tips emerge, is a masterpiece of simple solid tectonics, applied to the design of a functional item. Set out on the flat, as three simple intersecting circles, the schema yields a much tamer result. The relief ornament on the Danebury piece recalls that on the junction pieces of the Snettisham gold torc (Clarke 1954, pls XV, XVI). This bold relief treatment thus seems fairly closely related to the Snettisham goldworkers' style of the early to mid 1st century BC. Variants of this decorative style were to be seen in both gold and baser metals fairly widely over southern Britain, mainly in the 1st century BC, worked in both solid metal and thin sheet (Jope & Jacobsthal 1984, pl 127, map). The origins of this style, with all its bold relief and at its best with long probing inquisitive leaves spun off from a knop, mainly in miniature and much of it in gold, are still not entirely clear, though the work of the earliest coin-die makers in Britain in the last decades of the 2nd century BC may have had some influence.

Decorative attachments (1.40–1.47)

Eight items are classed here as decorative attachments: four are circular, two rectangular, and two triangular. Of these two (nos 1.40, 1.45) come from cp 3 contexts, one (1.42) from cp 6, and one (1.46) from cp 8. The others are not from dated contexts.

All have rivet holes suggesting attachment to wood or, more likely, to leather but no 1.40 is clearly part of a composite item of some kind.

Bronze U-sectioned bindings (1.48-1.53)

Seven fragments of U-sectioned bronze bindings have been recovered (1.48-1.53), one undated, two from a sterile layer in the very top of a cp 3 pit, and four from cp 7 and 8 contexts. One fragment (1.49) ended in a button terminal which survived largely intact. This piece belongs to Piggott's group VI scabbards — his Bredon type (Piggott 1950, 22, 28) found predominantly in the south-west of Britain. We need not, however, accept his 1st century AD date since the Danebury example is unlikely to be much later than *c* 100 BC. Whether or not these items are scabbard bindings is still unproven; the asymmetry at the 'chape' end is odd. The other fragments of U-bindings could be scabbard bindings but other functions should not be ruled out.

Amorphous fragments of bronze sheet (1.54–1.70)

Leaving aside plaques of sheet bronze of which the shape can be recognized and which were presumably decorative, 45 items of sheet bronze were found some of which were broken into fragments. Of these eighteen are illustrated; the rest, which are entirely formless, are listed on fiche 9, frames B5–8. Of the 45 pieces three are from cp 3 contexts and three from cp 4–5 contexts; the rest are all from late contexts (cp 6–8).

Some pieces, with small rivets or rivet holes (eg nos 1.54–1.59), were probably attached to leather and may have been decorative. Other, larger pieces were probably parts of vessels. This is certainly true of 1.62 with two dome headed rivets which conform closely to bronze vessels of the types found at Glastonbury and Spettisbury. The rather thicker pieces (1.67, 1.68) are less likely to be from vessels but may be bindings or attachments to wood or leather.

Bronze rods or nails (1.71–1.78)

Eight bronze rods were found coming mainly from cp 7 contexts. They vary in section but two were definitely circular and one of these, with expanded head, was presumably a nail. Some of the other fragments could have come from nails or rivets, while other pieces could be waste.

Other bronze items (1.79–1.87)

Several unique items were found at Danebury. They may be listed as follows:
1.79 Cylinder terminal: undated ?Roman
1.80 Decorated bronze stud: undated ?Roman
1.81 Heavy ring and shank: cp 7
1.82 Segmented ring possibly a decorative head hinged to a pin: cp 3
1.83 Wheel ring ?pin head: cp 3
1.84 Hinged fitting: cp 3
1.85 Tube fragment: cp 8 or later
1.86 Tool with triangular working end: cp 6
1.87 Large domed rivet head: cp 7
All have been described in detail in fiche 9, frames A9–B4. The quality of nos 1.82, 1.83, and 1.84, all of cp 3, is noteworthy.

7.1.5 Objects of iron (Figs 7.8-7.26)
by Lyn Sellwood

The iron objects found at Danebury have been divided into groups and are described in the following order:

  hook-shaped cutting tools
  knife blades

saw blades
socketed chisels and gouges
tanged chisels
socketed adzes and picks
ferrules
files
tools manufactured from small iron rods
ploughshares
horseshoes and horseshoe nails
latch lifter
currency bars
spearheads
arrowhead
hilt guard and chape
linch pins
sheet iron fittings
collars and rings
strip bindings
bucket fittings
discs
nails, rivets, and wedges
miscellaneous iron objects

Details of the individual illustrated items are given in fiche 9, frames B9–E8. A few iron scraps, not illustrated or described here, are listed on fiche 9, frames E9–F14.

Hook-shaped cutting tools (2.1–2.24)

Twenty-four hook-shaped cutting tools have been found distributed chronologically as follows:

cp	number	relative frequency
1-3	4	1.0
4	0	0
5	1	1.8
6-7	2	2.6
7-8	14	11.5

It was decided to group this collection of artefacts together under a general heading. The conventional alternative would have been to classify them more specifically as sickles, billhooks, reaping and pruning hooks; but this prejudges function in a way that fails to reflect the variety inherent within the collection. This being said, a number of constant characteristics can be identified. All the tools possess a curved cutting blade and, with only a few exceptions, the single sharpened edge was found on the concave, inner side. All were designed for attachment to a handle, most probably wooden, and most have a terminal formed by two wing-shaped flanges folded over to form a socket. Some were attached to the haft by means of a rivet or rivets, others by means of a bent back tang. It has also proved possible to subdivide the tools using size as a criterion. For this purpose, only the eleven complete or near complete specimens were considered, but the results are of relevance to the entire collection. The measurements of height were taken perpendicularly from the base of the socket to the highest point on the crest of the blade. The second measurement was taken at right-angles to this and was positioned to encompass the maximum width. The height range of the smallest artefact was between 57 and 81 mm; the widths fell between 49 and 66 mm while the weight range was from 15–29 gm. The measurements of the larger group were more diverse and if the body of material available for study had been larger, it is probable that an intermediate group would have emerged. The height range for this class was between 80 and 169 mm; the widths occupied the span between 107 and 154 mm,

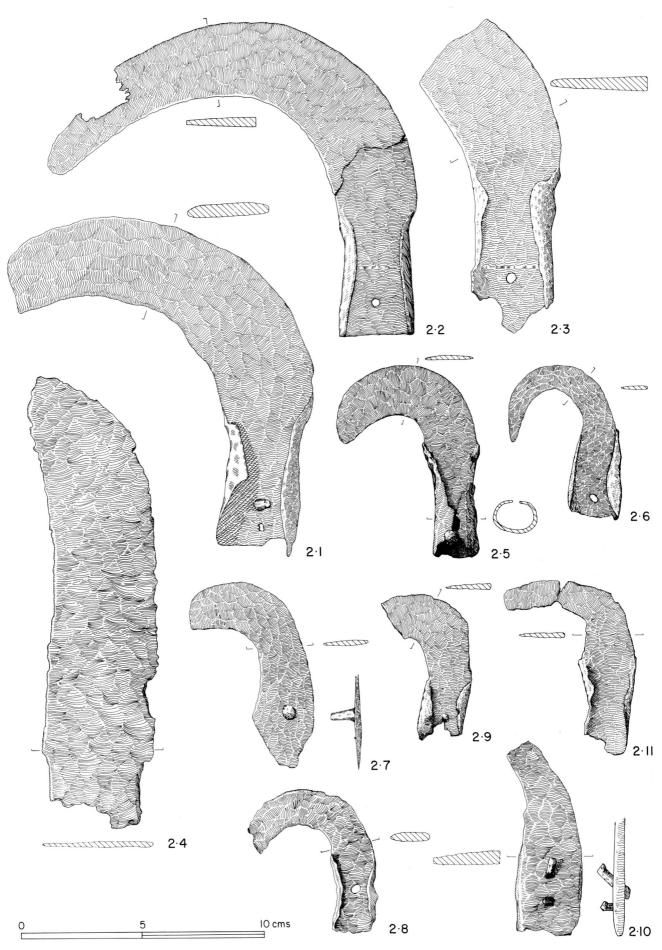

0   5   10 cms

Fig 7.8   Iron objects

2·1 2·2 2·3 2·4 2·5 2·6 2·7 2·8 2·9 2·10 2·11

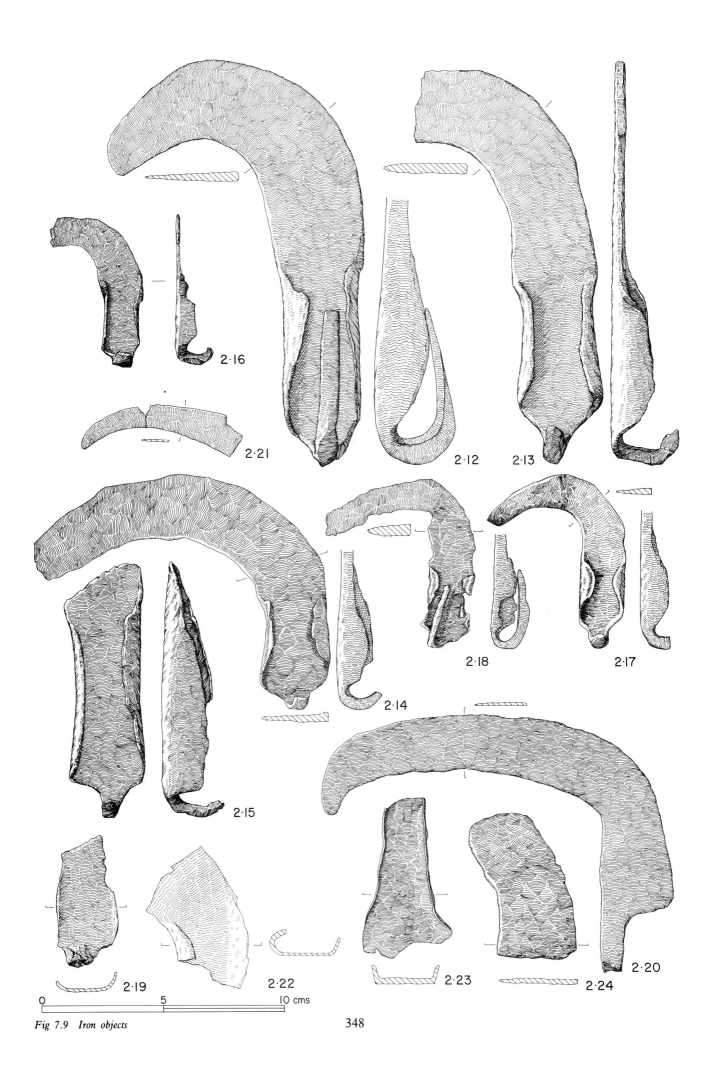

2·16

2·21

2·12

2·13

2·18

2·17

2·14

2·15

2·19

2·22

2·23

2·20

2·24

0   5   10 cms

Fig 7.9 Iron objects   348

while the weights varied from 47–201 gm. The two size groupings bear no correlation to the division between tanged and riveted terminals.

The 24 implements from Danebury form the largest collection from any Iron Age site in Britain. The most substantial number after this is from Glastonbury (Bulleid & Gray 1917, 358), where eight 'billhooks' and six 'reaping-hooks' were recovered. Six were found during excavation at Hod Hill (Richmond 1968), and another seven were published in the Durden collection of antiquities from the same site (Brailsford 1962). Five come from Barbury Castle, Wilts (MacGregor & Simpson 1963), and four from Hunsbury, Northants (Fell 1936, 56). Other sites have produced one or two examples.

The Glastonbury tools differ from those found at Danebury in two principal respects:

1 Gray records that 'they appear frequently to have been double-edged' (Bulleid & Gray 1917, 367), but no sections are published so the observation cannot be verified.
2 The tools range in size from 215.9 mm to 279.4 mm, and are thus larger than any of the tools from Danebury.

The six tools from Barbury (MacGregor & Simpson 1963, 394) compare much more closely with the Danebury size range, at least in respect of height. Three of the tools correspond closely with the smaller Danebury group (measuring 71, 67, and 71 mm), while the remaining three are comparable with the larger group (151, 147, and 140 mm).

A detailed study of this tool type has been published by Rees (1979, ii, 450–685). She distinguishes four major typological characteristics dealing with forms (tanged and socketed tools) and with function (reaping and pruning hooks). While the morphological distinction is quite valid, the functional division was less convincing and, as Rees admits, there is a gradation from one form to another. Because of this reservation, the Rees scheme was not adopted for the Danebury collection.

Function
It may be presumed that the variety of form witnessed by the hook-shaped cutting tools represents adaptations to specific activities. The two elements which comprise the metallic part of the tool are the terminal and the blade.

Terminals
All the tools, with the possible exception of 2.20 (which is in any case incomplete), terminate with two features, a socket formed by flanges and a rivet or tang. These elements combine to ensure that the metal blade remains firmly attached to the haft, whether the direction of movement is up and down or from side to side. It is reasonable to suggest that the tanged tools were specially designed to sustain a downward pulling and cutting movement because the tangs are wider and stronger than rivets, and because they not only pierce transversely through the haft but are folded back at an angle parallel with the socket, providing a firmer attachment.

Blades
Only two of the tools from Danebury are possibly double-edged (in marked contrast to Glastonbury). It is difficult to understand why a tool of this type, clearly designed to cut in a single direction, would need to be equipped with a double-edged blade.

The blades of the Danebury sample are the feature most subject to variation, and range from the tight curve of 2.6 to the almost straight line of 2.18, 2.20, and 2.21. The more curved variety may have been intended for pruning, while the straighter examples were more suited for reaping, but these distinctions do not correspond with size variations which must also reflect on function.

The small-sized group includes both the highly-curved and the much straighter blades. It is difficult to envisage tools of this size used in scything operations but some of the more curved specimens would have been well adapted for such tasks as stripping foliage and twigs from the poles used in the manufacture of wattle or for cutting leaf fodder, the tanged terminals providing the necessary rigidity for tools used in this way. None of the larger tools is quite so highly curved as 2.6; and while many may well be regarded simply as sickles, the range of form present in this group probably reflects a variety of usage.

Knife blades (2.25–2.41)
Eighteen iron knife blades were found at Danebury. Their chronological distribution is as follows:

cp	number	relative frequency
1-3	3	1.0
4	0	0
5	0	0
6	1	1.9
7-8	11	12.1

With one exception, 2.25, the iron knife blades from Danebury are clearly intended to be mounted either on or within a handle, most probably of wood or antler. Four morphologically distinct groups can be identified:

1 Knives in which the blade and handle are forged in one piece
2 Knife blades terminating with a tang for insertion into a handle
3 Knife blades with rivet holes either through the blade or tang, designed for the attachment of handle plates
4 Knives with a socketed terminal

Classes 1 and 4 are represented by one example each (2.25 and 2.37 respectively).

Class 2 displays a considerable variety of blade shape but certain other characteristics are more consistent; all but one have a tang which continues in an approximately straight line from the upper non-sharpened edge of the blade. 2.33 is alone in having a centrally placed tang and a double-edged blade. Three principal blade forms have been identified:

a parallel sided (eg 2.26)
b blades with a straight upper edge and a lower edge which tapers from the base to meet the upper at the point (eg 2.28, 2.30)
c blades with a concave upper edge and a convex lower cutting edge (eg 2.31, 2.32)

Class 3 comprises only three examples, two of which are incomplete. Despite this, certain formal distinctions and similarities can be identified. 2.34 possesses a riveted tang which is clearly differentiated from the blade. In the case of 2.36, the blade and tang are integral. All three examples within this class have two centrally placed rivets and slight raised flanges on the edges of the tang or base of the blade. Both examples on which the blade can be seen are curved.

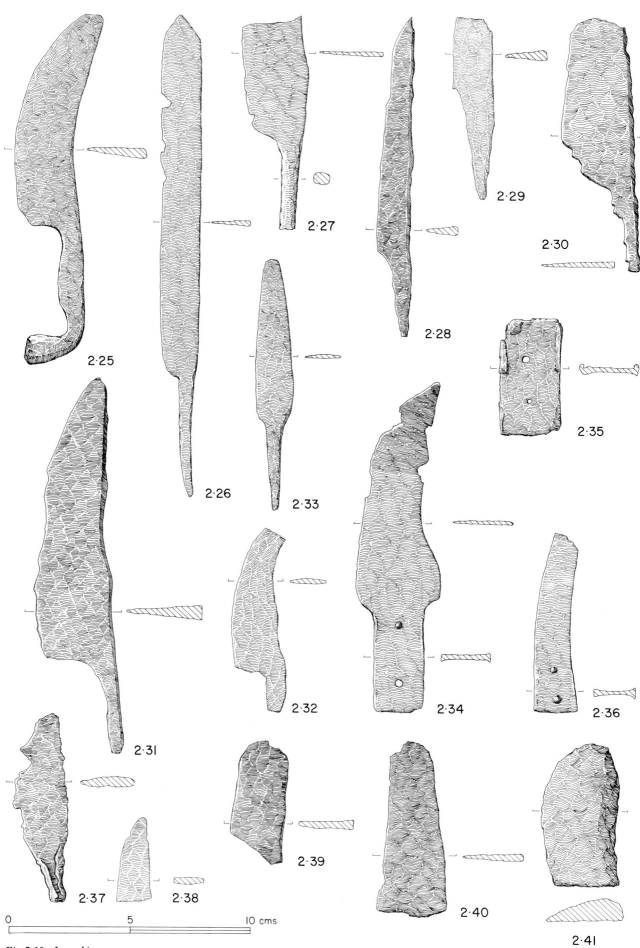

2·25
2·26
2·27
2·28
2·29
2·30
2·31
2·32
2·33
2·34
2·35
2·36
2·37
2·38
2·39
2·40
2·41

0   5   10 cms

Fig 7.10 Iron objects

Class 4, represented by a single example (2.37), has a narrow socketed terminal. The handle, which this would have accepted, must have been insubstantial; hence the status of this object as a knife may be questioned. The blade however is distinctly knife-shaped with a single cutting edge.

No comprehensive study of iron knives has been published. Fell, in her reassessment of the knives from Hunsbury, distinguished two major types: 'handles are either narrow tangs, or broad and riveted' (1936, 65). Other sites have produced smaller collections: thirteen from Glastonbury, ten from Maiden Castle, and four from All Cannings Cross. The knives from Hunsbury measure between 50.8 and 127 mm in length, and are thus rather smaller than the Danebury artefacts which measure between 75 and 192 mm. The largest knife from Glastonbury measures 279.4 mm, considerably longer than any specimen from the other sites. The variety of shape evidently reflects the wide range of function to which knives could be put.

Saw blades (2.42, 2.43)

Two iron saw blades were found at Danebury. 2.42 was from a cp 7–8 context. The other was unphased.

The single complete saw (2.42) consists of two elements, a blade and a riveted tang. This latter was obviously designed for attachment to a handle, presumably of wood. The blades of both saws have backward slanting teeth, which show that they were designed to cut on the backward stroke. Although 2.43 is incomplete, the two blades are of quite different size: 2.42 measures between 40 and 18 mm in width while 2.43 ranges from 22–25 mm. In both cases the teeth have been set so that the cut would be wider than the blade to allow easy working. This is more pronounced in 2.43. No 2.42 is of particular interest because the blade has been repaired by a welded scarf joint in antiquity. The overlap, necessitated by the repair, shows the original length to have been more considerable than the 353 mm which it now measures.

Saws occur rarely on Iron Age sites. Four were found at Glastonbury (Bulleid & Gray 1917, 385), three at Hunsbury (Fell 1936, 66), and two at Maiden Castle (Wheeler 1943, 274). The Glastonbury saws varied from 119–458.5 mm in length. The three Hunsbury saws were all quite short, measuring 190.5, 165, and 120.6 mm. Both the Maiden Castle saws were of small size. One saw from Glastonbury was found complete with wooden handle of ash to which it was riveted, while one example from Hunsbury was still attached to an antler plate. The size range apparent in the Danebury saws corresponds most nearly with the Glastonbury group. All four sites are consistent in producing saws with backward slanting teeth, although Gray does record an example of an Iron Age saw from Hod Hill which possessed teeth slanting in the opposite direction (Bulleid & Gray 1917, 372). Saws of this kind would have been useful for cutting across the grain of small timbers such as branches, wattle poles, posts, and planks.

Socketed chisels and gouges (2.44–2.46)

Three of these tools were found at Danebury, two from cp 7 and one from cp 5 contexts.

All three tools have a solid shaft and a hollow socket. In each case the socket was made by folding two edges of metal together to form a cone with a straight seam along one side. 2.44 had been worked at the top to form a collar which projects from the bottom of the cone. All were presumably designed to be mounted on a shaft. The solid tip of the shaft was worked to form the desired blade, whether chisel or gouge. Metallographic analysis has revealed that the blade of 2.46 was composed of three strips of metal welded together, and that the strip which formed the cutting edge had the highest carbon content. Deliberate hardening of the blade is a common feature with this genre of tool. The measurements of the three items are sufficiently similar to suggest that they were made by highly skilled craftsmen to a specified size. The lengths measure 168, 177, and 176 mm. The weights are also very close: 160.0 gm, 171.9 gm, 169.5 gm.

Socketed chisels and gouges are rare on Iron Age sites. Four gouges of this type were found at Glastonbury, but only two are closely similar to those from Danebury. Two socketed gouges were found at All Cannings Cross (Cunnington 1923, 125), and two socketed chisels came from Hunsbury (Fell 1936, 66). Traces of wooden handles were found within some of the Glastonbury socketed gouges (Bulleid & Gray 1917, 386) and Cunnington noted remains of a wooden handle in one from All Cannings Cross.

It is generally assumed that these chisels and gouges were for woodworking. The metallographic evidence from Danebury indicates that particular care was taken to harden the blades of these and other woodworking tools, while the metallic composition of knives and sickles was quite different. This observation combined with the evidence of the considerable skill involved in the production of the tools and their precise similarity in size (from Danebury at least) might well indicate that they were manufactured by specialist smiths.

Tanged chisels (2.47, 2.48)

Two tanged chisels were found, one from a cp 1–3 context and one from cp 7.

2.47 was found complete with its antler handle. The iron blade and tang are integral, and form an approximately triangular shape. The cutting edge measures 29 mm across. The second chisel, 2.48, is incomplete but has a square-sectioned tang and a much narrower blade which measures only 12 mm across at the point of fracture.

Seven tanged chisels were found at Hunsbury (Fell 1936, 66) but these are neither illustrated nor described in detail. The largest is said to have measured 298 mm and was thus much longer than the complete Danebury speciment 2.47, which has a length of 86 mm. The sizes of the remaining six were not published. Two tanged chisels were found at Maiden Castle (Wheeler 1943, 272 and fig 89, nos 3 and 4) but neither compares closely with the Danebury specimens.

It may be assumed that both of these chisels were intended for wood- or boneworking.

Socketed adzes and picks (2.49–2.51)

Three tools of this kind were found at Danebury: 2.49, a complete adze from cp 7, 2.50, a complete pick head from cp 6, and 2.52, the socketed terminal of an adze or pick from a cp 7 context.

The objects are composed of two elements, a solid blade and a socketed head, designed to accommodate a haft. The complete adze 2.49 measures 133 mm overall, and has a downward sloping blade which terminates in a flared cutting edge 54 mm in width. The irregular socket is approximately oval in form. The pick measures 210 mm overall, and also has a downward sloping blade which in this case terminates in a tip with a blunt point. It also has an irregular oval socket.

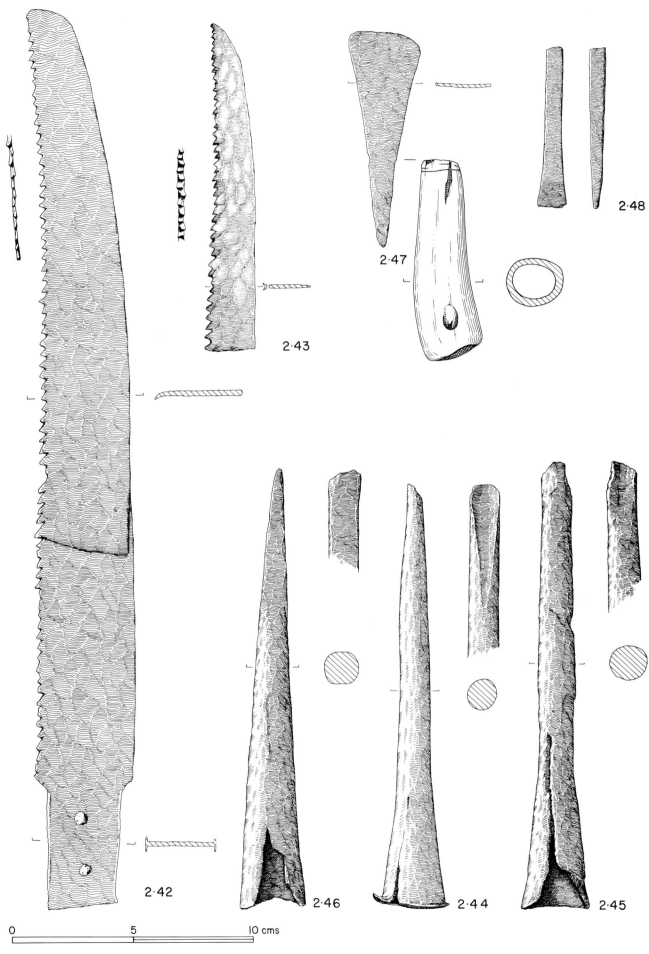

2·43

2·47

2·48

2·42

2·46

2·44

2·45

0   5   10 cms

Fig 7.11 Iron objects

352

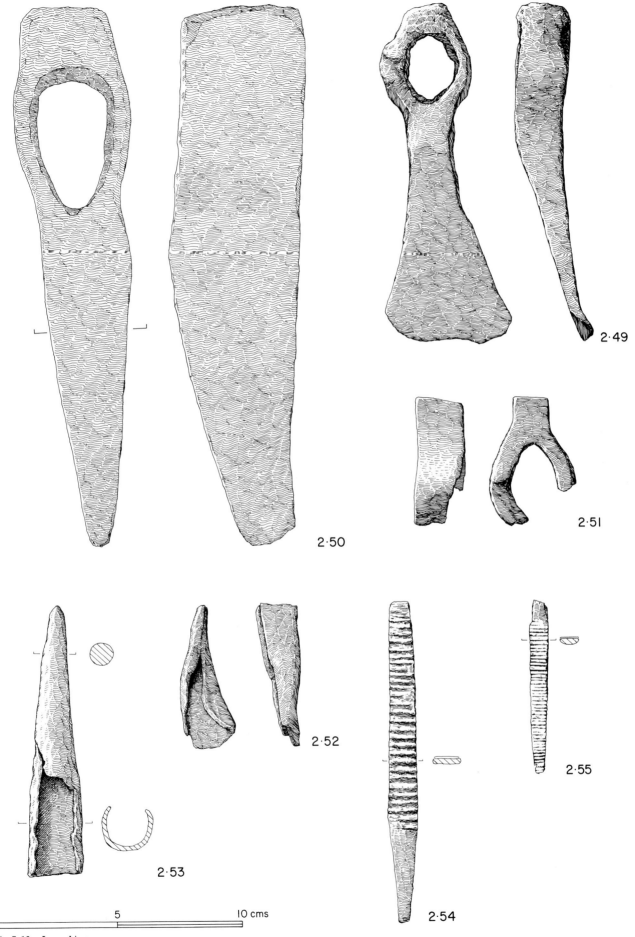

0   5   10 cms

Fig 7.12   Iron objects

2·49

2·50

2·51

2·52

2·53

2·54

2·55

Adzes do not occur frequently on Iron Age sites. Seven were recorded at Glastonbury (Bulleid & Gray 1917, 373), two with hafts *in situ*. These provide exact parallels with the Danebury specimens 2.49 and 2.51. Three complete and one fragmentary adze heads came from Hunsbury (Fell 1936, 66). Three were found at Hod Hill (Brailsford 1962, 13; Richmond 1968, 137). Pick heads are rare. Two examples were recorded from Hod Hill (Brailsford 1962, 14 and fig 13; Richmond 1968, 138). One example, 943, is similar to 2.50 from Danebury, but whereas the former has a double point the latter possesses only a single point.

Adzes were probably used principally as woodworking tools, but tool marks on the sides and bottoms of pits show that adzes and picks were also used to dig away the chalk.

Ferrules (2.52, 2.53)

Two iron ferrules were found in cp 7 contexts.

2.52 is an irregularly-shaped, socketed ferrule terminating in a point of rectangular section. Its socket is designed to accommodate a flat, pointed haft. 2.53 is more substantial and has a tapering circular socket. The solid point is elongated.

Iron ferrules do not feature widely in assemblages of Iron Age material. Two were found at Glastonbury, but both of these were apparently cylindrical. Two are mentioned in the report on the Durden collection from Hod Hill (Brailsford 1962, P 19, K 35 and 36) but without description. A single ferrule came from the excavations at the site (Richmond 1968, 39) but is not described.

It is probable that 2.52 was part of a tool, functioning as a binding. 2.53 was presumably fitted with a shaft, and may well have been either a spear butt or the pointed head of a digging stick. Such a tool was certainly used to construct postholes.

Files (2.54, 2.55)

Two iron files were found at Danebury, both from cp 7 contexts.

The Danebury files are composed of two elements, a blade scored with a series of cuts on one surface, and a tang. The complete file, 2.54, has a length of 129 mm. Both were clearly intended to fit within some form of handle. 2.54 is quadrangular in section, is widest immediately above the tang, and tapers in both directions. 2.55 is plano-convex in section with cuts in the convex surface, and again attains its maximum width at the base of the blade. It tapers more than 2.54 and terminates in what is almost a point. The exact form of the tang cannot be estimated. The gauge of the ridging is coarser on 2.54 than on 2.55.

The largest assemblage of Iron Age files comes from Glastonbury lake village where seven were recovered. Two were present in the Durden collection of antiquities from Hod Hill (Brailsford 1962, 14). A considerable size range is evident at Glastonbury. The files are comparable with the Danebury examples in form, and vary in length from 72–242 mm, and in width from 6–19 mm. Two of these files have quadrangular sections, while another two are plano-convex. The two files from Hod Hill measure 196.8 mm and 171.4 mm and are thus rather larger than the single complete example from Danebury.

The gauge of the file may be presumed to reflect the material it was designed to work. A metallographic analysis of the Danebury tools reveals that 2.54 had an enhanced carbon content which may have been an attempt to harden the metal (p 435). It was also suggested that the Danebury files, with their relatively widely spaced cuts, were intended for work on wood or bone rather than on metal.

Tools manufactured from small iron rods (2.56–2.68)

Thirteen tools belonging to this general category were found at Danebury. One came from a cp 3 context, but all others belong to cp 7–8.

These tools vary in form, and an attempt to categorize them rigidly would probably be misleading. Simple tools of this sort could well have been manufactured as required, each individually designed for a specific purpose. Certain general types can nevertheless be identified. 2.56, 2.57, 2.58, and 2.59 all appear to be awls. Example 2.58 was definitely intended for insertion within a wooden handle since mineralized wood was preserved, and this is possibly true of others. The points of 2.56 and 2.57 are square-sectioned while those of 2.58 and 2.59 are round. 2.56 and 2.58, with maximum diameters of 8 mm and 7 mm, are much more substantial than 2.57 and 2.59 which have diameters of 5 and 5.5 mm. Nos 2.60, 2.61, and 2.62 may all be classified as chisels. They have in common round sections and a blade formed by hammering one end of the rod. The width of the single complete blade, 2.60, measures 3 mm. This tool is the only complete example and is 135 mm in length. One cannot be sure whether these tools were designed to fit within handles but 2.62, with a square butt, may have had a handle. 2.67 is the only iron needle from the site. It is of much more substantial size than any of its bone counterparts. The precise function of 2.63, 2.64, 2.65, and 2.66 is unknown, but they may have been punches. 2.68, with one chisel-like blade and one curved flat terminal, appears to have been designed for a very specific range of functions.

Tools of this simple form are surprisingly rare on Iron Age sites. Four awls are recorded from All Cannings Cross (Cunnington 1923, 122, pl 19, no 7; 130, pl 20, nos 6, 7, and 8). Pl 19, no 7 has traces of a wooden handle on the tang; of the remainder, two have square and one has a round section. Pl 21, no 6 provides a close parallel with 2.58 from Danebury. The single awl illustrated from Hod Hill (Brailsford 1962, 14, fig 13, G 26) is close to Danebury 2.59. Two awls were found at Glastonbury (Bulleid & Gray 1917, 388). One of these, I 43, had a circular section. Both Glastonbury tools were shorter than all but 2.58 from Danebury. The single small chisel recorded from Maiden Castle is not paralleled at Danebury. Another single example came from Hod Hill (Brailsford 1962, 14, fig 13, G 27). This was close in form to the Danebury specimens but had a slightly wider blade. Four iron needles also came from this site (*ibid*, 18, pl XII, nos K 18, 19, 20, and 21). None of those illustrated is equivalent in form to 2.67.

It may be assumed that the iron awls were used for more heavy duty purposes than their bone counterparts (perhaps working the toughest grade of hides); some may even have been employed as punches in wood or metalwork. Tools 2.63–66 may also have been metalworkers' equipment. The small chisels are presumably woodworking tools. The iron needle may have been used in an activity which demanded more strength than a bone needle would provide.

Ploughshares (2.69–2.71)

One ploughshare bar and two ploughshare tips come from Danebury. The bar is from a cp 6 context, while

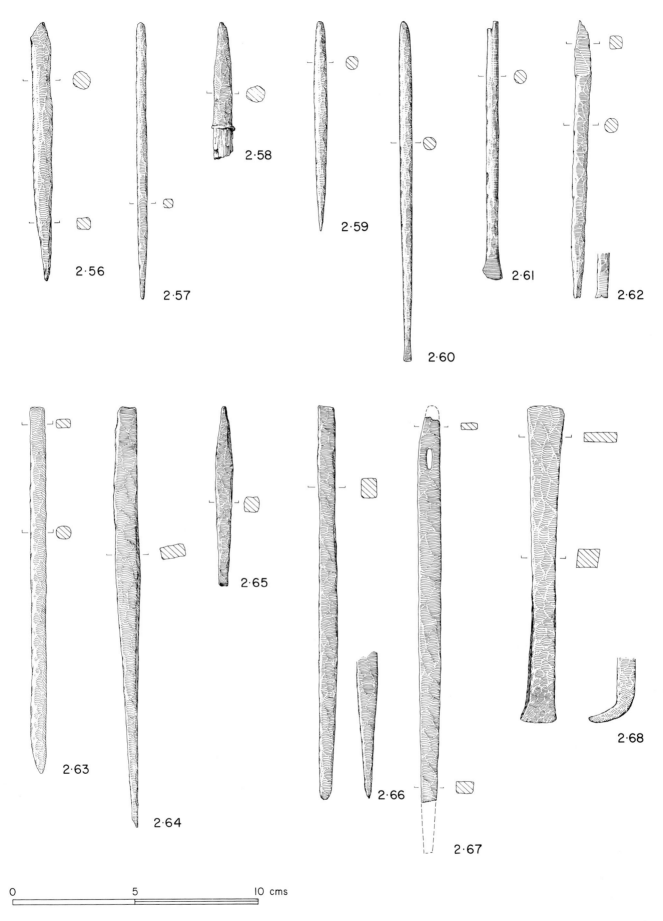

2·56
2·57
2·58
2·59
2·60
2·61
2·62
2·63
2·64
2·65
2·66
2·67
2·68

0   5   10 cms

Fig 7.13 Iron objects

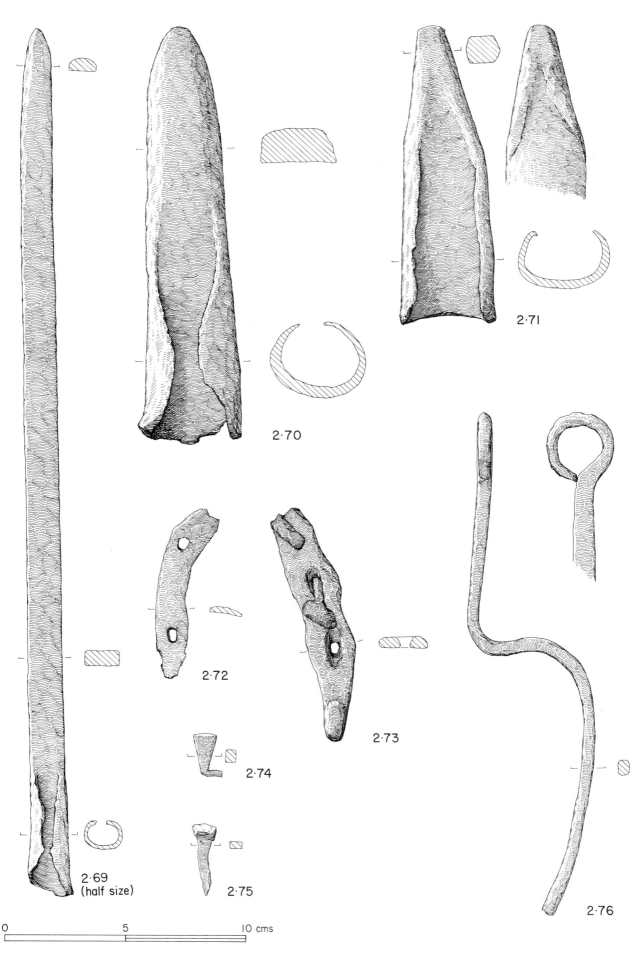

2·70

2·71

2·72

2·73

2·74

2·69
(half size)

2·75

2·76

0   5   10 cms

Fig 7.14 Iron objects

both share tips come from cp 7 pits. The bar (2.69) is complete and measures 690 mm in length. It terminates at one end in a flat rounded point and at the other in a socket formed by beating the two flanges of metal around a former until they almost touch in the centre. The shares, 2.70 and 2.71, are shorter and made from bars of similar size. 2.70 has a point which closely resembles that of 2.69 and the socket is formed in an identical manner. 2.71 is composed of the same elements as 2.70, but the point has been formed by pinching both sides of the bar together, and the two flanges are thinner, shallower, and less curved than those of either 2.69 or 2.70. 2.70 and 2.71 measure 165 and 118 mm in length. The bars range in width from 35–42 mm. In maximum thickness they vary from 11–15.5 mm.

The two most detailed studies of such bars and share tips are those by Allen (1967, 307) and Rees (1979). The Allen article is principally concerned with the complete ploughshare bars and the question of whether or not they should be regarded as currency. He draws attention to the fact that ploughshare bars differ considerably in form from either sword- or spit-shaped currency bars, and also expresses the belief that the share bars tend not to be found in hoards, a form of deposit which accounts for most of the extant sword- and spit-shaped bars. Although Allen distinguishes three principal types of plough bar, winged, tapered, and leaf-shaped, his criterion for answering the vexed question of whether or not such bars were functional is one of size alone. He concludes that the group of larger bars (to which 2.69 belongs) might have functioned as votive representational ploughshares, since large numbers have been recovered from the Thames and from the Welsh bog deposit of Llyn Cerrig Bach.

Rees' detailed study divides the finds of possible iron ploughshares on typological criteria. Her two major groups, socketed shares and tanged shares, each have three subdivisions.

2.70 and 2.71 belong to Rees' group 1a, the most commonly found in Britain (1979, 50). 2.69 is of Rees' group 2a, eighteen of which derive from Romano-British contexts (1979, 58). These bars occasionally show wear on their points and are found frequently in small hoards (contrary to Allen's view of them) accompanied by equivalent numbers of coulters, a fact which suggest that they were functioning ploughshares.

Of the three dozen or so ploughshares from Britain, five (of Rees' type 1a) were found in Iron Age contexts at Hunsbury (Fell 1936, 66). The Hunsbury shares measured on average 127 mm in length and 60.3 mm in width. They are thus rather shorter than 2.70 but correspond well with 2.71. Both Danebury specimens are narrower than their Hunsbury counterparts. Two iron ploughshare tips (Rees 1a) were found at Gussage All Saints (Wainwright 1979, 104, fig 80, no 1084, fig 81, no 1022). Neither showed much similarity to the Danebury specimens. A single iron ploughshare tip was recovered during excavations at Hod Hill (Richmond 1968, 137, no 9, pl 41). This example is morphologically similar to 2.70. A ploughshare tip from Slonk Hill, Sussex (Rees 1979, 156, fig 51 b) is almost identical to 2.71 from Danebury.

Horsehoes and horseshoe nails (2.72–2.75)

Two discoveries of iron horseshoe fragments and seven separate finds of possible horseshoe nails were made at Danebury. The two fragmentary horseshoes are from soil accumulations within the entrance, but were unassociated with the Iron Age gate stratigraphy. Nail 2.74 was from the soil filling of a slot of building RS1, but could easily have been intruded into the fill as a result of worm, animal, or root action. The remaining two stratified examples (sf 369 and 301) were found in the uppermost layers of pits, in contexts liable to disturbance. 2.75 is from an undated posthole within the interior. Small finds 435, 304A, and 304B were unstratified. Thus none of these items has a clear Iron Age context.

The larger of the two horseshoe fragments, 2.73, has three countersunk rectangular depressions, each pierced by a circular hole. Two fiddle-key nails were found *in situ* and a third was discovered in association with the shoe. The shoe, which is of lobate form, terminates in a calkin. The second shoe is much slighter and is morphologically quite different from the first. The two nail holes which survive are rectangular in form and are only slightly countersunk. The calkin is not visible, probably as a result of corrosion, but the shoe is clearly plain in outline. The two horseshoe nails, 2.74 and 2.75, are both of fiddle-key type.

No finds of horseshoes have been made in indisputedly Iron Age contexts. The problem of dating has received considerable discussion (Ward 1941, 9.28; Ward Perkins 1941, 144–9). All that can safely be said is that while horseshoes may have been in use in the pre-Roman Iron Age, conclusive evidence is wanting, and Danebury adds nothing to the debate.

Latch lifter (2.76)

A single latch lifter was found at Danebury, in a cp 7 context. It comprises two elements, a ring-headed terminal and a rod or arm with a curved sickle-like outline. The piece was not complete, but measured 195 mm in length.

In the Glastonbury lake village report, Gray lists finds of 52 iron latch lifters from Iron Age or Roman sites (Bulleid & Gray 1917, 376). Only one of the artefacts was discovered in the excavations at Glastonbury, and they are similarly rare in most of the major Iron Age site collections. Hod Hill is unique in producing seven from the Durden collection (Brailsford 1962, 18, 19, pl XII) and another four from the excavations, although one of these was from a Roman context (Richmond 1968, 27, 31, 41, 115).

The element of the latch lifter which is subject to most variety of form is the terminal. In most cases, as at Danebury, this is ring- or loop-shaped, but in a number of examples the tool terminates in a straight tang which was obviously designed for insertion within a handle.

These objects are generally assumed to have been used to lift the latch on the inside of a door or to open locks with a single wooden tumbler.

Currency bars (2.77–2.99; Figs 7.15–7.18)

Twenty-four complete and fragmentary iron currency bars were found at Danebury. Twenty-one of these (all largely complete) were deposited as a hoard in a cp 7 context close to the rampart sectioned in the 1969 trench. One of the three remaining fragmentary bars was found in P149 producing eleven sherds of nondescript pottery of cp 1–3 date while both others were from cp 7–8 contexts. Because of the paucity of distinctive pottery from P149 the cp 1–3 date cannot be regarded as reliable.

All the currency bars are of the sword-shaped variety, with a blade of more or less even thickness which tapers towards a rounded point. All except one example, 2.99 (a fragment of blade), have a hilt which has been formed by pinching both edges of the bar together to create a socket. These sockets vary considerably in shape, but no

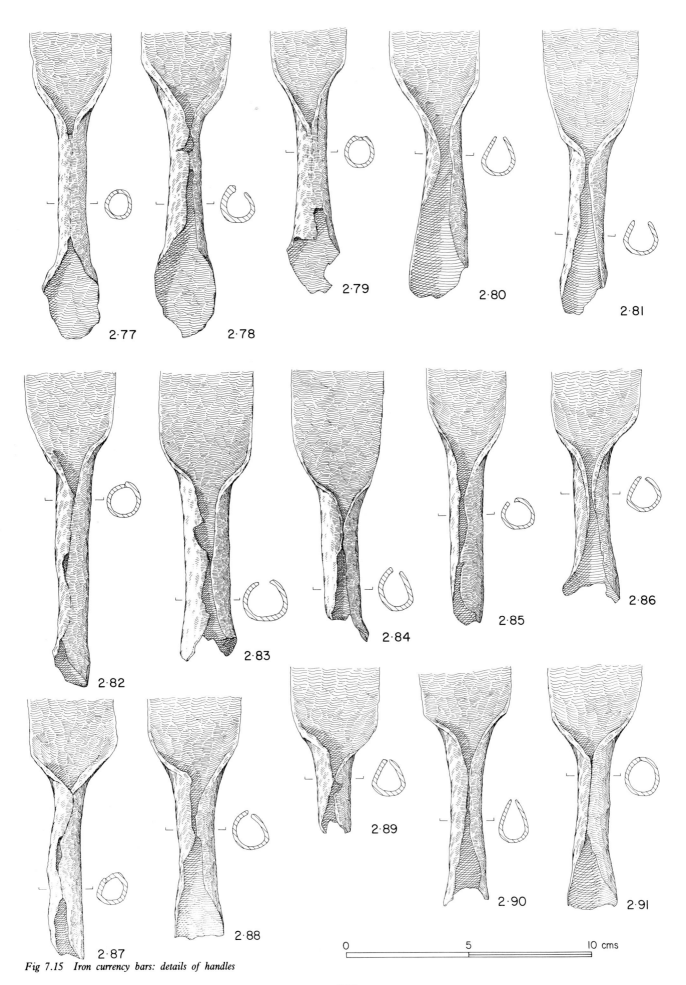

2·77

2·78

2·79

2·80

2·81

2·82

2·83

2·84

2·85

2·86

2·87

2·88

2·89

2·90

2·91

Fig 7.15   Iron currency bars: details of handles

0   5   10 cms

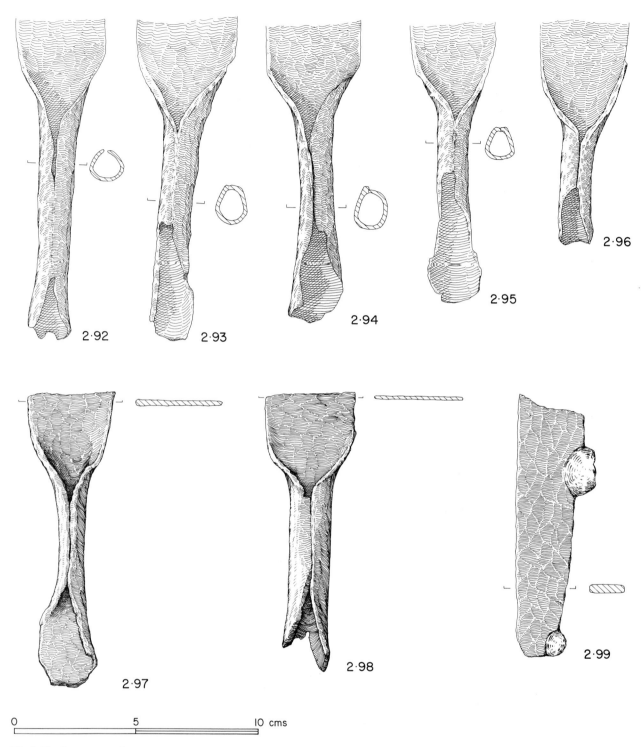

2·92 2·93 2·94 2·95 2·96

2·97 2·98 2·99

0   5   10 cms

Fig 7.16 Iron currency bars

valid typological distinction can be made. A metallographic examination conducted on a transverse section from the 'handle' of one of the Danebury bars revealed that the socket 'was formed in the last stage of working when the bar was cooling from the anneal' (Hedges & Salter 1979, 164). Some of the bars contain splinters of mineralized wood within their sockets. The hoard was found packed tightly against the edge of a pit, and it could thus be ascertained that the wood did not project beyond the haft. The suggestion that the pieces of wood represent not handles but formers, around which the metal was beaten, seems likely in this context (Cunliffe 1971, 251).

Despite the fact that each bar was individually forged, and that all have suffered some corrosion, the spans of size and weight are remarkably compact. Although lengths vary from 765–840 mm, 88% of the bars fall within the 50 mm spread from 770–820 mm. The widths of the bars vary by only 4 mm, and range from 36–40 mm. The weights recorded for the Danebury bars are between 388 and 492 gm, a difference of only 104 gm. The average weight is 452.9 gm. The assessments of weight and thickness are the least satisfactory because they are most subject to alteration by corrosion. It must also be noted that few bars are absolutely complete. Between 1,100 and 1,500 currency bars have been

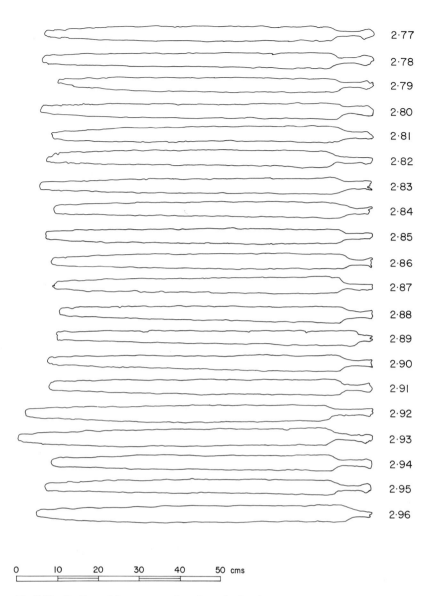

2·77
2·78
2·79
2·80
2·81
2·82
2·83
2·84
2·85
2·86
2·87
2·88
2·89
2·90
2·91
2·92
2·93
2·94
2·95
2·96

0   10   20   30   40   50 cms

Fig 7.17   Outlines of iron currency bars from the hoard

recovered from more than twenty sites in Britain (Allen 1967, 307). Despite this impressive total, these artefacts have received relatively little attention. The three most significant recent studies are by Tylecote (1962), Allen (1967), and Hedges and Salter (1979).

Tylecote's study omits to differentiate the bars by form, and consequently he is unable to make fine divisions in respect of size or weight. While providing a salutary warning about the problem of rusting which 'makes the accurate recording of weights somewhat meaningless' (1962, 207) he is nevertheless able to distinguish two generalized groups by weight. The first clusters around 652 gm, and the second around 312 gm. He also observes that a high proportion of the bars fall within the length span 690–890 mm. Allen refines the study of currency bars by defining three principal types: sword-shaped, spit-shaped, and ploughshare. In his analysis, only the sword- and spit-shaped bars — homogeneous in size and weight and hoarded in substantial numbers — meet the requirements of the term currency. The ploughshare bars are generally found in isolation and are of very diverse form. Among the sword-shaped bars, the category to which the Danebury group belongs, Allen distinguishes two types, those with partially closed hilts

and those with hilts made into a continuous tube. While Allen admits that bars vary individually, and that no clear geographical or chronological distinction exists between the types, he believes that they probably reflect different production sites, even if these operate on a very localized scale.

His maps of the distribution of sword-shaped bars reveal the major concentration rather to the west of Danebury, although a cluster of hoards occurs very close to the site, actually from the environs of Winchester (Allen 1967, 309, 327). He identifies the bars as a feature of the pre-Belgic Iron Age of the 1st century BC and observes that there is no chronological overlap between currency bars and coins.

The Hedges and Salter (1979, 163) metallographic analysis of the currency bars from three sites — Danebury, Beckford (Worcestershire), and Gretton (Northants) — indicates that there is a striking typological, metallographical, and chemical similarity within each hoard and that the three sites indicated three separate, non-overlapping regions, which would support the view that each site had its own particular single supply.

Sword-shaped currency bars have frequently been found in hoards. The majority of these were discovered during

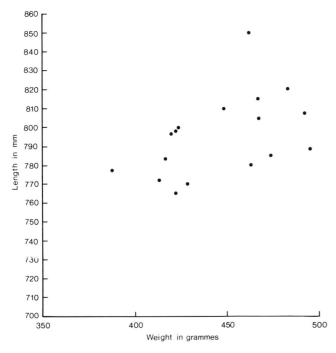

Fig 7.18 Sizes of currency bars from the hoard

ciently accurate to have a role as currency. In support of his contention, he quotes a series of measurements from extant Iron Age swords (1962, 211) which correspond very closely with those of the 'currency' bars.

Allen, while stressing the very localized character of the bars (a factor which is likely to account for slight variations in weight from site to site), is quite prepared to accept them as a form of currency functioning in the way that Caesar describes.

As Tylecote is aware, the question of the mood/bar equation cannot be settled until detailed metallographic studies are available for Iron Age swords. Some of the bars which he recorded were obviously of an unsuitable weight and size for conversion into swords, and he considered that these might have been intended for the manufacture of other types of implement or weapon.

The assertion that the primitive smith would have been unable to produce bars of sufficiently accurate measurements for them to be acceptable as currency is not endorsed by the evidence from Danebury.

It seems likely, therefore, that the bars had a distinct value recognized by the community. Some may have been made into swords but the majority were probably used by local smiths to cut up and forge into a variety of items at will. That the bars were being cut up at Danebury is shown by the three fragments, not belonging to the hoard, which had clearly been cropped from complete bars.

the 19th or early 20th century and contain somewhere between eight and twenty bars. A few much more substantial finds have occurred, including the 147 bars from Salmonsbury, near Bourton-on-the-Water, found in 1860 (Allen 1967, 328). The majority of these early finds are ill recorded (details summarized in Allen 1967, 324) and for this reason, and because the Danebury bars are the only ones to have been examined at first hand, the summaries and conclusions of Tylecote and Allen have been used to provide comparative data.

The Danebury currency bars, with an average weight of 452 gm, do not correspond well with either of Tylecote's weight groups but fall somewhere in between. The detailed weight analysis of the Danebury bars showed, contrary to Tylecote's general assertion, considerable similarities within the group. This may be because the bars were very well preserved and carefully conserved soon after exposure. It could in fact be suggested that each of the Danebury bars represents a measure of one and a half Celtic pounds of 308.9 gm; but until a wider data base is available, little more can be made of this correspondence.

Allen's claim for the two distinct types of sword-shaped currency bars is not supported by the morphological evidence from Danebury. While some of the bars undoubtedly belong under one or other of the categories which he outlines, the vast majority are of an indeterminate nature.

The sword-shaped and other iron bars were first considered as a form of currency because of an often quoted passage from Caesar's Gallic War (V, ch 12), which has been translated as stating that the Britons used iron bars of specific weights, *taleae ferreae*, as a means of exchange on a par with the early gold and bronze (actually potin) coins.

Tylecote proposes that the sword-shaped iron currency bars — and possibly some of the others — were intended to function principally as sword moods. He is of the opinion that it would have been impossible for the primitive smith to manufacture bars of a weight suffi-

Spearheads (2.100–2.103)

Four socketed iron spearheads were found at Danebury, 2.102 from a cp 3 context, 2.101 from cp 6, and 2.100 from cp 7. No 2.103 was unstratified. It is of interest that one of the most sophisticated artefacts, no 2.101, possessing midrib and closed socket, was from the later period of occupation.

2.100 and 2.101 have closed sockets and blades with raised central midribs. 2.100 is much the larger of the two, measuring 173 mm in overall length whereas 2.101 is a mere 110 mm long. The blade of 2.100 is decorated by two small bronze rivets exactly opposite each other and on either side of the central rib. 2.103 is a leaf-shaped, open-socketed spearhead, formed from a flat sheet of metal. 2.102 is fashioned in the same way as 2.103, but has been made from a saw blade, with the serrated teeth evident along one side of the blade and along the inner edge of the right hand flange. 2.101 has two pairs of rivet holes through the socket. A single pair of rivet holes is visible through both flanges of 2.103.

The largest collection of spearheads comes from Hod Hill. Seventy-nine of these are published in the Durden collection (Brailsford 1962, 5, 6, pls V, VI). Three principal types were identified, one of which may have been a cavalry lance. The second largest group of spearheads — all certainly of Iron Age date — came from Hunsbury (Fell 1936, 66). Twenty were discovered, and amongst these three principal types were isolated: 'the small javelin-head, the long narrow spearhead with the slight mid-rib, and the broad leaf-shaped form with the distinct mid-rib'. Neither of the two Danebury ribbed spears can be fitted into these categories. One example from Hunsbury (pl A, no 1), presumably of the first type identified, is apparently similar to 2.103 from Danebury, but no section is provided. Three spearheads (unillustrated) come from Glastonbury (Bulleid & Gray 1917, 360) and five were found at Maiden Castle (Wheeler 1943, 278), although only three of these were from the late Iron Age levels and none provides an exact parallel with the Danebury pieces.

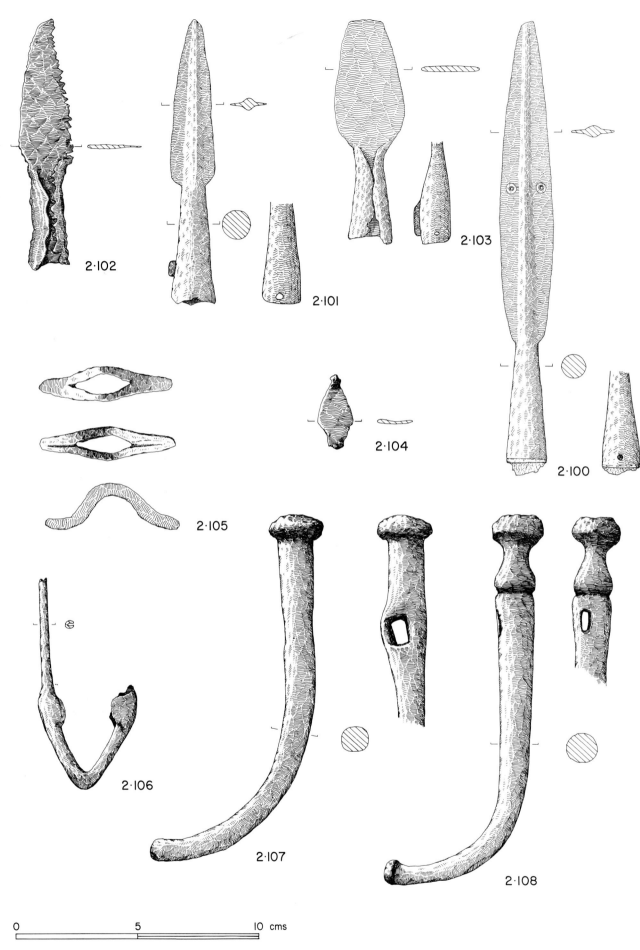

2·102

2·101

2·103

2·104

2·100

2·105

2·106

2·107

2·108

0   5   10 cms

Fig 7.19 Iron objects

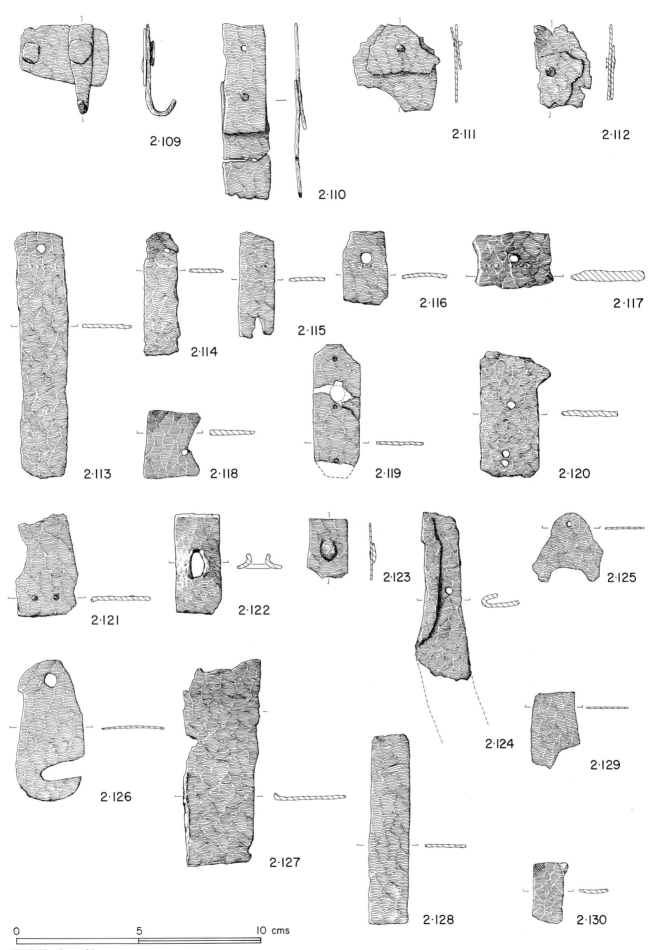

2·109

2·110

2·111

2·112

2·114

2·115

2·116

2·117

2·113

2·118

2·119

2·120

2·121

2·122

2·123

2·124

2·125

2·126

2·127

2·128

2·129

2·130

0   5   10 cms

Fig 7.20 Iron objects

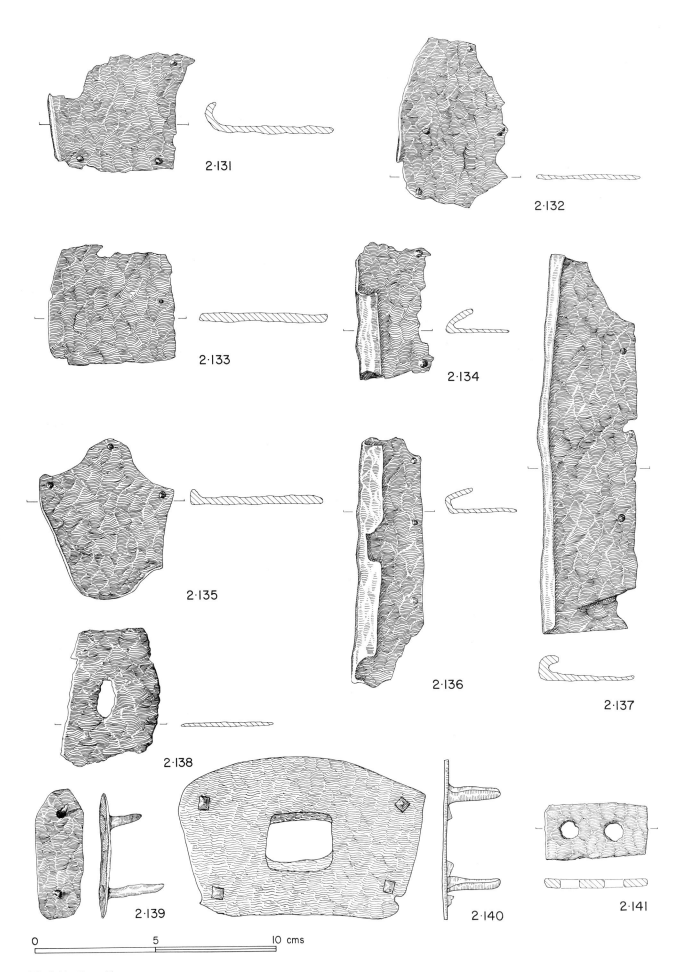

2·131

2·132

2·133

2·134

2·135

2·136

2·137

2·138

2·139

2·140

2·141

0   5   10 cms

Fig 7.21   Iron objects

364

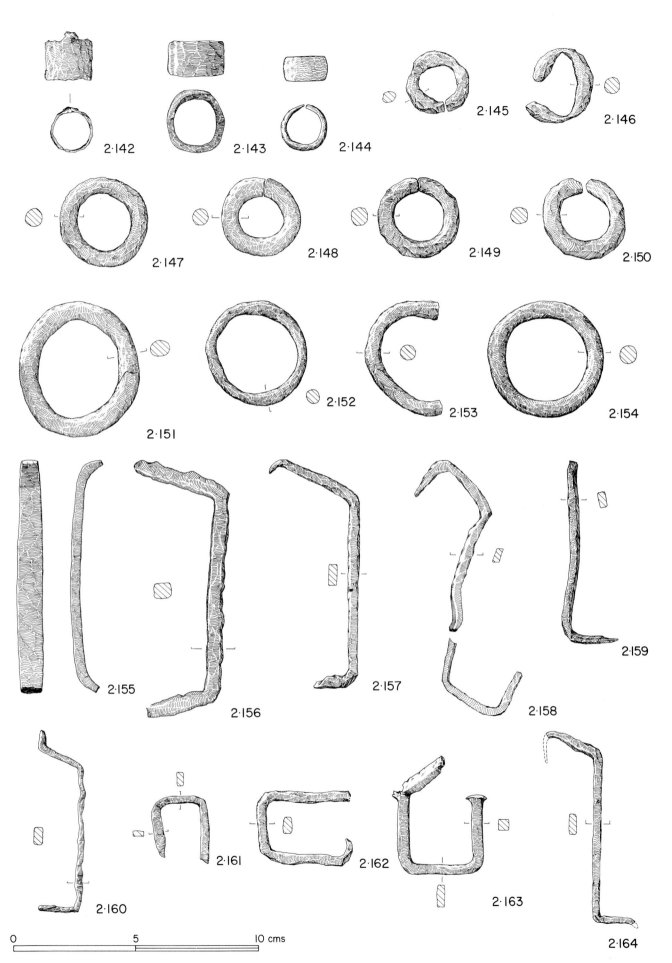

2·142   2·143   2·144   2·145   2·146

2·147   2·148   2·149   2·150

2·151   2·152   2·153   2·154

2·155   2·156   2·157   2·158   2·159

2·160   2·161   2·162   2·163   2·164

0   5   10 cms

Fig 7.22   Iron objects

365

It is possible that 2.100 is a Saxon weapon. It compares well with Swanton's type B2 spear (1976, 39), displaying in fact the continental Nydam-style midrib, wider at the lower part of the blade and seeming to emerge directly of a piece with the socket. Although Swanton gives no examples of Nydam spears decorated with copper-alloy rivets, a number are known with an inlaid pattern of silver, copper, and brass wires. This type of weapon dates to the early migration period, late 4th or 5th century AD.

Arrowhead (2.104)

A single example of a tanged iron arrowhead was found at Danebury, from a cp 7 context.

The arrowhead is manufactured from a flat sheet of iron. The approximately triangular blade has a long, buckled point. The tang is broken a short distance from the base of the blade, and the piece measures 28 mm in surviving length.

Arrowheads of this type are extremely rare from Iron Age sites. The only parallel from a major site collection is a single example discovered at Maiden Castle (Wheeler 1943, fig 88, no 9 and 272). This arrowhead is also made from sheet iron and terminates with a tang, but differs from the Danebury example in being barbed.

Hilt guard and chape (2.105, 2.106)

One example each of an iron hilt guard (2.105) and chape (2.106) were found at Danebury, from separate cp 7 contexts.

2.105 is formed from two narrow rectangular-sectioned iron bars, pinched together at either end and separated by a gap at the upward-curving midway point. This is an example of Piggott's group II guards, which are found on swords of Hunsbury type (Piggott 1950, 5–10, figs 2–4, and pp 25–6 for list of group II weapons and their fittings). The guard was designed to fit over the tang of a sword or dagger and bed down on the edge of the blade.

Another example of a sword or dagger is represented by the iron scabbard chape 2.106. This piece comprises a pointed terminal whose arms expand into rounded mouldings and continue as a narrow binding. The chape, like the hilt guard, belongs to Piggott's group II Hunsbury type. Chapes are more commonly manufactured in bronze, and have a wide distribution throughout southern Britain.

Linch pins (2.107, 2.108)

Two well-preserved linch pins (2.107, 2.108) were found close together and in a cp 7 context on the floor of CS20. The Danebury pins are not identical in form. 2.107 is ornamented only with an expanded disc-shaped head, while 2.108 possesses a baluster knop terminal at its wider end and a simple disc-shaped expansion at the narrower terminal. The rectangular perforations through each shaft occupy an off-centre position, and are almost identical in size. The two lengths, allowing for the terminal of 2.108, are very similar (163 mm and 175 mm respectively) as are the weights (126.7 and 141 gm).

Linch pins are rare items on Iron Age sites, and it has not proved possible to find exact parallels for the Danebury pair. The majority of linch pins from the British Isles have iron shanks and bronze terminals. They are widely distributed about the country. Two, with copper-alloy coated terminals, were found recently not far from Danebury at Old Down Farm, Andover (Davies 1981, 124, fig 29, nos 16 and 17). The only pair of linch pins

made entirely of iron came from Danes Graves, Yorks (Stead 1979, 45). These are not identical in form to either of the Danebury specimens, having squarish terminals. Stead refers to only one other example of an iron linch pin from Britain, found at Norfolk, but he quotes a number of continental parallels from the La Tène I cart burials in Champagne. The baluster-knop expansion of 2.108 occurs on many of the British linch pins which have bronze terminals.

The close proximity of the Danebury pins, and their similar size, suggests that they represent a pair, possibly from a chariot or cart.

Sheet iron fittings (2.109–2.141)

Thirty-three objects of this type were found at Danebury. Their chronological distribution is as follows:

cp	number	relative frequency
1-3	4	1.0
4	0	0
5	0	0
6	3	4.2
7	23	19.0

Three fittings came from contexts which have no ceramic phase.

In addition to the chronological concentration within cp 7–8 many of them are found together in the same pit or layer:

P79	2.113, 2.114, 2.120, 2.124, 2.127
P814	2.111, 2.115
P891	2.131, 2.132, 2.133
P911	(from the same layer) 2.117, 2.128
Layer 200	2.109, 2.116

All the objects within this category are manufactured from thin sheet iron. The majority possess one or more rivet holes, and a number have upturned flanges. Their general character is apparent from the illustrations. It is possible that 2.109–2.112 may have functioned as iron attachments on leather-backed body armour. The concentration of many items within the same pit presumably indicates that all were attached to some form of organic material at the time of deposition, but does little to illuminate a more specific function.

Collars and rings (2.142–2.154)

Thirteen objects in this category were found at Danebury, one each from cp 1–3, cp 4, and cp 6, three from cp 5, and six from cp 7–8 contexts. One ring was unstratified. A pair of rings of similar size (2.147, 2.149) were found in Trench 18, layer 20. Another pair of rings, in this case of different sizes (2.148, 2,151), were found within layer 10 of P1078.

2.142, 2.143, and 2.144 are morphologically distinct from the rest of the collection. They are much deeper and have a thinner section, and may be regarded either as rings or collars. The remaining rings display a considerable variation in size, which can be appreciated from the illustrations. Most are split-rings, but 2.151 has a distinct scarf-joint. 2.154 is unique among the specimens from the site in having two stop collars.

A number of the rings have been subjected to hard wear. This is apparent in the differential thickness and distortion of 2.145, 2.146, and 2.152. The two sets of paired rings may well have been attached to some organic material when they were finally discarded.

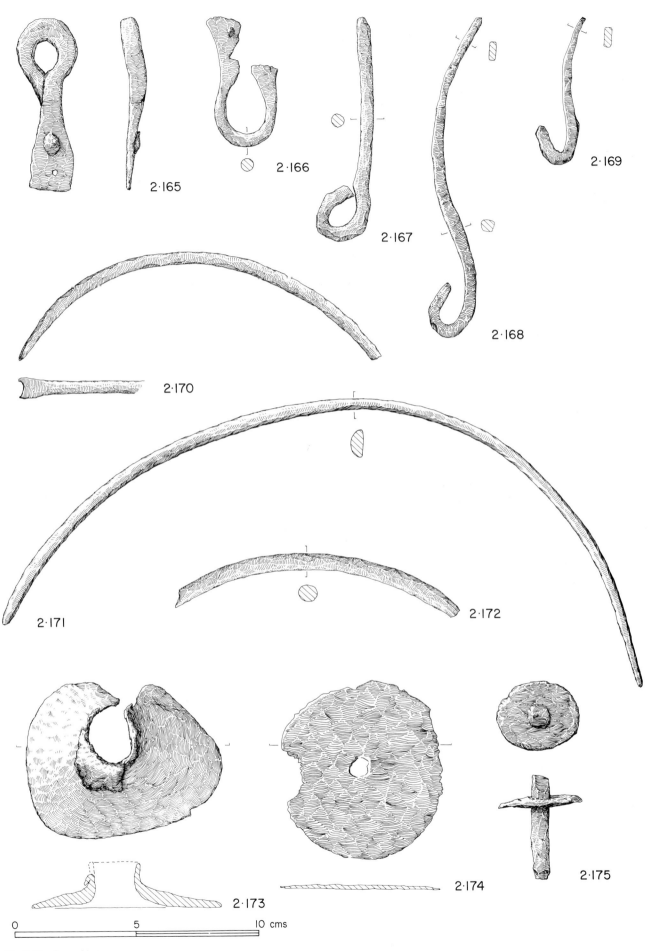

2·165

2·166

2·167

2·168

2·169

2·170

2·171

2·172

2·173

2·174

2·175

0   5   10 cms

Fig 7.23   Iron objects

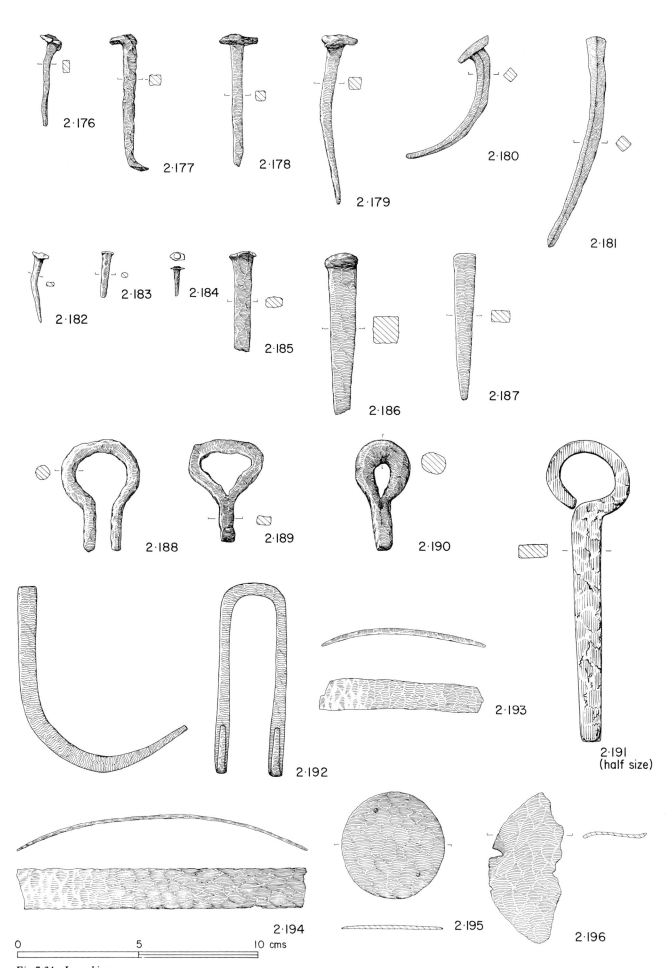

2·176

2·177

2·178

2·179

2·180

2·181

2·182

2·183

2·184

2·185

2·186

2·187

2·188

2·189

2·190

2·191
(half size)

2·192

2·193

2·194

2·195

2·196

0   5   10 cms

Fig 7.24 Iron objects

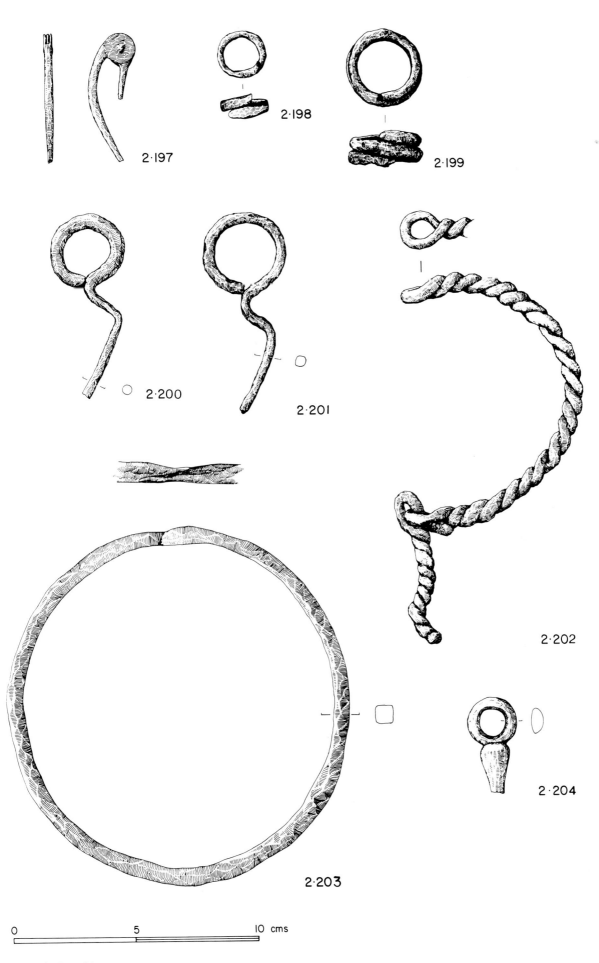

2·197

2·198

2·199

2·200

2·201

2·202

2·203

2·204

0   5   10 cms

Fig 7.25 Iron objects

369

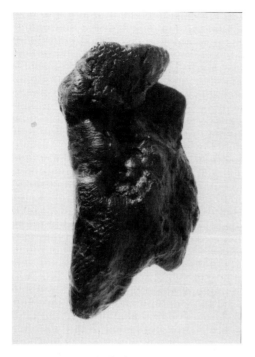

Fig 7.26 *Iron bloom (2.205). Scale 1:1*

Strip bindings (2.155–2.164)

Ten iron strip bindings or clamps were found at Danebury. 2.164 may possibly be better interpreted as a wall hook. One object was from a cp 6 context, seven came from cp 7, and the remaining two were from contexts which lacked ceramic phases. All these objects were manufactured from thin, rectangular-sectioned strips or bars of iron. Their variety of size is apparent from the illustration. The precise functions of these pieces cannot be determined.

Bucket fittings (2.165–2.172)

Eight iron objects, probably best interpreted as bucket fittings, came from Danebury. 2.165, 2.168, and 2.172 were from cp 6, while all remaining objects belong to cp 7 contexts.

2.165 and 2.166 are riveted loop attachments. 2.167, 2.168, and 2.169 are lengths of handle which terminate in either an open or a closed loop. 2.170 is a piece of handle with a fragmentary flattened terminal at one end, while 2.171 and 2.172 are lengths of handle broken at both ends.

Bucket fittings are rare from Iron Age sites, but a precise parallel for the fragmentary terminal of 2.170 was found at Bury Wood Camp, Wilts (King 1962, 198, fig 6).

Discs (2.173–2.175)

Three flat, approximately circular discs of metal, all perforated with a central hole, have been found at Danebury. All three were from cp 7 contexts.

The objects vary in size and detail. The circular hole in 2.173 had been punched through from one side. The method of perforation resulted in a raised flange on the upper surface. 2.174 is a completely flat disc, with a central circular perforation. 2.175 is ovoid and has a tang through the central perforation. It may be presumed that the variety of forms reflects different functions, although

it is not possible to be precise about these. An exact parallel for 2.174 was found at Spettisbury Rings, Dorset (Gresham 1939, 123, pl VI, no 5).

Nails, rivets, and wedges (2.176–2.187)

Seven iron nails, two rivets, and three wedges were found at Danebury. All these objects were unassociated with other finds.

Two of the nails were from cp 3 and one came from each of cp 4, 5, and 7. Both rivets were from cp 7 contexts and the two wedges from datable contexts also belonged to this latest ceramic phase. All the complete nails have square or rectangular-sectioned shanks and irregularly-shaped heads which project beyond the shanks on all sides. The two rivets have circular sections. All threee wedges have square or rectangular sections and heads which slightly overlap the shanks.

Miscellaneous iron objects (2.188–2.205)

Objects of uncertain function (2.188–2.196)

Nine of the Danebury iron objects have been included under this heading. All derive from cp 7 contexts. 2.188–2.190 possess ring-headed terminals, but the variety of shafts suggests different functions. 2.188 was probably a staple, 2.189 a hook, and the exact usage of 2.190 and 2.191 is uncertain. 2.192 is a double-armed hook, which like 2.191 was found in association with the charred wooden paddle or shovel 9.1. Nos 2.195 and 2.196 are flat circular discs, the former possessing two rivets for attachment. 2.193 and 2.194 are slightly curved strips of metal which may have functioned as bindings, perhaps from wooden buckets. A precise parallel for the hook 2.189 has been found at Rope Lake Hole, nr Kimmeridge (Henig, pers comm). 2.191 is very similar to an object from Hod Hill (Richmond 1968, pl 42), also of unspecified function.

370

Personal ornaments (2.197–2.202)
Seven items of iron which may be regarded as personal ornaments have been found.
2.197 Iron fibula (cp 7) with a hinged pin retained between two circular plates. Hinged pins of this kind are a feature of involuted brooches of which this may be an example.
2.198, 2.199 Spiral finger or toe rings (cp 7–8). Type not uncommon in southern Britain. See, for example, Glastonbury (Bulleid & Gray 1911, pl XLI) though rings of this kind are usually made of bronze.
2.200, 2.201 Ring-headed pins (cp 3) of the general type discussed in detail by Dunning (1934). The Danebury examples are close in form to those found at All Cannings Cross (Cunnington 1923, pl 20, no 4, pl 21, nos 2–4) and Maiden Castle (Wheeler 1943, 267 and fig 87, nos 5, 6).
2.202 Twisted iron 'torc' (cp 7). Objects of this kind are unusual but a very close parallel is published from Spettisbury (Hawkes 1941). The Danebury example retains part of a section which would have closed the gap between the two ring terminals suggesting that it may have been a gang chain of the kind found at Llyn Cerrig, Anglesey, and Bigbury, Kent.

Chariot or cart fittings (2.203, 2.204)
Two iron objects which may possible be chariot fittings have been found at Danebury, 2.203 from a cp 6 and 2.204 from a cp 7 context. 2.203, a complete iron ring with a scarf join, may be the nave hoop from a chariot. Similar objects have been found in the Arras burials (Greenwell 1905, 279) and at Hunsbury (Fell 1936, 67, pl IVB, no 5). 2.204 is a ring-headed terminal of bronzed iron which may come from a linch pin. Two such pairs with copper-alloy coated terminals were found at Old Down Farm, Andover (Davies 1981, 124, fig 29, nos 16 and 17).

Iron bloom (2.205)
Large amorphous fragments of iron, probably an iron bloom, of approximately 75 by 35 by 25 mm. Weight 221.5 gm. One surface retains marks suggestive of textile or matting on to which the hot bloom may have been placed. There is some evidence to suggest that the bloom was in the process of being cut by hammer and chisel when it was discarded.

7.1.6 Objects of bone and antler (Figs 7.27–7.40)
by Lyn Sellwood
The objects of bone and antler are discussed under the following headings:

combs of bone and antler
toggles of bone and antler
needles
gouges
awls, splinters, and points
tools manufactured from sheep long bones
antler handles
rings of bone and antler
objects manufactured from split cattle-size rib bones
miscellaneous worked bone
manufacturing waste: antler
manufacturing waste: bone

All bone artefacts are described in the microfiche (fiche 10, frames A2–D12). The majority are illustrated but those which are not are given the small find numbers after the group heading.

Combs of bone and antler (3.1–3.29)
Thirty-nine whole or fragmentary bone and antler combs were found distributed chronologically as follows:

cp	number	relative frequency
1-3	8	1.0
4	3	2.9
5	0	0
6	3	2.1
7-8	24	9.8

Although numbers are comparatively small, the increase in frequency of artefacts during the last phase is noticeable.

Of the 39 complete or fragmentary combs, ten were manufactured of bone, while the remainder were antler. This preference for antler is evident among other site collections and probably results from an appreciation of the relative strengths of the two materials, antler being the more resilient (MacGregor & Currey 1983). Most Iron Age weaving combs comprise three separate sections, the butt, the shaft or handle, and the teeth. Few combs from Danebury are complete, but a comparison of three which are reveals a size range of between 93.0 mm and 153.0 mm in length. The width of the combs, measured immediately below the dentate end, displays less variety. The widest measures 36.0 mm and the narrowest 25.0 mm.

The teeth, which vary in number between six and twelve, are cut parallel with the long axis of the comb, and are rectangular in section at the base where they join the shaft, tapering towards the apices. The ends of the teeth have frequently become rounded in section and pointed through wear. The interdentate notches are most often narrow and V-shaped, but occasionally are wider and U-shaped. In some instances, all the teeth have been cut to the same length, but in others those towards the centre of the comb are distinctly longer than those at the two edges. It is not altogether apparent whether this results from design or simply from wear.

The shaft of the comb is usually wider at the dentate end than immediately above the butt. It can be either plano-convex or concavo-convex in section and while normally straight sided is sometimes curved in the natural shape of the piece of bone or antler.
The butt or terminal of the comb is the element most subject to variation. In a few examples, it is integral with the handle, but in most it is present as some form of enlargement. The commonest butt form at Danebury is square or rectangular, but there are single examples of circular and ovoid terminations.

While Iron Age weaving combs display a limited number of forms, the decoration, within certain well-defined limits, is extremely varied. The principal motifs employed are:

1 the incised straight line
2 the 'compass' drawn ring-and-dot motif

The first appears frequently either as single or multiple arrangements of the following:

a lines running transversely across the comb
b lines forming a zig-zag pattern
c cross-hatched lines
d combinations of the above

371

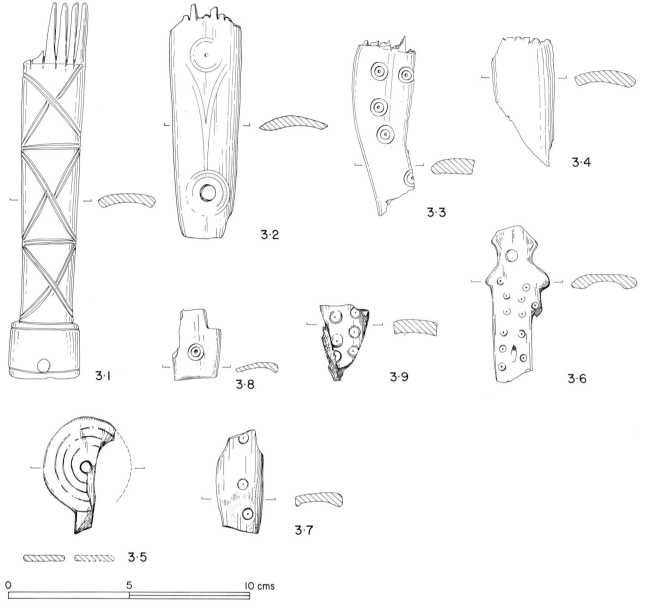

Fig 7.27 Bone combs

The ring-and-dot motifs vary considerably in size and depth of relief, and a variant of this form can comprise as many as four concentric circles. They are sometimes utilized as:

a the principal decorative device, either symmetrically or haphazardly arranged
b a motif which fills in the spaces in the field which have first been defined by the linear decoration. It is frequently the case that even when the circular components relate to a carefully positioned linear design, they are applied with no particular regard to this.

The range of decorative motifs presumably reflects to some extent the limits imposed by the material; but present evidence does not suggest that patterns were standardized to any degree. The number of combs with precisely similar decoration and form is extremely small.

In order to determine whether the decorative motifs on the Danebury combs show any change over time, decoration was examined in relation to ceramic phase (Table 36).

The numbers involved are too small for the findings to be of much significance. The total decorative range occurs only in ceramic phases 1–3 and 7–8, but these are numerically better represented than the remaining groups. The prevalence of circular motifs in cp 7–8, contrasted to their rarity in earlier ceramic phases, may well be of importance.

Table 36   Decoration in relation to ceramic phase

Ceramic phases	1-3	4	5	6	7-8
Undecorated	4	–	–	1	8
Linear decoration	2	2	–	2	3
Circular decoration	1	–	–	–	13
Combination of linear and circular	1	1	–	–	1

372

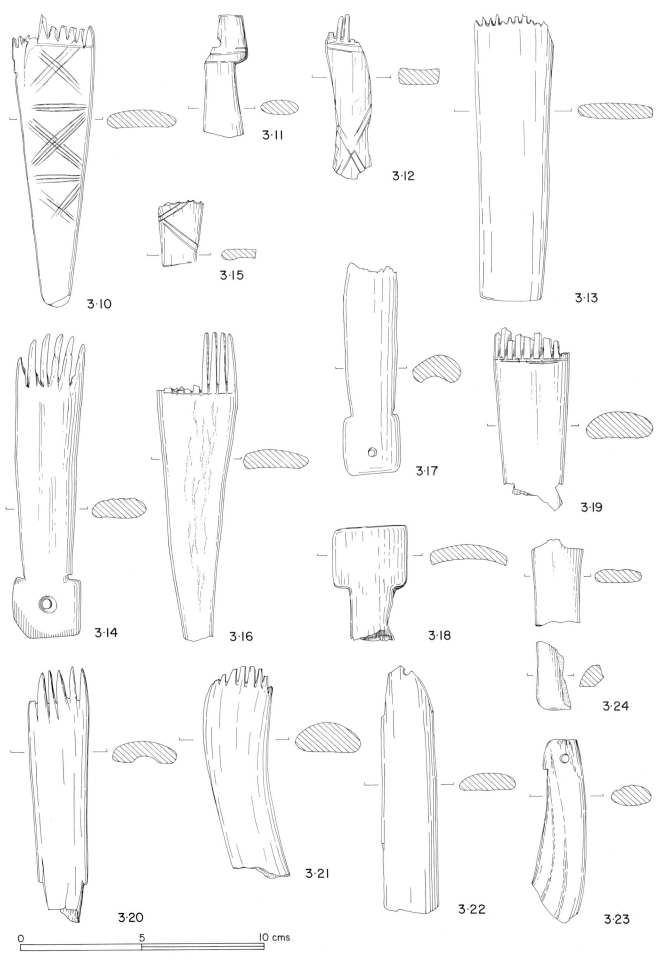

3·11

3·12

3·15

3·10

3·13

3·17

3·19

3·14

3·16

3·18

3·24

3·20

3·21

3·22

3·23

0   5   10 cms

Fig 7.28   Antler combs

373

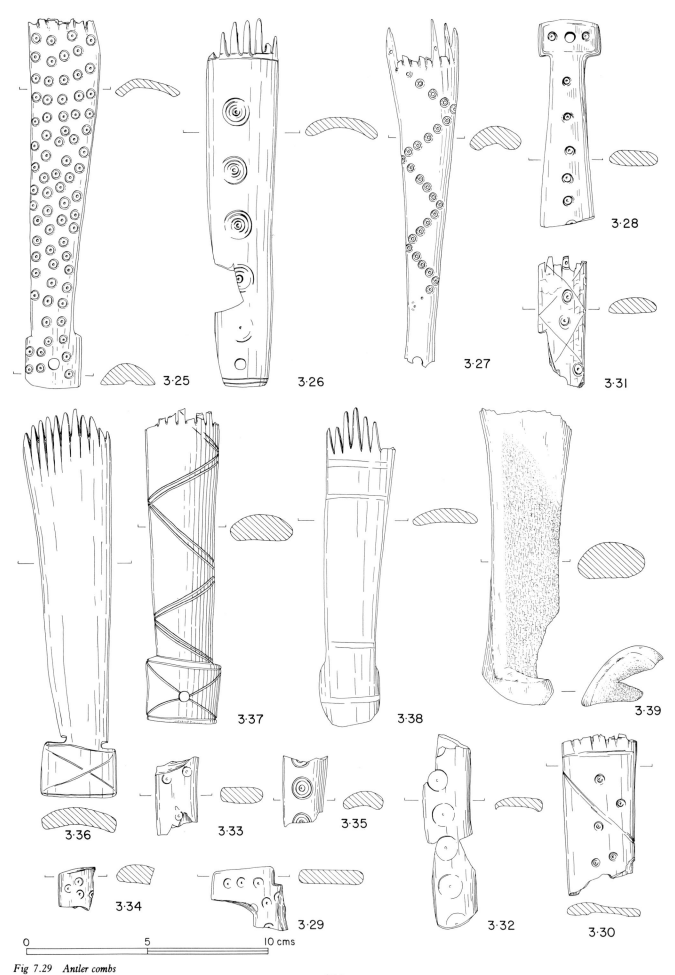

3·25 3·26 3·27 3·28 3·31

3·36 3·37 3·38 3·39

3·34 3·33 3·35 3·29 3·32 3·30

0   5   10 cms

Fig 7.29 Antler combs

374

Table 37 The relationship between butt form and ceramic phase

Ceramic phases	1-3	4	5	6	7-8
Square or rectangular enlargements	1	–	–	2	8
Butt and handle integrated	4	–	–	–	–
Handle tapers sharply towards butt	–	–	–	–	2
Ovoid enlargement	–	1	–	–	–
Circular enlargement	1	–	–	–	–
Miscellaneous	–	–	–	–	2

Table 38 The relationship between site and form

	Meare	Glastonbury	Maiden Castle	Danebury
Angular/pointed terminals	18	1	1	0
Oval or round enlargement	19	5	3	2
Square or oblong enlargement	2	5	0	10
No enlargement worth mentioning	66	43	18	3
Dentate at both ends	6	5	0	0

Table 37 was prepared in order to determine whether there was any correspondence between butt form and chronological horizon (none was found at Maiden Castle).

The small number of artefacts again prevents firm conclusions being drawn, but certain observations may be valid. The most common butt form from Danebury, the square or rectangularly enlarged terminal, spans the entire chronological horizon — with the exception of cp 4 — and concentrates in cp 7–8. The combs which have a butt integral with the handle are found only in cp 1–3. The very rare circular and ovoid terminals are confined to the two earliest phases. The two examples of combs in which the shaft tapers sharply towards the butt belong to the final ceramic phases; the actual form of the terminal is unknown.

Wear patterns (Fig 7.29)
The wear patterns on the Iron Age 'weaving combs' are likely to provide the best evidence of function. The dentate ends of the combs are obviously most relevant to such a consideration, and the Danebury excavations have provided 21 specimens in which this section of the comb is extant.

Most of the combs from the site bear signs of general wear, such as a polished surface and teeth which have become rounded in section and pointed towards the apices. There are nevertheless certain other commonly occurring patterns of wear which provide a more specific idea of the way in which the artefact was employed. The most frequent pattern involves the breakage of all or the majority of the teeth on a level with, or a little above, the shaft of the comb. We cannot be sure that breakage did not occur after the combs were discarded; but the most vulnerable areas are the apices of the teeth and the extreme outside teeth, and it seems likely that these would have been the most susceptible. The apparently simultaneous fracturing of all the teeth has occurred in nine examples from the site, and in a further two cases the majority of teeth are missing. This high frequency encourages the view that the breakage pattern results from use.

Another form of wear shows in the breakage and subsequent wearing smooth of the extreme left hand tooth or two teeth. This pattern is evident on five of the sample, and on another specimen it has occurred on the two extreme right-hand teeth. Sometimes wear has resulted in the teeth being recut. Five Danebury combs show signs of this, although it must be admitted that this sort of modification can only be detected on decorated examples, where the new interdentate notches can be seen to interrupt the design.

Eight combs have quite distinct transverse wear grooves running across either the upper or lower surfaces of the teeth, or in rare instances on both. In addition to this, five of the number have lateral wear on the teeth. This shows up as a slight indentation on the side of the tooth which runs at right-angles to the long axis of the comb.

On a further two combs, obvious indentations occur on the stumps of broken teeth which are situated at the outside edge of the implement. These indentations are worn backwards in the direction of the shaft.

Three of the Danebury combs possess central teeth which are markedly longer than the outer ones, while in five cases the teeth are all of approximately similar length. Only one comb with uniformly short teeth has been found on the site and this example was apparently in the process of having its teeth lengthened before it was abandoned.

The majority of combs show considerable — and on occasion a very high degree of — polish resulting from usage. This is most evident on the handle and butt, and on any raised points of the upper surface of the comb.

Comparisons
The aim of this section is to set the Danebury bone combs in context by comparing them with a selection of similar combs. Three site collections have been chosen, Glastonbury and Meare, because of their large size, and Maiden Castle because the conditions of excavation allowed the combs to be put into a chronological framework. In addition, the fifteen combs in the Ashmolean Museum's collection were considered. These were examined in detail at first hand, and as a group constitute a 'random' selection which gives some idea of the range of combs found in the counties of Oxfordshire, Berkshire, Northamptonshire, Wiltshire, and Sussex.

The classification of combs has occupied archaeologists since the first large bodies of material were collected. The division proposed in the Glastonbury report (Bulleid & Gray 1911, 274–7) was based entirely on an assessment of the decorative terminals. The same scheme was followed in the Meare volume (Bulleid & Gray 1948, 61–89) and at Maiden Castle (Wheeler 1943, 297–303). Wheeler felt constrained to comment that the divisions have 'no evolutionary or other significance', but were 'convenient in the absence of any more significant scheme' (ibid, 298). That the groupings have no significance is not altogether correct. Table 38 presents the relative numbers of types (as defined by Bulleid and Gray) at the four sites under consideration.

Although the samples from the two hillfort sites are small, it is interesting to observe that Danebury with its high percentage of combs with a square or oblong terminal is quite unlike the three other sites. Moreover, the range of forms is wider at Glastonbury and Meare than at either Danebury or Maiden Castle, although this may merely reflect the discrepant sample series.

In a recent paper, Hodder and Hedges (1977) have proposed a scheme for examining Iron Age weaving combs which takes into account both form and decoration, but omits chronological distinctions. When the Danebury combs are examined in accordance with the scheme, the most significant fact to emerge is that sixteen of the collection belong to one of the defined decorative

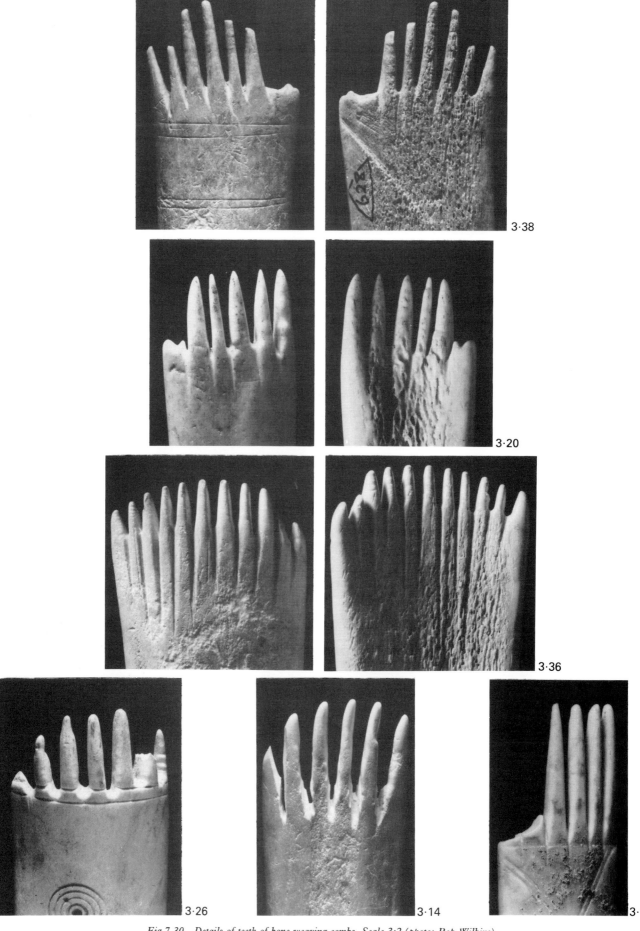

Fig 7.30   Details of teeth of bone weaving combs. Scale 3:2 (photo: Bob Wilkins)

Table 39 Comparative data on size

	Danebury	Maiden Castle	Glastonbury	Meare
Longest comb	153	–	218	222
Shortest comb	93	–	105	102
Average	–	–	155	145
Greatest width across teeth	36	–	49	42
Smallest width across teeth	25	–	26	21
Average	29	–	35	31
Greatest number of teeth	12	11	15	12
Smallest number of teeth	6	7	5	6
Average	8	8	9	9

All measurements in millimetres

groupings. The overall impression given is that the Danebury assemblage lies, for the most part, to the east of the concentrations of each relevant group. In some cases the Danebury combs were the most easterly outliers, while in other instances they fitted well into the overall distribution patterns, although these often covered such large regions that their usefulness is seriously in doubt. The authors concluded from the exercise: 'The general picture that emerges . . . is one of different scales of localization of comb types . . . . It is frequently the case that the most similar combs occur together on the same site' (*ibid*, 24). This confirms the conclusion presented in Table 38, in which classification into groups was determined by an analysis of formal elements alone.

Table 39 offers comparative morphological data on the combs from the four sites. Measurements were omitted from the Maiden Castle publication. The value of such a table is limited and, indeed, it may conceal more than it reveals. The functional differences apparent from wear patterns and from other details will not necessarily be complemented by variations in size. The broad similarities revealed in the table may reflect a uniformity of function; but it should be remembered that size is limited by the choice of material.

The Danebury and Maiden Castle combs have the smallest range of size, while those from Meare and, in particular, Glastonbury show a much greater variation. This hints that the lake villages may have a greater selection of forms than the two hillforts, but again it may simply reflect the fact that the sample is larger.

The Danebury combs are the most homogeneous, not only in size but also in other aspects of form. The teeth are all of approximately similar size (only one or two examples are extremely worn), and the interdentate notches are mostly V-shaped, although U-shaped examples do exist. At Maiden Castle, a distinction emerges between short-toothed combs — some with very wide interdentate notches — and long-toothed combs. The widths of the teeth display greater variety than was apparent at Danebury. The Meare and Glastonbury samples show a range of forms only paralleled by the collection in the Ashmolean Museum. The double-ended combs occur in all three collections, and often possess teeth of differing gauges at either end. The long- and short-toothed distinction is again valid, but the numbers of teeth and their size are more various than at either Danebury or Maiden Castle.

The only body of published data with which the wear patterns of the Danebury combs can be compared comes from the lake villages of Glastonbury and Meare. These two samples are numerically much larger than that from Danebury, comprising 89 and 130 combs respectively, but the wear patterns are very similar. These patterns were observed in reasonable detail but are not always recorded with precision; for example, transverse wear grooves are noted, but their exact position on the comb is not always stated. Lateral wear is seldom recorded *per se*, but a number of combs are described as having teeth which are blunt at the apices, an observation which may well reflect this form of use.

A number of general observations included in the two reports may also be relevant to wear. For example, it is noted that the teeth of some of the combs had 'entirely broken', but since no details are given, it remains unclear whether or not such breakage was simultaneous.

Most of the observations of wear accord very well with the Danebury sample. A considerable percentage of the combs from the lake villages have been worn to a semicircular outline at the dentate end; that is to say that the centrally positioned teeth are distinctly longer than those at the outer edges. Another pattern common to all three sites is the breakage of one or two teeth on the outside edge of the comb. The most commonly observed wear pattern at both Glastonbury and Meare is the transverse grooving across the lower surfaces of the teeth. Sixteen cases were noted at the former site, and eight at the latter. Only two examples from Glastonbury and one from Meare have transverse wear exclusively on the upper surface of the teeth, while one example from each site displays wear on both faces. Only one case of lateral wear is explicitly noted at Meare, and none occurs at Glastonbury.

The Danebury collection is of comparable size to that from Maiden Castle. Twenty-three combs are drawn and described, but wear patterns are generally omitted from the discussion. Only a single case of transverse grooves on the lower surface of the teeth is explicitly commented upon. It is however possible to suggest from the illustrations that as many as ten of the sample suffered the simultaneous fracturing of all or most teeth. Eight combs from the hillfort possess teeth which are almost identical in length, while four combs display the semicircular wear on the teeth which has been described above.

In addition to the evidence from the three published reports, the fifteen Iron Age combs in the Ashmolean Museum's collection were examined as a source of comparative data (from sites in the south Midlands and Wessex). Two specimens from this collection had apparently fractured across the teeth in a single movement. Three of the combs have transverse wear on the lower surfaces of the teeth, and a further comb showed signs of lateral wear. A single case of lateral and transverse wear occurring on the same comb was noted.

It has been observed that the wear patterns on the combs must provide the surest indication of their function. An assessment of these patterns is particularly necessary in a case such as this, in which experts have presented radically conflicting views. Ling Roth (1934, 132) denies that the combs could have been used in conjunction with the loom for two principal reasons: first the concavo-convex section of the combs would draw the warp threads out of position during the beating-in process; and secondly, the friction caused by the roughness of the cancellous tissue, which is frequently exposed on the lower surfaces of the comb, would make use of the implement unpractical. Hodder and Hedges (1978, 19) conducted experiments with the combs which endorsed Roth's findings.

Another recent experiment was conducted to investigate the use and efficiency of the warp-weighted loom (Reynolds 1972). This produced results quite opposite to those already outlined. The weaver in this instance found that 'the bone weaving comb proved far better for its job than the dinner fork he normally used on this type of loom — no great pressure falls on the tool since it is only used to push the weft roughly into position before it is beaten firmly into position by the weaver's sword' (*ibid*, 19)

Much of the controversy surrounding the possible use of these combs is centred upon the nature of the artefact's section, whether concavo-convex or plano-convex. Ling Roth objects that the illustrations of a comb actually in use in the Glastonbury report (Bulleid & Gray 1911, 269) is misleading on a number of scores. Not only is the comb being used upside down, beating downwards as opposed to beating upwards as is the case with warp-weighted looms, but the comb is perfectly plano-convex in section. As Roth rightly observes, many of the combs from the site are in fact concavo-convex. All the central American weaving combs which are often quoted as the nearest parallels to those in question are, in Roth's opinion, 'more or less flat and have a more open dent head than any of the Glastonbury instruments' (1934, 137).

Wild is in no doubt that the Iron Age combs were used as beaters-in in the weaving process since 'identical tools are used in Central America today' (1970, 66), but he omits to comment on the decidedly concavo-convex nature of many of the combs, and describes them as plano-convex in section.

Crowfoot (1945, 158), on the other hand, sees positive advantages in the concavo-convex sections, believing that the way in which such an implement would thrust the warp threads apart would be useful in countering the tendency of the web on the warp-weighted loom to 'waist' in towards the centre. Such waisting was also noted in the Reynolds experiment, but the remedy in this case — one which on paper at least sounds much more plausible — was to increase the tension on the outside threads, which should in theory prevent the distortion.

Very little has been written concerning the functional implications of the wear patterns noticed on so many of the combs. The only published explanations for the high percentages of broken teeth suggest that the combs were used in skin-dressing activity which would have entailed very rough usage (Roth 1934, 138). One hypothesis, which would explain the breakage of the combs during the weaving process, involves the suggested conjunction of comb and sword to pack the weft threads more efficiently against the warp. It is proposed that one or, more probably, a number of combs could be wedged parallel with the weft, and be driven up against it by a sword beater operated within the shed. This method of beating-in would be advantageous in cases where there was significant friction between warp and weft, for example where the weave was very coarse. The friction would help the combs to stay wedged in the warp before being struck by the beater; presumably only combs with fairly long teeth could be used in this way. Continuous usage in the manner described might be expected to result first in transverse wear grooves on one or both surfaces, and eventually in the large-scale breakage of the type which is so common.

Another possible explanation for the appearance of parallel grooves on the teeth would be to suppose that the comb was turned on its side, so that the teeth were at right-angles to the weave, and used in the manner of a pin beater in the space between the warps. This sort of action might be invoked to explain the frequent breakage and subsequent smoothing of the outside teeth which would of course sustain most of the pressure.

Transverse grooves vary considerably in character. Often they occur as fine incised lines across the teeth, but in a few instances — particularly towards the tips of the teeth — they are evident as much more substantial hollows. Whether the first form of wear is an early stage of the second, or results from a different sort of usage, has not yet been determined.

If the combs were employed as traditionally envisaged — inserted into the weave at right-angles to the warp and parallel with the weft — then one might well expect more signs of lateral wear. Grooves which may be assumed to result from such wear occur on only two combs from Danebury. While nearly all the combs show considerable rounding and polishing of the apices of the teeth this could result from a number of varied activities.

Some of the combs have parallel wear grooves which occur on combinations of upper and lower teeth. To explain this pattern, it could be suggested that the combs were used in the manner outlined above, between warp threads which were strung very close together. In order for the comb to be inserted, it would have to be tilted, which would occasion wear particularly on the teeth towards the edge, on which the comb would pivot. As the comb was slid up the warp, both surfaces would come into contact with the threads. The comb could also be used in this way to separate out the warp threads before the insertion of a heddle.

A few of the Danebury combs have wear grooves on their teeth which do not appear to run parallel, and in some cases it seems possible that the grooves on every alternate tooth are parallel. This might suggest that the combs were being used as traditionally envisaged beaters-in on some rather coarse weaves in which only alternate warp threads are in the same plane. In a few cases, the wear grooves do not appear to run parallel in any arrangement. The explanation for this patterning remains elusive.

The Danebury combs are distinct from the other collections examined in two principal ways. First, the most common butt form at Danebury is distinctly uncommon at the other sites, and secondly the Danebury collection is very much more homogeneous with regard to form.

The first difference may well have only geographical significance in that the two lake villages and Maiden Castle are nearer to one another than to Danebury, and this proximity is reflected in stylistic traits. The second point of difference is much more significant. The range of comb forms is more restricted at Danebury than at any of the other sites or collections examined. This may perhaps imply that a specialist kind of weaving, or only part of the full range of the weaving process were taking place at the site. The question will be considered in more detail below (pp 438–9).

Toggles of bone and antler (3.40–3.65)
(not illustrated: small finds 678 and 1273)
Twenty-eight bone and antler toggles were found, distributed chronologically as follows:

cp	number	relative frequency
1-3	3	1.0
4	0	0
5	1	2.6
6	5	10.4
7-8	20	24.6

The majority of toggles were manufactured from hollow sections of either bone or antler (sixteen were identified as bone, twelve as antler, and in a single case the material was indeterminate). Eight of the toggles were made from the long bones of cattle, while four were from equivalent

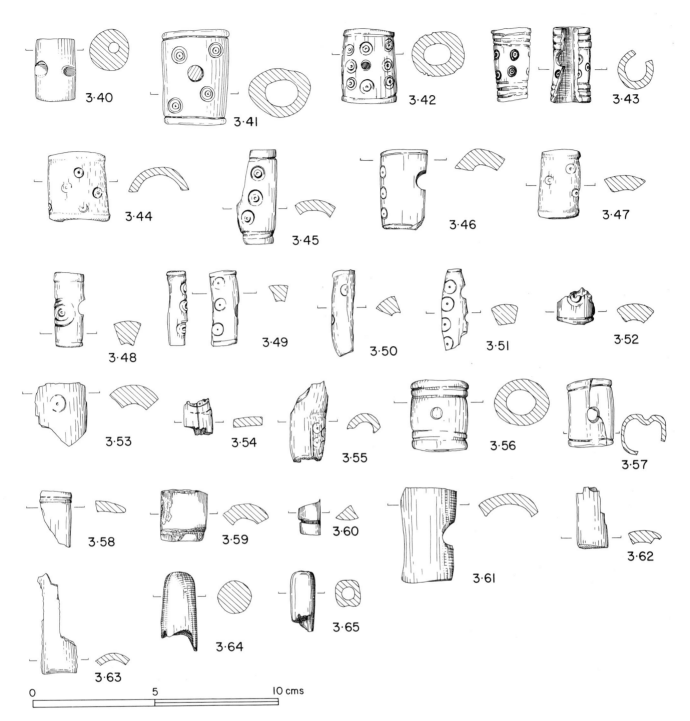

Fig 7.31 Bone and antler toggles

bones of sheep. Three of the antler toggles were manufactured from a section of tine, and one of these was solid rather than hollow. All have at least a single perforation, most frequently through one wall but occasionally through both. No 3.51, though fragmentary, had at least three holes.

The toggles vary in section; some are almost circular, others ovoid, and a few sub-rectangular. This range of shape should be borne in mind when diameter measurements are compared. The internal diameter measures between 7 and 16 mm, while the external measurement varies from 14.5 to 30 mm. The average thickness of the toggle wall is c 5 mm. The artefacts range in length from 2.35–42 mm. Fourteen were within the bracket 23.5–

30.5 mm, while a further four measured between 33.5 and 42.0 mm.

Decoration is circumscribed. The most common method of ornament involves the accentuation of the two ends (either by creating raised ridges or by incising grooves) and the application of ring-and-dot motifs to the body. Eleven are decorated in this way and one is inscribed with a triple ring-and-dot motif. Four examples were decorated only with one or more incised grooves, parallel with the two ends, but since only one was complete, the others may have had additional decoration which has not survived. Of the remaining fragments, some are decorated with ring-and-dot motifs, but eight are undecorated.

86% of the toggles have been burnt to some degree. Relatively few are calcined and it is therefore possible that burning was controlled. Burning changes the colour from light beige or grey to dense black and this may have been considered aesthetically desirable.

Wear patterns

Nearly all the toggles display considerable polish as a result of wear, but on all complete or near complete toggles a more specific wear pattern is apparent. The outer surface, in line with the perforation and parallel with the long axis, has been worn quite hollow in some cases and is flattened in others. This wear presumably results from friction either with a cord or thong or with the object to which the toggle was attached.

Only seven examples of breakage across the perforation were recorded, indicating that stress was not significantly greater at this point than elsewhere.

Comparisons

Toggles have been recovered in surprisingly small numbers from the major published Iron Age sites, and the Danebury collection is unparalleled in size. Croft Ambrey (Stanford 1974, 176) and Maiden Castle (Wheeler 1943, 309) have produced one toggle apiece. Two came from All Cannings Cross (Cunnington 1923, 77) and another two — similar to the Danebury specimens in name only — came from Gussage All Saints (Wainwright 1979, 113). Four examples apiece were retrieved from excavation at the cave of Borness, Kirkcudbrightshire (Corrie *et al* 1873–4, 496) and from Hunsbury hillfort (Fell 1936, 72). The largest collection comes from the lake village of Glastonbury (Bulleid & Gray 1917, 406, 460). Five from this site were described as 'button or dress fasteners', four were designated 'toggle-like fasteners', and those which have most in common with the Danebury sample are described as ferrules.

The majority of comparable finds were undecorated, but the small number of decorated examples are similar to the Danebury sample. The toggle from Hunsbury (Fell 1936, 72) is ornamented with a raised collar at either end and with ring-and-dot motifs, and is thus identical with the most common Danebury decoration. Toggle H20 from Glastonbury (Bulleid & Gray 1917, 461, pl LXVI) is decorated with a series of concentric circles which correspond with the triple ring-and-dot motif noted on 3.48 from Danebury; and the 'ferrule' H266 (*ibid*, 463, pl LXVI) was ornamented with a ring-and-dot design.

Function

Few observations have been made concerning the wear patterns on toggles, but the function is generally assumed to be that of a fastener. Cunnington (1923, 77) refers to a toggle from Borness, Kirkcudbrightshire, which was found with two bone pegs within it. From this she suggests an alternative function as runners on fishing lines. The majority of toggles are not, however, found in association with such pegs.

The size difference apparent in the Danebury collection, most noticeably between narrow bone toggles made from sheep bones and the much larger specimens from cattle bones or antler, may well reflect a functional distinction. The wear pattern data neither support nor refute this suggestion. The toggles with a single perforation were presumably employed in a slightly different fashion from those with two or more. It may also be proposed that the differential size of the perforation reflects upon the usage even if all are regarded as fasteners. The evidence of wear

patterns on the Danebury toggles supports the traditional view of the toggle as a fastener.

Needles (3.66–3.100)

Thirty-eight bone needles were found with a chronological distribution as follows:

cp	number	relative frequency
1-3	6	1.0
4	1	1.3
5	4	4.9
6	6	5.6
7	21	11.6

All needles were manufactured from splinters of bone, pointed at one, and frequently at both, ends. The complete or near complete examples range in length from 58–90.6 mm, with an average of 73 mm; the shaft thickness varies from 1–1.5 to 3 or 4 mm. The range of thickness was measured for each individual needle with the following results:

16.6% showed a variation of 0.5 mm
36.6% showed a variation of 1.0 mm
43.3% showed a variation of 1.5 mm
3.5% showed a variation of 2.0 mm

Most needles are rounded in section, with a tendency to flatten at the head. A few unworn or slightly worn examples are sub-rectangular along the entire length of the shaft.

Only about one third of the needles are complete, but none has more than a single perforation or eye. The eye varies from a circular to an elongated oval in form. Most needles have an eye which is placed a short distance from the head end, but in a few cases the perforation is central.

On the basis of these morphological observations, the needles were divided into five groups.

Class 1 (3.68-3.74)
Double pointed needle in which the element comprising the head and eye is shorter than the length of the shaft. The head itself flares out sharply from the shaft.

Class 2 (3.75–77)
Double-pointed needle in which the head and shaft are more or less integral, but the eye is situated towards the head end.

Class 3 (3.78, 3.79)
Double-ended needle in which both ends are pointed and the eye is centrally positioned.

Class 4 (3.80, 3.81)
A single-ended, blunt-headed needle. The eye is placed well towards the head end.

Class 5 (3.82)
A bodkin — a large needle with an angular head. The eye is placed squarely within the enlargement.

Classes 1 and 2 are the most common. Only one example of Class 5 is known, but seventeen of the needles were too fragmentary to be classified. Needles of Class 1 span the entire chronological range. The two needles from class 2 belong to cp 7, as do those from class 3. The bodkin also belongs to cp 7. The numbers involved are obviously too small for any conclusions to be drawn; but it is possible

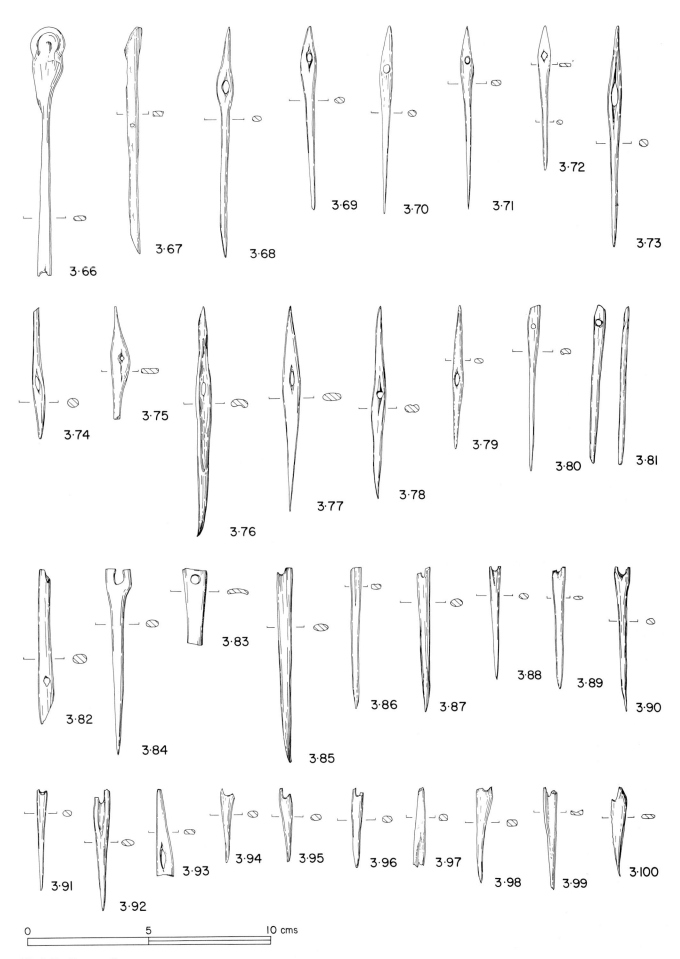

3·66 3·67 3·68 3·69 3·70 3·71 3·72 3·73

3·74 3·75 3·76 3·77 3·78 3·79 3·80 3·81

3·82 3·83 3·84 3·85 3·86 3·87 3·88 3·89 3·90

3·91 3·92 3·93 3·94 3·95 3·96 3·97 3·98 3·99 3·100

0   5   10 cms

Fig 7.32 Bone needles

that a greater range of forms was available within the final ceramic phase.

Wear patterns

The most common signs of wear are rounding of the shaft towards the tip and an overall polish. In fourteen cases the needle has broken across the eye, and in another ten the tip is missing. These two areas would be the most vulnerable to friction. In two examples the point was resharpened, another factor indicative of the tendency of this section to blunt or break. Nine of the collection have an upward curve at one or both ends. While in some cases this was probably a deliberate creation, designed with a specific function in mind, in others the feature may well be the result of continued friction on the under-surface of the curve. Five of the needles display a slight transverse grooving on a level with the eye. This pattern presumably reflects the way in which the threads or sinews were pulled against the needle. In three further cases the eye was misshapen, which may again result from friction with the thread. Seventeen needles have rather irregularly shaped shafts. This unevenness may have been present before use, but it is at least as likely that some of the hollowing results from wear, and is indicative of points along the shaft which were held most frequently.

Comparisons

Attempts have been made to classify the bone needles in the reports from Glastonbury (Bulleid & Gray 1911, 1917), All Cannings Cross (Cunnington 1923), and Maiden Castle (Wheeler 1943). Among the 40 needles from the Lake Village, Gray identified five classes, only two of which have typological significance, Class A, 'those having ring heads, with eyes more or less circular . . . and having little bone between the eye and the tip of the head' and Class B, 'a more or less pointed head extending from 4–17 mm beyond the eye, which is not always round'.

Forty-one needles were discovered at All Cannings Cross, all of Glastonbury class A. Twenty-five needles were illustrated in the Maiden Castle report, where they were grouped according to a modified version of the Glastonbury typology. Needles of both A and B type were found at the fort, and Wheeler observes that type A needles are a specifically Iron Age B feature.

None of the Danebury needles are of Glastonbury Class A, but Danebury classes 1–3 fall within Class B. The class 5 'bodkin' is almost identical with a needle from Maiden Castle (Wheeler 1943, XXXV B, no 8).

Function

It is probable that functional distinction is reflected by the various types of needle from Danebury, although the overall homogeneity of width and thickness must be stressed.

Certain differences, which may or may not have functional implications, cut across the groupings outlined above. The upward curve of one or both ends is present on some but not all of the needles from classes 1, 2, and 3, as is the full range of eye forms. This variety may reflect specialist uses within each group. It is possible, for example, that sinews were threaded through larger, more ovoid eyes, while wool and nettle fibres were used in conjunction with round perforations. Alternatively, finer fibres, whatever their nature, might have been used with the needles which possessed small rounded eyes. Of the five classes noted at Danebury the following observations may be made:

Class 1 The head, although pointed, is quite distinct from the shaft, so it is unlikely that the needle would have been used as a truly double point, in the manner of class 3. The strong wide head may possibly have been used for piercing or for re-establishing a hole in the fabric prior to the insertion of the needle. The enlarged head would surely be a disadvantage if used on any fine or closely woven fabric.

Class 2 In this group the head, while shorter than the shaft, is more or less integral with it. The needle might therefore perform a similar function to class 1 but friction would be considerably reduced.

Class 3 The double-ended needle. Wheeler proposed that this type of needle would have performed efficiently if used in conjunction with a loom, for darning in loose ends (1943, 307). It could also be employed in any situation where two pieces of fabric required to be joined, since the needle could be efficiently passed back and forth without the necessity of turning the fabric over.

Class 4 These two needles would have the advantage of classes 2 or 3 in that the head and shaft are more or less integral. Both have a circular eye which is perhaps another reflection of the rather finer material with which they were used.

Class 5 This bodkin would be particularly suited, as with a modern needle of the same type, for running threads through a casing, or indeed for any activity in which it was not required to pierce the fabric.

Gouges (3.101–3.138)

Thirty-eight bone gouges were found. Their chronological distribution is as follows:

cp	number	relative frequency
1-3	15	2.0
3-4	1	1.9
5	1	1.0
6	6	4.5
7-8	14	6.1

The term 'gouge' applied to this type of bone implement is unfortunate because it implies a chisel-like function for which there is no evidence. Moreover, it masks a variation in form which may reflect different functions. In general the tools were made from sheep long bones (95% of the examples from Danebury are in this category) which have an oblique diagonal cut across the shaft in a longitudinal direction, exposing the medullary canal. The tip in nearly all examples is sharply pointed, but may be worn to a variety of shapes. The butt of the tool is formed by the distal or the proximal end of the bone. In some instances the end was left intact, while in others it may have been trimmed, bored, or perforated. The majority of Danebury gouges were made from sheep tibiae, and of this number twelve are composed of the shaft and distal end while seven comprise the shaft and proximal end. The length of the complete or nearly complete tool varies from 60–176 mm, with the average somewhere over 100 mm.

Previous attempts to classify gouges have concentrated on the form and variations of the non-utilitarian end of the tool. In the case of the Danebury gouges, it was found that these secondary characteristics failed to correlate with the form of the pointed end or with the wear patterns. It was thus decided to ignore previous classifications and to divide the Danebury gouges into groups based on a consideration of point-form and wear pattern.

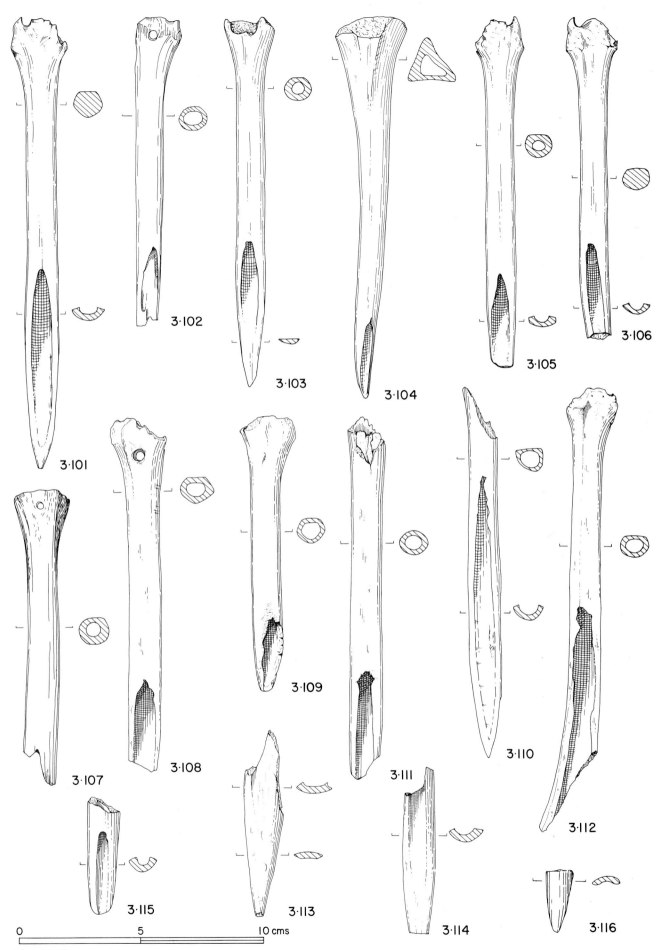

3·101
3·102
3·103
3·104
3·105
3·106
3·107
3·108
3·109
3·110
3·111
3·112
3·113
3·114
3·115
3·116

0   5   10 cms

Fig 7.33   Bone gouges

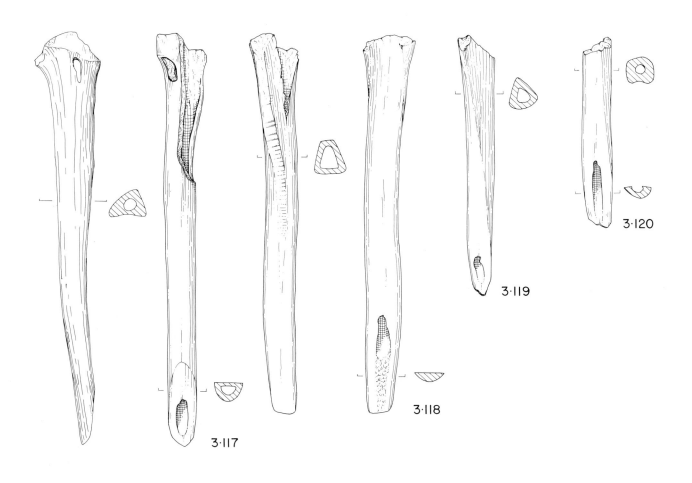

3·117

3·118

3·119

3·120

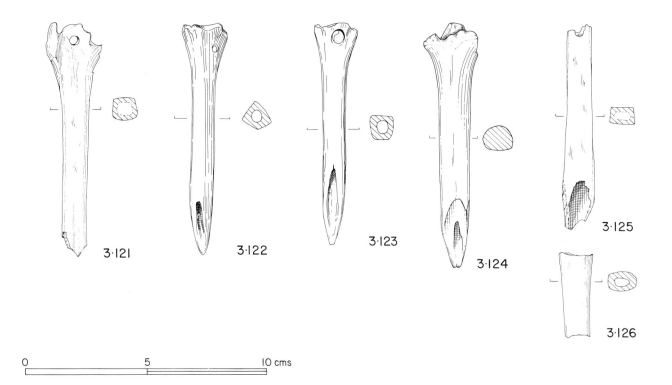

3·121

3·122

3·123

3·124

3·125

3·126

0   5   10 cms

Fig 7.34 Bone gouges

Class 1 (3.101–3.116)

Tools with long, pointed terminals and with raised flanges at either side. The extreme tip of the tool is a thin, flat point. All except two of this group were formed from sheep tibiae, ten of which comprised the shaft and distal end while two were fashioned from the shaft and proximal end.

Class 2 (3.117–3.120)

Essentially similar to class 1, but with the point displaying a different form of wear. In all cases the point and lower surface of the shaft have been worn absolutely flat on the same plane through friction (the point is much shorter than is common in class 1). Three of the four tools in this class were made from the shaft and proximal end of sheep tibiae. The fourth was manufactured from a sheep metatarsal.

Class 3 (3.121–3.126)

Gouges with much shorter shafts than the tools of classes 1 and 2. The shafts have generally been squared and the ends are sharply pointed.

In addition to the three main classes there are two general categories. The first comprises tools of which only the shaft survives and the diagnostic features are therefore missing; the second comprises six miscellaneous examples:

3.133 A fragmentary bone gouge made from the shaft and proximal end of a sheep metacarpal. The deliberately hollowed shaft has an artificial taper just above the point of fracture.

3.134 An extremely short gouge, complete except for the tip, which measures 60 mm overall surviving length. The piece was manufactured from the distal end of a sheep tibia, which had been artificially hollowed and perforated through both sides.

3.135 A fragment of sheep metatarsal comprising the proximal end and part of the shaft. The end has a single irregular perforation which pierces through one side. The bone had been bored and is broken across the shaft. In its original form, the tool may have functioned as a bobbin or as an awl or gouge. It has been included here because the end of the shaft was subjected to considerable post-fractural wear.

3.136 A fragmentary bone gouge made from a sheep tibia. The shaft had been hollowed and there are signs of a perforation through the proximal end. A large sliver of bone had broken from one side of the point, and the tool had subsequently been shaped to a sharp point by a diagonal cut.

3.137 A fragment of bone gouge manufactured from a hollowed sheep metatarsal. A countersunk perforation pierces both sides of the proximal end. The shaft has broken just below the proximal end across a knife cut or chop. The maximum surviving length is 36 mm.

3.138 This is one of only two tools within the group of gouges which was made from a cattle or horse bone, in this case a metapodial. The bone was split longitudinally and has a single perforation through the proximal end. It is untypical of the gouges and has been included here by virtue of its gouge-like end. One side of the point has been quite rounded by wear, but overall the bone displays scant signs of usage.

Wear patterns

In class 1 the most commonly occurring wear pattern is a very high degree of polish on the tip, particularly on the underside, and an overall sheen. In four examples the point has broken but subsequent wear has occurred. In three cases the tool has broken across the perforation at the distal or proximal end. On two examples from this group, if the tool is viewed from the upper side, a small indentation can be seen at the right-hand side of the tip.

In the case of class 2 tools the diagnostic wear pattern results in a flattening of the gouge point, and sometimes part of the shaft, on a level plane. All have blunted ends which have been broken and subsequently worn. The highest level of wear occurs at the tip. All four have broken in some way at the non-utilitarian end, possibly as a result of hollowing or perforation.

As in the case of the other classes, the most common wear pattern on class 3 tools is an overall polish, particularly at the tip. Two of the tools have broken across the point and a third is blunted. Three have broken across the perforation and another has fractured across both ends of the shaft. Two show distinct wear at the point which results in one instance in the shaft having a hollowing at either side of the tip when viewed from above, and in the other case in a slight transverse hollowing on the underside of the tip.

Of the shafts five have fractured completely across both ends, while the sixth has broken across the narrow end of the shaft and has a partially intact proximal end. Most show a degree of wear polish.

In this miscellaneous group, two examples have been broken across the shaft and in one of these cases wear has occurred subsequent to fracture. The tip of the point has broken from one further example, and in a fourth a sliver has been detached from the pointed end. In two specimens the end has broken across the perforation. The atypical horse or cattle shaft tool has wear polish on one side of the point, but otherwise shows little sign of usage.

Comparisons

A section in the Glastonbury report (Bulleid & Gray 1917, 419–21) was devoted to a discussion of the 65 gouges manufactured from the tibiae of sheep or goats. Most attention was focused on the non-utilitarian qualities of the tool, such as trimmed epiphyses and longitudinally bored shafts. This concern resulted in part from Bulleid's belief that the gouges were attached to wooden handles by means of the transverse perforations which many possess. One tool, B 151, was found with a wooden shaft *in situ*. One hundred and twenty-three similar tools were found at All Cannings Cross (Cunnington 1923, 84–7) and Cunnington also subscribed to the idea that in general the tools were designed for attachment to a wooden shaft. One of the gouges from the site was found to contain an iron pin, and the author quotes examples of bone gouges associated with iron or bone rivets from Wookey Hole, Somerset and Hanging Langford Camp, Wilts (*ibid*, 86).

Bulleid and Gray (1917, 420–1) divided the Glastonbury gouges into eight classes, based as much on the degrees of wear which they displayed as on typological or functional distinctions. Cunnington recognized five classes at All Cannings Cross. In this case the division was based exclusively on a consideration of the non-utilitarian aspects of the tools.

The 70 tools from Maiden Castle were classified in accordance with Cunnington's five-fold division (Wheeler 1943, 303–4). The author concluded that 'the generalisation that gouges with distal butts are normally Iron Age A, whilst those with proximal butts are of Iron Age B, may be regarded as established'.

The Danebury gouges, divided in accordance with the form of the point and the type of wear to which it had

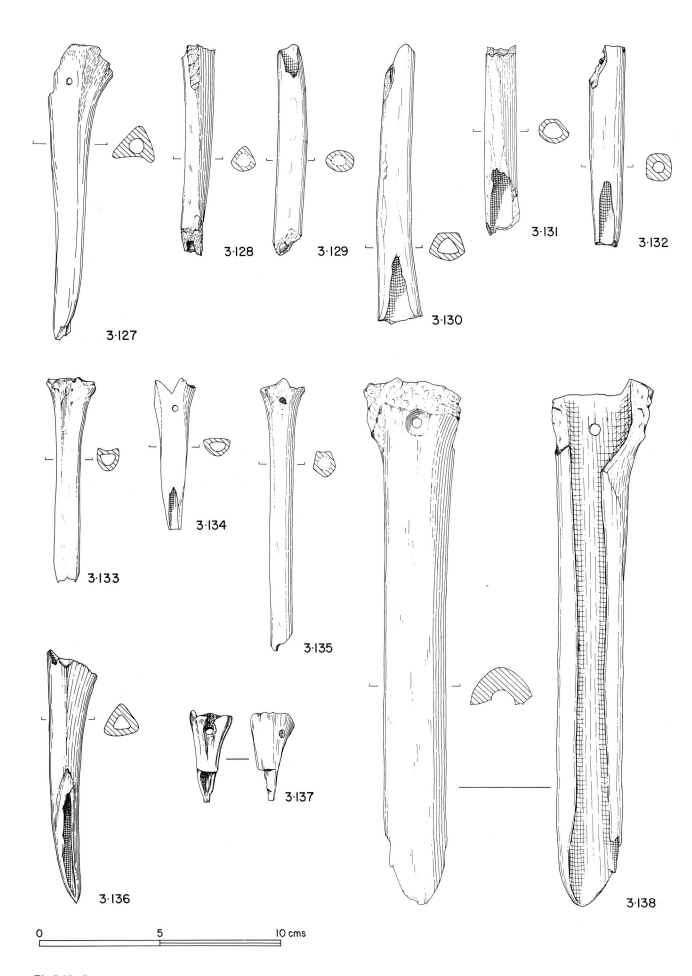

3·128

3·129

3·131

3·132

3·127

3·130

3·134

3·133

3·135

3·136

3·137

3·138

0   5   10 cms

Fig 7.35 Bone gouges

been subjected, show no clear-cut correlation between the date of the implement and the form of the butt. One of the most detailed discussions concerning the functions of the bone gouges is contained in the All Cannings Cross report (Cunnington 1923, 86). Cunnington's interpretations are many and varied and include spoons for feeding young children, pins, skewers, shuttles for weaving (which she rejects), and lance heads. She also quotes ethnographic parallels showing that similar tools were used to dress reindeer hides. Wheeler, however, preferred to see them as weaving shuttles, some with and some without the wooden handle attachment.

While there is admittedly an 'all-purpose' character to these tools, the three main classes at Danebury display peculiar design qualities which presumably fitted them for different tasks. It may also be observed that the tools in classes 1 and 2 appear to have demanded a special selection of the bones. Some of the wear patterns on the tools from classes 1 and 3 indicate that these may have functioned as pin-beaters in the weaving process. The tools of class 2 were evidently subjected to considerable pressure against a resistant surface, and it could be that they were used in hide dressing. The tools could indeed have functioned as shuttles, although Cunnington's objection that the rough distal or proximal butts would snag the weave cannot be lightly dismissed. The two metacarpal and metatarsal tools classified under the miscellaneous category would have been more suited for this form of work than the more bulky tools fashioned from the proximal ends of tibiae.

None of the Danebury gouges was found associated with rivets of bone or iron or with any other form of handle attachment. While it is possible that they were fitted with handles, it is difficult to envisage any function which would necessitate this. It is possible that the wooden splinter found inside the gouge at Glastonbury had actually been used to hollow the shaft.

Awls, splinters, and points (3.139–3.176)

These three categories of tool have been grouped together because they may all have been employed in a similar manner. This being said, a number of different categories can be distinguished. Of the 37 tools included under the general heading, nineteen are awls, eight are sharpened splinters, and three are points. The awls are distributed in chronological terms as follows:

cp 1/3	4 awls
cp 4	1 awl
cp 5	1 awl
cp 6	1 awl
cp 7/8	9 awls

The general grouping has been further divided, on morphological criteria, into seven sub-classes. None of these has any particular chronological significance, although it may be observed that the majority of tools derive from later contexts.

Class 1 (3.139–3.144)
Awls fashioned from the shaft and the proximal end of the bone. The shaft was sometimes split longitudinally, but this is not always the case. The bones used for these tools are quite varied, and while sheep account for most, one was manufactured from a horse metapodial and one from a cattle ulna. In all cases the butt is formed by the complete or near complete proximal end of the shaft. The fragment of point, 3.144, is almost identical to 3.141 and

has hence been included in this class. The size range and thickness of point varies considerably.

Class 2 (3.145–3.153)
Awls manufactured from a splinter of shaft bone, which frequently includes part of the proximal or distal end as the butt. The pointed end of the tool is sharp, but widens quite quickly. All these tools were made from sheep long bones.

Class 3 (3.154–3.157)
Awls made from bone splinters which vary in size and character. The common factor is a long, needle-like point rounded in section.

Class 4 (3.158-3.165)
Splinters of a variety of different bones and sizes, which were sharpened at one end to form a point.

Class 5 (3.166–3.170)
Fragmentary points which may or may not derive from awls. Four of the number are sharp and rounded in section. The point is missing from 3.169 but it is unusual in having a trapezoidal section.

Class 6 (3.171–3.173)
The three tools in this section can be loosely classified as points. Two were made from cattle shaft bone and the third from a splinter of sheep shaft bone. 3.171 is plano-convex in section. The point was broken from the tool, but it continued in use subsequent to the fracture. 3.172 is circular in section, and again the tip was broken and wear had occurred after the time of fracture. 3.173 is complete, and the more pointed end was neatly squared across.

Wear patterns
The wear patterns on these tools are essentially similar. The point almost invariably has the highest polish, and is mostly quite sharp although sometimes worn to a rounded profile. There were ten cases in which the tip had broken from the shaft, three in which the tip had broken but the tool had been reused, and six instances of breakage further up the shaft. The tools in class 6 displayed a more even wear polish than is usual.

Comparisons
Relatively little has been written concerning these tools. They are in general found less frequently than the gouges. The excavations at Glastonbury (Bulleid & Gray 1917, 404) produced only five awls and twelve splinters with worked points.

Fifteen awls derive from Maiden Castle (Wheeler 1943, 308). Thirteen of this total were made from the split bones of ponies, while two were from sheep shafts. The tools were apparently spread across the entire chronological sequence, although it is interesting to note the very high degree of standardization relative to the Danebury collection.

Function
The general function of an awl is to pierce or bore a hole in some softer substance, and today such tools are most frequently employed in leatherworking. The large range of shapes encountered at Danebury is likely to reflect at least a degree of functional distinction. It might be suggested that the tools of class 3, with long needle-like points, could be used on densely woven fabrics or leather where the shape of the tool would not create undue

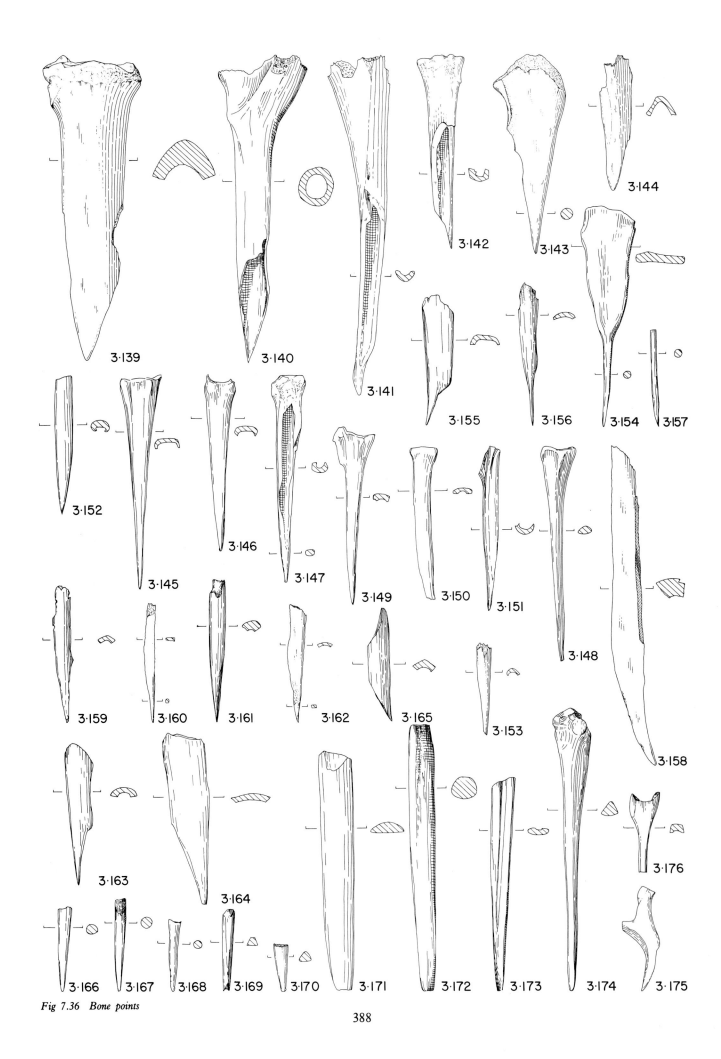

Fig 7.36 Bone points

388

friction nor leave a large hole in its wake. The high degree of wear and breakage evident at the pointed end of the tool must indicate that even if the function was not to pierce, the pointed end was used almost exclusive of any other area.

Some of the smaller 'awls' could have functioned as pins for holding clothing together, although few have an overall polish or a high degree of finish. 3.174 with its overall wear and uncharacteristic point might well have been used in this way.

The tools of class 6 may have functioned as modelling tools, since both ends have been subjected to wear and wear polish is evident across the entire surface.

Tools manufactured from sheep long bones (3.177–3.198)

Tools manufactured from sheep shaft bones occur frequently at Danebury. This section excludes all tools which belong to the categories of awls, pin-beaters, or gouges, and concentrates firstly on those which may have functioned as spindles, bobbins, or spools, and secondly on the worked shafts of indeterminate function.

In the first category, five morphologically distinct classes can be recognized:

1 Tools with a transverse perforation which is bored through the centre of the shaft
2 Tools with transverse perforations which occur elsewhere
3 Tools on which two opposite surfaces of the shaft have deeply incised grooves which run parallel with the long axis of the bone
4 Tools with transverse grooves on either side of the shaft
5 Artificially hollowed shafts with proximal ends intact

A few tools can be classified under more than one class.

Class 1 (3.177–3.180)
All of the tools in this class were made from sheep metacarpals. All three complete examples have unfused distal ends, and range in size from 82–106 mm. All the tools have a centrally placed, transverse perforation. 3.179 was unfinished since only one side of the bone was completely perforated and a slight hollow on the opposite side indicates that it was intended to pierce the entire shaft. In three cases the diameter of the perforation measures 3.5 mm. In the fourth specimen, the countersunk perforation measures 5 mm at its outer and 2.5 mm at its inner edge. Striated wear marks are visible on the shaft of 3.178.

The only tool which shows any degree of wear polish is 3.178. 3.180 has broken across the perforation which may indicate that the tool was subjected to some stress.

Class 2 (3.181–3.185)
This class is less homogeneous than class 1 and includes a variety of different bones and types of perforation. 3.181 is manufactured from a complete sheep radius with a perforation below each epiphysis. 3.182 is also fashioned from a radius, but only the proximal end survives intact; although this is pierced through in exactly the same place as 3.181, it cannot be asserted that this tool served a similar purpose. It could equally well have functioned as a gouge or awl.

3.183 is made from a complete sheep metatarsal which was deliberately hollowed and has a perforation through one side of the proximal end. Two deep grooves, on opposite sides of the shaft, run parallel with the long axis

of the bone. 3.185 is also fashioned from a sheep metatarsal, but in this case only the shaft and the proximal end remain. The shaft has been squarely cut with a knife above the distal end, possibly during butchery. The proximal end of this tool is pierced through both sides with holes of different diameters. 3.184 is again a tool made from a sheep metatarsal. The shaft has been roughly broken above the distal end, and the bone, which was deliberately hollowed, has a single perforation through one side of the proximal epiphysis.

A quite considerable degree of wear polish is evident on the surfaces of 3.185 and 3.182, while 3.184 has been highly polished. Breakage has occurred across the perforation of 3.183, 3.184, and 3.182 and indicates that the tool was subjected to stress. Some wear polish is apparent on the broken end of the shaft of 3.184.

Class 3 (3.186–3.187)
This class comprises three small finds, one of which, 3.183, is already listed under class 2 by virtue of its transverse perforation. Two of the tools were made from complete bones, a metacarpal and a metatarsal. The third is also from a metatarsal, but its original form cannot be guessed, since only a short section of shaft remains. All three have deep grooves which occur on opposite sides of the shaft and run parallel with the long axis of the bone. The grooves measure c 1 mm in depth and vary from 1.5–6 mm in width. A limited degree of wear is evident on all three tools.

Class 4 (3.188)
This tool is composed of a complete sheep metacarpal which has a V-shaped groove cut on both sides of the shaft. The grooves are set opposite one another and are nearer the distal than the proximal end. Parallel indentations caused by wear are apparent within each groove and along the length of the shaft.

A high degree of wear polish is evident in places, but the surface is considerably weathered.

Class 5 (3.183, 3.184, 3.185, 3.189, 3.190)
The first three are also included in class 2 because of their transverse perforations. All five are manufactured from sheep metatarsal bones. The proximal end is complete in all cases. All have been longitudinally bored. One example has the grooves parallel with the long axis of the bone which characterize class 3. Knife cuts which may be consistent with butchery are visible along the shaft of 3.183. Three tools from this group have broken above the distal end; one was cut with a knife above this point and the remaining example is complete. Striated wear marks are visible on the surface of 3.184.

Refer to class 2 above for details of wear on 3.183, 3.184, and 3.185. 3.189 displays some wear polish.

78% of the tools classified as bobbins were dated to cp 7.

Comparisons
The most detailed study of the tools made from sheep shaft bones which may have functioned as bobbins is published in the Glastonbury report (Bulleid & Gray 1917, 423–7). The Glastonbury collection compares quite closely with that from Danebury in range of form, although in number it is much greater. Seventeen implements from Glastonbury (Class A) compare exactly with those from Danebury class 1. The 63 tools which constitute Class E at Glastonbury are paralleled by two within class 2 from Danebury. The four which comprise Glastonbury Class F have their counterpart in a single example from Danebury class 2. The 65 tools from the

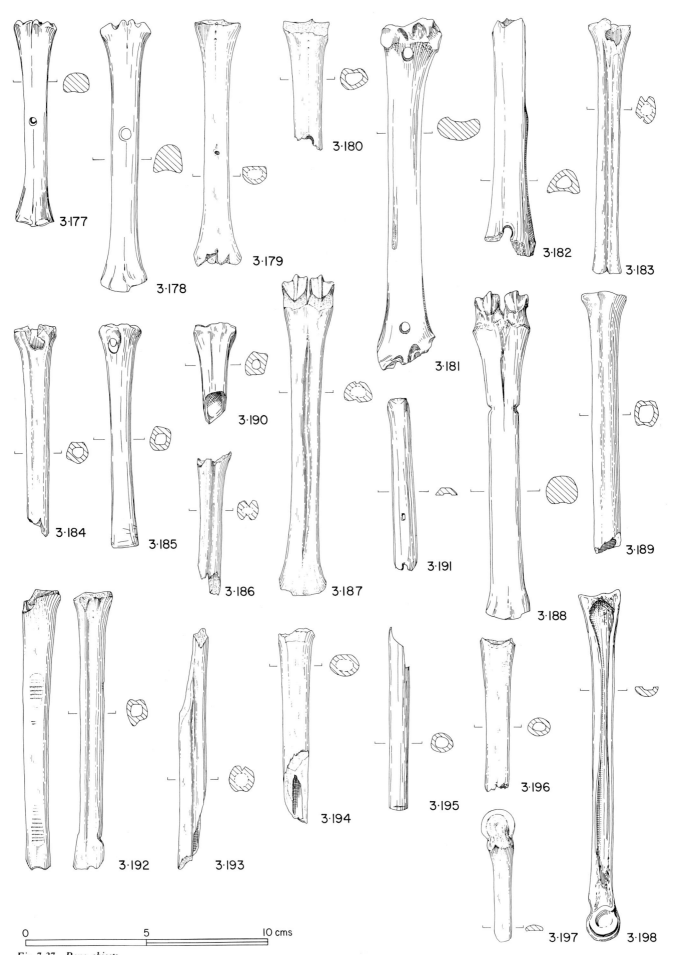

3·177
3·178
3·179
3·180
3·181
3·182
3·183
3·184
3·185
3·186
3·187
3·188
3·189
3·190
3·191
3·192
3·193
3·194
3·195
3·196
3·197
3·198

0   5   10 cms

Fig 7.37 Bone objects

390

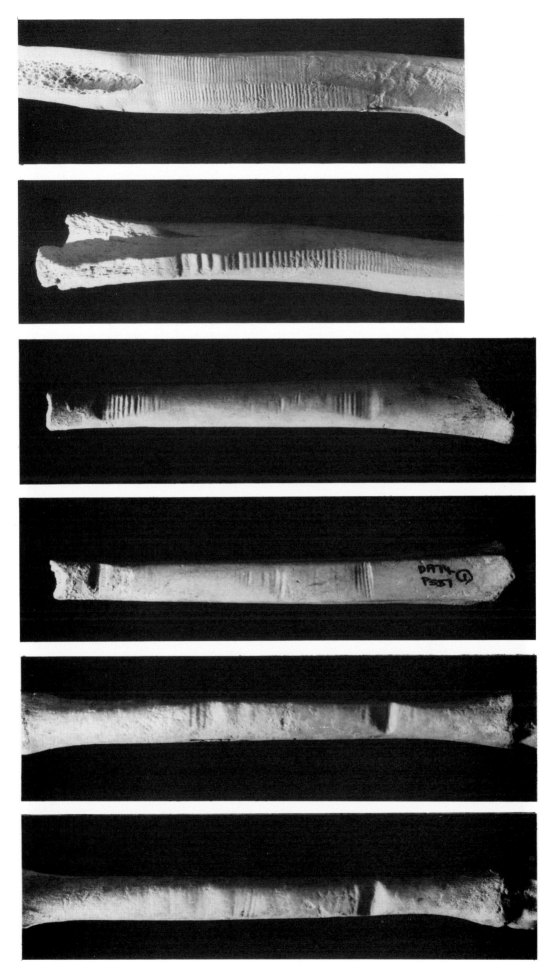

Fig 7.38 Grooved and scored bone. Scale approx 3:2 (photo Bob Wilkins)

lake village Class D are equivalent in form to group 5 at Danebury. The transverse grooving, characteristic of Danebury class 4, and the longitudinal grooves of class 3 were not noted at Glastonbury. The Danebury class 4 piece is precisely paralleled at All Cannings Cross (Cunnington 1923, 891, pl 9, no 18) and by two examples from Maiden Castle (Wheeler 1943, pl XXXV A, nos 4 and 5). The two examples from Danebury and All Cannings Cross were made from metatarsals while those from Maiden Castle were from metacarpals.

Function

Speculation concerning the use of the Glastonbury tools was confined to those which were either completely or partially bored in a longitudinal direction. It was postulated that these were utilized in the weaving process either as spindles — with a metal pin inserted — or as bobbins (Bulleid & Gray 1917, 423–7).

Wild groups together a variety of tools with transverse and longitudinal borings under the heading of bobbins, arguing that they might well have been used to hold 'spun yarn at some stage between spinning and warping. Perhaps the contents of several spindles were wound on it. The end of the thread could be fastened through the central hole' (1970b, 34).

The function of the Danebury tools cannot be determined with certainty. All or only some may have functioned as bobbins, and the variety of forms may well reflect different uses. It is quite possible that ends of yarn were tied through any or all of the perforations. Where longitudinal grooves exist, it is possible that the first few metres of thread would be wound along the groove to prevent slippage, before being wound in any other convenient way. The yarn could have been attached first of all through the hole in the proximal end of 3.185, or knotted and wedged in between the epiphyses on the distal end of 3.187. The transverse grooves of 3.188 may also have functioned as a convenient point at which thread could be attached without slipping. While it is possible that the longitudinally perforated bones were designed for use with spindles, there is no wear evidence from Danebury to support this. The hollowing of the bone may result from it being considered desirable to clean out the marrow before employing the bone as a tool.

Miscellaneous

A number of pieces of worked bone of indeterminate function have been grouped together under this heading. These pieces are often fragmentary and while most display signs of wear, a few while evidently worked show no wear and might perhaps be better regarded as manufacturing waste.

3.191 is a fragmentary shaft with two perforations which cut through one side of the bone. It is possible that this was a bobbin, but the incomplete condition of the piece does not allow certainty.

3.192 is again in a category of its own. It comprises an almost complete metatarsal bone which bears no sign of having been deliberately hollowed, but which had transverse wear striations along its length. This too may have been used as a bobbin, or may have been inserted between the warp threads on the loom.

3.193 is a sheep metatarsal of which only a fragment of shaft survives. This was artificially squared and shows signs of having been split at either end. This splitting has the appearance of accident rather than design. One face of the shaft has a groove 1 mm in depth and 1.5–2 mm in width. It is possible therefore that this piece was utilized in the manner of the class 3 tools, although none of these had been artificially shaped.

3.194, 3.195, and 3.196 are all hollow sections of sheep shaft bone. Two of them have been identified as tibiae. Two are broken across at either end, while the third has broken at one end and is carefully cut at the other. The cut end displays considerable smoothing and wear polish. There was no sign that anything had been inserted through these shafts, and their function is uncertain.

Two of the tools were made from shaft bones which had been neatly split in half along the longitudinal axis. One of these was a metatarsal and the other a metapodial. The metatarsal, 3.198, was complete in length and had no further working but was evenly polished over the entire surface area. The fragmentary sheep metapodial, 3.197, comprised the distal end and part of the shaft. The rounded end of the shaft showed most wear, but the precise function of the piece remains uncertain.

The tools within this category were distributed fairly evenly across the chronological span, although none belonged to cp 4.

Antler handles (3.199–3.202)

Four of these were found at Danebury. Three belong to cp 7–8 while 3.201 comes from cp 1–3. Nos 3.199 and 3.200 were manufactured from hollowed sections of beam, 3.201 is from a section of hollowed tine, and 3.202 was manufactured from the tip of a tine which had been partially hollowed and which has a square socket at the narrower end. 3.199 is ovoid in section, while 3.200 and 3.201 are approximately circular. Both ends of 3.200 have a similar diameter, 3.199 tapers from 30 to 23 mm across, while 3.201 ranges from 23 to 15 mm. 3.199 is ornamented with a single groove, parallel with the edge at the wider end, and with three parallel grooves, each separated from the outer by raised ridges, at the narrower end. 3.200 has a single wide groove, parallel with the edge at the base of the handle. The surface of the beam has been left in its original state on the body of these two handles. 3.201 is smoothed and polished and has three incised parallel lines running around the handle at the base of the socket, while 3.202 has a smooth surface but is otherwise undecorated. 3.201 was found with a tanged iron chisel in situ.

Forty-one antler handles derive from the excavations at Glastonbury (Bulleid & Gray 1917, 455). The majority of these did not have sockets but rather slits into which the tanged blade could be inserted. Nine of the tools were socketed, but none provide exact parallels with the Danebury group. Eighteen antler handles were found at All Cannings Cross (Cunnington 1923, 106, 107). All of these were socketed, and a number were exactly similar to 3.202. No antler handles were noted in the Maiden Castle report.

All four Danebury tools show signs of iron corrosion within their sockets. 3.201 was the socket of a chisel-like blade which was found in situ. 3.202, with its small square socket, may also have functioned as the handle for a chisel, or a graving tool or awl. The beam handles were evidently used in conjunction with much more substantial shafts.

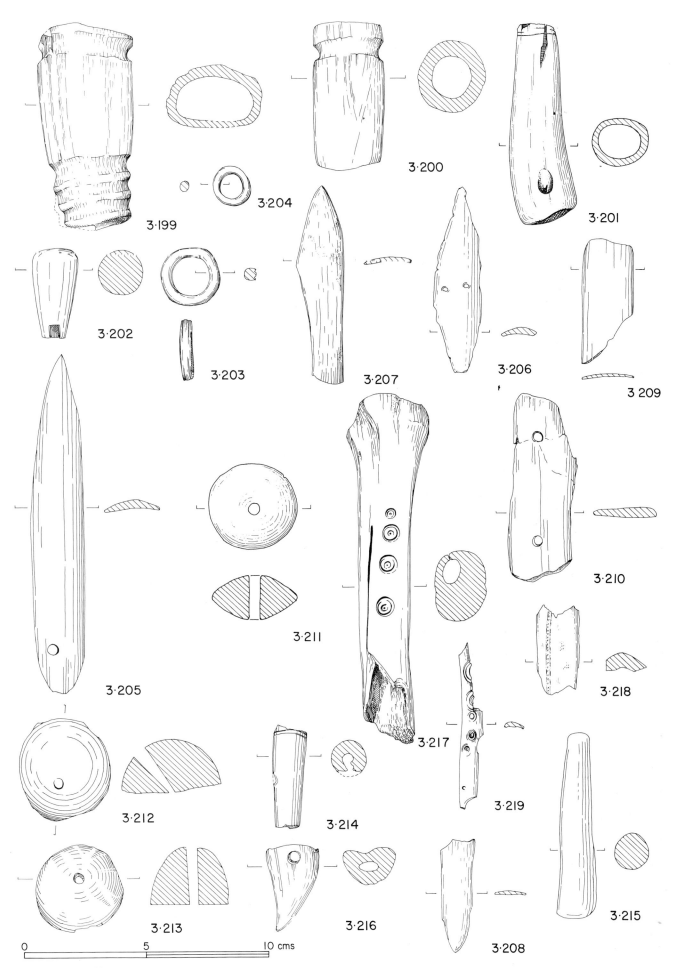

3·199

3·200

3·201

3·202

3·203

3·204

3·205

3·206

3 209

3·207

3·208

3·210

3·211

3·212

3·213

3·214

3·215

3·216

3·217

3·218

3·219

0   5   10 cms

Fig 7.39 Bone objects

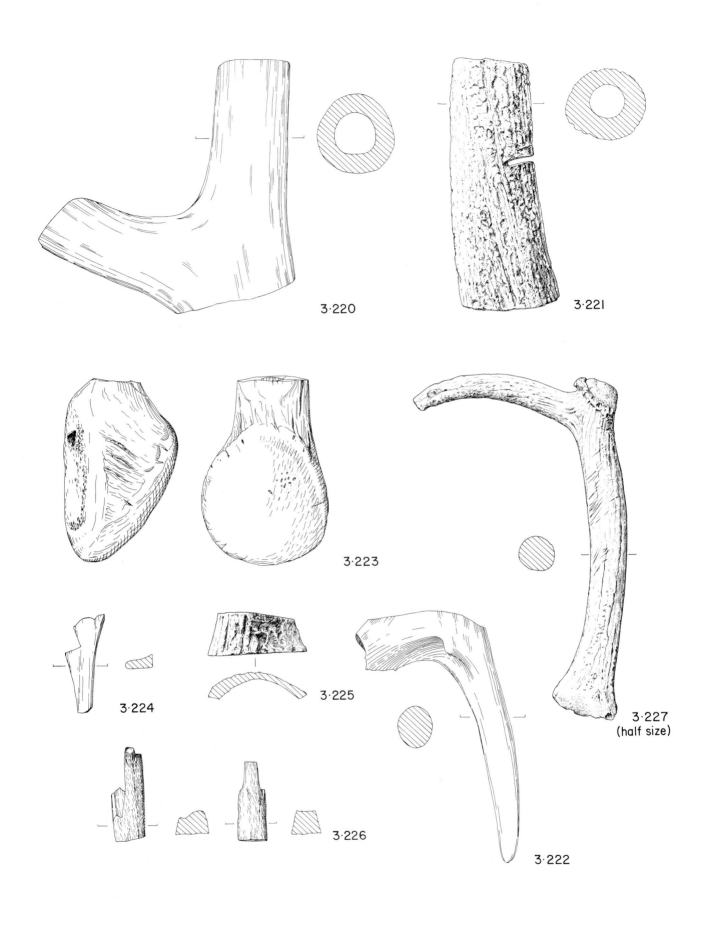

3·220

3·221

3·223

3·224

3·225

3·226

3·227
(half size)

3·222

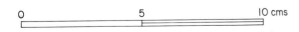
0   5   10 cms

Fig 7.40 Sawn antler

Rings of bone and antler (3.203–3.204)

Two small bone and antler rings were found at Danebury, the antler piece from a cp 6 context, the bone from cp 7.

The antler ring (3.203) is the more elaborate of the two, and is of a size to have been worn as a finger ring. It is decorated by two parallel incised lines, and has been burnt, possibly for aesthetic effect.

The bone ring (3.204) is much smaller, and while it could conceivably have been worn by a child, might equally well be an attachment for leather or textile, possibly functioning as some sort of fastening.

The wear on the antler ring, which involves the flattening of the piece at one point on the circumference, would be consistent with wear on the finger.

Objects manufactured from split cattle-size rib bones (3.205–3.209)

Five objects of this category were found. All belong to the two earliest phases, cp 1–3 and cp 4.

The objects display a variety of forms, but all have in common the fact that they were manufactured from a split section of cattle rib bone. 3.205 and 3.207 have carefully pointed ends, and 3.205 is pierced towards its blunter end. 3.206 and 3.208 are formed into roughly shaped points and 3.206 is pierced through in two places in an approximately central position. The surviving end of 3.209 is neatly squared off. Only two of the artefacts, 3.205 and 3.206, are complete, and both of these display perforations. It is possible that 3.207 and 3.208 were also perforated originally, but this must remain uncertain. Cunnington records 27 similar objects from All Cannings Cross (1923, 74, 75). All complete examples were perforated with holes at one end. It seems possible that 3.206 and 3.207 may have functioned as netting needles. 3.210 was perhaps utilized rather differently, as some form of modelling tool or burnisher.

Miscellaneous worked bone (3.210–3.219)

3.210 Shaped cattle rib bone perforated in two places. Broken in two places but one break shows subsequent wear. Both upper and lower surfaces are polished. Function unknown.

3.211–3.213 Bone and antler spindle whorls, one from cp 1–3, two from cp 7–8. Both were made from the heads of cattle femurs and were perforated, 3.212 through the centre and 3.213 diagonally. 3.212 showed evidence of wear sheen. 3.211 was manufactured from antler and was of truncated biconical form.

3.214 Tip of antler tine broken across a transverse perforation. Decorated with two roughly parallel incised lines. Well smoothed. Possibly a toggle or cheek piece.

3.215 Tip of antler tine sawn across the shaft. Polished by wear on all surfaces. Function uncertain but may have been a handle.

Not illustrated: small find 977. Tine fragment, worn.

3.216 Perforated male pig's upper canine.

3.217 Worked fragment of cattle long bone decorated by a series of three double and one single ring-and-dot motifs. The decoration was proabably applied after breakage and wear since the motifs are sharp. Possibly a tool broken and later used as a trial piece. Nine similar polished bones of horse and cattle have been found (small finds 422, 449, 450, 1400, 1416, 1417, 1418, 1421), all but one (cp 6) from cp 7–8 contexts. 'Polishing bones' of this kind are known from Glastonbury (Bulleid & Gray 1917, 414) but their precise function remains unknown.

3.218 Decorated cattle bone.

3.219 Decorated sheep bone.

Not illustrated: miscellaneous fragments of worked bone, small finds nos 93, 507, 518, 870, 1276, 1425.

Manufacturing waste: antler (3.220–3.227)

Eight pieces are included within this category. All except two derive from the last phase of Iron Age activity on the site, cp 7–8.

3.220 and 3.221 are both sections of sawn antler beam. 3.220 comprises a section of beam and brow tine, which was sawn across at the junction of the two, and separately across the beam and tine. The beam was completely hollowed, mostly by work from the beam rather than from the junction end. The tine was partially hollowed, again by working towards the junction. It may thus be suggested that the intention was to remove the portions of beam and tine and to manufacture, perhaps, a handle and a toggle. It is obviously easier to hollow such sections when they are still attached to the junction than when they have been detached.

3.221 is a section of hollowed beam, which was sawn neatly across at either end. A further saw cut penetrates rather less than halfway across the shaft. It seems probable that the piece was being cut in preparation for working as either one or two toggles. The reason for abandonment is not apparent.

3.222 is a piece of antler which was sawn across the junction of the tines. One tine has been removed, but the other remains intact. The surviving piece is smooth and highly polished, but this may have occurred through natural wear.

3.223, while probably best regarded as manufacturing waste, also appears to have served an independent function. It is a portion of the shed, sawn from the beam, which has had the burr removed and which has been pierced as if for suspension.

3.224, 3.225, and 3.226 are all offcuts of antler, none of which have been subjected to wear subsequent to their detachment.

3.227 could be regarded as an antler 'pick'. It is an antler beam, shed, and burr tine. A series of diagonal knife cuts are visible along the length of the beam while the end of the tine appears to have been subjected to a use resulting in the detachment of large slivers.

Manufacturing waste: bone

Six examples of proximal or distal ends of bone sawn or cut from shafts have been found; five are sheep (three proximal and two distal ends) and one is the unfused distal end of a cattle metatarsal. Two come from cp 4, three from cp 5, and one from cp 7–8. (Not illustrated: small finds 506, 1404, 1431, 1452, 1453, 1454)

All have been detached from the shaft by knife or saw cuts, and cut marks are frequently visible on the surviving piece of shaft below the point of removal. Only one piece, 1404, shows any further working, and this was pared and filed to present an artificially square section.

The pieces may have derived from the manufacture of a number of different products. In the case of the sheep shaft bones, these might be bobbins, toggles, gouges (particular 1404), or needles. The cattle shaft might have been used during manufacture of a comb, ferrule, or handle.

Other varieties of bone manufacturing waste include small finds 191, 192, 275, 501, 1401, 1455, 1456 (not illustrated).

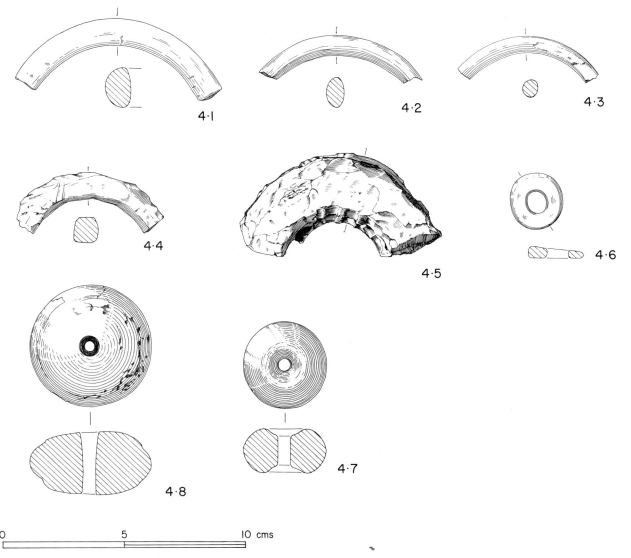

Fig 7.41 *Objects of Kimmeridge shale*

7.1.7 Objects of Kimmeridge shale (Fig 7.41)
by Barry Cunliffe

Eight objects of Kimmeridge shale were discovered, three finished bracelets (two of cp 3 and one of cp 7), two bracelet roughouts (one of cp 5 and one of cp 6), two spindle whorls (both cp 7), and a bead (unphased). The collection is limited and biased towards the later phase of occupation. Items of Kimmeridge shale are comparatively widespread in the Iron Age. The presence of two roughouts suggests that Danebury, in common with other sites, was receiving at least some products in a semi-finished state; it is not however known whether the roughouts were imported in this form or whether they were made on site from blocks of unworked shale.

7.1.8 Beads of amber and coral (Fig 7.42)
by Barry Cunliffe

Three amber beads were found in pits of cp 3, cp 6, and cp 7. All were fragmentary and two had been drilled after breakage presumably to facilitate repairs. Two can be regarded as beads, with comparatively restricted central perforations, the third is more correctly regarded as a ring.

Amber appears to have been a rare commodity in the British Iron Age. It is seldom found on settlement sites and even from the comparatively rich Glastonbury assemblage only five pieces were recorded. The fact that two of the three Danebury examples show signs of mending is a reflection of the value of the material.

The one fragment of perforated coral, possibly a bead, from a cp 3 context is also a rare find.

7.1.9 Beads of glass (Fig 7.43)
by Julian Henderson

Eight glass beads were discovered in the excavations.
6.1 Cobalt blue, undecorated. Guido group 7. Unphased.
6.2 Cobalt blue, undecorated. Guido group 7. Ceramic phase 7.
6.3 Cobalt blue, undecorated. Guido group 7. Ceramic phase 4.
6.4 Cobalt blue fragment. Unphased.
6.5 Blue matrix with blue wavy decoration. Guido group 5B. Ceramic phase 7.
6.6 Pale blue matrix with yellow decoration. Guido group 5A. Ceramic phase 7.
6.7 Blue matrix with blue and white decoration. Guido group 7A. Ceramic phase 6.

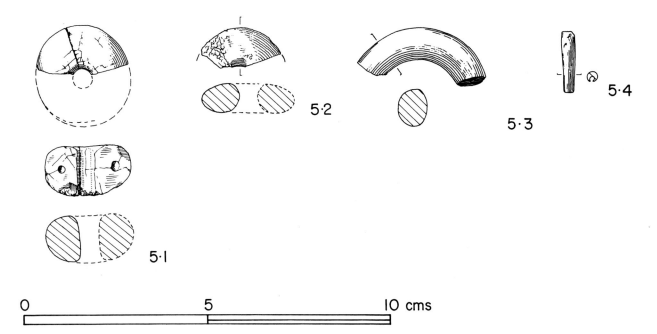

Fig 7.42 Beads of amber and coral

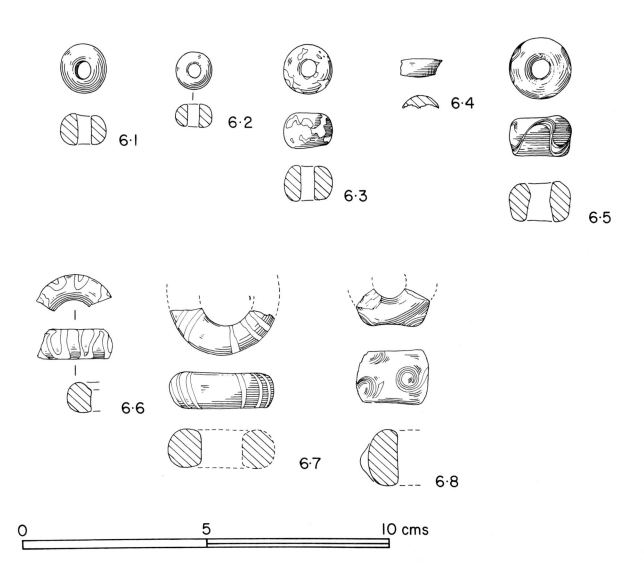

Fig 7.43 Beads of glass

6.8 Cobalt blue with white spiral decoration. Guido group 6. Ceramic phase 7.

The detailed report (fiche 10, frames E4–F2) discusses the typology and the non-destructive chemical analysis by x-ray fluorescence of the glass beads. The technology of bead manufacture is also considered, involving the three principal methods of producing beads mainly with the use of a mould: gathering, winding, and spinning glass. There is no direct evidence for glassworking at Danebury and certainly none for glassmaking. It is interesting to note that at present we only have significant evidence of glassworking, in archaeological and analytical terms, from one southern British Iron Age site, that of Meare Lake Village, Somerset (Henderson 1980; 1981). The concentration of characteristic bead types bears this out (Guido 1978).

Although British hillforts may be considered to be of high status amongst Iron Age site types on the grounds that their construction would involve many man-hours and a high level of organization (Cunliffe 1978, 243), it is perhaps surprising that only limited evidence for specialized industry on any scale has been found during their excavation. Meare Lake Village can probably be treated as a lower status site in these terms, and it was probably defendable from its situation in a marshy environment (Orme *et al* 1981, 67). It did however produce ample evidence for a concentration on various specialized crafts. The small Dorset Iron Age farmstead at Gussage All Saints has also produced a large volume of debris from the production of horse-riding equipment (Spratling & Wainwright 1973; Spratling *et al* 1980). With these two examples of specialized industrial sites at our disposal from southern England it becomes apparent in our present state of knowledge that perhaps prior to the foundation of *oppida* in 'Belgic' areas, specialized industries were centred on relatively small-scale settlements.

7.1.10 Objects of baked clay
by Cynthia Poole

A number of objects made from baked clay were discovered at Danebury. The following categories have been defined and are described in order below:

   slingshots
   perforated clay balls
   beads
   perforated clay reels
   spindle whorls
   clay weights
   metalworking accessories

Full descriptions of the individual objects will be found in fiche 11, frames A2–B5.

Slingshots (7.1–7.11; Fig 7.44)

There are eleven manufactured clay slingshots from Danebury. Except for one from an undated context, all belong to the final phase of occupation: one from cp 6 and the rest from cp 7. Their spatial distribution covers most of the site, though four occur relatively close to the east entrance.

There are two types of slingshot. The most common is ovoid in shape and pointed at both ends. They would appear to be more consistent in size than weight. The length measures between 40 mm and 50 mm and the diameter between 27 mm and 31 mm. The weights cover a greater range from 30 gm to 50 gm. The sample however is scarcely large enough to judge whether any particular weight was preferred. All this type were made from fabric J and except for one were baked.

Of the second type only three occur. These take the form of a spherical clay ball measuring from 35 mm to 40 mm in diameter. Two are complete and weight 39.5 gm and 42.2 gm.

Similar clay slingshots occur commonly on Iron Age sites such as Maiden Castle, Glastonbury, All Cannings Cross, Gussage All Saints, and Yarnbury Castle. The examples from Yarnbury are closest in size to those from Danebury, being of the same length and only a few millimetres less in diameter. The examples from both Glastonbury and All Cannings Cross are noticeably smaller than the Danebury slingshots. Those from Glastonbury measure 35–40 mm by 20–22 mm and those from All Cannings Cross 30–40 mm by 18-25 mm.

It is possible that this difference in size reflects a difference in use. It may be that the smaller examples from Glastonbury and All Cannings Cross were used for hunting game, such as birds, whilst those from Danebury and Yarnbury were being used as an offensive weapon either in defence or attack of the hillfort. It is also noticeable that these slingshots are all dated to the latest phase of occupation, when other evidence suggests the settlement was more subject to attack.

Perforated clay balls (7.12–7.15; Fig 7.44)

Four partially perforated clay balls have been found at Danebury. They date to cp 4, cp 5, cp 6, and cp 7 and all were found relatively close together in the southern area of the site. They are approximately spherical but of quite varying sizes: the larger two measure 33 mm and 20 mm in diameter and weigh 30.3 gm and 7.6 gm, whilst the two smaller measure 10 mm and 11 mm and weigh 0.8 gm and 1.49 gm. The largest is made of fabric J and the others of an unspecified clay. The partial perforations measure 3.5 mm and 4.0 mm in diameter and appear to taper to the inside. The two small balls have been flattened on the side from which the hole was made, and it has worn right through in both these cases.

These objects are very similar to ones found at Glastonbury and All Cannings Cross. The flattened surface and the tapering perforation seem to be typical features. The smaller of the Danebury balls would appear to be unusually small, as they fall between 16 mm and 35 mm in size from other sites. Their function is uncertain, though it has been suggested that they were used as pin heads. This is a distinct possibility for the smaller of the Danebury balls, but seems unlikely for the larger examples. It is possible that they may have functioned as weights on a bowdrill, although one might have expected a heavier device to be used for this.

Beads (7.16–7.17; Fig 7.44)

Two clay beads have been found at Danebury dating from cp 5 and cp 7. The smallest bead is barrel-shaped and measures 9 mm, whilst the other is spherical and measures 23 mm. The perforation in the latter is placed slightly off centre.

Beads mostly of the spherical variety have been found at Gussage All Saints. They were presumably used as a form of personal adornment.

Perforated clay reels (7.18–7.30; Fig 7.45)

Thirteen perforated clay objects of the same type were found together immediately outside the wall of building CS7/8 in a phase i (cp 7) context. They are all made of fabric J, mostly burnt red or black. Six are complete and of the others only one is badly damaged. Ten are cylindrical, two of these rather barrel-shaped, while the

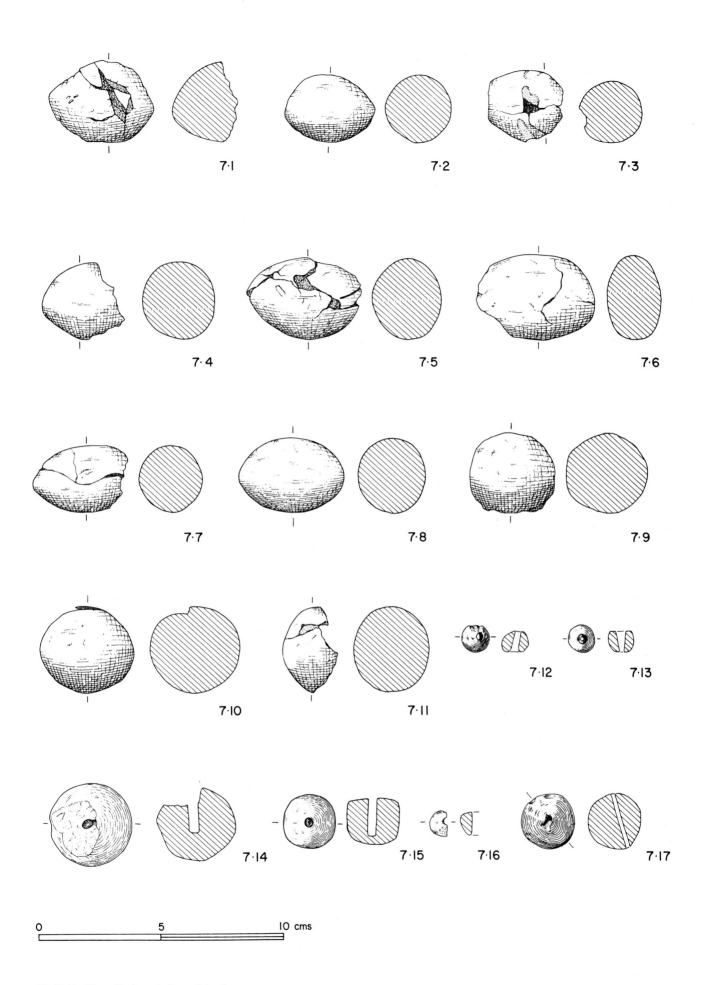

7·1

7·2

7·3

7·4

7·5

7·6

7·7

7·8

7·9

7·10

7·11

7·12

7·13

7·14

7·15

7·16

7·17

0   5   10 cms

Fig 7.44 Clay slingshots, balls, and beads

399

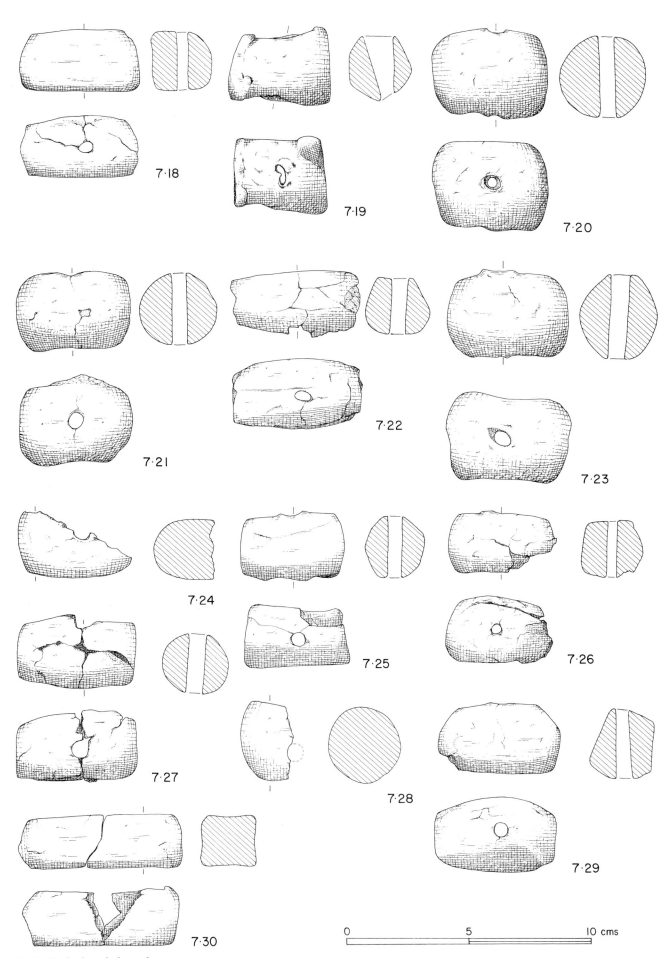

7·18

7·19

7·20

7·21

7·22

7·23

7·24

7·25

7·26

7·27

7·28

7·29

7·30

0   5   10 cms

Fig 7.45 Perforated clay reels

other three are rectangular in section. All, except one which measures 71 mm, are between 42 mm and 53 mm in length. The diameters measure from 23 mm to 34.5 mm, whilst the rectangular ones have widths varying from 20 mm to 26 mm. The rectangular ones tend to be long and thin compared to the others. All the objects have a circular perforation measuring from 5 mm to 8 mm in diameter, which is centrally placed and pierces the object at right-angles to the length. The complete objects weigh from 35.9 gm to 69.5 gm; it is estimated that all the damaged ones would fall within this range.

No exact parallels have been found from other sites. The function of these objects is not obvious, but it seems likely they were all used together and the perforation was presumably intended for some form of suspension. The weights do not appear to cluster about any particular figure, so it seems unlikely that they were intended for measurement.

Spindle whorls (7.31–7.50; Fig 7.46)

There are a total of eighteen spindle whorls made of baked clay and one pierced pottery disc, which could be either a spindle whorl or a small weight. Of these, five come from undated contexts. The rest come from pits dating to ceramic phases 3–7 and one posthole dating to stratigraphic phase e of the 1971 stratified deposits. They are fairly evenly distributed throughout all periods. Spatially their distribution covers most of the site, though there is a slightly denser concentration in the central southern area.

Three basic shapes, which have slight variants, can be recognized.

Type 1 is cylindrical having straight sides and flat ends. There are three examples of this type, as well as one that has convex sides making it barrel-shaped and another that is of a dumbbell form. These all occur in the earlier phases from cp 3–5.

Type 2 is disc-shaped and can be subdivided into straight-sided, curved, and angular. The first two forms are not represented amongst the clay spindle whorls (but examples may be found amongst the chalk ones). The angular type is thickest in the middle with the flat ends converging towards the edge, where the sides are straight and narrow — a cross between disc-shaped and biconical. Two examples of this form occur, one from cp 6 and one undated.

Type 3 is the most common and can be subdivided into two, one being spherical, sometimes with flattened ends, and the other biconical, being more angular at its greatest width. There are eleven examples of this type, occurring in all ceramic phases.

The perforation through the spindle whorl is always centrally placed or nearly so. It is usually a straight cylindrical hole, probably formed by a stick when the clay was wet. This is supported by 7.37, where three attempts were apparently made to get the position right, and 7.47 where two attempts were made. Most of the perforations measure 5–8 mm in diameter, though some are slightly wider at the edges, which is probably due to wear in most cases. There are only two genuine hourglass-shaped perforations: 7.44 has the hole tapering from 5 mm at the outside to 3 mm in the middle and 7.50 tapers from 11 mm on one side to 3 mm in the middle and widens to 10 mm at the other side. This shape must have been formed by drilling out the perforation after the clay had dried. Clearly the perforation in the pottery disc had also to be drilled.

The sizes of the spindle whorls cover a wide range, in which the distribution shows preference for no particular size. The diameters measure from 25 mm to 48 mm and the depths from 18 mm to 36 mm and all that is obvious is that both factors tend to increase together.

The weights vary from 12 gm to 83 gm, though the smallest one may be a bead and the largest is the pottery disc. There do seem to be two possible groupings according to weight; one concentration is from 18-28 gm and another from 44-49 gm. However all forms occur in both groups and the sample is too small to be sure of any real significance in the distribution.

Nearly all the spindle whorls are made of a sandy clay fabric. Thirteen are made from fabric A, three from fabric F, and two are of clay, one of which is fabric K. They were all fired or baked and it seems likely that this was deliberate as no unbaked examples have been found. However there is a possible unfinished spindle whorl in fabric K. It takes the form of a flat circular disc measuring 28 mm in diameter and 11 mm in depth with a central perforation of 6 mm.

There is no proper decoration on any of the spindle whorls. The marking on 7.35, an irregular indentation round the centre of the spindle whorl, may be regarded as an attempt at decoration.

Clay spindle whorls occur on many Iron Age sites, though often fairly sparsely. Maiden Castle produced only one clay spindle whorl, spherical in form. Gussage All Saints produced five, both spherical and cylindrical, as well as ten pottery discs. There are larger collections of clay spindle whorls from All Cannings Cross (34), Glastonbury (42), and Meare (41).

All Cannings Cross has a similar range of shapes and sizes as Danebury, as well as some additional forms such as a hemispherical shape (similar in shape to the bone spindle whorls from Danebury). The major difference noticeable with those at All Cannings Cross is that several of the cylindrical spindle whorls are decorated, usually by ridges or incisions round the circumference and sometimes additionally on the ends. Those from Glastonbury are largely spherical or disc-shaped.

The Danebury collection is similar to those from most other sites, except in their lack of decoration. All excavators accept that they were used as spindle whorls and no alternative uses have been suggested except to say that some of the smallest may be beads, which may also be the case at Danebury.

Clay weights (7.51–7.69)

A total of 62 clay weights, mostly incomplete fragments, have been found at Danebury. Of these seven come from cp 3 contexts, five from cp 4, four from cp 5, fifteen from cp 6, nineteen from cp 7, eight from cp 8, and four were undated. Their spatial distribution on site shows them to be fairly evenly scattered, though there is a greater concentration from the stratified deposits on the north side of the site. There are also two contexts, pits 110 and 863, where several have occurred together. The majority of the weights have been found in pits, though a small number also occurred in layers and other features. Seven different types may be distinguished, but of these six types occur only once or twice each.

Type 1 (7.51–7.64; Figs 7.47, 7.48)

This is the most common type and accounts for 51 examples, of which 31 are only small fragments, mostly single corners. There are possibly some small pieces in the daub samples that could not be positively identified as weights, owing to a lack of any distinguishing characteristics. Of the other twenty only five are complete or nearly so and half or more survives of the

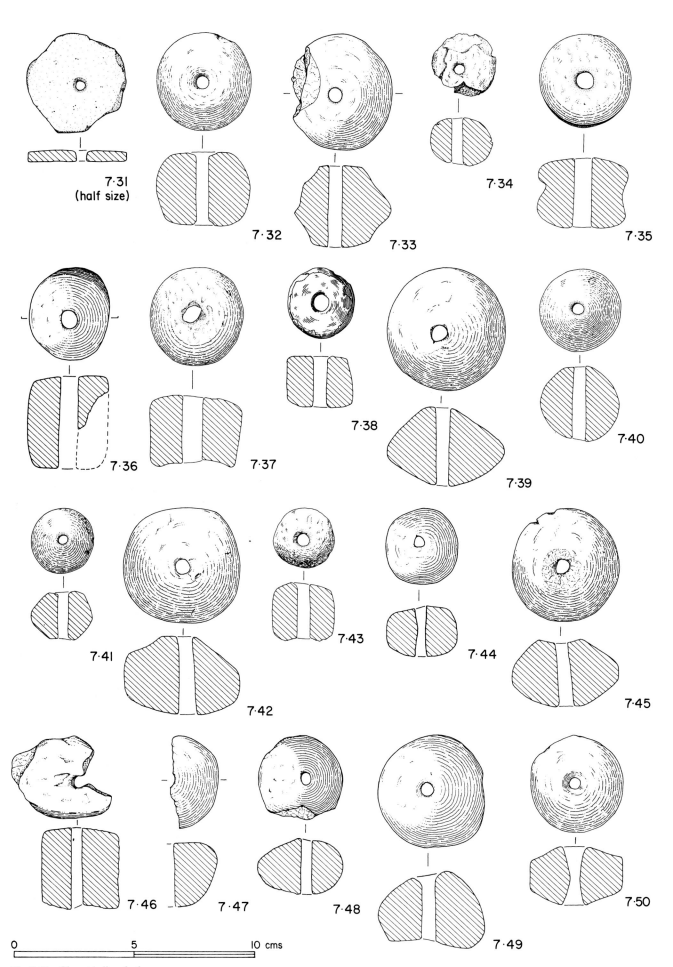

7.31
(half size)

7.32

7.33

7.34

7.35

7.36

7.37

7.38

7.39

7.40

7.41

7.42

7.43

7.44

7.45

7.46

7.47

7.48

7.49

7.50

0   5   10 cms

Fig 7.46   Clay spindle whorls

402

remaining fifteen. They occur throughout the occupation of the site.

The weights are triangular in shape, usually with rounded corners. It has been possible to measure the length of at least one side of eighteen weights, and these range from 120 mm to 200 mm, with most falling between 130 mm and 150 mm. Only four examples are complete enough to have all three sides measured and this shows that one side is often marginally shorter than the others; eg 7.59 measures 185 mm, 185 mm, and 175 mm along its sides, and 7.52 measures 145 mm, 145 mm, and 140 mm. The possibility that the weights were not usually equilateral may suggest that one corner was regarded as the top.

The width could be measured on 38 examples and the measurements were evenly distributed between 49 and 80 mm with one as wide as 85 mm. In general the greater widths coincide with the longer sides, though not necessarily as one with a side of 130 mm has a width of 75 mm.

The weights for the complete examples are 1875 gm, 1675 gm, 1450 gm, and 1017 gm, whilst others of which over three-quarters survive weigh 1634 gm, 1162 gm, 1107 gm, 1389 gm, 1428 gm, and 1175 gm. These can only indicate the range of weights, as the sample is too small to show if any particular weight norm or norms were desired.

Each of the corners was pierced by a hole from side to side. The diameters of these perforations range from 8 mm to 18 mm, though they are mostly 11 mm or 12 mm. It is clear that these perforations were made with a small stick pushed through the soft clay before it dried. Several examples show that the perforations were sometimes made from both directions resulting in an oval hole. The perforations of 7.64 were made in two attempts resulting in a figure of eight shape, with the diameters measuring 14 mm and 16 mm on one and 19 mm and 16 mm on the second.

There are three examples where there is an additional fourth perforation. 7.53 has two parallel perforations across one corner, both measuring 9 mm in diameter. They diverge slightly from 6 mm to 10 mm apart. 7.55 has part of a second perforation across one corner, 10 mm in diameter and about 60 mm long. This example was clearly misplaced and had not been completed. Similarly 7.56 has a second narrow hole across one of its corners running parallel to the main perforation but measuring only 6 mm in diameter. The most likely explanation for these extra holes is that the first perforation was wrongly positioned and subsequently altered.

The fabric most commonly used to make the weights was E, which was used for 25, followed by K (10), and D (6) with a few made in A, B, C, F, and J. Nearly all were baked to some extent, but the degree to which they were fired is very variable and one cannot be certain that the baking was deliberate rather than accidental.

Type 2 (7.65; Fig 7.48)

There are three examples of this type, two of which were found in P658 (cp 3), and the other in a cp 7 context. They are also triangular in form, but do not have the three perforations characteristic of type 1. The two found together are very similar, both being made from coarse fabric C and both being fairly small. The better preserved of the two, 7.65, is almost complete except for the loss of one corner and part of the base. The base measures 130 mm in length and the width is 65 mm thick. It survives to a height of 85 mm and it is likely that only 20–30 mm are missing from the top. It weighs 737

gm. There is only a single hole 6 mm in diameter perforating the top corner through the triangular faces, not the sides. In the second example the perforation measures 16 mm in diameter. The third weight (sf 1766) is similar though only part of the corner survives. It has concave sides and looks as though it may have been more pyramidal in shape. The single perforation is 8 mm wide.

Type 3 (7.66; Fig 7.48)

There are fragments of two examples of this type surviving and both come from the corner of a triangular object. 7.66 is 105 mm wide and weighs 1130 gm. Small find 609 measures over 80 mm in thickness and weighs 108 gm. They are made of fabric A and K respectively. Both of these pieces have very angular corners unlike type 1 and there are no signs of any perforations. One comes from a cp 7 context and one is undated.

Type 4 (7.67; Fig 7.48)

There are two examples of this type from cp 3 and cp 5 contexts. Both examples are only corner fragments and so their overall form remains uncertain. They appear to be the ends of oblong or cylindrical weights. 7.67 is roughly rectangular in section and 65 mm thick, with a perforation 10 mm in diameter. Small find 1359 has a very rounded top and is 80 mm thick. The perforation through it is much larger than on other weights, measuring 25 mm by 30 mm. Both were made of fabric D and baked.

Type 5

There is only one example of this type from a cp 7 context (sf 1752). Only the base remains, which is 70 mm in diameter, and the sides survive to a height of about 25 mm, where the weight measures 85 mm in diameter. It looks as though it was roughly hemispherical in shape, in fact more like some of the stone weights than other clay weights. As the top does not survive, it is not known whether there was a perforation.

Type 6 (7.68; Fig 7.48)

There are two examples of this type, which are characterized by having a notch or groove cut in part of the surface. They are otherwise dissimilar in shape, as sf 1771 is rather like a cube with rounded corners and 7.68 is oblong. The former has a deep V-shaped notch 18 mm deep and 33 mm wide, whilst the latter has a shallower groove 9 mm deep. Both would be sufficient to hold the objects if suspended by tying a rope round them, rather than through a perforation.

Type 7 (7.69; Fig 7.48)

There is only one example of this type from a cp 7 context.

It is roughly circular measuring about 150 mm in diameter and about 80 mm thick. It weighs 2080 gm and was made of fabric E and baked. There is no evidence that it was suspended, as there are no perforations or grooves, but it could still have been used as a weight in the same way as a paperweight.

There are no signs of wear on any of the weights, though many of the triangular examples have broken along the perforations, which are obvious weak points and would have been liable to break before obvious wear patterns developed. Evidence of wear would have helped to assess whether the type 1 weights were suspended by one or more perforations at a time.

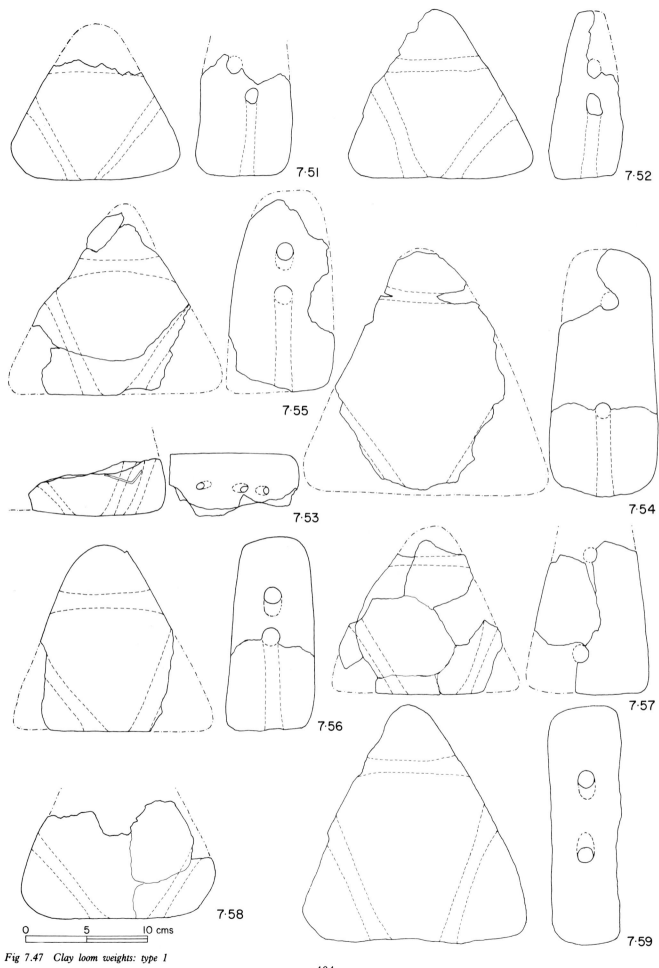

7·51

7·52

7·55

7·53

7·54

7·56

7·57

7·58

7·59

0   5   10 cms

Fig 7.47 Clay loom weights: type 1

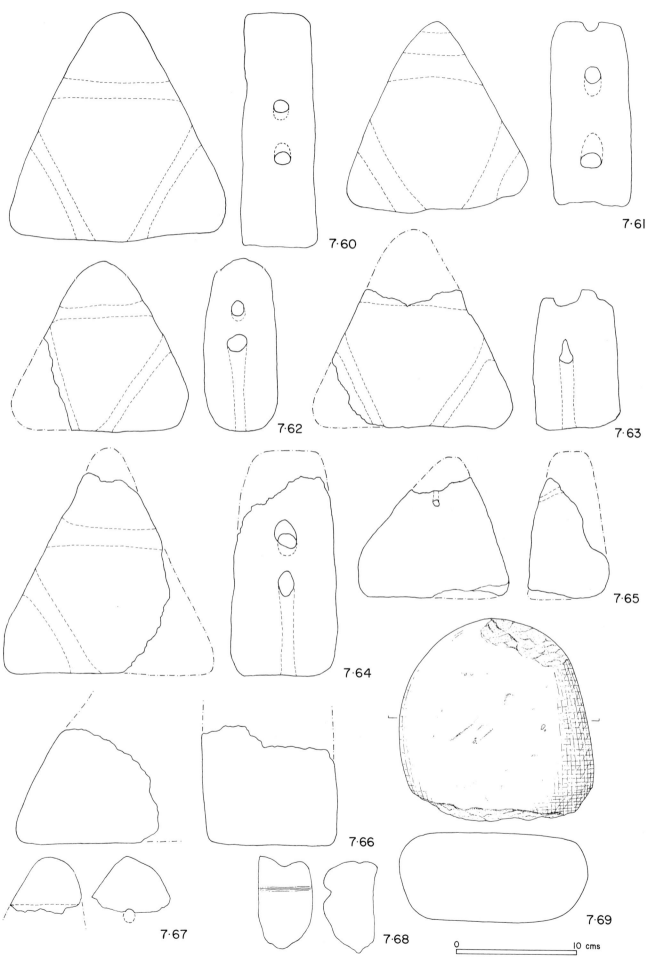

Fig 7.48 Clay loom weights: type 1, 7.60–7.64; type 2, 7.65; type 3, 7.66; type 4, 7.67; type 6, 7.68; type 7, 7.69

7·60

7·61

7·62

7·63

7·64

7·65

7·66

7·67

7·68

7·69

0   10 cms

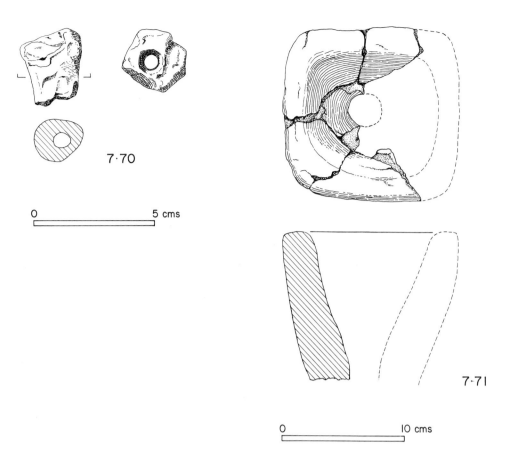

0   5 cms

7·71

0   10 cms

Fig 7.49 Clay metalworking accessories

Triangular and cylindrical or oblong weights have been found on many other Iron Age sites; the triangular weights are usually the more common, as at Danebury. Many sites have produced only a small number of examples. Maiden Castle produced 25 of which seven were oblong with one perforation, while the rest were triangular with three perforations, one across each corner. These included four examples of very large triangular weights, measuring *c* 200 mm along each side, *c* 90 mm wide, and weighing *c* 3.5 kg. These seem more comparable to the Danebury type 3 weights.

From Glastonbury, 42 weights were found of triangular, cylindrical, and pyramidal shape, of which the triangular were the most frequent. They were mostly perforated by two holes, and less frequently by three or one. By comparison, at Danebury there is no evidence of two-holed examples. The triangular weights from most sites fall within the same size and weight range as those from Danebury.

Cylindrical weights are also commonly found, though nearly always in small numbers and often in late Bronze Age contexts; the triangular weights seem to have replaced them. At Danebury there are, however, many chalk weights of a cylindrical form and it is possible that the material changed but the functional type continued.

The usual interpretation of clay weights on Iron Age sites is that they were loom weights, used to keep the warp threads tense on an upright loom. This was the conclusion reached at Glastonbury, where groups of triangular weights were commonly associated with large numbers of weaving combs. The explanation is reasonable, but if they were loom weights it is not clear why the triangular form needed three perforations, when one would have been quite adequate. It is of course possible

that each perforation was used in turn till it broke, giving the weight a longer life span, but this seems a somewhat elaborate explanation. Moreover the small perforations, of 10 mm or less, would have been too constricted to get many warp threads through. The cylindrical chalk or clay weights would in practice have made far more suitable loom weights than the triangular examples. On balance, however, some indoor activity, such as weaving, is likely, since not all the weights were fired, which would preclude them being left outside in wet weather.

The other types of weight, which occur in small numbers at Danebury, were probably not types repeatedly manufactured, but were perhaps made for single instances of need. They may have been used in weighing down hay or thatch; the heavier examples would have made suitable door or gate weights.

Metalworking accessories (7.70, 7.71; Fig 7.49)

Ceramic metalworking accessories fall into three categories:

Crucibles

Four fragments of small crucibles have been found, one in cp 4/5, two in cp 6/7, and one in cp 7 contexts. The fabrics are described in detail by Hilary Howard (fiche 11, frames C2–3). The crucibles are of the sub-triangular form commonly found in Iron Age contexts and were probably used for melting bronze.

Tuyère nozzle (7.70)

Perforated nozzle of baked clay (fabric J) measuring 26 mm in diameter tapering to 18 mm. The hole measures 11 mm tapering to 7 mm. It may be the nozzle of a tuyère but it shows no sign of intensive heating. From a cp 5 context. Another fragment of what was probably a tuyère was found in a cp 7 context (see fiche 11, frame C3).

Possible bellows guards

Fragments of four similar objects of which the one illustrated (7.71) is the best-preserved example (the others are small finds 610, 1753, 1776). In general form the objects are funnel-shaped with a square mouth and flat lip. They taper towards the base which in no case survives. All are made in fabric G. Two come from cp 7 contexts, the other two are undated.

Similar examples have been found at Glastonbury (Bulleid & Gray 1911, XLIX, D30) and Little Woodbury (Brailsford 1949, 160, fig 4). It is quite possible that they were guards designed to protect the bellows from the intense heat of the furnace.

7.1.11 Objects of stone
by Lisa Brown

The objects made from stone are divided into categories and described in the following order:

the imported stone
stone weights
whetstones
quernstones
chalk marl discs
chalk weights
chalk spindle whorls and other perforated chalk discs
miscellaneous chalk objects
sling stones

Relevant descriptions and other details will be found in fiche 12, frames A2–G8.

The imported stone

Almost 3000 fragments of stone were recovered from the excavations between 1969 and 1978. Only about 700 of these could be definitely identified as representing an object (quern, weight, whetstone, or thatch weight) but many showed evidence of working and it is probable that even those with no surviving worked faces represent fragments of broken objects. Few unworked lumps of stone large enough for fashioning a quern or weight were found, and this indicates that most of the stone objects were brought to the site in finished form. The lack of substantial evidence for stoneworking on the site supports this argument, though some of the stone was obviously reused.

The percentages of each stone type were computed on the basis of the number of fragments. Although it was obvious that many fragments may have joined, each was counted separately.

Danebury is situated on the chalk downland some distance away from any source of hard stone, apart from flint and various pebbles. All other stone, therefore, would have been brought to the site, implying organized transport, and, in some cases, widespread exchange contacts.

Most of the imported stone fell into one of three main groups: greensands, Tertiary sandstones, and gritstones (including Millstone Grit). Greensand is by far the largest group, representing approximately 78% of all the stone. At Gussage All Saints and nearby at Balksbury, most of the greensand was found to be the tougher, coarser Lower Greensand (Wainwright 1979, 89–90) whereas at Danebury, most was Upper Greensand. This raises some interesting questions when one considers the proximity of Danebury to Balksbury and the basic unsuitability of

Upper Greensand for the job of grinding. If the harder Lower Greensand were available from the same general sources why should the softer Upper Greensand have been preferred at Danebury?

The Upper Greensand would almost certainly have come to Danebury either from the Shaftesbury or the Westbury area, both about 30–50 km away to the west. Upper Greensand does outcrop at equally close sources — 30 km away to the north and 40 km to the east around Alton — but, for ease of transport, the western sources seem more likely. The Nadder, Solent, Avon, and Test River complexes would have been convenient means for transporting this heavy material.

The smaller amount of Lower Greensand is also, for the same reason, likely to have come from the western sources. There are small outcrops near Shaftesbury in the Vale of Wardour 40 km away, and in the area around Devizes about 50 km away. A closer source is to the east where there is a substantial outcrop at the western end of the Wealden anticline, and some may have come from there.

The Tertiary sandstones, including some of the ferruginous sandstone, would almost certainly have been obtained from the closest source — the Hampshire Basin a few kilometres to the south. This group represents about 10% of the imported stone and was used for making saddle querns, rubbing stones, and whetstones, but only rarely for rotary querns. A small quantity of the ferruginous sandstone may have come from the Westbury area.

The third group, the gritstones, comprised about 2.5% of the stone. It is possible that all the gritstones, including Millstone Grit, were derived from the Millstone Grit and Culm Measures in the Mendips about 80 km distant where there is a small outcrop. The next closest sources for Millstone Grit, apart from S Wales, would be Devon (about 130 km away) or Derbyshire/Yorkshire (over 200 km away). Some of the gritstones may be Tertiary gritstones from the Hampshire Basin.

Worked chalk formed quite a high proportion of the stone but has not been considered on the same terms as the other stone since much of it was locally available. All of the Lower Chalk and chalk marl which were used to make the loom weights would probably, however, have come from the western outcrops in the Vale of Wardour-Warminster area. The white chalk is obviously local.

All other stone types represent less than 1% each of the imported stone. Table 40 gives stone type, number of fragments, percentage based on fragment count, most probable source, and approximate distance of source from Danebury.

The odd 2% of stone from uncertain sources includes fine hard quartzites and Permian/Triassic and Palaeozoic sandstones. Some of these could well have come from the Hampshire Basin and others from the Somerset/Devon area where the Permian/Triassic sandstones outcrop in a band running north-south. Several limonite nodules were also found on the site and have been included in the final category.

The picture presented by the wide variety of stone types found at Danebury is one of organized transport and contact with areas possibly as far distant as 200 km. Most of the stone, however, would have come from the nearest outcrops of hard stone 20–50 km away. In fact, it was usually the smallest objects — whetstones and, occasionally, weights — which were made from the materials least easily obtainable. The variety of stone used and the distance of source diminish in relation to the size of the object.

Table 40　Quantification of foreign stone

Stone type	Frags	%	Probable source	Distance
Greensand	2299	78.0	Shaftesbury, Westbury, Vale of Wardour	30-50 km
Tertiary Sandstones	277	9.43	Hampshire Basin	10-40 km
Gritstones	79	2.69	E Mendips and (?) Yorkshire	80 and ?200 km +
Chalk and Marl	155	5.28	Local and Vale of Wardour	Local and 40 km
Carboniferous Limestone	17	0.58	Mendips	80 km
Mudstones	12	0.41	Bristol area/Somerset or Purbeck	65 km +
Sarsen	9	0.31	Wiltshire	30 km
Purbeck Limestone	6	0.20	Purbeck or Vale of Wardour	40 km +
Shale (Rhaetic and Lias)	6	0.20	Bristol area	80 km
Red Sandstone	4	0.14	Devon/Somerset	80 km +
Igneous Rock (Syenite and Gabbro)	3	0.10	South-west Britain ?Drift	160 km +
Lias Limestone	2	0.07	Shepton Mallet area	65 km
Bembridge Limestone	1	0.03	Isle of Wight	50 km
Quartz Conglomerate	1	0.03	Bristol area	80 km +
Other	64	2.18	uncertain	

Stone weights (Figs 7.50–7.52)

Thirty-six stone objects were recovered from the excavation, in whole or fragmentary form, sharing sufficient characteristics to suggest that they may be classed together and may have functioned as weights.

Eight stone types were identified. Twenty-four (67%) of the weights were made from greensand, four (11%) from Tertiary white sandstone, two (5%) from Carboniferous limestone, and one each (3%) from hard grey marl, grey limestone, Bembridge limestone, Carboniferous sandstone, brown sandstone, and quartz conglomerate.

Four morphological types were distinguishable called here W1–W4. Several examples of W1, W3, and W4 possessed a means of suspension, either in the form of an iron ring or an integral knob. In other examples, the attachment no longer survived, but iron staining, holes drilled for taking iron rings, or broken knobs were present. In the tables (fiche 12, frames A2–11), this information is recorded under the column marked 'attachment'. With a few exceptions, the weights were carefully shaped and finished.

Type W1 (8.1–8.10; Fig 7.50)
Weights of this category are half-spherical (bun-shaped) with a base which is round in section. The diameter range is 110–160 mm with the exception of one smaller stone (75 mm). The variety of stone used in their manufacture is fairly wide, but half (five of the ten) are of Upper Greensand. Six of the weights possess an iron hook, or evidence that one existed (for details see fiche 12, frames A2–3).

Type W2 (8.11–8.13; Fig 7.50)
Only three weights could definitely be assigned to this category. They are taller than W1 types, straight or steep-sided, with an unperforated, rounded top. The base section is sub-rectangular and there is no apparent means of suspension (for details see fiche 12, frames A4–5).

Type W3 (8.14–8.21; Fig 7.51)
These are very similar to type W2 but the top may be flattened and all show evidence of a means of suspension (apart from one stone which has a broken top). Five of the eight are of Upper Greensand (for details see fiche 12, frames A4–5).

Type W4 (8.22–8.23; Fig 7.51)
There are two weights in this category. The distinctive feature is a knob shaped from the top of the stone. Both are large and heavy. No 8.23 (quartz conglomerate) is well finished with a neat, circular knob, whereas 8.22 is much more crudely fashioned. Its 'knob' could more aptly be described as a wide groove around the top of the stone (for details see fiche 12, frames A4–5).

Of the thirteen remaining weights which are too fragmentary to reconstruct, two are identifiable as Type W1, and one is probably Type W2.

Most of the weights were recovered from pits and the majority are dated to ceramic phases 7–8. The exceptions are sf 787 (cp 6), and sf 86, which has a ceramic phase date of 4, but this is based on only two diagnostic potsherds found in the pit and the actual date of the pit may therefore be later. There is a problem with one weight which was found in two pieces (sf 752 and sf 765) which join to form a complete weight. Two separate contexts are recorded for the two halves, one in a ceramic phase 3 and one in a ceramic phase 7 pit (both well

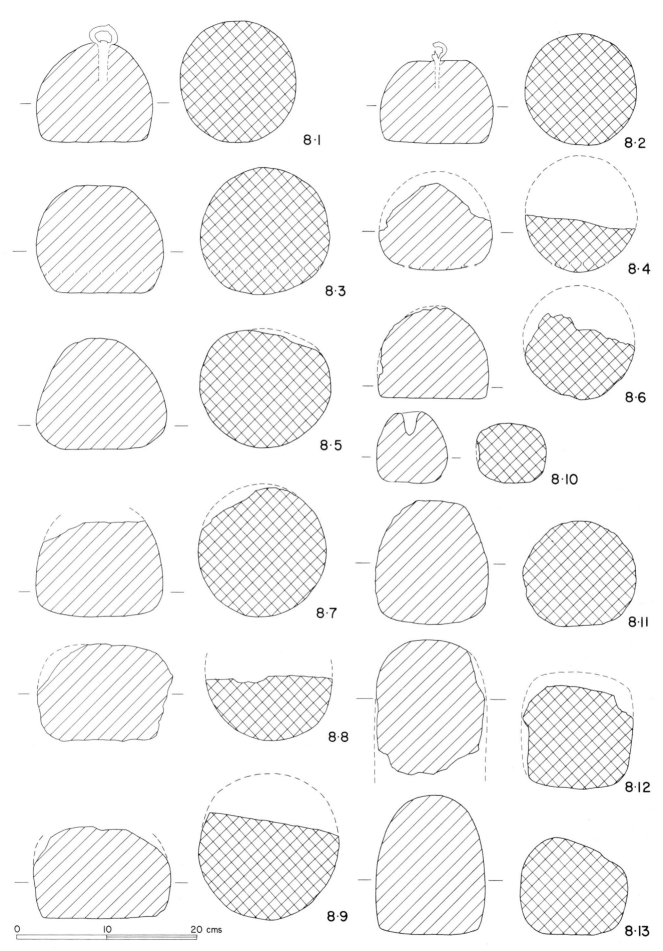

8·1

8·2

8·3

8·4

8·5

8·6

8·7

8·10

8·8

8·11

8·9

8·12

8·13

0   10   20 cms

Fig 7.50 Stone weights: types W1 and W2

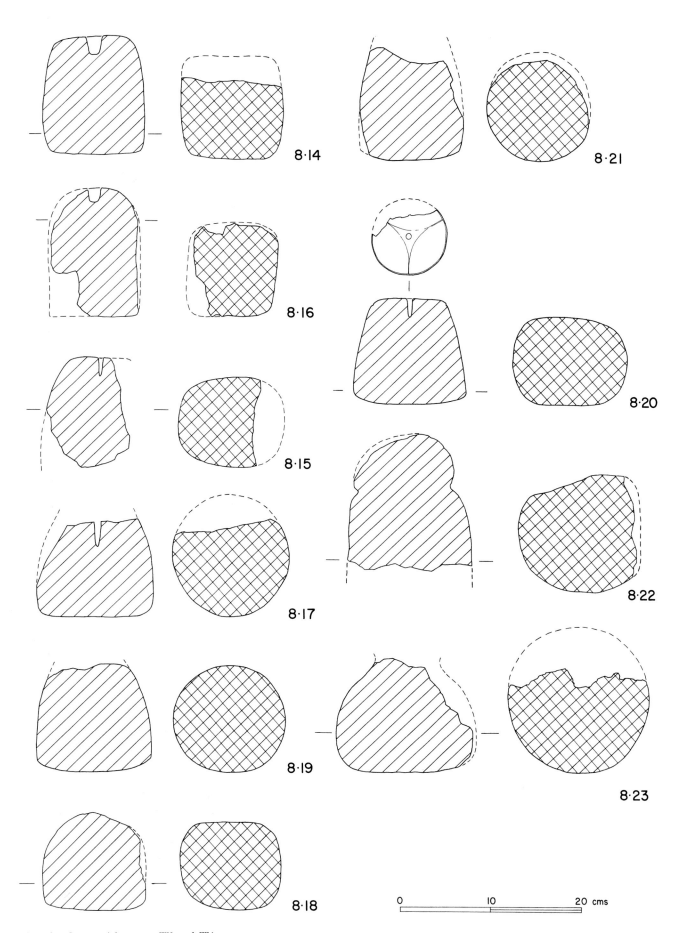

8.14

8.21

8.16

8.15

8.20

8.17

8.22

8.19

8.23

8.18

Fig 7.51   Stone weights: types W3 and W4

0   10   20 cms

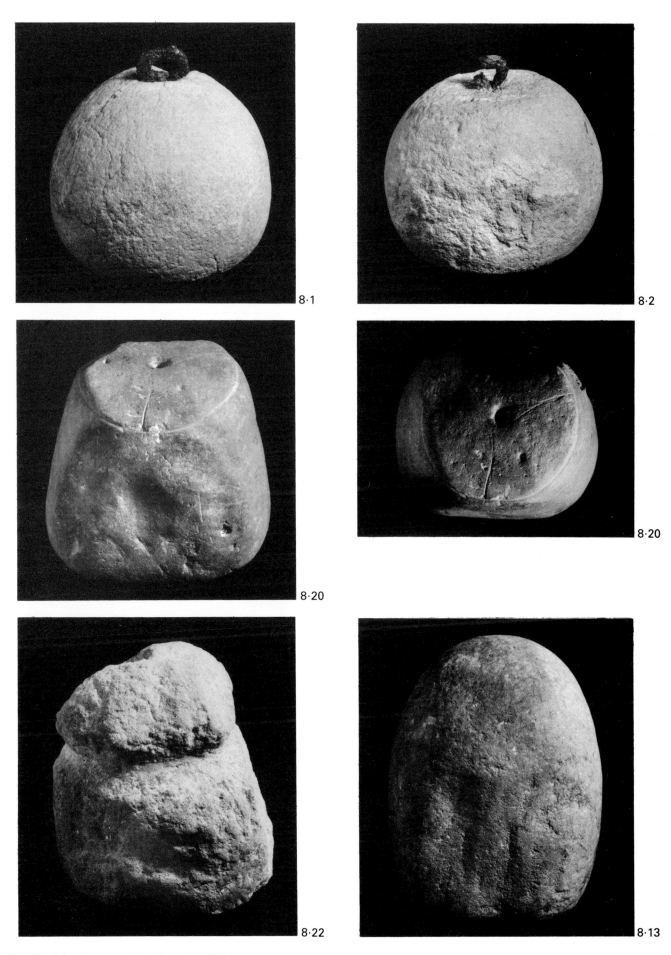

8·1

8·2

8·20

8·20

8·22

8·13

Fig 7.52   Selected stone weights (photo: Bob Wilkins)

411

TABLE 41 Stone weights

Small find number	W^1 (gm)	W^2 (gm) + 5%	V^1 (ml)	V^2	D
98	2195.8	2240.839	975	995	2.2521
247	1870.7	2735.928	800	1170	2.3384
226	1602.4	2031.300	710	900	2.2570
536	565.5	642.600	220	250	2.5704
684	1317.2	1499.862	685	780	1.9229
418	2478.0	2802.239	1070	1210	2.3159
1385	2168.0	2617.764	940	1135	2.3064
633	2737.5	3067.870	1160	1300	2.3599
616	1842.3	2344.755	825	1050	2.2331
634	1894.7	2499.877	1080	1425	1.7543
752 + 765	2624.0	2631.000	1330	1333	1.978
1245	1681.7	2165.163	800	1030	2.1021
1163	1468.5	2889.570	620	1220	2.3685
1133	2067.0	4133.948	910	1820	2.2714
1248	2171.0	4342.000	895	1790	2.4257
683	1115.4	1861.803	665	1110	1.6773
1165	1142.2	2514.992	520	1145	2.1965
761	883.3	2065.206	355	830	2.4882
1263	2066.5	2932.469	1050	1490	1.9681
787	2820.0	3384.000	1250	1500	2.2560
86	3004.9	3004.9	Complete weight		
905	1587.9	1587.9	Complete weight		
978	2406.5	2406.5	Complete weight		

directly and volume (V^1) measured by volumetric displacement of water. The original shape of the weight was then carefully reconstructed in plasticine and the new volume (ie its original volume) was measured (V^2). Using the formula original weight (W^2) = D x V^2 it was possible to arrive at an accurate assessment of the original weight. A margin of error of 10% of the added weight has been assumed. The assessments are given in Table 41. No allowance has been made for the weight of the iron attachment hook and it is, of course, impossible to assess what margin of error was tolerated by the manufacturers.

If the weights are arranged in a simple order of increasing heaviness no clusterings appear to suggest standard weight sets and if the four morphological types are considered separately the sample size is too small. Thus it must be concluded that there are too few weights to allow a weight unit to be derived from the objects themselves.

The next stage was to test an *a priori* unit to see whether the derived weights bore any relation to it. For this purpose the presumed 'Celtic' weight standard of 638 gm was used (another standard of 309 gm is also thought to have been used at the same period). A statistical test, Fisher's Exact, Chi Squared tested the null hypothesis that the derived weights did not cluster around multiples of 63.8 gm. It was found, however, that the weights did correlate fairly well with multiples of a figure such as 63.8 gm ± 10% and ± 25%, but that there was no significant correlation at a finer level of ± 5% (for details of test see fiche 12, frames A7–11). It is therefore possible that there is a link with the 638 gm unit, but, bearing in mind the possible errors in reconstruction and manufacture, this cannot be certain. Furthermore, the question remains why such inexplicable multiples of a basic unit, whatever it may have been, were used.

The same procedure was used to test the 309 gm weight standard, with different results. This time it was found that the weights correlated as well with 30.9 gm ± 5% as with ± 10% and 25%. It is possible, therefore, that the Danebury weights may have been part of a system of weights using 309 gm as a standard.

dated). Since the contexts are both well below the levels in the pits which could be assumed to be disturbed, it must be assumed either that the weight is a cp 3 artefact half of which ended up in a later pit, or, more likely, that one half was mislabelled in processing the finds.

The 1975–77 excavations at Winklebury Camp produced two certain and one possible stone weights, all unstratified (Smith 1977, 108, 113). Two, which most closely resemble Danebury Type 1, are made from white sandstone and have remains of iron hooks in the top. One is smooth and carefully finished, the other roughly pecked to shape. They weigh 2.6 kg and 3.7 kg respectively, and both are unstratified. The third stone resembles Type 2 and is made from greensand. It is well finished with a pecked surface and weighs 3.1 kg (context not given in report). No other published examples of weights have been found in a survey of the literature.

The possibility exists that the weights are, in fact, balance weights. If so they might be expected to conform to a standard pattern of measurement. To test this hypothesis it was necessary first to establish as many of the original total weights as possible. Three specimens were intact and could be weighed directly; a further twenty were sufficiently complete for the original weights to be reconstructed. The procedure adopted was based on elementary physics, using the formula density = weight divided by volume. First the density of each example was established using weight (W^1) measured

Whetstones

Thirty-eight whetstones were discovered (for a full listing see fiche 12, frame A12). None appears to have been deliberately shaped. Most are large, waterworn pebbles, and are generally long and flat in shape. In a few instances a fragment broken from a larger stone has been used. None of the Danebury examples has a drilled hole for taking a string or thong, but many have been broken and may originally have had such holes.

Of those to which ceramic phases could be assigned, seven come from cp 1–3 contexts, five from cp 4, four from cp 6, and twenty from cp 7. Eighteen different stone types were employed of which the most common were hard, fine-grained sandstones. Igneous rocks used include one example each of syenite, gabbro, and basalt; other exotics include black slate, mudstones, and Devonian red sandstones. All could, in theory, have been collected from drift or beach deposits but not from the immediate territory of Danebury. A high proportion of the more unusual stone types were found in pre-cp 5 contexts.

Quernstones (Figs 7.53–7.57)

The site produced 592 fragments of stone utilized in the manufacture of rotary and saddle querns. Of this number 120 fragments representing 54 saddle querns and 36

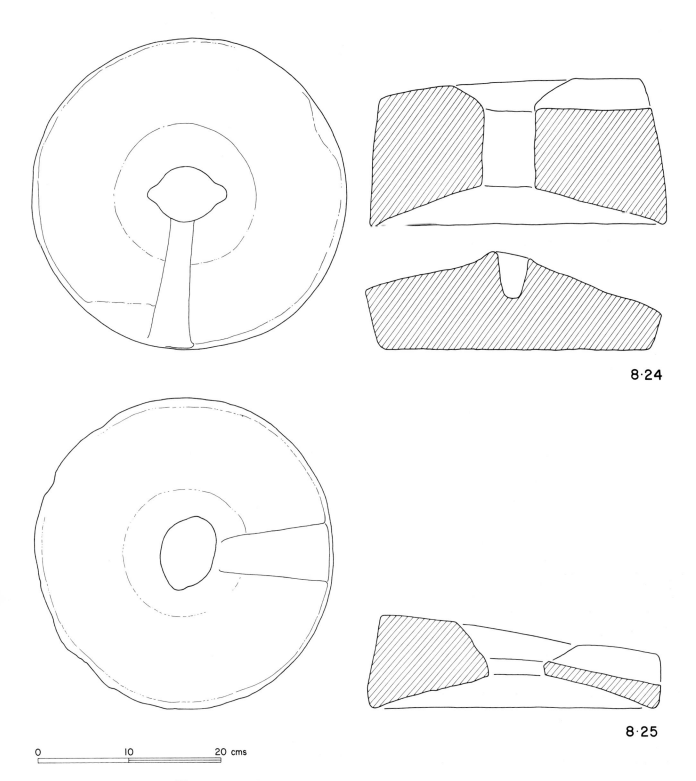

8·24

8·25

0   10   20 cms

Fig 7.53   Rotary querns: type R1

413

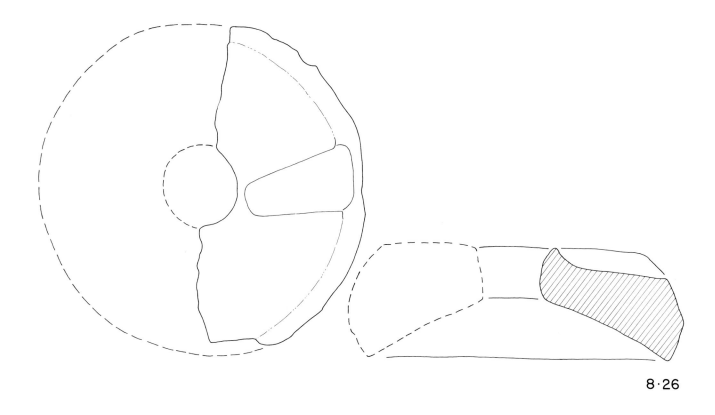

8·26

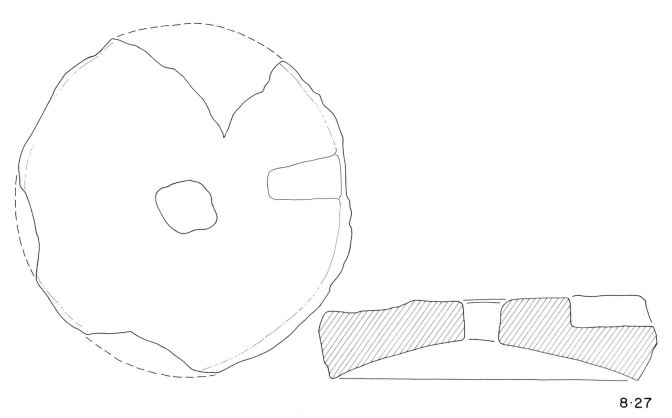

8·27

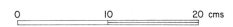

0   10   20 cms

Fig 7.54   Rotary querns: type R2

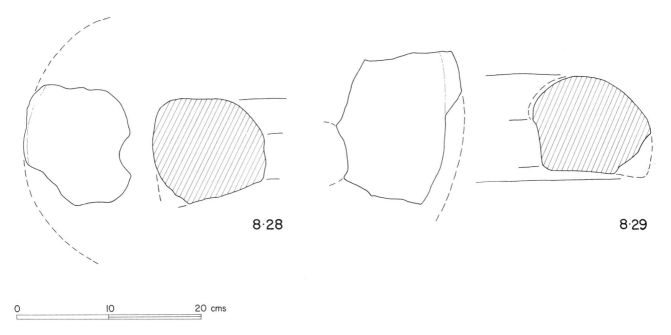

8·28

8·29

0   10   20 cms

Fig 7.55   Rotary querns: type R3

fragments representing 29 rubbing stones were recognized. Of the remaining fragments 360 were from rotary querns, of which 82 were certainly lower stones, and 48 fragments (representing 32 complete querns) could be identified as one of five types of upper stone. The remaining 232 rotary quern fragments were mostly from upper stones but were too fragmentary to identify as a particular type. A final category consisted of 74 fragments identifiable as querns but unrecognizable as belonging definitely to one form or another (rotary or saddle)

Most of the stone falls into three main groups: greensand, Tertiary sandstones, and gritstones (especially Millstone Grit). The greensand predominates and by far the highest proportion is Upper Greensand. The common use of Upper Greensand for querns at Danebury is not easy to understand considering its basic unsuitability for the job of grinding (F W Anderson, pers comm) and must be put down to availability of raw material and proximity of sources. Even so, this does not explain the preference for Upper as opposed to Lower Greensand when the two are available from the same general sources. At Balksbury and Gussage All Saints the harder Lower Greensand was preferred for the manufacture of querns. The Danebury examples of Lower Greensand seem to have come from at least one of the same sources — the Vale of Wardour.

The stone types and sources are discussed in greater detail in a general section on all the stone recovered from Danebury (pp 407–8).

Detailed listings of all querns will be found in fiche 12, frames A13–B5).

Rotary querns

Upper stones
Five forms were distinguished and are called R1–R5.
R1 (8.24–8.25; Fig 7.53) The characteristics of this type include a flat or slightly concave upper surface. The stones are generally well finished with vertical or diagonal tooling apparent on the curved outer edges. A hopper is invariably present and is usually in the shape of

a funnel. The handle would have been held in a groove at the top of the stone and the groove intersects the central cavity and/or hopper. The cavity may be either a simple oval shape or oval with small vertical slots at either end. The diameters of querns of this type range from 200 to 380 mm but most are in the 300–340 mm range. Of fifteen examples, all but one are of greensand, the exception being of Feldspatic Grit. Type R1 querns would fit into the category Curwen called the Sussex type, with their flat tops, conical grinding surface, and radially projecting handle groove (Curwen 1937; 1941).

R2 (8.26–8.27; Fig 7.54) The general shape of this type is similar to that of R1 but the handle groove terminates before reaching the central cavity and no hopper is present. Querns of this type are not as well finished as those of Type R1 and some have no finish at all, being roughly cut to shape. Their general characteristics, however, do conform to the Sussex type. Diameters range from 280 to 380 mm but only three of six examples were complete enough to allow for diameter measurement. All six are made from greensand.

R3 (8.28-8.29; Fig 7.55) A beehive (or domed) top characterizes this type, along with an apparently small diameter and a fairly rough finish. The grinding surface is generally semispherical. None of the four examples preserves complete central perforations, handle sockets, or grooves; in consequence the means of fixing the handle is uncertain. Since, however, the top is not flat enough to take a groove, a socket in the side (as in Type R4 below) can probably be assumed. None of the stones was complete enough for exact determination of the diameter, but the general size and shape seems smaller and more compact than the other types. All four querns are greensand.

R4 (8.30–8.31; Fig 7.55) Querns of this type are large and heavy with diameters of 400 to 420 mm and surviving heights up to about 220 mm. The central cavity is oval in shape and the handle would have been held in a socket about halfway down the side of the stone. The hopper is basin-shaped with well-defined and fairly steep sides forming a rounded ridge about the periphery of the stone. The grinding surface is usually semispherical. The basic characteristics of this type and of Type 3 conform

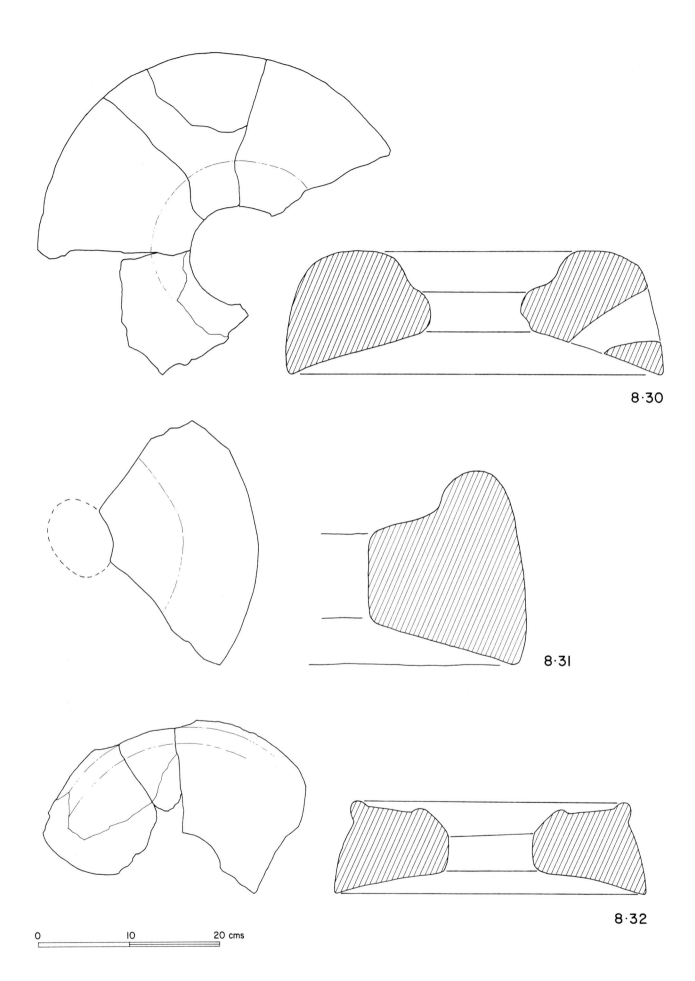

Fig 7.56 Rotary querns: types R4 (8·30, 8·31) and R5 (8·32)

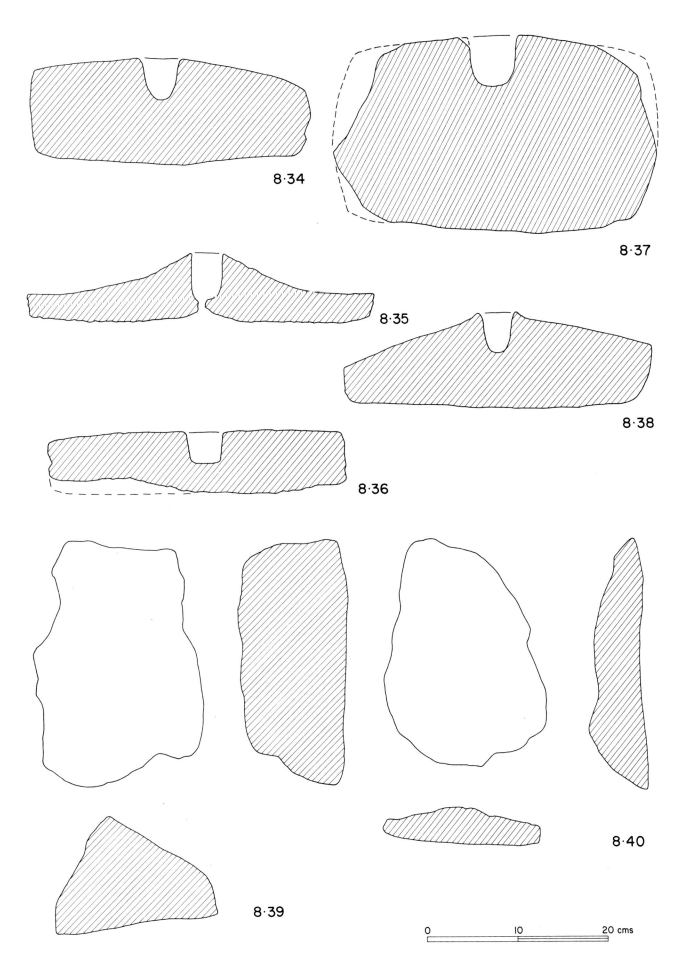

8·34

8·37

8·35

8·38

8·36

8·39

8·40

0   10   20 cms

Fig 7.57 Rotary querns, lower stones, and saddle quern

417

Table 42 Quern sizes

mm	Greensand	Pink ss	Millstone Grit	Brown ss	Grey ss
220	1				
280-300	1				
300	2				
320	4				
320-340	1				1
340	3				
350	1				
340-360	1				
360	6			1	
360-380	1				
380	4				
380-400	2	1			
400	3	2	2		

to Curwen's Wessex type (Curwen 1937; 1941). Of six examples, four are of greensand and two of Millstone Grit. Two lower stones of Millstone Grit with the same diameter size have also been recovered, one from the same feature as one of the upper stones (P110), so the two probably go together.

R5 (8.32; Fig 7.55) Only one example of this type has been recovered from the site. The quern has a flat upper surface (as R1 and R2) but with a small ridge around the top. Another ridge of the same size defines the edge of the hopper and the stone is well finished. Only half the quern survives and this shows no evidence of a handle slot or socket. The diameter is 340 mm and the material is Upper Greensand. Although essentially a variation of R1 type, it was thought necessary to place the stone in a separate category because of the distinctive ridges.

Lower stones (8.33–8.37; Fig 7.57)
Of the lower stones recovered 59 were made from greensand (almost 77%). Of the remainder, nine fragments were of pink sandstone, four of Millstone Grit, two of brown sandstone, and one each of white sandstone, grey sandstone, and sarsen. Thirty-six of the stones were complete enough to allow a measurement of diameter. Table 42 shows the results.

The fact that Millstone Grit was used for larger querns is obvious not only here but also in the typology of upper stones (see Type R4). The Tertiary sandstones (white, pink, brown, etc) seem only rarely to have been used in the manufacture of rotary querns, but Table 42 indicates that when pink sandstone was used it was for larger querns, whereas the general size of the white and brown sandstone examples is more in keeping with the average smaller size of the greensand querns.

It was possible only in one case definitely to match a lower stone with an upper (sf 350). It is likely, however, that the Millstone Grit examples match with examples of upper stones of Type R4 — the large, heavy form. In all cases except two (sf 46 and sf 808) the lower stones display the convex shape characteristic of Curwen's Wessex and Sussex types (Curwen 1937; 1941). Of the

two exceptions, which display the flat grinding surface of the Hunsbury type (Curwen 1941), one is one of the large pink sandstone examples and the other (sf 46) is a smaller and rather fragmentary greensand quern.

Since all the upper stones (Types R1–5) have the angled grinding surfaces of the Wessex and Sussex types, it is difficult to say whether the two lower stones with flat surfaces definitely represent examples of the Hunsbury tradition or whether they happened to wear in a peculiar manner. In any case, it did not seem that the presence of these two stones warranted the creation of a Type R6 rotary quern which had no upper stones to represent it.

The saddle querns and rubbing stones (8.38-8.39; Fig 7.57)

Saddle querns and rubbing stones represent about 30% of querns from the site. There are two basic types of saddle querns: small, oval-shaped stones, usually displaying some degree of finish and usually in greensand, and larger, block-shaped querns with less evidence of shaping and often made in pink or white sandstone.

The variety of stone used in the manufacture of saddle querns and rubbing stones was much greater than in the case of rotary querns. The same basic range of materials was used (ie greensand and Tertiary sandstones) but the percentage of greensand is lower than in the case of rotary querns. For the saddle stones greensand represents 79% and for rubbing stones 42%, in comparison with 89% greensand for rotary querns. There are no examples of saddle stones or rubbing stones made from Millstone or other gritstones whereas these form a noticeable if not high percentage in the rotary type. The variety of stone is especially notable in the rubbing stones where a rare example of Devonian red sandstone is present along with the more commonly occurring sarsen and Tertiary white, pink, and ferruginous sandstones.

Chronology

The notion that the use of the saddle quern ceased with the early Iron Age (Curwen 1937) and was completely superseded by the rotary quern does not seem to hold true on the basis of the evidence from Danebury and from Balksbury and Gussage All Saints (Wainwright 1979, 89). When all the querns are dated on the basis of ceramic associations the pattern appears to indicate a continuous though definitely declining use of saddle querns throughout the Iron Age occupation of the hillfort. Of the datable examples of saddle and rubbing stones, 73% fall into the ceramic phase range earlier than cp 7, but the remaining percentage is too significant to be said simply to represent residual material.

The later appearance of rotary querns is, however, quite clear. All examples of Types R2–R5 are of ceramic phases 7 or 8. The only complete quern (sf 350) came from the top layer of a pit which was given a ceramic phase 3 date on the basis of a very small number of early sherds and must, therefore, be considered unreliable. The earliest, reliably dated, rotary quern (a Type R1) appears in a cp 5 context. There are also three examples of the type from cp 6 pits. These form only a small proportion of the Type R1 querns, however, and the general date of that type seems compatible with that of Types R2–R5. In terms of real chronology this would suggest that the rotary querns were beginning to be introduced no earlier than the 4th century BC. The argument based on the evidence from Gussage All Saints (Wainwright 1979, 89) that rotary querns were introduced much earlier in the Iron Age is, therefore, contradicted by the Danebury chronology.

Fig 7.58 Chalk marl disc (scale 1:4)

Chalk marl discs (8.40–8.42; Fig 7.58)

Thirty-six large discs made from chalk marl were recovered from the excavations. Some were perforated, others not, but the majority were so fragmentary that there was no evidence either way. In many cases, even the diameter could not be ascertained.

The number of discs per ceramic phase is as follows: cp 3 — 5 (13.9%); cp 6 — 6 (16.7%); cp 7 — 20 (55.5%); cp 7/8 — 1 (2.8%); cp 8 — 1 (2.8%); undated — 3 (8.3%). Thirty-four were found in a total of 27 pits, the remaining two coming from postholes.

On the basis of the more complete examples, the diameters range from 215–380 mm and the height from 35–75 mm. Some are not quite circular, having slightly sub-rectangular faces. In one or two cases, part of the outer, circular edge has been chopped straight. Most of the discs appear to have been initially carefully shaped, the outer edges having been neatly cut, probably with a metal blade. In one case (sf 431), a blade mark 7 mm wide was visible on the outer surface. Toolmarks frequently survive within the perforations, which appear to have been cut from one side with a small gouge or awl. The toolmarks are frequently weathered, but not worn smooth as though something had been inserted into the perforation. Frequently, one face has been worn very smooth whilst the other is rough and weathered, with layers of marl peeling away. In most cases the outer edges and/or the rougher surface have been extensively burnt. There is sometimes evidence of burning around the perforation as well.

No close parallels to these objects have been found in the published literature. It was at first thought that they may be flywheels of the type found at Hod Hill (Richmond 1968, 17, pl 2B) made from lias limestone. Since, however, some are definitely not perforated, and since even those which are do not have the right sort of wearmarks, on balance, this is highly unlikely. Neither are there any wearmarks which would indicate that they were tied or suspended to be used as rick weights or thatch weights. It is apparent, however, that they were consistently in use in a context where burning or smoking occurred. The fact that many have one weathered and one unweathered side indicates that they lay flat on one side. The pattern of the burning suggests a function as some sort of oven or kiln lid, but this cannot be clearly demonstrated by the rather meagre evidence so far recovered.

Chalk weights (8.43–8.56; Figs 7.59, 7.60)

One hundred and forty-four chalk weights were recovered from the excavations. Four were found in postholes, five in layers, and 135 in a total of 58 pits. Twenty-five of the pits produced more than one weight, the maximum number found in one context being fourteen.

The number of weights per ceramic phase is as follows: cp 1/3 — 37 (25.7%); cp 4 — 15 (10.4%); cp 5 — 4 (2.8%); cp 6 — 4 (2.8%); cp 7 — 76 (52.8%); cp 8 — 3 (2.1%); undated — 5 (3.4%).

The distribution patterns of the weights are distinguished more by obvious blank areas than by concentrations. The two most apparent blanks are the areas above the line of the main road in the 1969–75 excavated area, and the western part of the area at the northern end (grid north) of the site. The distribution plot appears otherwise to be fairly uniform and is not very informative. Occasional clusters of two or three pits containing weights seem to be insignificant. In two cases weights' were associated with circular structures, CS7 and CS5, the latter sharing a context with a chalk spindle whorl, and in nine pits weights were found with chalk spindle whorls.

There is a very wide morphological range. At one end of the scale are weights which have been very carefully shaped and finished and at the other are natural chalk fragments, unmodified apart from a countersunk perforation at one end. The shapes are difficult to describe in some cases, especially those in the latter category, but a general range of types can be characterized as follows: triangular (or roughly triangular), pyramidal, sub-rectangular, wedge-shaped, pear-shaped, cylindrical, diamond-shaped, oval, shouldered, and completely irregular. Usually, the most deliberately shaped weights are triangular, and several roughouts of this type were found. The most common shapes were triangular, sub-rectangular, and wedge-shaped.

All of the weights have countersunk perforations, usually at one end of the stone, but, in a few cases, centrally placed. A favoured position for the perforation seems to have been 25–60 mm from the top edge. The diameters of the perforations were measured at three points, the two ends and the centre. The narrowest perforation was 15–7–15 mm, the widest end measurement was 70 mm, and the widest central measurement 32 mm. The majority fell midway between the two extremes.

The size and weight varied considerably. The minimum height measured was 120 mm, the maximum 260 mm. The weight ranged from 873.8 gm to 3200.0 gm (on the basis of complete examples only), but most weighed between 1 and 2 kg. In several of the pits, including P264, 530, 542, and 1026 which contained more than one weight, the evidence suggests that the discarded weights were part of a set because their weights in grams relative to one another are so close (p 422). It is significant, however, that in these cases there is rarely a correlation between shape and weight.

Wearmarks/toolmarks

Toolmarks are frequently preserved on the weights, especially in the case of roughouts and particularly within the perforations. The toolmarks within the perforations clearly indicate that in most, if not all, cases the holes were countersunk, often resulting in an hourglass shape. In many cases, the workings from the two sides did not meet properly, and a sort of 'dogleg' shape resulted. The marks suggest the use of a small pointed implement,

419

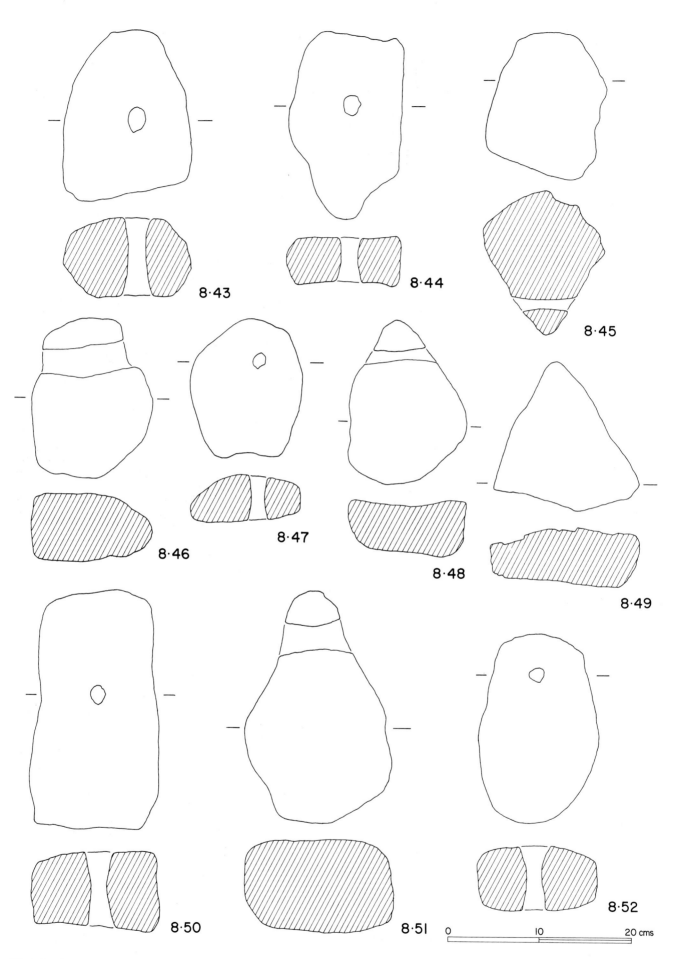

8·43

8·44

8·45

8·46

8·47

8·48

8·49

8·50

8·51

8·52

0   10   20 cms

Fig 7.59 Selected chalk weights

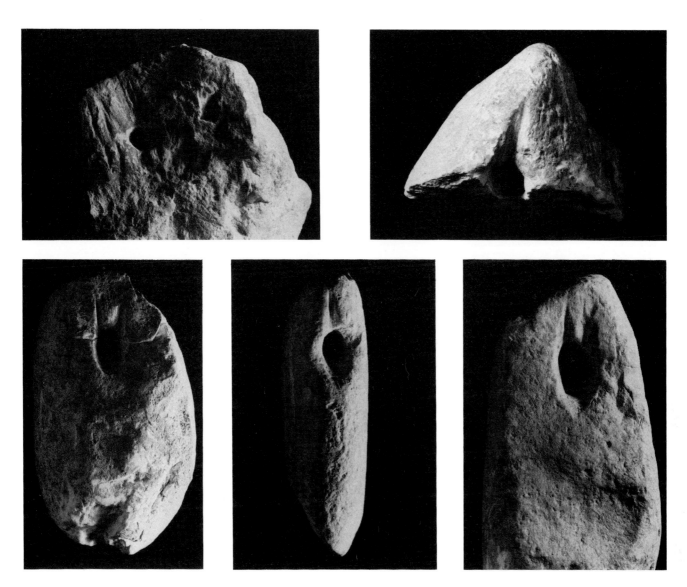

Fig 7.60 Chalk weights showing wear marks and tool marks (scale approx. 1:2; photo: Bob Wilkins)

perhaps some sort of awl, in most cases, and a gouge of varying widths in others. The marks from these tools normally run lengthways along the perforation, and are best preserved on the base and sides, which are usually less worn. In a very few cases there is evidence that a narrow, flat blade was used to finish the perforation, both across its length and around the edges, where circular striations suggest a turning or coring motion.

Far fewer toolmarks survive on the outer surfaces of the weights, which are often battered and weathered. The marks most frequently surviving are adze marks (generally 20–50 mm wide) and parallel scoremarks produced by a similar pointed implement to that cutting the perforation. This tool seems to have been used to give a final finish because it often overlies blade/adze marks. Three triangular roughouts (sf 446 A, B, C), almost certainly for weights, show clearly the process of shaping. In all three cases the initial shaping was done by a flat blade 10–15 mm wide, and secondary finishing was done with an adze, whose marks cut across the first ones at right-angles. In a very few cases, the evidence indicates that a fragment of chalk was roughly chopped to shape by a large blade, perhaps an axe of some sort.

Wearmarks were frequently preserved on the weights, chalk being an ideal material for recording wear. The marks record, to a surprising degree of detail, the means of suspending the weights. In the majority of cases, wear grooves rise vertically, or at a slight angle, from the top of the perforations. The grooves frequently take the following pattern: on one side, double parallel wear grooves, usually 3–5 mm wide and 7–10 mm apart, emanate from the top edge of the perforation; on the other side a single groove, frequently wider and less distinct, also rises vertically. In one case the groove could be traced to the top of the stone. This pattern of wear suggests that a looped string or narrow rope was passed through the perforation.

The wear pattern does, however, vary. Sometimes there are double grooves on both sides, or single on both. Often only one side shows signs of wear. In some cases, a wide, fan-shaped mark indicates suspension by a loose group of strands rather than a string. Often, the evidence is no more specific than a faint rub mark and smoothness on the outer top edge of the perforation. Generally the top of the interior of the perforation shows a great deal more wear than the base and sides.

421

In two cases (sf 267 and sf 391), a wear groove runs horizontally around the side of the stone from the side of the perforation. There is no evidence, however, from the Danebury collection as a whole, to substantiate Cunnington's theory (1923) that chalk weights were, as a rule, suspended horizontally rather than vertically. Unlike the Danebury weights, those from All Cannings Cross (and other examples in Devizes Museum) had wear marks at the base rather than the top of the perforation.

Sometimes the wearmarks are clear enough to preserve the impressions of individual strands or twists of fibre. In the case of sf 668, nine individual strands could be counted.

Comparisons

The range of forms is closely comparable to the Maiden Castle and Hod Hill examples. Wheeler has attempted roughly to classify the Maiden Castle collection by morphological type, and his five types all have close parallels within the Danebury group. Richmond describes the Hod Hill weights as matching Wheeler's types in some instances. Neither, however, can see any chronological significance in the different types, and this is also the case at Danebury.

Wheeler and Richmond do not specifically discuss wear patterns, but in one of the illustrations from Maiden Castle (Wheeler 1943, fig 100, no 6) the double vertical wear grooves show clearly.

Function

In the initial stages of the examination of the chalk weights, it was assumed that they did not all serve the same function. It seemed reasonable to think that the smaller and generally well-finished examples were loom weights, especially those which resembled the triangular clay loom weights in shape and form. Alternative uses for the larger, cruder examples might be thatch weights, rick weights, or door weights. Further examination has indicated that there is no real evidence to show that any of the weights were other than loom weights. The possibility that some served other functions cannot be completely discounted.

Ethnographic and archaeological studies have shown that loom weights vary enormously in shape and size, from small, rounded stones with circumscribed grooves for taking the warp to large, unshaped perforated fragments. The Danebury weights fit easily within the range. Ethnographic parallels from Scandinavia suggest a means of suspension which would have produced exactly the wear patterns preserved on the Danebury weights. Hoffman (1964) describes loom weights used in the present century in Norway and in Scotland. A string or small rope was passed through the perforation and tied loosely. The warp threads would then have been tied to this 'handle' rather than passed through the perforation itself. Alternatively, a looped string was passed through the perforation and its single strand then tied to a bunch of warp threads. These two systems could have produced both the double and single, and the single and single wear groove patterns found on the Danebury stones. Occasionally, warp threads were tied directly to the weight, as suggested by the wear on two or three of the weights.

A second point concerns the weight (in grams) of the objects. Hoffman describes modern weavers in the process of setting up a piece of work on a warp-weighted loom. In order to achieve the correct tension on each shed, it was necessary to weigh each stone and select a matching set to attach to the warp. The weight range of the Danebury collection varies enormously, but it was found in several cases that a group of weights recovered from the same context could be considered a set (or sometimes two sets) on the basis of their relative weights. The best example is a set of seven complete weights from P264, which have a weight range of 1986.4 gm to 2210.0 gm. Pits 530, 542, and 1026 produced smaller, but similar sets.

On the basis of the wear patterns and the weight of the objects, it seems reasonable to regard the function of these objects as loom weights for a vertical loom. Perhaps the different sizes were used to produce varying products, but Hoffman has also shown that the use of heavy stones did not mean that a fine cloth could not be produced.

The weights are individually described in fiche 12, frames B9–C14.

Chalk spindle whorls and other perforated chalk discs (Figs 7.61, 7.62, nos 8.57–8.69)

The excavations produced 53 chalk spindle whorls. Included in this category are several objects which, although similar in general shape and manufacture to the main body of whorls, are of a size which suggests that they were too large for spinning. It is possible that they are either drill weights or even small flywheels. Since, however, it is difficult to know where to draw the line in terms of size and weight, these objects are included with the spindle whorls, and the doubtful ones noted in the 'comments' section of the catalogue (fiche 12, frames D1–4).

The number of whorls per ceramic phase is as follows: cp 1/3 — 5 (9.4% of the total); cp 3/4 — 1 (1.9%); cp 4 — 1 (1.9%); cp 5 — 3 (5.7%); cp 6 — 4 (7.5%); cp 7 — 25 (47.2%); cp 7/8 — 1 (1.9%); cp 8 — 5 (9.4%); undated — 8 (15.1%).

Forty were recovered from pits, two from postholes, and the remainder from layers. In all, 34 separate pits produced spindle whorls.

The spindle whorls were scattered fairly uniformly (and sparsely) over the excavated area of the fort, although there was a slight concentration in the area closest to the east entrance. The only significant concentration was a group of five cp 7 spindle whorls (sf 114, 78, 151, 292, 187) found in five separate pits which were close together, located in an area to the south of Road 1. Another spindle whorl (sf 111) was found in a well-dated cp 3 pit close to this same group. Two were associated with round houses CS20 and CS5. It is not surprising that no particular areas of the site seemed to be devoted to spinning since it is a 'portable' activity.

The chalk spindle whorls do not display a wide morphological range. They are basically disc-shaped (ie with a larger diameter than height measurement). There are variations within this general type range. Some have convex faces, some one flat face and one convex, some are much thicker than others, and some almost oval in section. These variations seem to depend a great deal more on quality of finish than deliberate design. Those with the best finish are generally the flattest and have either neatly rounded or sharply angled outer edges. Some of the whorls are very crudely shaped, with no attempt made to produce even surfaces. The disc shape of the chalk spindle whorls is interestingly different to that of the clay examples, which are usually biconical or round (or oval in section). There are no stone whorls from Danebury (except for two Kimmeridge shale examples), but the chalk whorls are of a similar range of shape to stone versions found, for example, at Glastonbury.

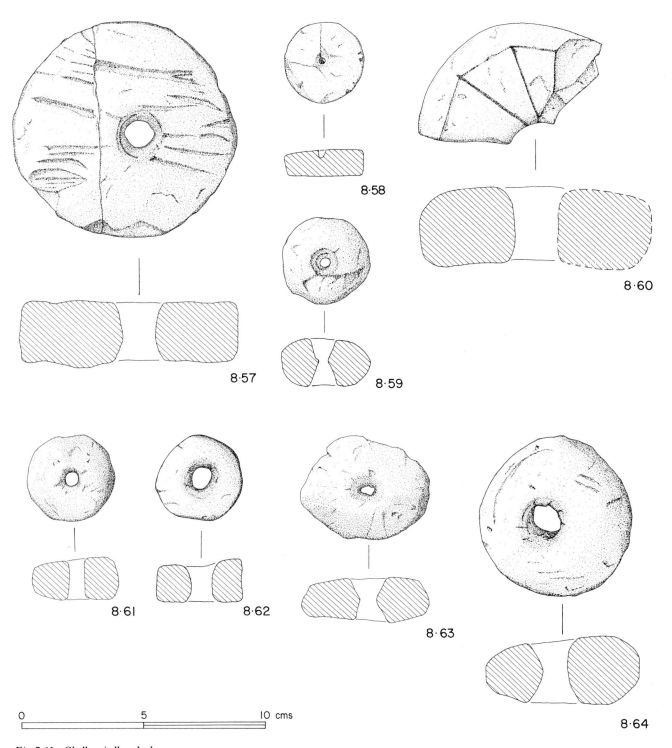

8·58

8·60

8·57

8·59

8·61

8·62

8·63

8·64

0   5   10 cms

Fig 7.61   Chalk spindle whorls

A second characteristic shared by all but a possible one or two of the objects is a centrally-placed, countersunk perforation, which often has an hourglass-shaped section. In several examples the perforation is slightly off-centre, and, in one instance, the maker obviously abandoned the product because the two initial perforations do not meet. In one or two cases the perforation appears to have been cut from one surface only.

Two spindle whorls are decorated, but both are fragmentary, so the total design can only be assumed. One motif consists simply of an incised circular line centring around the perforation, located about halfway between the outer edge and the perforation (sf 930). The second consists of an incised circle near the outer edge intersected by incised lines (spokes) radiating from the perforation (8.60).

The size of the spindle whorls ranges from a diameter measurement of 25 mm to one of 160 mm, and their weight ranges from 6.5 gm to 1246.8 gm. The diameter (measured at a central point) of the perforations varies from 3–33 mm. It is considered that those with an overall diameter greater than approximately 100 mm and a weight over 300 gm are more likely to have served a different function. Sf 1383, especially, a perforated,

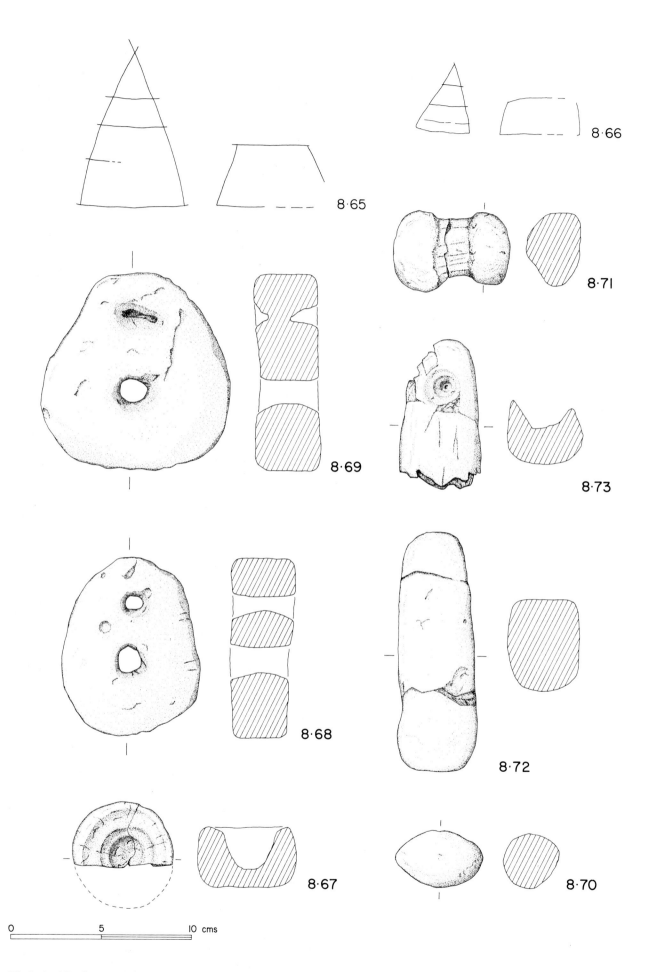

8·65

8·66

8·71

8·69

8·73

8·68

8·72

8·67

8·70

0   5   10 cms

Fig 7.62   Miscellaneous chalk objects

discarded roughout, is far too large and heavy to serve the purpose of a conventional spindle whorl.

There is no apparent correlation between the finer differences in size and shape and the ceramic phase of the context containing the whorls. Furthermore, when two or three are found together in one context, there are no particular similarities between them.

Wear patterns

Most of the spindle whorls are very worn and/or weathered, and several are burnt, resulting in a paucity of clear toolmarks. In those cases in which toolmarks are preserved (generally in unfinished examples), the marks indicate the use of a small, pointed implement 1–2 mm wide to cut the perforation, sometimes with the additional use of a flat blade of some description to turn the outer edges with a circular motion. In eight cases, flat blade marks, measuring 20–50 mm, are preserved on the outer surfaces, and, in one case each, narrow gouge marks and point marks, used to make the perforation, survive.

None of the spindle whorls manifests specific wear patterns. In all cases, excluding the unfinished examples, the interior of the perforation has been worn completely smooth, and the presumed original hourglass shape sometimes worn nearly vertical. This could easily be accomplished by frequent jamming and twisting of the whorls onto the spindles to make them hold. Even in the case of the larger discs thought not to be spindle whorls, the wear is similar. There is no evidence of any having been suspended. If they were used as small flywheels they would presumably have suffered similar wear to that sustained by spindle whorls.

Comparisons

In general size and shape, the Danebury spindle whorls are similar to the range found at Hod Hill, All Cannings Cross, and Maiden Castle (although Maiden Castle produced a more extensive range of elaborate shapes and decoration). The disc shape with countersunk perforation seems to be the general pattern. Furthermore, the range of decoration is similar. Spindle whorls with incised circles and/or radiating lines were found on all three sites. Unfortunately, none of the published examples were accompanied by descriptions of toolmarks or wear, but on the basis of the illustrations, the wear within the perforations, the general finish of the stones (usually fairly rough), and their present condition are similar. In considering the larger class of objects (mentioned earlier), Cunnington (1923) described a perforated disc approximately 130 mm in diameter, and mentioned that it seemed too large and heavy to have been used as a spindle whorl, but did not suggest an alternative use.

The Danebury assemblage of chalk spindle whorls is rather modest, but large enough to give a general range of shape and size. Considering the size of the smallest examples (25–30 mm in diameter), it is unlikely that many were missed in excavation. Since chalk was not the only material used in their manufacture (clay, bone, and possibly wood were also used), a sufficient number were recovered to indicate that spinning/weaving constituted a substantial part of the domestic activity on the site, especially in the later period.

Miscellaneous chalk objects (Fig 7.62, nos 8.65–8.73)

Worked chalk blocks with graffiti:
8.65 and 8.66 Two crudely worked chalk blocks were found in the same context, which, although differing in size, share a number of characteristics. Both have a crudely hollowed surface, and, on equivalent faces, a small incised triangle which is divided into four parts by parallel lines. A second symbol, a trapezoid, is found on different faces on the two stones. The context probably represents the top of a pit (P13) buried beneath the south hornwork of the entrance. The chalk blocks were amongst chalk rubble covering an ox skull and leg bone.
8.67 Carefully worked small bowl/cup.
8.68 and 8.69 Two flat, pear-shaped objects, perforated through the narrow end and through the centre; one unfinished.
8.70 Single chalk sling shot.
8.71 A small 'dumb-bell' shaped object, burnt.
8.72 Carved phallus, 120 mm in length.
8.73 Small carved cylindrical object, possibly phallic, with a small hole cut near the top and a long hollow along the length.

Six other chalk objects of miscellaneous form are described in fiche 12, frames E1–3.

Sling stones

Many thousands of water-worn oval and spherical pebbles, conventionally called sling stones, have been found at Danebury. The largest single deposit was a group of 11,000 found in pit 911 just inside the main gate in 1976. That many of the pits in the vicinity of the gate contained quantities, and that several thousand were found in the excavation of the east entrance, particularly along the flank of the north inner hornwork, strongly suggests that the pebbles were used as missiles for defensive purposes. Chronologically they are found in pits of all periods but the quantity increases dramatically in cp 7.

In 1977 a sample of 1,000 sling stones was collected from cp 7 pits close to the entrance. Mr C E Everard of the Department of Geography, Queen Mary College, London, undertook to examine them in order to ascertain their origins. His detailed report will be found in fiche 12, frames E4–98, on which the following comment is based.

An assessment of the weights of the Danebury sample, considered in relation to samples collected at random from local Tertiary pebble deposits, reveals that a considerable degree of selection occurred. The vast majority of Danebury stones fall within the weight range 29.5–109.5 gm. The only comparative archaeological data derive from Maiden Castle, Dorset, where considerable numbers of sling stones were recovered. The recorded weight range of these is between ½–2 oz (14.17–56.69 gm) with the majority gravitating towards the heavier end of this scale. The discrepancy between the weight of the Danebury and Maiden Castle samples might be of ballistic significance, perhaps indicative of the manner in which they were used, whether singly or in groups.

It was hoped that the detailed analysis of the Danebury specimens would provide precise information about the source from which the stones were derived. In practice the somewhat homogeneous nature of the pebble deposits in the vicinity of the site means that this aim could not be realized. While the *in situ* flints within the chalk of the hill itself are morphologically quite different from the sling stones, it is not impossible that Danebury was at one time capped with a small outlier of Tertiary pebbles which has since been either removed or else severely disturbed.

The nearest known sources of suitable stones are the gravel terraces of the River Test, although it should be noted that pebbles do not dominate these deposits. One

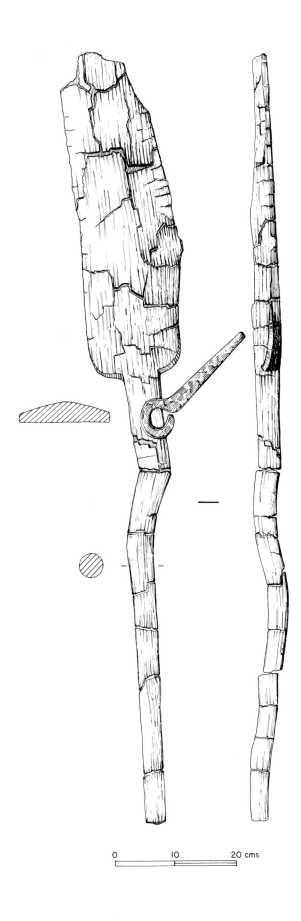

Fig 7.63 Oak shovel

location which contains a preponderance of stones of the right size and shape lies in Harewood Forest 8 km from Danebury.

The main pebble beds of the Hampshire Basin are to be found as lenses within certain horizons in the Reading Beds, the London Clay, and the Bagshot Sands. Since Reading Beds clay was certainly transported to Danebury for use on the site, it is by no means improbable that the two commodities were derived from the same source and imported together.

7.1.12 Wooden shovel or paddle (Fig 7.63)
by Barry Cunliffe

On the bottom of pit 925, of cp 7 date, a number of large pieces of wood, converted to charcoal, were found. Of these one, small find 9.1, survives largely intact and in good shape. The object, made from a single piece of oak, consists of a blade and a handle. The handle is of circular section, 710 mm in length, and increases in diameter from the end (34 mm) to the junction with the blade (60 mm). The blade now measures 520 mm long by 160 mm wide and is 34 mm in maximum thickness. Originally it appears to have been parallel-sided but intense burning at the tip and on one side has destroyed the original shape of the end. Other characteristics will be apparent from the illustration. Several iron objects (2.140, 2.192) were found in close proximity and one (2.191) was rusted on to the charcoal of the handle. The iron fittings do not appear to have been part of the wooden object.

The remarkable preservation of the item is probably due to the fact that it caught fire and continued to burn very slowly after chalk and soil had fallen on to it damping down the intensity of the blaze.

Iron Age parallels for the Danebury object are difficult to find, the closest being a wooden shovel from the salt mines of Hallstatt (now in the Naturhistorisches Museum, Vienna; for convenient illustration see Kromer 1963, Taf 61). The Hallstatt example is of broadly similar shape with a handle c 470 mm in length and a parallel-sided blade measuring c 420 by 156 mm. It differs from the Danebury object in that its handle is somewhat shorter and the shoulders of the blade, where it joins the handle, are more sloped.

The intended function of these objects is uncertain. The Hallstatt example is generally considered to be a shovel. The Danebury example could well have been used in this way, perhaps to shovel grain. Alternative uses, as a paddle, baker's pallet, or even a stirrer for clay in the conical clay pits, cannot be ruled out.

7.1.13 Briquetage containers (Figs 7.64, 7.65)
by Cynthia Poole

Briquetage containers, or coarse clay vessels associated with the salt industry, have been found at Danebury. The briquetage amounts to 1,119 sherds, weighing 4974 gm. It is found throughout the occupation of the fort, though 68% of it occurs in cp 7 and cp 8 contexts as compared to 8½% from cp 1–3, 12½% from cp 4 and cp 5, and 7½% from cp 6.

Most of the briquetage was deposited as a few broken sherds in the pits, though a few fragments were found in postholes and a larger proportion in the stratified deposits. Most of the material is fairly evenly spread across the fort. Some groups are noticeably larger than others and five of these from the 1978 stratified deposits are concentrated quite close together. However, their contexts vary from cp 4 to cp 7 in date and one cannot be sure that there is any significance in their concentration in the one location.

0   10   20 cms

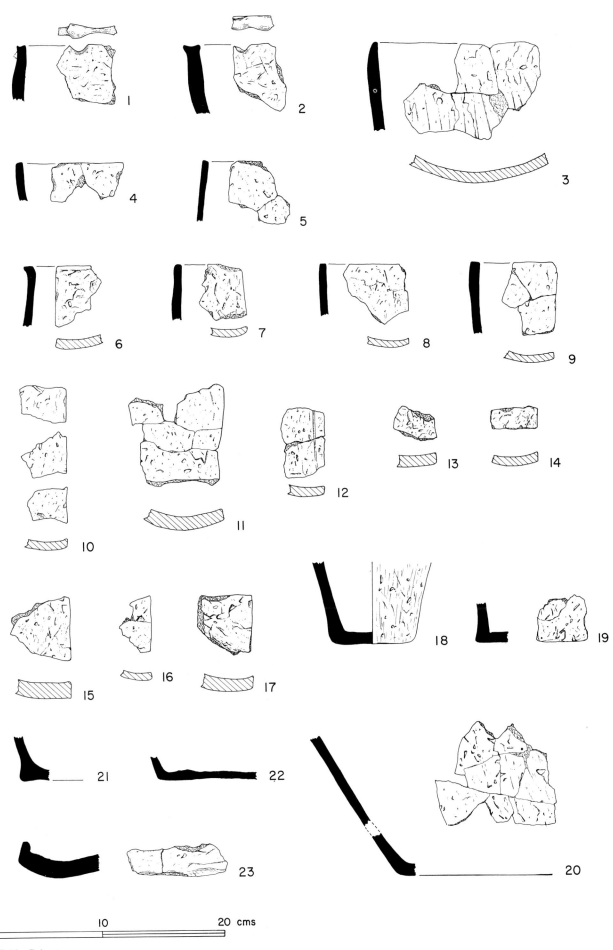

Fig 7.64   *Briquetage*

0   10   20 cms

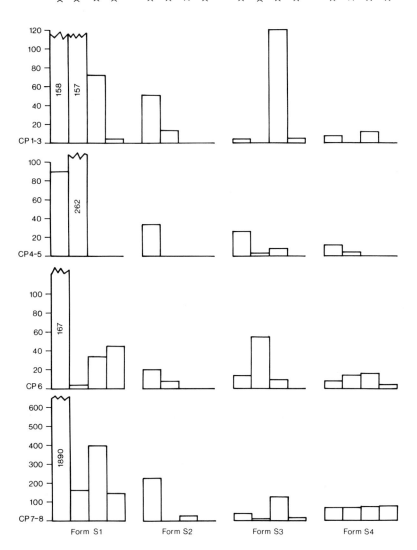

Fig 7.65   *Quantification of briquetage by period, forms, and fabric; form S4 includes all fragments of uncertain form*

Three different forms could be defined, but a small number of pieces were too fragmentary to be assigned to any particular form. It has also been possible to define four different fabrics.

The forms

Form 1 (Fig 7.64, 3–17,19,20,23)
This takes the shape of a cylinder, left open at one end and with a flat base enclosing the other. The rim at the open end usually tapers to a point or is sometimes rounded. It appears that the normal practice was to cut these vessels in half before firing, as one usually finds the flat straight edges at right-angles to the moulded rim. The thickness of the walls varies between 4 mm and 15 mm, but they most commonly measure 7–8 mm. The base is usually thicker, 10 mm-15 mm.

There are several fragments from the base of the cylinder (eg br 10, 11, and 23). These show the base to be flat with an angular edge, sometimes slightly splayed, on the outside, but curved inside. These pieces indicate an external diameter of 80 and 140 mm (Fig 7.64, 19, 20, 23).

Most fragments however come from the walls of the containers. There are four groups, which each contain substantial amounts of a cylinder, though it has not been possible to establish whether both halves are represented. Enough fragments have come from pit 32 (br 14–20, Fig 7.64, 6, 10, 17) to make it likely that two half-cylinders are present. They indicate diameters of *c* 80, 100, 140 mm and *c* 160 mm. Pit 994 has produced a substantial part of a half-cylinder (br 56, Fig 7.64, 20), which has a diameter of 140 mm and a length greater than 170 mm. There are also large numbers of broken fragments of one or more cylinders from layers 496 (br 66, 67, Fig 7.64, 11) and 497 (br 68, 69). It has been possible to join several of the rim fragments together and the diameters measure 160 and 120 mm, though no more than 110 mm survives as a continuous length.

A large quantity of briquetage from layer 410 (br 70, Fig 7.64, 3) has also been partly reconstructed. Several pieces of the top rim, tapering to a point, survive and indicate a diameter of 200 mm. At least 75 mm of the length survives. But the base fragment measures only 140 mm in diameter, indicating more a bucket or barrel shape. The sherds are thicker than normal, measuring 10–12 mm.

428

Most cylinder fragments indicate a diameter of 100–140 mm, though a small number are outside this range measuring 80, 160, or 200 mm.

Many of the cylinder fragments show evidence of the vertical cut edge through the container. Some pieces (eg br 42 from pit 640) have two cut edges at right-angles. Most of the cut edges are straight and flat but jagged edges in some cases suggest that they were not always cut right through. In some cases the edge is wider than the rest of the wall (eg pit 334, br 30, and pit 553, br 36).

This form is the most common accounting for 81% of all sherds. Half of these are in fabric 1, a quarter in fabric 3 (most of this accounted for by layer 410), followed by fabric 2 (largely layers 496 and 497), with only a small amount in fabric 4.

Form 2 (Fig 7.64, 18)
This form is closest in shape to a flower pot or bucket. It has a flat base with straight sides flaring out slightly. The best example comes from pit 231 (br 25), which produced part of a flat base with a diameter of c 100 mm and the sides beginning to flare out at an angle. The walls are 11–12 mm thick and survive to a height of 70 mm. The total height is unknown and no rim survives. There is no evidence to suggest that it was cut in half like form 1.

This form accounts for only 3.5% of the briquetage and most of it is in fabric 1, though small numbers also occur in the other fabrics.

Form 3 (Fig 7.64, 21, 22.1, 2)
This form is a type of rounded bowl, possibly hemispherical in shape, though most of the fragments found are fairly small so the precise size and shape are not certain. Some pieces are as thin as 4 mm or 5 mm, though most are 7 mm-13 mm thick. There are a number of rim fragments which have been flattened with finger depressions, eg pit 264 (br 26–28) and layer 423 (br 61, Fig 7.64, 1). These rim fragments suggest a diameter of c 180 mm.

Some pieces of base probably belong to these bowls. From pit 872 (br 47, 48, Fig 7.64, 22) comes an almost complete flat base, 120 mm in diameter. An angle piece of the base and side from pit 895 (br 50, Fig 7.64, 21) has a diameter of 120–130 mm.

This form accounts for 7½% of the briquetage sherds. It is most commonly in fabric 3, and less often in the other fabrics.

The fabrics

Fabric 1
This fabric is characterized by its organic temper. Its colour is usually red or reddish-yellow on the surface and dark grey or black inside. It is normally very fissile and porous from the large quantities of chaff used as temper, as evidenced by the impressions and occasionally charred remains left. (The impressions have not yet been identified.) Some pieces have additional tempering material in very small quantities, in particular shell fragments and fine quartz sand. The chaff temper usually remains dominant, though it may decrease in amount when other materials are used. This fabric was used for 47½% of the briquetage and for all forms.

Fabric 2
The distinctive feature of this fabric is that the clay is silty or contains very fine sand. In addition it nearly always contains a small amount of chaff temper from the impressions. There are also small quantities of other materials such as quartz grains or shell fragments in some instances. It is fairly porous though not as much as fabrics 1 and 4. This fabric was used for 18% of the sherds and for all forms.

Fabric 3
This fabric is characterized by the coarse quartz sand temper. It is usually red or reddish-yellow in colour. In addition to the sand it may also contain very occasional small quartz pebbles and other rock fragments or a little chaff temper.

This fabric was used for 27½% of the briquetage and for all forms. However, it is noticeable that it was used more often than the other fabrics for form 3.

Fabric 4
The major characteristic of this fabric is the large quantity of shell temper. Its colour is normally yellowish-red or brown on the outside, though black or grey inside. The broken angular shell fragments normally measure 1–2 mm in size, though may be up to 7 mm in size. The shell source has not yet been identified, but it could be either marine, freshwater, or fossil. Most of the examples also contain a little chaff temper, which makes it fairly porous, and a few fragments contain quartz grains.

This fabric is the rarest type, accounting for only 5½% of the briquetage. It was used for all forms, but mostly for form 1.

Surface treatment
The surfaces are normally plain and smooth, though it is possible to see very fine striations on some pieces, which may be the equivalent of 'brush marks' mentioned on briquetage from other sites. On the pieces of a large cylinder from layer 410 (br 70, Fig 7.64, 3) there are wide vertical ridges, similar to the 'finger-pasting' on a piece of 'Fitzworth' trough from Godlingston Heath, Dorset. The direction of drag of the markings suggests that the purpose was to assist in welding together coils of clay used in forming the cylinder. The only other surface treatment is finger-tipped indentation made around some of the rims of the hemispherical bowls (Fig 7.64, 1 and 2).

Discussion
The most likely sources for Danebury briquetage are the salt-producing sites along the Dorset and Hampshire coasts. Few of the known sites, however, can be definitely assigned to the Iron Age. Farrar (1963) describes briquetage from Wyke Regis, Dorset, which dates to the 1st century BC. Most of the recognizable fragments look like base angles for straight-sided vessels. He also mentions that none of the Dorset briquetage, either Iron Age or Roman, is particularly porous or includes any traces or chaff. It is generally sandy, which would suggest that only those pieces made of fabric 3 at Danebury may come from Dorset.

Calkin (1948) reports sherds from Kimmeridge of cylindrical jars 3-4 ins (70–100 mm) in diameter and ¼-½ in (7–13 mm) thick. The height is not known but often exceeds 4 ins (100 mm). They had been cut in half before firing, though not always right through. These jars are clearly equivalents of form 1 from Danebury, though most of the Danebury examples are slightly larger. Also from Kimmeridge came fragments of small open bowls of hemispherical shape about 140–180 mm in diameter at the rim and 100–120 mm in diameter at the base, sometimes with a hole deliberately near the base.

These bowls seem very similar to the small fragments from Danebury described as form 3, which is often in a sandy fabric and so could have come from the Dorset area. From Warsash, Hampshire (Fox 1935) comes briquetage of a cylindrical shape with splayed-out circular bases up to 5 ins (130 mm) in diameter. The evidence from this and other sites that the bases of cylinders sometimes splayed out suggests that forms 1 and 2 at Danebury may not be valid distinctions, but further evidence is needed to confirm this. Much of the briquetage from the Hampshire coast is tempered with chaff, which makes this a more likely source for much of the Danebury briquetage. Further detailed examination of the fabrics could help in pinpointing the sources more closely.

Riehm (1961) has shown by experiment that the tempering was related to the function. At Halle, Germany, the brine was evaporated in non-porous containers and subsequently dried into uniform cakes in small, mass-produced, standard containers of porous chaff-filled clay made in a goblet shape. The salt was evidently marketed in these small containers. The porous containers split if used for boiling brine, while a low temperature of 60°-70°C was most suitable for drying the salt firmly in the porous goblets. The porous fabric, and in some case holes for draining, assisted this final process. Riehm thought that the British cylindrical jars were used for this final stage and for transporting the salt. Farrar however disputed this, as there seemed no way of easily transporting them cut in half; he thought it more likely that they were used as evaporating troughs. However this seems unlikely for the Danebury briquetage because the half cylinders are open at one end, they are mostly made of a porous fabric unsuitable for heavy heating, and the containers have clearly been transported some distance from the salterns. Why the cylinders were cut in half before firing is not clear unless it was to facilitate division into two equal half-measures. They could have been held together during transport by tying with string.

7.2 Metallurgical analyses

7.2.1. Introduction

It has not, hitherto, been conventional to undertake analyses of copper alloy and iron objects from Iron Age sites. It was felt, however, that the large collection of comparatively well-dated objects from Danebury warranted close examination in order to demonstrate the potential of Iron Age metallurgical studies. The reports offered here by Dr Northover and Mr Salter are the first results of a programme of analysis designed to examine the technological, economic, and social aspects of metallurgy in the British Iron Age.

7.2.2 Analysis of the bronze metalwork
by Peter Northover

At the time of writing samples from 59 bronze objects from the excavations at Danebury have been analysed. They include the dispersed bronze hoard (Cunliffe & O'Connor 1979 and above pp 335–40) and Iron Age objects in both cast and sheet form. The analyses were carried out on the CAMEBAX automated electron probe microanalyser in the Department of Metallurgy and Science of Materials, University of Oxford. The results of these analyses are listed in Table 118. Comparative analyses for the Bronze Age metalwork are given in Table 119. The Iron Age analyses represent the longest series available from Britain at the present time; there are insufficient others to make a comparative table meaningful although other analyses will be mentioned. The Tables will be found in fiche 13, frames A3–10.

Bronze Age

Most of the Bronze Age material derives from a disturbed hoard dating effectively from Late Bronze Age III (Ha C), although including earlier objects.

The hoard contains three objects, two small axes and a rapier, dating from before the Late Bronze Age. Early objects in late hoards are not unknown and it might be reasonable to find such objects in collections of scrap. All three are appropriate to the Hampshire area and have compositions typical of their periods. The As/Ni impurity pattern of the two Early Bronze Age axes was widespread in the British Isles and on the Continent at the time but could, in this case, derive as much from a British source as any other. The impurity pattern of the rapier and the associated high tin content are typical of Taunton metalworking and the transition to Penard metalworking in the southern half of Britain. The metal was almost certainly imported and the tin content is typical of the immediate source area in France.

Several deposits contemporary with the Late Bronze Age material have been analysed although too few to give an

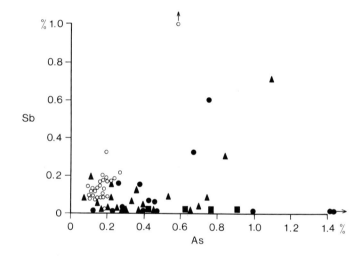

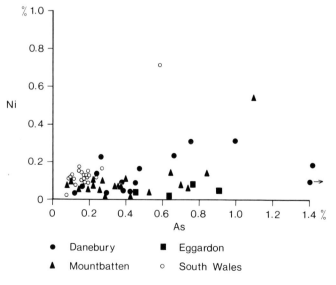

Fig 7.66 Plots of antimony (Sb) against arsenic (As) and nickel (Ni) against arsenic for Late Bronze Age III bronzes

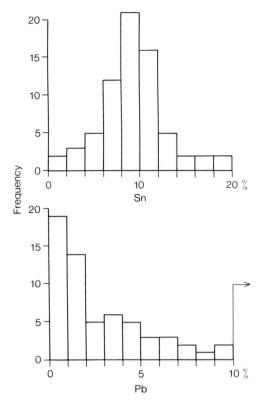

Fig 7.67   The tin (Sn) and lead (Pb) content of Late Bronze Age III bronzes

overall view of the metallurgy of the period. Nevertheless they are still sufficient to demonstrate an appreciable variety in the metal resources available and in use at the time.

The metal types were examined by plotting scatter diagrams of Sb against As and Ni against As (Fig 7.66). Encouragingly the two plots divide the material up in the same way. On the Sb/As plot the Llynfawr and Cardiff hoards from south-east Wales concentrate in a small area between 0.1% and 0.3% As and Sb

They form a similarly tight cluster on the Ni/As diagram. On the other hand the Danebury material as well as the Eggardon hoard are by comparison largely antimony-free. Two interesting exceptions are the two small 'chisels' from Danebury which have analyses very similar to the south Wales types. The finds from Mount Batten, in the south-west of England, are rather more a mixture of the two types.

Immediately we can recognize a difference between the metal in use in southern Wales and that in central southern England; that in use in south-western England shows features of both. The south Welsh type with As/Sb/Ni (probably Ag although the instrument used for these analyses had a rather high detection limit for Ag) is very similar to the metal in use in the preceding Ewart Park phase in this area although the overall levels of impurities are slightly lower. Much of the metal presumably derives from Ewart Park scrap with a relatively small addition of other metals. This continuing circulation of metal of the same type probably relates to the relative absence of any very large hoards of the period which might signify 'dumping' of bronze.

The metal in southern England presents greater problems of interpretation. Traditionally the area was dependent on the Continent for its bronze stocks but there is some evidence (Northover & Pearce forthcoming) to

suggest that local production from south-west England was beginning to make an appreciable contribution to metal stocks during the Ewart Park period. However the evidence must still be regarded as equivocal. The metal presumed to be typical of south-west England has arsenic as its principal impurity with low levels of cobalt, nickel, iron, and silver; antimony is generally absent; the cobalt content, although low, is usually about equal to or greater than the nickel content and can also be present in Co/Fe/As inclusions. This metal, generally alloyed with 9–12% tin, was produced throughout most of the Bronze Age in south-west England. On present evidence it was not until the Late Bronze Age that the metal was carried far from the Devon/Cornwall area. Unfortunately similar metal occurs in Atlantic France but most available results do not include the cobalt. On the evidence of a few obvious imports, such as the Breton socketed axes, cobalt levels in the coppers and bronzes used in France at this time were insignificant but at present we cannot be certain. The best we can do is to suggest that the metal used in southern Britain contains imported material as well as new production from British sources and residual scrap from earlier periods. It may become possible, as more analyses are accumulated, to group metal by alloy type as well. At present (Fig 7.67) we can say that the majority of the material is in the range 9–13% tin and 0–6% lead. Overall levels of lead are lower than in the preceding Ewart Park phase; it is possible that the lead present is largely residual and that lead additions were not a regular feature of the metallurgy of the period. Exceptions to this rule are of course the Breton socketed axes while some other tools have above average lead. The high lead in the Breton axes is associated with low tin in the bronze matrix; this association suggests that some of the bronze cake at Mount Batten also derives from such a source.

Iron Age

Of the 40 Iron Age samples taken, two proved to be entirely corroded. The remaining 38 can be looked at in various ways: according to ceramic phase, whether sheet or cast, by alloy type, or by impurity pattern.

Initially the impurity patterns provide the most inform-

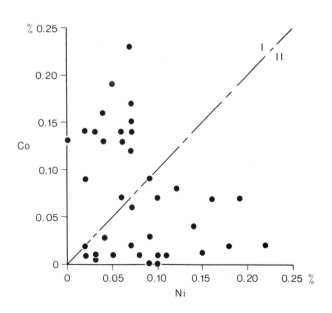

Fig 7.68   Plot of cobalt (Co) against nickel (Ni) for Iron Age bronzes from Danebury showing division into Class I and Class II analyses

431

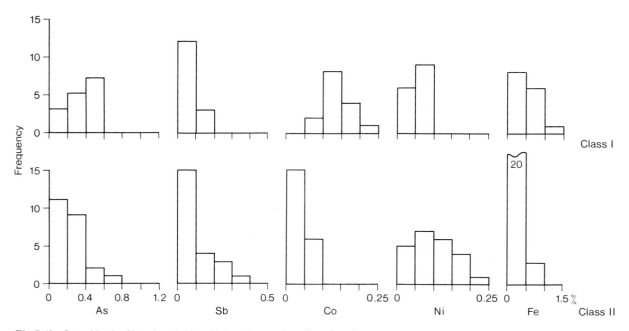

Fig 7.69   Impurities in Class I and Class II Iron Age analyses from Danebury

ation. One very significant feature is the number of compositions in which the cobalt content is greater than the nickel. This feature is very unusual in prehistoric metalwork analysed to date so the first division was made into Class I with Co>Ni and Class II with Co<Ni (Fig 7.68). This done, other elements were compared between the 15 objects in Class I and the 23 in Class II. Besides the reversal of the Ni and Co distributions between the two groups (Fig 7.69) Class I is associated with higher levels of arsenic and iron than Class II while Class II has antimony as a significant impurity which is largely absent in Class I.

This combination of arsenic and no antimony with cobalt, nickel, and iron, sometimes with more cobalt than nickel, we have already suggested as being typical of bronze production in the Bronze Age in south-western England. In the Iron Age material we are discussing here these effects are emphasized. A possible source for them would be the use of a mixed copper/iron ore for the production of copper and iron. The minerals concerned would probably be something like chalcopyrite with some arsenopyrite. Arsenopyrite had been observed to contain significant cobalt impurities (Jenkins in Northover & Burgess forthcoming). The necessary conditions for the coproduction of iron would account for the increase in the iron content above the levels typical of the Bronze Age where iron removal was very efficient. The increases in cobalt and arsenic can be closely associated with this increase in iron. These observations are especially significant in the light of the occurrence of similar impurities in some of the ironwork from the same contexts at Danebury.

The separation of the bronze into the two classes decribed above can be correlated with the chronological sequence of ceramic phases and with the division of objects into sheet metal and castings and other fabrications.

Class I metal occurs in all phases from which bronze has been examined. The material from ceramic phase 3 is too insecurely assigned to that phase and too small in quantity to allow any further comment. Class I metal is most prominent in ceramic phase 7 where it occurs in five

out of seventeen objects. However, four out of those five are sheet while only six out of the twelve Class II analyses in ceramic phase 7 are of sheet. Overall fourteen out of fifteen Class I objects are of sheet while eleven of the 23 Class II analyses are from non-sheet products. In ceramic phase 8, after the period of maximum use of the site, only one out of six analyses is of Class I even though most of the objects are of sheet type. There appears to be no significant variation in tin content between the two classes given the corroded state of many objects. Lead additions are not apparent even in the small cast objects although the metal from which the sheet had been manufactured could originally have been leaded. The zinc content of analysis Da 47 is completely ambiguous. Such zinc contents (about 1%) are very rare in British prehistory but are not completely unknown; on the other hand the date of ceramic phase 7 is such that an element of zinc-containing metal could have been in circulation in Britain, although probably of Continental origin.

We have already associated the production of Class I material with the south-west of England. The additional association with ironworking would not be incompatible with this. We cannot at present suggest an origin for the Class II metal. It is remarkably similar to much Late Bronze Age material which would perhaps suggest a continuing import of bronze and some mixing with British bronze. The possibility of the recovery in the Iron Age of Late Bronze Age material cannot be ruled out.

Clearly in the 2nd century BC (ceramic phase 7) more than one type of bronze was available and there was certainly some degree of specialization in the industry. With the great lack of comparative material we can make no comment at present about the possibilities of bronze-working in the Danebury area. However the chronological variation in the abundance of the two composition groups indicates changes in the pattern of bronze use.

The distinctive nature of the Class I compositions makes them easy to spot when they appear, for instance, in three out of four samples from the bronze decorations on a sword, sword chape, and dagger scabbard from the Thames at Standlake (Northover unpublished). The iron sword from Standlake shows the Danebury high cobalt iron type. A possible Class I analysis occurs as far afield as the Breiddin hillfort, Powys. There the Iron Age metalwork differs in having appreciable lead content except for this particular analysis which matches other Class I analyses in this respect. A fragment of bronze sheet from Mount Batten possibly of Iron Age date also has a Class I analysis (Table 119).

These Iron Age analyses serve to demonstrate the importance of bronze analysis in Iron Age contexts and the possibilities of obtaining information about the operation of the industry.

Sources of analyses

All listed analyses except for Llynfawr and Cardiff hoards by J P Northover in Department of Metallurgy and Science of Materials, University of Oxford. Those two hoards analysed by J P Northover for Board of Celtic Studies, University of Wales at UCNW, Bangor.

Analyses of Standlake hoard by J P Northover and C J Salter at Oxford. Breiddin analyses by Dr P T Craddock at British Museum Research Laboratory, London.

7.2.3 Metallurgical aspects of the ironwork
by Chris Salter

Up to the present date only a small number of studies of the chemical composition of Iron Age artefacts from British contexts have been carried out (Haldane 1970; Hedges & Salter 1979). These have usually involved a relatively small number of objects, from a number of different sites. The purpose of such studies was to determine whether there was any significant inter-site variation in the chemical composition which could act as a means of tracing the trading of iron. The examination of the Danebury ironwork forms part of a second stage in the examination of British Early Iron Age iron. Danebury has provided a fairly extensive collection of metal from different periods and from a wide range of different types of objects from the same site. This has made possible a more extensive sampling programme than is usual with many British Iron Age sites. Altogether 74 objects have been sampled from a total of 278 iron objects examined so far. Unfortunately the time required in cutting, polishing and analysing the samples has been too great to allow a higher sampling rate.

Details of the analyses will be found in Tables 120–5 in fiche 13, frames B1–C7.

Methods

The sampling of each object was carried out by cutting two parallel or two inclined slits using a thin abrasive wheel (wheel thickness 0.3 mm). When two inclined slits were used the sample was freed when the two slits intersected. However, in the case of the parallel slits it was often necessary to drill a hole between the bases of the two slits with a fine high speed drill to allow a fine jeweller's saw blade to be inserted. The sample could then be sawn free. When the sample was free, it was mounted in an electrically conductive resin together with two or three other samples. The samples were then ground and polished in the usual manner for metallurgical examination, with abrasive papers and diamond pastes, down to a final polish using 0.25 micron diamond paste.

The sample was then transfered to the CAMEBAX Electron Microprobe for analysis. The analysis took place in three stages. The first stage analysed the metal at five or six different places on the sample for the elements cobalt, nickel, copper, arsenic, phosphorus, and sul-

phur. The concentration of these elements tended to be low, that is between 0.5 weight percent and the detection limits. Thus, high beam currents and long counting times had to be used (90 nannoamps and 100 seconds) to collect sufficient X-ray counts to obtain statistically significant results. This meant that it required between one and one-and-a-half hours to analyse a single sample for these elements. The next stage was to select five or six representative slag inclusions. Those inclusions containing only iron oxides were rejected from the analysis as virtually all the other elements segregated out of this phase. Once the inclusions were found, they were analysed for the elements sodium, magnesium, aluminium, silicon, phosphorus, sulphur, potassium, calcium, manganese, and iron using the Kevex energy dispersive detector. The results were corrected using the Kevex Magic V correction program. The analysis of the inclusions could be carried out in between fifteen and twenty minutes per sample. Finally, the same inclusions were analysed at high beam currents and long counting times for the elements titanium, vanadium, chromium, strontium, and barium.

After removal from the microprobe, the samples were etched in a 4% nital solution to reveal the microstructure, and finally, the hardness of the samples was determined using a Vicker's Pyramid hardness tester. Table 122 (fiche 13, frame C4) gives a full listing of the analytical results obtained. It should be noted that those results marked * were analsed only for Co, Ni, Cu, As, P, and S because they were too corroded to be able to find any metal or inclusions, so the corrosion products were analysed instead. Those marked ** are the results of the analysis of only one or two inclusions, and therefore may not be representative of the whole object. Table 121 (fiche 13, frames C2–3) correlates the analysis reference number (ie D101, etc) with the site find numbers, the type of object, and the ceramic phase of the context where it was known.

The inclusions

Fig 7.70 illustrates a typical microstructure of an early Iron Age artefact. The darker elongated particles are the slag inclusions. These inclusions occurred in varying proportions of the total surface area of sampled section, the proportion varying from virtually zero in some artefacts to about 5% of the surface area in the 'currency' bars. The analyses performed have shown that there were a number of different classes of inclusions. They could be divided as follows:

1 Those composed mainly (95% or greater) of oxides of iron
2 Those composed mainly of silicon dioxide (90% or greater)
3 The rest, of 'normal' compositions. These have a wide range of composition and structure, and a single inclusion could contain up to three distinct physical phases.

The first two types of inclusions were in general eliminated from the study as it was found that they tended to be relatively pure and free from the minor elements which proved to be important in distinguishing the various groups. The inclusions of type one probably formed during the welding or forging of the artefact, by the oxidization of some of the metal. The inclusions of type two probably represent unreacted quartz grains. These could just possibly have come from the original ore, or it is more likely that they were added as a flux

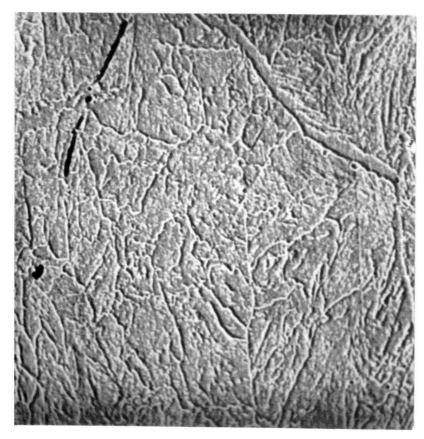

Fig 7.70   Photograph showing a line of fine slag inclusions (top to centre left) in a matrix of iron. The iron was etched in a 2% Nital solution to show the presence of grain boundaries and carbides

during the welding process. When such a grain reacts further with the surrounding iron it can become impossible to distinguish this type of inclusion from those originating from the initial smelting slag. This, therefore, is a possible source of variation that could broaden the group distribution.

The phases present in the 'normal' slag inclusions were, for the most part, the same as those described by Morton and Wingrove (1969; 1972) in bulk Roman and medieval smelting slags. However, in a few currency bars the aluminium content became high enough for hercynite to form. The morphology of these inclusions would be described better by the phase diagram used by Todd and Charles (1978). Most of the inclusions fell into the Morton and Wingrove regime, which consists of the iron silicate fayalite (Fe_2SiO_4), the iron oxide wustite (FeO), and a glass of roughly anorthitic composition ($CaAl_2Si_2O_8$). When the average compositions are plotted on a three component phase diagram (Fig 7.71) similar to that used by Morton and Wingrove, it can be seen that the compositions do not lie in the same areas as the groups defined by those authors. Groups A to C on Fig 7.71 are Morton and Wingrove's groups, where group A represents the compositions of Roman bulk slags formed from rich ores, Group B represents medieval smelting slags formed from rich ores, and Group C those medieval slags formed from poorer Carboniferous nodular ores. It can be seen that the plot of the Danebury inclusions lies further away from the anorthitic part of the diagram and more towards the wustite corner. This could be the result of two processes. Firstly, the reaction between the original slag inclusions and the surrounding metal during forging resulted in

more iron dissolving in the inclusions. The second possibility is that the inclusions were selectively enriched in iron oxides during the forging process. There is some evidence that the wustite phase is more resistant to deformation than the other phases with higher silica contents. This would make it more difficult to expel wustite-rich inclusions from the metal during forging.

Metallography

The metallography of the samples largely reflects the influence of phosphorus on the rate of diffusion of carbon into iron. The relationship was, in general, that where there was a high phosphorus content the carbon content was low. The analysis showed that there was a wide range of phosphorus contents in the metal, from below the detection limit to just above one weight percent. This element would have had some hardening effect of its own on the metal, but it could not have been hardened by quenching and tempering in the way that carbon hardened iron could. The observed carbon contents had a similar range of values, but only rarely were the carbon contents above 0.3 to 0.4 weight percent. Etching also revealed the presence of nitride particles which would have increased the hardness above the value expected from the carbon content. Thus, the presence of these additional elements explains the variations in the hardnesses measured (from 85 to 225 VPN) in those samples with a carbon content below 0.1 weight percent.

The hardest samples were found to be those with the higher carbon contents, but very few samples showed signs that the carbon had been deliberately diffused into the metal. The structures observed were, in the main, of

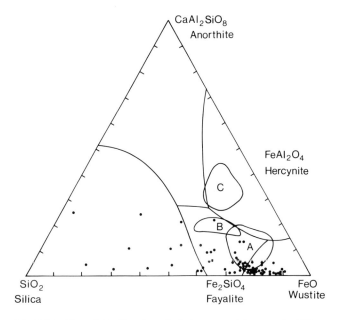

Fig 7.71 Plot of the Danebury inclusion compositions on the Silica-Wustite-Anorthite ternary phase diagram

rather large grain sizes (8 or less per mm) and the presence of spheriodized carbides would suggest that the annealing had been carried on for longer than required for the optimum mechanical properties. Occasionally, a Widmannstaten structure was observed indicating that the metal had been slowly cooled from the austenitic range.

It was noticeable that all the currency bars were of relatively high phosphorus contents (mean 0.314) and thus could not have been easy to harden. However, there were a number of objects with much lower phosphorus contents, presumably because the metal used was smelted from a different ore. This low phosphorus metal would have been much easier to harden than the currency bar metal. It seems clear, therefore, that the people of the hillfort had access to both types of metal and could have chosen to use the low phosphorus metal when they needed to produce artefacts with high strengths. The artefacts from Danebury provided no evidence for the selection of the most appropriate metal for carburization. The artefact that showed the greatest hardness was chisel 2.48 (D157/D158) which had a hardness of 415 VPN at the blade, together with a phosphorus content of 0.74 weight percent.

Objects like this chisel are the most interesting metallurgically, as they would often have had to withstand testing mechanical conditions. Thus, they are the most likely to have been hardened. Table 122 (fiche 13, frame C4) gives a list of the artefacts from those sampled that were likely to have been carburized. This Table shows that the chisels were definitely hardened. The blade of 2.48 (D157/8) had a hardness of 415 VPN against 309 for the shaft of the same object. Not only had the blade been carburized, it had also been quenched, as the structure was a coarse moderate carbon martensite. The socketed chisel 2.46 (D139) had a different method of construction, in that the blade consisted of three strips of metal welded together. The strip that formed the cutting edge had the highest content of 0.8 weight percent, which gave a hardness measurement of 329 VPN. This indicates that this tool again had a quenched blade. The other two strips of metal had much lower carbon contents and were not significantly hardened.

The above tools were obviously woodworking tools. Another chisel was, however, either a general purpose or a metalworking tool. The hardness of the blade of this tool was recorded at 272 VPN, and the shaft recorded at 121 VPN. The carbon content of the blade was 0.3–0.5 weight percent, whereas the content of the shaft was about 0.08 weight percent.

These chisels show that the smiths of ceramic phase 7 could control the properties of the metal to produce suitable microstructures. On the other hand, their choice of starting material was not always the best. This is shown by the high phosphorus content in the chisel D157/8, which would have considerably slowed down the carburization process.

The structures of the other artefacts in Table 121 (fiche 13, frames C1–3) are all rather similar, in that when there were any carbides present they were in the form of spherical particles or partially spheriodized pearlite. The sickles were, unfortunately, often completely corroded, but those that had some metal remaining did not have hardnesses greatly above the normal range shown by the whole collection. The slag stringers of sickle 2.5 (D130) showed that the blade consisted of thirteen to fourteen different layers of metal welded together. This could have been an attempt to improve the properties of the metal. However, it is just as likely that the layering was a relic of the original structure of the bloom of iron from which the object was made. The currency bars often show the same type of structure, with between four and eight strips of metal welded together. It has been suggested that the currency bars represent an intermediate stage in the manufacturing process between the original bloom and the final finished product. It would not, therefore, be surprising to see a similar structure in any artefact manufactured from such a currency bar.

The sample of 2.5 (D130) was in fact much softer than an earlier sickle 2.3 (D154)(ceramic phase 3) which had a high phosphorus content and a hardness of 230 VPN. The knives showed a similar variability in their hardnesses. This suggests that no deliberate hardening was carried out. There were a number of files in the collection (2.55, 2.54 (D133, D172)), one of which, 2.54, had an enhanced carbon content (D172), whereas the other did not. This may or may not be indicative of the tools having been hardened, because a file only requires a thin surface layer or 'case' of carburized material to confer all the hardness required. Such a thin layer of carburized material is likely to have been removed by corrosion leaving no other evidence of hardening. Probably the degree of hardening required would have been low, because the spacing of the teeth (10–13 per 25 mm) was rather large to be used on metal. It is much more likely that such tools were used on materials such as wood and bone.

In summary, it seems that the smiths of ceramic phase 7, at least, had sufficient skill to convert wrought iron into a reasonably good hardened steel when this was required for hard-wearing tools. However, they did not seem able to distinguish between metal with high and low phosphorus levels, although both types of metal were available at Danebury. The level of skill shown in the production of the chisels was well above that shown in the production of most of the other artefacts. It is possible that the occupants of Danebury tolerated knives and sickles that became blunt quickly, but required woodworking tools that stayed sharp. If that was the case, all the tools could have been manufactured at the hillfort. Another possibility is that the woodworking tools were manufactured by a specialized toolmaker skilled in the production of hardened tools. If this was the case it would seem unlikely that the hillfort would create sufficient demand for the full-time employment of such a smith. It would also seem unlikely that a skilled smith would have been satisfied by the repair attempted on the saw 2.42 (D173/4). The broken blade had been scarf-welded together, but there was no attempt to reduce the double ·thickness of metal. Therefore, although the blade was in one piece, the saw would have been useless as it would have stuck every time the weld crossed the saw cut. Thus, there seems to be tentative evidence of the presence of two different levels of blacksmithing skill.

Compositions

Table 120 (fiche 13, frames B1–12) gives the average compositions of the inclusions and the metal for each sample taken from the Danebury ironwork. The reason for performing the analysis was the hope that it would be possible to detect chemical differences between different groups of iron artefacts from the same site. The possible sources of such chemical differences would have been the use of different ores or different techniques to produce the metal. Certain elements such as silicon and iron would not be expected to help distinguish such groups, as the whole smelting operation was designed to separate these elements. Nevertheless, the proportions of these elements in bulk slag would have been a function of the efficiency of the smelting operation. However, on the scale of the inclusions found in early iron objects, the proportions of these two elements would only be a function of proportions of the different phases present.

Some elements such as sodium, titanium, and sulphur (S in the metal) showed no grouping other than that of a distribution around a single centre. There were other elements that showed distributions around more than one centre. These elements were Mg, Al, P, S, K, Ca, Mn in the inclusions and Co, Ni, Cu, As, P in the metal. Of particular interest were the concentrations of the elements Co and Ni in the metal, as these elements were found at relatively high levels in some artefacts, even though they are not commonly distributed amongst the British geological formations.

By plotting histograms of the elemental distributions and multidimensional analysis it was possible to define a group by the parameters given by Table 123 (fiche 13, frame C5). Table 124 (fiche 13, frame C6) gives a list of those samples that belong to the group. The samples marked * failed to fulfill the manganese condition because the sample was too corroded to be able to find an inclusion. Table 124B gives the two samples that fulfilled most of the conditions specified in Table 123 except that they contained more than the limit of copper. Table 124C gives the analysis obtained from the Standlake sword (from the Ashmolean Museum). This sample also contained no inclusions.

The compositions of this group of artefacts are so unusual that it should be possible to trace the metal back to the original ore. However, the geological regions of Britain where one would expect to find cobalt and nickel-rich iron ores are distant from Danebury. The regions are the south-west of England, west of Dartmoor, the Snowdonia area of Wales, and a few regions further afield. Although it is possible that these areas were the source of the metal, it is reasonable to look for some ore source closer to Danebury. Unfortunately, there are few analyses of the uneconomic iron ore bodies. Those there are, such as Lamplugh 1920, do not give values for the elements important in this study. Another source of geochemical information is the *Wolfson geochemical atlas of England and Wales* (1978), which gives the results of an

extensive programme of analysis of stream sediments. This atlas shows, as expected, that the Chalk uplands are low in iron. However, the nearby Tertiary basins of Hampshire and Berkshire together with the Weald of Sussex and Surrey are rich in iron. In these areas there is considerable evidence for the use of the iron ores from Roman times (Gibson-Hill 1976).

The Wealden clay around Horsham and Crawley is known to contain thin bands of ironstone nodules (Worssam 1964; 1972) which are of particular interest. This is because the stream sediments in the area, underlain by the Wealden Clay to the west and north of the Wealden Sands of the High Weald, are recorded as containing well above the average amounts of the elements cobalt and nickel. The manganese levels in this region are also above average. Table 125 (fiche 13, frame C7) shows that the stream sediment survey concentrations are much lower than those found in the metal and the slag inclusions of the group of ironwork from Danebury. This is not surprising, however, as the stream sediment analysis measured the concentrations of the elements concerned in a detritus derived from all the surrounding rock types. The iron ore used is likely to have enhanced concentrations of these elements compared with the surrounding rocks. This ore would have been used directly in the smelting process and the elements cobalt and nickel would have been enriched in the metal relative to the slag. The manganese on the other hand would have been slightly segregated to the slag inclusions. The factors governing such segregations are complex and yet have to be investigated fully. It is not, therefore, possible to calculate if the levels of these elements recorded by the sediment survey could have given rise to the levels recorded at Danebury. Taking all this into consideration, it appears that the Wealden Clay ironstones are the most likely source of the iron used in the high cobalt group of artefacts.

The rest of the iron in the Danebury collection may well also have come from other Wealden iron ores, such as those found in the High Weald. However, at the moment, not enough is known about the detailed composition of early British iron artefacts to be able to delineate other definite regional compositional groups.

7.3 Manufacturing activities

In addition to a wide range of domestic activities such as the preparation and storage of food and the building of defences, storage structures, and houses, the inhabitants of Danebury were engaged in a number of other productive activities reflected now in specialized tool kits and in the various residues discovered during the excavation. The tools have been described, according to the material of which they were made, in the preceding section while residues have been considered in various places in the report, including the microfiche supplement to this section (fiche 13, frames D1–E6). In the following paragraphs therefore we bring together the salient facts in a brief discussion designed to summarize the evidence for manufacturing activities.

7.3.1 Metalworking

Evidence for metalworking is not extensive. That both bronze and iron were being worked on the site is, however, clear. The bronze hoard (pp 335–40) is likely to reflect a collection of scrap metal brought together for exchange or for resmelting some time in the 7th or 6th centuries BC at a very early stage in the life of the community. The only other direct evidence for bronze-

Fig 7.72 Distribution of metalworking debris

working consists of four small bronzeworking crucibles from the late period of occupation (cp 6–7). Several other items of equipment may, however, have been used in bronzeworking. Two fragments of tuyère have been recovered, one from a cp 5 and one from a cp 7 context, together with four clay funnels which may have been guards for bellows (pp 406–7 and fiche 11, frame C3). Two of the four were from dated contexts and belonged to cp 7. Tuyères and bellow guards could equally well have been used for iron smithing as for bronzework.

Evidence for ironworking comes in various forms. The hoard of currency bars and the three fragments of cut-up currency bar belonging to cp 7 (pp 357–61) imply that iron was brought into the fort in ingot form for forging into tools and weapons, but the one fragment of an iron bloom, also from a cp 7 pit (p 371), shows that preformed ingots were not the only way in which raw iron reached the site.

While the currency bars were presumably imported to Danebury the bloom raises the question of whether or not iron was actually smelted on the site. A quantity of slag and other furnace debris found during excavation was examined in detail (report by Chris Salter in fiche 13, frames D6–E6). Two principal types of slag were defined: high density slag and low density slag. The samples of high density slag subjected to analysis contained a high iron content (25–60%) and must therefore have resulted from an ironworking process,

most probably forging rather than smelting. Slags of this kind are found in cp 1–3 and cp 7 contexts. The low density slags had a lower iron content and also contained appreciable percentages of copper. The most likely explanation is that they were furnace linings from furnaces used both to forge iron and melt copper-based alloys. Low density slags were found in all phases. The excavation also produced a surprising quantity of iron sulphide nodules and limonitic fossils, both occurring naturally in the chalk. The possibility that they were collected off the fields for smelting is to some extent supported by the fact that a number had been roasted — a necessary preliminary to iron extraction. In summary, conclusive proof of smelting is not forthcoming although it is conceivable that the high density slags may be the waste from such a process.

A spatial presentation of metalworking debris is offered in Fig 7.72 divided into the early (cp 1–4) and later (cp 6–8) periods. Few generalizations can be made from so small a sample but in both periods metalworking activity appears to concentrate in the area south of the main road. The virtual absence of debris immediately north of the main road in the early period is interesting and may reflect the restricted use of this area for the storage of grain. The distribution breaks down in the later period. Perhaps the most significant general observation is the comparatively wide extent of metalworking in both periods.

437

Fig 7.73 Distribution of textile equipment. Material plotted includes bone and antler combs, bone gouges, tools manufactured from sheep shaft bone, clay and chalk spindle whorls, clay and chalk weights. More than one category or item may be represented by each spot

Phase 1–4

Phase 6–8

0 10 20 30 40 50 Metres

7.3.2 Pottery manufacture

The possibility that pottery may have been made on the site has been considered elsewhere (p 244). In the absence of permanent kiln structures in this period the only evidence likely to have survived is prepared clay and wasters. Both have been found in some quantity at Danebury but interpretation is not straightforward. The clays could have been, and indeed probably were, used for a variety of purposes including the manufacture of loom weights, the building of ovens and hearths, and the daubing of walls (Vol 1, pp 110–23). The over-fired vessels, on the other hand, found in ceramic phases 4 and 5 may have resulted from one or more conflagrations (p 248). On balance, however, pottery manufacture, at least in cp 4 and 5, is a strong possibility since the over-fired forms are of a very restricted range of types and the clays brought to the site were very carefully mixed and tempered in puddling pits to a standard much finer than that needed for structural daub.

7.3.3 Textile manufacture
by Lyn Sellwood

Textile manufacture is attested by a wide range of artefacts including 62 clay loom weights, 144 chalk loom weights, 18 clay spindle whorls, 53 chalk spindle whorls, 39 bone and antler combs, 38 bone gouges, and 22 tools made from sheep bone of the kind that may have been used in the weaving process. In order to present the data spatially two maps were produced (Fig 7.73), one showing all artefacts of cp 1–3 and cp 4, the other items of cp 6–8 (omitted from the plans were artefacts of cp 5 and the few found in layers as opposed to pits).

In the earlier period material appears to have been scattered thinly but evenly across the excavated area with the exception of a blank in the eastern parts of zones N3 and N4. In zone S1 the only finds were ten chalk weights in three pits; otherwise there were no particular concentrations. There were six features in which two or more kinds of artefacts were associated, the most prolific producing a comb, a spindle whorl, three clay weights, and a gouge.

In the later period (cp 6–8) a difference can be seen between the southern zone where the material was clustered, and the northern zone where the artefacts were more scattered. In zone S2 a close-spaced group of five pits produced two chalk weights, one clay weight, three chalk and three clay spindle whorls, a bone comb, and another bone tool. Another cluster of pits in zone S3 yielded four chalk weights, one chalk and one clay spindle whorl, two bone gouges, and two bone combs. Within the house CS7/8 there were found two chalk spindle whorls, two chalk weights, and two bone combs. Chalk and clay weights were associated in four instances and there were fifteen occasions when two or more different items of textile equipment were found in single pits.

These general observations do little more than emphasize the quantity of spinning and weaving equipment on the site and reflect its more prolific occurrence in the later period. The significance of the associations and locations, if any, will only become apparent when material from a larger sample of the fort is considered statistically, as is hoped will appear in a subsequent volume.

The artefacts listed above reflect both spinning and weaving. At Danebury there were 71 spindle whorls and 206 weights, a ratio of 1:2.9. If we examine certain other broadly contemporary sites a series of interesting figures can be derived. At Maiden Castle the numbers would

438

appear to be 59 spindle whorls and 233 weights (assuming all those found were recorded in the report), a ratio of 1:3.9 — a figure not unlike Danebury. For non-hillforts the figures are rather different. At Meare 216 spindle whorls were recorded. The number of loom weights is unclear but the report implies that comparatively few were found. At Glastonbury there were 232 spindle whorls and only 52 complete or fragmentary weights. The All Cannings Cross report listed 93 whorls and 13 complete or near complete weights, while at Gussage All Saints period 1 produced 8 weights and 2 whorls, period 2, 7 weights and 2 whorls, and period 3, 10 weights and 13 whorls.

Although these figures can hardly be regarded as a satisfactory sample, bearing in mind geographical and chronological variables as well, the overall impression given is that artefacts of spinning were more common on settlements while weaving equipment was more prevalent in hillforts The tentative observation may prove to have a wider relevance.

7.3.4 Bone and antler work

The manufacture of bone and antler tools and ornaments is likely to have been carried out continuously on a domestic basis. Bone would have been widely available as butchery waste while shed antlers could have been gathered from woodlands nearby. A certain amount of manufacturing debris and offcuts has been recovered and gives some idea of the simple processes involved (pp395–6 with supporting fiche).

7.3.5 Ornaments of rare materials

The possibility that ornaments were being manufactured at Danebury may be briefly considered. Unfinished armlets of Kimmeridge shale (p 396) show that a limited quantity of shale was reaching the site in roughout form. Similar roughouts on sites some distance from the Purbeck source (at for example Glastonbury, Hengistbury Head, and Maiden Castle) imply that shale was being exchanged as semi-finished objects and may even have had a value as currency. Once at Danebury the roughouts were probably intended to be finished.

The single fragments of coral (p 396) might possibly be regarded as raw material brought in for ornamental purposes.

Consideration of the glass beads has raised the question of glassworking (pp 396–7) but the evidence for bead manufacture on the site is tenuous in the extreme and is best regarded as unproven.

That so little evidence for the manufacture of ornaments can be detected from the considerable area excavated strongly suggests that items of this kind were generally made elsewhere and imported.

7.3.6 Other handicrafts

There can be little doubt that a wide range of domestic skills was employed in the fort. The archaeological evidence for timber structures shows that hurdlemaking and carpentry were extensively practiced (see for example Vol 1, pp 113–15) while the relevant tool kit of axes, adzes, hammers, saws, gouges, chisels, knives, and cutting hooks is well represented.

Other crafts such as leatherworking, basketry, and netting are implied by needles, awls, and knives of the appropriate kind. Of the many other skills that were probably practiced, tanning, dying, the preparation of drugs, tattooing, etc, we are entirely ignorant.

Bibliography

Alcock, L, 1971 Excavations at South Cadbury 1970, *Antiq J*, **51**, 1–7
Allen, D F, 1944 The Belgic dynasties of Britain and their coins, *Archaeologia*, **90**, 1–47
————, 1961 The origins of coinage in Britain, in *Problems of the Iron Age in southern Britain* (ed SS Frere), 97–308
————, 1967 Iron currency bars in Britain, *Proc Prehist Soc*, **33**, 307–35
————, 1968 The Celtic coins, in *Hod Hill*, **2**, *Excavations carried out between 1951 and 1958* (I A Richmond), 43–57
Anon, 1950 Antimony in the ceramic industry, *Ramsdens Bull*, 24
Bamford, C R, 1977 *Colour generation and control in glasses*, Amsterdam
Bersu, G, 1940 Excavations at Little Woodbury, Wiltshire, Part 1, The settlement revealed by excavation, *Proc Prehist Soc*, **6**, 30–111
Bertin, E P, 1970 *Principles and practice of X-ray spectrometric analysis*, New York
Biek, L, & Bayley, J, 1979 Glass and other vitreous materials, *World Archaeol*, **11**(i), 1–25
Boswell, P G H, 1916 The stratigraphy and petrology of the Lower Eocene deposits of the north-eastern part of the London basin, *Quart J Geol Soc*, **71**, 536–88
Brailsford, J W, 1949 Excavations at Little Woodbury, Wiltshire. Part 4, supplementary excavation 1947, and part 5, the small finds (with appendices), *Proc Prehist Soc*, **15**, 156–68
————, 1962 *Antiquities from Hod Hill in the Durden Collection. Hod Hill*, **1**
Briard, J, 1965 *Les dépôts Bretons et l'Age du Bronze Atlantique*, Rennes
Briard, J, & Verron, G, 1976 *Typologie des objets de l'Age du Bronze en France*, fascicule 3–4, *Haches*, Société Préhistorique Française, Commission du Bronze, Paris
Brill, R H, 1970 The chemical interpretation of the texts, in *Glass and glassmaking in ancient Mesopotamia* (A L Oppenheim et al), 105–8
Britton, D, 1963 Traditions of metalworking in the Later Neolithic and Early Bronze Age of Britain, part 1, *Proc Prehist Soc*, **29**, 258-325
Broholm, H C, 1946 *Danmarks Bronzealder*, **3**, Copenhagen
————, 1953 *Danske Oldsager*, **4**, Copenhagen
Bulleid, A, & Gray, H St G, 1911 *The Glastonbury Lake Village*, **1**
————, & ————, 1917 *The Glastonbury Lake Village*, **2**
————, & ————, 1948 *The Meare Lake Village*, **1**
Burgess, C B, 1968a The Later Bronze Age in the British Isles and north-western France, *Archaeol J*, **125**, 1–45
————, 1968b Bronze Age disks and rapiers as illustrated by examples from Durham and Northumberland, *Trans Architect Archaeol Soc Durham Northumberland*, **2**,1, 3–26
————, 1969 Some decorated socketed axes in Canon Greenwell's collection, *Yorkshire Archaeol J*, **42**, 267–72
————, 1974 The Bronze Age, in *British prehistory* (ed C Renfrew), 165–232
Burgess, C B, Coombs, D, & Davies, D G, 1972 The Broadward complex and barbed spearhead, in *Prehistoric man in Wales and the west; essays in honour of Lily F Chitty* (eds F Lynch & C B Burgess), 211–83
Burgess, C B, & Cowen, J D, 1972 The Ebnal hoard and Early Bronze Age metalworking traditions, in *ibid*, 167–81
Bushe-Fox, J P, 1915 *Excavations at Hengistbury Head, Hampshire, in 1911–12*
Calkin, J B, 1948 The Isle of Purbeck in the Iron Age, *Proc Dorset Natur Hist Archaeol Soc*, **70**, 29–59
Callander, J G, 1921 A Bronze Age hoard from Glen Trool, Stewartry of Kirkcudbright, *Proc Soc Antiq Scot*, **55**, 29–37
Case, H J, 1966 Were Beaker-people the first metallurgists in Ireland?, *Palaeohistoria*, **12**, 141–77
Carke, R R, 1951 A hoard of metalwork of the Early Iron Age from Ringstead, Norfolk, *Proc Prehist Soc*, **17**, 216–25
————, 1954 The Early Iron Age treasure from Snettisham, Norfolk, *ibid*, **20**, 27–86
Clay, R C C, 1924 An Early Iron Age site on Fifield Bavant Down, *Wiltshire Archaeol Mag*, **42**, 457–96
————, 1925 An inhabited site of La Tène date on Swallowcliffe Down, *ibid*, **43**, 59–93
Coles, J M, 1968-69 Scottish Early Bronze Age metalwork, *Proc Soc Antiq Scot*, **101**, 1–110
Coombs, D, 1979 The Figheldean Down hoard, Wiltshire, in *Bronze Age hoards: some finds old and new* (eds C B Burgess & D Coombs), 253–68
Cope, T H, 1902 Note on the titaniferous iron-sand of Porth Dinalleyn, *Proc Liverpool Geol Soc*, **11**, 208-19
Corrie, A J, Clarke, W J, & Hunt, A R, 1873–4 Notice of a cave at Borness, *Proc Soc Antiq Scot*, **10**(ii), 476–99
Cotton, M A, & Frere, S S, 1968 Ivinghoe Beacon excavations, 1963–5, *Rec Buckinghamshire*, **18**, 187–216
Cowen, J D, 1933 Two bronze swords from Ewart Park, Wooler, *Archaeol Aeliana*, 4 ser, **10**, 185–98
Crowfoot, G, 1945 The bone gouges of Maiden Castle and other sites, *Antiquity*, **19**, 157–8

Cunliffe, B W, 1971 Danebury, Hampshire: first interim report on the excavation 1969–70, *Antiq J*, **51**, 240–52

Cunliffe, B W, 1978 *Hengistbury Head*

Cunliffe, B W, & O'Connor, B, 1979 The Late Bronze Age hoard from Danebury, Hampshire, in *Bronze Age hoards: some finds old and new* (eds C B Burgess & D Coombs), 235–44

Cunnington, M E 1923 *The Early Iron Age inhabited site at All Cannings Cross farm, Wiltshire. A description of the excavations and objects found by Mr and Mrs B H Cunnington, 1911–1922*

Curwen, E C, 1937 Querns, *Antiquity*, **11**, 133–51

————, 1941 More about querns, *ibid*, **15**, 15–32

Das, H A, & Zonderhuis, J, 1964 The analysis of electrum coins, *Archaeometry*, **7**, 90–7

Davies, S M, 1981 Old Down Farm, Andover, Part 2, *Proc Hampshire Fld Club Archaeol Soc*, **37**, 81–165

Dekówna, M, 1980 *Szkło w europie wczesnośredniowiecznej wroklaw*: Polska Akademia Nauk, Instytut Historii Kultury Materialnej

Dieck, A, 1976 Tatauierung in vor- und fruhgeschichterlichen zeit, *Archäologisches Korrespondenzblatt*, **6**, 169–73

Dudley, D, & Jope, E M, 1965 An Iron Age cist-burial with two brooches from Trevone, North Cornwall, *Cornish Archaeol*, **4**, 118-26

Dunning, G C, 1934 The swan's-neck and ring-headed pin of the Early Iron Age in Britain, *Archaeol J*, **91**, 269–95

Ehrenberg, M, 1977 *Bronze Age spearheads from Berkshire, Buckinghamshire and Oxfordshire*

Eustace, G W, 1923 An Early British bronze from Sussex, *Antiq J*, **3**, 142–4

Farrar, R A H, 1963 Note on prehistoric and Roman salt industry, *Proc Dorset Natur Hist Archaeol Soc*, **84**, 137–44

Fell, C I, 1936 The Hunsbury hillfort, Northants, *Archaeol J*, **43**, 57–100

Folk, R L, & Ward, W C, 1957 Brazos River Bar, a study in the significance of grain size parameters, *J Sediment Petrol*, **27**, 3–27

Forbes, R J, 1957 *Studies in ancient technology*, 5, Leiden

Fourdrignier, E, 1876 *La Gorge Meillet*, Paris

Fowler, E, 1960 The origins and development of the penannular brooch in Europe, *Proc Prehist Soc*, **26**, 149–77

Fox, C F, 1935 Salt works at Hook, Warsash, Hants, *Proc Hampshire Fld Club Archaeol Soc*, **8**, 105–9

Gibson-Hill, J, 1976 Further excavations of a Romano-British ironworking site at Broadfields, Crawley, West Sussex, *Bull Inst Archaeol*, **13**, 79

Giessler, R, & Kraft, G, 1942 Untersuchungen zur frühen und älteren Latènezeit am Oberrhein und der Schweiz, *Ber Röm-Ger Komm*, **32**, 20–115

Gillam, J P, 1958 Roman and native AD 122–197, in *Roman and native in northern Britain* (ed I A Richmond), 60–90

Gray, H St G, 1966 *The Meare Lake Village*, 3 (ed M A Cotton)

Gray, H St G, & Bulleid, A, 1953 *The Meare Lake Village*, 2

Greenwell, W, 1905 Early Iron Age burials in Yorkshire, *Archaeologia*, 2 ser, **10**, 251–324

Gresham, C A, 1939 Spettisbury Rings, Dorset, *Archaeol J*, **96**, i, 114–31

Grimes, W F, 1951 *The prehistory of Wales*

Guido, M, 1978 *The glass beads of the prehistoric and Roman periods in Britain and Ireland*

Haevernick, T E, 1960 *Die Glasarmringe und Ringperlen des Mittelund Spätlatènezeit*, Bonn

Haldane, W, 1970 A study of the chemical composition of pre-Roman ironwork from Somerset, *Hist Metall*, **4**,2, 53–66

Harbison, P, 1969 The axes of the Early Bronze Age in Ireland, *Prähistorische Bronzefunde*, 9,1 Munich

Hawkes, C F C, 1940 A Celtic bronze from Bury Hill Camp, *Antiq J*, **20**, 121

————, 1941 An iron torc from Spettisbury Rings, Dorset, *Archaeol J*, **97**, 112–14

Hedges, R E M, & Salter, C J, 1979 Source determination of iron currency bars through the analysis of slag inclusions, *Archaeometry*, **21**,2, 616–75

Henderson, J, 1977 *A technological study of blue glass beads with special reference to some from Meare Lake, Somerset*, unpub BA thesis, Queen's Univ Belfast

————, 1980 Some new evidence for Iron Age glassworking in Britain, *Antiquity*, **54**, 60–1

————, J, 1981 A report on the glass excavated from Meare Village West 1979, *Somerset Levels Pap*, **7**, 55–60

————, J, 1982a Glass and the manufacture of prehistoric and other early glass beads. Part 2: archaeology and experiment, *Ir Archaeol Res Forum*, **6**, in press

————, J, 1982b X-ray fluorescence of Iron Age glass: the chemical investigation of a prehistoric industry, PhD thesis, Univ Bradford, in press

Henderson, J, & Warren, S E, 1981 X-ray fluorescence analyses of Iron Age glass: beads from Meare and Glastonbury Lake Villages, *Archaeometry*, **23**,1, 83–94

Henshall, A H, 1950 Textiles and weaving appliances in prehistoric Britain, *Proc Prehist Soc*, **16**, 130–63

Hodder, I, & Hedges, J W, 1977 Weaving combs — their typology and distribution with some introductory remarks on date and function, in *The Iron Age in Britain — a review* (ed J Collis), 17–28

Hodson, R F, 1968 *The La Tène cemetery at Münsingen-Rain*, Berne

————, 1971 Three Iron Age brooches from Hammersmith, *Brit Mus Quart*, **35**, 50–6

Hoffmann, M, 1964 The warp-weighted loom, *Studia Norvegica*, **14**

Jenkins, D A, forthcoming The analysis of Welsh copper ores, in *Welsh Bronze Age metallurgy* (eds J P Northover & C B Burgess)

Jockenhövel, A, 1971 Die Rasiermesser in Mitteleuropa, *Prähistorische Bronzefunde*, **8**,1, Munich

Jope, E M, 1960 The beginnings of La Tène ornamental style in the British Isles, in *Problems of the Iron Age in Southern Britain* (ed S S Frere), 69–83

————, 1961 Daggers of the Early Iron Age in Britain, *Proc Prehist Soc*, **27**, 307–43

Jope, E M, & Jacobsthal, P, 1984 *Early Celtic art in the British Isles*

Jope, E M, & Wilson, B C S, 1957 A burial of the first century AD near Donaghadee, Co Down, *Ulster J Archaeol*, **20**, 73–95

King, D Grant, 1962 Bury Wood Camp, report on excavations, 1960, *Wiltshire Archaeol Mag*, **210**, 185–205

Krämer, W, 1958 *Manching: ein Vindelikisches Oppidum an der Donau*, Römisch-Germanische Kommission des Deutschen Archäologischen Instituts zu Frankfurt am Main, Berlin

————, 1960 The oppidum of Manching, *Antiquity*, **34**, 191–200

Kromer, K, 1963 *Hallstatt. Die salzhandelsmetropole des ersten Jahrtausends vor Christus in den Alpen*, Vienna

Kunkel, O, 1961 Zur Frage Keltischer Glasindustrie, *Germania*, **39**, 322–9

Lamplugh, G W, 1920 *Special report on the mineral resources of Great Britain*, **20**, 226

Lins, P A, & Oddy, W A, 1975 The origins of mercury gilding, *J Archaeol Sci*, **2**, 365–73

MacGregor, A G, & Currey, N D, 1983 Mechanical properties as conditioning factors in the bone and antler industry of the 3rd–13th century AD, *J Archaeol Sci*, **10**, 71–7

MacGregor, M, 1976 *Early Celtic art in north Britain*

MacGregor, M, & Simpson, D D A, 1963 A group of iron objects from Barbury Castle, Wilts, *Wiltshire Archaeol Mag*, **58**, 394–482

Mackenson, M, 1974 Die älteste keltische Gold- und Silberprägung in England, *Jahr für Nummismatik und Geldgeschicte*, **24**, 7–63

Mays, M, forthcoming *A social and economic study of the Durotriges, with particular reference to coinage (c 150 BC-AD 150)*, DPhil thesis, Oxford

Moore, C N, & Lewis, E, 1969 A hoard of Breton socketed axes from Nether Wallop, *Proc Hampshire Fld Club Archaeol Soc*, **26**, 19–20

Moore, C N, & Rowlands, M J, 1972 *Bronze Age metalwork in Salisbury Museum*

Morton, G R, & Wingrove, J, 1969 The constitution of bloomery slags, Part 1, Roman slags, *J Iron Steel Inst*, **207**, 1556–64

————, &————, 1972 The constitution of bloomery slags, Part 2, Medieval slags, *ibid*, **210**, 478-87

Müller, S, 1897 *Nordische Altertumskunde*, **1**, Strasburg

Müller-Beck, H, & Ettlinger, E, 1962–3 Die oppida von Bern, *Ber Röm-Ger Komm*, **43-4**, 108-55

Nash-Williams, V E, 1933 A late bronze hoard from Cardiff, *Antiq J*, **13**, 299–300

Nauer, G, & Kny, E, 1978 *Zur numerischen Klassification römischer Gläser aufgrund ihrer Elementgehalte*, paper presented at the meeting of the Projectgruppe 'Glas', Bonn, 13 March 1978

Northover, J P, & Pearce, S M, forthcoming *The metallurgy and metalwork of the Bronze Age in south-west England*

Oddy, W A, & Hughes, N J, 1972 The specific gravity method for the analysis of gold coins, in *Methods of chemical and metallurgical investigation of ancient coinage* (eds E T Hall & D M Metcalf), 75–84

Orme, B J, et al, 1981 Meare Village West 1979, *Somerset Levels Pap*, **7**, 12–69

Payne, F G, 1948 The plough in ancient Britain, *Archaeol J*, **104**, 82–111

Peacock, D P S, 1967 The heavy mineral analysis of pottery: a preliminary report, *Archaeometry*, **10**, 97–100

Pellat, A, 1919 Bead-making in Murano and Venice, *J Roy Soc Arts*, **24**, 600–10

Piggott, C M, 1946 The Late Bronze Age razors of the British Isles, *Proc Prehist Soc*, **12**, 121–41

Piggott, S, 1950 Swords and scabbards of the British Early Iron Age, *ibid*, **16**, 1–28

———— (ed), 1981 *The agrarian history of England and Wales*, **1**, 1

Planck, D, 1980 Die abschliessende Untersuchung in der Spätkeltischen Viereckschanze von Fellbach-Schmiden, Rems-Murr-Kreis, *Archäologische Ausgrabungen*, 1980, 50–9

Rees, S E, 1979 *Agricultural implements in prehistoric and Roman Britain*

Reynolds, P J, 1972 Experimental archaeology, *Worcs Archaeol Newsl*, **9**, 1–13

Richmond, I A, 1968 *Hod Hill*, **2**, *Excavations carried out between 1951 and 1958*

Riehm, K, 1961 Prehistoric salt boiling, *Antiquity*, **35**, 181–91

Rodwell, W, 1976 Oppida and the rise of Belgic power in south-eastern Britain, in *Oppida in barbarian Europe, papers presented to a conference at Oxford, October 1975* (eds B W Cunliffe & R T Rowley), 181–376

Rooksby, H P, 1962 Opacifiers in opal glasses through the ages, *GEC J Sci Technol*, **29**(1), 20–6

Roth, H Ling, 1934 *Studies in primitive looms*, repr

Rowlands, M J, 1976 *The production and distribution of metalwork in the Middle Bronze Age in southern Britain*

Savory, H N, 1980 *Guide catalogue of the Bronze Age collection*, Cardiff

Sayre, E V, 1963 The intentional use of antimony and manganese in ancient glasses, in *Sixth international conference on glass: advances in glass technology* (eds F R Matson & G E Rindone), 263–82, New York

Scheers, S, 1977 *Traité de numismatique Celtique*, **2**, *la Gaule Belgique*, Paris

Sellwood, D G J, 1963 Experiments in Greek minting technique, *Numis Chron*, 7 ser, **3**, 226–30

Smith, K, 1977 The excavation at Winklebury Camp, Basingstoke, Hampshire, *Proc Prehist Soc*, **43**, 31–130

Smith, M A, 1959 Some Somerset hoards and their place in the Bronze Age of southern Britain, *ibid*, **25**, 144–87

Spratling, M G, & Wainwright, G M, 1973 The Iron Age settlement of Gussage All Saints, *Antiquity*, **50**, 109–30

Spratling, M G, *et al*, 1980 An Iron Age bronze foundry at Gussage All Saints, Dorset: preliminary assessment of technology, *Proc sixteenth international symposium on archaeometry and archaeological prospection*, 268-92

Stanford, S C, 1974 *Croft Ambrey*

————, 1981 *Midsummer Hill, an Iron Age hillfort on the Malverns*

Stead, I M, 1968 An Iron Age hill-fort at Grimthorpe, Yorkshire, England, *Proc Prehist Soc*, **34**, 148-90

————, 1979 *The Arras Culture*

Swanton, M J, 1976 *A corpus of pagan Anglo-Saxon spear-types*

Theophilus C R Dodwell (ed), 1961 *De diversis artibus*

Todd, J A, & Charles, J A, 1978 Ethiopian bloomery iron and the significance of inclusion analysis in iron studies, *J Hist Metall Soc*, **12**,2, 63–87

Turner, W E S, & Rooksby, H P, 1961 Further historical studies based on X-Ray diffraction methods on the reagents employed in making opal and opaque glasses, *Jahrb Röm-Ger Zentralmus*, **8**, 1–6

Tylecote, R F, 1962 *Metallurgy in archaeology*

Vouga, P, 1925 *La Tène*, Leipzig

Venclova, N, 1978 The origin of the La Tène glassware in Bohemia, *Annales du 7ᵉ Congrès international d'étude historique du verre*, Berlin-Leipzig, 123–8

Wainwright, G J, 1970 The excavation of Balksbury Camp, Andover, Hants, *Proc Hampshire Fld Club Archaeol Soc*, **26**, 21–56

————, 1971 A fortified settlement at Walesland Rath, *Britannia*, **2**, 48-108

————, 1979 *Gussage All Saints. An Iron Age settlement in Dorset*

Wamser, G, 1975 Zur Hallstattkultur in Ostfrankreich, *Ber Röm-Ger Komm*, **56**, 1–178

Ward, G, 1941 The Iron Age horseshoe and its derivation, *Antiq J*, **21**, 9–27

Ward Perkins, J B, 1939 An Iron Age linch pin of Yorkshire type in Cornwall, *ibid*, **19**, 64–7

————, 1941 The Iron Age horseshoe, *ibid*, **21**, 144–49

Werner, J, 1955 Die Nauheimer Fibel, *Jahrb Röm Germ Zentralmus Mainz*, **2**, 170–95

Wheeler, R E M, 1943 *Maiden Castle, Dorset*

Wild, J-P, 1970a Button-and-loop fasteners, *Britannia*, **1**, 137–55

————, 1970b *Textile manufacture in the northern Roman provinces*

The Wolfson geochemical atlas of England and Wales, 1978

Worssam, B C, 1964 Iron working in the Western Weald, *Proc Geol Ass*, **75**, 529–46

————, 1972 Iron ore workings near Horsham, Sussex, and the sedimentology of the Wealden Clay ironstone, *ibid*, **83**, 37–55

8 Population and behaviour

8.1 The deposition of the human remains
by Lucy Walker

8.1.1 Types of burial practice

The bones from a minimum number of 70 people were excavated from 98 storage pits, 2 postholes, and 10 stratified contexts behind the ramparts. The assemblage appears to break down into six main deposition categories:

A Whole bodies (in single or group burials)
B Incomplete skeletons (individual depositions)
C Multiple, partially articulated skeletons in charnel pits
D Skulls or frontal bones
E Pelvic girdles
F Individual bones, and bone fragments

The term 'deposition' has been used as a convenient label for all the deposits of human remains, but the division of the assemblage into 'deposition categories' is intended to distinguish between the different rites involved. Throughout the text, the term 'inhumation' is only used when discussing deposition category A, ie the burial or inhumation of whole, articulated bodies.

The distinct nature of the assemblage within each category would suggest that we are witnessing performances of a fundamentally different kind, but the main distinction appears to be in the treatment of the body after death:

1 Inhumation whilst the body is still articulated and probably before the flesh has seriously begun to decay.
2 The deposition of various parts of one or more skeletons, after the flesh and often most of the connecting tissues have decayed; with one exception, the skeletal debris does not exhibit any traces of violent dismemberment.

The dumping of several partially articulated skeletons and skulls into one layer in one pit (category C) has been considered as a fundamentally different performance to the deposition of individual, incomplete skeletons in any one layer in a pit (category B) although the initial treatment of the bodies prior to their final deposition may be similar. The depositions of skulls (D) and pelvic girdles (E) have been considered separately from the rest of the individual bones and bone fragments (F) on the grounds that they are likely to reflect socially distinct performances; this is suggested by classical references to the symbolic importance of the skull to the Celts (p 462), and by the fact that one of the pelvic girdles exhibits the only evidence of butchery in the entire assemblage. This does not imply, however, that the rest of the bones in Category F do not necessarily have their own distinct cultural/social associations.

8.1.2 Treatment of the data in the burial assemblage

It is apparent from classical sources and Irish texts that the Celtic peoples believed in the existence of an 'afterworld', in the transmigration of souls, and in the efficacy of manipulating the relationship between these two worlds (see Ross 1967; Piggott 1969; Chadwick 1970 for a review of the material).

In order to elucidate more about Iron Age mortuary traditions in this region, the burial assemblage at Danebury was analysed with a view to identifying common themes and disposal patterns within the data, particularly in terms of the treatment of the body. Hooper has provided anatomical and pathological information for all the bones (below, 8.2), and a description of each deposition placed within its archaeological context is presented in catalogue form in microfiche (fiche 14, frame B4–fiche 15, frame A10).

Each deposition has been assigned a number and a letter designating 'deposition category' as defined above. Indexes facilitate the association of deposition numbers with pit numbers and vice-versa, and an introductory paragraph in the microfiche explains the form of the catalogue. The depositions are presented in sequence according to pit number. The location of each pit is indicated by a grid reference. There follows a description of the age and sex of the skeleton, with anatomical details of the bones present and any pathological comments. The articulation, position — including depth of burial — and orientation of each deposition are presented, together with plans and photographs, wherever possible. Finally there is a brief description of the archaeological context, with any associated data such as special animal deposits, animal bones, pot sherds, and small finds.

Index 3 (fiche 14, frames A10–12) lists all the depositions chronologically within their categories A-F, with associated pit numbers, pit forms, and where possible the age and sex of each body represented. This latter information is not possible for most of the individual bones in category F. In the main text section 8.1.3 places the assemblage at Danebury in its wider cultural context, and includes some comments about the association of human bones with storage pits and their backfills. There follows a discussion on the main themes which emerge within each deposition category and within the assemblage as a whole, including the chronological and spatial distribution of the depositions in the hillfort, comments on the population represented in the burial record, and a final section which summarizes a few of the main points, taking a general look at the assemblage within the framework of what is known about Celtic ideology and suggesting some possible interpretations of the data. Specific references to the Celtic practice of head-hunting are included at the end of the appropriate section dealing with the deposition of skulls (p 462).

8.1.3 Burial tradition

Cultural framework

In spite of the diversity of the assemblage of human remains at Danebury, their one common attribute, namely their presence in the fillings of storage pits within the settlement area, suggests that the whole may be seen, in the wider context of Iron Age mortuary practices, as being part of a tradition of pit burial recognized in central southern England. The deposition of human remains in storage pits occurs 'in those areas of higher ground where the construction of storage pits is an integral aspect of the local economic system' (Whimster 1981, 8; distribution plan, 9).

The most common or most frequently recognized type of pit burial is the simple inhumation of one or more bodies, but the presence of incomplete skeletons and various parts of the anatomy has also been recognized on an increasing number of Iron Age settlement sites (Whimster 1981, 177–89).

Ten % of the storage pits so far excavated at Danebury contained human remains. The practice occurs throughout the occupation of the hillfort, from the earliest period, beginning in the 6th century BC. This is considerably earlier than has so far been recognized on other Iron Age sites. For a discussion of the chronological distribution see below, pp 456–7.

In the context of large areas of Great Britain where there is so far little evidence for the mortuary rites of the pre-Roman Iron Age, it should be stressed that the tradition of interment in storage pits is recognizable because of the survival of 'below-ground' features for archaeological investigation. The destruction of 'above-ground' data, almost certainly including further mortuary evidence, should be borne in mind. At Danebury, where there is no surviving stratigraphy above the chalk bedrock except behind the ramparts, there was one surviving inhumation in a feature other than a storage pit (gully 67, surrounding circular structure CS9 of cp 3) and bone fragments from ten deposits in the quarry hollow.

Storage pits, associated artefacts, and refuse

The tradition of depositing human remains in the secondary fillings of disused storage pits was for long not recognized as a formal mortuary ritual primarily for two reasons, both of which are characteristic of the assemblage at Danebury:

1 The bones were deposited in storage receptacles within the settlement area, rather than in specially dug graves in confined cemetery zones.
2 The inhumations and other depositions were never accompanied by grave-goods in the accepted sense of the word.

The depositions are therefore generally characterized by a mode of treatment which appears to involve the minimum expenditure of energy, and a complete absence of any surviving, overt demonstration of wealth or rank in the form of durable artefacts.

Although there are exceptions, such as pit 374 whose large boat-shape does not resemble any other Danebury pit form, and pit 383, a small oval pit (both of which were probably excavated for the primary function of inhumation), the human remains are usually found deposited in the most common of the pit form types, notably the 'bath-tubs' and the 'beehives'. These are primarily associated with grain storage. Human remains are also found in cylindrical pits, and there is one bone fragment in a conical pit, possibly originally used for storing clay.

The general tradition appears to be one of depositing human bones with other refuse in receptacles which have a primary economic/agrarian function.

Whatever the symbolic distinction between the different deposition assemblages at Danebury, the final deposition in features with a primary occupational/domestic storage function, and a secondary function as a receptacle for refuse, suggests a strong cultural association which is not present in burials in specially prepared graves.

There appears to be little to distinguish the general refuse and backfilling processes of the pits with human bones — inhumation or otherwise — from those without: a combination of natural silting and deliberate backfills of occupation and domestic waste, including burnt debris, animal bones, and pot sherds. Many of the depositions however were buried with, or interleaved between,

deliberate tips of debris, a closer analysis of the contents of which might reveal crucial refuse patterns and associations. Although a general description of associated debris is included with each deposition in the catalogue, more detailed work on the pot sherds and bone fragments is required before common associations may emerge (see the bone report, p 540).

Apart from pot sherds and animal bone fragments, the most commonly associated objects are quern stone fragments, which occur in at least twenty contexts, predominantly in the sediments associated with bone fragments (F), although they also occur with inhumations (depositions 6, 27, and 43–45), one skull (deposition 11), and one pelvic girdle (deposition 47).

Other objects comprise loom weight fragments, spindle whorl fragments, bone needles, a variety of iron objects including a sickle, and some slag in pit 79. There was a bone comb with the adult male inhumation in pit 1015 (deposition 46). The pattern of retrieval of these small finds, however, does not appear to deviate from contexts without human bones, and their association may well be casual rather than deliberate. On the other hand, they are likely to reflect the spatial distribution of activities, which may be relevant to the associated deposition of human remains.

The association of 'special animal deposits' is more difficult to evaluate; there are human depositions of all categories with and without such deposits, and similarly there are numerous special animal deposits without human bones.

The cultural implication of the association of human remains with the refuse in a storage pit may well be of a general, rather than a particular nature.

8.1.4 Deposition categories

Deposition category A: inhumations (Figs 8.1, 8.2)

Twenty-five bodies were excavated from nineteen pits and one gully. The earlier pits tend to be bath-tub shaped, and the later beehives, although a single adult female (deposition 22 of cp 5) and two foetal/neonatal infants (depositions 17 and 18 of cp 6) were buried in shallow, circular pits, 497 and 430. Deposition 16 was crammed head first into a small oval pit, 383; and pit 374 (cp 3), with an unusual sequence of depositions in contiguous layers, was a large boat-shaped excavation quite distinct from the usual Danebury forms. Gully 67 (cp 3) surrounded building CS9. The deposition of a child in the gully and a neonatal infant in a pit within the structure may well have been contemporary, and associated with the abandonment of the building (deposition 58, gully 67; deposition 31, pit 857) (see p 457).

Age and sex

The bodies represent all age groups within a range of 0–45 including eleven adult males, five adult females, two children over 10, two infants under 5, and five foetal/neonatal infants. The age of each inhumation may be extracted from Index 4 (fiche 14, frames A13–B3). The adult males are predominantly in the 25–35 age bracket, although there are three under 25 and one possibly over 40. Both the females in group burials are under 25, whereas two of the three single inhumations are somewhat older, between 30 and 40.

Looking at the whole assemblage, the preponderance of adult males and the relatively small number of fertile women and newborn infants would suggest that we are looking at a biased sample of any 'normal' or stable

Fig 8.1   Inhumation burials: 1, deposition 24 in P587; 2, deposition 23 in P582; 3, deposition 12 in P343; 4, deposition 22 in P497; 5, deposition 6 in P84; 6, deposition 46 in P1015 (photos: Mike Rouillard)

Fig 8.2a Inhumation burials: depositions 28, 29, 30 in P829 (photo: Mike Rouillard)

Fig 8.2b Inhumation burials: charnel pit with depositions 48–57, 162, 164, and inhumation 49 in P1078 (photo: Mike Rouillard)

Fig 8.2c   Inhumation burials: deposition 14 in P374 (photo: Mike Rouillard)

population structure. This is particularly exaggerated in the early and middle occupation phases; there are no female inhumations belonging to cp 3 or 4, and only one in cp 5. The balance changes in cp 7 when there are four females and only two males.

Burial practice
The tradition of inhumation in the fillings of storage pits was practised from the earliest occupation period, and continued through to the latest, up to the early 1st century BC. There appears to have been a preference for deposition in the lower half or bottom of the pit, although one single adult was deposited in the top of a bath-tub pit (deposition 6 of cp 3) and one triple and two single burials occur in the middle or upper half of their respective pits. Sometimes the bodies were interleaved

between two layers (depositions 19, 23, 24), others were buried within a deposit (depositions 6, 22, 27), and a few appear to have been left exposed, to be covered by chalk shatter and erosion silts (depositions 28-30, 43–45).

Although the relatively simple treatment of the body clearly distinguishes this group from the other depositions on site, there are a number of variations within the assemblage which suggest that it should not be seen as an entirely homogeneous group. These include the distinction between solitary and group inhumations, the treatment of the body in the pit, and the presence of special animal deposits with some of the inhumations.

Solitary and group inhumations
The most obvious distinction in the burial record is that between solitary and group burial. There are fourteen

446

Fig 8.2d Burials: depositions 33–42 in charnel pit P923 (photo: Mike Rouillard)

Fig 8.2e Burials: deposition 20 in P448 (photo: Mike Rouillard)

solitary, one double, two triple, and two group inhumations; these latter are inhumations within the same layer. Pit 430 (cp 6) contained two neonatal infants — possibly twins. Pit 829 (cp 6) contained three adult males, and pit 935 (cp 7) contained one adult male, one young adult female, and a child — possibly a family group. In addition, pit 374 (cp 3) contained two inhumations and an incomplete skeleton in contiguous layers; the crouched body of an infant was interleaved between the bottom inhumation of the extended, prone body of a young adult male and the incomplete remains of an adult above (depositions 14, 13, 61). Pit 1078 (cp 7) contained a fully articulated contracted female skeleton (deposition 49) in the same layer as a heap of partially disarticulated skeletons. She was, however, spatially separated from them, tucked under the overhang of the beehive pit.

The single inhumations include six males, three females, two children, and three neonatal infants.

The group depositions tended to be in the larger storage pits, but it is possible that pit 374 was excavated for the primary purpose of burial. It contained the only recorded extended body of an adult from a pit on an Iron Age site (deposition 14); all the other bodies are to some extent flexed or contracted.

The group inhumations may be seen as 'deviations' from the more common solitary burial rite, and the recurrence of three burials grouped together (see also the deposition of three incomplete child skeletons in pit 120, cp 8) may suggest a symbolic association not intended with the solitary depositions. It must, however, be emphasized that each triple deposition appears to be quite distinctive. Apart from pit 374, the group inhumations occur in the later occupation phases. Indeed, when considering the entire mortuary assemblage at Danebury, it is apparent that all the triple or multiple depositions occur in the later phases (p 456).

Treatment of the bodies

Buried or exposed

A repeated characteristic, reinforcing the distinction between solitary and group burials, is the tendency deliberately to bury the single body within the pit. In the group burials, the bodies appear to have been left exposed in their pits, to be sealed by natural erosion silts and chalk shatter. This is incidentally also true of the bodies in the charnel pits 923 and 1078.

The presence of sling stones in pits 935, 923, and 1078 suggests that there may be a correlation between the exposure of bodies and hostile treatment. This may be endorsed by the apparently casual position of the bodies in pit 935, in contrast to the more formal placement of some of the solitary burials. At the same time, however, the absence of sling stones and the more formal placement of the three bodies in pit 829 imply that we may be witnessing quite distinct rituals.

Apart from the group depositions, the foetal/neonatal infants — with the exception of deposition 19 in pit 437 — were also left exposed in their pits, rather than deliberately buried. It may, therefore, be possible to infer that clear distinctions were made between the treatment of solitary child/adult burials and the infant and group inhumations. This should be borne in mind when looking at further patterns of deposition.

Body position

There is no information available for four of the foetal/neonatal infants, nor the child in gully 67. Apart from deposition 16, which was crammed head first into a small oval pit, and deposition 14, fully extended and prone on the bottom of pit 374, the bodies may be divided into two main groups, according to the degree of contraction of their limbs.

1 Those whose limbs are tightly crouched or contracted against the body, in such a manner as to suggest that they may have been bound thus prior to deposition. Of the eleven bodies in this group, eight were placed on their sides (depositions 6, 13, 19, 21, 23, 28, 29, 49), two on their back (depositions 22, 30), and one on his front (deposition 24).
2 Those whose limbs are more lightly — even casually — flexed. Of the seven bodies in this group, four lie on their back (depositions 12, 43, 44, 46) and three on their front (depositions 27, 25, 45) although their limbs may be flexed to one side.

Table 43 indicates the manner of deposition of 19 of the 25 inhumations, giving the age and gender of the body, the side to which it is contracted or flexed, its orientation position, and depth of burial in the pit. Orientation is determined by a line drawn from the centre of the pelvis to the crown of the skull (Whimster 1981, 14).

The apparently casual manner of deposition of some of the skeletons in group 2 might suggest a less formal deposition ritual than that involved with the more tightly contracted bodies. But this need not be the case, and the awkward deposition of a male body head first into pit 383 (deposition 16) should probably be regarded as exceptional and not part of the more standard inhumation tradition.

The most homogeneous group of burials consists of those lying on their sides with the limbs tightly contracted against the body: group 1a. They occur in both solitary and group inhumations. Within this group, however, there appears to have been another distinctive ritual which involved depositing the tightly contracted body under the overhang of the pit so that it lay hidden, tucked away, and facing the wall. The concealed position of these bodies (depositions 6, 19, 23, 49) contrasts sharply with the other inhumations where the bodies were placed more centrally in their pits, in a more 'dominating' position. The concealing of the body is a ritual seen in both the early and later periods; the two early depositions are an adult male and a neonatal infant, and the two later ones are females.

Within group 1a it is apparent that the three early depositions, 6, 13, and 19, were placed on the left side,

Table 43 Inhumations (category A)

Details of the deposition of nineteen bodies, including body position, orientation, and depth of burial. The inhumations are listed chronologically within groups defined according to the articulation of the skeletons (see p 442 and Figs 8.1–8.3)

	Deposition number	Pit number	cp	Sex	Age	Orientation	Position	Depth of burial in pit
1: Contracted								
1(a): on side	6•	84	3	♂	30-40	NE	Facing E, on left side, under SE overhang of pit	Top
	13x	374	3	—	c 3	NNE	Facing E, on left side, in centre of pit	Middle
	19•	437	5	—	0	SW	Facing NW, on left side, under NW overhang of pit	Middle
	28△	829	6	♂	25-35	W	Facing S, on right side, at W edge of pit	Upper
	29△	829	6	♂	25-35	NW	Facing SW, on right side, at E edge of pit	Upper

448

Table 43   Inhumations (category A) *continued*

	Deposition number	Pit number	cp	Sex	Age	Orientation	Position	Depth of burial in pit
1: Contracted								
1(a): on side	21•	489	7	♀	+35	S	Facing E, on right side at SE edge of pit	Upper
	23•	582	7	♀	25-35	NNW	Facing SW, on right side, under NW overhang of pit	Bottom
	49○	1078	7	♀	21-25	SW	Facing SE, on right side, under SE overhang of pit	Middle
1(b): on back	22•	497	5	♀	25-35	NW	Facing SE, with hands crossed on chest, knees bent to left, in centre of pit	Lower
	30△	829	6	♂	30-40	N	Facing W, legs bent over front of body, in centre of pit	Upper
1(c): on front	24•	587	3	♂	30-40	NNW	Facing SW, hands crossed under abdomen, legs contracted at knee, feet either side of pelvis	Bottom
2: Flexed								
2(a): on back	12•	343	3	♂	25-35	NW	Facing W, legs flexed to left (W), head in centre of pit, feet against side	Lower
	43△	935	7	♂	25-35	ESE	Facing N, legs flexed to left (SW), on E side of pit	Lower
	44△	935	7	♀	17-25	SSE	Facing SW, legs flexed to right, in centre of pit	Lower
	46•	1015	7	♂	20-25	WNW	Facing N, one leg extended, one leg contracted to right (W), head in centre of pit, feet and pelvis against side.	Bottom
2(b): on front	27•	807	6	♂	17-22	N	Head facing ground on right front side, legs flexed to left (W), in N half of pit	Lower
	25•	620	7	—	c 5	SE	Facing NE, on right front side, legs flexed to left (E), head against S side of pit	Bottom
	45△	935	7	—	10-12	WSW	Facing S, on right front side, on W side of pit	Lower
3: Extended								
	14x	374	3	♂	17-25	SW	Prone, facing SE (left), legs slightly flexed to left, extended along full length of pit	Bottom

Key   •   single inhumation
△   group inhumation in one context
x   single inhumation stratigraphically separated from another inhumation in same pit
○   single inhumation in charnel pit (Category C)
cp   ceramic phase

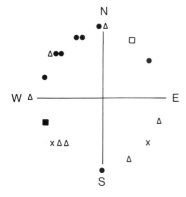

- ● Solitary adults
- △ Grouped adults
- × Solitary infants
- □ Grouped infants
- ■ Grouped child

Fig 8.3 Orientation of inhumations

whereas the later ones, depositions 28, 29, 21, 23, and 49, were all placed on their right sides. Similarly, the bodies in group 2b are all late depositions on their right front sides. There may well be a real chronological distinction between the preference for the left and the right side, but the numbers are too small to be reliable.

Of all the inhumations, including those lying prone, only one — deposition 27, pit 807 — was placed with the head facing down into the ground; all the other heads were facing sideways. It has been suggested that the deliberate placement of the head facing down into the ground may be associated with an attempt to prevent the transmigration of the soul of the dead person. Presumably the converse would also apply. The placing of the hands near the mouth — most common with the tightly contracted bodies on their sides — may also be related to similar beliefs.

Orientation
Looking at the inhumations whose orientations have been recorded (Table 43) it is clear that while there seems to have been an overall preference for the western rather than the eastern side of the north/south axis, bodies were placed with their heads in almost every direction.

A more coherent patterning may be detected when looking at the solitary and group inhumations. The adult, solitary inhumations (depositions 6, 12, 22, 23, 24, 27, 46) are all orientated in the northern arc, between WNW and NE, with only deposition 21 deviating to the south. Although there are exceptions, the infants and group burials have a preference for the southern rather than the northern arc (Fig 8.3).

This pattern reinforces distinctions within the inhumation assemblage which have already been detected in other aspects of the deposition process.

Associated objects
The general absence of ornaments might imply that the bodies were deposited without clothes, although some of the more tightly contracted skeletons may have been bound or swathed in cloth (eg depositions 6, 23, 49). The presence of organic material and a metal attachment close to the wrists of deposition 22 (pit 497) suggests that her hands may have been tied together on her chest.

Deposition 24 (pit 587) had a large flint and chalk block placed on the right-hand side of his back (he was lying

on his front) and deposition 46 (pit 1015) was surrounded by large flints and chalk blocks placed around the body and between the limbs. This skeleton was a young adult male with a defective hip joint which in life would probably have caused him to limp. Sling stones were present in the triple burial pit 935.

Special animal deposits
These are associated with six of the inhumations: three single burials and one triple burial. The foetal/neonatal infant, deposition 19 in pit 437, was buried with a neonatal calf, interleaved between the same layers but at the other side of the pit. A broken cattle skull was deposited in the layer sealing deposition 24, a solitary adult male in 587. Pit 1015 had large amounts of sheep skull bone in layers 2 to 8, including seven around deposition 46. The three bodies in pit 935, depositions 43, 44, and 45, were associated with a broken ox skull, an almost complete horse skull, and a horse lower limb. There was also a fairly large proportion of cattle skull bone in the same pit (layers 1 and 6). Deposition 49 was associated with the heap of bodies and animal bones in the charnel pit 1078, including part of a foetal/neonatal pig, a horse skull, and a large amount of sheep and cattle skull bone.

Deposition category B: individual incomplete skeletons

This group of interments involves the burial of single, incomplete skeletons. The depositions contrast sharply with the inhumations of category A in the manner of treatment of the body: whereas the latter were apparently deposited shortly after death before the flesh had decayed, in the normal practice of inhumation, the incomplete skeletons clearly underwent an intermediary period of decay, resulting in the 'loss' or 'removal' of certain parts of the body prior to deposition. There is no evidence of butchery or dismemberment whilst the flesh was still on the bones; we are apparently witnessing a less violent but more complex ritual involving the decomposition of the flesh and, to varying degrees, the connecting tissues, before the bones were interred.

There are at least seven depositions within this category which may be divided into three sub-groups according to the degree of articulation and the parts of the anatomy present or absent in the pit:

  i Articulated skeleton without skull and arms: depositions 3 and 10
  ii Skull, fragmentary torso, and disarticulated limbs: depositions 7, 8, and 9
  iii Mixed assemblage from one body: depositions 60 and 61

Style Bi: articulated skeleton without skull and arms
Both of these skeletons appear to have been in a minimum state of decay when buried, in that they were still articulated even though the skulls and arms were absent. The manner of their deposition was, however, quite distinctive: deposition 3 (pit 37), a male aged 14–16 years, was dumped in a heap at the bottom of the pit, above the primary silt. Also present was a scatter of animal bones which included a cattle scapula, and some isolated human bones from another skeleton(s), including a mandible, right tibia, and two cervical vertebrae. These were buried in a thin tip of occupation debris which included pot sherds and lumps of daub.

Deposition 10 (pit 266), a (?)female aged 20–30 years, was laid out on a layer of charcoal and ash near the top of the pit. Her spinal column and sacrum had been removed from the pelvis and laid around her feet and lower legs. These were extended in such a manner as to suggest that they were at least partially articulated, although the right fibula was not present. Her right scapula and left clavicle were also absent.

The removal of the skull and arms of each skeleton was probably deliberate; the scapula and clavicle of deposition 10 may have been included in the process. The presence of so many isolated long bones in pits on the site possibly implies an interest in certain parts of the anatomy for purposes other than simple burial, and one may therefore infer that the right fibula of deposition 10 was also deliberately removed.

As the source of life, the head was an important symbol to the Celts. Its removal from the body may be seen in either a primitive or ritual context.

Both depositions belong to the early phase of occupation in the hillfort, cps 3 and 4 respectively.

Style Bii: skull, fragmentary torso, and limb bones
The three interments in this group are all children. They are clearly distinguishable from Bi in that the skulls are present and the skeletons are much more fragmentary: in all three cases the pelvic girdles are absent and there are no complete lower limbs. Only one deposition includes an articulated arm.

Deposition 9 (pit 149 of cp 1–3) includes a skull and mandible, one thoracic vertebra, and ribs of a (?)male child aged about 12 years. The bones were deposited in the top of the pit with occupation debris and burnt flints.

Depositions 7 and 8 (pit 120 of cp 8) were located in contiguous layers of the same pit. Deposition 7 includes a skull (less mandible), one cervical and fragments of five thoracic vertebrae, and the left femur of a child about 8 years old. Deposition 8 includes a skull and mandible, vertebrae, ribs, and the right arm of a (?)female aged 14–17 years. They were both sealed by chalk shatter and erosion silts, suggesting that the bones were left exposed after deposition. In this instance, the presence of the teeth marks of a carnivore on the femur of deposition 7 suggests that the burial remains may have been modified; dogs may remove bones entirely as well as chew the ends.

Deposition 7 was more fragmentary than 8. The child was younger and the connecting tissue may have decayed sooner. This is endorsed by the absence of the mandible from the skull, whereas it is still attached on depositions 8 and 9.

Deposition 9 belongs to the earliest occupation phase whereas 7 and 8 belong to the latest phase of the fort.

Style Biii: mixed assemblages from one body
Deposition 61 (pit 374 of cp 3) includes a small skull fragment, ribs, sternum, right patella, left ulna, and articulated right forearm with hand of an adult. Burial 60 (pit 120 of cp 8) includes the left humerus, scapula, clavicle, and fibula of a child aged about 5 years. Both depositions overlie two other interments in their respective pits, and were deposited with tips of occupation debris, including flints and daub. Deposition 61 was also associated with burnt organic debris, overlying a crouched infant (deposition 13) and extended adult inhumation (deposition 14). The combination of two distinct interment rites in one pit is not common in the assemblage. Deposition 60 overlies the two children of Bii in pit 120.

Special animal deposits
These occurred in Pit 120, depositions 7, 8, and 60. Deposition 60 was buried with a dog skull. There was also a complete lamb skeleton at the base of the pit, and a relatively large amount of sheep skull bone in all layers.

The emphasis on the single skeleton in each deposit and the articulation of some of the bones suggest that the interments were not redeposited old and dry bones from past disturbed inhumations. Instead we appear to be witnessing distinct mortuary rites whereby the removal or loss of certain parts of the anatomy, and the interment of the remaining parts of the skeleton, is the final process of a more complex ritual which is not archaeologically visible. There may even be a crucial if general relationship between the absence of particular bones in these deposits and their presence as isolated depositions in other pits.

Deposition category C: charnel pits
Pits 923 and 1078, large beehive-shaped pits belonging to the late occupation period, cp 7, contained the mixed skeletons and skulls of ten and eleven bodies respectively. In both cases the bodies were dumped with animal bones, and special animal deposits, into the pits when they were already partially dismembered. The presence of sling stones may even suggest that the skeletons were stoned in the pits while they were left exposed for a period, but less dramatic explanations are more likely.

When excavated the bodies were found to be in a varied state of articulation, some of the bones being very scattered and mixed.

It was therefore extremely difficult for Bari Hooper to match up all the skeletal material with any degree of certainty, and in both pits there was a more complicated mass of bones than the catalogue might imply, with a number of scattered limbs and skulls not necessarily attributable to the same bodies.

Despite these problems, Hooper has identified:

Pit 923, depositions 33–42:
  i Almost complete skeleton of a female child/adult
  ii Partial skeleton of one female aged 25–30 and four children, two in their teens and two about 10 years old
  iii Four male skulls, aged 20–25, 35–40, 35–45, and 40–50 respectively

Pit 1078, depositions 48-57 and 162:
  i Complete skeleton of a female aged 21–25; deposition 49 has been included in the inhumation category, as the manner of treatment of her body appears to be entirely different, and she was tucked under the side of the pit, away from the main pile of skeletons. Complete skeleton of a child aged 10–14
  ii Almost complete skeleton of a male aged 25–35 years
  iii Partial skeletons of a female 20–30 years, a male over 40 years, and a child 10–12 years
  iv Skulls of three children, two under 10, and one between 8 and 12 years old, and one male over the age of 30
  v Fragmentary thoracic vertebrae of an infant c 4 years old

The assemblage is dominated by children over the age of 8 years and adult males in an older age bracket than in the other assemblages at Danebury.

There is no evidence of butchery or violent dismemberment of limbs, and the manner of the deposition of the bodies suggests that they were thrown into the pit after the flesh had largely decayed, in which process limbs,

Table 44 Skulls (category D)

Deposition number	Pit no	cp	Sex	Age	Bones present	Depth of burial in pit
32	906	3	♂	25+	Frontal bone with part of parietals	Middle
20	448	5	♂	17-25	Skull minus mandible	Upper
26	639	6	♂	25-35	Skull minus mandible	Lower
1	23	7	—	7-9	Fragmentary skull plus mandible	Middle
2	27	7	♂	25+	Left frontal bone and zygomatic arch	Bottom
4	62	7	♂	25+	Frontal bone	Bottom
5	78	7	♀	16+	Cranium minus jaws	Bottom
11	287	7	♂	−40	Frontal bone	Middle

skulls, and torsos have naturally separated from each other. The whole process suggests that the bodies were deposited or exposed elsewhere for a period prior to burial, but the varying states of articulation of the different skeletons implies that the bodies were in varying degrees of decay when deposited in their pits. Both pits contained carbonized grain and ash in the bottom. In pit 1078, this layer was subsequently sealed by further deposits of burnt debris before the bodies were deposited. It was finally backfilled with more burnt debris after the bodies had been exposed for a period. The bodies in pit 923 were interleaved between the layers of chalk shatter and erosion silts and the backfilling process appears to have been more intermittent than with pit 1078.

Special animal deposits
There is a remarkable similarity in the animal bones deposited with the skeletons in both pits: both contained a young pig, a horse skull, and a large amount of sheep skull bone. In pit 923 there was also an articulated lower horse leg in the middle of the pit; in pit 1078 the foetal/neonatal pig was only a partial carcass. There was also a large amount of cattle skull bone in the same layer. Both pits included animal deposits in layers other than those with the skeletons. Pit 923 included a partial horse skull and a cattle skull in layers above and below respectively, and pit 1078 included a sheep skull fragment and dog skull above, with a broken sheep skull below the human burial layer.

Both pits contained an unusually wide range of special animal deposits in association with the human bones.

There are only two such instances of multiple deposition in storage pits so far excavated at Danebury, and they do not appear to be paralleled elsewhere. Both belong to the later period, and possibly reflect the increase of stress at this time.

Deposition category D: skulls and frontal bones
Eight pits were found to contain a single skull or large part of a skull in the backfill. Table 44 indicates the age, gender, parts of the skull present, and the depth of burial in each context. They are listed according to the ceramic phasing of the pits.

Six of the eight depositions are adult males. There is one skull of a child, and one adult female cranium. The child's skull still has an attached mandible suggesting that the connecting tissue had not entirely decayed, and that it was fresher when deposited than the other skulls, which are without mandibles. It is also possible that the female cranium may not belong to this group; if the five thoracic vertebrae and rib fragments (deposition 91) in the same context come from the same body she would fit more easily into category Bii.

Five of the skulls, including the child and female, belong to the later occupation phase 7. The other three occur in cps 3, 5, and 6 respectively. This might suggest an increase in popularity for this ritual, but the numbers are too small to be reliable and the removal of depositions 1 and 5 would weaken the case still further.

There appears to be no clear preference for deposition at the top, middle, or bottom of the pits, although at least three in cp 7 were deposited at the bottom, on the primary silt or fill. All the skulls however were deposited with deliberate tips of debris; the fill around the female cranium contained carbonized grain, and several included animal bones.

Special animal deposits
Four contexts (with depositions 2, 5, 11, 26) included a relatively large amount of sheep skull bone. Deposition 2 was also associated with two articulated lower limbs of a horse and a pair of horse mandibles. Four of the pits included animal skulls in contexts other than those with human skulls; pits 27 and 78 both contained a broken sheep skull near the top. Pits 287 and 906 both contained a cattle skull, the former at the base of the pit. Pit 906 also had a pig skull at the base of the pit in the same context as a human skull fragment.

Sheep appear to be the most commonly associated animal in the later occupation phase, whereas cattle occur in one early and one late context, and pig is only seen in the early context. Given the emphasis on animal skull bones, the presence of articulated lower horse limbs with the adult male skull in pit 27 (cp 7) is unusual in this assemblage. The same bones occur with other human depositions in pit 923 (the charnel pit) and pit 935 (group burial of three skeletons in category A).

Hooper suggests that only one of the skulls — deposition 11, the oldest male in pit 287 — suffered from detectable severe head injuries. These need not have been fatal, but death followed quite soon after the injury as there is no

452

Table 45 Pelvic girdles (categoryE)

Deposition number	Pit no	cp	Sex	Age	Bones present	Depth of burial
62	16	3	♀	−30	Fragmentary pelvis	—
47	1020	3	♂	18-25	Fragmentary pelvis with femur heads: butchered	Bottom
64	900	3	♂	15-20	Pelvis with five lumbar vertebrae	Middle
63	94	7	—	c 6	Fragmentary pelvis and femur head	Bottom

evidence of healing (p 471). Three of the skulls, depositions 20, 26, and 32 have distinctive small scars, possible caused by branding or cauterization. These scars are also seen on ten other skulls in the burial assemblage (p 469).

The condition of the male, and possibly the female, skulls suggests they were deposited in their pits long after the flesh had decayed. As already mentioned (p 442) the skull was an important symbol to the Celts, and it is possible that here we have archaeological evidence to support the classical references to the practice of head-hunting — the removing of the heads of the slain during battle (Polybius, *Hist*, III, 67; Diodorus Siculus, 29, 4–5; trans Tierney 1960, 250; Strabo, IV, IV, 5; trans Tierney 1960, 209), and the value of skulls as trophies for display (Silius Italicus, IV, 215; Lucan, I, 447; Livy, XXIII, 24). The further evidence of skull fragments in pits supports the contention that skulls were being kept for particular purposes on the site.

The skull is an ambiguous symbol, however, and its removal from the body and use as a trophy may not only be associated with victory and contempt for the enemy, but also with the veneration of ancestors and lineage; it may therefore have a dual function, serving both as an object of profound contempt or of great value.

If the skulls were trophies for display, they clearly no longer served that purpose when deposited in a pit, and one cannot disregard the possibility that these old and dry skulls were ultimately discarded in convenient receptacles with or without ceremony.

On the other hand, as a symbol for the source of life, power, and regeneration, the deposition of a skull in the backfill of a disused storage pit may be seen as a propitiatory act, associated with the regeneration of crops or even livestock. This suggestion may be supported by the association with special animal deposits, also predominantly skull bones (see p 443 for a discussion of the symbolic association of human remains in corn storage pits).

Deposition category E: pelvic girdles

Single, fragmentary pelvic girdles were found in four pits, three of which belong to the earliest occupation period and one to the latest.

Table 45 indicates the bones present, the age and gender of the body from which they come, the depth of burial, and the ceramic phase of each deposition.

The pelvic girdles belong to one adult female (cp 3), two males (one child/adult and one young adult (cp 3)), and one child aged c 6 years (cp 7).

Depositions 47 and 63 were placed on the primary silt at the bottom of the pit whereas deposition 64 was deposited when the pit was already half full. All the bones are associated with tips of occupation debris including animal bones and pot sherds; deposition 64 was sealed by a tip including large quantities of charcoal and burnt flints.

Deposition 47 is distinctive among this group, for several reasons; it is the only one in the entire assemblage with clear evidence of butchery — the pelvis and femur heads were cut away from the torso and legs whilst the flesh was still on the bones. It is impossible to know whether this was done pre- or post-mortem but the details of the damage are described and discussed by Hooper, p 471. This butchered pelvis was associated with a bone fragment from another body (the right innominate bone of a child aged about 5 years), and a broken pig skull. There were also three fragments of saddle quern stone in the surrounding fill, and the whole burial layer was sealed with puddled chalk.

There were no special animal deposits with any of the other pelvic girdles.

The other bones appear to have been naturally disarticulated from the torso presumably after the flesh and connecting tissues had decayed; deposition 64 also includes five lumbar vertebrae. Deposition 63 however includes a femur head with the girdle, and the shaft had been snapped from the head prior to deposition. The bones had been gnawed by a carnivore, possibly a dog, suggesting that they may have been exposed somewhere on site whilst still fresh.

The process of decay and separation of the pelvic girdle from the torso suggests that there may be a crucial relationship between the treatment of some bodies after death and the presence or absence of particular parts of the anatomy in the final process of deposition. There were no pelvic girdles present in the assemblages of Bii and Biii, and the snapping of the shaft from the femur head of deposition 63 is reminiscent of similar evidence among the assemblage of bone fragments in category F.

The question of whether the significance of the presence of a pelvic girdle in a storage pit lies in the act of deposition and the symbolic association with the pit and associated refuse, or whether it lies elsewhere in the archaeologically irretrievable layers of activity on site prior to deposition, is relevant to all the deposits of parts of the anatomy.

The ambiguity of the separation of the pelvic girdle from the body is, however, reminiscent of a similar ambiguity with the separation of the head. Whereas in one context it may be seen as a primitive act towards an individual person, in another, where the individual persona may no longer be relevant, it is not inconceivable that it may be used in an act of propitiation, possibly as a symbol of

Table 46 The distribution of human remains throughout the occupation of the hillfort

Ceramic phase		1-3	4-5	6	7	7/8	?	number of contexts	% age of total number of contexts
Deposition category	A	8	2	3	6	0	1	20	12.8
	B	3	1	0	0	3	0	7	4.5
	C	0	0	0	2	0	0	2	1.3
	D	1	1	1	5	0	0	8	5.1
	E	3	0	0	1	0	0	4	2.5
	F	40	11	17	34	8*	5	115	73.7
Number of contexts		55	15	21	48	11	6	156	
% age of total number of contexts		35.25	9.6	13.5	30.7	7.0	3.8		

*There are three instances of bones in category F deposited in cp 8 in the top layer of earlier pits.

fertility and regeneration, and thus its association with a storage pit might be particularly significant (pp 461–2).

Deposition category F: individual and fragmentary bones

Individual and fragmentary bones representing a minimum of thirteen people were excavated from 116 contexts in 77 pits, two postholes, one gully, and ten layers in the quarry hollows behind the ramparts. Table 46 indicates the number of contexts with bone fragments in each ceramic phase. They occur in more contexts than all the other depositions combined, representing 73.7% of the total number of contexts with human remains on site.

They usually occur as solitary bones, although small bones such as vertebrae, phalanges, and metatarsals tend to be found with several of the same or in combination with a long bone. They may be found in the same pit with human remains from other deposition rites, but there are only four instances when they occur in the same context (layer): pit 37 (4) with deposition 3 (B), pit 78 (10) with deposition 5 (D), pit 430 (2/3) with depositions 17 and 18 (A), and pit 1020 (3) with deposition 47 (E).

In the past, these individual bones, frequently found in storage pits, ditches, ramparts, and sediments of Iron Age sites, have normally been considered to be residual from accidental disturbance of older graves. Although this may be the case for some of them it seems an inadequate explanation for much of the assemblage at Danebury for four reasons: (i) They tend to occur as solitary bones rather than the haphazard scatters one might expect from the disturbance of older graves. (ii) The pattern of distribution of parts of the anatomy appears to deviate from what one might expect if all parts of a skeleton were randomly distributed throughout the sediments on site. (iii) The bones have been subjected to various agents of attrition, which are difficult to explain if they are merely residual from earlier graves. (iv) In the context of the other burial assemblages within the settlement, it may be that particular parts of the anatomy were used for a variety of different purposes.

Fig 8.4 indicates the distribution of the different parts of the anatomy throughout the occupation of the hillfort from cp 3–8. Skull fragments and long bones, particularly the femur, occur more frequently than any other part of the body. (This is also apparent at Gussage All Saints,

Dorset (Wainwright 1979, 24).) There are also more right long bones than left ones. Some parts of the anatomy are very infrequently represented, particularly parts of the torso, and others do not appear at all. These biases appear to hold true in all phases, although there are more smaller bones, eg teeth and vertebrae, in cp 7, and no bones from the torso at all in cp 6. The bias may be partially explained by the distinctive appearance of skull fragments and long bones which may enhance the likelihood of their retrieval during the process of excavation.

The visible evidence is also partially explained by the fracturing of many of the long bones into at least two parts, and the multiple fracturing of skulls, which considerably reduces the actual number of complete long bones and skulls represented in the archaeological record. Fig 8.5 indicates the number of long bones which occur either as complete bones, or as shafts only, end only, or as a shaft with one end. Hooper suggests that in many cases the bones were fractured while still fresh and green (pers comm). Many of the skull fragments are small, indicating a considerable degree of attrition prior to deposition, and eleven skull fragments, two femora, and a phalange were found to be burnt or partially burnt. The possibility that some human bones were actually burnt to ashes would alter the survival pattern of any bone assemblage still further.

When considering other agents of attrition which might considerably alter the survival pattern, it may be important to note that seven bones, including six long bones (four femur and two tibiae) and one skull fragment, show evidence of having been gnawed by carnivores, probably dogs. This would have occurred only when the bones were still fresh, and suggests that some human bones were available to scavenging dogs soon after death. Binford and Bertram have shown how dramatically the archaeological record may be distorted by various agents of attrition, and particularly by bone-gnawing dogs (1977, 77–111). It is quite feasible that they might entirely consume many of the smaller flesh-carrying bones, and even the ribs (Hooper, pers comm). This possibility may be supported by the relatively frequent survival of hand and feet bones and vertebrae — the least flesh-supporting parts of the anatomy — and the scarcity of ribs and shoulder blades.

At the same time, however, it may be important to consider the 'removal' or 'loss' of certain parts of the anatomy in some deposition assemblages at Danebury, and their presence as individual parts of the anatomy in

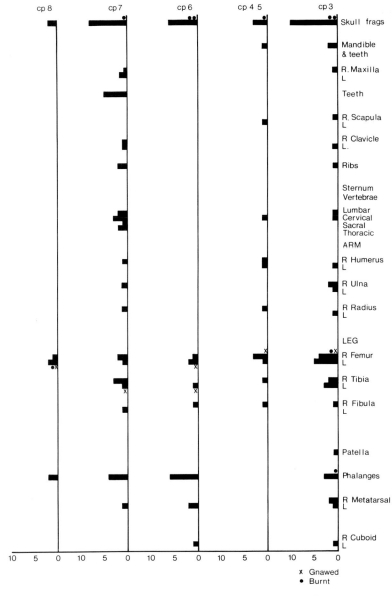

Fig 8.4 *The anatomical distribution of the bone fragments in category F*

others, particularly skulls, pelvic girdles, and limb bones. It may be remembered in this context that not only the skull and arms were missing from deposition 10 (pit 266) but also the right fibula. Only the shaft of the right fibula was present with the other bones in pit 374 (deposition 61), and the head of the femur with the pelvic girdle in pit 94 (deposition 63) had been snapped from the shaft.

The fracturing of long bones while still fresh remains enigmatic, but comparison with evidence from other sites suggests that we may be witnessing deliberate breakage soon after death. None of the bones have holes bored through them or are worn smooth in particular places in such a manner as to suggest reuse as ornaments or tools, as seen at several sites such as Ham Hill, Somerset (Taunton Mus Collection, A.1753, unpublished) or Lidbury, Wiltshire (Cunnington 1919, 35 and pl X, 10; Whimster 1981, 185). Nor is there any evidence that these bones were treated in the same way as bones of meat prepared for food, as suggested by the 'unmistakeable knife cuts' on the distal end of a humerus at Croft

Ambrey, Herefordshire (Stanford 1974, 220). Only one bone has a couple of knife cuts, and these are not reminiscent of such practices (Hooper, pers comm). There is no evidence of human gnawing marks on any of the bones.

Dunning suggested that two radius bones, an ulna and the right femur of a young adult female, at Salmonsbury, Gloucestershire had all been broken intentionally 'soon after death, and after the dismemberment of the body for the purpose of extracting marrow' (1976, 116–17, and pl XI). This may be considered a possibility for the fractured long bones at Danebury, but until the fracture patterns are looked at more closely, it may only be suggested rather than stated. It would be beneficial to compare the fractures of the bone assemblage at Danebury with the different patterns of marrow-bone breakage discussed and illustrated by Binford (1981, 148-63).

It is clear that the individual bones and bone fragments have been subject to a variety of agents of attrition. Some may have been used for specific purposes, others may simply be residual from older graves or other mortuary

455

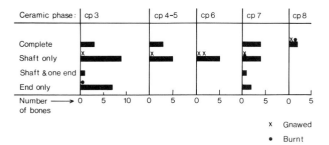

Ceramic phase:	cp 3	cp 4-5	cp 6	cp 7	cp 8

Complete
Shaft only
Shaft & one end
End only

Number ⟶ of bones

x Gnawed
• Burnt

Fig 8.5 Attrition of long bones: the presence of complete and fractured bones with an indication of how many have been gnawed by carnivores or burnt

rites (p 454). They are found both in deliberate tips of debris of a wide variety of occupational/domestic refuse (for details, see each context in microfiche) and in layers of erosion silts and chalk shatter. The latter association might suggest that some of the bones could have washed into the pits with surface debris. The diversity of the processes leading to final deposition in a pit, however, is well illustrated by the variety of associations between burnt bones and unburnt debris, and unburnt bones and burnt debris. The burnt femurs in pits 761 and 908 and skull fragments in pit 337 were all associated with burnt debris, suggesting they may have been burnt in the same process. The burnt skull fragments in pits 428 and 906, however, had no similar association with burnt debris, suggesting that the human bones may have been combined with the refuse at a more 'neutral' stage. Similarly, many of the other bones which exhibit no traces of burning were deposited in tips with burnt debris.

The whole assemblage illustrates how the complexities of the formation of the archaeological record must be more clearly understood before it may be interpreted. It would seem however that Danebury has an unusually large amount of individual bones on the site (Whimster, pers comm) and whatever the attritional processes, be they human or otherwise, the presence of these bones in disused storage pits and other features should be looked at within the framework of the other mortuary rites performed on the site.

8.1.5 Chronological factors in burial practice

Table 46 indicates the distribution of each deposition category throughout the occupation of the fort, as determined by the ceramic phasing of the pits. It is apparent that the inhumation of whole articulated bodies (A) and the deposition of individual bones and bone fragments (F) occur in all phases. The burial of individual incomplete skeletons (B) occurs in the earliest periods, and again in the 2nd century BC; both headless, armless articulated bodies (Bi, depositions 3 and 10) occur in the early period. The deposition of skulls occurs most frequently in the later occupation phase, but also in

the early and middle periods. Three of the four pelvic girdles were deposited in the earliest period, and the fourth in cp 7. Both charnel pits belong to this later period.

Taking the assemblage as a whole, the deposition of human remains in storage pits is seen most often in the early period (cp 1–3), the 6th to 5th centuries. They occur less often in the middle period (cp 4–6) but are again more numerous in the later period, up to the 1st century BC (cp 7–8).

When comparing the number of burial pits with the total number of pits in each period, however, it is evident that, owing to the disparity in the number of storage pits within each period, the practice of inhumation and the deposition of human remains in storage pits occurs relatively much more frequently in the later period at Danebury, reaching a peak in the late 2nd to early 1st century BC. This is illustrated in Table 47 which indicates both the total number of pits and the number with human remains in each ceramic phase. According to these figures, 6.7–6.8% of the pits in cp 3–5 contain inhumations and human remains. There is a rise in frequency in cp 6 to 13.0% and a further dramatic increase in cp 7 to 20.12%. The highest frequency of 42.85% may relate more to a historic event in the 1st century BC than an occupation phase.

The significant increase in the relative number of pits with human remains in the later period is paralleled by an increase in the number of inhumations and depositions per 'burial' pit. The data in Table 48 indicate a slight rise from a relative frequency of 1.29 to 1.5 per pit in cp 3–5, a further increase to 1.76 in cp 6, and a much larger rise to 2.16 depositions per pit in cp 7. They rise again slightly in cp 7/8. Whereas there is only one group burial in cp 3–5, there are six in cp 6–7: three triple and one double inhumation, and the multiple depositions in two charnel pits.

Against this background may also be seen an increasing tendency to bury the human remains with special animal deposits; 29.0% of the 'burial' pits in cp 7 also contained special animal deposits as opposed to only 11.0% of the pits in cp 3. 86.0% of the depositions in categories A–E in cp 7 were associated with special animal deposits, as opposed to 13.0% of those in cp 3.

The tradition of pit burial, particularly inhumations, in central southern Britain has so far only been recognized from the late 4th to early 3rd century BC, reaching its peak of popularity in the hundred years prior to the Roman conquest (Whimster 1981, 191). Although the variety of the Danebury data is on present evidence unusual, it is clear however that the increasing frequency of the deposition of human remains up to the late 2nd to early 1st century BC accords with data from other sites in this region. On the other hand, the practice occurs much earlier on this site than has so far been recognized elsewhere. It thus provides significant mortuary data for the earlier Iron Age in this region, for which there has been an even greater lacuna than for the later period,

Table 47 The % age of pits with human bones, according to the total number of pits in each ceramic phase

Ceramic phase	1-3	4-5	6	7	7/8
Total number of pits	531	147	100	154	7
Pits with human bones	36	10	13	31	3
%		6.7	6.8	13.0	20.12	42.85

Table 48 The frequency of depositions per 'burial' pit in each ceramic phase including all categories A–F

Ceramic phase	1-3	4-5	6	7	7/8
Number of depositions	48	15	23	67	7
Number of pits	36	10	13	31	3
Relative frequency	1.29	1.5	1.76	2.16	2.3

highlighting the ancestry of those rites which have been recognized in the later period.

The size of the early assemblage is related to the large number of storage pits dated to the early period, which make up 56.25% of the total number for the entire occupation of the fort. The implication is that the tradition of pit burial may be seen as early as storage pits occur on Iron Age sites in this area.

8.1.6 The spatial distribution of human remains

When considering the distribution of pits containing human bones within the fort we should remember that we are looking only at data from a transect across the site and an area around the entrance.

Given the differential distribution of pits, it may be said that there are no large areas without pits containing human bones, but that within the deposition categories there do appear to be certain distributional biases. Figs 8.6–8.9 illustrate the spatial distribution of each deposition category.

All but four of the inhumations, six of the seven single, incomplete skeletons, and both charnel pits are distributed north of the main track, whereas six of the eight skulls and three of the four pelvic girdles are distributed in the southern area. The pits with fragmentary bones are distributed throughout the area but tend to occur more frequently around the zones of the post structures — they are particularly concentrated between the two rows of post structures in the southern area between tracks 1 and 2 — and less frequently around the surviving areas of occupation stratigraphy behind the northern rampart. There are, however, four pits with fragmentary bones actually situated within the circular structures in the northern area, and several located in and around the occupation area behind the eastern rampart. Two pits were situated under the rampart extension near the east entrance, and in the entrance forecourt. There do not appear to be any distinct zoning patterns relating to particular parts of the anatomy.

The four inhumations south of the main track are all single adult burials, two belonging to cp 3 and the other two to cp 7. The rest of the inhumations are mostly distributed in the area between the post structures and the occupation zone behind the northern rampart, although the triple burial pit 935 is closer to the main track, adjacent to the occupation zone behind the eastern rampart. Whereas the single adult inhumations are distributed in the northern and southern area, all the neonatal, infant, and group burials are in the northern zone. The neonatal infant, deposition 31 (pit 857), in the upper layers of a pit within the circular structure CS9, and the child, deposition 58 in the gully surrounding the structure, were both associated with the abandonment of the building prior to the extension of the northern rampart in Danebury period 4. Pit 829 with the triple inhumation of three adult males was the first recognizable feature in the quarry hollow following the extension to the rampart. This area was subsequently covered with occupation structures.

One decapitated interment, deposition 3 (pit 37), is situated in the southern zone close to the single adult inhumations. The other interments in category B are located north of the main road, but considerably south of the structures behind the northern rampart. There are none near the south-east entrance.

The charnel pits are strategically placed close to the main road, pit 923 almost adjacent and pit 1078 beside a track which forks off it.

The skulls are predominantly distributed in the southern area between the rows of post structures, with which they are largely contemporary. The pelvic girdles are similarly distributed, and span a wide zone across the inside from the east entrance. If one compares the distribution of the inhumations with the other deposition practices B-E, whereas the former appear to have a closer spatial relationship with the surviving occupation zones behind the rampart, the latter appear to avoid them, with the pits with skulls and pelvic girdles particularly clustering around the southern area which is most densely occupied with post structures.

Chronology

The spatial distribution of pits with human bodies and bones within ceramic phases 1–3, 4–5, 6, and 7–8 are illustrated in Figs 8.6 and 8.7. The deposition categories are differentiated by the category letter. (See Table 46 for the chronological distribution of the deposition categories, and p 456 for a discussion of the relative frequency of depositions in each phase.)

In the earliest occupation phase cp 1–3 (Fig 8.6) the distribution of pits with human bones is apparently unaffected by the preponderance of storage pits in the northern half of the fort. They appear to avoid the central area around the main road, and there are only two pits in the far northern area, both within structure CS9. The inhumation in the surrounding gully also belongs to this phase. There were two pits with bone fragments under the rampart extension in the south-east. The pits in cp 4–5 (Fig 8.6) are lightly distributed over the central area, including one pit with fragmentary bones immediately inside the east entrance, contrasting with the pit distribution in cp 6 (Fig 8.7) which is predominantly in the northern area, including the zone behind the rampart. Pit 829, the triple inhumation, belongs to this phase. Pit 807, with the inhumation of a single adult male, distinctive as being the only body placed with the head face down rather than sideways, is located about 15 m south of the entrances of contemporary circular structures. The two pits in the entrance forecourt, P9 and P10, belong to cp 5 and 6 or 7. In cp 7 (Fig 8.7) the pits are widely distributed across the northern area, and slightly more clustered in the south, respecting the distribution of the post structures. Two pits with bone fragments flank the sides of the east entrance. The skulls and bone fragments are deposited in much larger storage pits than the two inhumations in the southern area.

8.1.7 The population structure of the skeletal remains

The number of skeletons represented in the entire assemblage, including the individual bones (category F), amounts to a minimum of 70 individuals. About 23% of the fort was excavated between 1969 and 1978 and therefore one might assume that if the site was 'totally' excavated, it might yield the remains of a minimum of 300 individuals. Even if one raised this figure to 500, while the sample would be large in terms of what has so far been found on other Iron Age sites, we are unlikely to be witnessing the mortuary rites of the entire population of the hillfort over a span of 500 years.

Bearing in mind the relative lack of archaeological evidence for Iron Age funerary rites, it is important to attempt to clarify what segments of the population may be represented by the surviving depositions. Since it is to be expected that different mortuary rites will be biased towards particular elements of the population, it was felt

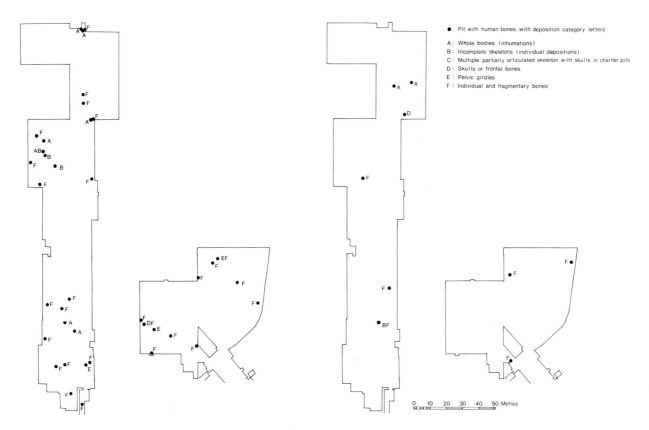

Fig 8.6   *Spatial distribution of pits with human remains in ceremic phases 1–3 (left) and 4, 5 (right)*

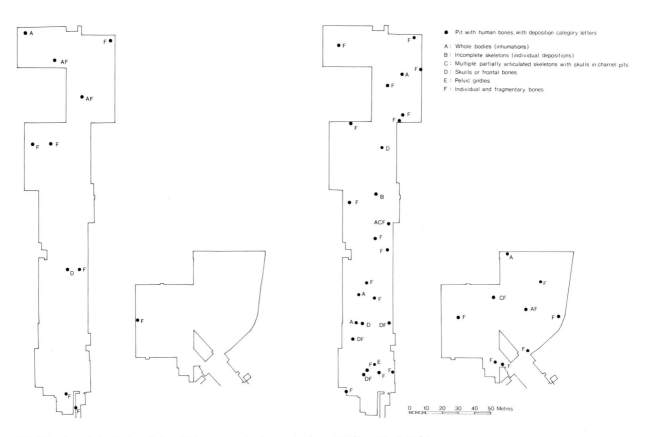

Fig 8.7   *Spatial distribution of pits with human remains in ceremic phases 6 (left) and 7, 8 (right)*

458

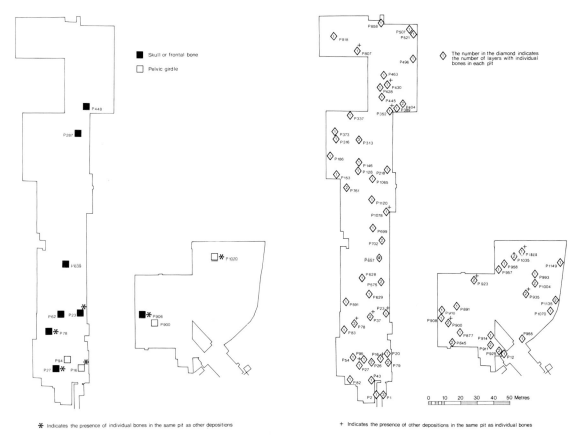

Fig 8.8 Spatial distribution of pits with human remains in deposition categories D: skulls or frontal bones, and E: pelvic girdles (left); individual and fragmentary bones (right)

Fig 8.9 Spatial distribution of pits with human remains in deposition categories A: inhumations (left); B: incomplete skeletons, and C: charnel pit (right)

Table 49 The distribution of the 'population structure' of the skeletal remains within categories A-E

		A	B	C	D	E	number of bodies/skeletons	% age of total number
				Deposition categories				
Adult 16+	♂	11	0	7	6	2	26	40.6
	♀	5	1	3	1	1	11	17.2
	unsexed	0	1	0	0	0	1	1.5
Child 8-16		2	4	8	1	0	15	23.4
Child 5-8		1	1	1	0	1	4	6.25
Infant −5		1	0	1	0	0	2	3.1
Foetal/neonatal		5	0	0	0	0	5	7.8
Number of bodies/skeletons		25	7	20	8	4	64	
% age of total number		39.0	11.0	31.25	12.5	6.25		

inappropriate to attempt to analyse the assemblage in the manner described by Acsádi and Nemeskeri (1970, 60–72) and Hassan (1981, 103–9), but certain points do emerge from a more straightforward comparison of the data.

Owing to the difficulties in ageing and sexing much of the fragmentary bone material, the bones in category F will be excluded from the following discussion, although it is evident that both sexes and all age ranges are represented.

The 64 depositions in categories A-E represent 38 adults: 26 males, 11 females (including two probable females), and one unsexed; 19 children of which 15 are between the ages of 8 and 16 and four between the ages of 5 and 8; two infants under 5; and five foetal/neonatal infants. The distribution of these groups within the deposition categories is illustrated in Table 49. For the specific age of each skeleton or partial skeleton see Index 4, (fiche 14, frames A13–B3).

Looking at the assemblage as a whole, it is evident that the burial record is dominated by adult males (40.6% of the total number of bodies represented) and children between the ages of 8 and 16 (23.4%). Adult females represent only 17.2% of the total number of bodies, and under 30.0% of the adults. Hooper comments on the relatively small number of neonatal infants and infants under 5 (p 464).

Table 49 clearly illustrates the biases within each category. Adult males predominate in categories A (inhumations), E (pelvic girdles), and particularly D (skulls). They are represented equally with children over the age of 8 in charnel pits (C). They are mainly in the 20–35 year age range, although there are some older men, particularly in the charnel pits. Inhumation is the most common rite (11 out of the total of 26), and they are not represented at all in category B (individual incomplete skeletons).

Inhumation is also the most common rite for the adult females (5 out of 11), but they are represented in all the deposition categories, including three (excluding one inhumation) in the charnel pits. The two oldest females aged 30–40 are single inhumations. The younger ones are either in the group burials or part of other deposition rites.

Children are represented in all deposition rituals, but predominantly in B and C. 80.0% of the children in both these categories are over the age of 8; there are no single skulls of a child under the age of 8. Neonatal infants have not been found in deposition rituals other than inhumations (A), although they are represented among the fragmentary bones (F).

More bodies are subject to the rite of inhumation than any other single rite, and in the light of evidence from other sites with the same pit burial tradition (Whimster 1981), this may be considered to be the most 'normal' of the rituals witnessed at Danebury. The preponderance of adult males, and relatively small number of adult females, children, and infants, however, would suggest that even this more 'normal' rite was biased towards certain elements of the population. This is particularly reinforced when looking at the solitary inhumations, which may well be more 'standard' than the group burials.

68.5% of the adults, both in the total burial assemblage and among the inhumations, are male. The implication that most fertile women were being buried elsewhere or disposed of in another manner is supported by the fact that a stable population could not have been maintained with the ratio of women to the population represented in the burial record, inhumations or otherwise. This imbalanced ratio is particularly exaggerated in the early and middle occupation periods of the hillfort.

There are also very few children buried on the site in the early and middle occupation period (Index 4, fiche 14, frames A13–B3). Moreover, since 57.7% of the children, including infants, are between 8 and 16 years old, not normally the most death-susceptible age group, it may be inferred that those represented on site had been specifically chosen for deposition within the settlement. The nature of the burial evidence would support this implication: the two inhumations may be regarded as 'special' in that one was from a triple inhumation with an adult male and young adult female (Pit 935, deposition 45), and the other was in the gully surrounding the early circular structure CS9 and associated with its abandonment (gully 67, deposition 58). The other children between the ages of 8 and 16 were all involved in mortuary rites B and C: individual, incomplete skeletons, and charnel pits.

The combination of a low ratio of fertile women, infants, and young children reinforces the suggestion that they may have been buried elsewhere, and with this in mind it may be significant that at Gussage All Saints, a conventional farming settlement in Dorset, of the eight skeletons excavated and dated to the Iron Age settlement phases 1 and 2 (up to the 1st century BC), seven were neonatal or very young infants and one was an adolescent female. There were no older children or adult males. It may also be significant that while there were a number of individual bones and bone fragments from the pits and enclosure ditch belonging to phase 2, the mortuary assemblage is much smaller and less diverse than the assemblage at Danebury (Wainwright 1979, 20, 24).

8.1.8 Discussion

In this final section, some of the major points which emerge will be summarized and possible interpretations of the data suggested, within the framework both of Iron Age mortuary traditions and what is known about Celtic ideology. Some anthropological comparisons will also be offered.

Ten % of the pits excavated up to 1978 within the settlement area of the hillfort contained human remains. These range from the inhumation of complete bodies (the most common rite) to the deposition of partial skeletons and individual parts of the anatomy. They reflect different rituals within a framework of two fundamentally distinct ways of treating the human body, involving a) deposition soon after death, and b) deposition after an intermediate period of decay. The latter is inferred from the lack of evidence of violent dismemberment of limbs while the flesh and connecting tissues were still present, and the varying degrees of articulation of the skeletal debris.

None of the depositions are associated with grave goods in terms of, for example, metal or ceramic vessels or jewellery. But although their presence is often understood to be associated with a belief in the afterlife and/or the status of the individual, Ucko (1969, 262–77) reminds us that to be buried without grave goods was not necessarily a negative statement about either of these factors.

The minimum number of individuals represented in the burial record is 70; given that about 23% of the total area has been excavated, this figure should be multiplied by 4 or 5 to give some idea of the total number of individuals deposited in storage pits. Since the total in no way matches the reasonable expectations of deaths over a 500 year period, it seems likely that we are witnessing minority rites reserved for particular occasions or particular individuals, inside or outside the community.

It may be inferred that the different rites reflect socially distinct performances, and that the status of the individuals represented may to some extent be reflected in the rite in which they are involved. This is corroborated by the biased population structure within each deposition category.

If it is accepted that we are not witnessing the funerary rites of the majority of the population, the treatment of the bodies other than the inhumations may give a clue to the majority rite which still eludes us. Some bodies had clearly undergone a period of decay before parts of them were deposited in pits, and during this time some of the skeletons were vulnerable to scavenging dogs; what percentage of these bodies actually survives is totally unknown.

The disposal of human bodies and skeletal material with occupation and domestic refuse in storage pits within the settlement area is characteristic of Iron Age society in a region of central southern England where the construction of storage pits is an integral part of the economy of the settlement (Whimster 1981, 5–10).

It may be suggested that, because the inhumed bodies and other human remains had been excluded or 're-moved' from what may have been the normal funerary rite, they were considered as separate from the rest of the population. In this context, it may be significant to note that the Asante tribe in West Africa used to bury certain elements of their society in their refuse middens, and by so doing denied the bodies the normal ritual and ceremony reserved for their lineage. The people who were treated in this way, ie dumped in a place of refuse and broken debris, were considered to be damaged or incomplete beings, and included babies, children pre-puberty, infertile women, witches, criminals, and those who met inauspicious deaths, for example by snake-bite or drowning. By denying them the normal funerary rituals and associating them with the refuse, their spirits were removed from general circulation and the purity of society and lineage was thereby better preserved (McLeod 1981, 36–8).

Although we know little about the details of Celtic religion and ideology, Caesar states that the core of druidic teaching was that the soul did not die but passed into another body (Chadwick 1970, 150); in that case, special treatment of those considered to be outsiders, damaged, or incomplete, would not have been unlikely. It might be appropriate to see some of the inhumations as 'outcasts' of this kind, but the diversity and complexity of the burial assemblage, and the different rites practiced, would imply several distinct social responses which cannot easily be explained and whose very ambiguity suggests complex cultural associations.

The most obvious ambiguity lies in the deposition of human remains with refuse in disused storage pits. On the one hand, the association with refuse might be considered to imply disregard, contempt, or even punishment, as with the Asante tribe. On the other hand, deposition in a storage pit, a symbol of the economic safety, well-being, and even power of the community may be seen as an expression of the involvement of an ancestor or a member of the lineage with the continuity of agricultural production (Bradley 1981, 234).

Given the nature of the human remains at Danebury, it seems valid to explore the possibility that we are witnessing the archaeological remains of Celtic ritual and secular activities involving human subjects for purposes other than simple burial: practices which are referred to by classical authors as well as in certain Irish texts. Literary and iconographic evidence for activities such as human sacrifice, votive burial, head-hunting, and even cannibalism have been examined (Kendrick 1927; Tierney 1960; Ross 1967; Piggott 1969; Chadwick 1970). Some classical writers refer to Celtic sanctuaries where gods were worshipped and humans sacrificed (Caesar, I,1, 33–4; Lucan; Tacitus, XIV, 30; Chadwick 1970, 142–51); the ritual killing of prisoners taken in war, criminals, or even entirely innocent victims, either by burning or by other methods such as stabbing, strangulation, drowning, or dismemberment (Athenaeus, IV,1; Diodorus Siculus, V,32, 6; Caesar, VI,16, 4–5; Strabo, IV,IV, 5; trans Tierney 1960, 196); the removal of the heads of the slain during battle and their display as trophies in homes and temples (Polybius, *Hist*, III, 67; Diodorus Siculus, 29, 4–5; Strabo, IV,IV, 5; Lucan, I, 447; Livy, XXIII, 24; Whimster 1981, 185–6); and finally, cannibalism, mentioned by Strabo, as being practiced by some tribes, including the Celts, in times of siege or famine, when harsh conditions made the practice expedient (Strabo, IV, 5; Whimster 1981, 184).

Several of these classical references may well be propaganda against the 'barbarians' outside the Empire, but

Whimster has considered the archaeological evidence in an attempt to discover whether traces of these activities survive in the archaeological record of the British Iron Age (1981, 177–89).

Clearly motivation is not easy to distinguish in the archaeological record and evidence of sacrifice or deliberate killing by stabbing, strangulation, or drowning is unlikely to manifest itself on the excavated bones. Indeed, the causes of death are not generally visible in the burial record; Hooper discusses the skull wounds but suggests that the assaults received by deposition 11 (pit 287), for example, need not have been fatal, even though death followed soon after. Deposition 30 (P829) and 50 (P1078) had both received heavy blows, the former with a blunt instrument and the latter with a sharp bladed sword. In both cases, however, the wounds showed signs of healing and were clearly not the immediate cause of death. The skull of deposition 49, also in the charnel pit 1078, had four holes in the vault made by a pick-like instrument, but although the bones were fresh when the wound was inflicted, it was not possible to tell whether they occurred just before or just after death.

When considering the Iron Age inhumations in the waterlogged peat deposits in Denmark, the state of preservation of the bodies enabled the excavators to detect that several had died of strangulation or by having their throats cut; neither of these methods would leave detectable traces on the skeletal material normally available to the archaeologist (Glob 1969).

Similarly, the ritual burning of bodies would leave little detectable trace unless the ashes and charred remains were deliberately preserved, in archaeologically surviving features. The survival of a few burnt bones in pits on site is not enough evidence to support the classical references to state sacrifices, such as those described by Caesar when discussing the Gauls: 'Some tribes have colossal images made of wickerwork, the limbs of which they fill with living men; they are then set on fire, and the victims are burnt to death' (I,1; trans Handford). It has been suggested that the burial of human or even animal bones in the backfill of a storage pit or other features may have served as a formal closure offering when the feature concerned had fulfilled its original function (Fox & Wolseley 1928, 451). The possibly strategic placement of bones in the top or bottom of pits is frequently witnessed at Danebury. Similarly the inhumation of a child in the backfill of a circular gully surrounding building structure CS9, and the burial of a neonatal infant in the top layers of a pit inside the same structure (depositions 58 and 31), may well have been votive offerings associated with the final abandonment of the building.

Within the same tradition, but in a rather different context, the burial of three adult males in pit 829, the earliest recognizable feature in the quarry hollow on the northern side of the fort following the rebuilding of the rampart in Danebury period 4, may represent a foundation offering on completion of the rampart heightening (Cunliffe, 1976, 210). The pelvis of a pig, an animal often associated with feasting, was associated with the bodies in the same layer. This area was subsequently occupied with domestic buildings and storage pits, with which the burial of a young adult male (deposition 27, pit 807) about 10–15 m south of the entrances of the buildings was contemporary.

The Celtic interest in the head as an object of social and ideological significance and the archaeological evidence for head-hunting have already been commented upon (p 453). The considerable variety of deposition rites involving different parts of the anatomy would support the contention that the human body may have symbol-ized a number of different meanings to the community, there being a strong cultural association between the individual/social personality and the physical body. The manipulation and use of certain parts of the anatomy may have ranged from propitiatory acts to social symbols such as talismans and heirlooms, or even to symbols of dominance and power over another community.

The presence on Iron Age sites of dismembered skeletons and bone fragments that were broken when still fresh has encouraged some archaeologists to consider the possibility that we are witnessing the residue of cannibalistic practices (Dunning 1976, 116–17; Stanford 1974, 220). As already mentioned, Strabo observed that the Celts did practise cannibalism in time of extreme necessity, for example during periods of siege when regular food supplies were inadequate (Strabo, IV.5; Whimster 1981, 184). A significant motive other than hunger for the practice of cannibalism is that which involves the belief that 'consumption of part of an enemy may be taken to symbolize the extent to which he and his people have been subjugated' (Whimster 1981, 184); or, as among the Asmat of New Guinea, the practice was intended to bring peace to warring societies on the grounds that the eaters became symbolic kinsmen and even blood relations of those they had fought and were then consuming (Zegwaard 1959; Whimster 1981, 184). Whimster points out that, in the case of the Asmat and other tribes, cannibalistic practices tend to be closely linked with head-hunting activities. It might not therefore be totally inappropriate to consider the possibility that the Celts did practise cannibalism for similar purposes, particularly as the physical body appears to have served so many symbolic functions for the community.

On the other hand, although it is not impossible that marrow was extracted from some bones (p 455), there is only one example of butchery in the entire assemblage (the pelvic girdle and femur heads, deposition 47, pit 1020), only one bone fragment with small knife marks, and no evidence of human teeth marks or gnawing. If these people were manipulating the corpses of their enemies as a symbol of their authority, or even kinship, it is more likely that we are witnessing rituals whereby the removal of the head and dismemberment of the body after the flesh had decayed were less extreme but equally effective methods, which did not require the flesh to be actually ingested.

Seen in these terms, the increasing frequency of the presence of human remains in disused storage pits on the site, reaching a peak in the late 2nd – early 1st century BC, may be an indicator of an increase in warfare and social tension during that period.

Anthropological studies have suggested that in some societies there is a crucial link between the belief that the relationship between the living and the afterworld may be controlled by the manipulation of a corpse, and the custom of secondary burial involving a transitional period during which the body rots and the bones become free of flesh, prior to final deposition (Van Gennep 1960; Hertz 1907; Huntington & Metcalf 1979, 8–15). In this intermediary period between life and death, the corpse is a model for the soul, both being formless, stateless, and an object of dread until the liminal period is terminated, usually by a ritual confirming the arrival of the soul in the land of the ancestors and marking the reestablishment of normal relations among the survivors. In Borneo the end of the intermediary period is marked by a feast, 'during which the remains of the deceased are recovered, ritually processed and moved to a new location' (Hertz 1907; Huntington & Metcalf 1979, 14–15). In such cases it would not be surprising to see the faunal remains buried with the corpse. Pig, for example, is an animal often associated with feasting, and at Danebury special pig deposits were found in both the charnel pits and with the butchered pelvic girdle. There was also the pelvis of a pig with the three inhumations in pit 829.

Although those three bodies had clearly not undergone a transitional period of decay prior to final deposition, it does seem to be a process common to much of the assemblage of human remains at Danebury, and it is possible that some of the depositions should be viewed in this context.

Hertz showed that in some societies there is a strong symbolic link between the liminal concepts of growth and decay whereby the secondary burial of a corpse after a period of putrescence may be associated with agricultural–fertility rituals within the community, strongly connecting the practice of secondary burial with that of sacrifice (Hertz 1907; Huntington & Metcalf 1979, 15). This might endorse the possible connection between the 'secondary' burials witnessed in the archaeological record and the literary references to sacrificial and propitiatory rituals, on the grounds that under certain circumstances the manipulation of corpses is symptomatic of a belief that the continuity of life is ensured by the control of the passage of the dead.

It has been suggested that the practice of secondary burial particularly as a propitiatory act is often associated with phases of social transition (Turner 1967), and it is possible that at Danebury the practice of depositing decomposed bodies or individual parts of the anatomy in disused storage pits may well be related to periods of social and economic stress, or even seasonal transitions — the latter being marked by important festivals in the Celtic calendar. If this was the case, the evidence again suggests an increase in stress in the later period both at Danebury and in the region as a whole, and this behaviour may well be as closely connected with the treatment of the corpses of the enemy as with the treatment of members of the community.

Although the burial assemblage at Danebury may be seen within the wider context of the tradition of pit burial in a region of central southern Britain, a comparison of the data with other sites in this region, particularly with the human remains at Gussage All Saints, Dorset (Wainwright 1979, 20, 24), suggests that the burial assemblages may vary according to the type and rank of settlement. Whereas inhumation in storage pits is clearly practiced on a wide variety of sites, the elements of the population involved in these rites do not appear to be consistent (Whimster 1981, appendix A1, 198–225). Similarly, the diversity of the rites practised at Danebury may reflect the functionally distinct role of a major hillfort, with possibly a greater emphasis on major community rituals in comparison with the more domestic interests of conventional farming settlements.

Until more Iron Age sites within this region are extensively excavated and published, it is difficult to estimate to what extent, or in what way, the burial assemblage at Danebury is unusual and therefore indicative of the special role of such a site within the organization of Iron Age social and settlement hierarchy.

Acknowledgements

I would like to express my thanks to Roger Thomas and Rowan Whimster for their helpful discussion after reading the first draft of this text, and to Alison Wilkins for drawing up the plans. I am particularly grateful to Rowan Whimster for the timely publication of his thesis (1981).

8.2 Anatomical considerations
by Bari Hooper
8.2.1 Introduction
The skeletons were found to be in fairly good condition, soil erosion having had little effect upon them except for deposition 6 (and the solitary Beaker burial). As is common with bones that have been interred for a long period in chalky soil, they were found to be light and friable. Several skulls and a few bones were received in damaged condition having disintegrated whilst being lifted from the soil or during the subsequent washing process. Where possible the broken skulls were reconstructed, but with some this proved to be an impossible task, the pressure of the superincumbent earth having distorted the pieces. In all 43 complete, partial, and reconstructed skulls were examined, but only twenty of these were complete enough to yield anything like a full set of measurements, too few to justify any attempt at an elaborate statistical analysis. A further complicating factor in examining the skeletons was the ancient disturbance that those from pits 923 and 1078 had been subjected to. Even after the long and tedious task of sorting the bones from these two pits had been completed, some skulls could not be matched with any real degree of certainty to the appendaged remains.

In several pits no complete burials were found, only a few token bones or fragments. Some of these disarticulated remains appear to have been lying about the site, or perhaps had only been lightly buried or concealed before finally being consigned to the pits. Claw-like scratches and the teeth marks of rodents and carnivores support this hypothesis. The carnivorous assaults, which seem to have been the work of dogs, must have taken place whilst the bones were fresh enough in nutritious matter to attract them. Post-mortem breaks in some of the odd long bones exhibit typical fresh bone fracture patterns. A few skull and other bone fragments show evidence of their having been in fires.

The total mass of bones from all of the pits represents a *minimum* of 70 individuals. The bones in deposition categories A-E (pp 443–54) represent 38 adults, including 26 males, 9 females, 2 probable females, and 1 unsexed, 19 children, 2 infants, and 5 foetal-neonatal infants.

8.2.2 Estimation of age at death
The estimations of the age at which each individual died were based upon the criteria listed below:

Immature individuals
  i the development of the dentition
  ii the degree of union of the epiphyses

Mature individuals
  iii the degree of attrition of the molar teeth
  iv the condition of the spheno-occipital suture of the skull
  v age changes in the pubic symphysis
  vi senile skeletal changes
  vii the amount of osteoarthritis present

i The general sequence of eruption of the deciduous and permanent dentitions (see standard dental textbooks) provides a reasonably accurate guide to the age of individuals from six months until the end of the first decade of life. From about the age of twelve years the chance of error increases as individual variations and sex differences become greater.

ii The average times of appearance of the primary and secondary centres of ossification and fusion of the

Table 50 Mean age at death

Combined males and females	males	females
28.69 years	29.48 years	26.5 years
(37)	(26)	(11)*

*The two probable females are included in this figure.

Table 51 Percentage distribution of ages at death of children and infants

Age in years	number	%
0 – 2	5	19.2
2 – 4	2	7.7
4 – 6	2	7.7
6 – 8	2	7.7
8 – 10	4	15.38
10 – 12	4	15.38
12 – 14	2	7.7
14 – 16	4	15.38
16 – 18	1	3.84

epiphyses have been well charted by several authors (Smith & Simpson 1956; Brothwell 1963).

iii The wearing down of the cusps of the teeth is a normal process affecting all peoples. This process was greatly accelerated in earlier populations by the fibrous nature of their diet and the inclusion of fine grit from quern stones in their food (p 473). Brothwell (1963), working upon the assumption that the rate of wear of the molars in British populations has changed little from the Neolithic to the medieval period, produced a chart of tentative age classifications based upon molar attrition.

iv The spheno-occipital suture is usually closed by the 25th year. Of all the skull sutures it is the only one considered reliable as an age indicator.

v From the beginning of the second decade of life the pubic symphysis commences to change its form at the symphyseal face. McKern and Stewart (1957) in a study of American males devised a method of evaluating the phases of change in terms of combinations of their component parts. They chose three components each subdivided into five developmental stages, which when combined as a formula for any pubic symphysis yields an age range for the individual.

vi Senile skeletal changes include thinning of the skull vault, loss of the teeth and absorption of the alveolar margins with subsequent diminution of the jaws, and fusion of the manubrium with the sternum. The predominant changes of senility are pathological.

vii Osteoarthritis as a degenerative disease is commonly found in the bones of people in middle and later life. The amount of disease present when combined with other aging criteria provides a rough guide to the period of life in which the individual died, ie middle or advanced age.

Using the above criteria, the age at death of each individual was estimated. The mean age at death of the whole group of adults is shown in Table 50.

The earlier age at which the females died may be explained as a natural consequence of the dangers inherent in child-bearing. These figures may be compared with averages based upon 221 Roman epitaphs from Britain: males 34.6 years, females 27.8 years, combined males and females 32.5 years (Acsádi & Nemeskéri 1970).

The five foetal/neonatal infants (Table 51) could not be aged with any certainty. The size and development of three of them suggests that they were not full-term infants. It is doubtful if any of them, even if born alive, lived very long, a few weeks at most. To include them in Table 51 they were each arbitrarily given an age of twelve weeks.

On present evidence 57.7% of the children died between 8 and 16 years. This is the sort of figure that might be expected for the 0–2 years period, the most hazardous time of infancy in any early population. This may suggest that many infant burials have been lost through soil erosion or through failure to detect them during the excavation. Neither of these possibilities is very likely given the nature of the chalky soil and careful excavation techniques employed. A stronger possibility is that the dead infants were disposed of elsewhere, or perhaps in a

different manner. If their bodies were burnt or even just left exposed upon the ground surface there would be nothing left to find today. Any brittle remains left after cremation would in the course of time have become scattered and disintegrated, and any corpse left abandoned upon the earth would have fallen prey to scavenging animals and birds. Carnivores, probably dogs, which do seem to have scavenged the site on occasions (see introduction) would have been capable of devouring even the bones of an infant. If an allowance were made for these missing infants the percentage would take on a more 'normal' appearance for a prehistoric group, ie a half or more of the infants dying in the 0–2 years period. This would also have the effect of making the life expectancy from birth for these people very low indeed.

8.2.3 Determination of sex

Theoretically, where a complete skeleton is available for examination it should be a relatively simple task to inspect the bones that most emphasize sexual dimorphism and to pronounce a verdict as to its sex. In practice the overlap in morphological range between the bones of the two sexes can lead to some skeletons being only tentatively classified as to their gender. The following bones are particularly important in sexual diagnosis:

The pelvic girdle Because of its marked adaptation for child-bearing the pelvic girdle is the most reliable indicator of sex. Its most important sexual characteristics are (i) the greater sciatic notch: in the female it is wide and shallow; in the male narrow and deep. (ii) the pre-auricular sulcus: this groove is generally present in the female, sometimes unilaterally. (iii) the pubic symphysis: the depth is generally greater in the male. (iv) the acetabulum: in the male it is larger; in the female it is slightly forward facing as well as smaller. (v) the pubic bone: it is usually larger in the female, but more robust in the male. (vi) the sacrum: in the female it is wider and relatively shorter than in the male.

The skull In the male the skull is generally larger with more prominent muscular markings. The supra-orbital ridges, mastoid processes, and external occipital protuberances are more developed, the palate and mandible larger.

The vertebral column In the male the vertebrae are generally larger, especially the atlas and lumbar segments.

Long bones The femur, tibia, and humerus in the male are

Table 52   Stature estimates: means and range of adults

Sex	Number	Mean	Range
Male	15	164.474cm	156.958 – 175.034cm
Female	7*	(156.428cm)	(150.43 – 160.240cm)

*One of the probable females is included in this figure

generally more rugged with stronger muscle markings and broader heads.

Using the above criteria, 25 males and 7 females were identified. Two other adults were found to have intersexual characteristics, but were probably females. Because of the immature development of their bones only a small number of the children were sexually classified (see individual burial descriptions in fiche 14, frame A4–fiche 15, frame A10).

8.2.4   Estimation of stature

The stature estimates given below in the burial description and in Table 52 were all calculated using the formulae of Trotter and Gleser (1952; 1958). The regression equations which comprise this method were devised from the examination of a large number of American whites. Despite the obvious inherent difficulties within a system that estimates the stature of a prehistoric European group based upon a formula developed from a modern North American group, it is widely agreed among anthropologists that Trotter and Gleser's formulae are the best at present available.

All estimates are subject to a standard error of ± 35mm. The mean and range of estimated heights is shown in Table 52.

8.2.5   Skeletal adaptation

At least nine of the adults (five females, three males, and one unclassified odd tibia) were found to have 'squatting facets'. These upturned extensions upon the anterior articular surface of the lower tibiae are thought to result from habitually resting in a squatting position with the joint in extreme dorsiflexion. They are frequently reported in Anglo-Saxon skeletons, but are rare among urban Romano-Britons, the latter more civilized people being presumably more familiar with the use of chairs and benches.

In one instance (deposition 29) the facet is upon the right leg only, indicating a unilateral squat, with the opposite leg probably outstretched to maintain balance. In the case of deposition 46, a male with a defective hip joint, the squatting facet upon the right leg is more strongly marked than that upon the left. The hip defect may have forced the individual to adopt a modified squatting stance, thus reducing the dorsiflexion of the left ankle joint.

8.2.6.   Epigenetic variants

A number of minor morphological variants occur in every system of the body, especially in the skull. Berry and Berry (1967) have shown that most of these variants are genetically determined, resulting from the normal processes of development rather than disease or external influences as was formerly thought. The frequency of any particular trait in a given race is constant and in closely related races similar. This fact provides a useful method for comparisons of ethnic groups within a major race.

Many of the skull variants are to be found in the facial bones and at the base of the skull, two areas often found to be deficient in the Danebury material. Because of these deficiencies the only variants recorded here were those that occur in the cranium, ie wormian bones (extra sutural ossicles), metopism, and parietal foramina. The commonest of these morphological traits are wormian bones along the lambdoid suture. Of 40 skulls examined with the back of the skull complete, 20 (50%) were found to have wormian bones (this figure does not include a single instance of an inca bone — an extra bone being created in the occipital through it being divided into two parts). Other wormian bones noted were two parietal notch bones (5%) and one ossicle at the bregma (2.5%). Metopism, the division of the frontal bone by a continuation of the sagittal suture from bregma to nasion, is a fairly common retention of a childhood feature. Two examples were noted (5%). Small parietal foramina are sometimes found close to the sagittal suture just above the lambda. In life they transmit a small branch of the occipital artery or a minor emissary vein. Seventeen skulls were found to have them (42.5%).

Brothwell (1963) in a study of the percentage frequencies of these traits in different populations found that for the Iron Age/Romano-British group the percentages were as follows: wormian bones 71.03%; parietal notch bones 36.04%; metopism 9.71% (parietal foramina were not recorded in his survey).

8.2.7   Pathology (Fig 8.10)

Manifestations of osteoarthritis were found in the spines of six of the men and two of the women. Of the nine recognized forms of arthritis, osteoarthritis is the most common, affecting mainly people in middle and later life. A degenerative joint disease, it is characterised by erosion of the articular cartilage with consequent narrowing of joint space; subchondral sclerosis; and the production about the articular margins of cartilaginous excrescences which have a tendency to ossify and in severe cases to restrict or totally immobilize the joint. These typical features are direct consequences of wear and tear initiated in many cases by some predisposing factor, especially trauma. The most common focus of affection is the spinal column where osseous changes take place at the posterior intervertebral joints and sometimes at the anterior margins of the vertebral bodies. Some of the eight individuals with osteoarthritic spines at Danebury have additional outbreaks of the disease elsewhere in their bones. Deposition 23 is the most seriously affected, the anterior margins of the lumbar vertebrae showing both attrition and formation of osteophytes. Deposition 6 may also have been as badly affected; despite soil erosion having destroyed much of the spine, what remains suggests a fairly serious attack. The remaining six individuals are only mildly affected, much less so than a group of Anglo-Saxon agriculturalists would have been. This might be an indication that the Danebury people were subject to less physical labour than later farming groups. This tentative hypothesis is supported by an absence at Danebury of osteoarthritis of the knee and elbow joints, two articulations that generally received strenuous usage in agricultural societies.

Deposition 21, a woman of above 35 years of age, has an arthritic right hip (Fig 8.10). The disease was still in an early stage of development when she died, and although it would have caused her some pain and limitation of movement she would not have been immobilized. Had she lived longer, the condition would undoubtedly have

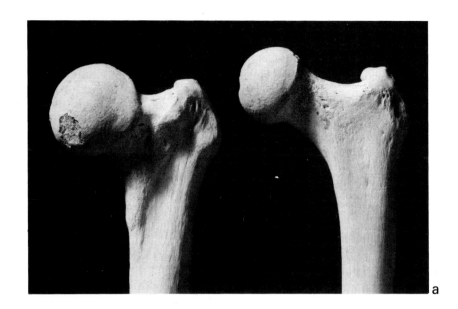

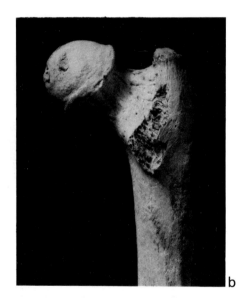

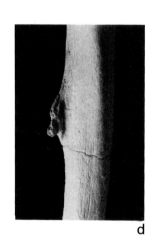

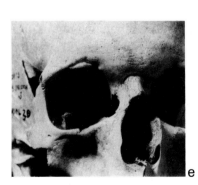

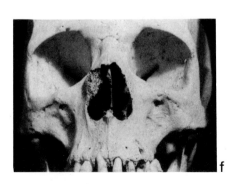

Fig 8.10   Details of pathological conditions and injuries: (a) left femur showing mushroom-shaped head and reduced angle of neck (left) in comparison with normal femur (right); deposition 46. (b) early stages of osteoarthritic lipping in the head of a right femur; deposition 21. (c) osteomyelitis at the left ankle showing sinus cavity; deposition 12. (d) exostosis ('rider's bone') on the right femur shaft; deposition 16. (e) healed injury on supra-orbital margin of right orbit; deposition 30. (f) inflammatory disorder in right lateral wall of nasal cavity; deposition 32. (g) right clavicle showing two small notches cut into it. All at 1:2 (photos: Bob Wilkins)

progressively worsened until ankylosis and fixed deformity supervened.

A less common site for the disease is the acromio-clavicular joint, one example being found in the right shoulder of the woman in deposition 23. Regular abrupt movements like those made when using a heavy tool against an unyielding object can cause this type of lesion. The unilateral focus suggests that the usage was consistent and right-handed, perhaps caused by wielding a one-handed type of tool rather than a spade. A single-handed mattock or pick being used upon a very hard ground could well have caused the stress to the joint which led to the disease. This same woman, and the man in deposition 28, were also affected at the metatarso-phalangeal joint of the great toe. This condition, known as *hallux rigidus*, can be induced by walking and working over rough ground or by stubbing the great toe against a hard object. Another important cause is *pes planus*, or flat foot, a condition in which the longitudinal arch of the foot is flattened so that when standing the weight of the body is borne upon the sole of the foot instead of the three normal support points. In this position the great toe is flexed and the metatarsal becomes horizontal, leading to the degeneration of the metatarso-phalangeal joint and subsequent osteoarthritis. No sign of *hallux valgus*, another deformity of the great toe, was found, indicating that cramping footwear was not worn by these people.

Depositions 29 and 30 both have osteoarthritic changes at the temporo-mandibular joint. Malocclusion, dislocation, vigorous mastication, and unilateral dental disease can all lead to this condition.

Deposition 46, a young man of 20–25 years, has a deformity of the left hip, the femur head being mushroom-shaped and the shaft of the neck having an angle of 110°. The neck shaft angle in the adult is normally about 125°. The appearance and position of the displaced femur head is diagnostic of Perthes' disease (osteochondritis of the femoral capital epiphysis), an affliction of childhood that generally occurs between the ages of 5 and 10 years, running its course in about two years. Its aetiology is still unknown, but a localized interference with the blood supply may well be a cause (Adams 1971). In a typical case of Perthes' disease the femur head becomes temporarily softened and being subject to the stresses of weight-bearing becomes deformed. Eventually the bone is revascularized and hardens, but the deformity remains, usually persisting for life. During its average two-year cycle of activity the disease causes pain in the groin and thigh. As a self-limiting disorder with a strong tendency to spontaneous recovery it has no long-term effect upon the general health, but the sufferer may well be left with the legacy of a slight limp and some limitation in the range of leg movement. The abnormally shaped femur head tends to predispose the joint to osteoarthritis in later life.

Deposition 23, the woman already mentioned above, was afflicted in life by several disorders which when considered individually are not particularly unusual, but together add up at first sight to a possible case of leprosy. However, after careful consideration of the evidence, this possibility was rejected, even though an apparently high number of leprous characteristics were found to be present. The reasons for suspecting leprosy in the first place and for finally rejecting this hypothesis need stating at some length, for if it were a case of leprosy it would be an important discovery. Contrary to popular belief very few examples of leprous skeletons have been found in British remains in any period.

The principle lesion in the skull of this burial is an inflammatory reaction within the right lateral wall of the nasal cavity and in the associated conchae. Moller-Christensen (1961), in an extensive study of medieval Danish lepers' skeletons, found many chronic nasal conditions, and suggested that there might be a causal connection between them and leprosy. He listed it among seven highly characteristic features of the disease (which need not necessarily all be present in any one individual) as follows: 1 Atrophy of the maxillary alveolar process, beginning in the prosthion region and proceeding upwards to the base of the nasal spine and symmetrically, resulting in the loosening and possible loss of the incisors. 2 Atrophy of the anterior nasal spine, ranging from slight but well-defined reduction through to complete obliteration. 3 Inflammation of the superior and inferior surfaces of the hard palate. On the superior surface the changes are of a destructive or reactive nature, or a combination of both. Those on the inferior surface are usually seen as a deepening and multiplication of the small palatal pits, especially around the middle palatine suture. 4 Inflammation of the nasal septum and conchae. 5 Inflammation of the lacrimal bone and groove and the frontal maxillary process. 6 Inflammation of the roof of the orbits — *usura orbitae*. 7 Inflammation of the maxillary sinus.

Apart from the nasal inflammation already described, an examination of the sites of these changes revealed the following: 1 The maxillary process is atrophied and the central incisors are loose within their sockets. 2 The anterior nasal spine is very slightly reduced. 3 The superior surface of the hard palate is unchanged, but the inferior surface is inflamed. 5 The right lacrimal groove has some very small pinpoint perforations. 6 *Usura orbitae* I° is present. 7 The maxillary sinus appears to be unchanged. From this it will be seen that five out of the seven changes were found in the skull. These changes are normally associated with others in the extremities of the skeleton, especially at the metatarso-phalangeal joint of the great toe. In this instance a periostitic inflammation of the lower end of the right fibula is coupled with osteoarthritic changes to the joints of the great toes. This combination of skull and skeletal changes constitutes the evidence upon which the initial suspicion of leprosy was founded. But when these characteristics were re-examined the strong element of doubt that arose finally culminated in the rejection of the leprosy hypothesis. To begin with, the atrophic condition which loosened the incisors and reduced the anterior alveolar margin is probably the same periodontal infection that caused the loss of the molars. In Moller-Christensen's medieval lepers the molars were not affected, the bone destruction being limited to the incisor region. The inflammation of the inferior surface of the palate may also be a consequence of periodontal disease. The most important stumbling block to the supposed diagnosis of leprosy is undoubtedly the lack of reactionary changes upon the superior surface of the hard palate, for according to Moller-Christensen (1961), 'the inflammatory changes of the hard palate constitute the basic pathology of this condition (leprosy). They must always be present for a diagnosis of leprosy to be made. The other conditions, atrophy of the anterior nasal spine and maxillary alveolar process may not always be present.' The other changes in the skull, the pin-point perforations of the lacrimal groove, and the I° *usura orbitae* may well be symptomatic of other disorders, the latter being fairly commonly found in early skeletal remains (p 468). this leaves only the original nasal inflammation that suggested a possible diagnosis of leprosy in the first place. Moller-Christensen found inflammatory nasal reactions in all of the 99 skeletons at Naestved, Denmark, which he diagnosed as being leprous. He therefore assumed, as stated above, a causal relationship between leprosy and chronic nasal inflammation. He did however qualify this by pointing out that chronic rhinites can also be a consequence of other causes. The failure to establish the basic pathology of leprosy, ie an inflammatory change of the *superior* surface of the hard palate, must indicate another cause for the nasal infection. In this instance that cause remains unidentified. As regards the changes in the lower extremities, the lesion in the fibula is the result of a sprained ankle and those at the metatarso-phalangeal joints of osteoarthritis.

A pit-like lesion in the right femur of deposition 29 may be a chronic bone abscess, a localized form of chronic osteomyelitis. This same skeleton has another cavity in the costal tuberosity of the left clavicle. A more certain diagnosis of osteomyelitis may be made in the case of the sinus aperture at the distal end of the left fibula of deposition 12, a consequence of an ankle injury (see below). A small sinus aperture and groove in the right tibia of depostion 21 may also be attributed to an early state of the disease. The commonest infecting organism of osteomyelitis is staphylococcus pyogenes aureus. Children between the ages of 3 and 12 years are the most common victims, but adults are not immune from attack. The onset of the disease usually follows, as in the case of deposition 12, from a previous recent injury. In some cases the trauma is preceded by some general blood infection, or by one of the more common fevers.

The origins of the groove-like lesions in the humeri of deposition 46 are more problematical. The fact that both bones are affected, albeit one more than the other, close to tendon insertion points, seems to indicate a post-traumatic infection. The lesions are unlike the sinus apertures associated with acute and chronic osteomyelitis, and their cause remains unidentified.

Another problem is the left calcaneum found with depostion 10. This bone has an area of osseous destruction upon one of its articular surfaces, a manifestation of some osteolytic malignancy within the foot. Bone destroying disorders of this kind are extremely difficult to identify, especially since the rest of the bones of this foot are missing. In fact there was so much post-mortem disturbance in this pit that there can be no certainty that the calcaneum even belongs to this burial.

A large cavity at the level of the third and fourth sacral vertebrae of the sacrum of deposition 40 may be an abcess. Since this burial is of a woman, it could be evidence of a puerperal infection.

The skull of deposition 52 is slightly hyperostotic. The relatively advanced age of this man (40+) might indicate that this condition is an early stage of Paget's disease (osteitis deformans), a slow progressive disorder of unknown origin. Among the symptoms of Paget's disease are surface changes in the skull entailing a steady deposition of fine porous bone throughout the whole thickness of the calvarium. Other characteristic changes take place in the long bones, especially in the tibia, which becomes thickened and deformed. Unfortunately in this case there is no appendaged skeleton to examine. It should also be noted that none of the long bones from any part of pit 1078 in which this skull was found are in any way diagnostic of the disease. Hyperostosis of the skull can also be a feature of certain blood disorders.

Eight skulls (four children, one child/young adult, and three adults) have slight cribrous pitting of the parietals. The perforations are elongated and radiate from the primary centres of ossification. Angel (1967) considered this type of pitting to be healed 'osteoporosis'. He argued

Table 53 Frequency of usura orbitae

Depositions	Sex	Age	Degree of severity	
			right	left
2	♂	25+		I°
4	♂	25+	I°	I°
8	♀	14–17	I°	I°
9	?	c12	I°	I°
13	?	c3	I°	I°
14	♂	17–25	I°	I°
16	♂	25–35		I°
22	♀	25–35	I°	I°
23	♀	30–40		I°
25	?	c5	I°	I°
28	♂	25–35	I°	I°
29	♂	25–35	I°	I°
34	?	8–10	★	I°
36	?	14–18	I°	I°
37	♂?	16–20	I°	★
38	♂	20–25	II°	II°
45	?	10–12	I°	I°
52	♂	40+		III°
54	?	10–12	III°	III°
55	?	8–9	II°	II°
56	?	6–7	I°	I°
57	?	8–12	I°	I°
58	?	c15	I°	I°

★orbit missing

that symmetrical osteoporosis of the parietals (which he calls porotic hyperotosis) is a consequence of an hereditary anaemic disorder such as thalassaemia. This inherited disease, being dependent upon a recessive gene, varies in frequency between families in areas where it occurs. The same author (1964) describes similar but more dense perforations upon the skulls of prehistoric Greek children, skulls which have also undergone other changes, including a thickening of the diploic marrow space, None of the osteoporotic Danebury skulls has any appreciable thickening.

A much more common type of osteoporosis is the condition known as *usura orbitae*. This manifests itself as strainer-like perforations in the roof of the orbits. Twenty-three (47.9%) of the Danebury adult and children's skulls in which one or both orbits were available for inspection were found to be affected by this condition (see Table 53). Orbital osteoporosis was first fully described by Welcker (1888) under the name of *cribra orbitalia*, and since then it has been noted worldwide in much early skeletal material. Despite its frequency its origins are still unknown and subject to considerable speculation. Henschen (1956) concluded after exhaustive research that insufficient nutrition must have been a causative factor. Wells (1964) drew attention to its high frequency among children and suggested that it might be due to an unidentified deficiency disease. He also mentioned another theory which attributes it to panophthalmia, a generalized infection of the eye. Moller-Christensen (1961) divided *usura orbitae* into three categories or degrees of severity:

468

I° in which the affected area covers up to 0.5 x 0.5 cm
II° in which this area covers up to 1 x 1.5 cm
III° in which the affected area is very large

This classification has been adopted for the present report. He states that the condition is always bilateral in occurrence. In the present author's experience this is not invariably so. In the Saxon cemetery at Portchester (Hooper 1976) one of the seven cases found was unilateral, and in the present group from Danebury there are three such examples. Moller-Christensen suggests that the perforations may be ascribable to an enlarged infected lacrimal gland. In his investigation of a medieval leper cemetery at Naestved, Denmark, he found bilateral *usura orbitae* in 69% of 99 leprous skeletons. This high incidence caused him to speculate upon the possibility of a causal relationship between *usura orbitae* and leprosy. However this may be, it should be noted that the frequency of the condition in non-leprous skeletons is not small; Brothwell (1963) gives the following frequencies for British material: Iron Age/Romano-Britons 35%, Anglo-Saxons 27.64%, and 17th century Londoners 15.38%.

Many of the Danebury skulls have very small osteomata upon their surfaces. These compact miniature neoplasms are composed of dense hard tissue, from which they are sometimes termed 'ivory exostoses'. The dense sub-periosteal bone is deposited through the eruption of osteoblasts at a single point perhaps caused by some pathological irritation. The exact nature of their origin is still uncertain, some authors preferring to regard them as epigenetic variants (Brothwell 1959). The compact osteoma is usually a singular phenomenon, but multiple osteomata are far from uncommon. The Danebury examples are much smaller than those usually noted, the largest being only 8 mm in diameter, and most are difficult to see without the aid of powerful side lighting. This lighting revealed a finely 'blistered' surface in over half of the skulls where one or more osteomata were present. Whether these 'blisters' are a form of incipient osteomata or a consequence of some unidentified pathological process could not be determined.

Three osteomata were also noted upon long bones, two measuring 7 x 4 mm and 6 x 4 mm upon the medial surface of the midshaft of the right tibia of deposition 29, and another upon the right tibia of deposition 10. These are probably scars resulting from the ossification of sub-periosteal haemorrhages following injuries to the bones at these points. Heavy blows from blunt instruments or kicks can cause this type of traumatic osteoma.

Other changes noted upon the long bones, particularly the tibia, take the form of linear impressions. The occurrence of these grooves upon pathological specimens has led to a variety of interpretations being offered for them. Some early workers thought they were caused by surgical intervention (Wakefield & Dellinger 1936; 1937), but in recent years they have been recognized as vascular channels (Wells 1963). In most cases these vascular sulci are of non-pathological origin, but Wells suggests that when the grooves are tortuous upon an otherwise normal bone, they may have been caused by arteriosclerotic vessels.

The fourth lumbar vertebra of deposition 23 and the fourth and fifth lumbar vertebrae of a fragmentary pelvis and lower spine in layer 4 of pit 900 have detached neural arches. Defects of this nature are known as spondylolysis, an anomaly of the lower spine in which the posterior part of the vertebral arch is separated from the rest of the bone, the deficiency being effected by fibrous tissue. This defect was formerly thought to be congenital but trauma is now believed to play a part in its origin. Uncomplicated spondylolysis can cause lumbar back pain, but symptom is generally absent. It is frequently found in association with *pes cavus*, or claw foot, an accentuation of the longitudinal arch of the foot. A complication that can arise from the defect is the slipping or complete rupture of the fibrous tissues allowing the vertebral body and superior articular processes to move forward, leaving the detached neural arch in normal articulation with the sacrum. This forward displacement is one of the three varieties of spondylolisthesis. No evidence of such spontaneous displacement was found here.

The fifth lumbar vertebra of deposition 43 also has a defective neural arch. In this case it is firmly united at the left side, but at the right the bony continuity is interrupted between the superior and inferior articular processes by a thin join. This partially defective vertebra is associated with an anomalous sacrum in which the laminae of the third, fourth, and fifth sacral vertebrae have failed to unite, leaving an open canal. The laminae of the first and second sacral vertebrae have met, but the join running along the median sacral crest is still patent. Congenital gaps in the vertebral column occur in the lumbar vertebrae in modern Britain in about 1:1000 births (*spina bifida*) and they constitute one of the major neurological disabilities of today. Deficiencies of the sacral laminae are much less common, and when they do occur are usually situated at the level of the fifth or fourth and fifth vertebrae (*hiatus sacralis*). More rarely the whole of the sacral canal remains open (MacCurdy 1923; Brothwell 1963). In the present instance it may be presumed from the age of the individual, 25–35 years, that the anomaly had little or no effect upon his well-being.

An exostosis upon the right femur of deposition 16 is of post-traumatic origin, a direct consequence of tearing of part of the Adductor longus muscle and the underlying periosteum. The angle at which the osseous outgrowth is projecting indicates that part of the broad aponeurosis (flattened tendon) has become ossified. The Adductor longus muscle, which as its name suggests, adducts the thigh and rotates it laterally, is subject to much strain in those who ride a great deal. In horsemen it is not uncommon for it to become ruptured by the sudden gripping of the saddle with the thighs. This rupture may occur at the pubic bone where the muscle originates or, as in this instance, at the femur where it terminates. The resulting ossification of the injury is commonly called a 'rider's bone'. In all probability this individual was a regular horseman, and, according to the evidence of his heels, not inactive in pedestrian activities as well. Reactive changes at the insertion points of the Achillis tendon in both of his heels tell of recurring strains being placed upon them. The Achillis tendon, the thickest and longest in the body, is common to both Gastrocnemius and Soleus muscles, the main plantar-flexors of the ankle joint. Apart from being essential to standing, these muscles are used in walking, jumping, and dancing. Over-vigorous pursuit of any of these activities puts a heavy strain upon the Achillis tendon, causing it in some instances to rupture. Three other individuals (depositions 6, 23, and 28) suffered similar strains to the Achillis tendon. One of them, deposition 6, a man, had also strained the tendon of his right Sartorius muscle probably in a fall. This same man also had the misfortune to strain the tendons of the Quadriceps femoris muscles at their patellar attachments in both legs, the right more than the left. The Quadriceps tendon is sometimes torn

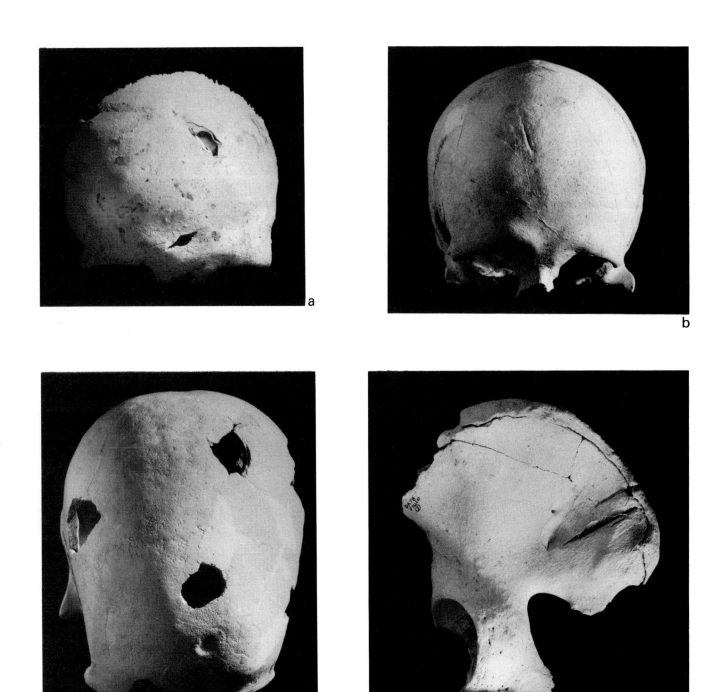

Fig 8.11 Details of injuries: (a) puncture and impact injuries on frontal bone; deposition 11. (b) healed sword wound on frontal bone; deposition 50. (c) holes in vault of skull. The edge of the fourth hole in the left parietal can just be seen at the lower right side of the photograph. In the centre of the frontal bone is a crater-like scar whose cause was not determined; deposition 48. (d) sword cuts and impact fractures on the left ilium; deposition 47. All at 1:2 (photos: Bob Wilkins)

470

away from the patella by an unexpected flexion force being opposed by a contraction of the Quadriceps muscle, especially in the elderly. In the present instance the damage is not so severe, the tendons having been apparently subjected to a recurring strain perhaps through some occupational activity involving the regular flexing of the knee joints.

The man in depostion 12 also suffered the consequence of accidental leg injuries. Inflammatory traumatic reactions at the left tibiofibular, talofibular, and talotibular joints and interosseous ligamental insertion point upon the fibula tell the story of a badly sprained ankle, perhaps accompanied by the cracking of the lateral malleolus. A stumble upon uneven ground with the lateral rotation of the ankle could have caused this injury. A sinus aperture at the base of the interosseous crest of the fibula indicates an early stage of osteomyelitis, almost certainly a direct consequence of the trauma. The right ankle was also sprained on some occasion. The woman in deposition 23 suffered similar ankle injuries in addition to the other pathological changes already mentioned above.

The skull of deposition 48, a man above 30 years of age, was incomplete when received and in fragmentary condition. Subsequent reconstruction revealed the presence of four holes in the vault. One hole, 24 x 18 mm, is in the frontal bone, another, 40 x 30 mm, is in the right parietal bisecting the temporal line, and the third, 30 x 22 mm, is in the top of the left parietal. The full extent of the fourth hole in the left parietal could not be determined as most of this side of the skull is missing. Two of the holes have depressed fractures of the lamina externa at their margins. Impact flake scars and larger margins of the holes on the lamina interna indicate that the bone was in fresh or relatively fresh condition when the injuries were inflicted. Whether the wounds, which were made with a pick-like instrument, were inflicted before or after death could not be established. The skull must have been lying upon the surface or partially exposed at some time, for the broken edge of the left parietal had been gnawed by a rodent, probably a mouse.

The odd frontal bone classified as deposition 11 also bears witness to a violent assault being made upon it. In this instance three serious wounds were made. The first was inflicted with a sharp weapon which appears to have been reinforced with a central ridge (Fig 8.11). The weapon, perhaps the point of a spear or heavy knife, pierced both laminae and caused a hairline crack to extend from the lower edge of the wound down through the superciliary arch and into the left orbit. The second wound was again made with a pointed weapon, causing a depressed fracture 25 x 13 mm in the lamina externa. The weapon did not penetrate through to the brain cavity, but the force of the blow detached a flake of bone 35 x 26 mm from the lamina interna. The third injury up against the coronal suture about 60 mm to the right of the bregma is in the form of a slight depressed fracture of the lamina externa, with a hairline crack extending about 37 mm from it towards the sagittal suture on the outside and 50 mm inside. Fine striae upon the surface of this wound seems to indicate a heavy glancing blow rather than a direct downward stroke. This injury would have extended to the missing right parietal. None of the injuries, if they were inflicted during life, need necessarily have caused immediate death, but the lack of any sign of healing shows that death must have followed within a very short time.

Deposition 50, a man in the 25–35 years age range, was struck upon the centre of the frontal bone with a sharp-bladed weapon, almost certainly a sword. The blade made a 35 mm cut into the bone, about half of this length actually penetrating the lamina externa to the diploe. The lamina interna was not breached. The failure of the weapon to reach the brain and the lack of infection about the wound led to good healing and recovery. The degree of healing suggests that the assault must have taken place several weeks, perhaps even months, before death. One rib of this man was also found to have been fractured and healed.

A violent frontal assault also seems to have taken place upon the man in deposition 30. The attack with what appears to have been a blunt weapon resulted in the man receiving a heavy blow over the right eye which removed an 11 x 2.5 mm sliver of bone from the supra-orbital margin. The fragment was not completely detached, the roof of the orbit holding it in position. The wound healed, but the bone sliver did not properly reunite to the arch (Fig 8.10). The follow-through movement of the weapon after striking the edge of the orbital margin would have continued into the eye, severely damaging or destroying it.

A small osseous protruberance below the left orbit of another male, deposition 28, may be an ossified haematoma arising from a blow in the face at this point.

The pelvic girdle classified as deposition 47 bears evidence of crude but effective butchery used to cut it away from the trunk and to remove the legs. It was not possible to determine whether the legs were removed before or after the pelvic girdle was cut from the spine, but the practicalities of the operation would suggest that they were removed first. Despite the fragmentary condition of the remains, several interesting points about the butchery technique can be made together with some tentative speculations as to how it was carried out. It is impossible to know how many men were involved in the gruesome task of dismemberment, but in order to avoid qualifying sentences referring to the butcher(s) with he/they, all such references below are in the singular. It is assumed that the victim was dead when the operation was commenced.

The removal of the legs could have been achieved once the overlying muscles had been cut and stripped back, by carefully severing the ilio-femoral and associated ligaments with a sharp knife, thus enabling the femoral heads to be removed from the acetabula. But not surprisingly in view of the clumsy butchery described below, this was not done; the butcher instead resorted to the crude expedient of hacking through the upper ends of each femur shaft with a combination of longitudinal and horizontal chopping strokes (Figs 8.11, 8.12). The cuts upon the underside of the right femur (Fig 8.12) suggest that having severed the surrounding muscles and tendons, the butcher manipulated the leg laterally within its socket and attempted to cut through the base of the femur neck. But instead of directing his strokes across the long axis of the neck, he mistakenly struck horizontally into a wide part of the bone. Alternatively, this and other cuts, one of which almost removed the greater trochanter (Fig 8.12), were made during the removal of the overlying muscles. The final cutting through of the shaft of the right leg cannot be seen, the bone having suffered some post-mortem damage. The left femur was sliced through longitudinally (Fig 8.12a-b), the bone being almost completely cut through before being snapped off by forcefully applying lateral pressure. Three other cuts upon this bone may be abortive attempts at severing the shaft or, as is more likely, made in removing the overlying structures.

The freeing of the pelvic girdle from the spine must have begun with the cutting through of the muscles and soft

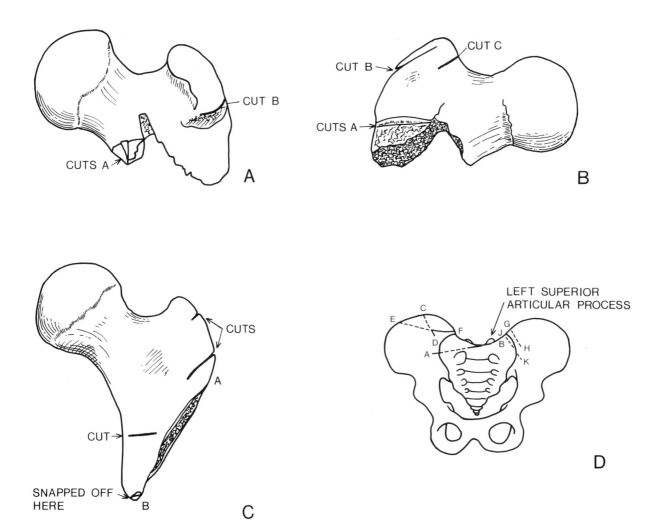

Fig 8.12   Details of cuts marks on human bones of deposition 47: (a) posterior aspect of right femur: (b) anterior aspect of right femur; (c) anterior aspect of left femur; (d) pelvis

tissues and removal of the lower organs of the trunk. Once this had been achieved, the operation to part the pelvic girdle from the spine was effected by chopping through the first sacral vertebra (Fig 8.12). The cutting stroke A-B, perhaps the first of two or three strokes, struck the ventral surface of the vertebra just below its promontory and sliced obliquely downwards and backwards cutting off the left superior articular process at its base. The natural anterior curve of the spine at this point and the angle of the cut from front to back indicates that the blow must have been struck at approximately a right-angle to an imaginary horizontal line drawn through the spinal column with the body lying upon its back or, as is more likely, upon its left side. Part of the blade of the weapon just touched the right ilium at A, indicating that this stroke alone was insufficient to sever the backbone having been aimed too low. Other blows C-D and E-F, aimed perhaps from behind in an effort to severe the muscles of the lower back, were made before the task was successfully accomplished. Two much less destructive cuts G-H and J-K upon the external surface of the left ilium were certainly struck from behind, with the body now probably lying face downward (Fig 8.11). Stroke G-H cut through the iliac epiphysis, but stroke J-K only opened the surface of the bone, indicating that the last stroke was made with the point of the weapon, or it would have touched the epiphysis had it been made

with the long edge of the blade. These two cuts, the impact of which fractured the bone surface, would have severed part of the broad tough gluteal aponeurosis covering the Glutaeus medius muscle situated here. These last two cuts were probably made as part of the operation to sever the upper thigh muscles.

The narrowness of the cuts and the impact fractures upon the ilium indicate that a thin-bladed weapon of relatively heavy weight was used by the butcher. A sword rather than an axe or knife would seem to have been his chosen instrument.

Much less dramatic cuts probably made with sharper knives were found upon bones in depositions 4, 45, and 46. Deposition 4 consisting only of a frontal bone of a male above 25 years of age has a very small cut upon the right supra-orbital margin just above the zygomatic process. Deposition 45, a child of 10–12 years, has a very small nick out of the left parietal, and deposition 46, a male aged 20–25 years, a similar cut above the left orbit. None of these tiny cuts show any signs of healing, but whether they were pre- or post-mortem lesions could not be determined. If the latter, they were inflicted in antiquity, not in the course of the present excavation. One definite example of ancient post-mortem damage is a right clavicle found in layer 2 of pit 925. This bone has

472

two small cuts upon its superior surface. The cuts take the form of shallow notches and were quite obviously deliberately made.

8.2.8 Dental pathology

The dentition of the Danebury inhabitants was found to be generally well developed except for some overcrowding and in some cases a tendency towards microdontia of the third molars. The overcrowding of the teeth of deposition 14 resulted in malocclusion causing very severe wear to the lingual surfaces of the upper incisors. Six individuals were found to have microdontic upper third molars; this congenital anomaly has been noted in teeth from the Neolithic period onwards and its present frequency is about 0.5% among Europeans (Brabant 1967). Hypodontia, the congenital absence of one or more teeth, was noted in five individuals. According to Salzmann (1957) the order of frequency for missing teeth is as follows: third molars, maxillary lateral incisors, maxillary or mandibular second premolars, mandibular central incisors, and maxillary first premolars. At Danebury depositions 6 and 12 are missing their lower third molars, deposition 26 the upper third molars, deposition 16 the upper left first premolar, and deposition 44 the upper right lateral incisor, the canine taking its place (behind the canine is the socket of a lost tooth, either a supernumerary or a deciduous tooth retained late). Third molars (and lateral incisors) as the commonest form of hypodontia have been studied more than any other teeth, revealing varying frequencies in different populations. Brothwell et al (1963) give a frequency range of 0.2–25% for all populations, with 10.8% for the French, Belgian, and British Neolithic, and 7% (mandibles only) for Anglo-Saxons. The frequency of missing third molars from 27 adult specimens (23 complete jaws, 3 maxillae, and 1 mandible) at Danebury is 4.93%. The causes of hypodontia may include disease and nutritional and endocrine disturbances, but heredity appears to be the most important determinant.

The upper jaw of deposition 24 has a supernumerary tooth between the left canine and the first premolar; a corresponding socket at the right must have held a similar tooth which was shed shortly before death. These additional teeth contributed to the overcrowding noted in this dental arch.

The physiological wearing away of the substance of the teeth during mastication is known as dental attrition. This wear normally occurs upon the occlusal surfaces of the back teeth and to a lesser extent upon the edges of the incisors. For the people of Danebury and other prehistoric groups this attrition process was greatly accelerated by the accidental inclusion of fine grit in their food from the use of lava-stone querns. A tough fibrous diet requiring vigorous mastication is another likely causative factor. The greatest amount of occlusal attrition occurs upon the earliest erupting teeth; thus the first molar will be subjected to longer wear than the second and third molars. In an older person this will be less apparent, the later erupting teeth having had ample time to become almost as worn as those erupting first. Occasionally the wear is very excessive resulting in oblique planes of abrasion as in deposition 38. Cooke and Rowbotham (1968) explain this phenomenon as being largely due to the range of movements allowed by the temporomandibular joint and the differing size and shape of the two dental arches. Depositions 43 and 50 have grossly worn incisors and canines with pulp cavities exposed. The attrition here has been so rapid that secondary dentine has been unable to form fast enough to repair the damage. Wear of this nature can result from malocclusion of the jaws, as in deposition 13, or it can develop where an individual is suffering from painfully diseased back teeth and is chewing his food with his incisors. Another cause of rapid wear that should not be discounted is the use of the teeth in occupational tasks. Eskimo women, for instance, sometimes have abnormal wear upon their incisors from their habit of softening leather hides and thongs by chewing them (Pedersen 1949).

The obviously low standard of dental hygiene at Danebury encouraged the deposition of calculus upon the teeth of several individuals. In most cases the deposits are of the supragingival variety and not excessive. A notable exception to this is deposition 21, a female whose upper molars are coated with dysfunction calculus, her jaws having lost most of their masticatory functions through the painful condition of her diseased molars, which in the course of time were shed. The chemical composition of these calculus deposits is mainly of calcium, and in some cases it might have afforded the teeth some protection from caries. It also had the adverse effect of irritating the gingival tissues and thus initiating gum diseases.

The living teeth are supported in the alveolar bone by surrounding soft tissues. These supporting systems of bone and tissues constitute the periodontium, and any inflammatory changes to this brought about by trauma or infection are known as periodontal disease. Periodontal infection is commonly observed in early human remains, but its frequency is probably underestimated in most reports, for minor inflammations do not affect the underlying bone. It is only the more serious infections that lead to a recession of the alveolar margins with consequent loosening and loss of the teeth. A conservative estimate of the frequency of periodontal disease in the Danebury jaws is 18.5%, with at least 70 teeth being lost through this cause.

Dental caries was found in 7.15% of the remaining 950 teeth. The disease was noted mainly in the cervical regions of the molars, but examples were found in all teeth except the lower lateral incisors and canines. Apart from five deciduous molars, all of the carious teeth are of the permanent dentitions. The causes of caries differ from one population to another, but diet seems to be the prime causative factor. No specific nutrient is consistently identified with the disease, but fermentable carbohydrates lodging between the teeth seem to be strongly associated with it. The percentage of carious teeth at Danebury may be compared to Brothwell's percentage of about 10% for the British Iron Age (1963). His frequency graph for British populations shows a steady rise from 2% c 1500 BC to 10–12% in the Iron Age/Romano-British population; after this it drops to 6% for the Anglo-Saxons before climbing steeply to above 20% for modern Britain.

Acknowledgments

I wish to express my thanks to Mr David Silver of Saffron Walden, Essex, for his valuable comments upon the dental pathology, and to Miss Brigid Hooper of Wicken Bonhunt, Essex, Mr and Mrs Bob Langley of Hare Street, Hertfordshire, and Miss Gillian Pasternak of Lucy Cavendish College, Cambridge, for assistance in sorting and classifying the material. And especially I should like to thank Mr John Monk of Wicken Bonhunt for the many long hours spent in reconstructing skulls and providing much other practical assistance.

Bibliography

Acsádi, G-Y, & Nemeskéri, J, 1970 *History of human life span and mortality*, Budapest

Adams, J C, 1971 *Outline of orthopaedics*

Angel, J L, 1964 Osteoporosis: thalassemia?, *Amer J Phys Anthrop*, n ser, **21**, 369

————, 1967 Porotic hyperostosis or osteoporosis symmetrica, in *Diseases in antiquity* (eds D Brothwell & A T Sandison), 378–89, Springfield

Berry, A C, & Berry, R J, 1967 Epigenetic variation in the human cranium, *J Anatomy*, **101**, 2, 361

Binford, L J, 1981 *Bones: ancient men and modern myths*

Binford, L J, & Bertram, J B, 1977 Bone frequencies — and attritional processes, in *For theory building in archaeology, Essays on faunal remains, aquatic resources, spatial analysis and systemic modelling* (ed C J Binford), 77–153

Brabant, H, 1967 Palaeostomatology, in *Diseases in antiquity* (eds D Brothwell & A T Sandison), 546, Springfield

Bradley, R, 1981 Economic growth and social change: two examples from prehistoric Europe, in *Economic archaeology* (eds A Sheridan & G Bailey), 231–8

Brothwell, D, 1959 The use of non-metrical characters of the skull in differentiating populations, *Ber 6 Tag Dtsch Ges Anthrop Kiel*, 103–9

————, 1963 *Digging up bones*

Brothwell, D, Carbonell, V M, & Goose, D H, 1963 Congenital absence of teeth in human populations, in *Dental anthropology* (ed D Brothwell), 179–90

Chadwick, N K, 1970 *The Celts*

Cooke, C, & Rowbotham, T C, 1968 Dental report, part 3, in *The Romano-British cemetery at Trentholme Drive, York* (L P Wenham), 201

Cunliffe, B W, 1976 Danebury, Hampshire: second interim report on the excavations, 1971–5, *Antiq J*, **56**, 198–216

Cunnington, M E, 1919 Lidbury Camp, *Wiltshire Archaeol Mag*, **40**, 12–36

Dunning, G C, 1931 Salmonsbury Camp, Gloucestershire, *Antiquity*, **5**, 489–91

————, 1976, Salmonsbury, Bourton-on-the-Water, Gloucestershire, in *Hillforts, later prehistoric earthworks in Britain and Ireland* (ed D W Harding), 76–118

Fox, C F, & Wolseley, G R, 1928 The early Iron Age site at Findon Park, Findon, Sussex, *Antiq J*, **8**, 449–60

Glob, P V, 1969 *The bog people*

Hassan, F A, 1981 *Demographic archaeology*

Henschen, F, 1956 Zur Paläopathologie des Schädels—über die Sog. Cribra Cranii, *Verh Dtsch Ges Path*, 39 tag

Hertz, R, 1907 Contribution à une étude sur la répresentation collective de la mort, *Année Sociologique*, **10**, 48–137

Hooper, B, 1976 The Saxon burials, in *Excavations at Portchester Castle*, **2** (B W Cunliffe), 235–61

Huntington, R, & Metcalf, P, 1979 *Celebrations of death, the anthropology of mortuary ritual*

Kendrick, T D, 1927 *The Druids: a study in Keltic prehistory*

Lisowski, F P, 1967 Prehistoric and early historic trepanation, in *Diseases in antiquity* (eds D Brothwell & A T Sandison), 651–72, Springfield

MacCurdy, G G, 1923 Human skeletal remains from the highlands of Peru, *Amer J Phys Anthrop*, **6**, 217–329

McKern, T W, & Stewart, T D, 1957 *Skeletal age changes in young American males*, 179ff, Natick

McLeod, M D, 1981 *The Asante*

Miles, A E W, 1971 Age assessment from the dentition, *Brit Dent J*, **130**, 4, 163

Moller-Christensen, V, 1961 *Bone changes in leprosy*, 51 ff, Copenhagen

Moller-Christensen, V, & Sandison, A T, 1963 Usura orbitae (Cribra Obitalia) in the collection of crania in the Anatomy Department of the University of Glasgow, *Path Microbiol*, **26**, 175–83

Pedersen, P O, 1949 The East Greenland Eskimo dentition, *Medd Grønland*, **142**, 1–256

Piggott, S, 1969 *The Druids*

Ross, A, 1967 *Pagan Celtic Britain: studies in iconography and tradition*

Salzmann, J A, 1957 *Orthodontics, principles and prevention*, Philadelphia

Smith, S, & Simpson, C K, 1956 *Taylor's principles and practice of medical jurisprudence*, 16 edn, **1:IV**

Stanford, S C, 1974 *Croft Ambrey*

Tierney, J J, 1960 The Celtic ethnography of Posidonius, *Proc Roy Ir Acad*, **60** (C), 189–275

Trotter, M, & Gleser, G C, 1952 Estimation of stature from long-bones of American whites and negroes, *Amer J Phys Anthrop*, **10**, 463–514

————, & ————, 1958 A re-evaluation of estimations of stature based on measurements of stature taken during life and long-bones after death, *ibid*, **16**, 79–123

Turner, V, 1967 *The forest of symbols*, New York

Ucko, P J, 1969 Ethnography and archaeological interpretation of funerary remains, *World Archaeol*, **1**, 2, 262–77

Van Gennep, A, 1960 *The rites of passage* (trans M B Vizedom & G L Caffee), Chicago

Wainwright, G J, 1979 *Gussage All Saints. An Iron Age settlement in Dorset*

Wakefield, E G, & Dellinger, S C, 1936 The probable adaptation of utilitarian implements for surgical procedures by the 'Mound Builders' of Eastern Arkansas, *J Bone Joint Surgery*, **18**, 434–8

————, & ————, 1937 Artefacts found among the remains of the 'Mound Builders', *Bull Inst Hist Medicine*, **5**, 452–60

Welcker, H, 1888 Cribra Orbitalia, ein ethnologisch-diagnostiches Merkmal am Schödel mehrerer Menschenrassen, *Archiv Anthrop*, **17**, 1–18

Wells, C, 1963 Cortical grooves on the tibia, *Man*, **137**, 112–14

————, 1964 *Bones, bodies and disease*

Whimster, R, 1981 *Burial practices in Iron Age Britain. A discussion and gazetteer of the evidence c 700 BC-AD 43*

Zegwaard, G A, 1959 Headhunting practices of the Asmat of New Guinea, *Amer Anthrop*, **61**, 1020–59

9 Environment and economy

9.1 The Danebury environment

by Barry Cunliffe

It is a not unreasonable assumption that the Danebury community utilized the immediate environment of the fort for raw materials and for other resources bearing upon the productive needs of the population. Some remarks about the potential of the environment are therefore appropriate before the actual archaeological evidence of utilization is considered in the specialist reports to follow. Questions of territorial boundary are best left to the more speculative section of this report (pp 550–4) but for the purposes of the present discussion we will assume that the greater Danebury territory includes much of the land between the Rivers Test and Bourne and from the Dean Hill syncline to the high Downs north of Andover.

The availability of drinking water presents a difficult problem. So far the excavation has yielded no direct evidence of dew ponds or of rain water conservation but the fort is not far from a permanent water supply in the Wallop Valley and we may assume that much of the water needed for domestic purposes would have been carried to the site daily. At present the closest source, at Nether Wallop, is a fraction over 2 km from the south-western entrance of the fort, but allowing a higher spring line in the Iron Age, water may well have been obtainable from a subsidiary spring in the valley immediately west of the fort less than 1½ km away, ten minutes walk.

If one includes the Tertiary clays exposed in the Dean Hill syncline to the south of the site, the landscape around the fort may be divided into five ecological zones.

1 The flood plains The chalkland rivers flow in flood plains floored with alluvium and fringed in places by narrow gravel terraces. Some are only a few metres across, others, like the Test, are up to 1 km wide. As a resource the flood plain environment has much to offer. The narrow gravel terraces, fertilized by chalk hillwash, provide excellent crop-growing areas, while the flood plain itself, suitably managed, will yield rich crops of hay and browsing pastures for cattle. Fish and birds abound. In addition, reeds, rushes, and willow for thatching, wattlework, and basketry are widely available. There can be little doubt that the Test valley was a much prized and extensively utilized environment essential to the well-being of the community.

2 The watered downland Most of the Danebury region was gently undulating chalk downland but with different potentials. It is worth making a distinction between the downland within, say, 1 km of the nearest permanent water supply and the higher downs beyond the 1 km limit. The actual boundary is of course purely arbitrary but, bearing in mind that cattle have to be watered twice a day and tire if driven long distances, land within easy reach of permanent water supply is clearly better suited to cattle rearing than higher and drier pastures. One would therefore expect cattle to have been concentrated within easy reach of streams and rivers. Dew ponds and minor springs no longer flowing would have completed the picture but such fine detail is now beyond recovery.

3 The dry downland Away from permanent water supply the downland would have been less suitable for cattle but

would have been perfectly satisfactory for sheep and goats whose water intake is much less.

Both types of downland were well suited to cereal growing. Much of the region was covered with a light loamy soil, slopes were not excessive, and altitude, always below 200 m, would not have been a limiting factor; wheat and barley would, theoretically, have flourished almost everywhere — only the maintenance of fertility would have been a consistently significant limiting factor. Proper fallowing and manuring, by manipulating flocks and herds, would probably have ensured adequate fertility throughout the period here concerned.

4 Isolated woodlands How much of the downland was under plough in the Iron Age there is no way yet of assessing, but if the Iron Age use is reflected in the distribution of 'Celtic fields' then arable land was very extensive. There are, however, areas which would not have been easy to plough — the thick clay-with-flints capping to some of the hills and the steep scarp slopes. Areas of this kind may well have been carefully maintained and cropped as woodland to provide a wide range of woodland products from timber to medicinal herbs and fungi. The timber needs of the hillfort community alone would have been considerable (p 552) but of the more esoteric products we are entirely ignorant. Nor' should we forget that pannage for pigs would have been an essential facility.

5 The clay lands In contrast to the downland zones a totally different environment is provided by the outcropping band of Tertiary rocks of the Dean Hill syncline 7–8 km south of Danebury. Since only Reading Beds clay and London clay are exposed the syncline can be treated as a single zone of clay land, the only variation being occasional patches of superficial plateau gravel. In all probability the clay zone retained its woodland cover forming a band 3 km wide and 16 km long across the southern edge of the Danebury territory. Like the isolated woodlands the forest zone would have provided a wide range of woodland products together with extensive pannage. Both types of clay were also transported to the site in quantity for constructional work and possibly for pottery manufacture. It is not impossible that the pebble beds were a source of sling stones for the defenders of the fort.

The diagram, Fig 9.1, sums up the distribution of resources immediately available to the fort, but it is merely a pale reflection of an immensely complex picture the detail of which we can never know. Nor is it possible to be precise about the mechanisms of exploitation. Danebury lies in the centre of a densely settled landscape; we can only suppose that exploitation involved the peasant communities in an intricate pattern of production and exchange some aspects of which will be considered later.

Finally something must be said of productivity over and above the needs of self-sufficiency. The Danebury environment was not remarkable for its productive potential; moreover, it appears to have had no rare materials suitable for international exchange but the landscape would have allowed animal and agrarian commodities to have been produced in surplus. Cattle on the hoof, cereals, and woollen goods could all have been produced for exchange. These are matters to which we shall return after reviewing the site evidence.

○
DANEBURY

Zone 1 – flood plain

Zone 4 – woodland

Zone 2 – watered downland

Zone 5 – forest

Zone 3 – dry downland

0   5   10 Kms

Fig 9.1 The major micro-environmental zones in the Danebury region

9.2 Land snail analysis

by J G Evans

Samples for snail analysis were taken from four groups of loci during the area excavation of 1975:

1 Pre-bank soils

2 Soils and occupation levels associated with the hut floors. On the whole these pre-date the pits that were sampled with the exception of pit 829 which may be contemporary with or earlier than the hut levels (see Table 54 for details)

3 Pits. Eight pits were sampled (see Table 55 and the relevant pit section drawings for sample details)

4 Layer 200. Hillwash sealing pits and hut levels (see Fig 4.114 for position of samples)

The results of analysis have been presented in tabular (Tables 54, 55) and histogram (Figs 9.2, 9.3) form. In the Tables the details of each sample are given. The histograms, on the other hand, are to some extent a subjective assessment of the results. In Fig 9.2 all the pit data are presented in one diagram in terms of both absolute and relative abundance, the order being roughly chronological with the earliest at the bottom of the diagram. In many of the samples total numbers are too small to be meaningful in percentage terms other than, possibly, in the broad ecological groupings on the right-hand side. In Fig 9.3 assemblages from selected horizons are presented in approximately chronological order, again with the earliest at the bottom. In this case all the results are in percentage terms, and certain samples have been amalgamated.

Table 54 Molluscs from layers, 1975

	pre-bank soils		soils/occupation levels													layer 200					
sample number	79	78	62	69	23	33	43	22	71	70	44	56	11	57	1	72	73	74	75	76	77
dry weight (kg)	1.0	1.0	0.5	1.0	0.5	0.5	0.5	0.5	1.0	0.5	0.5	0.5	0.5	0.5	0.5	1.0	0.75	0.75	0.75	0.75	0.75
Pomatias elegans (Müller)	7	5	–	–	–	–	–	–	–	–	–	–	–	–	–	–	–	–	–	–	–
Carychium tridentatum (Risso)	–	–	–	–	–	3	–	–	1	–	–	–	–	–	–	20	5	3	2	1	1
Cochlicopa lubrica (Müller)	–	–	–	–	–	3	–	–	–	–	–	–	–	–	–	2	–	–	–	–	–
Cochlicopa lubricella (Porro)	1	–	–	–	–	3	–	–	–	1	–	–	–	–	–	4	1	–	–	1	–
Cochlicopa spp	8	2	–	–	–	3	6	–	–	–	–	–	–	1	1	34	4	–	–	–	1
Vertigo pygmaea (Draparnaud)	3	–	–	1	–	–	–	–	–	–	–	–	–	–	–	4	1	1	1	–	–
Pupilla muscorum (Linné)	55	106	18	43	34	131	73	–	18	5	6	9	10	12	1	6	7	6	2	6	6
Lauria cylindracea (da Costa)	–	–	–	–	–	–	1	–	–	–	–	–	–	–	–	–	–	–	–	–	–
Vallonia costata (Müller)	18	365	5	22	34	28	73	–	17	2	8	1	6	2	7	81	39	42	48	17	6
Vallonia excentrica Sterki	100	250	2	6	5	21	7	3	1	3	–	2	–	–	–	9	11	12	6	73	5
Ena obscura (Müller)	–	–	–	–	1	–	–	–	–	–	–	–	–	–	–	1	–	–	–	–	–
Punctum pygmaeum (Draparnaud)	–	–	–	–	–	–	–	–	–	–	–	–	–	–	–	4	–	–	–	–	2
Discus rotundatus (Müller)	–	–	–	–	1	–	9	1	1	1	–	1	–	1	–	14	1	1	1	–	–
Vitrina pellucida (Müller)	–	8	–	–	–	–	–	–	–	–	–	–	–	–	–	2	–	1	–	–	1
Vitrea contracta (Westerlund)	–	1	–	1	–	–	–	–	1	–	1	–	–	–	–	11	5	6	1	–	–
Aegopinella nitidula (Draparnaud)	–	–	–	–	–	–	–	–	–	–	–	–	–	–	1	10	–	–	–	–	–
Oxychilus cellarius (Müller)	2	–	–	1	1	1	6	1	1	–	1	1	1	–	–	27	3	2	2	–	–
Limacidae	1	2	–	2	3	–	–	1	1	–	–	–	1	1	–	7	8	1	2	–	–
Cecilioides acicula (Müller)	–	–	–	1	1	–	–	1	1	–	–	–	–	–	–	–	–	–	–	–	–
Clausilia bidentata (Ström)	1	1	–	1	1	–	–	1	–	–	–	–	–	–	–	1	+	–	1	–	1
Helicella itala (Linné)	21	20	3	3	2	6	1	1	1	–	2	1	–	–	1	3	10	11	13	4	6
Trichia hispida (Linné)	1	82	4	7	6	3	72	1	10	7	1	–	1	1	–	60	18	21	35	43	17
Cepaea hortensis (Müller)	–	–	–	–	–	–	–	–	–	–	–	–	–	–	–	1	–	–	–	–	–
Cepaea spp, Arianta	3	2	–	–	–	–	–	–	–	–	–	–	–	–	–	5	2	–	2	1	–

Land mollusca from horizons other than pits, in approximate order of age; + = non-apical fragment; nomenclature after Waldén 1976

477

Table 55 Molluscs from pits, 1975

pit	800				807					813								814		815	818		819			829
layer	10	8	6	3	5	4	3	2	1	10	9	8	7	6	5	3	2	1b	1t	3	5	1	2	1	1t	3
dry weight (kg)	0.5	0.5	0.5	0.5	1.0	1.0	0.5	0.5	1.0	0.5	0.5	1.0	0.5	0.5	1.0	0.5	0.5	0.5	0.5	0.5	0.5	0.5	1.0	1.0	0.5	0.5
Pomatias elegans (Müller)	–	–	–	–	1	–	–	–	–	–	–	–	–	–	–	–	–	–	–	–	–	–	–	–	–	–
Carychium tridentatum (Risso)	–	–	–	–	1	1	33	6	18	4	–	–	–	–	–	4	86	38	83	–	–	48	3	26	28	–
Cochicopa lubrica (Müller)	–	–	–	–	–	–	–	1	–	–	–	–	–	–	–	–	–	4	4	–	–	–	–	–	–	–
Cochicopa lubricella (Porro)	–	–	–	–	–	–	14	9	6	–	–	1	–	–	4	4	19	16	10	–	–	15	2	–	11	1
Cochicopa spp	–	–	–	–	–	–	50	48	21	–	–	7	–	–	–	9	96	56	80	–	–	71	3	22	27	–
Vertigo pygmaea (Draparnaud)	1	–	–	–	–	4	12	7	8	2	–	–	–	–	–	–	4	10	10	–	–	17	–	–	1	1
Pupilla muscorum (Linné)	–	3	4	2	6	4	2	20	18	8	10	95	3	7	34	–	3	10	5	43	1	9	31	9	10	33
Vallonia costata (Müller)	–	3	–	1	5	8	119	90	48	1	2	39	–	2	26	23	143	186	164	53	1	186	30	45	66	29
Vallonia excentrica Sterki	2	–	2	1	1	–	5	4	8	2	–	6	1	–	5	1	11	4	3	–	–	–	8	46	–	6
Ena obscura (Müller)	–	–	–	–	–	–	4	1	1	–	–	–	–	–	–	–	–	4	6	–	–	4	–	–	1	–
Punctum pygmaeum (Draparnaud)	1	–	–	–	–	1	12	9	2	–	–	–	–	–	–	–	2	11	11	–	–	18	–	2	2	–
Discus rotundatus (Müller)	–	–	–	–	–	1	26	6	5	–	–	–	–	–	–	5	64	24	14	1	1	26	7	14	22	2
Vitrina pellucida (Müller)	–	–	–	–	–	–	10	5	2	–	–	2	–	–	1	1	13	12	11	–	–	7	–	2	–	–
Vitrea contracta (Westerlund)	–	–	–	–	–	1	37	28	17	–	–	–	–	–	2	2	31	13	21	–	–	31	3	12	8	–
Nesovitrea hammonis (Ström)	–	–	–	–	–	–	–	–	–	–	–	–	–	–	–	–	3	2	4	–	–	1	–	1	1	–
Aegopinella pura (Alder)	–	–	–	–	–	–	?1	–	–	–	–	–	–	–	–	–	–	–	–	–	–	–	–	–	–	–
Aegopinella nitidula (Drap)	–	–	–	–	–	–	19	11	15	–	–	1	–	–	2	2	18	10	10	17	–	17	1	9	13	–
Oxychilus cellarius (Müller)	–	–	–	–	–	11	29	13	9	–	–	1	–	1	1	4	46	65	35	8	1	38	4	16	24	–
Limacidae	–	–	–	–	–	–	2	1	–	–	–	1	–	–	2	1	1	4	1	–	–	3	–	9	8	13
Cecilioides acicula (Müller)	–	–	–	–	–	–	–	1	1	–	–	–	–	–	–	–	–	–	–	–	–	–	1	–	3	–
Clausilia bidentata (Ström)	–	–	–	–	–	–	4	6	4	–	–	–	–	–	–	–	4	7	5	6	–	4	1	+	4	–
Helicella itala (Linné)	1	–	–	–	2	5	1	4	1	–	–	7	–	–	5	1	1	3	–	–	–	1	5	3	1	7
Trichia hispida (Linné)	–	2	1	–	4	14	53	44	36	–	1	7	2	3	14	16	48	82	44	8	–	76	23	22	32	15
Arianta arbustorum (Linné)	–	–	–	–	–	–	5	7	1	–	–	–	–	1	1	1	4	4	7	–	–	–	–	–	1	–
Cepaea spp, *Arianta*	–	–	–	–	–	–	–	–	2	–	–	–	–	–	1	–	2	6	3	–	–	16	–	2	–	–

Land mollusca; + = non-apical fragment, t = top, b = bottom; nomenclature after Waldén 1976

478

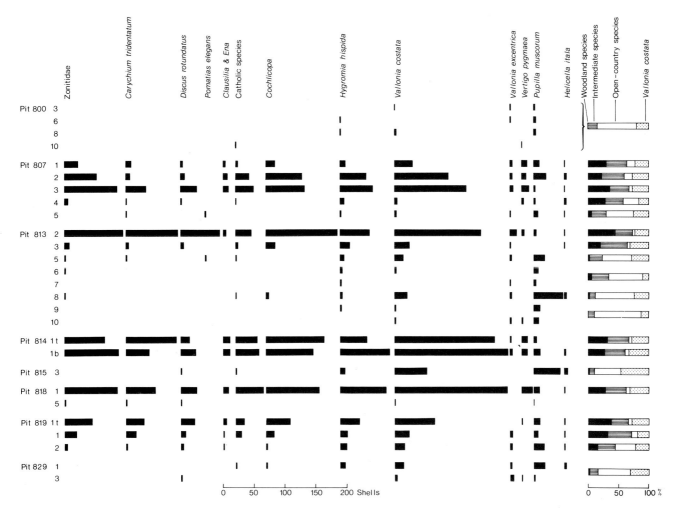

Fig 9.2 Molluscan assemblage from the pits, 1975

I will outline the main features of the results first of all then discuss the succession as a whole.

9.2.1 Pre-bank soils

Context/layer	Sample number
310	78
315	79

Sample 79 came from a layer that may pre-date any of the major Iron Age constructional activities on the site such as pit digging, hut building, and rampart erection. 78 was from a layer that, adjacent to the sampling point, sealed two pits, 860 and 858. Both assemblages were of open country type with practically no shade-loving species at all. Notable was the presence of *Pomatias elegans* which is otherwise virtually absent from the later assemblages.

9.2.2 Hut levels

The main features of these assemblages are their totally open country nature and the consistently high abundance of *Pupilla muscorum*. In this latter feature they contrast with the assemblages from the pre-bank soils.

9.2.3 The pits

These merit individual consideration although it can be said generally that, where there are long sequences, there is a tendency for the assemblages to become increasingly dominated by shade-loving species towards the top. They are considered in roughly chronological order, and as presented in Fig 9.2.

Pit 829

Assemblages were sparse in numbers and of open country type.

Pit 819

The assemblages show a succession from open country halfway up the fill to shaded near the top.

Pit 818

The lowest sample, although from fine sediment, was virtually devoid of shells. The assemblage from close to the top was of woodland type.

Pit 815

The single assemblage from the upper levels of the fill was of open country type.

Pit 814

The two assemblages from the upper levels of this pit were almost entirely of woodland type.

479

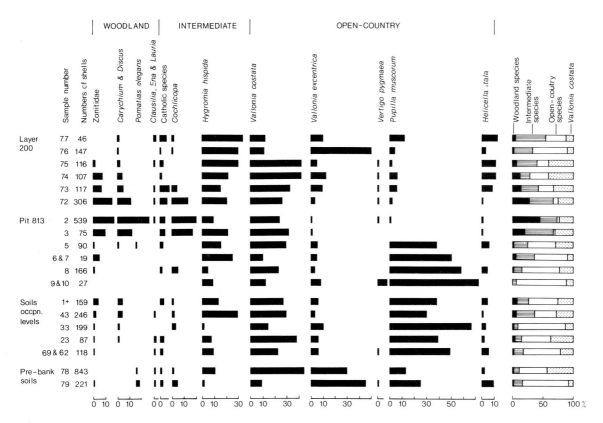

Fig 9.3 Molluscan assemblage sampled in 1975, arranged in chronological order with the latest at the top

Pit 813

The lengthy sequence from this pit showed a transition from an open country assemblage at the base to a woodland one at the top.

Pit 807

A similar, although shorter, sequence to that of pit 813, and with a slightly less wooded aspect in the upper two samples.

Pit 800

Snails were very sparse but all were consistently of open country type.

9.2.4 Layer 200

Six samples in a vertical sequence were taken from this layer. The assemblages showed a progressive change from woodland to open country.

In interpreting the assemblages it is necessary to decide the extent to which their composition is determined by the special nature of the deposit or feature in which they occur. For example, the fact that the assemblages in the lower and middle (and in some cases upper) levels of the pits are of fairly open country type in spite of often slow infilling implies the absence of refugia in the immediate vicinity and the existence of widespread conditions of open country. By the same token, the occurrence of woodland assemblages within the upper levels of some pits suggests a pretty widespread episode of woodland regeneration and not an immediately local response to the pit environment. The differences between the various pit sequences and especially the fact that some do not contain woodland assemblages at all could be due either to age differences (the precise dating relationships of most are uncertain) or to facies differences.

In the case of the other assemblages it is to be noted that, when arranged in chronological order (Fig 9.3), there is a reasonably sensible succession of assemblages, with good correlation between the uppermost sample of the assemblages from one group of features and the lowermost of the succeeding group. On the whole, major faunal breaks take place *within* the sequence of assemblages from any one group of features. It is gratifying, therefore, that, as at Rams Hill (Evans in Bradley & Ellison 1975), snail assemblages from a variety of contexts may reflect overall land use in some cases.

Four series of assemblages have been arranged in chronological order diagrammatically in Fig 9.3. Only one pit sequence, the longest and whose stratigraphical position is reliable, has been included. From this we can recognize several snail assemblage zones which from the earliest to the latest are:

an open country assemblage (pre-bank soils, samples 79 and 78)

an open country assemblage in which *Pupilla* predominates (hut levels and pits, pit 813, samples 5 to 10)

an assemblage in which woodland species predominate (pit 813, samples 2 and 3; layer 200, sample 72)

an assemblage in which there is an increasingly open country element (layer 200, samples 73 to 77).

As already discussed, it is likely that these assemblages reflect the environment of the site as a whole and to some extent its surrounds and we can therefore propose the following environmental sequence:

1 An episode of open country, probably grassland. The presence of *Pomatias elegans* suggests some relict scrub cover. The virtual absence of woodland species, however, indicates this to have been at the most

480

sparse, and the open country nature of the environment to have been longstanding. Pre-hillfort environment.

2 An episode of open country and much bare ground as hinted by the high *Pupilla* zone. This coincides with the hut levels and the lower infill of the pits.

3 An episode of woodland regeneration when presumably there was little activity on the site. This almost certainly belongs to the period of hillfort abandonment during the 1st century BC.

4 An episode of woodland clearance and possible tillage. This is probably equivalent to the 'ceramic phase 8 activity' in the later part of the 1st century BC.

Acknowledgements

Acknowledgement is made to the Danebury Archaeological Trust and Hampshire County Council for financial help. The snail analyses were done by David Leighton.

9.3   The woodlands and their use

by Cynthia Poole

The existence of woodland must inevitably be inferred, since the woods themselves no longer exist, nor is it known where they were and what area they covered. The evidence used to assess the type of woodland utilized includes archaeological features such as postholes, stakeholes, and wattle impressions, which indicate the size and amount of timber used (Vol 1, pp 110–22), and charcoal, which shows the species of tree brought to the site.

There are 153 charcoal samples, of which 75 have been identified (29 by Carole Keepax of the Ancient Monuments Laboratory and the rest by Cynthia Poole), 8 used for radiocarbon dating without first being identified, and 4 lost, leaving 66 still available for examination. Further samples may be available when some soil samples have been floated for carbonized material. Thirty-six samples come from contexts of cp 3 date and 54 from cp 7

contexts, whilst the other phases have between 10 and 22 samples each.

The number of occurrences of different species has been based on the number of identifications from different contexts, not from the amount within a context. A detailed list of the contexts and species identified for each ceramic phase appears on fiche 13, frames F2–6.

The information from the species identifications is summarized in Figs 9.4 and 9.5. Fig 9.4a shows the numbers of each species identified for each ceramic phase, whilst 9.4b presents this information as a percentage. Fig 9.5 shows the number of samples in each phase and how many have been identified. Nearly all available samples from cps 4, 5, and 6 have been identified, but only 25% from cp 3, 37% from cp 7, and 36% from cp 8.

The hazel includes identifications described as hazel/alder, but definite identifications of alder are separate. Willow includes willow/poplar. Hawthorn type includes a number of species of *Pomoideae* such as *Pirus malus*, *P. communis*, *Crataegus sp.*, and *Cyclonia oblonga*, whose wood cannot be easily separated. *Prunus sp.* may include *Prunus avium* (wild cherry), *Prunus spinosa* (blackthorn), or *Prunus padus* (bird cherry).

The figures show a wider variety of species in the early period, even though only eight samples have been examined. In the middle phase of cps 4 and 5 the rarer species are not present, but start appearing again in cps 6 and 7. However, over twice as many samples have been examined in both of the later phases than in cp 3, which suggests that although the less common species occur it is not in the same numbers as in the early phase.

Oak is the species most often identified and three-quarters of the identifications indicate that the oak came from mature trees. Ash and elm, which occur consistently throughout the occupation, are nearly always from mature trees. Nearly all the minor species, which occur sporadically except for maple, are from mature trees rather than small branches or stems. Most hazel, hawthorn, and maple, and some oak are what may be

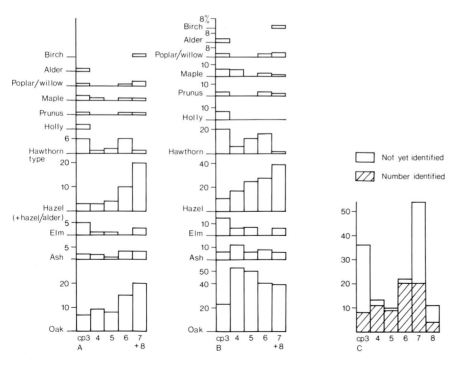

Fig 9.4   Charcoals: (a) the number of species identified in each phase and the number of samples identified in each phase; (b) the information of above (including the number of samples identified) shown as a percentage for each phase

481

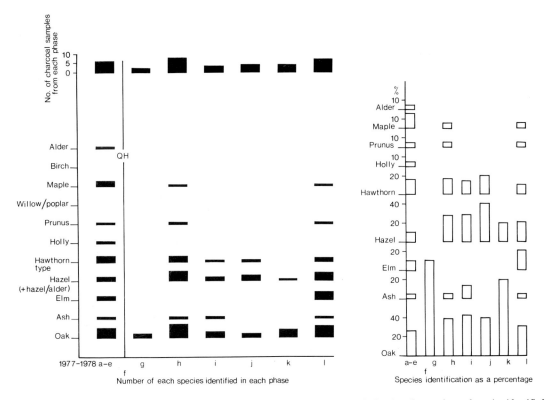

Fig 9.5 *Charcoals: the samples from the stratified deposits excavated in 1977–78 showing the numbers of species identified in each stratigraphic phase*

described as 'twiggy', coming from small stems or branches. Hazel apparently shows a dramatic increase in occurrences in the later period and is the only species to show any real change in amount, though from the percentages oak apparently decreases slightly.

In general the charcoal suggests that oak was an important constituent of woodland, probably mainly as a standard tree. Where charcoal has been found in postholes and is thought to be from the posts themselves, eg PS1 (phs 3624, 3627, 3628, 3629), gate-posts (phs 16, 20, 26), and phs 3613 and 3619, these have all produced oak charcoal suggesting that this was the major timber tree. Oak was also the wood used for the large wooden paddle and associated wooden objects found in P925 (p 426). According to Rackham (1980) oak has always been the commonest timber tree used for buildings in the historical period and its qualities were no doubt recognized in the Iron Age. In historical records and present woods ash is the next commonest timber tree after oak, though in old buildings elm is more often used after oak, and ash is rare. Both ash and elm charcoal has been found at Danebury though in much smaller quantities than oak, but there is no definite evidence for its structural use. The only recorded use of ash at Danebury was as a spindle found within the perforation of a spindle whorl.

The smaller sized oak charcoal may represent either the 'lop-and-top' from timber trees, utilized as firewood, or alternatively it may be underwood, as oak may form a major constituent of woodland in this way. The underwood would have been important for fencing, hurdles, wattle, thatching wood, and fuel.

The charcoal evidence at Danebury suggests that the major underwood species was hazel. Nearly all of this has come from small stems averaging about six years, but varying from three to nine, where the growth rings could be counted in total. Moreover several carbonized wattles associated with the wall daub were all identified as hazel

(or hazel/alder). Leaf impressions on the daub also look like hazel, though they are insufficiently clear to make the identification certain. Over half the maple comes from immature examples, suggesting that this also may have formed part of the underwood. According to Rackham, ash, maple, and hazel in varying combinations form the dominant underwood in a large proportion of woodland today, which commonly has standard oak trees but seldom oak underwood. It is possible that this type of woodland was being utilized at Danebury.

'Hawthorn type' is the only other species found consistently through all phases in any quantity. This identification includes both hawthorn species as well as other rosaceous trees such as wild apple and pear, which are difficult to separate. Thus the charcoal may represent any one of these trees occurring in the woodland. However apple and pear are relatively rare, while hawthorn is commonly associated as underwood with the ash-maple-hazel type of woods. Alternatively it may represent hawthorn occurring in hedgerows or as a pioneer tree-forming scrub in abandoned fields. Nearly all the hawthorn charcoal comes from small stems and branches and it was probably mainly utilized as fuel. There is however one piece of worked wood of unknown use from P1133, which was identified as hawthorn type.

It seems almost certain that the woodland utilized at Danebury was managed. The study of the structural timber (Vol 1, pp 110–22) showed that a variety of wood was needed for structures while smaller poles were required for wattles and the stake-built walls of round houses. The numbers of postholes and stakeholes found on the site suggest that large quantities of timber were needed on the settlement. Some of the radiocarbon dates (eg from PS1 and the main gate) indicate that timber was reused, suggesting that wood was a valued resource not to be wasted. In a landscape where even many of the steeper hillsides retain evidence of field lynchets, the woodland must have been relegated to the most marginal land, making it a scarce commodity, and would have been managed to make the best use of the available resources. The underwood must have been coppiced and the evidence of the wattle impressions in the daub supports this.

It is hoped that further, more detailed, work on the charcoal may provide more information on the utilization of wood and the composition of the woodland from which it was obtained and on how the woods may have changed during the occupation of Danebury.

9.4 The plant remains
by Martin Jones
9.4.1 Introduction

Background

During the course of investigations at Danebury, a number of radical changes have occurred in the attitude of archaeologists towards, and their understanding of, plant material from archaeological contexts. In the '50s and '60s, recognizable plant debris was thought to occur only sporadically in archaeological deposits and was generally dealt with on an *ad hoc* basis. In the survey conducted by Helbaek (1952), for example, actual plant material constituted no more than a marginal source of information on early crops in southern Britain, and the bulk of the information was derived from impressions in pottery. This illusion of the rarity of plant material was dispelled for the lower Rhine Valley by Knörzer (1971) who observed that carbonized material was ubiquitous in the deposits he examined, and that its apparent rarity was due instead to the difficulty of discerning the material with the naked eye. The rich dark deposits that were brought on Helbaek's attention were merely an unusual extreme of a far commoner phenomenon. A range of flotation methods aimed at extracting this extensive body of data were outlined in the early seventies (Jarman *et al* 1972; Williams 1973) and their deployment in the Upper Thames Valley and elsewhere (Jones 1978a; 1981) clearly demonstrated that Knörzer's conclusions on the widespread occurrence of plant material could be extended to southern Britain.

These changes are reflected in the way in which plant assemblages have been approached at Danebury itself. In the early seasons, the sporadic occurrence of dark rich deposits of carbonized plant material was noted, and these proved to be dominated by carbonized cereal grains. This body of material constituted the entire plant record of the site until the 1978 season, when in the light of the developments discussed above, it was decided to examine the whole range of archaeological contexts on the site for plant assemblages, whatever their apparent 'richness'. Thus in the 1978 season, a strategy was implemented to examine the total distribution of plant material, and assess its implications for an understanding of the hillfort and crop-related activities associated with it.

Method

It has been argued elsewhere (Redman 1975; Jones 1978b) that a sampling programme should, wherever possible, make use of any prior knowledge of the way in which the material being sampled is distributed, and use this knowledge either to stratify the sampling population or else as a basis for purposive sampling. Where such knowledge does not exist, the more appropriate course is random sampling.

In the case of Danebury, the only prior knowledge of the distribution of plant material was of the occasional occurrence of extremely rich pure assemblages amongst the deposits. It was decided to conduct a purposive examination of any such assemblages that might be encountered, and implement a programme of random sampling for the remaining deposits. The sampling population was stratified according to feature type, and two sampling strata, the layers beneath the ramparts and the pits, were examined. A sample was randomly selected from each of the layers and from each context within a 10% random sample of the pits. In each case, the sample size was two buckets, or approximately 25 litres of sediment. The author is grateful to Ms C Poole for supervising this sampling programme and for performing the subsequent flotation of the samples.

The flotation and laboratory procedure followed Jones (1978a, 97); each sample was floated over tap water and the floating material collected in a sieve of 500 μ mesh-aperture, and air dried. According to the quantity of floated material, either the whole sample or a random sub-sample was scanned at x20 magnification, using a Meopta G11P stereo microscope. All carbonized fragments other than wood were picked out and identified as far as possible, by comparison with the author's own reference material and material from the Oxford University Botany School Herbarium.

The material thus collected was examined in order to examine the following aspects:

i the floristic composition of the assemblages
ii The distribution of carbonized material within features
iii The distribution of carbonized material between features
iv The nature of the special 'rich' samples
v The processes behind these qualitative and quantitative parameters

9.4.2 The floristic composition of the assemblages

The economic plants

The assemblages are dominated by the grains of two species of cereal, *Triticum spelta* (spelt wheat) and *Hordeum polystichum* (hulled six-row barley), the first of which is the more abundant (see Tables 56, 57). There are, in addition, sporadic occurrences of *Triticum dicoccum* (emmer), *Triticum aestivocompactum* (bread/club wheat), and *Corylus avellana* (hazelnut). A number of other taxa, for example *Daucus carota* (wild carrot), may have served as a food source, but may equally well have existed solely as weeds. This may also apply to some of the grass species represented (see p 429).

The two main species of cereal would appear to display the same genetic characters as those evident in the Ashville material (Jones 1978a, 103). Some intact fragments of barley ear from the rich deposit at the base of pit 1078 allow some further comment to be made on the genotype of this cereal. The well-preserved specimen in Fig 9.6 exhibits a relatively lax ear in which the grains, pales, rhachillae, awns, and even the vestigial glumes are visible. The specimen has densely hairy rhachis margins and glumes, and the rhachillae, which are about a quarter of the length of the grain, bear long silky hairs. The lemma spicules are largely confined to the nerves but also occur intervenally.

The general composition of the crop species represented does not appear to fluctuate through time.

Table 56 The carbonized seeds. Total numbers of seeds identified from each feature with the exception of sample 1870 from pit 1078 (see Table 59)

				cp 3										cp 4	cp 5				cp 6				cp 7		cp 8
Pits	450	514	554	1012	1022	1031	1045	1048	1060	1092	1098	1109	1131	1011	1058	457	458	472	478	547	1041	1074	460	1057	1078
CEREALS																									
Triticum (wheat)																									
T. spelta (spelt wheat)	2	2	1	12		1					2		5			1		4	2	3		6	1		82
T. aestivo-compactum (bread/club wheat)																						1			1
hexaploids NFI	8	4	1	73	17	15	1	2	2	1	16	1	20	26	2	7	3	17	11	16	18	59	9	8	215
T. dicoccum (emmer)				1						1				2						1	2	4			3
NFI	10	5	1	22		8			2	6	19		19	7	2	6	1	19	4	9	7	27	16		70
total *Triticum*	20	11	3	108	17	24	1	2	4	8	37	1	44	35	4	14	4	40	17	29	27	97	26	8	371
Hordeum (barley)	18	2	3	61	2	5	3		3	3	9		24	1	4	2	1	21	14	1	13	27	12	5	44
cereals NFI	29	14	4	126	4	31	7	3	8	15	24	2	67	13	17	12	3	35	20	7	27	29	13	14	79
OTHER TAXA																									
Boraginaceae																									
Lithospermum arvense (corn gromwell)				18										4						2					
Caryophyllaceae																									
Cerastium sp. (mouse-ear)															1										
Silene alba (white campion)				18				1																	
Silene nutans (Nottingham catchfly)				1																					
Stellaria media (chickweed)							1																		
NFI	1			2		1			1				1	1				2				1			
Chenopodiaceae																									
Atriplex patula (common orache)				1									4												
Atriplex patula/hastata (orache)	3		1						1	1			19												
Chenopodium album (fathen)																							1		
Chenopodium sp. (fathen/goosefoot)	2			6						1	1		5										2		
NFI										1											1				
Compositae																									
Chrysanthemum segetum (corn marigold)																	1				1				

484

Table 56 *continued*

Pits	450	514	554	1012	1022	1031	cp 3 1045	1048	1060	1092	1098	1109	1131	cp 4 1011	cp 5 1058	457	458	472	cp 6 478	547	1041	1074	cp 7 460	cp 7 1057	cp 8 1078
Tripleurospermum maritimum (scentless mayweed)	1																	1			1				
NFI				40						1			3		1			3		1	1	1			
Corylaceae																									
Corylus avellana (hazelnut)				1		2													1						
Cruciferae NFI										1			2			2					1				
Cyperaceae																									
Carex sp. (sedge)				1																					
Eleocharis palustris (spike rush)				3									1										1		1
Fumariaceae																									
Fumaria officinalis (fumitory)										1								1						1	
Graminae																									
Agrostis tenuis (common bent)																	2	1	5	1					
Avena sp. (wild oats)	1			26	1	1				3		1	16	2	1	2	2								17
Bromus mollis/secalinus (soft brome/chess)	5	2	1	231	8	17			10	9	3		48	29	3	4		6	3	9	8	5	6		65
Bromus sterilis (sterile brome)																						1		1	5
Festuca sp. (fescue)				1													1	1			1				1
Poa sp. (meadow grass)		1		122	4	5			2				2		5		1		1	2	4		1	1	
NFI	3	1		54	4				3	6	1		19	16	1	8	1	7	4	6	1	3	9	1	9
Labiatae																									
Mentha sp. (mint)				2																			1		
Leguminosae																									
Trifolium sp. (clover)				2	2	2							8				1	1		1					
Vicia/Lathyrus sp. (vetches)				2		1	1			1			1			1	1	1			1		1		1

485

Table 56 *continued*

Pits	450	514	554	1012	1022	1031	cp 3 1045	1048	1060	1092	1098	1109	1131	cp 4 1011	cp 5 1058	457	458	472	cp 6 478	547	1041	1074	460	cp 7 1057	cp 8 1078
Papaveraceae																									
Papaver sp. (poppy)				22									2												
Plantaginaceae																									
Plantago lanceolata (ribwort plantain)			2										5							3	1			1	
Polygonaceae																									
Polygonum aviculare (knotgrass)						1												1							
Polygonum convolvulus (black bindweed)				1					3				7					1							
Polygonum sp.													1												
Rumex acetosella (sheep's sorrel)		2		5				1		1			11							3					
Rumex sp. (dock/sorrel)				9		1							42	1		1		2	1	1	2	1	1		
NFI													2												
Ranunculaceae																									
Adonis annua (pheasant's eye)				2																					
Ranunculus acris/bulbosus/repens (buttercup)					1	1			1				3		1						1				
Rosaceae																									
Aphanes arvensis (parsley piert)				2																					
NFI											1													1	
Rubiaceae																									
Galium aparine (goosegrass)	1			17		1			1	1			27	1	3		3	4	1	3	4		6		2
Galium sp. (bedstraw)				1		1												1					1		
Sherardia arvensis (field madder)	3			8		1			2	1			12	1		1			2	1	2		1		1
Scrophulariaceae																									
Euphrasia/Odontites sp. (eyebright/bartsia)	1	1	3			1																			

486

Table 56 *continued*

Pits	450	514	554	1012	1022	1031	cp 3 1045	1048	1060	1092	1098	1109	1131	cp 4 1011	cp 5 1058	457	458	472	cp 6 478	547	1041	1074	cp 7 460	1057	cp 8 1078
Umbelliferae																									
Daucus carota (wild carrot)				1																					
Torilis nodosa (knotted hedge parsley)				1																					
Torylis/Anthriscus sp. (hedge/cow parsley)				3						1			9						1						
NFI				1									2						1						
Urticaceae																									
Urtica urens (annual nettle)				31						1			4								1				
Valerianaceae																									
Valerianella dentata (lamb's lettuce)				5			2			1			10				2				1	1		1	
Violaceae																									
Viola sp. (violet/pansy)																									
NFI	15	10	1	278	7	26	4	1	17	11	7	1	169	12	16	3	4	12	10	6	18	5	11	18	10
number of cereal grains per 100 seeds	64	61	70	24	50	49	58	63	27	38	84	78	24	42	44	56	35	68	65	48	52	89	55	51	82
total number of seeds counted	104	44	10	1225	46	123	19	8	56	69	83	9	572	117	57	50	24	142	79	77	100	171	93	53	606

Table 57 The carbonized fragments other than seeds and wood. Total numbers of fragments identified from each feature with the exception of sample 1870 from pit 1078 (see Table 59)

	450	514	554	1012	1022	1031	cp 3 1045	1048	1060	1092	1098	1109	1131	cp 4 1011	cp 5 1058	457	458	472	cp 6 478	547	1041	1074	cp 7 460	1057	cp 8 1078
Triticum sp. glumes	22	17	3	1239	24	55	6	2	29	30	17	4	167	77	17	17	9	78	51	89	25	62	38	15	44
internodes (brittle rachis)				31		5					1		4				1			1		1			
internodes (tough rachis)				1									3												
awns											1											1			
Hordeum internodes				34	1		1			1	1		4	2		1				1	1		3		
floret base				1																1					
culm nodes	1			1		1					1														
Avena awns														1											

487

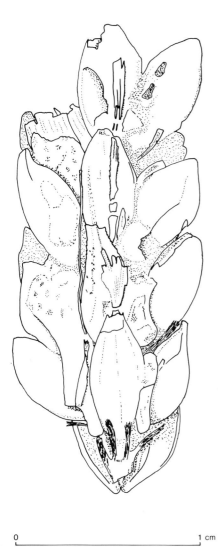

Fig 9.6 Intact fragment of hulled six-row barley from the base of pit 1078

from Iron Age deposits in the Upper Thames Valley (eg Jones 1978a; Lambrick & Robinson 1979).

As would be expected, many of the taxa present are ecologically consistent with the type of well-drained cultivated land which would dominatc the chalkland catchment of Danebury. Indeed at least half of the taxa present have already recolonized the reconstructed Iron Age arable field on chalk soils at Little Butser in the first few years of its establishment (information from the author and P J Reynolds). Striking similarities also exist with the contemporary palaeofloras from the nearby farmstead sites at Micheldever Wood and Winnall Down (Monk & Fasham 1980). While taxa such as *Galium aparine*, *Rumex* spp., *Tripleurospermum maritimum*, and *Chenopodium* spp. are associated with disturbed ground on a variety of soil types, the occurrence of *Urtica urens*, *Fumaria officinalis*, *Papaver* sp., *Bromus sterilis*, *Aphanes arvensis*, and *Silene nutans* all point to the free-draining, well-aerated nature of chalkland soils (Clapham *et al* 1962).

However, not all the taxa present share these ecological characteristics. While *Ranunculus* sp. and *Mentha* sp. are certainly found on chalk soils, these genera are usually associated with moist conditions. Two other taxa of moist soils, *Eleocharis palustris* and *Carex* sp., would certainly not share the same habitat as the 'free-draining ground' taxa above. Two further species, *Rumex acetosella* and *Chrysanthemum segetum*, are associated with acid soils rather than the very alkaline chalk-derived sediments. Thus, as well as the expected 'free-draining ground' series of taxa, the Danebury palaeoflora contains 'damp-ground' and 'acid-ground' components that require some explanation (Table 58).

As has already been mentioned, one of these species, *Chrysanthemum segetum*, has also been identified at Micheldever Wood, and here it may be related to boulder clay soils overlying the chalk. The nearest stretches of clay-with-flints to Danebury are at 3–4 km to the east and

The weedy species

At least 40 plant taxa are represented in the assemblages in addition to the economic plants cited above (Tables 56, 57). Of these the great majority are familiar as weeds of arable land, and many are found in conjunction with cereals in carbonized assemblages in many parts of northern Europe (eg Jones 1978a; van Zeist 1974). Certain of these taxa are of particular interest as Quaternary records.

Adonis annua (Pheasant's eye) (Fig 9.7), of which two seeds occur in pit 1012, is perhaps the most surprising record. Unlisted by Godwin (1975), and considered to be a relatively recent introduction from southern Europe or south-west Asia by Clapham *et al* (1962), this species must now be regarded as a well-established member of the British flora.

The single seed of *Silene nutans* (Nottingham catchfly) (Fig 9.7), also from pit 1012, is the first Flandrian record of this species.

The only other pre-Roman record of *Chrysanthemum segetum* (corn marigold) (Fig 9.7) known to the author is from the nearby contemporary site of Micheldever Wood (Monk & Fasham 1980). *Valerianella dentata*, which is listed as a Roman introduction by Godwin (1975), occurs relatively frequently in the Danebury deposits, as it does

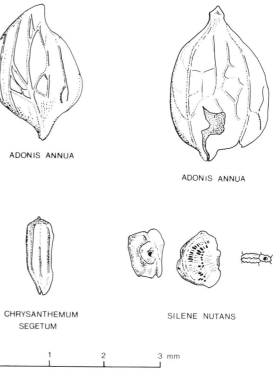

ADONIS ANNUA

ADONIS ANNUA

CHRYSANTHEMUM SEGETUM

SILENE NUTANS

Fig 9.7 Selected macrofossils (see opposite)

488

Table 58 Weed ecotypes identified from Table 56
(See text pp 488–9 for explanation)

1　Free-draining ground
　　Aphanes arvensis
　　Bromus sterilis
　　Fumaria officinalis
　　Papaver spp.
　　Silene mutans
　　Urtica urens

2　Damp ground
　　Carex spp.
　　Eleocharis palustris
　　Mentha sp.
　　Ranunculus cf. *repens*

3　Acid ground
　　Chrysanthemum segetum
　　Rumex acetosella

catchment area that could account for the taxa in question, the riverside loams and gravel soils that occur at Thruxton and at various points along the course of the Test and its tributaries. The carbonized seeds of these taxa associated with the cereal assemblages from Danebury, and presumed to be derived from the weeds of the cereal field, would therefore suggest that the cereals that arrived within the fort originated not only from the well-drained alkaline soils in the immediate vicinity of the fort, but also from the low-lying valley loams and gravel soils scattered around the presumed perimeter of its territory.

Two further points about the weedy species may be added: the presence of autumn-germinating weeds such as *Galium aparine*, which would suggest that at least some of the cereal crop was autumn sown, and the diversity of seeding heights among the weeds, which suggests that the harvest was taken at ground level.

north of the site. Some further clarification may be provided by Townshend 1904. As well as noting the common occurrence of many of the general weeds and the 'free-draining ground' component, this record of the Hampshire environment prior to the herbicide era notes the common occurrence of *Eleocharis palustris* and *Chrysanthemum segetum* around Thruxton, a village 8 km to the north of Danebury on the Pill Hill Brook, a tributary of the Test. This area also interestingly yields records of two other species in the Danebury palaeoflora that are now rather uncommon, *Lithospermum arvense* and *Adonis annua*. It would of course be foolish to suggest that a source of the Danebury palaeoflora was located at Thruxton; indeed the clustering of records at this location is most likely to result from the distribution of 19th century natural historians. What the records do show is the existence of an ecozone in the Danebury

9.4.3　The distribution of carbonized material within features

The clear stratification of deposits filling the pits at Danebury provides an ideal opportunity to examine distribution of plant material within individual features. Three pits that exhibited a well-defined sequence of deposits were selected, and the samples from each deposit analysed. The results of the analysis are shown in Fig 9.8.

The figures clearly demonstrate how material is not evenly distributed through the profile, but instead tends to occur at a far higher frequency in the basal deposits. There are three possible explanations for this: the material could have tended to move down the profile through the action of rain or faunal activity; the material in the upper layers could have been more vulnerable to post-depositional destruction; or the activities producing

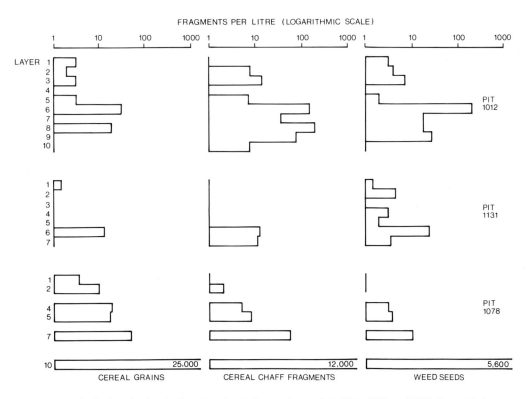

Fig 9.8　*The distribution of grain, chaff, and weed seeds between layers of pits 1012, 1131, and 1078. Layer 1 is the uppermost layer in each pit. 'Cereal chaff fragments' are defined as the sum total of the fragments listed in Table 57, with the exception of awns, which fragment into such small portions that numerical estimates are impossible*

489

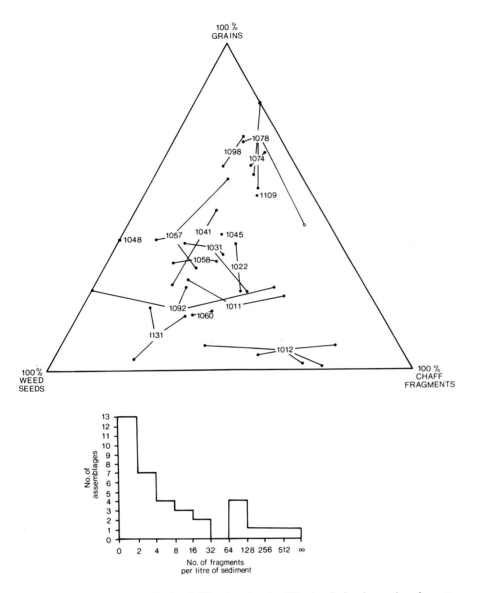

Fig 9.9 *Above: composition of grain, chaff, and weed seeds within pits, displayed as a triangular scattergram in which individual dots represent individual layers within pits. Cereal chaff fragments are defined as in Fig 9.8, and proportions of each component are estimated as percentages of the sum total of fragments of grain, chaff, and weed seeds in the assemblage. Below: histogram of fragment density*

refine in the deposits could have changed as an individual pit was filled.

Whilst attention has been drawn (Keepax 1977) to the possibility of the first process in archaeological contexts in general, the finer details of the observed distributions suggest that this factor is not responsible for the vertical variation. While there is a general increase in the plant material as one moves down the profiles, they are occasionally intercepted by a 'sterile' layer, for example pit 1012 layer 4, which clearly had very little material to start with, but which also did not receive material from higher layers. It seems likely that vertical movement only affects fresh seeds which are durable enough to survive faunal movement.

The second possibility is far more probable. Carbonized plant material is mechanically vulnerable to such factors as ingestion by earthworms and freezing and thawing of soil water, processes that are more prevalent near the surface. The relative state of preservation of individual fragments supports the idea that material near the surface had suffered mechanical destruction.

The third possibility is more difficult to assess and is better considered in the light of the whole assemblage than of one component alone.

The figures also suggest that while the density of material is greater at the basal levels, the relative proportions of grain, weeds, and chaff remain broadly similar through the profile. Thus chaff fragments form numerically the most abundant component in pit 1012, weeds in pit 1131, and cereal grains in pit 1078, and this also holds generally true for individual layers. It may be noted in passing that this consistency through the pit profile does not seem to be apparent in pit profiles from the nearby contemporary farmstead at Winnall Down (Monk & Fasham 1980). Nor is this consistency apparent at Danebury itself in the specific floristic make-up of the weed assemblages in each layer. The implications are that at Danebury a particular pit would seem to have collected refuse from a particular crop-related activity, but that the source material which was subjected to these activities did not necessarily remain constant while the pit was being filled up.

490

9.4.4 The distribution of carbonized material between features

On the basis of the more intensive examination of the main body of pit material towards the lower layers in each pit, up to three layers of each pit were examined. The relative proportions of cereal grains, weeds seeds, and chaff fragments in these layers and from the layers sealed beneath the rampart are shown in Figs 9.9 and 9.10. It becomes immediately evident from Fig 9.9 that the consistency of overall composition within individual pits observed for the three pits examined in detail holds true for the pit assemblages in general.

Dennel (1974) has argued that variations in composition such as those evident in these data reflect the different crop-processing activities from which the carbonized debris is derived. Thus the chaff-rich assemblages in pit 1012 would have derived from threshing and winnowing activities, the weed-rich assemblages in pit 1131 from seed cleaning, and the grain-rich assemblages in pit 1078 from storage and usage of the final product. It may be deduced that each of these activities was taking place within the hillfort.

9.4.5 The nature of the special 'rich' samples

Non-random samples were taken from three pits, 1065, 1078, and 1089, on account of the visible concentrations of carbonized grain within them; pit 1078 was selected for intensive study.

The lowest layer in pit 1078 was composed almost entirely of carbonized seeds and chaff, and the layer immediately above was entirely composed of grey ash. This sequence would result from a small fire in which the oxidising conditions on the outside of the fire would produce a mineral ash, while the reducing conditions in the core would produce elemental carbon. The preservation of this sequence indicates that the plant material was carbonized *in situ* and that the deposit therefore represents the material that was being stored in the pit. A careful scrutiny of the deposit might well yield valuable information about the storage function of such pits.

The material was analysed in two ways. First, the whole body of the material was spread out over gridded paper and separate sub-samples randomly selected, weighed, and scanned. This procedure allowed the composition of the whole deposit to be estimated (Table 59). Secondly, a fragment of the deposit was removed intact and excavated under a microscope in the laboratory in order to establish the exact state in which the material was stored. This 'micro-excavation' was achieved by laying the fragment in a sorting tray under a cellulose sheet on which a centimeter grid had been marked. The fragment was then scanned at 20 magnification through the grid and the alignment of each seed or chaff fragment drawn. The layer of seeds and chaff fragments was then prised away with dissecting needles, the carbon dust obscuring the next layer blown away with a photographer's lens brush, and the process repeated. Each layer was itself

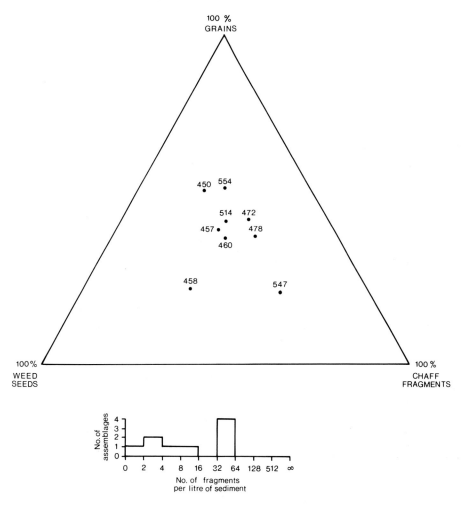

Fig 9.10 As Fig 9.9, for layers under the rampart

491

Table 59 The means and standard errors of the various components of sample 1870 (the bottom layer of pit 1078), estimated from six random sub-samples

Total weight of sample = 4640 gm
Mean weight of individual sub-sample = 1.78 gm

Triticum (wheat)	per gm	estimated total
grains	32 ± 11	$1.46 \times 10^5 \pm 0.53 \times 10^5$
glume bases	15 ± 6	$(7.1 \pm 2.8) \times 10^4$
brittle rachis internodes	0.11 ± 0.18	524 ± 813
tough rachis nodes	0.057 ± 0.14	267 ± 653
awn fragments	1.8 ± 2.0	$(8.3 \pm 9.1) \times 10^3$
Hordeum (barley)		
grains	2.2 ± 0.95	$(1.03 \pm 0.44) \times 10^4$
internodes	0.22 ± 0.40	$(1.03 \pm 1.9) \times 10^3$
Cereals NFI		
grains	2.7 ± 2.88	$(1.3 \pm 1.3) \times 10^4$
culm nodes	0.055 ± 0.14	258 ± 631
Non-cereal seeds	15 ± 12	$(6.96 \pm 5.79) \times 10^4$

Breakdown of non-cereal seeds	Total no from six sub-samples combined
Avena sp.	17
Bromus mollis/secalinus	47
Bromus sterilis	5
Bromus sp.	12
Graminae NF1	4
Galium aparine	1

scanned and each component recorded (Fig 9.11). In addition, any evidence of germination among the cereal grains was noted, in order to test the hypothesis outlined by Reynolds (1967; 1974) concerning methods of below-ground storage. Reynolds argues that the most effective method of storage is as follows: the grain is stored fresh in a sealed pit, and the germination of an outer skin of grains creates the anaerobic environment that conserves the bulk of the stored grain.

The results of these examinations are shown in Table 59 and Fig 9.12. From the random sub-samples it is apparent that the whole assemblage is dominated by cereal grains, and grains of spelt wheat probably account for three-quarters of the seeds by number. Smaller quantities of six-row barley, emmer, and bread/club wheat are also present, as well as a narrow range of weeds which are mostly large-seeded grasses.

It is evident from both the context and the composition of the assemblage that it derives from the stored product of certain crop processing activities. The question of which processes the material was subjected to may be elucidated by the finer details of the assemblage. The preponderance of large-seeded grasses among the narrow range of non-cereal seeds may be explained in at least two ways. It may be that size-dependent seed-cleaning processes had been employed, allowing only the large seeds to remain in the crop. It may alternatively be that the grass seed was purposely included to bulk up the harvest, a possibility that has often been suggested for the main non-cereal component, *Bromus* spp. (Hubbard 1975; Jones 1978a). The truth could also lie somewhere between these two explanations. Whatever the cause of the presence of these few non-cereal taxa, there can be no doubt that the method by which the vast majority of weedy taxa listed in Table 56 were excluded must have been extremely efficient.

The exclusion of the majority of weed taxa from this sample is not mirrored in the exclusion of chaff. The most common recognizable chaff fragments in carbonized assemblages of this date are the bases of glumes of the hulled wheats (*Triticum spelta*, *T. dicoccum*, *T. monococcum*). In this sample the number of glume bases is a little less than half the number of hulled wheat grains. In view of the ratio between glumes and grains in the fresh plant, this implies that only 40–60% of the chaff was removed. The incomplete nature of the threshing process is also reflected in the condition of some of the grains, a few of which are still intact on fragments of ear. A particularly well-preserved fragment of six-row barley is illustrated in Fig 9.6. While the micro-excavation showed that the majority of grains were detached from their ears, a number of the grains are clearly orientated as they were in the spikelet. By contrast to the glume bases, stem and rhachis nodes occur at an extremely low frequency, suggesting a fairly complete removal.

It may be concluded that at the time of storage, most types of weed seeds and almost all of the cereal stems had been removed, but that the grains had only been partially dislodged from their spikelets. Storage at such an intermediate stage of processing is best understood in the light of the major crop component, spelt wheat. While the spikelets of this cereal easily fragment from the ear the grains are fairly difficult to loosen from the spikelets.

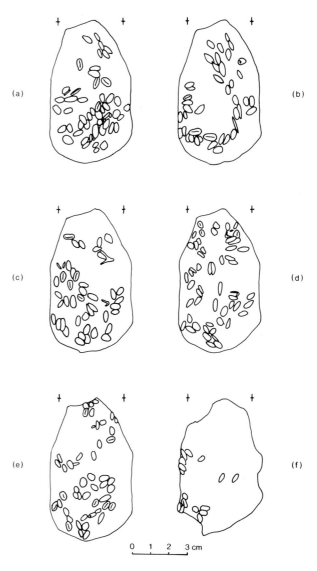

Fig 9.11 Plans of successive layers of micro-excavation of basal deposit 1870 in pit 1078. Layer a is adjacent to pit floor, and b, c, d, and f successive layers above it (see pp 491—3 for explanation)

492

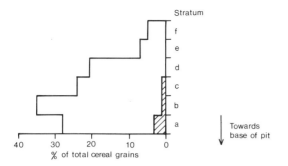

Fig 9.12 Percentage of cereal grains showing some signs of germination in the layers of grain shown in Fig 9.11. Open bars represent grains showing greater heat-damage around the germ area, and hatched bars represent grains with an extended radical, both indicative of germination. Notation as in Fig 9.11

This cereal consequently has an intermediate form in the processing sequence not shared by modern bread wheats (cf Hillman 1981, 131), which are easily threshed in a single process, and it would appear that the spelt was being stored at this intermediate stage.

The first point that may be deduced from the micro-excavation about the actual storage of this crop mixture is that the wheat and barley are well mixed. In other words, there is no evidence that variation in the wheat grain: barley grain ratio between different strata is anything other than random ($X^2 = 5.37$ at 5 degrees of freedom).

The second point is that the variation in ratio between germinated and non-germinated grains between the layers is unlikely to be attributable to chance ($X^2 = 55.2$ at 5 degrees of freedom). Instead the proportion of germinated grains appears to be significantly lower in the micro-layers furthest from the pit wall. This pattern is in accord with the method of storage outlined by Reynolds (1967; 1974) and it is therefore suggested that the assemblage under consideration derives from material stored in this manner.

9.4.6 The processes behind these qualitative and quantitative parameters

Having considered the qualitative and quantitative aspects of the data, some general inferences may be drawn about the kinds of crop-related activities they represent, and the systemic relationships between them. Ideally one would like to comment on the source of the material, the transformations it undergoes within the hillfort, and its subsequent destiny, and the inferences are here discussed under these three headings.

The source of the material

The best indicator of the source of the carbonized assemblages is the composition of the weedy component, which may act as an ecological monitor of the fields in which the crops grew. Whilst a large number of the weeds represented may well have grown in the chalky rendzinas in the immediate vicinity of the hillfort, the presence has already been noted of weeds that are more likely to have grown in the river valley soils of the Test, and in particular the loamy and gravelly soils flanking the Anton to the north. The occurrence of these weeds demonstrates that the hillfort was receiving cereal crops from throughout its territory at all stages of its development. It is evident from the paucity of culm nodes in the assemblages that the ears had been separated from the straw prior to entering the activity system from which refuse deposited within the hillfort derived.

Cereal processing within the hillfort

Both the quantity and the ubiquity of carbonized cereal and weed debris in the deposits indicate that cereal processing was occurring at a substantial level throughout its development. The material is as ubiquitous as at the Ashville site in the Upper Thames Valley (Jones 1978a) which was interpreted as a farming settlement geared strongly towards arable production. The mean density of carbonized fragments in the deposits is a little higher than at the Ashville site, and considerably higher than at other farmsteads in the Upper Thames Valley which show less emphasis towards cereal crops. It may also be of significance that the range of fragment densities within the deposits and the extremes of fragment composition (Fig 9.9) are substantially greater than at any one of these individual farmsteads.

However, the comments of Monk and Fasham (1980, 333) on the cereal weed ratios from Winnall Down and Murphy's (1977) survey of plant material from a number of nearby contemporary sites serve to emphasize that caution should be applied assuming that crop-processing activities in the Iron Age were organized in similar ways in Hampshire and in the Upper Thames Valley. Until more sites are approached with probabilistic sampling strategies compatible with the strategies employed at Danebury and in the Upper Thames Valley, all that can be said is that a broader range of activities seems to be represented within the hillfort at Danebury than within any one of a series of contemporary farmsteads in the Upper Thames Valley.

To aid the identification of cereal-related activities within Danebury, and their systemic interrelationships, an attempt has been made to subdivide the assemblages according to the principal characteristics outlined in previous sections. While intermediate assemblages may exist, three broad subdivisions are clearly evident, and these are described below.

Group 1

Including layers 457, 458, 460, 472, 478, and 514, and pits 1022, 1031, 1045, 1048, and 1058.

Characteristics
  i Cereal grains, chaff fragments, and weed seeds occur in numerically similar quantities.
  ii The fragments occur at low densities within the deposits.
  iii Weed ecotypes (see Table 56) are not mixed in individual assemblages.

Interpretation
These may be seen as the low density scatters of primary refuse (Schiffer 1976) from individual households handling harvests derived from restricted ecozones.

Two subgroups may be isolated: 1a comprising layer 460 alone, which derives from a relatively damp ecozone; and 1b comprising layers 458 and 472 and pit 1045 deriving from relatively dry ecozones.

Group 2

Including layers 450 and 554, and pits 1074, 1078, 1098, and 1109, and also comprising the large number of deposits of almost pure carbonized cereal debris encountered from time to time throughout the course of excavations at Danebury.

Characteristics
  i Cereal grains dominate the assemblages.
  ii Grasses are well represented among the weeds.
  iii The fragments often occur in large quantities.

493

Interpretation

These assemblages presumably derive from the end-products of cereal processing, in which seed-cleaning has efficiently removed all but the large-seeded grass weeds.

Two distinct subgroups are probably involved. The majority of assemblages are presumably the secondary refuse from handling the cereal product and may be designated 2a. However, pit 1078 and the whole range of almost pure assemblages which may be designated 2b must derive from a separate depositional activity. They presumably relate to the specific destruction of the cereal product by fire, for example as a means of storage-pit sterilization, which is most probable in the case of pit 1078. This is similar in principle to what Schiffer would designate as *de facto* refuse and provides the most direct evidence of a particular process in the crop-related system. It has been argued above that the deposit at the base of pit 1078 reflected storage after seed-cleaning but before the chaff was completely removed.

Group 3

Including layer 547 and pits 1011, 1012?, 1041, 1057, 1060, 1092, and 1131.

Characteristics

i Cereal grains comprise a minor component of the assemblage.
ii Barley is often well represented among the cereal grain.
iii Weed ecotypes are mixed in individual assemblages.

Interpretation

These assemblages presumably derive from the combined waste product of several harvests processed together. The association with barley is rather enigmatic, especially since the high proportion of chaff in some of these assemblages is dominated by the glumes of wheat, and may either suggest that the crop-cleaning debris is being adding to barley as a basis for animal feed, or that the handling of barley is linked to crop-cleaning in some more subtle way.

Two subgroups may be isolated: those in which weed seeds dominate the assemblage, designated 3a and including pits 1041, 1057, 1060, and 1131; and those in which chaff fragments dominate the assemblage, designated 3b and including layer 547 and pit 1012.

These various groups of assemblages thus furnish evidence of the collection, cleaning, storage, and threshing within the hillfort itself of crops harvested from throughout the territory. It is also apparent that harvests from different ecozones were cleaned and threshed together. A further point may be deduced from the tendency for assemblages in different layers within the same pit to belong to the same assemblage group, even though they might be floristically distinct from one another (Fig 9.9 and pp 489–91). This would suggest that the zone for which a particular pit was serving as a refuse depository was the site of a specific crop-related activity. The activities associated with, for example, pit 1012 whilst it was being backfilled were specifically the threshing of cereals. By contrast the activity associated with pit 1131 whilst it was being backfilled was specifically cleaning.

From these latter points, it may be deduced not only that these processing activities were taking place, but also that they were taking place in specialized activity areas (in contrast apparently to the local farmstead sites) to which harvests from a number of sources were directed.

The subsequent destiny of the cereal product

In contrast to the considerable evidence discussed above for processes to which the harvested crops were subjected within the hillfort, relatively little may be inferred about their subsequent destiny. One point is however clear from the evidence of processing outlined above: any cereals that moved out of the hillfort would have done so in a fully processed state. This point must follow from the integral nature of cleaning and threshing in the system of handling harvest outlined above.

It further follows that archaeological contexts related to the destiny of cereals handled by the hillfort would contain assemblages composed almost entirely of cereal grains and more or less free of weeds and chaff. This is put forward as a working proposition that may be tested in the excavation of sites that may have been receiving cereals from the hilltop, through such mechanisms as trade and redistribution. It has been argued elsewhere (Jones in press) that pastoral sites in the Upper Thames Valley, though receiving cereals, were not receiving them in this form, and were instead receiving cereals in the form in which they would have left the Ashville-type farmstead rather than the Danebury-type hillfort. However the elucidation of the subsequent destiny of cereal crops handled within the hillfort requires more archaeobotanical evidence than is currently available, and must await the careful scientific examination of appropriate contexts in the future.

The systemic relationships between crop-related activities

The activities described above may be placed in a logical sequence and this has been done in the form of a flow diagram in Fig 9.13. Cereal harvests derived from the whole territory were brought into the hillfort by individual households. By the time some of the material entered domestic fires and became incorporated into primary refuse deposits, the cereal ears had already been separated from the straw, though these ears had only been partially fragmented and were still mixed with the seeds of field weeds. These crops were collected together and processed communally in specialized activity areas. Three distinct processes prior to consumption are here described as 'cleaning', 'storage', and 'threshing'.

'Cleaning' in this sense involved the removal of most of the weed seeds and some of the chaff from the cereal grains. Whatever the process, it was not forceful enough to fragment intact sections of the ear, and it was either inefficient at removing the larger grass seeds or was specifically designed not to remove them. Crop-sieving is a process consistent with these observations.

It was in this state that the grain was stored underground in pits. It had undergone no process that would hinder its germinability, such as parching or threshing (cf Percival 1921, 327), and could therefore serve as seed-corn the following year. The state of the cereal grain burnt *in situ* at the base of pit 1078 is consistent with the storage mechanism described by Reynolds (1967; 1974).

Either directly after cleaning, or after a period of storage, the remaining chaff could be removed from the grain. There is no evidence to suggest how this threshing was accomplished, though in the case of spelt wheat flailing alone would have been insufficient to liberate the grain, which needed to be loosened by parching (Helback 1952) or soft milling (Percival 1921).

The various destinies of the fully processed grain are difficult to define at this stage, though the evidence from pastoral farmsteads in a different ecosystem, the Upper Thames Valley, are inconsistent with a model of redis-

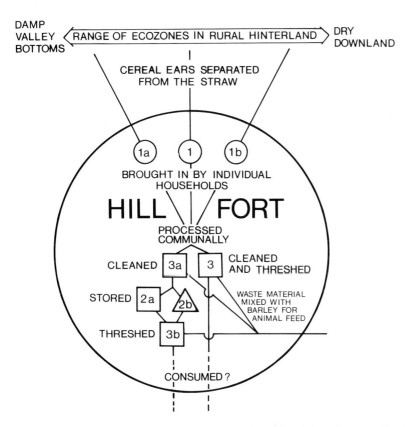

Fig 9.13 Flow diagram showing suggested systemic relationships of the various crop-related activities reflected in the data (see p 494) for explanation of the notation used)

tribution of cereals from a Danebury-type hillfort to such farmsteads. The cereal grains, of course, constituted only a part of the useful product of a cereal harvest, and two other parts have been mentioned in this report. The cereal straw was separated from the ears prior to the generation of cereal-related refuse within the hillfort, and while the assemblages provide no further indication of its usage, it would have been produced at an equal tonnage to the grain crop, and served amongst other things as an important resource for building construction. There is evidence of the waste material from cleaning and threshing, and the suggestion is made that this part may have been mixed with barley as the basis of animal feed.

9.4.7 Changes through time

The assemblages discussed in this section span ceramic phases 3 to 8 in the hillfort sequence.

As far as the main crop taxa are concerned, the variation between assemblages is insufficient to indicate any substantial change through time. The relative proportions of spelt wheat, emmer wheat, and six-row barley remain similar throughout, with wheat grains occurring with two or three times the frequency of barley grains, and spelt predominating among the wheats.

Virtually all the weed taxa encountered in the assemblages are already present in cp 3, the only exceptions being *Chrysanthemum segetum*, the single seed of which occurs in a cp 6 context, and *Chenopodium album* identified to species level only in cp 7, though almost certainly a major component of the *Chenopodium* sp. found in earlier phases.

Neither does the division of assemblages into three groups, on the basis of quantitative and qualitative characteristics, seem to reflect any temporal trend. Group 1 assemblages may be found in cps 3, 5, 6, and 7, group 2 assemblages in cps 3, 6, and 8, and group 3 assemblages in cps 3, 4, 6, and 7.

In the light of these points, it would appear that the conclusions drawn in this section as a whole are equally applicable throughout the period represented by cps 3–8.

Acknowledgement

The analysis was conducted as part of a research programme investigating the ecological and archaeological implications of selected arable plant assemblages, funded by the Science Research Council and under the supervision of Dr S R J Woodell and Mr D Britton, to whom the author extends his thanks.

9.5 Animal husbandry

by Annie Grant

9.5.1 Introduction

Although interest in the environmental aspects of archaeology has grown greatly over the past fifteen or so years, there are few published analyses of animal bone material from British sites of the Iron Age that are anything other than simple species counts, generally based on inadequate numbers of recovered bones. There are a few notable exceptions, which will be discussed in a later section of this analysis, but archaeozoology still has to prove itself as a proper study by providing the kind and depth of information which allows an appreciation of man's relationship to his animals and to his environment and which cannot be provided solely by an analysis of his settlements and artefact forms.

With the recovery of nearly 140,000 animal bones and bone fragments in the first ten years of excavation at Danebury, a unique opportunity has been provided for an analysis of the bone material at a level of detail that has rarely been possible for other British sites excavated to date. Such a large sample of bone material has also provided the opportunity to expand and refine methods of analysis and interpretation. The aims of this analysis of the Danebury bone material are: to investigate the size, form, uses, and management of the domestic animals kept by the people who inhabited the hillfort; to determine the role of wild animals; to examine any changes that took place during the occupation of the site; to examine the possible environmental effects of long-term occupation of a single site; to investigate, if possible, the relationship between meat and non-meat food resources; to assess the status of Danebury in terms of its self-sufficiency or dependence on other communities; to examine all aspects of the man–animal relationship in terms of both practical and ritual behaviour; to place Danebury in a wider context by assessing the relevant evidence from other contemporary sites; and to develop methodologies to further the above aims.

It is implicitly assumed that the bone material recovered from Danebury is, in the main, domestic refuse, thrown into disused storage pits or onto the ground surface and thus incorporated into the occupation layers that built up against the ramparts. This assumption is examined in more detail in a later part of the analysis.

The analysis of the bone material has been divided into two sections. Part one, published in this volume, looks at the overall nature of the bone material and discusses the animals kept and utilized by the hillfort's inhabitants and the nature of the animal husbandry practices. It examines changes in the husbandry practices and in other man–animal relationships over the period of occupation of the site.

In part two, to be published in a later volume, a more detailed examination is made of particular aspects of the animal bones, such as the size of the animals, the butchery techniques used, the incidence of animal diseases, and the pattern of bone deposition. An attempt is made to integrate the animal bone evidence with other classes of archaeological evidence and there will be a discussion of the methodological research and developments that have been carried out during the analysis of the bone material. Finally, the animal husbandry and all other aspects of man–animal relationships at Danebury will be discussed in the context of comparable evidence from other British Iron Age sites and from sites in continental Europe.

9.5.2 The condition of the bone material

The bone material recovered during excavation was generally in very good condition, demonstrating that soil conditions at the site were conducive to good bone preservation. In fact many of the bones were in such 'fresh' condition that if they had not been recovered from secure archaeological contexts they might have been thought to have been only recently deposited. The only exceptions were a small percentage of bones that had eroded surfaces, consistent with their having lain on the surface of the ground for some time prior to their eventual burial, and a further small percentage that had been damaged by the root action of the beech trees planted on the hilltop in the 19th century. These bones had a distinctive appearance — they were generally stained a purple colour through contact with the roots and partial destruction of the bone itself had resulted in some instances.

The condition of the bones was recorded and its implications are discussed in Part II of the analysis.

Much of the bone material was fragmented and although most of this fragmentation had occurred in the past, some was due to excavation and post-excavation breakage.

9.5.3 The recovery of the bone material

The actual excavation of the site was, as is common on British excavations, mainly in the hands of volunteers, ranging from beginners to highly skilled diggers. Sieving was not a routine part of the normal process of excavation, although some deposits were sieved for the retrieval of molluscs and seeds and two small-scale sieving experiments were carried out on site. Judging only by the size of bones recovered and other subjective measures, the impression was that recovery was better at Danebury than at, for example, Portchester Castle (Grant 1975a, 378). The nature of the soil at Danebury, the fact that Danebury was excavated in the summer months when the soil is generally drier than in the spring months when much of Portchester was excavated, and the more restricted use of heavy tools for excavation at Danebury may all have contributed to the apparently better recovery.

However, the results of two small-scale sieving experiments, carried out by the present writer and Ms J Startin in 1972 and 1973, suggest that complacency about recovery standards is not in order. The work of Payne (1972) has shown fairly convincingly that at sites where sieving is not a routine part of the excavation technique, material of all kinds is lost during excavation. In order to assess the amount and the nature of the material likely to have been lost, sieving experiments were set up whereby the spoil resulting from normal excavation was sieved and the numbers of finds recovered from the sieved spoil were compared with the numbers of finds recovered during excavation (Payne 1972). Table 60 gives the results of the two experiments carried out. In 1972, the present writer supervised the dry sieving of the spoil from one complete layer within a pit, using a 3mm mesh sieve. In 1973, Ms Startin supervised the wet sieving of the spoil from one half of a complete pit and from one complete layer of another, using a series of 5mm, 3mm, 1.5mm, and 0.7mm mesh sieves. The results of the experiments appear alarming for all species, but a closer examination of the nature of the material recovered from the sieved spoil for the larger animals (cattle, sheep, pigs, etc) showed that it consisted almost entirely of loose teeth, small bone fragments, and small bones such as the phalanges of sheep, pigs, and dogs. We can thus predict

Table 60 The results of on-site sieving experiments

Species	Recovered in trench N*	Recovered in sieve N*	Total N*	Percentage lost %
1972				
Sheep	30	34	64	53
Cattle	2	1	3	33
Pig	1	1	2	50
Dog	1	0	1	0
Horse	0	0	0	0
Bird	0	2	2	100
Fish	0	1	1	100
Small mammal	3	50	53	94
Unidentified	0	2	2	100
Total	37	91	128	71
1973				
Sheep	102	4	106	4
Cattle	29	1	30	3
Pig	22	0	22	0
Dog	2	0	2	0
Horse	3	0	3	0
Bird	0	0	0	0
Fish	0	1	1	100
Small mammal	0	17	17	100
Unidentified	0	0	0	0
Total	158	23	181	13

*Bones counted when part of epiphysis (fused) or the fusion surface (unfused) of the shaft was present. Teeth counted when half or more present.

that these small bones will be under-represented in the bone material. In any calculation of the proportional representation of species, the figures may show some bias in favour of the larger animals (cattle and horses) and against the smaller animals (sheep, pigs, and dogs).

The rate of loss of the small mammal, fish, and bird bones is much more serious, and strongly suggests that the bones of these species collected during excavation cannot be considered a representative sample. For this reason and for others discussed elsewhere, a detailed examination of the small mammal bones has not been undertaken. The numbers of bird bones recovered must be considered to underestimate their importance at the site and the sample recovered is likely to be biased in favour of the larger bird species. Only six fish bones were recovered during the ten seasons of excavation, but since two of these were recovered from sieved material it is clear that an evaluation of the significance of the fish remains cannot be made without larger-scale sieving on site.

9.5.4 The provenance of the bones

The vast majority of the bone material was recovered from the chalk-cut features such as pits, postholes, and gullies. Most of the rest of the bone material came from the occupation layers that built up against the ramparts within the fort and a further small amount of material was recovered during the excavation of the defences themselves. A full discussion of the differences in the bone material found in various contexts and an evaluation of the significance of these differences is given in the second part of this analysis, but it is important at this stage of the discussion to give some details of the way that the animal bones were distributed on the site.

If the average number of bone fragments recovered per pit for each phase of occupation is calculated, clear differences are shown. In the early phase, the average

number of bones and bone fragments per pit was 57, in the middle period 105, in the early part of the late phase 136, and in the later part of the late phase 312, demonstrating a continuous increase over the period of occupation (Fig 9.14). Moreover, within each phase, the average number of bones per pit is greater for pits near the ramparts than for pits near the centre of the fort. This information is particularly relevant to an understanding of the distribution of animal burials and other 'special' deposits in pits (see pp 533–43).

9.5.5 Identifying and recording the bones

Work on the identification of the animal bones from Danebury began in 1971 and has continued (although not without interruption) until the present day. Inevitably, over this length of time, methodological changes and changes in the recording systems used have been made, so that complete consistency in all aspects of the recording cannot be claimed. However, changes have been changes of detail rather than of any radical kind.

For several seasons, the majority of the preliminary identifications of the animal bones were made by the writer on site while the excavation was being carried out. This proved to be a valuable exercise. It allowed the writer to gain an understanding and appreciation of the site itself, the local environment, and the archaeology and archaeological problems of the site. It was also possible to some extent to monitor the recovery of the animal bone including carrying out the sieving experiment described above, and to examine *in situ* some of the animal burials and other unusual finds. Another important benefit of working on site was that it encouraged a dialogue between excavator and specialist that allowed each to gain a better understanding of the problems and priorities of the other and to understand the kinds of questions that each was asking about the site.

Examination of the bone material recovered during later seasons of excavation was carried out away from the site. By 1978, when the dimensions of the problems posed by the task of analysis of such a large number of bones was understood, it was decided that the detailed analysis of the bone material would only be feasible with the aid of a computer. Thus a recording system, designed for computer analysis, was devised by the writer. Identifications made prior to the development of this system were transferred from the old records to the computer system,

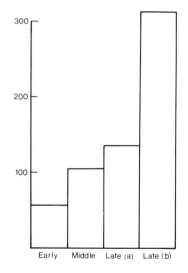

Fig 9.14 Average number of bones per pit

497

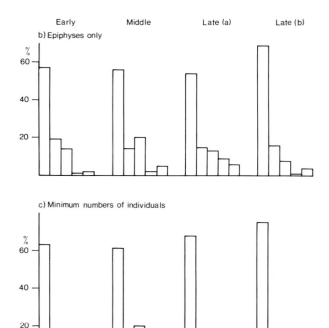

b) Epiphyses only

c) Minimum numbers of individuals

S C P D H   S C P D H   S C P D H   S C P D H

S Sheep
C Cattle
P Pig
D Dog
H Horse

Fig 9.15 Percentages of species represented

which was slightly more detailed than the previous recording system but not otherwise incompatible. The computer recording system used is described in detail elsewhere (fiche 16, frame A2).

Of nearly 140,000 bones and bone fragments recovered approximately 40%, consisting of small fragments and chips of bone, were not identified. This may seem a high percentage compared to, for example, the percentage at Portchester Castle (Grant 1975a), where only 19% of the recovered bone was not identified. However, the higher percentage of unidentified bone at Danebury is thought to reflect the better recovery of bone at Danebury already discussed, and it does not reflect any particular problems of identification.

Bones of the following species were identified: sheep, goat, cattle, pig, horse, dog, cat, red deer, roe deer, fox, and badger. Fish and bird species were also identified. The numbers of bones of each and their relative proportions in the bone sample are shown in Tables 61, 62, and 63, and Fig 9.15, which serve as basic reference points for much of the following discussion. Separate figures are given for different types of context, and for the different phases of occupation. Three methods are used to calculate the relative proportions of species (see below).

After preliminary identification, all the bird and some of the small mammal bones were sent to Ms Jennie Coy of the Southampton Faunal Remains Project and her report is included in this first part of the bone analysis. The small mammal bones have not been analysed in detail, partly because of the poor recovery of small bones at Danebury and partly because there is evidence of extensive rabbit burrowing in some parts of the site. This means that among the small mammals that might have found their way down rabbit burrows, it is not always possible to distinguish between Iron Age and intrusive animals.

9.5.6 Methods of analysis

The methods of analysis used in this discussion are, in the main, those that have been used by the writer for other analyses of bone material such as the animal bone from Portchester Castle (Grant 1975a; 1975b; 1978b). Only a brief outline will be given here, with more detail only given where new methods have been used. The second part of this report will discuss methodological problems and research in more detail.

The representation of the species

The identification of the animal bones provides evidence for the presence of various species at Danebury. However, it is important for any kind of overall analysis of the animal husbandry to quantify the bones of each species so that their relative importance can be assessed. The methods used to determine the relative proportions of the bones of the species represented were the 'epiphyses only', 'total fragments', and 'minimum numbers of individuals' methods fully described in the analysis of the Roman bones from Portchester Castle (Grant 1975a, 379). The only difference between the method as described for Portchester and that used for Danebury was in the exclusion from the 'total fragments' count of axial metapodials and axial phalanges, because of the unequal numbers of such bones in the skeletons of different species. The numbers of these bones are listed separately in Table 61. Further discussion of methods of calculating the relative proportions of species and of their various merits and biases will be given in part two.

The representation of skeletal elements

Calculations of the proportional representation of skeletal elements show, for each species, the pattern of bone representation, from which information can be obtained relevant to the interpretation or recognition of rubbish disposal practices, butchery techniques, bone use for tool manufacture, marketing of or supply with partial animal carcasses, recovery rates for different bone elements, and differential survival of bone elements. The methods used here are broadly those used for the Portchester Castle report (Grant 1975a, 384), but further refinements have been developed for the Danebury material.

The order in which the skeletal elements are shown in the histograms of the skeletal element representation of sheep, cattle, and pigs (Figs 9.16, 9.21, 9.24) is the order in which the elements are *expected* to occur assuming that all elements were once equally represented on the site. This order, with the elements expected to be best represented on the left and those that are expected to be least well represented on the right, takes account of bone density, age at epiphyseal fusion, and size. Further discussion of this method of analysis will be included in part two of the report.

For many of the species represented, a figure called the 'minimum percentage loss' is calculated. If, for example, 100 mandibles are recovered, representing a minimum of 50 animals, and the other skeletal elements together only account for a total of 40% of the rest of the skeletons of these 50 animals, the minimum percentage loss would be 60%. This figure allows comparisons to be made between the representation of skeletal elements of different species and in different phases of occupation.

NB At the time of writing this first part of the analysis of the Danebury bone report, the full analysis of the butchery practices and of the incidence of bone gnawing by dogs has not yet been completed. Both butchery and bone gnawing are expected to have affected the pattern of

Table 61 The species represented (by total fragments method)
Layers, trenches, features, slots, gullies, and postholes

Species	Early N	Early %	Middle N	Middle %	Late(a) N	Late(a) %	Late(b) N	Late(b) %	Undated N	Undated %	Total N	Total %
Sheep†	580	61	470	60	1534	66	3368	60	1676	54	7628	60
Cattle	190	20	150	19	335	14	1295	23	665	21	2635	21
Pig	148	15	108	14	404	17	630	11	250	8	1540	12
Dog	9	1	5	1	19	1	100	2	334	11	467	4
Horse	27	3	37	5	38	2	168	3	113	4	383	3
Red deer	0		0		0		6		40	1	46	
Roe deer	0		0		0		1		1		2	
Bird	1		9	1	9		22		28	1	69	1
Cat	0		0		1		0		1		2	
Fox	0		0		0		6		1		7	
Badger	0		0		0		0		1		1	
Fish	0		0		0		0		0		0	
Total (a)	955		779		2340		5596		3110		12780	
Skull bone	154	12	92	9	309	9	583	8	261	6	1399	8
Ribs	166	13	158	15	697	21	1108	15	682	17	2811	17
Misc★	5		6	1	9		25		14		59	
Total (b)	1280		1035		3355		7312		4067		17049	
Unident	971		804		2210		6304		3168		13457	

Pits

Species	Early N	Early %	Middle N	Middle %	Late(a) N	Late(a) %	Late(b) N	Late(b) %	Undated N	Undated %	Total N	Total %
Sheep†	6053	56	3485	57	3075	55	14206	67	367	52	27186	61
Cattle	2534	23	980	16	952	17	4241	20	75	11	8782	20
Pig	1648	15	1136	19	704	13	1444	7	99	14	5031	11
Dog	128	1	142	2	483	9	367	2	134	19	1254	3
Horse	129	1	261	4	235	4	703	3	15	2	1343	3
Red deer	7		5		2		31		1		46	
Roe deer	3		1		0		2		6	1	12	
Bird	209	2	83	1	151	3	146	1	1		590	1
Cat	15		40	1	3		11		4	1	73	
Fox	125	1	1		4		3		0		133	
Badger	41		0		0		11		0		52	
Fish	0		2		0		3		1		6	
Total (a)	10892		6136		5609		21168		703		44508	
Skull bone	2051	12	1079	12	982	12	4198	13	87	8	8397	12
Ribs	3441	21	1912	21	1692	21	6562	20	300	27	13907	21
Misc★	85	1	110	1	75	1	105		3		378	1
Total (b)	16469		9237		8358		32033		1093		67190	
Unident	10466		5425		4854		19627		460		40832	

All features

Species	Early N	Early %	Middle N	Middle %	Late(a) N	Late(a) %	Late(b) N	Late(b) %	Undated N	Undated %	Total N	Total %
Sheep†	6633	56	3955	57	4609	58	17574	66	2043	54	34814	61
Cattle	2724	23	1130	16	1287	16	5536	21	740	19	11417	20
Pig	1796	15	1244	18	1108	14	2074	8	349	9	6571	11
Dog	137	1	147	2	502	6	467	2	468	12	1721	3
Horse	156	1	298	4	273	3	871	3	128	3	1726	3
Red deer	7		5		2		37		41	1	92	
Roe deer	3		1		0		3		7		14	
Bird	210	2	92	1	160	3	168	1	29	1	659	1
Cat	15		40	1	4		11		5		75	
Fox	125	1	1		4		9		1		140	
Badger	41		0		0		11		1		53	
Fish	0		2		0		3		1		6	
Total (a)	11847		6915		7949		26764		3813		57288	
Skull bone	2205	12	1171	11	1291	11	4781	12	348	7	9796	12
Ribs	3607	20	2070	20	2389	20	7670	20	982	19	16718	20
Misc★	90	1	116	1	84	1	130		17		437	1
Total (b)	17749		10272		11713		39345		5160		84239	
Unident	11439		6229		7064		25931		3628		54289	
											138528	

†Sheep and goat
★Axial and abaxial metapodials and phalanges
Numbers of bones of individual species expressed as percentages of total (a)
Numbers of skull bones, ribs, and miscellaneous bones expressed as percentages of total (b)

Table 62 The species represented ('epiphyses only' method)
Layers, trenches, features, slot, gullies, and postholes

Species	Early N	%	Middle N	%	Late (a) N	%	Late (b) N	%	Undated N	%	Total N	%
Sheep†	184	58	166	54	558	62	1172	58	683	54	2763	57
Cattle	69	22	51	17	125	14	466	23	251	20	962	20
Pig	43	14	48	16	174	19	260	13	110	9	635	13
Dog	4	1	3	1	10	1	31	2	155	12	203	4
Horse	14	4	31	10	31	3	71	4	43	3	190	4
Red deer	0		0		0		0		1		1	
Roe deer	0		0		0		0		0		0	
Bird	1		8	3	5	1	20	1	29	2	63	1
Cat	0		0		1		0		1		2	
Fox	0		0		0		3		2		5	
Badger	0		0		0		0		0		0	
Total	315		307		904		2023		1275		4824	

Pits

Species	Early N	%	Middle N	%	Late (a) N	%	Late (b) N	%	Undated N	%	Total N	%
Sheep†	2867	57	1546	56	1374	54	6534	69	200	51	12521	62
Cattle	938	19	381	14	385	15	1489	16	28	8	3221	16
Pig	710	14	540	20	335	20	726	8	42	12	2353	12
Dog	43	1	44	2	224	9	130	1	68	19	519	3
Horse	101	2	140	5	144	6	406	4	2	1	793	4
Red deer	0		0		0		4		0		4	
Roe deer	0		0		0		0		6	2	6	
Bird	189	4	68	2	94	4	144	1	1		496	2
Cat	13		42	2	1		11		3	1	70	
Fox	96	2	1		0		0		0		97	
Badger	31	1	0		0		5		0		36	
Total	4988		2762		2557		9459		350		20116	

All features

Species	Early N	%	Middle N	%	Late (a) N	%	Late (b) N	%	Undated N	%	Total N	%
Sheep†	3051	57	1712	56	1932	56	7706	67	883	54	15284	61
Cattle	1007	19	432	14	510	15	1955	17	279	17	4183	17
Pig	753	14	588	19	509	15	986	9	152	9	2988	12
Dog	47	1	47	2	234	7	171	1	223	14	722	3
Horse	115	2	171	4	175	5	477	4	45	3	983	4
Red deer	0		0		0		4		1		5	
Roe deer	0		0		0		0		6		6	
Bird	190	4	76	2	99	3	164	1	30		559	2
Cat	13		42		2		11		4		72	
Fox	96		1		0		3		2		102	
Badger	31		0		0		5		0		36	
Total	5303		3069		3461		11482		1625		24940	

†Sheep and goat

Table 63 The species represented (minimum numbers of individuals)

All features

	Early N	%	Middle N	%	Late (a) N	%	Late (b) N	%	Total* N	%
Sheep†	130	63	84	61	111	68	470	75	815	70
Cattle	30	15	18	13	17	10	72	11	137	12
Pigs	33	16	27	20	24	15	70	11	154	13
Dog	5	2	3	2	7	4	9	1	24	2
Horse	8	4	6	4	5	3	15	2	34	3
Total	206		138		164		656		1164	

†Sheep and goat
*Excluding undated features

bone survival, so some of the apparent anomalies in the representation of skeletal elements may be clarified when these two analyses have been completed.

Ageing methods

An assessment of the age at death of the animals whose bones are found is of vital importance to an understanding of the animal management practices, the animal products that were of most importance, the agricultural efficiency as reflected by the ability to overwinter animals, natural mortality and the effect of disease, and the seasonality or permanence of the occupation of the hillfort. The methods used here to assess age at death are an analysis of the tooth eruption and wear of the domestic

Table 64

Phase	Ceramic phase	Approx date BC
Early	1-3	550-450
Middle	4-5	450-400
Late (a)	6	400-300
Late (b)	7-8	300-100/50

Note that the late phase has been divided into two subphases for some analyses

animals (Grant 1975a, 437–50; 1978a; 1983b) and an assessment of the epiphyseal fusion data (Grant 1975a, 393–6; Watson 1978). Correlation of bone fusion and tooth eruption data was possible particularly where complete animal skeletons were recovered. This will be discussed in detail in part two.

Metrical analysis

Measurements were taken on the bones of the domestic species whenever the condition of the bones allowed. Analyses of these measurements were made for several purposes: to assess the general size of the Danebury animals; to detect any size changes or changes in the variation within the animal populations during the period of occupation of the site; to assess the nutritional status of the animals; to determine the sexual structure of the animals; and to separate the sheep from the goats.

A description of the measurements taken and full details of the measurements themselves are given on microfiches 16: A8–17: E2. Full discussion of the metrical data will be given in part two.

Statistical testing

Wherever applicable, non-parametric statistical tests were used to test the validity of apparent differences between sets of observations. A range of tests was used to suit particular situations.

9.5.7 The dating of the animal bones

One of the main aims of the animal bone analysis was to determine any changes in any aspect of the man–animal relationships that occurred during the long period of occupation of the hillfort. Thus, it was important to distinguish between bones from different phases of occupation as determined by the ceramic phases assigned to the pottery found in association with the animal bone. Table 64 shows the correlation between the ceramic phases and the phase divisions used in discussion of the animal bones.

Inevitably there are some dangers inherent in such a divison into phases on a single site, since bone material from, for example, an early phase, cannot *per se* be distinguished from bone material from a later phase and some mixing due to disturbance such as rabbit burrowing may have occurred. However, since the majority of the bone material was recovered from pits that have been dated to a single phase and were generally cut discretely into natural chalk, the likelihood of bone from different phases of occupation having been mixed seems to be small, at least for the bone found in pits.

Some bone material could not be assigned to a specific phase within the Iron Age occupation of the site. Some of this bone came from pits that contained little or no pottery, but the majority of the unphased bone came from postholes, gullies, and other shallow features, and from the defensive ditches.

9.5.8 The domestic animals

Sheep

Since the separation of sheep bones from goat bones is notoriously difficult, these two species are generally treated together. However, metrical analysis of the Danebury material strongly suggests that very few goats were kept at Danebury and so much of the following discussion is specifically limited to sheep. Goats are discussed separately below.

The evidence

Overall, almost two-thirds of the bones recovered were identified as sheep bones. Figures for the four phases of occupation at the site show a slight but significant increase in the percentage of sheep bones found over time, from 57% in the early phase to 68% in the late (b) phase (Table 62). Slight differences in the representation of sheep bones in the pits and in the other features are evident, but these will be discussed in detail at a later stage.

Sheep bones were found widely distributed over all the excavated area and occurred in every kind of feature. In each context, sheep were almost always the best represented species.

There were, amongst the more typical domestic refuse in the pits, a number of complete or partial sheep skeletons. In all, 24 burials were identified, which are 3% of the calculated minimum number of individuals (Table 89, Fig 9.31). Finds of complete skeletons have made possible some correlations between tooth wear and epiphyseal fusion and have given some indication of the sequence of epiphyseal fusion.

Analysis of the representation of the most important skeletal elements is given in Table 65 and Fig 9.16. In each period, the best represented bone element was the mandible — this has been true of the sheep bones from every large sample studied by the writer. All other bone elements were fairly well represented and the pattern of bone element representation shown in Fig 9.16 broadly fits the expected pattern of bone element representation (see p 498). The bone elements that are best represented are those that fuse early in the animal's life and are formed of compact bone, while those that are least well represented are those that fuse late in the animal's life, have low density, and are small in size. Some anomalies in this general picture are seen. The particularly young average age of the Danebury sheep population (see below) is likely to have had a marked effect on the survival potential of bones that fuse late in the sheep's life, since comparatively few of the Danebury animals were skeletally mature. A factor that was not taken into account when the expected frequencies of bones were determined was the use of bone as a raw material. This is discussed in detail below, but it is clear that some bones, such as the tibias and the metapodials, were used in preference to other bones for tool manufacture. This may explain the relatively poor representation of the proximal metapodials.

The evidence of the bone element representation, however, strongly suggests that the bones recovered from the excavation are reasonably representative of the remains of whole animals. There is no suggestion that we have in the excavated area overall a particular abundance of butchery waste or food debris, and even the relatively fragile bone of the skull is fairly well represented. When a more detailed analysis of the spatial distribution of the animal bones is undertaken, differences in the types of deposits found in different areas of the site may emerge.

Table 65 Sheep: representation of skeletal elements

	Early N	Early %	Middle N	Middle %	Late (a) N	Late (a) %	Late (b) N	Late (b) %
Horn core	132	51	83	50	120	54	461	47
Upper orbit	98	38	82	49	112	50	402	41
Lower orbit	77	30	47	28	73	33	236	24
Maxilla	103	40	68	40	130	59	499	51
Mandible	260	100	168	100	222	100	980	100
Scapula D	130	50	72	43	82	37	430	44
Humerus P	66	25	45	27	35	16	156	16
Humerus D	184	71	93	55	133	60	557	57
Radius P	161	62	65	39	96	43	437	45
Radius D	118	45	44	26	69	31	323	33
Ulna P	115	44	61	36	48	22	298	30
Metacarpal P	140	54	67	40	89	40	329	34
Metacarpal D	119	46	62	37	71	32	245	25
1st phalange	337	32	199	30	200	23	581	15
2nd phalange	140	13	92	14	80	9	259	7
3rd phalange	85	8	49	8	34	4	101	3
Pelvis	147	57	85	51	102	46	466	48
Femur P	98	38	70	42	49	22	258	26
Femur D	76	29	59	35	56	25	236	24
Tibia P	106	41	41	24	50	23	202	21
Tibia D	189	73	79	47	106	48	447	46
Calcaneum	116	45	73	43	70	32	281	29
Astragalus	128	49	92	55	88	40	314	32
Metatarsal P	128	49	70	42	113	51	341	35
Metatarsal D	107	41	47	28	59	27	215	22
Atlas	71	55	27	32	38	34	178	36
Axis	40	31	21	25	30	27	136	28

Key: P proximal; D distal; % = % of the greatest number in each phase. Corrections made when there are more or fewer than two bones per skeleton

Already a preliminary analysis of a random sample of the features excavated in 1978 suggests that some pits contained particularly high percentages of bones with a low meat yield, whereas some of the layers against the ramparts contained particularly high percentages of the main meat-bearing bones.

The pattern of bone element representation is broadly similar from phase to phase, but one difference is clear. If the figures for the minimum percentage loss (see p 498) are calculated for each phase, there is a clear change over time. In the early period the minimum loss was only 55% but there was a steady rise to a figure of 66% in the late (b) period (see Fig 9.28). These figures for Danebury sheep are quite low when compared, for example, to Roman Portchester, where the minimum loss of sheep bones was 76–80%, and Odell (Grant 1983a), where the

loss was 87%.

The evidence for the age of the sheep is presented in Table 66 and Fig 9.17 and 9.18. Since the mandible was in all periods the best represented bone element and seems, for sheep at least, to have a relatively high survival potential, the eruption and wear of the mandibular teeth (Fig 9.18) probably offer the best indication available of the age structure of the sheep population represented by the bones recovered from the excavated area. Not all the mandibles recovered could be assigned to a particular MWS (mandible wear stage, Grant 1975a; 1983b). Fig 9.18 includes only those mandibles that could be assigned to a single MWS or where the MWS could be confidently estimated to within two or three stages.

The age structure as indicated by the analysis of tooth eruption and wear shows a remarkably consistent pattern

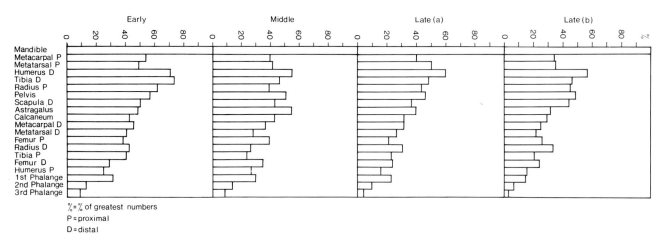

Fig 9.16 Sheep: skeletal element representation

Table 66   Sheep: bone fusion

Approx age at fusion*	Bone	Early F	Early UF	Early %F	Middle F	Middle UF	Middle %F	Late (a) F	Late (a) UF	Late (a) %F	Late (b) F	Late (b) UF	Late (b) %F
10 mths	Humerus D	132	51	72	64	28	70	102	31	77	411	147	74
	Radius P	124	40	76	46	20	70	69	37	65	319	117	73
	Scapula D	66	45	59	31	24	56	39	25	60	226	100	69
1½-2¼ yrs	Tibia D	86	104	45	35	43	45	54	50	52	199	240	45
	Metacarpal D	33	69	32	17	37	31	15	44	25	63	143	31
	Metatarsal D	34	55	38	11	29	28	21	28	43	61	113	35
2½ yrs	Ulna	16	36	31	18	16	53	12	27	31	48	97	33
2½-3 yrs	Calcaneum	44	66	40	25	42	37	31	32	49	102	134	43
	Radius D	27	86	24	11	34	24	18	51	26	101	217	32
	Femur P	34	66	34	33	37	47	18	36	33	86	181	32
3-3½ yrs	Humerus P	16	50	24	18	31	37	13	25	34	45	115	28
	Femur D	31	44	41	18	40	31	25	30	45	86	142	38
	Tibia P	45	62	42	13	27	33	18	34	35	78	128	38

Key: *Silver 1969; P proximal; D distal; F fused; UF unfused; %F percentaged fused

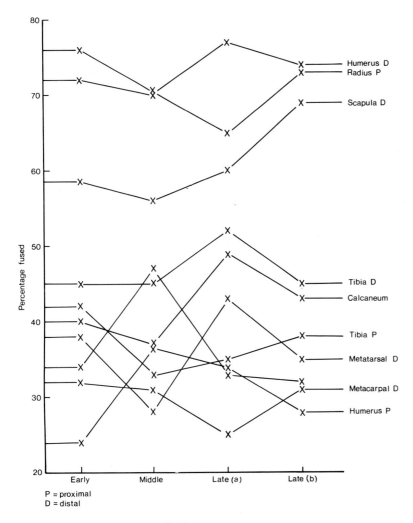

P = proximal
D = distal

Fig 9.17a   Sheep: bone fusion all phases

503

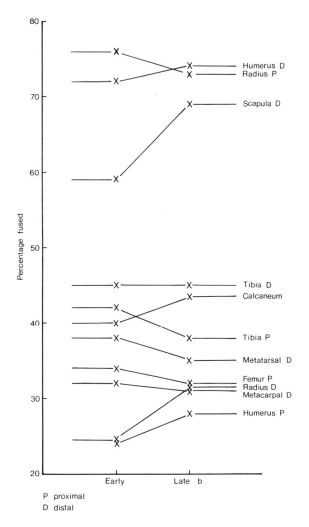

Percentage fused

80			
70		Humerus D / Radius P	Scapula D
60			

X — Humerus D
X — Radius P
X — Scapula D
X — Tibia D
X — Calcaneum
X — Tibia P
X — Metatarsal D
X — Femur P / Radius D / Metacarpal D
X — Humerus P

Early   Late b

P proximal
D distal

Fig 9.17b Sheep: bone fusion early and late (b) phases

over the four phases of occupation. Two-tailed statistical tests showed that there were no significant differences in the MWS distribution for the four phases. However, a one-tailed test indicated that there were fewer mandibles from young animals in the middle phase than in the early phase. No other significant differences were noted.

Discussion of the tooth wear data is hampered by an as yet imprecise knowledge of the relationship between MWS and real age. As more evidence becomes available and a more detailed picture emerges, it may become easier to assign approximate ages to tooth wear stages. At the present time, for a variety of reasons that will be discussed in detail in the later sections of the analysis, it would seem that MWS 8–10 may represent animals of approximately one year in age. If this is the case, we have evidence that a reasonably high percentage of the sheep whose mandibles were recovered were around one year old or younger at death. Approximately one-third of the mandibles may have come from animals that were little older than one year at death (MWS 1–9) and about half the mandibles from animals under about 18 months (MWS 1–13). In each period, peaks in the MWS distribution occurred at stages 1, 5, and 9/10. We may tentatively suggest that these represent new-born lambs, lambs of approximately six months, and lambs approximately one year old. The next peak in the MWS distribution occurs at stages 19–21, which must represent

juvenile animals, perhaps of around two years. Seventeen % of the mandibles were at MWS 14–27, which may represent the majority of animals over approximately 18 months but not yet fully mature. The next peak occurs at stage 31/32. These must be animals whose long bones are almost entirely fused and whose molar teeth are all fully erupted and in wear, and for whom an age of approximately 3½–4 years is suggested by bone fusion and tooth eruption data (Silver 1969). Thirty-four % of the mandibles were between stages 28 and 49 and may be from animals between approximately 3½ years and 7 or 8 years of age. Fig 9.19 attempts a correlation between MWS and actual age at death. It must be stressed that the absolute ages are to some extent speculative, especially for older animals, but it gives some idea of the possible absolute age structure of the sheep whose bones were recovered.

The bone fusion data are presented in Table 66 and Fig 9.17 which compare the proportions of fused and unfused bone elements in the different phases of occupation. To make Fig 9.17 clear, only certain bone elements have been included; these are the well-represented elements and include elements that fuse at different periods in the animals's life. The bone fusion data broadly confirm the tooth wear evidence. The fusion data suggest that under 30% of the sheep were skeletally mature at death and that at least 25% of the sheep died before any of the main long bones had fused (ie were, on Silver's (1969) figures, under 8–10 months). One interesting pattern emerged from the analysis of the bone fusion data, which was not apparent from the tooth wear evidence. Although the percentages of fused bone are for several bone elements similar in the early and late (b) phases (Fig 9.17 (b)), for several bone elements much higher percentages of fused bones were recovered in the late (a) period and much lower percentages of juvenile animals (Fig 9.17 (a)). However, statistical comparisons of the MWS sequence thought to relate to the period in the animal's life when epiphyseal fusion was taking place have revealed no differences in the MWS distribution between the four phases. The sample size of the middle and late (b) periods is significantly smaller than for the early and the late period and since the mandibles must, on the evidence from Table 65, be much more representative of the sheep at Danebury than the long bones, no conclusions are drawn from the anomalies in the bone fusion data for the middle and late (a) phases, at least until bone from further seasons is analysed and more information is available.

Evidence from the bone fusion data as shown in Table 66 and Fig 9.17 and from finds of complete sheep skeletons suggests that the earliest fusing bone for sheep is not the scapula, as suggested by Silver (1969), but the distal humerus. The Danebury data also suggest that the metapodials fuse sequentially rather later than Silver's figures imply and that the metatarsals in fact fuse before the metacarpals. However, as the metapodials were fairly commonly used in boneworking (see p 506), if more fused than unfused metapodials were used, the bone fusion figures would be distorted. In the second part of the bone analysis, bone fusion sequence and the correlation between tooth wear stages and bone fusion will be investigated using the evidence from the complete skeletons found at the site. No further speculation can be made in the present state of knowledge.

Full details of the measurements taken of the sheep bones are given in microfiche 16, frames A8–G2, with a summary in Table 67. The full metrical analysis is still being undertaken, but preliminary analysis suggests that the Danebury sheep were small and slender-boned. For

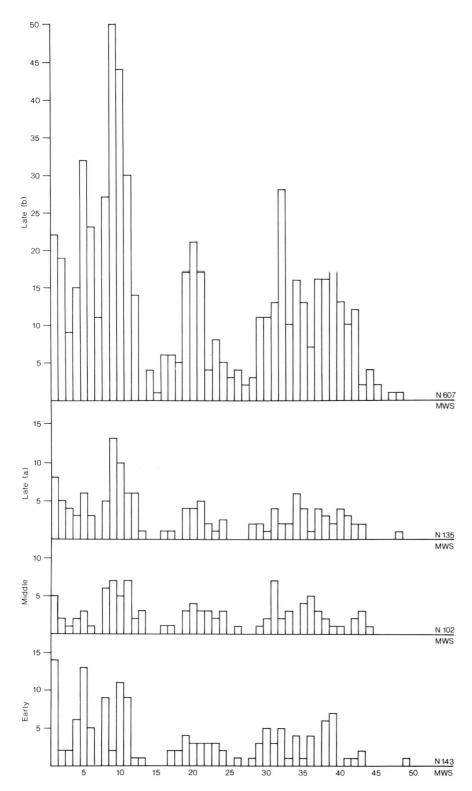

Fig 9.18 Sheep: mandible wear stages (MWS)

most bone measurements, comparisons between the four phases of occupation suggest that there were no changes in the size of the sheep throughout the occupation of the hillfort. For a small number of measurements there is a suggestion of some size reduction over the period of occupation, but until this has been more fully investigated and the sexual composition of the bones has been determined, this will not be further discussed.

The vast majority of the sheep skull fragments bore small horn cores and we may assume that the sheep were horned in both sexes. However, skull fragments were found that suggest the presence of some hornless sheep and one example was found of a skull fragment from a four-horned animal. All but two of the examples of hornless sheep were dated to the late (b) phase, the two exceptions being of middle phase date. The four-horned

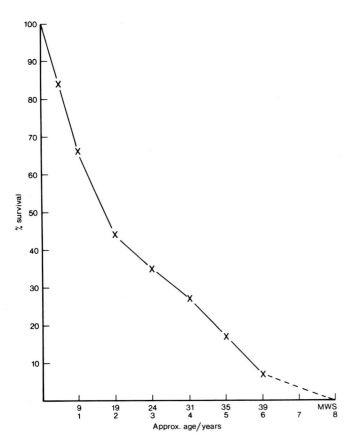

y-axis: % survival (100, 90, 80, 70, 60, 50, 40, 30, 20, 10)

x-axis:
MWS: 9 19 24 31 35 39 — MWS
years: 1 2 3 4 5 6 7 8

Approx. age/years

Fig 9.19 Sheep: survival curve based on estimated correlation between mandible wear stages (MWS) and absolute age

example was also of late (b) date.

Many of the sheep bones had cut marks on them, clearly resulting from the butchery of the animals after slaughter. The butchery technique generally was one where a sharp knife was used to cut through the ligaments at the joints. A constant butchery pattern and technique was apparent and this is currently being analysed.

Don Brothwell is making a detailed investigation of the evidence for diseases in the animal population, but one aspect of the health of the sheep which was striking was the high incidence of periodontal disease of the mandibles and maxillae in the jaws of mature animals. Fig 9.20 shows the MWS distribution of the older animals and the incidence of recorded examples of periodontal disease. Overall, 33% of mandibles with MWS above stage 28 and 53% with MWS above stage 35 have periodontal disease, the incidence of disease being highest in the late (b) phase.

Sheep bones were fairly commonly used as a raw material for the manufacture of tools and other objects, the tibias and metapodials being the most commonly used bones (Table 87). Cut marks were found around the bases of some horn cores, suggesting that the horns may also have been used as a raw material, but these marks were not very common. The average length of the sheep horn cores was only 68 mm, which suggests that the horns were of small size. The find, in a single posthole, of five sheep horn cores together with 35 antler fragments, interpreted as raw material for object manufacture, suggests a similar use for the horns.

Interpretation

The chalk downlands have traditionally been associated with sheep farming. The shallow light soil covering the Hampshire downland is of medium quality and generally

Table 67 Sheep: bone measurements

Bone	Measurement	Range (mm)	$\bar{x}$ (mm)	SD	CV	N
Scapula	dw	22-33	27	1.7	6.1	223
Humerus	l	105-131	119	8.4	7.1	14
	dw	22-33	25.6	1.5	5.7	421
Radius	l	123-165	140	7.9	5.6	63
	pw	23-34	26	1.6	5.9	184
	shw	12-17	14	1.2	8.5	57
Metacarpal	l	93-135	116	8.0	6.9	90
	pw	16-23	19	1.2	6.4	156
	dw	19-26	22	1.5	6.7	117
	shw	9-15	11	1.3	11.5	84
Femur	l	163-170				2
	dw	26-40	33	2.8	8.5	51
Tibia	l	167-202	187	9.2	4.9	22
	dw	19-28	22	1.3	5.7	289
	shw	9-15	12	1.1	8.9	58
Metatarsal	l	106-150	126	7.5	5.6	104
	pw	15-20	17	0.9	5.5	121
	dw	19-24	21	1.1	5.5	121
	shw	8-12	10	0.9	8.6	96
Calcaneum	l	42-59	48	2.8	5.9	160

Key: $\bar{x}$ mean; SD standard deviation; CV coefficient of variability; N number; l length; pw proximal width; dw distal width; shw minimum shaft width
Definition of measurements given on microfiche 16, frames A4–7

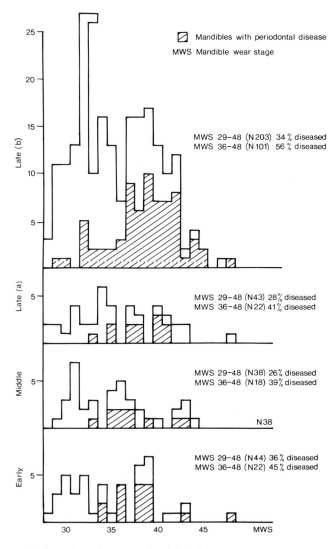

Plot labels:

MWS 29–48 (N203) 34 % diseased
MWS 36–48 (N101) 56 % diseased

MWS 29–48 (N43) 28% diseased
MWS 36–48 (N22) 41% diseased

MWS 29–48 (N38) 26% diseased
MWS 36–48 (N18) 39% diseased
N38

MWS 29–48 (N44) 36% diseased
MWS 36–48 (N22) 45% diseased

☒ Mandibles with periodontal disease
MWS Mandible wear stage

Fig 9.20 Sheep: incidence of periodontal disease

classified as being suitable for barley and sheep (Ordnance Survey 1944). Documentary evidence from the medieval period and beyond shows that the sheep flock was the pivot of chalkland husbandry, providing both wool and fertilizer for the ploughland (Jones 1960). Although the agricultural improvements of the 18th century led to increasing numbers of cattle being kept on the chalk, the downs were still considered primarily sheep country and therefore it is not surprising that the animal bone evidence for Danebury clearly shows that the livestock economy was centred on sheep.

The Danebury sheep were small and probably relatively slender animals, and the available evidence would suggest that they were generally horned in both sexes. A small number of finds of hornless sheep skulls and one example of a four-horned skull may be evidence of separate types of animals, but they could have resulted from genetic mutations within a horned population. The Soay sheep, presently to be found feral only on the Scottish island of St Kilda, are thought to be the closest living relatives of the Iron Age domestic sheep. Primitive domestic sheep are likely to have had predominately hairy rather than woolly coats and to have shed their hair in an annual moult. The gradual change from such primitive animals to animals with a woolly coat that grows continuously and can be sheared may have been

happening in the Iron Age period. To some extent, the change may have happened gradually in Britain through selection by man of those sheep where genetic mutation led to a retention of the fleece, though Wild (1970) has suggested that the Belgae might have imported a type of sheep with a fine woolly fleece. Thus, the change to sheep types with finer, woollier fleece may in Britain have owed more to foreign imports than to developments of the native sheep. In the lack of any other evidence — and there are very few finds of wool dating to the Iron Age (Ryder 1981a) — we must assume that the Danebury sheep are likely to have had coats of a hairy type which were shed naturally in an annual spring moult. To ensure the minimum loss of wool, the Danebury shepherds may have plucked the hair in the manner that was used in Scotland with native Shetland sheep until recent times (Ryder, 1981b). The so-called bone weaving combs that are found ubiquitously on Iron Age sites may have been used to pluck wool from the sheep. It is significant that there were no finds of shears at Danebury.

The clearest indication we have of the nature of the Danebury sheep husbandry is in the evidence for the age at death of the animals. However, such evidence can only tell us about the sheep that died, were killed, or were eaten in the hillfort itself, and does not necessarily give an accurate reflection of the animals kept on the chalk downlands around the fort. One of the most striking aspects of the age structure shown by the MWS distribution is the very high incidence of remains of very young animals — approximately one-third of the animals represented in the bone debris died within their first year of life. Perhaps as many as 50% were under 18 months and a significant number of deaths occurred in the neonatal period or within the first few months of life. Studies on the feral Soay sheep of St Kilda (Grubb 1974) show neonatal mortality as high as 20–45%, but these are animals living in a climate much harsher than at Danebury and there is no human involvement in their management. Medieval records, however, also suggest high neonatal loss (Trow-Smith 1957) and even on a modern sheep farm in a bad year losses can be as high as 20% (Speedy 1980). Although the environment at Danebury is certainly not nearly as harsh as on the Hebrides, the chalk land produces grass of only medium quality and modern winter food supplements such as turnips and sugar beet would not have been available.

In his study of the plant remains from Danebury (p 489), Jones has suggested that the harvest was taken at ground level and we may assume that once the cereal had been processed, some or most of the waste and straw was dried for use as animal fodder. Some crops may even have been grown specifically for animal feed. However, the cattle and horses kept at Danebury are likely to have made greater demands on the stocks of animal fodder than the sheep, as neither cattle nor horses can easily survive the winter on chalk downlands without supplementary feeding. If enough of the downland was available to the Danebury shepherds for winter grazing, the sheep could have survived the winter with little or no food supplements, as do many of the Welsh hill sheep today. However, the sheep will inevitably have suffered some loss of condition during winter months, and this would have made the pregnant and nursing ewes and their lambs particularly vulnerable, so that neonatal mortalities may well have been very high.

The presence of the bones of so many young animals, including complete skeletons of neonatal lambs, suggests that lambing may have taken place within the hillfort area. Pregnant and nursing ewes and lambs would have been easy prey for predators such as wolves and foxes if kept on the open downs. We have no certain evidence of the presence of wolves in the environment but they are known to have survived in Britain until the medieval period. Fox bones were found amongst the bone debris and may represent predators killed while attempting to steal lambs, young animals, or chickens. Bringing the pregnant ewes into the protected area of the hillfort for the lambing, and perhaps the period immediately before and after lambing, may have reduced the risk to young animals both from predators and from difficult unattended births. The ewes could have been given what supplementary food was available and this may have minimized the death of ewes at this period. If sheep milk was utilized, and with a high infant mortality there may have been a reasonable amount of surplus milk available, ewes could have continued to be brought into the fort for milking. Some (male) lambs may even have been killed in order to ensure a good milk supply.

The prime object of any flock management system, where the livestock is required for wool, meat, manure, or milk, must be at least to maintain the size of the flock, and, especially if there is human population expansion, even to build it up. A ewe will not lamb before her second year, or perhaps even her third year, and within a flock fertility may be quite low. Trow-Smith (1957) quotes fertility figures of 60–90% from medieval evidence. A ewe may thus be expected to produce only 4–5 lambs in her lifetime, and, if neonatal losses are high and 50% of her lambs are male, it would seem likely, in order to ensure that each ewe leaves a breeding ewe to replace her, that few female lambs would be deliberately killed. Even under modern hill farm conditions, the majority of ewe lambs born must be reared since they barely equal in number the natural rate of loss in the breeding flock (G Davies, pers comm).

If animals are being bred for meat, it is meat animals whose bones one would expect to find particularly well represented in the bone debris, and yet a relatively low proportion of the Danebury animals would appear to have been of an age for optimum meat production. The group of MWS from 17–27 with a peak at MWS 19–21 may represent animals killed for meat, but only 17% of the mandibles fall within this group. The peak at MWS 9 might represent one year olds killed after they had been fattened up on the spring grass. Such animals will have provided only a small amount of food compared to modern animals of the same age, but if food was in relatively short supply, even very young animals might have been eaten. Alternatively, deaths of animals at this age could reflect the culling of animals that were too weak and sickly after the winter to have been of much further economic use, or even natural mortalities at this period. We may assume that many of the animals deliberately killed at this time were males or castrates.

We have as yet no clear indication of the sexual structure, although it is hoped that further analysis of the bone dimensions may give some indication of the sex of the sheep. We may nevertheless assume that castration was carried out. Very few rams are required for breeding purposes — medieval figures suggest that one ram would serve on average 35–50 ewes (Trow-Smith 1957) — and uncastrated males present a management problem and are more susceptible to winter mortality as they tend to lose condition during the rut. Boyd and Jewell (1974) show that during the rutting period from mid September to mid October, the rams spend much less time grazing than the ewes, and that the rams expend a great deal of energy during the rut. Thus, even without any firm evidence of castration, we may assume that the majority of male lambs were castrated.

Approximately a third of the sheep found at Danebury seem to have been mature animals, past the optimum age for meat production, and the best interpretation of this age group would be that they represent ewes kept for breeding purposes and ewes and wethers kept for wool. Although wethers generally provide the best quality wool, many of the wool flock may have been ewes, because females will have had to be preserved to ensure adequate numbers of lambs to maintain the size of the flock.

If wool was an important requirement, animals would not have been slaughtered until they had gone too far back in condition to be of any further economic use. Thus, what we may have at Danebury in the domestic refuse are the animals that were too old, too weak and sickly, or of the wrong sex to have been of further use to the community. This may account for the high incidence of periodontal disease amongst the mandibles from adult sheep. Animals with broken mouths and periodontal diseases would have been just the ones to be culled and slaughtered. Such animals would not have been wasted and, as butchery marks even on the bones of very mature animals show, almost all animals were ultimately utilized for food. The speculative mortality curve (Fig 9.19) shows a fairly steady mortality of mature animals such as one might expect to have resulted from regular culling of sick or weak animals and natural mortalities each year. Peaks in the actual MWS distribution may suggest that although the death rates were fairly steady when calculated on an annual basis, the majority of deaths may have occurred at particular times of year, such as at the end of the winter when natural mortalities tend to be high and at the end of the summer when some animals had clearly not gained enough weight to survive the winter.

Mortality patterns as determined from tooth wear or epiphyseal fusion data are usually interpreted in terms of kill-off patterns (Payne 1973) but this assumes that the bones we have at an occupation site are an accurate reflection of the composition of the live flock. We may only have a partial record of the deaths occurring in the animal population. If the sheep were grazed on open downland, some of them may have fallen prey to predators and others may have been in such poor condition when they died or so far away from the hillfort that it would not have been worthwhile bringing the carcass back to the fort for consumption.

In interpreting mortality patterns, the assumption is often made that the majority of deaths represent a controlled and deliberate management policy. In practice, the restrictions imposed by factors beyond the control of an Iron Age shepherd, such as shortage of food, incidence of disease, loss of animals to predators, low fertility, and high neonatal mortality, may have greatly restricted the choices available to the farmers.

So far, the sheep have been discussed in terms of their production of meat, milk, and wool, using the evidence of the age at death of the sheep. Evidence to support the contention that wool was a valued product is found in the loom weights, spindle whorls, and weaving combs that are discussed in another section of this volume (pp 438–9). Wool seems to have been spun and woven within the hillfort, and wool or finished woollen products may even have been traded to other communities, perhaps those whose environment did not favour the large-scale rearing of sheep. However, there is one product of sheep for which we have no direct evidence, but which may well have been one of the most crucial of the flock's byproducts, and that is manure. On shallow light soil, cereal growing soon robs the soil of its fertility and, in a primitive farming system, the only way to keep up the fertility of the soil is to manure it. Thus, sheep must have been a vital part of the agricultural system and may have been folded on the arable land after harvest to eat the stubble and refertilize the soil at the same time.

Sheep bones seem to have been utilized as raw materials for tool and object manufacture (see Table 87) and horn may also have been used, though there is less evidence for the working of sheep horn than cattle horn. The horn cores found at the site suggest that the sheep horns were only of relatively small size and so may not have been particularly prized for hornworking. However, the find in a single posthole of five sheep horn cores with 35 red deer antler fragments interpreted as raw material for manufacturing purposes suggests a similar function for the horns.

The finds of whole skeletons of sheep in the pits can be interpreted variously. Those of neonatal animals add weight to the suggestion that lambing took place within the fort. Finds of slightly older lambs and of juvenile and more mature animals may also be interpreted as natural mortalities, perhaps victims of diseases that made the carcasses distasteful or hazardous for consumption. Alternative interpretations of the burials are discussed in a later section which evaluates their possible ritual significance.

A detailed comparison between the Danebury economy and that of other Iron Age sites will be made when all the analyses of the bone material are completed. Preliminary comparisons between the MWS distributions of Danebury, Ashville (Wilson 1978), and Odell (Grant 1983a) showed that although the Ashville and Odell distributions were not significantly different from each other, they both differed from the Danebury MWS distribution, particularly in their relative scarcity of the remains of very young sheep. However, both Ashville and Odell are situated in environments very different from the chalk downlands of Hampshire. The MWS distribution of two sites close to Danebury in similar environmental positions, Balksbury and Old Down Farm (Maltby 1981) showed closer affinities with the Danebury distribution, although at neither site was the high proportion of very young animals paralleled, and the MWS distributions were still significantly different from the Danebury MWS distribution. The Balksbury MWS distribution suggested rather more animals between one and two years and other peaks in the distribution occurred at slightly later stages than were seen at Danebury. However, as at Danebury, the majority of the sheep at Balksbury and Old Down Farm seemed to have been either young or mature, with relatively few juvenile animals represented. At these sites, and at Ashville too, sheep predominated, although at Ashville cattle were much better represented than at Danebury, reflecting environmental differences between the site on the Oxfordshire gravels and the sites on the Hampshire downlands. At Odell, cattle and sheep bones were found in similar proportions. A survey of the available evidence for the rest of England has shown the importance of sheep on Iron Age habitation sites in a variety of environments. Comparisons are inevitably hampered by differing conditions of preservation and variable quality of excavation, but more detailed comparisons between the Danebury material and that from such sites as Balksbury and Old Down Farm are likely to be profitable and informative.

Goats

The evidence

Evidence for the presence of goats at Danebury was revealed by a metrical analysis of the metapodials. This process is used to separate sheep from goats (Boessneck et al 1971). A clear separation between what was interpreted as the sheep and five specimens of goat was seen in the metacarpal measurements, and similarly four examples of goat metatarsals were identified. Apart from one undated specimen all the goat bones were dated to the early period of occupation. Two metacarpals and two metatarsals identified as belonging to goat came from a single complete skeleton, confirming its identification as a goat. One metacarpal and two metatarsals came from a single layer within a pit, suggesting that those bones may also have come from a single animal. Thus, the five goat metacarpals suggest the presence of four goats, three from the early phase and one undated specimen, and the metatarsals the presence of two goats, one certainly and the other probably the same goats as are represented by the metacarpals.

The only other certain evidence of the presence of goat is ten horn cores, including two from a complete skull, from a maximum of seven individuals, of which two were dated to the early phase, one to the middle phase, one to the late (a) phase, and three to the late (b) phase. This suggests that the presence of goat was not in fact restricted to the early phase of occupation. If the number of goat horn cores identified is calculated as a percentage of the total numbers of sheep and goat horn cores (see Table 65) it is clear that goat was present in very small numbers, since 2% of the horn cores were identified as goat in the early and middle phases, and less than 1% in the two late phases.

Interpretation

The scarcity of finds of goat bones indicates that goat was not of economic importance at Danebury. Even allowing for the fact that some goat bones may have been misidentified as sheep, the evidence of the horn cores and metapodials suggests that only a very small proportion of the animals were goats. The post-cranial evidence suggests that goats were restricted to the early phase, but the presence of horn cores in all four phases suggests that this was not in fact the case. We may perhaps deduce that goats were slightly more common in the early phase than in the later phases of occupation.

The available evidence shows that remains were found in only small numbers, if at all, on the majority of Iron Age sites. Goats are better adapted to rough mountainous country in temperate regions than to cold wet English winters. Ryder (1981b) points out that they are less docile than sheep and less suitable for keeping in large herds. However, since, as Ryder suggests, they can easily be kept tethered, they may have been kept in small numbers at Danebury to supply milk, either for drinking or for making butter and cheese. In other respects, as suppliers of hair or meat, they are generally inferior to sheep, although they can eat a wider variety of foodstuffs than sheep.

The single complete skeleton of a mature goat (see Fig 9.33) and the goat skull are discussed below with the special deposits.

Table 68   Cattle: representation of skeletal elements

	Early N	Early %	Middle N	Middle %	Late (a) N	Late (a) %	Late (b) N	Late (b) %
Horn core	33	55	14	39	16	47	78	54
Upper orbit	27	45	11	31	12	35	62	43
Lower orbit	37	62	13	36	10	29	66	46
Maxilla	33	55	7	19	9	26	53	37
Mandible	53	88	22	61	18	53	144	100
Scapula D	47	78	36	100	34	100	129	90
Humerus P	28	47	16	44	10	29	41	28
Humerus D	54	90	24	67	32	94	126	88
Radius P	44	73	29	81	33	97	127	88
Radius D	32	53	19	53	15	44	57	40
Ulna P	40	67	23	64	20	59	108	75
Metacarpal P	54	90	16	44	24	71	65	45
Metacarpal D	35	58	13	36	20	59	61	42
1st phalange	104	43	27	19	52	38	149	26
2nd phalange	93	39	22	17	24	18	108	19
3rd phalange	61	25	12	8	24	18	61	11
Pelvis	60	100	24	67	23	68	113	78
Femur P	36	60	12	33	21	62	61	42
Femur D	28	47	12	33	14	41	38	26
Tibia P	24	40	9	25	14	41	48	33
Tibia D	35	58	24	67	26	76	103	72
Calcaneum	23	38	20	56	19	56	82	57
Astragalus	49	82	23	64	27	79	89	62
Metatarsal P	45	75	11	31	16	47	81	56
Metatarsal D	31	52	9	25	12	35	68	47
Atlas	28	93	8	44	9	53	55	76
Axis	11	37	2	6	8	47	41	57

For key see Table 65

Cattle

The evidence
Approximately one-fifth of the animal bones were identified as cattle bones. The proportions of cattle bones fluctuated slightly over time, cattle being best represented in the earliest and latest periods of occupation. In the middle and late (a) phases, cattle bones are slightly less common (Tables 61, 62; Fig 9.15).

Like sheep bones, cattle bones were found widely distributed over the whole excavated area and were found in all types of feature. Fourteen cattle burials were found in pits, accounting for 10% of the minimum number of individuals represented for the whole period of occupation (Tables 63, 89). All but three of these burials were of young calves.

The representation of cattle skeletal elements is shown in Table 68 and Fig 9.21. The patterns of bone element representation shown in Fig 9.21 are very close to the expected patterns and clearly suggest that the cattle bones found at Danebury are the remains of whole animals. There is no evidence of a preponderance of either butchery waste or of the meat-bearing bones and all parts of the body are well represented, including the skull. The only major anomaly is the poor representation of metapodials, particularly proximal metapodials, in all but the early period.

The finds of worked bone include objects made of cattle metapodials (Table 87). These dense, straight bones are a natural choice as raw material for boneworking. This use of metapodials may explain the lower than expected frequencies of these bones amongst the domes-

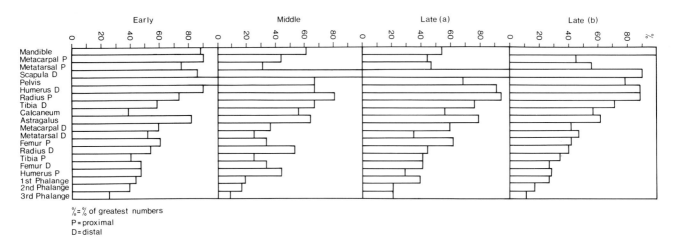

Fig 9.21   Cattle: skeletal element representation

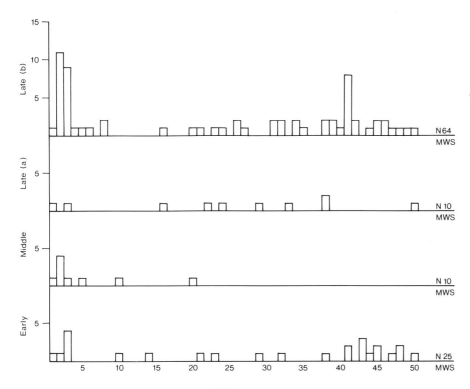

Late (b)   N 64
            MWS

Late (a)   N 10
            MWS

Middle   N 10
            MWS

Early   N 25
            MWS

Fig 9.22a   Cattle: mandible wear stages (MWS)

tic refuse. There were no bone objects made from identifiable cattle metapodials in the early period, when metapodials were well represented, although some of the small objects, such as bone needles, could have been made from splinters of metapodial shafts. The pattern of bone element representation remains broadly the same from phase to phase. The middle and late (a) periods show a slightly less consistent pattern, but in these periods far fewer bones were recovered than in either the early or the late (b) periods. The figures for the minimum percentage loss for each period show, as they did when calculated for sheep bones, a rise from the early to the late phases. However, the highest loss was in the middle phase, where the figure was 57%, as compared to 39% in the early phase and 47% in the late phases (Fig 9.28).

The evidence for the age of the cattle is shown in Table 69 and Figs 9.22 and 9.23. The mandible was the best represented bone element in the late (b) phase and was very well represented in the early phase. However, in both the middle and late (a) phases, mandibles were not the most common skeletal elements and so we have no way of knowing how representative of the age of the cattle those mandibles that were found might be. Unfortunately, post-mortem tooth loss in cattle seems to be a particular problem, and many of the mandibles found could not be assigned to a precise MWS. Fig 9.22 (a) gives the MWS of those mandibles that could be given a precise MWS or that could be confidently estimated to within two or three stages. However, far more of the mandibles that, because of the loss of one or more molar

Table 69   Cattle: bone fusion

Approx age at fusion*	Bone	Early			Middle			Late (a)			Late (b)		
		F	UF	%F	F	UF	%F	F	UF	%F	F	UF	%F
10 mths	Scapula D	29	6	83	20	8	71	26	3	90	82	15	85
18 mths	Humerus D	37	14	73	19	4	83	27	3	90	111	15	88
	Radius P	36	7	84	22	6	79	30	3	91	116	11	91
	1st phalange	67	37	64	18	9	67	45	7	87	128	21	86
	2nd phalange	60	32	65	14	8	64	20	2	91	95	10	90
2-2½ yrs	Metacarpal D	14	17	45	7	7	50	8	9	47	37	13	74
	Tibia D	20	14	59	15	9	63	21	5	81	90	11	89
	Metatarsal D	11	14	44	3	5	38	8	1	89	45	12	79
	Metapodial D	7	1		3	2		6	0		18	2	
3½ yrs	Calcaneum P	5	17	23	2	12	14	3	9	25	17	23	43
	Femur P	20	15	57	6	6	50	11	10	52	43	18	70
3½-4 yrs	Humerus P	11	17	39	8	8	50	6	3	67	24	17	59
	Radius D	13	19	41	7	11	39	8	6	57	35	21	63
	Ulna P	2	20	9	5	4	56	1	6	14	10	14	42
	Femur D	16	12	57	3	9	25	7	7	50	23	15	61
	Tibia P	11	13	46	2	7	22	7	8	47	31	17	65

For key see Table 66

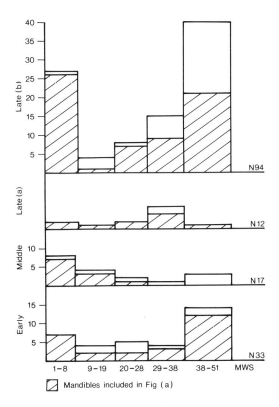

Fig 9.22b Cattle: mandible wear stages (MWS), including fragmentary mandibles

teeth, could only be imprecisely aged were from mature animals than from immature animals. In Fig 9.22 (b) the MWS are grouped in such a way as to allow the inclusion of the majority of the mandibles recovered with molar teeth present. Clearly, an assessment of the age structure of the cattle should take account of these damaged mandibles; in the late (b) phase particularly, the number of mandibles of mature cattle was almost doubled by the inclusion of the damaged mandibles, whereas there was only one damaged mandible from a very young animal. Of course, the survival pattern of the bones of very young animals is likely to mean that the MWS distribution is still biased, in this case in favour of older animals and against younger animals.

The small number of mandibles recovered from the middle and late (a) periods makes meaningful comparisons between the MWS distributions difficult. Statistical testing in fact showed no significant differences between the MWS distributions of any phase. In all phases, there were significant numbers of young animals. In the late (b) phase, just under one-third of the mandibles were at MWS 8 and below, and as Fig 9.22 (a) shows, the majority of these mandibles were from very young calves, with mandibles at stages 1–3, ie where the first molar was only just erupting through the bone of the mandible. Mandibles from older calves and juvenile animals were only rarely found in any phase, and the majority of the cattle had wear stages of 29 or above. The relatively small number of aged mandibles recovered, and the rarity of complete juvenile or mature cattle burials, has made correlations between tooth wear and epiphyseal fusion difficult. However, one skeletally mature cattle burial has a MWS of 38, which confirms the view that MWS 38–51 represent fully mature animals of approximately four years or older. In the early phase 42% and in the late (b) phase 43% of the mandibles were between MWS 38 and 51. The 12% and 15% of mandibles in the early and

late (b) phases respectively which were between MWS 29 and 38 are likely to represent the older juvenile animals, including those just reaching full maturity.

Epiphyseal fusion data shown in Table 69 suggest that between about 40% and 55% of the cattle bones were from mature animals, and that approximately 10–20% of the bones were from very young animals. The correlation between the age at fusion of the earliest fusing bones and the MWS is not clear, as none of the calf burials was of the appropriate age. MWS 1–8 may represent animals up to about one year of age and thus may include animals in whom some or all of the early fusing bones had already fused.

Although there were no significant differences between the MWS distributions in the early and late (b) phases, Fig 9.23 shows that for all the best represented bone elements a higher percentage was fused in the late (b) period than in the early period. The figures for the middle and late (a) periods were not included because of the relatively small numbers of cattle bones recovered in these phases. Some anomalies in the sequence of bone fusion suggested by the figures in Table 69 and Fig 9.23 are evident. The very high percentage of fused distal tibias in the late periods is difficult to explain and one can only assume that particular survival factors were acting against the recovery of unfused distal tibias in the late periods, although Fig 9.21 shows that distal tibias were in fact rather better represented in the late periods than in the early period. The sequence of bone fusion suggested by the figures for the early period implies that the metapodials fuse later than the proximal femur, but in the late (b) period the sequence is reversed. Since the metapodials and femurs have been shown to have been used for bone tools (Table 87) the fusion data for these bones may be biased. However, the possibility that the metapodials may not fuse at the time suggested by Silver (1969) will be further investigated.

The measurements taken on the cattle bone are given in microfiches 16: G3–17–B7, and are summarized in Table 70. The cattle were small animals by modern standards, but they included some animals that were fairly large by Iron Age standards. However, the majority of the measurements could be considered fairly typical of Iron Age cattle. Calculations of shoulder height using Foch's

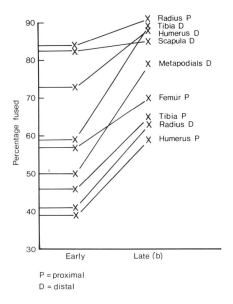

Fig 9.23 Cattle: percentages of fused bones in the early and late (b) phases

Table 70 Cattle: bone measurements

Bone	Measurement	Range (mm)	x̄ (mm)	SD	CV	N
Horn core	l	100-180	137	24.5	17.9	7
Scapula	max dw	51-77	60	4.6	7.7	81
Humerus	l	209-250	230	12.0	5.2	7
	dw	62-83	73	4.9	6.7	67
Radius	l	216-289	247	16.7	6.8	21
	pw	61-89	72	5.5	7.6	72
	shw	29-41	35	3.2	9.3	13
Metacarpal	l	163-188	174	7.3	4.2	34
	pw	43-61	52	4.1	7.8	49
	dw	48-67	56	4.8	8.5	46
	shw	26-34	30	2.6	8.6	27
Femur	l	286-312	295	10.6	3.6	5
	dw	60-95	81	9.3	11.5	8
	shw	27-32	29	2.0	6.9	3
Tibia	l	295-335	314	13.4	4.2	9
	dw	49-62	55	3.1	5.7	96
	shw	28-37	34	2.3	6.9	9
Metatarsal	l	182-235	202	10.8	5.3	32
	pw	37-48	43	2.7	6.3	46
	dw	44-59	50	3.8	7.5	41
Calcaneum	l	108-126	117	5.4	4.6	17
Astragalus	l	41-65	57	4.3	7.5	94

For key see Table 67

(1966) figures suggest animals of approximately 0.9 m to 1.20 m in height. The horn core dimensions put the cattle in the 'short-horned' (Armitage & Clutton-Brock 1976) group. None of the measured horn cores was small enough to suggest 'small-horned' cattle. Calculation of the metacarpal shaft and distal indices using Howard's (1963) method to determine the sexes of cattle bones failed to reveal clear groupings that could be interpreted as sexual groupings.

Comparisons between phases are generally hampered by the small number of measurable bones. Most tests revealed no differences between the size of the cattle in the four phases of occupation, but for a few bone dimensions differences were apparent. Further seasons of excavation will add to the numbers of measurable cattle bones, and when the full metrical analysis has been completed more informed interpretation of the bone dimensions will be possible than at present.

A distal radius and two femur shaft fragments were found that were considerably larger in size than any of the other cattle bones found at Danebury. They appear to be of *Bos primigenius* dimensions, the radius having a distal width of c 97 mm. All three bone fragments were in extremely eroded condition, quite untypical of the majority of bones at Danebury. The bones with which they were found were not eroded, and it is suggested that these bones may not be contemporary with the rest of the animal bones. The find of, for example, the Beaker burial shows that the site was used before the Iron Age, and so it would be unwise to interpret these bones as evidence for the presence of *Bos primigenius* in southern Britain in the Iron Age.

Many cattle bones had cut marks on them. While on the sheep bones the cuts were almost always fine knife cuts, the cattle bones had both knife cuts and cuts that seem to have been made by a heavier tool such as a chopper.

Cattle bones were made into bone objects, the most commonly used bones being the metapodials and the femurs (Table 87). Several horn cores had been chopped at the base suggesting the removal of the horn, presumably for hornworking. Although more common than on sheep horn cores, cuts on cattle horn cores were relatively rare.

Interpretation

If the animal bones found in the mainly domestic contexts of the hillfort interior are representative of the animals kept by the hillfort inhabitants, cattle were clearly kept in much smaller numbers than sheep. The chalk downlands, so suitable for sheep, provide a much less suitable environment for the rearing of cattle, both because the grass is of relatively poor quality and because cattle need access to water. A heavy milking cow such as a modern Friesian may drink as much as twelve or fourteen gallons of water per day and, although we can assume that a small Iron Age cow could survive on rather less than this, access to water is an important requirement for cattle keeping. The chalk downland, is however, cut by rivers; 3.5km to the east of Danebury is the valley of the Test, while 3 km to the west is the Wallop Brook, a tributary of the Test which joins it some 6 km to the south of the fort. The water meadows and lush grasslands on either side of the Test would have provided excellent pasture for cattle, even if the downland immediately surrounding the fort was not suitable for permanent cattle pasture.

The cattle themselves seem to have been of a short-horned variety and were of small size. There is little evidence of the hair type or colour of Iron Age cattle, as finds of skin and hair are very rare (Ryder 1981b).

The comparatively large numbers of mandibles from very young calves suggest that calving, like lambing, may have taken place within or near the hillfort. Calves, like lambs, are vulnerable to predators such as wolves and even in a protected environment there would have been neonatal losses. Pregnant cows may have been stalled throughout the winter months. Although a small cow can survive on grass for the spring, summer, and perhaps even the autumn months, during the winter the pregnant cows and even the oxen and bulls would almost certainly have required supplementary feeding. On a modern grassland farm, a maintenance ration for a cow, merely to keep her alive, would be about 18 lbs of hay per day in the winter (Watson 1938). It is likely that some part of the crops would have been grown as food for the cattle in the winter months, but other foodstuffs, such as leaves, may have been utilized.

In the spring and summer months, the river valley

meadows and the watered downland would have provided lush grass. We have evidence for the exploitation of the river valley areas in the presence of weeds that are likely to have grown in loamy and gravelly soils (pp 488–9).

The small numbers of mandibles from juvenile animals at the optimum age for meat yield suggest that the rearing of cattle was not focused towards meat production. The majority of the cattle mandibles were from animals that, on all the available evidence, must have been mature or even old. Many of the problems that faced the shepherds must also have faced the cattle herdsmen and in order to ensure the maintenance of the herd, cows may only have been killed when barren or diseased. Apart from cows kept for breeding purposes, the rest of the herd may have been oxen, whose main use would have been as draught animals, used for general cartage and particularly as plough animals. Medieval records (Trow-Smith 1957) suggest that plough teams may have been made up of steers and females — cows that had failed to become pregnant or were in the early stage of pregnancy. A castrated male can be trained for drawing the plough from around two or three years old, and the herd may have included animals who were being trained in order to maintain the plough team. The animals whose bones were found in the rubbish pits at Danebury were probably animals that had ceased to be useful for breeding or draught purposes and were slaughtered and eaten, perhaps after a period of fattening up.

Cattle manure, like sheep manure, would inevitably have been utilized and if cattle were stalled for any period, the manure could have been carted out to the fields. Cows' milk would have been of most value for feeding the calves. In primitive cattle the cow does not generally produce milk beyond the time when the calf is weaned. However, cows that lost their calves could have provided milk for human consumption.

The finds of objects made from cattle bones show that the cattle, like the sheep, were utilized even after death. The hide particularly may have had great value for many purposes, from clothing or armour to buckets.

Preliminary comparisons with other Iron Age sites have been made. Cattle bones are inevitably more common on lowland sites such as Odell (Grant 1983a), where 30% of the animal bones from the Iron Age occupation were cattle bones, and Ashville (Wilson 1978), where the figure is 30–40%. At Gussage All Saints (Harcourt 1979) on the edge of a similar downland environment and at a lower altitude, 20–30% of the farm species represented were cattle.

Comparisons between the MWS of the cattle from Danebury and Odell showed strikingly different patterns. At Odell, the Iron Age MWS distribution is almost the reverse of the Danebury distribution, with the majority of cattle mandibles at stages representing juvenile animals, and relatively few very young or mature animals represented. The MWS distribution of Iron Age cattle from Odell, Ashville, and Barton Court Farm (Wilson 1978) showed no significant differences and suggests a similar exploitation and management of cattle at these three lowland sites. The Danebury cattle MWS distribution was, however, very similar to the distribution from the two chalk downland sites of Winnall Down and Balksbury (Maltby 1981). Both sites had relatively high proportions of mature animals and young animals, with few juveniles, although at neither site was the proportion of very young animals seen at Danebury matched. Differences between the age distribution of animals found at these chalkland settlements and those from the settlements on lower ground may indicate differences in cattle management techniques in different environments.

However, the possibility emerges that there may have been specialization in different aspects of cattle rearing at different sites. Animals born and weaned at some sites may have then been moved to farmsteads in lower-lying areas, where the pasture would have been more suitable for cattle rearing, particularly for young growing animals whose nutritional requirements were high. If a settlement served as a breeding centre, one would expect to find mainly the bones of very young animals and the older breeding cows, together with the animals required for agricultural purposes. The interpretation of Danebury as a possible cattle breeding centre is, in the present state of knowledge, only speculative and other interpretations of the evidence are possible.

More information is needed, particularly to enable comparisons between upland and lowland sites in the same areas to be made, and further analysis of the sexual composition of the cattle bone assemblage at Danebury and other sites is also vital. The settlement site at Meon Hill, little more than 2 km from Danebury but less than 1 km from the river, would be an ideal site on which to test this hypothesis. Unfortunately, the excavation of this site (Liddell 1935) was on a small scale. The writer has reexamined the surviving bones and, although they suggest a higher percentage of cattle bones than at Danebury, no conclusions can be drawn from such a small sample, especially when there is no way of knowing how representative the surviving bones are of those that were originally present.

Pigs

The evidence

The proportion of pig bones found at Danebury varied from approximately one-tenth to one-fifth over the period of occupation. Pig bones were most common in the middle phase, and were significantly rarer in the late (b) phase than at any other period (Tables 61, 62, 63; Fig 9.15). Pig bones were widely distributed over the excavated area and, like sheep and cattle bones, were found in every type of feature. Twenty-two pig burials were recorded, 14% of the calculated minimum number of individuals (Table 89). Eleven of these burials were dated to the middle phase of occupation, 41% of the minimum number of individuals for that period. Fourteen of the total number of pig burials were very young animals, while eight were older animals.

The representation of skeletal elements is shown in Table 71 and Fig 9.24. All parts of the skeleton were represented, but as at the majority of sites examined by the writer, the mandible was the best represented element. The patterns of bone element representation in Fig 9.24 show some departures from the idealized pattern of representation. Most notable is the very poor representation of metapodial bones in all phases of occupation. This might be interpreted as suggesting that the bone assemblage was lacking in the parts of the skeleton that would have been discarded as butchery waste, but if this were the case other bones, such as phalanges, distal tibias, calcanea, astragali, and distal radii, would also be expected to be rare, whereas such bones were in fact relatively well represented. Sheep and cattle metapodials were also relatively uncommon, but this was explained by the use of the metapodials of these species for bone tools. Pig bone is rather porous compared to the bone of sheep or cattle and is not generally used for bone tools — only one tool made from

Table 71 Pig: representation of skeletal elements

	Early N	Early %	Middle N	Middle %	Late (a) N	Late (a) %	Late (b) N	Late (b) %
Upper orbit	39	59	14	26	31	65	71	51
Lower orbit	4	6	3	6			5	4
Maxilla	61	92	40	75	48	100	123	88
Mandible	66	100	53	100	48	100	139	100
Scapula D	38	58	25	47	37	77	81	58
Humerus P	24	36	17	32	11	23	20	14
Humerus D	34	52	30	57	25	52	70	50
Radius P	36	55	31	58	27	56	53	38
Radius D	23	35	24	45	13	27	24	17
Ulna P	42	64	29	55	29	60	79	57
Metacarpal P	38	29	34	32	25	27	47	17
Metacarpal D	36	27	30	28	26	27	35	13
1st phalange	84	32	62	29	57	30	83	15
2nd phalange	47	18	38	18	31	17	55	10
3rd phalange	33	13	28	13	25	14	19	4
Pelvis	34	52	27	51	30	63	59	42
Femur P	28	42	19	36	11	23	11	8
Femur D	25	38	23	43	21	44	19	14
Tibia P	25	38	19	36	10	21	21	15
Tibia D	39	59	29	55	24	50	65	47
Calcaneum	44	67	17	32	19	40	43	31
Astragalus	30	45	21	40	28	58	37	27
Metatarsal P	39	30	19	19	21	23	36	13
Metatarsal D	38	29	18	17	23	25	27	10
Atlas	23	70	10	38	8	33	22	32
Axis	9	27	2	8	4	17	7	10

For key see Table 65

a pig bone was found. Allowing for the fragile nature of pig bone, and the young average age of the pig population, the pattern of bone element representation must be assumed to reflect mainly survival and recovery factors, with only the poor representation of metapodials departing enough from the expected pattern to warrant any other explanation. None can, however, be offered at the present time. Table 71 shows that pig skulls, particularly upper jaws, were well represented.

The figures for the minimum percentage loss for each phase of occupation are, from the early to the late (b) period, 56%, 62%, 59%, and 70%, showing an increasing disproportion between the best represented element and the other bone elements; this is clearly visible in Fig 9.28.

The evidence for the age at death of the pigs whose bones were found at Danebury is presented in Table 72 and Figs 9.25 and 9.26. Mandibles were the most common

skeletal element in all phases, and so it is hoped that the age of the mandibles is representative of the age of the pigs whose bones were found at Danebury.

From Fig 9.25 it is clear that many of the mandibles were from very young pigs that must have died in the neonatal period, and 17–38% were from pigs whose first molar had only just erupted through the bone (MWS 1-4). From Silver's (1969) data those animals may have been younger than 4-6 months and they were almost certainly well under one year of age. The highest proportion of young animals was found in middle period contexts and the lowest proportion in the early phase. In all phases except the early phase there were very few mandibles with wear stages above MWS 31, which coincides with the time when the third molar is just coming into wear. This implies that very few pigs were fully mature at death. In the early phase, significantly more mandibles from mature animals were found.

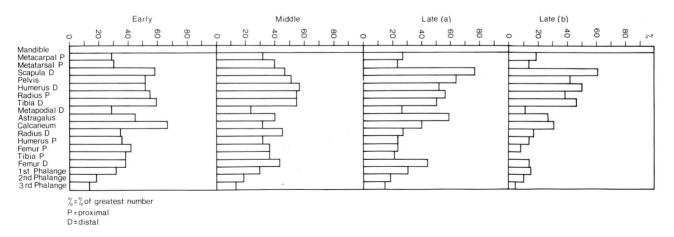

% = % of greatest number
P = proximal
D = distal

Fig 9.24 Pig: skeletal element representation

515

Table 72   Pig: bone fusion

Approx age at fusion*	Bone	Early F	Early UF	Early %F	Middle F	Middle UF	Middle %F	Late (a) F	Late (a) UF	Late (a) %F	Late (b) F	Late (b) UF	Late (b) %F
1 yr	Scapula D	13	14	48	9	12	43	18	8	69	45	13	78
	Humerus D	16	17	48	7	22	24	14	11	56	44	25	64
	Radius P	17	19	47	13	18	42	15	13	54	35	19	65
	2nd phalange	20	27	43	14	24	37	27	4	87	44	10	81
2-2¼ yrs	Metacarpal D	4	27	13	1	29	3	1	20	5	1	27	4
	Metatarsal D	3	29	9	2	15	12	4	18	18	4	17	19
	Metapodial D	8	16	33	0	18	0	2	9	18	5	20	20
	1st phalange	29	49	37	16	46	26	16	41	28	45	38	54
	Tibia D	8	32	20	8	20	29	12	12	50	26	37	41
	Calcaneum P	4	24	14	4	13	24	1	13	7	4	26	13
3½ yrs	Humerus P	1	23	4	4	14	22	1	7	13	3	17	15
	Radius D	2	21	9	1	23	4	0	14	0	3	20	13
	Ulna P	0	23	0	0	19	0	0	11	0	1	21	5
	Femur P	1	27	4	0	19	0	1	10	9	1	10	9
	Femur D	4	20	17	2	20	9	2	19	10	3	15	17
	Tibia P	3	23	12	1	18	5	0	11	0	1	17	6

For key see Table 66

Further differences between the MWS distribution from the early and late (b) phases can be seen. While in both phases there was a small group of mandibles at stages 6-10, in the early phase only 9% were between stages 13 and 24, while in the late (b) period over 30% of the mandibles were between these stages. Twenty-nine % of the early mandibles were between stages 25 and 31, compared to only 10% of the late (b) mandibles.

Differences between the MWS distributions of the early and late (b) phases were confirmed by statistical tests, which also suggested that there were no differences between the MWS distribution of the middle, late (a), and late (b) phases.

The bone fusion data were examined to confirm the impression that fewer young animals and more old animals were found in the early phase than in the late (b) phase, but as Fig 9.26 and Table 72 show, the bone fusion figures suggest quite the opposite. Fig 9.26 excludes the middle and late (a) phases because of the relatively small numbers of bones found in these periods. For almost all the bone elements, there are higher percentages of unfused bones in the early period than in the late period. The bone fusion and the tooth wear figures for the early phase are not in fact inconsistent, given the nature of the bone material and the sample size, whereas there is less consistency between the two sets of data for the late (b) period. The only reasonable explanation of this anomaly is that the factors which led to the much higher percentage loss figures for the late period (70% compared to 55% in the early period) have disproportionately affected the survival of the bones of young animals, which are of course much more vulnerable to breakage and decay than fused bones of more mature animals.

The complete pig skeletons found at Danebury have given some indication of bone fusion order and of the correlation between tooth wear and bone fusion. The sequence of bone fusion in young animals seems to be

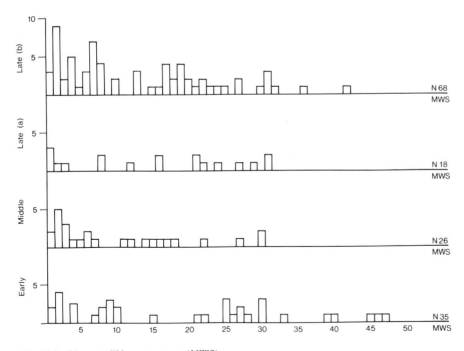

Fig 9.25   Pig: mandible wear stages (MWS)

516

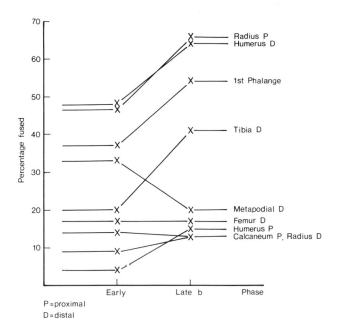

Fig 9.26   Pig: percentages of fused bones in the early and late (b) phases

P = proximal
D = distal

by diet than bone development (McCance *et al* 1968). Unfortunately, relatively few of the bones of the pigs were complete enough for measurements to be taken. This was partly due to poor survival of pig bone, but also to the fact that the majority of pig bones from the site had unfused epiphyses and thus could not be measured. Table 73 summarizes the pig bone measurements, and full details are given in microfiche 17, frames B8–C11. Apart from metapodials, only one complete measurable long bone was found—a tibia. Calculation of the shoulder height, using Teichert's method (1969) gave a figure of 0.7 m, suggesting small animals by modern standards. The measured bones suggest that the Danebury pigs were typical for the Iron Age. There was no certain evidence from the bone measurements of the presence of wild boar, although some very large canines were found which may have come from large male pigs. But until further investigations have been made of the range of sizes of such teeth in domestic pigs, it has been assumed that wild boar was not present.

Butchery marks were common on the bones of pig, and although they were mostly fine knife cuts, occasional cuts that resulted from the use of a heavier tool were noted.

Pig bones do not seem to have been used for toolmaking, the one exception being a pig fibula, which had evidently been chosen because of its natural shape. A perforated upper canine had evidently been used as an ornament.

variable. In some pigs, the proximal radius, distal scapula, and pelvis had fused before the distal humerus, while in others the distal humerus was one of the earliest fusing bones. In one pig, two-thirds of the second phalanges had fused before the distal humerus, but in another pig the distal humerus had fused before the second phalanges. There were fourteen examples of skeletons with MWS from 1 to 9 and in none of these was any of the early fusing group of bones fused (see Table 72). Silver's fusion ages for pig bones would suggest that MWS 1-9 represent animals of less than one year of age. In one skeleton with mandibles at MWS 16/17, the distal humerus and scapula were fused, but the proximal radius was unfused, and in another skeleton with the mandibles at MWS 19, the distal scapula, proximal radius, distal humerus, and pelvis were all fused, and all other bones, including the second phalanges, were unfused, suggesting animals of little more than one year of age, if Silver's ages of bone fusion are used. Absolute ageing of pig mandibles will always be difficult because the varied diet of pigs means that animals of the same age but fed on different kinds of food may have very different degrees of wear on their teeth. Tooth eruption may be less affected

Interpretation

Pigs are remarkably adaptable animals, surviving and breeding in a variety of environments ranging from their natural woodland and grassland habitats to urban back-yards. They are omnivorous and can thus be fed on a wide range of foodstuffs. However, if pigs are not to compete with man for food, they require forested or wooded areas for autumn and winter feeding, and pastures with rough grass and bracken for spring and summer feeding. The pigs may have been turned onto the stubble after the sheep and cattle since, with their ability to root out food from under the soil, they could utilize the last traces of edible material that the sheep and cattle could not reach. Although the extent of the woodlands near Danebury during the Iron Age is uncertain, as Cunliffe has shown (p 475) there are soils within the surrounding area that could have supported forest or woodland growth.

Interpretation of the economic value of pigs to the hillfort is more straightforward than for sheep or cattle. Pigs provide only two main products — meat and manure.

Table 73   Pig: bone measurements

Bone	Measurement	Range (mm)	$\bar{x}$ (mm)	SD	CV	N
Scapula	dw	26-37	32	2.3	7.0	54
Humerus	dw	29-42	37	2.3	6.2	54
Radius	pw	24-30	26	1.4	5.1	32
Metacarpal	l	65-75	71	3.0	4.2	10
	dw	13-16	14	0.8	5.3	6
Femur	dw	41-45	43	1.3	3.1	7
Tibia	l	179				1
	dw	25-32	28	1.5	5.3	38
Metatarsal	l	69-85	78	4.8	6.1	12
	dw	13-16	14	0.9	6.0	11
Calcaneum	l	69-79	72	3.7	5.2	5

For key see Table 67

Their great value to man is in their ability to transform a wide variety of normally inedible organic matter, including such things as acorns which are poisonous for most creatures, into first class protein. Then, as a byproduct, they produce manure of the highest quality; there is no animal that enriches the soil as quickly and as lastingly as a pig. Thus, any husbandry system for pigs will have two main aims: to ensure that there are sufficient breeding animals to keep the herd at the required size, and to rear the rest of the pigs to an age where there is the maximum yield of meat for the minimum expenditure of food and effort.

The tooth wear evidence suggests that pigs may have been bred inside the fort. The incidence of the bones of very young animals might suggest a fairly high infant mortality, but relatively high mortality is common in modern farm conditions. Since even unimproved pigs will produce litters of five or six piglets twice a year, maintaining the size of the pig population should not have presented as many problems as maintaining the size of the sheep flocks or cattle herds. Roast sucking pig is known to have been a delicacy at least from Roman times, and even animals that died in the neonatal period may have been eaten.

In all periods, many of the mandibles came from juvenile animals. These animals are likely to have been the males, probably castrated for ease of management, and females surplus to breeding requirements, fattened up sufficiently to provide meat for the community. Finds of the bones of older animals could represent sows killed at the end of their useful breeding life.

Although pig bones are not generally used for tool manufacture, the pig provides a range of byproducts once dead, including skin and bristles.

At other sites of the Iron Age, as at Danebury, pig bones are generally the third most commonly represented species. The age distributions too show the same general pattern, with few mature animals and high proportions of juvenile animals, although the mandibles of very young animals are rarely as well represented as at Danebury. More detailed comparisons between the MWS distributions of Danebury and Odell show that, while Odell and the Danebury early phase MWS distributions do not differ significantly, the Danebury late (b) phase MWS distribution is significantly different from that at Odell. In the absence of any other evidence from the Iron Age, comparisons were made with the pig MWS data for the Roman site at Fishbourne (Grant 1971). Again, the Danebury early phase did not differ from the distribution at Fishbourne, while the late (b) phase distribution was significantly different. This is discussed below when the changes in the economy over the period of occupation are considered.

Horses

The evidence

Horse bone accounted for only 3% of the bone recovered at Danebury (Table 62). The percentage of horse bones varied only slightly from period to period, although there is evidence of a very small but significant increase from the early period to the later periods of occupation.

Horse bones were found in all types of context and there seems to be no difference between the proportions found in pits and in other types of feature. It was thought possible that if a species was relatively rare, the bones of that species might be concentrated in a relatively small number of contexts. However, although only 3% of the animal bones found in dated pits were horse bones, 29% of the dated pits contained horse bones (Table 74 a). This suggests that horse bones were generally well distributed over the site. This is confirmed by calculating the average numbers of horse bones per pit containing horse bones (Table 74 b), which shows an average of only five bones

Table 74 Horse: distribution of horse bones in the pits

		Early	Middle	Late (a)	Late (b)	Total*
a)	*Percentages of pits with horse bone*					
	Pits with horse bone	71	38	37	110	256
	Pits with bone	492	139	98	162	891
	% pits with horse bone	14%	27%	38%	68%	29%
b)	*Average numbers of horse bones per pit (excluding pits with skull bone only)*					
	Horse bones ('total frags')	129	261	235	703	1328
	Pits with horse bone	65	38	36	105	244
	Average numbers horse bones per pit	2.0	6.9	6.5	6.7	5.4
c)	*Percentages of pits containing horse bone special deposits*					
	Pits with horse special deposits	11	4	3	17	35
	Pits with horse bone	71	38	37	110	256
	% pits with horse special deposits	15%	11%	8%	15%	14%
d)	*Percentages of pits containing horse bones and any type of special deposit*					
	Pits with horse bones and special deposit	24	13	12	52	101
	Pits with special deposits	49	25	22	65	161
	% pits with horse bones and special deposits	49%	52%	55%	80%	63%
e)	*Percentages of horse bones classed as special deposits (epiphyses only, therefore excluding skulls)*					
	Horse bones in special deposits	6	46	64	50	166
	Horse bones	101	140	144	406	791
	% horse bones in special deposits	6%	33%	44%	12%	21%

*Total of dated pits only

Table 75　Horse: representation of skeletal elements

	Early N	Middle N	Late (a) N	Late (b) N	Late (b) %
Upper orbit	10	6	1	17	59
Lower orbit	6	3	0	11	38
Occipital condyle	15	2	1	20	69
Maxilla	9	6	2	20	69
Mandible	6	4	8	21	72
Scapula D	7	5	8	20	69
Humerus P	3	2	7	7	24
Humerus D	2	3	5	7	24
Radius P	7	4	6	29	100
Radius D	4	5	7	22	76
Ulna	4	4	3	24	83
Metacarpal P	7	5	10	27	93
Metacarpal D	7	6	10	25	86
1st phalange	10	15	15	37	66
2nd phalange	5	8	7	21	38
3rd phalange	3	7	7	22	38
Pelvis	7	4	8	18	62
Femur P	4	6	4	13	45
Femur D	3	6	4	12	41
Tibia P	3	4	6	12	41
Tibia D	6	8	9	24	83
Calcaneum	4	7	5	13	45
Astragalus	3	12	7	24	83
Metatarsal P	1	10	5	15	52
Metatarsal D	1	12	7	10	34
Atlas	0	3	1	1	7
Axis	1	2	1	0	

For key see Table 65

per pit. Both calculations show an increase over time, and although this is partly related to the slight increase in the proportion of horse bones over the period of occupation, it must also reflect the significant increase from the early to the late (b) period in the average number of all animal bones per pit (Fig 9.14). These figures do hide a number of exceptions, where relatively large numbers of horse bones were found in pits. These are, in almost every case, pits where complete horse skeletons or articulated horse limbs were found. Three skeletons of mature horses (see Fig 9.30), representing 9% of the calculated minimum number of horses, and eleven articulated limbs (Fig 9.35) were found. In Table 74 e, the percentages of horse bones found as whole skeletons or articulated limbs (classed here as special deposits, a term which is discussed in detail in a later section) are calculated. A high percentage of the horse bones from the middle and late (a) periods were classed as special deposits, whereas in the late (b) and early periods, many fewer of the horse bones were found as whole skeletons or articulated legs.

Table 75 summarizes the evidence for the skeletal element representation. Analysis of such evidence is always difficult if only small numbers of bones are retrieved. Percentage figures have only been calculated for the late (b) phase, so that comparisons between the four phases of occupation are not really possible until we have larger numbers of horse bones. The pattern of bone element representation for the late (b) period is shown in Fig 9.27. The expected order of bone representation used is that used for cattle, since the expected order of bone representation has not yet been separately calculated for horses. The expected order assumes a rather higher percentage of immature animals than were found amongst the horses, so some anomalies may be due to the high percentage of the bones of mature animals. Most bone elements are well represented in the late (b) phase. The most conspicuous anomaly is the poor representation of the distal humerus, which is not easily explained. Horse metacarpals are well represented, but horse metatarsals occur rather less frequently. A small number of bone tools were made from the proximal ends of the metatarsals, but none of those found used the proximal end of metacarpals.

There is an apparent discrepancy between the evidence for the presence of horses in Table 63 and the number of horse skulls listed in Table 90. This is due to two factors. Firstly, the skull bone is very easily damaged and the orbit areas listed in Table 75 may have been damaged even on relatively complete skulls. Horse skull bone seems to be particularly fragile. Secondly, there is likely to have been some change in the detail used in recording skull bone from the very early seasons of excavation owing to the change in recording systems during the long

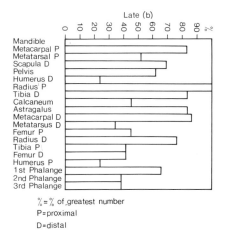

% = % of greatest number
P = proximal
D = distal

Fig 9.27　Horse: skeletal element representation (late (b) phase)

519

Table 76 Horse: bone fusion

Approx age at fusion*	Bone	Early F	Early UF	Middle F	Middle UF	Late (a) F	Late (a) UF	Late (b) F	Late (b) UF
9–12 mths	2nd phalange	5	0	8	0	7	0	21	0
13–15 mths	1st phalange	9	0	14	0	15	0	35	2
15–18 mths	Humerus D	2	0	3	0	5	0	7	0
	Radius P	7	0	4	0	6	0	28	1
	Metacarpal D	7	0	5	0	9	0	21	0
	Metatarsal D	2	0	11	0	4	0	5	0
18–24 mths	Scapula D	7	0	5	0	6	1	15	0
	Pelvis	6	0	3	0	5	0	18	0
	Tibia D	4	1	8	1	8	1	24	0
3–3½ yrs	Humerus P	3	0	2	0	4	2	7	0
	Radius D	4	0	5	0	5	2	21	1
	Ulna P	0	1	2	0	0	1	6	0
	Femur P	3	1	5	1	1	3	11	2
	Femur D	3	0	6	1	3	1	11	1
	Tibia P	2	1	4	0	4	2	12	0
	Calcaneum P	1	0	4	0	1	2	7	1

For key see Table 66

period over which work on the identification of the Danebury bones was carried out (see p 497). Thus, a count was also made of the occipital condyles for horse, since this part of the skull is dense and less easily broken than some of the other areas of the skull, although it is a part of the skull that is frequently damaged by butchery. The MNI figures for horse in the early phase (Table 63) were calculated for the number of occipital condyles recorded. Horse skulls seem to have been particularly common in the early phase, since seven complete skulls and three nearly complete skulls were found. In contrast, the minimum number of individuals calculated for the post-cranial skeleton suggest the presence of only four horses. Horse skulls were rather under-represented in the middle and late (a) periods, but in the late (b) period, although there was no significant discrepancy between the representation of skulls and the post-cranial skeleton, when the fragile nature of skull bone is taken into account, skull bone may be considered to be particularly well represented.

The figures for the minimum percentage loss for horse in the four phases of occupation are, from early to late (b) phase respectively, 68%, 54%, 48%, and 45%. The highest percentage loss is seen in the early period, whereas for sheep, cattle, and pigs the highest percentage loss was in the late (b) period. The high figure for the early phase clearly reflects the discrepancy between the numbers of skulls and the number of post-cranial bones just discussed.

The evidence for the age at death of the horses represented at Danebury is summarized in Table 76. The mandibular tooth wear method used to age the cattle, sheep, and pigs at Danebury has not yet been developed for horses. Silver's (1969) guide to the ageing of horses from the eruption of the teeth and the wear on the incisors has been used. The bone fusion evidence shows that a very high percentage of the horse bones found were fused. Even in the latest fusing group of bones, few unfused bones were represented, so that we may assume that the majority of the horses found at Danebury were mature animals. Although the sample sizes are small, differences in the ages of the horses in the four phases of occupation are suggested. In the early, middle, and late (a) phases, none of the very small numbers of unfused bones found were bones that fused before approximately 18 to 24 months (Silver 1969) and only a small percentage of the later fusing bones were unfused.

The figures for the late (a) phase include the complete skeleton of a horse (Fig 9.30). All epiphyses in the four earliest fusing groups (see Table 76) were fused, but all three in the latest fusing group were unfused, with the exception of the distal femur, which had nearly fused. The upper third molar was just erupting. Thus, an age of around three to four years is suggested for this animal.

In the late (b) phase, although the majority of the horse bones were fused, two first phalanges and one proximal radius were unfused, indicating the presence of at least one animal of no more than 15 months at death. The eruption and wear of the teeth confirm the bone fusion evidence, although very small numbers of jaws were found and they were particularly rare in the early, middle, and late (a) phases. In the early and middle phases, there were only two jaws that could be aged, one from each phase. One was from an animal of at least six years and the other at least seven years of age. In the late (a) period, there was evidence of two juvenile animals, one of about two to two and a half years, the other, the complete skeleton mentioned above, of about three to four years. The other three jaws were all from mature animals and one was probably at least ten years old at death. In the late (b) phase, we have evidence of age at death from nineteen jaws. Two were aged approximately three to four years, while the rest ranged in age from four years to over nine years. The most striking aspect of the Danebury horses is the complete absence of the remains of neonatal or very young animals, in marked contrast to the abundance of young sheep, cattle, and pigs.

The presence or absence of the canine tooth was used as a guide to the sex of the horses. Although some jaws were too broken for the sex of the animal to be determined, it would seem from the evidence available that the majority of horses at Danebury were male. Of the 29 jaws that were sexed, only seven (24%) were female. Mares were found in all phases of occupation, but the amount of evidence available does not allow comparisons to be made between the proportions of mares found in the four phases of occupation.

Full details of the measurements taken on the Danebury horse bones are given in microfiche 17, frames C12–D12, and are summarized in Table 77. There are few published horse bone measurements for the Iron Age, but as far as it is possible to tell the horses at Danebury seem to be of a comparable size to those found at other settlements in southern Britain. They were small by modern standards. Calculation of withers height using an adaptation of Kieswalter's (1888) method suggests horses of approximately 1.10 to 1.50 m, roughly equivalent in size to small ponies. Although only a small number of horse bones were found at Danebury, comparisons between the horses from the four different phases of occupation revealed some interesting differences. In all cases, the largest long bones were found in the deposits of the early and middle phases. Statistical testing of the significance of differences between the bones found in the early and middle phases compared to those found in the late phases showed that the metacarpals, tibias, and first phalanges of the earlier periods were significantly larger than the same bones in the late periods. Similarly, the distal widths of the humeri and metacarpals and the minimum shaft width of the metacarpals were greater in the earlier phases. What is also interesting is that the variation in the measurements for the early and middle period bones, measured by the coefficient of variability, was greater than that for the later bones. Unfortunately, there is not a statistical test that allows coefficients of variability to be compared, but such a consistent trend cannot be ignored.

Butchery marks were found on the bones of horse, as on the bones of other domestic animals at Danebury. Many of the marks were knife cuts, but some bones showed the use of a heavy chopping tool and one bone shaft had been sawn through.

Several worked horse bones were found on the site, the metapodials being the bones which seem to have been most commonly used (Table 87).

Interpretation

Horses were clearly of much less importance to the economy at Danebury than were any of the other animals already discussed. Horses can be kept in a wide range of environments, and so we can assume that it was not entirely for environmental reasons that so few horses were kept at the site. At Danebury, as at most other farming settlements from the Iron Age right through to the medieval period and later, horses would have been kept to provide a few limited but special functions. In most respects, a horse has no advantage over a cow. A cow can be used for traction, including pulling ploughs,

can provide meat, milk, and manure, and can convert cheap, relatively plentiful foodstuffs into protein. A horse can provide traction, but until the development of improved harnesses in the Saxon period (Trow-Smith 1957), it could only pull relatively light loads and was no use as a plough animal. A horse does not provide milk and, although it may provide meat and manure, it requires a more expensive diet to produce what the cow will produce much more cheaply. The only real advantage that a horse has over a cow is in its speed and ability to be trained and ridden; in all other respects, the cow or ox is a superior animal.

The evidence for the age of the horses at Danebury suggests that there was no breeding of horses actually on the site. The absence of the bones of any young foals is in marked contrast to the plentiful finds of young lambs, calves, and piglets. Moreover, the majority of the horses seem to have been male. This is a situation paralleled at other sites of Iron Age date. No bones of young horses were found at, for example, Gussage All Saints (Harcourt 1979), Old Down Farm (Maltby 1981), and Odell (Grant 1983a). In his discussion of the Gussage evidence, Harcourt made the suggestion that horses were not bred during the Iron Age but were periodically rounded up to be broken in and trained for riding, light traction, and as pack animals. The evidence from Danebury supports this suggestion. Horses are not generally ready for training until they are around two to three years of age. Almost all the horse bones from Danebury may have come from animals that were at least this age or older. The predominance of male animals in the horse population also makes it unlikely that what we have at Danebury is a breeding population. However, if horses were being rounded up, the males may have been selected preferentially.

If this interpretation of the horse bones is to be accepted, we must assume that herds of horses were living wild in the Wessex countryside. The horses at Danebury might then be more accurately classed with the wild than with the domestic animals. However, there is some evidence that during the latest phases of occupation at Danebury, there might have been a change in the relationship between man and horse. There is an increased incidence in the late phase of occupation of the bones of immature horses, and in the late (b) phase the presence of at least

Table 77   Horse: bone measurements

Bone	Measurement	Range (mm)	$\bar{x}$ (mm)	SD	CV	N
Humerus	l	250-257	252	2.3	0.9	4
	dw	65-75	69	2.8	4.1	12
Radius	l	274-324	299	13.5	4.5	15
	pw	65-81	72	3.9	5.1	16
	shw	30-35	33	2.0	6.1	9
Metacarpal	l	172-240	204	16.6	8.1	32
	pw	40-51	44	2.9	6.6	18
	dw	39-52	44	2.3	5.2	31
	shw	24-32	28	2.3	8.2	18
Femur	l	307-320	312	5.5	1.8	4
	dw	75-86	80	4.0	4.9	6
Tibia	l	292-343	313	16.1	5.1	14
	dw	58-71	63	3.1	4.9	32
	shw	31-39	35	2.3	6.6	10
Metatarsal	l	218-251	239	10.2	4.3	18
	pw	40-48	44	2.5	5.7	9
	dw	38-48	44	2.8	6.4	16
	shw	23-31	27	2.2	8.1	13
1st phalange	l	65-81	75	4.1	5.5	48

For key see Table 67

521

Table 78   Dog: distribution of dog bones in the pits

		Early	Middle	Late (a)	Late (b)	Total*
a)	*Percentages of pits with dog bone*					
	Pits with dog bone	49	34	20	72	175
	Pits with bone	492	139	98	162	891
	% pits with dog bone	10%	24%	20%	44%	20%
b)	*Average numbers of dog bones per pit (excluding pits with skull bone only)*					
	Dog bones ('total frags')	128	142	483	367	1120
	Pits with dog bone	47	33	20	70	170
	Average numbers dog bones per pit	2.7	4.3	24.2	5.2	6.6
c)	*Percentages of pits containing dog bone special deposits*					
	Pits with dog special deposits	3	4	4	7	18
	Pits with dog bone	49	34	20	72	175
	% pits with dog special deposits	6%	12%	20%	8%	10%
d)	*Percentages of pits containing dog bones and any type of special deposit*					
	Pits with dog bone and special deposits	10	9	9	37	65
	Pits with special deposits	49	25	22	65	161
	% pits with dog bones and special deposits	20%	36%	41%	57%	40%
e)	*Percentage of dog bones classed as special deposits (epiphyses only, therefore excluding skulls)*					
	Dog bones in special deposits	7	9	122	11	149
	Dog bones	47	44	224	171	486
	% dog bones in special deposits	15%	21%	54%	6%	31%

*Total of dated pits only

one animal of under 15 months is indicated. This by itself cannot be considered evidence for a change to horse breeding, but some further support can be given by the metrical analysis. In the early and middle periods, the horse bones were generally both larger and more varied in size than in the later phases. Within a free-ranging wild population, a fair amount of variation is to be expected, but once man is controlling the breeding of any species, there may be restriction of the natural variation as the genetic pool is effectively reduced. In terms of bone measurements, a reduction in size and in measures such as the coefficient of variability would not be an unexpected consequence of more restricted breeding.

We cannot consider that Harcourt's theory has been proved by the evidence from Danebury and much more evidence is required from other contemporary sites. It is possible that horses were being bred in the Iron Age, but that they were being bred by some communities and then traded. The capturing and breaking in of horses could itself have been a specialized task. However, when the bones from further seasons of excavation at Danebury are examined, it will be interesting to see if they further confirm or contradict these interpretations.

The very fact that an animal was of only restricted use to a community might have in some way given it an extra value that was not merely related to its economic function. Horses may have had value as status symbols and as animals involved in ritual sacrifice. Table 74 d shows that many of the pits that contained special deposits also contained horse bones other than those that were in themselves interpreted as special deposits. The high degree of correlation between horse bones and special deposits was confirmed by statistical testing. Although this correlation cannot easily be accounted for, it adds weight to the view that the horse was in some way a special animal. The special deposits themselves are discussed below.

The traces of butchery marks on the bones suggest that many of the horses came to the same undignified end as the rest of the domestic animals and provided meat for the community. Whether horses were generally or only occasionally eaten cannot be fully assessed until the analysis of the butchery has been completed. However, the discrepancy between the numbers of skulls and the numbers of other bones found in the early period may indicate that in some instances the skulls found their way into the pits as special offerings, while the rest of the carcass may have been abandoned elsewhere and was thus not found in the pits or layers containing predominantly bone waste from meat that had been eaten. Once dead, horses' skins may have been removed and tanned, and other byproducts such as hair may also have been utilized. Horse bone was certainly utilized (Table 87).

Dogs

The evidence

Dog bones, like horse bones, were found in only relatively small numbers at Danebury. Between 1% and 2% of the bones in all phases of occupation were dog bones except in the late (a) phase where a significantly higher proportion of dog bones was identified. Dog bones were found in similar proportions both in the pits and in the occupation layers.

Because of the relatively low number of dog bones recovered, a preliminary analysis of the distribution of dog bones was made, to see if they were concentrated in a small number of contexts. In Table 78a the percentage of pits with dog bones is calculated. The figures indicate that in each period there was a relatively high percentage of pits containing dog bone, the changes over time broadly reflecting changes in the general distribution of bone during the occupation phases, although if this is taken into account the figures for the late period are

Table 79   Dog: representation of skeletal elements

	Early N	Middle N	Late (a) N	Late (b) N
Upper orbit	4	2	4	8
Lower orbit	1	2	1	3
Occipital condyle	6	6	6	11
Maxilla	9	2	14	18
Mandible	6	3	7	18
Scapula D	5	2	9	13
Humerus P	2	1	8	9
Humerus D	3	1	6	10
Radius P	3	3	10	11
Radius D	1		10	7
Ulna	4	4	10	7
Metapodial P	7	21	67	70
Metapodial D	10	11	63	62
1st phalange	7	11	47	24
2nd phalange	4	2	33	5
3rd phalange	4		31	
Pelvis	5	4	10	14
Femur P	3		6	5
Femur D	3		9	6
Tibia P	1	2	8	8
Tibia D	1	4	6	12
Calcaneum	3	3	9	10
Astragalus	1	4	6	4
Atlas	4	1	3	4
Axis	1	2	4	9

P proximal; D distal

rather lower than for the other periods. These figures suggest that the dog bones, far from being concentrated in a small number of deposits, were fairly widely distributed over the site. This is further confirmed by the calculation of the average number of dog bones found per pit containing any dog bone. The figures are very low for all phases except the late (a) phase. Changes over time again relate to the general increase in the average number of bones found per pit (Fig 9.14) throughout the period of occupation. In the late (a) phase, however, the average number of bones per pit was very much greater than for the other three phases. The higher figures reflect the finds of a number of dog special deposits in this phase (Table 78e), but even in the pits that did not contain dog burials, the dog bones were usually concentrated in larger numbers than in the pits of the other three phases, where a much higher percentage of the pits contained only one or two dog bones. Eight complete or partial dog skeletons were found, one-third of the calculated minimum number of individuals.

Table 79 gives the numbers of each of the main skeletal elements found for the four phases of occupation. The small number of dog bones recovered do not allow a very detailed analysis. It would seem that all parts of the skeleton were fairly well represented in all phases of occupation. There was no evidence of the large discrepancy between the numbers of skulls and the post-cranial skeletons that was noted in the horse bones from the early phase.

The minimum percentage loss figures (Fig 9.28), which are of course much less useful when only small numbers of bone are found, suggest that a greater loss occurred in the early period than in the late period. This situation was paralleled in horse, but was the reverse of the situation for sheep, cattle, and pigs.

The bone fusion evidence summarised in Table 80 shows that in all phases young and mature animals were represented, although only in the middle phase was there any evidence for the presence of a dog under 6-7 months of age. There was no evidence for new-born animals.

Table 80   Dog: bone fusion

Approx age at fusion*	Bone	Early F	Early UF	Middle F	Middle UF	Late (a) F	Late (a) UF	Late (b) F	Late (b) UF
6-7 mths	Scapula D	4	0	1	1	8	0	13	0
8-10 mths	Humerus D	2	1	0	1	6	0	10	0
	Ulna P	1	1	2	0	9	2	6	0
	Metapodial D	6	1	9	2	52	11	55	6
11-12 mths	Radius P	3	0	3	0	8	2	11	0
	Radius D	1	0			8	2	5	2
13-16 mths	Tibia D	2	0	4	0	6	0	11	1
	Calcaneum	2	0	3	0	7	2	9	1
15-18 mths	Humerus P	2	0	0	1	6	2	5	3
18 mths	Femur P	1	2			4	2	2	3
	Femur D	1	2			7	2	3	3
	Tibia P	1	0	1	1	5	1	11	1

For key see Table 66

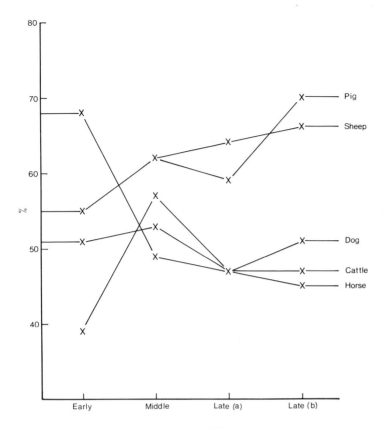

Fig 9.28   Minimum percentage loss (see p 498)

The dog bone measurements are summarized in Table 81 and full details are given on microfiche 17, frames D13–E2. The measurements suggest that there was a wide variation in the size of the dogs at Danebury, with quite small animals and large animals both represented. The lengths of the long bones fall within the range of measurements given by Harcourt (1974) for Iron Age dogs, the only exception being the smallest tibia. This was smaller than any of the Iron Age tibias included in Harcourt's study, but the femur for the same animal was within the range of femur lengths quoted by Harcourt. A particularly large dog is suggested by a tibia with a distal width of 28 mm.

Dog bones, like the bones of all the other species discussed so far, had butchery marks on them which suggested that dogs were eaten. The writer has the impression that butchery marks were not as common on the bones of dogs as on the bones of sheep, cattle, and pigs, but this impression will not be confirmed until the full analysis of the butchery has been concluded. There

was no evidence that dog bones had been used for toolmaking.

Many of the bones of all species had been gnawed, the gnaw marks being consistent with having been made by dogs. Finds of coprolites which could have been produced by dogs included large amounts of tiny bone splinters. A study is being made of the effect of dog gnawing on the survival of bone at Danebury, which may give some information on the behaviour of the dogs themselves.

Interpretation

Dogs seem to have been present at the majority of Iron Age sites in Britain, where they are generally assumed to have been kept as guard dogs, sheep dogs, and hunting dogs. We may assume that they were kept for these same purposes at Danebury, although, since there is very little evidence for hunting, this may have been the least important of their roles. The wide range of sizes of dogs may have related to particular types of animals being

Table 81   Dog: bone measurements

Bone	Measurement	Range (mm)	$\bar{x}$ (mm)	SD	CV	N
Scapula	l	126-132	129	2.8	2.1	2
	dw	26-32	29	1.9	6.6	10
Humerus	l	137-141	139	1.4	1.0	3
	dw	23-29	25	2.8	11.0	3
Radius	l	111-173	140	20.0	14.3	5
Tibia	l	102-185	155	21.4	14.0	10
	dw	18-28	22	3.0	13.6	7
Femur	l	107-155	141	19.8	14.0	4
	dw	27-32	30	1.5	5.0	5

For key see Table 67

524

chosen for particular functions. Harcourt (1974) suggests that many of the dogs may have been scavengers, who did not contribute a great deal to the community, but this can only be a matter for speculation. Dogs may have been fed on scraps and waste food not considered suitable for human consumption. The gnaw marks on bones provides some evidence of dog feeding habits. Dogs certainly seem to have provided food, even if only occasionally, and their skins may also have been utilized.

Although there is no evidence of neonatal dogs at Danebury, the bone fusion evidence suggests that young and juvenile animals as well as adults were present at the site. Dogs may have bred freely with little human intervention, except when the dog population became too large.

Like horse bones, dog bones were relatively frequently encountered as what have been termed special deposits (see below). Eight complete or partial burials and eleven skulls were found. However, there also seems to have been an association between dog bones and other special deposits (Table 78d). While only 20% of the pits at Danebury (Table 78a) contained dog bones, 40% of the pits with special deposits had dog bones in them. This association was confirmed by statistical testing and is discussed further below.

Cats
The evidence
A small number of cat bones were found in features dated to all four phases of occupation (Tables 61, 62). A complete skeleton of a young kitten was found in a pit of the middle phase, and twelve bones representing at least two individuals were found in a pit of the early phase. The rest of the finds ascribed to cat were isolated finds of one or two bones, mainly found in pits. Very few cat bones were found in the layers or other features. There were bones from both young and mature animals.

Interpretation
The distinction between wild and domestic cat is usually based on size, although there are obvious problems in making a distinction on this basis, especially when comparatively little is known about the wild population of cats in England in the post-glacial period. Finds of cat are rare on Iron Age sites, but several sites do record their presence. Examples are Budbury (Westley 1970) and Gussage All Saints (Harcourt 1979). At Gussage, almost all the bones were from immature animals and included a litter of five new-born kittens. Harcourt interpreted this predominance of young animals as evidence of domestication. Since the finds of cats at Danebury include young animals, we may consider that these cats too were domestic and may have lived on the site, catching the mice and voles that raided the corn storage pits.

9.5.9 Wild animals
Deer
The evidence
Bones from two species of deer were found at Danebury — red deer (cervus elaphus) and roe deer (capreolus capreolus). These two are the only species of deer certainly present in England in the Iron Age. Deer bones form a very small proportion of all bone remains found at Danebury, less than 0.2%. Of the two species, red deer were better represented than roe deer.

Of the 92 red deer fragments recorded in Table 61, only seven were bones or bone fragments, five were loose teeth, and the remaining 80 were fragments of antler. To the number of these antler fragments should be added the number of antler objects or fragments recorded as small finds (Table 87) in order to gain a more realistic impression of the total amount of antler found. Fifty-six worked fragments and manufactured objects of red deer antler are included among the small finds.

Roe deer remains occurred in even smaller numbers. A total of only fourteen are recorded in Table 61. Of these, seven were bones, one was a tooth, and six were antler fragments, including a shed base.

Thus, from the whole period of occupation at Danebury, there were only twenty bones, bone fragments, or teeth, and one antler pedicle and burr still attached to a skull fragment, that certainly came from dead deer. All the other antler fragments could have been obtained from shed antler and no hunting or killing of the deer need have been involved.

Most deer remains were found as single occurrences in widely distributed features. The only exceptions were a group of five roe deer fore- and hind-limb bones, probably from the same juvenile animal, found in an undated pit, and a collection of 35 antler fragments found in an undated posthole. There was no evidence from the occurrence of deer bone, as opposed to deer antler, to suggest that there was any change in the amount of deer hunting in any particular period of occupation.

Although, because of the small numbers involved, it is unrealistic to compare the percentage of deer bone finds from phase to phase, there does seem to be a change in the proportion of small finds made from antler in the four phases of occupation. In the early phase, 17% of the bone and antler small finds were made from antler, whereas in the late (b) period, 26% were antler, suggesting an increased importance or availability of antler in the latest phase of occupation, although the sample size again is rather small.

The only measurable red deer bone which was found was a complete metacarpal, listed in the appendix of measurements. It was within the range of sizes of deer metapodials found at gussage All Saints (Harcourt 1979). This site, broadly contemporary with Danebury, was only 45 km from Danebury and similar populations of deer could have been exploited by the inhabitants of both sites.

The finds of deer antler, together with the manufactured antler objects, suggest that antler may have had some importance as a raw material for tool manufacture. Of the total number of bone and antler small finds, 22% are made of antler. As a raw material, antler appears to have some distinct advantages over bone; although bone and antler are essentially made of the same substance, antlers are denser and stronger than bone as they have no haemopoietic tissue in the cancellous bone, so that a large space inside the centre of the bone is not required. The collection of antler fragments already mentioned may have been deposited for future use as the raw material for tools or decorative objects.

Interpretation
From the scarcity of deer bone found at Danebury, we must assume that hunting deer did not provide any significant contribution to the food requirements of the community. All the deer bones found could in theory have come from as few as two roe deer and three red deer.

Antler, however, seems to have had some value and was used in the manufacture of objects, particularly weaving combs and toggles. The particular strength of antler would have been an advantage for the weaving combs, which have fine teeth, and for the manufacture of toggles, where antlers provide a thicker and denser substance than can be obtained from any bone. The thickness of any solid bone object is limited by the thickness of the cortex, which even in cattle and horse bones would not allow the manufacture of a thick solid toggle. Thus, although bone would always have been readily available as a raw material, and was clearly utilized, for some objects antler seems to have been thought superior enough to have justified the effort expended in obtaining it. It has been suggested (Grant 1981) that deer antler may have been collected seasonally from areas known to be inhabited by deer, specifically for the manufacture of tools and decorative objects.

Badgers and foxes

The remains of wild animals are extremely rare at Danebury. The bones of the smallest mammals (voles, mice, hare, etc) and the birds are discussed by Jennie Coy (see pp 526–31). The small mammals are not included in Tables 61 and 62. The only other wild animal species present at Danebury are the deer, which have already been discussed, and badger and fox.

Fifty-three badger bones are included in Table 61. They were recovered from only three contexts. A single humerus was found in an undated layer; a large part of a single immature animal, including skull fragments, vertebrae, ribs, and part of the fore- and hind-limbs, was found in a pit of the early phase of occupation; part of a mature animal, including skull fragments and fore- and hind-limb bones, was found in a pit of the late (b) phase of occupation.

One hundred and forty fox bones are recorded in Table 61. Fox bones were found in a total of ten contexts. Five bones occurred in isolation in pits dated to the early, middle, and late periods, and one single bone was found in an undated posthole. Five bones were found in two layers of the late phase, and all the rest of the bones were found in two pits. A large part of a single immature animal, including vertebrae and bones from front and rear limbs, was found in a pit of the early phase, and three mandibles, three skull fragments, and an upper jaw were found in a single pit of the late (a) phase.

These finds of badger and fox bones are perhaps the remains of animals that were killed as pests or fell into open pits. One unusual and perhaps significant point is, however, worth noting: the immature badger and the immature fox both dated to the early phase were in fact found in the same pit. The significance of this can only be a matter for speculation, but it certainly seems surprising that two such unusual finds should both occur in the same pit and in the same layer within that pit. It is possible that these two animals were put in the pit as an unusual form of special deposit (see p 541) but since they were not found with any of the other more usual special deposits, they have not been included in that category.

The small mammals and amphibia

by Jennie Coy

Small bones retrieved by conventional means from 381 contexts were examined. The following species were identified in these contexts:

Amphibia
frog (probably common frog, *Rana temporaria*), *Rana* sp.
common toad, *Bufo bufo*

Table 82 Minimum numbers of rodents and lagomorphs (excluding rabbit)

	Early	*Middle*	*Late (a)*	*Late (b)*
Lepus	2	—	4	5
Apodemus	59*	30*	22	2
Mus	5	5	1	8
Arvicola	7	6	4	2
Microtus	38	11	27	79*
Total no samples involved	64	38	43	53

*Individual caches partly account for high figures

Mammals
mole, *Talpa europea*
weasel, *Mustela nivalis*
polecat or ferret, *Mustela putorius* sp.
wood mouse, *Apodemus sylvaticus*
possibly yellow-necked mouse, *Apodemus flavicollis*
house mouse, *Mus musculus*
water vole, *Arvicola terrestris*
short-tailed vole, *Microtus agrestis*
rabbit, *Oryctolagus cuniculus*
hare, *Lepus* sp.

The rabbit bones may be regarded as intrusive as this species probably did not spread to Danebury until after the Norman invasion (Corbett & Southern 1977). The polecat or ferret bone was found with rabbit bones and may be regarded as contemporary with them.

Frog and toad bones, like many of those of the small rodents, probably represent animals which fell into open pits.

Omitting the four species above and all contexts contaminated by rabbits the phased finds for the remaining species are detailed in Table 82. Some additional comments on these species are given below.

Hare

These sparse remains were examined carefully as there has been some discussion in recent years as to which species is represented on prehistoric sites in Britain. The brown hare, *Lepus capensis*, at least, is represented at Danebury with definite identifications of the species in both late phases.

Small rodents

The presence of house mouse, even in the early phase (pits 618, 921, and possibly 1043), is interesting.

Apodemus and *Microtus* are very common species today. The former has two species, *A. flavicollis* nowadays usually somewhat larger (Corbett & Southern 1977). Some of the individuals, in the middle phase and late (a) phase at least, are large enough to be suspected *flavicollis*. Remains of nine individuals were found together in middle phase pit 663 (layer 4) and altogether 40 individuals in layers 5, 6, and 7 of early pit 712. This suggests that *Apodemus* may have been living in the pits at some point; they are such excellent jumpers that only a very smooth-sided, steep pit, many feet deep, would trap them. An alternative explanation is that remains of bird pellets (probably from owls as *Apodemus* is nocturnal) accumulated here because there was a post used as a perch near the edge of the pit.

The high frequency of *Microtus* in the late phases includes caches of 28, 14, 12, and 11 individuals in pits 923 (layer 6), 884 (layer 4), 955 (layer 2), and 955 (layer

Table 83 Bird bones from the early phase

	skull & jaw	vertebrae	ribs	tracheal rings	sternum	coracoid	furcula	scapula	humerus	radius	ulna	carpometacarpus	wing phalanges	synsacrum & pelvis	femur	tibiotarsus	tarsometatarsus	foot phalanges	Total
goose												1							1
Anser sp.										1	2	1	1						5
duck			1		1					2	1	1			1				7
wigeon	1																1		2
teal									1										1
goosander						1													1
buzzard						2	1	2	2	3	2	1	2		2	2	1		20
kestrel											1								1
corncrake																	1		1
golden plover															1				1
kittiwake									1										1
wood pigeon									1		2	1							4
skylark									2		1								3
wagtail					1														1
redwing											1								1
house sparrow	1															1			2
jay					1														1
crow																1	1		2
raven	6	71			5	13	3	9	9	6	13	12	11	6	11	7	5	38	225
unidentified			8	3												1		1	13
Total	8	71	8	3	8	17	4	11	16	12	23	17	14	6	15	12	9	39	293

3), respectively. One theory for these accumulations is that they might be from the pellets of buzzard, *Buteo buteo*, and associated again with a post at the edge of the pit.

Buzzards today do scan their surroundings from a suitable perch and are great vole feeders. Again, though, this could be a pitfall effect through an open pit and voles would not be able to escape as easily as mice.

Water vole is present in all phases and is represented in the *Microtus* caches in pits 923 and 955 (one individual). Both theories of origin discussed for *Microtus* could apply to them.

Conclusions

The figures in Table 82 cannot in themselves do anything but indicate the presence of these species in all phases. The house mouse seems to be the earliest record so far for prehistoric Wessex. *Apodemus* and *Mus* would have been considerable pests of stored grain and might have actually lived in grain stores. *Mus* has the ability to survive on food with a very low water content.

More detailed study of these species and the integration of these results with the details of particular pits might give greater insight into the primary and secondary functions of these pits.

As indicators of the surrounding environment this material is less useful. It is difficult to make comparisons between phases with the samples we have and the possibility that bird pellets may be involved (first suggested by Jewell 1958) introduces a wider catchment area.

The bird bones
by Jennie Coy

A total of 804 bird bones was examined. Of these 796 could be phased and identifications for the early, middle, and late Danebury generalized phases are shown in Tables 83 to 86. Most bones came from pits and all but ten were the remains of wild birds. Bones of raven, *Corvus corax*, were a major contribution to these totals as this species was largely represented by whole skeletons or partial skeletons, especially wings. This caused the raw figures in the Tables to suggest a misleadingly high significance for raven in all phases and for buzzard (also represented by a partial skeleton) in the early phase. The account below therefore gives more detail of the numbers of birds represented by these bones.

Table 84 Bird bones from the middle phase

	skull & jaw	vertebrae	ribs	tracheal rings	sternum	coracoid	furcula	scapula	humerus	radius	ulna	carpometacarpus	wing phalanges	synsacrum & pelvis	femur	tibiotarsus	tarsometatarsus	foot phalanges	Total
Anser sp.											2								2
duck						1					1						1		3
Anas sp.																	1		1
teal					1														1
buzzard									1		1	1							3
quail						1													1
golden plover									1										1
kittiwake	1																		1
wood pigeon											1								1
skylark											1								1
redwing											1	1							2
shrike									2										2
starling									1										1
crow									1		1			1	1	2	1		7
raven	3	25	14		1	7	3	3	5	3	3	2	3	1	4	4	3	5	89
unidentified	1		1	30					1		2	1	1					1	38
Total	5	25	15	30	2	8	3	3	13	3	13	5	4	2	5	6	6	6	154

Table 85 Bird bones from the late (a) phase

	skull & jaw	vertebrae	ribs	tracheal rings	sternum	coracoid	furcula	scapula	humerus	radius	ulna	carpometacarpus	synsacrum & pelvis	femur	tibiotarsus	tarsometatarsus	foot phalanges	Total
fowl														1				1
goose												1						1
Anser sp.									1									1
duck					1			1										2
golden plover														1		1		2
song thrush									1									1
house sparrow	2																	2
crow						1		1	2	1	3			2	2	1		13
raven	6	50	14		3	8	3	4	9	2	3	2	4	6	8	5	13	140
unidentified				15													1	16
Total	8	50	14	15	4	9	3	6	13	3	6	3	5	9	10	7	14	179

Table 86 Bird bones from the late (b) phase

	skull & jaw	vertebrae	ribs	sternum	coracoid	furcula	scapula	humerus	radius	ulna	carpometacarpus	wing phalanges	synsacrum & pelvis	femur	tibiotarsus	tarsometatarsus	foot phalanges	Total
fowl	1							2						1	1	1		6
goose								1							2			3
heron								1	1	1								3
swan				1				1										2
duck									2	3	3	1						9
Anas sp.									1	1								2
wigeon									1	1								2
goosander															2			2
buzzard									1						2			3
red kite															1			1
peregrine	1																	1
black grouse									1	1								2
quail								1			1							2
corncrake					2			1		1				1	1	2		8
golden plover								2		2						1		5
kittiwake								1	1	1		1						4
wood pigeon										1								1
shrike								1					1					2
starling					1													1
jackdaw									1	1								2
rook										1								1
crow								4	3	6	2	1			1	2		19
raven	5	8	2	1	7	1	2	4	5	6	8	6	5	5	4	5	5	79
unidentified		6	2					1		1					1		1	12
Total	7	14	4	2	10	1	2	20	16	24	18	9	6	11	13	9	6	172

Species represented

Domestic fowl, Gallus sp. (domestic)

A single fragment of fowl femur in the late (a) phase is from P639, layer 1, a layer containing rabbit bones and therefore probably contaminated. All other fowl and suspected fowl bones are from the late (b) phase. This fits the picture so far obtained from Wessex Iron Age settlements with fowl appearing, presumably by introduction from Europe, in the Late Iron Age and Romano-British levels only (eg Harcourt 1979; Maltby 1981).

Ashdown (1979) has shown that bones of well-preserved pre-Conquest fowl found at Puckeridge, Herts, represent birds comparable in their high degree of sex dimorphism to the wild red jungle fowl. Detailed anatomical comparisons are not possible with the Danebury bones as these are fragmentary, eroded, and in three cases, although assigned to 'fowl', immature.

The fowl represented, however, are at the small end of fowl measurement ranges for Wessex.

The work of Thesing (1977) summarizes current views on the near-eastern origins of the domestic fowl, which was followed by their presence on Phoenician sites in Spain in the 8th century BC and Hallstatt–La Tène finds in central Europe. Despite the apparently late introduction into Wessex this species provides over half the bird bone finds in the area by the 1st and 2nd centuries AD.

Geese and swans

By contrast occasional large geese comparable in size with the wild greylag, *Anser anser*, are found from earlier Iron Age phases in Wessex and these are probably from domestic birds (eg Harcourt 1979; Maltby 1981). Danebury is no exception, having a wing bone of this species in the early phase, pit 229. All 'goose' bones in the Tables refer to this type of goose whereas those recorded as '*Anser* sp' more closely resemble the group of species somewhat smaller in size that are represented today in Hampshire by the overwintering white-fronted goose, *Anser albifrons*.

Riddell (1943), in discussing the use of goose quill feathers, makes the important point that domestic geese would decoy wild geese. Early phase pits 63A (layer 7) and 1135 (layer 4) both contained associated bones from a goose wing.

The swan humerus is identifiable to Whooper swan, *Cygnus cygnus*, now a scarce winter visitor to Hampshire.

Ducks

The identification of duck bones to species is difficult and accuracy depends upon the anatomical element represented. The bones referred to as 'duck' in all Tables are a very good match with the wild mallard, *Anas platyrhynchos*, but there is a possibility that they could have been either tamed or domesticated birds.

Some other duck bones are exact anatomical matches with the wigeon, *Anas penelope*, teal, *Anas crecca*, and goosander, *Mergus merganser*. The goosander coracoid in the early phase bore knife cuts. The wigeon represented by wing bones in the late (b) phase (pit 264, layer 5) showed skeletal pathology — considerable bony exostoses on the radius and ulna.

The remainder of the duck bones are ascribed to '*Anas* sp.' in the Tables and are probably from wild species comparable in size with wigeon.

The presence of goosander might indicate a visit to areas of deep inland water although we cannot rule out a coastal origin for all these species in the light of the kittiwake bones discussed below.

Birds of prey

The buzzard, *Buteo buteo*, and red kite, *Milvus milvus*, would have been formidable predators and scavengers and their occasional remains are found not only on rural Wessex settlements into the medieval period but in urban contexts. Early phase pit 949, layer 4, contained a partial skeleton of a buzzard and middle phase pit 1149 an articulated wing.

Falcon remains are an ulna of kestrel, *Falco tinnunculus*, and the beak of a peregrine falcon, *Falco peregrinus*, but these provide no evidence that falconry was practised at Danebury.

Edible species

Although all the Danebury bird bones were checked for butchery it was rarely found and we can only guess which birds were eaten. Apart from the fowl, geese, and ducks mentioned above a selection of game, waders, and small passerines is represented (Tables 83 to 86). Grey heron, *Ardea cinerea*, wing bones were in the late phase. Black grouse, *Lyrurus tetrix*, which survived in Hampshire at least until Gilbert White's time (Nicholson 1929), is occasionally found in archaeological material of all periods. Quail, *Coturnix coturnix*, and corncrake, *Crex crex*, are both represented, the latter as a partial skeleton; these species have become dangerously scarce in Hampshire only in relatively recent times. Golden plover, *Pluvialis apricaria*, cannot be taken as a seasonal indicator as they may have bred locally in the Iron Age; today they only visit in winter.

The presence of the kittiwake, *Rissa tridactyla*, a coastal species, in three of the four collections, suggests more than the occasional presence of an off-course migrant. There is a humerus in early phase pit 658, a mandible in middle phase pit 22 (layer 2), and in the late (b) phase an articulated wing from pit 23 (layer 6) and a wing digit from pit 620.

Anatomically kittiwake is very close to the common gull, *Larus canus*, which winters more widely inland, so that these bones were subjected to a most careful scrutiny. It was finally decided that the humeri, radius, and wing digit were marginally more like kittiwake than common gull. This and the fact that Bramwell identified kittiwake from an undated layer at the Iron Age settlement at Gussage All Saints (Harcourt 1979) suggests that they *are* probably kittiwake and therefore most likely of coastal origin; the species still breeds on the Dorset and Isle of Wight coasts. It may well have been regarded as a delicacy.

A very few bones of more common species were presumably either eaten or deposited in pits by chance because they died nearby. Some may have been brought in by domestic dogs but in fact only a raven coracoid and the black grouse wing showed any sign of canid gnawing. The remaining species represented include wood pigeon, *Columba palumbus*, skylark, *Alauda arvensis*, a wagtail, probably *Motacilla* sp., redwing, *Turdus iliacus*, song thrush, *Turdus philomelos*, and a shrike, probably the great grey shrike, *Lanius excubitor*, now only a winter visitor.

Of the occurrences of house sparrow, *Passer domesticus*, and starling, *Sturnus vulgaris*, some are from layers disturbed by rabbit burrowing but others are not. It must therefore be assumed that these two species were already sharing human settlements at this period.

Corvids

These remains are dominated by partial skeletons of the raven, *Corvus corax*. There are remains of eleven birds in the early phase, one with a pathological skeleton. One partial skeleton with cuts on the wing bones and the remains of a raven leg were assigned to the middle phase. In the late phases, two partial skeletons are in the late (a) phase and three partial skeletons and the remains of three wings in the late (b) phase.

Ravens frequent rubbish dumps and may pick at carcasses so that the high frequency of raven finds on Iron Age settlements in Wessex is not surprising. The large number of birds represented in just a few pits does suggest that nearby trees may have supported a considerable breeding colony of the birds although this should be seen in the context of the considerable time span of the Danebury occupation.

Other corvids represented are jay, *Garrulus glandarius*, jackdaw, *Corvus monedula*, rook, *Corvus frugilegus*, and crow, *Corvus corone*.

Information on modern distributions discussed above came from Cohen and Taverner (1972).

Conclusions

Most of the bones studied were from wild birds, especially raven, and we can only guess whether or not they were exploited in any way. Fowl, goose, duck, swan, and a number of the other birds would have been readily eaten. As can be seen from the Tables some of these birds are represented by wing skeletons, and in some cases referred to above bones were found in association. This may partly be the result of the strong ligamentation in the distal wing which kept the bones in association throughout the processes leading up to their deposition in the pits. Bogucki (1980) has suggested that a high incidence of these bones on some settlements may be due to their removal with a meat mass with bones intact, whereas other parts of the bird skeleton are more likely to have been fragmented during dismemberment.

A number of the birds mentioned above may have been overwintering rather than breeding locally and the several finds of kittiwake suggest that this was more likely to have been brought from a breeding colony on the coast.

The list of species from Danebury is surprisingly small as many more species of birds commonly breeding in Hampshire might have been expected. This suggests no deliberate and large-scale exploitation of the edible birds of the neighbourhood.

Acknowledgement
I am grateful to Graham Cowles and the Trustees of the British Museum (Natural History) for access to the collections for checking difficult identifications.

Note
The differences in the numbers of bird bones recorded in Tables 61 and 62 and Tables 83 to 86 are due in the main to differences in the counting procedures used by the writer and by Ms Coy. A small number of bird bones were inadvertantly included with the small mammal bones and thus were excluded from the computer analysis from which Tables 61 and 62 were compiled. The differences are unlikely to have affected any interpretations made or conclusions drawn.

Only 1% of the bones found at Danebury were bird bones, although we must assume that bird bones were under-represented in the excavated material because of their small size. Differences between the numbers of bones found in each of the four phases of occupation are not significant.

Fish
Only six fragments of fish bone were identified and for only one of these fragments could the species be determined. Jennie Coy kindly identified a single vertebra from a salmon (*Salmo* sp.). The discussion of the recovery of the bones from Danebury (p 496) shows that the number of fish bone remains recovered may have been a gross underestimate of the numbers of fish bones that were deposited on the site, since very little sieving was undertaken. We can be sure that fish bones were lost during excavation but we cannot, without much more sieving, show what the real contribution of fish to the faunal assemblage was likely to have been.

The Hampshire chalk streams are today particularly favoured by anglers, especially trout fishermen, and there is no reason to assume that streams other than the local ones were the habitat for a variety of species of freshwater fish in the Iron Age. However, the availability of a resource does not necessarily imply that the resource was exploited, as we have shown for the deer. Fish bone tends to be rare on archaeological sites until the medieval period, although the more frequent finds of fish bones on some Iron Age sites in marginal areas (eg Nor'nour (Turk 1968) and Skitten (Platt 1948)) show that this is not just a question of survival and recovery. Nor does it seem to relate to proximity to the sea. At Portchester Castle, situated on the tip of a peninsula, fish bones were absent in the Roman layers and rare in the Saxon layers (Grant 1975a;b). However, quite large numbers of fish bones were found in the medieval layers of the Inner bailey (Grant forthcoming).

9.5.10 Bone and antler as raw materials
The catalogue of small finds includes 259 objects made from bone or antler. The use of bone as a raw material obviously affects the representation of individual bone elements. If particular bones are frequently used in the manufacture of bone objects, the occurrence of these bones in the bone debris assumed to be food debris is thus likely to be reduced. In Table 87a the bone objects are analysed in terms of the bone elements that were utilized in their manufacture, and in Table 87b, the numbers of objects attributed to each species are given.

Clearly some bones were utilized much more frequently than others. Particularly favoured were the metapodials of sheep, cattle, and horses and the tibias of sheep. The metapodials of these species are straight solid bones with a relatively thick cortex, and are the obvious choice if strong, straight bone is required; sheep tibias have similar properties. With some bone objects, the natural shape of the bone was clearly exploited. Many of the objects identified as gouges had been made from the distal epiphyses and shafts of sheep tibias, the distal end being unworked and evidently used as a handle. The proximal ends of metapodials were also used as gouge handles. One example of a bone point made from a horse lateral metapodial was found the naturally pointed shape of this bone had been used to advantage, the only work required being a slight sharpening of the distal end.

On some bone objects the only working of the bone was in the form of decoration of the surface, the natural shape of the bone being more or less unaltered. The majority of these objects were sheep radii and metapodials.

With some objects, particularly the smaller objects such as bone needles, it was impossible to identify the bone from which the object had been made as thin splinters of bone had been used.

The bones of sheep, cattle, and horses seem to have been favoured for bone working. Only one example of an object made from a pig bone was found and that was one where the natural shape of the bone, a fibula, had been used with little alteration. Pig bone is more porous and splinters more easily than the bone of many other animals, so that it was probably not exploited to any extent.

Approximately a quarter of the objects were made from antler. Antler is a strong, dense substance that clearly has some advantages over bone (p 525) and seems to have been particularly chosen for weaving combs. Approximately 80% of the weaving combs were made from antler, the rest all being made from cattle or horse bone shafts. Other objects that were made from antler were toggles, rings, and handles.

No concentrations of bone or antler manufacturing waste were identified amongst the animal bone deposits, although some of the bone objects included amongst the small finds were interpreted as unfinished items. Bone tool waste can usually be distinguished from butchery waste by the nature and position of the cut marks, although the distinction is not always obvious. It is possible that there are concentrations of bone manufacturing waste in areas of the site as yet unexcavated, but it is also possible that bone tools were made relatively infrequently, as and when required. If this was the situation, the waste bone might be widely distributed and not easily recognized. In all periods, the number of bone objects was only 0.3 to 0.4% of the number of fragments recorded (Table 61b). Bone objects may, of course, have been lost away from the site or even traded. We have no way of knowing how representative of those that were made are those that survive. A find of 35 antler fragments and seven sheep horn cores in a single posthole may have been a store of raw material, deposited for later use.

The use of bone as a raw material for object manufacture is one of the many facets of animal exploitation that should be assessed as part of the whole picture of the

Table 87 Bone and antler as raw materials

a) bone elements utilized

Species	Bone element	Early	Middle	Late(a)	Late (b)	Total*
sheep	skull	1				1
	radius P				2	2
	D				1	1
	shaft				1	1
	metacarpal P	2	1	2	4	9
	D	1	3	1	2	7
	femur P	1				1
	tibia P		1	3	3	8
	D	6	3	1	5	16
	shaft	6		1	6	14
	metatarsal P	3	2		8	14
	D				2	2
	shaft	1	2	2	3	8
	metapodial D				1	2
cattle	ulna P				1	1
	metacarpal P			2	3	5
	femur P	1			1	2
	metatarsal P				1	1
	D				1	1
	shaft		1			1
	rib	3	1		1	6
pig	upper canine			1		1
	fibula		1			1
horse	metacarpal D				1	1
	metatarsal P	1			1	2
	metapodial D				1	1
	metapodial shaft				1	1
	lateral metapodial					1
sheep size	shaft	1	1	1	10	14
cattle size	shaft	10	2	1	18	32
unknown	shaft	8	5	12	30	56

b) number of bone objects made per species

Species	Early	Middle	Late (a)	Late (b)	Total*
sheep	19	12	9	33	77
sheep size	1	1	1	10	14
cattle	4	2	2	7	16
cattle size	10	2	1	18	32
pig		1	1		2
horse	1			4	6
red deer (antler only)	9	5	5	36	56
unknown	8	5	12	30	56
Total	52	28	31	138	259
% of bone fragments (total b in Table 61)	0.3	0.3	0.3	0.4	

*Total includes undated finds;   P proximal;   D distal

532

relationship between man and animals. It affects the interpretation of the survival of the bone elements but, just as importantly, reminds us that the use of an animal does not end at the cooking pot. Not only can the bone be utilized, but many other parts of the body, such as the hair, the sinews, the fat, and the stomach, whose exploitation leaves no trace in the archaeological record.

9.5.11 Ritual behaviour: the special bone deposits

When any ancient habitation site is excavated, the expectation is, assuming satisfactory soil conditions, that animal bones will be found and that these animal bones will be mainly the debris from the meals that the former occupants of the site ate. These expectations were fulfilled by the excavations at Danebury, as the analysis of the bone material has shown. However, during excavation, bones were recovered that, either through their associations with other bones or by the manner and site of their deposition, were singled out from the majority of the bone debris. This section discusses these 'special' deposits of bones and the light that they throw on particular aspects of behaviour at Danebury.

The evidence

Several categories of bone deposits were identified and classed as special deposits. They were:

1 Articulated or mainly articulated animal skeletons of young, juvenile, or mature animals
2 Complete or nearly complete animal skulls and, in the case of horses, complete mandibles
3 Articulated limbs

The species involved were usually sheep, cattle, pigs, horses, and dogs, but a single burial of a cat, and a skull and a burial of a goat were found.

Animal burials
The most important category of special deposits are the animal burials, but unfortunately an assessment of the total numbers of occurrences and of their completeness is hampered by the variable quality of excavation at the site. Whereas some animal skeletons were recognized by the excavators and were cleaned, drawn, and photographed, others were not recognized until partly removed or disturbed. Others were only recognized as possible animal burials during post-excavation analysis. Burials of neonatal animals are those that are most likely to have suffered this fate.

Thus, it is certain that some of the evidence has been lost, but it is also possible that, in an attempt to compensate, groups of bones have been interpreted as possible animal burials, when in fact they were only the remains of single animals that had been thrown together into a pit after they had been butchered and eaten. The definition of an animal burial for the purposes of this

Table 88 Special deposits: animal burials

	Early		Middle		Late (a)		Late (b)		Total	
	N	%	N	%	N	%	N	%	N	%
sheep										
MWS 1-5	4	32	2		3		8		17	
MWS 6†	2†		2		0		5		9†	
Total	6	32	4	19	3	23	13	62	26	35
cattle										
MWS 1-5	5		2		2		2		11	
MWS 6+	3		0		0		0		3	
Total	8	42	2	10	2	15	2	10	14	19
pig										
MWS 1-5	2		7		2		3		14	
MWS 6+	2		4		2		0		8	
Total	4	21	11	55	4	31	3	14	22	30
horse										
young	0		0		0		0		0	
juvenile + mature	0		1		1		1		3	
Total	0		1	5	1	8	1	5	3	4
dog										
young	1		0		0		1		2	
juvenile + mature	0		2		3		1		6	
Total	1	5	2	10	3	23	2	10	8	11
cat										
(young) Total			1	5						
All species										
young	12	63	12	57	7	54	14	67	45	61
juvenile + mature	7	37	9	43	6	46	7	33	29	39
Total	19		21		13		21		74	

† includes one goat

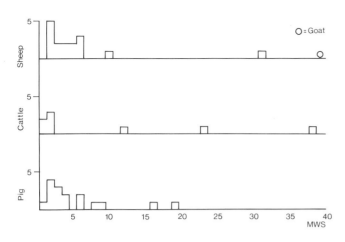

Fig 9.29   Animal burials: mandible wear stages (MWS) of the sheep, cattle, and pig burials

discussion is a group of bones, certainly or very probably found in articulation, representing a whole animal or at least a substantial part of a single animal, and usually showing no evidence of having been butchered. Divisions were made according to the known state of completeness of the burials and these are given with the catalogue of animal burials on microfiche 17, frames E3–8. For the purposes of the rest of this discussion, all the burials are treated together.

The animals represented in burials are all the domestic animals found at the site — sheep, cattle, pigs, dogs, horses, one goat, and one cat. Initially a division in terms of the age at death of the animals was made between those animals of MWS 5 and under, and those of MWS 6 and above. To some extent this division is arbitrary, as the same MWS for different species is unlikely to represent the same real age. However, the division was made to separate the very young animals from those that had lived longer than a few weeks or months.

Fig 9.30   A horse and a dog skeleton found in pit 321. Note that the head of the horse has been removed from the neck and placed at the edge of the pit near the dog

534

Table 89   Special deposits: animal burials; percentages of minimum numbers of individuals

	Early			Middle			Late (a)			Late (b)			Total		
	a	b	%	a	b	%	a	b	%	a	b	%	a	b	%
sheep	6+	130	5	4	84	5	3	111	3	13	470	3	26+	815	3
cattle	8	30	27	2	18	11	2	17	12	2	72	3	14	137	10
pig	4	33	12	11	27	41	4	24	17	3	70	4	22	154	14
horse	0	8		1	6	17	1	5	20	1	15	7	3	34	9
dog	1	5	20	2	3	67	3	7	43	2	9	22	8	24	33
Total	19	206	9	20	138	14	13	164	8	21	656	3	73	1164	6

Key: a = no of animal burials; b = % minimum no of individuals (MNI); % = % of MNI for each species; + includes one goat

Fig 9.31   A complete lamb skeleton on the base of pit 741. The jumble of bones at the top of the photograph is the remains of a dog, originally articulated but disturbed during excavation

535

Fig 9.32   A partly articulated juvenile cow skeleton associated with chalk blocks (pit 909)

Of the 891 pits that contained animal bone, 43 (5%) contained animal burials, and ten contained burials of more than one animal. Details of the numbers of animal burials are given in Table 88. Fig 9.30-9.33 illustrate respectively a horse and dog burial, a lamb, a juvenile cow, and a goat. Fig 9.29 gives the MWS distribution for the sheep, cattle, and pig burials. Not all the animal burials are included on this figure, as in some instances the mandibles were damaged or lost. Where this had happened, the burial was assigned to one of the two age groups shown in Table 88 by the size and state of fusion of the long bones.

The significance of apparent changes in the different phases of occupation is rarely conclusive, because of the relatively small number of occurrences in each phase. Of the 73 burials, 45 (62%) were burials of very young animals. There did not seem to be any differences in the proportions of young to older animals in the four phases of occupation. Of the six animal species represented, sheep and pigs were the most common, both as very young and as older animals. However, while the proportion of sheep burials in the pits was around one-third, approximately two-thirds of the animal bones from the site as a whole were sheep bones. This discrepancy between the proportion of sheep burials and the proportion of sheep bones is shown more clearly in Table 89, where the numbers of animal burials are shown as percentages of the minimum numbers of individuals calculated for each phase. Sheep burials form only 3% of the minimum numbers of individuals found at Danebury, whereas a third of the dogs were found as burials. Cattle and pig burials occurred in roughly the same proportion as did the minimum numbers of these species, when calculated for all phases of occupation; however, cattle burials were particularly common in the early phase; and in the middle phase, 41% of the minimum numbers of pigs found were as animal burials. The incidence of animal burials was highest in the middle phase, when a relatively high proportion of the dogs and horses were complete burials. The incidence of burials was lowest in the late (b) phase, when only 3% of the minimum number of individuals calculated were burials. However, dog burials accounted for a large proportion of the numbers of dogs represented.

Skulls
Although skulls are easily recognized during excavation, the thin, brittle areas of the skull are easily damaged, and

536

Table 90 Special deposits: skulls and horse mandibles

a) *Skulls*

	Early		Middle		Late (a)		Late (b)		Total‡	
	N	%	N	%	N	%	N	%	N	%
sheep	11	24	8	50	6	50	29+	38	54+	36
cattle	11	26	2	13	2	17	14	18	29	19
pig	12	24	2	13	3	25	13	17	30	20
horse	10	22	2	13	0		15	19	27	18
dog	2	4	2	13	1	8	6	8	11	7
Total	46		16		12		77		151	

b) *Horse mandibles*

	Early		Middle		Late (a)		Late (b)		Total‡	
mandibles	1	13	–		3	60	7	47	11	32

c)

	a	b	%	a	b	%	a	b	%	a	b	%	a	b	%
sheep	11	130	8	8	84	10	6	111	5	29+	470	6	54+	815	7
cattle	11	30	31	2	18	11	2	17	12	14	72	19	29	137	21
pig	12	33	36	2	27	7	3	24	13	13	70	19	30	154	19
horse	10	8	100★	2	6	33	0	5	0	15	15	100	27	34	79
dog	2	5	40	2	3	67	1	7	14	6	9	67	11	24	46
Total	46	206	22	16	138	12	12	164	7	77	656	12	151	1164	13

Key: a = number of skulls; b = minimum numbers of individuals; % = % of MNI for each species; ‡ = total of dated deposits only; ★ see p 538; + includes one goat

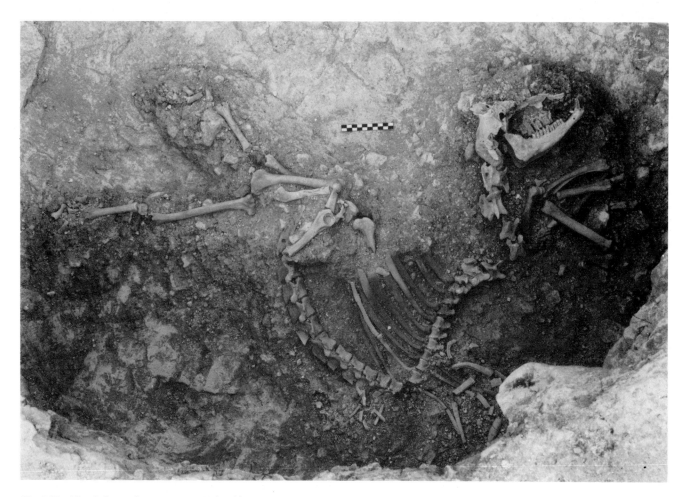

Fig 9.33 The skeleton of a mature goat (pit 455)

Fig 9.34 A horse skull found on the base of pit 389

the distinction between ordinary skull material deposited after butchery and the special deposits of skulls was not always clear. The distinction was made on the basis of the amount of skull surviving and the absence of butchery evidence. Special deposits of skulls were thus defined as including skulls that had clearly been deposited whole and skulls where a substantial amount had survived, any damage having probably or possibly occurred post-deposition. A complete horse skull on the base of a pit is illustrated in Fig 9.34.

Another special category was defined that related only to horses — isolated complete mandibles, where the left and right hand halves of the mandibles were still joined and the mandibles were substantially undamaged.

Special deposits of skulls were found in 99 (11%) of the pits at Danebury and horse mandibles were found in ten pits (1%).

In Table 90, the numbers of skulls of each species and the numbers of horse mandibles are shown. Sheep skulls form the largest category of skull deposits, but when the number of sheep skulls is calculated as a proportion of the minimum number of individuals for sheep, it is clear that only a small proportion of the sheep skulls became special deposits. Much larger proportions of cattle and pig skulls were found as special deposits. The number of horse skulls that were found was 79% of the calculated minimum number of individuals for horses and in the early and late (b) phases the proportion was 100%. No horse skulls were, however, found in the late (a) phase pits, although a complete horse burial and three horse mandibles were dated to this phase. The number of dog skulls was proportionately very high, especially in the early, middle, and late (b) phases.

The incidence of skull deposits was significantly higher in the early phase than in any other phase of occupation, all animals except sheep being particularly well represented among the skull deposits. Significantly fewer skulls were found in the late (a) period than in the late (b) period, but differences between the middle and late (a) phases are not statistically significant.

Horse mandibles seem best represented in the two late phases.

Fig 9.35 *An articulated horse leg, apparently cut from the rest of the body through the lower part of the humerus (pit 99)*

Articulated legs

The category of special deposits defined as articulated legs consists of several bones from a single animal leg, found in articulation within a pit. In this category, only those recognized during excavation are included. They can be divided into two groups, the first consisting of articulated bones that represent a substantial part of an animal's leg, including some of the main meat-bearing bones (ie the humerus and radius, or the femur and tibia). The second group consists of articulated bones from the lower part of the limb only (the carpals and tarsals and metapodials and phalanges). This group can be disputed as 'special' deposits, since it can be argued that such articulated bones could merely represent butchery waste — the cutting off and disposal of the parts of the carcass that bear very little meat.

An articulated horse limb is illustrated in Fig 9.35. The fore limb appears to have been severed from the rest of the body through the humerus shaft. Slight traces of butchery marks on some of the articulated limbs could be consistent with removal of the hide, although they could also have resulted from flesh removal. It is certainly difficult with this group of special deposits to be clear whether the bones were deposited with the flesh intact or only after a substantial amount of the flesh had been removed. There was, however, no evidence of any singeing of the bone, such as might have occurred if these limbs were the remains of large 'joints' roasted over a fire.

The incidence of articulated limbs is shown in Table 91. Only seven of the first category were found, of which four were horse limbs. A further eighteen articulated lower limbs were found, of which seven were from horses and eight were from sheep. Articulated limbs of both categories were found in all four phases of occupation.

Manner of deposition

In some instances, it was not only the nature of the bones themselves that distinguished them as special, but the location or associations of their deposition.

Although many of the deposits were found within layers of pits that did not appear to have any special features, some were found that had clearly been laid on the bases of what would appear to have been empty pits. Examples of all three main categories of deposits were found on the chalk bottoms of pits or within the primary silt. Fig 9.34 illustrates a horse skull and Fig 9.31 a lamb skeleton, both found on the bases of pits.

Table 91 Special deposits: articulated limbs

	Early			Middle			Late (a)			Late (b)			Total		
	a	b	a+b	a	b	a+b	a	b	a+b	a	b	a+b	a	b	a+b
sheep	0	3	3	0	4	4	0	1	1	2	0	2	2	8	10
cattle	1	2	3	0	0	0	0	0	0	0	0	0	1	2	3
pig	0	0	0	0	0	0	0	0	0	0	1	1	0	1	1
horse	0	1	1	1	0	1	1	1	2	2	5	7	4	7	11
Total	1	6	7	1	4	5	1	2	3	4	6	10	7	18	25

Key: a = articulated limbs including the upper limb bones; b = articulated lower limbs (carpals or tarsals, metapodials and phalanges)

A small number of burials were found closely associated with chalk blocks or sling stones. The horse skeleton found in pit 321 (Fig 9.30) was associated with approximately 50 sling stones and several chalk blocks, while the juvenile cattle burial in pit 909 was associated with four large chalk blocks (Fig 9.32). Again, the incidence of such deposits may in fact have been higher than currently recognized, since such information may have been lost during excavation.

Many of the animals appear to have been deposited in the pits as complete carcasses, and examination of the bones for butchery marks suggested that not even the skin had been removed prior to burial, although it is possible that skinning could have been done without leaving any traces on the bones. However, in some instances, there was evidence that the animals were not intact when deposited in the pits. The most notable example is the horse skeleton found with the dog skeleton in pit 321 and illustrated in Fig 9.30. The horse was mostly fully articulated, but one front and one back limb were slightly displaced. However, it is possible that this could have occurred if the burial was left uncovered or only lightly covered after deposition, and was disturbed when the carcass had partly rotted. However, the head seems to have been deliberately removed from the spine and was placed above the rear of the horse, next to the dog. The calf burial from pit 909 (Fig 9.32) was complete but not fully articulated. The head was not in articulation with the vertebral column, and the limbs, although partly in articulation, were displaced. The bones were examined for butchery marks, but none were found, except for fine knife cuts on one calcaneum and astragalus, common sites for butchery marks on the bones at Danebury.

A pig skeleton in pit 499 was in a fairly jumbled condition when found, but examination of the bones suggested that the animal may have been complete when deposited in the pit. We do not know what happened to a skeleton once it was deposited in a pit — whether it was covered over with a thick layer of soil or whether it was left uncovered or only thinly covered. If the latter was the case, skeletons that were complete when deposited could have been disturbed by scavengers such as dogs, foxes, birds, or even wolves. The jumbled nature of the bones of pig in pit 499 could have resulted from such post-deposition disturbance.

Animal special deposits and human bones
Many of the pits at Danebury contained human bones, which occurred as isolated bone fragments, groups of bones, isolated skulls, partial burials, and complete burials. The human bone remains have been discussed in detail elsewhere (pp 442–63). This section examines whether there was any association between animal deposits and human bones. Initially, associations between any human bone and any animal deposits within the same pit were examined.

Of the 93 pits containing human remains, 38 (41%) also contained animal special deposits. Statistical tests showed that this association was significantly higher than would be expected to have occured by chance. However, if the finds in each phase are analysed individually, the association was only significant in the early and late (b) phases.

Some association between animal and human deposits is thus suggested, but the precise nature of the association is not yet clear. Certainly, animal special deposits cannot be seen exclusively as part of a funerary ritual, as the majority of animal deposits were found in pits where there were no human bones. Even when animal deposits and human bones were found in the same pit, they were only rarely found in close association, although there are examples of human bones and animal deposits being found more closely associated. One explanation is that particular pits were marked out in some way and deposits of animal bones and human bone were made in them at different times during the period in which the pit was filling up with other domestic debris. The detailed analysis of the distribution of the animal bones presently being undertaken will examine the association between human and animal bone in more detail.

Animal special deposits and bird bones
Only a very small percentage of the bones recovered at Danebury were bird bones (Tables 61, 62) and even allowing for the relatively poor recovery of the bones of small animals, they cannot be considered a significant source of food. Nor can they be considered a representative selection of the birds living wild in southern Britain at this period, since the vast majority of bones were from a single species, raven (Tables 83–86). Bird bones could thus be considered as another form of special deposit and, to test this possibility, the association between bird bones and animal bone special deposits was examined. Although only 12% of the total number of dated pits at Danebury contained bird bones, bird bones were found in 34% of the pits that also contained animal special deposits. Statistical tests showed that in all periods except the late (a) period, the association between bird bones and animal bones in pits was very unlikely to have occurred by chance. However, when the association between bird bones and human bones was tested, no significant association was found.

Table 92   Special deposits: summary

	Early		Middle		Late(a)		Late(b)		Total*	
	N	%	N	%	N	%	N	%	N	%
Pits with animal bone	492		139		98		162		891	
Pits with special deposits	49		25		23		64		161	
Pits with animal burials	14	29	16	64	9	39	18	28	57	36
sheep burials	5	10	4	16	3	13	12	19	24	15
cattle burials	5	10	2	8	1	4	2	3	10	6
pig burials	4	8	8	32	4	17	3	5	19	12
horse burials			1	4	1	4	1	2	3	2
dog burials	1	2	2	8	3	13	2	3	8	5
cat burials			1	4					1	1
Pits with burials of more than one species	1	2	2	8	3	13	1	2	7	4
Pits with more than one burial	3	6	3	12	3	13	1	2	10	6
Pits with skull deposits	35	71	9	36	11	48	44	69	99	61
sheep skulls	8	16	6	24	6	26	25	39	45	28
cattle skulls	10	20	2	8	1	4	12	19	25	15
pig skulls	11	22	2	8	3	13	9	14	25	15
horse skulls	10	20	2	8			11	17	23	14
dog skulls	2	4	2	8	1	4	6	9	11	7
Pits with skulls of more than one species	5	10	4	16			15	23	24	15
Pits with more than one skull	8	16	4	16	1	4	18	28	31	19
Pits with complete horse mandibles	1	2			3	13	6	9	10	6
Pits with articulated legs	7	14	2	8	2	9	9	14	20	12
Pits with animal burials and skulls	3	6	2	8	1	4	5	8	11	7
Pits with animal burials and articulated legs	2	4					1	2	3	2
Pits with skulls and articulated legs	3	6	1	4			6	9	10	6
Pits with human bone and animal deposits	8	16	4	16	4	17	22	34	38	23
animal burials	1	2	3	12	2	9	6	9	12	7
skulls	7	14	3	12	1	4	17	27	28	17
complete horse mandibles					3	12	2	3	5	3
articulated legs							5	8	5	3
Pits with birds and animal deposits	9	18	9	36	4	17	21	33	43	27
animal burials	3	6	8	32	2	9	6	9	19	12
skulls	6	12	2	8	2	9	15	23	25	15
articulated legs	3	6					4	6	7	4
Pits with human bone and bird bone	4		3		3		13		23	

*Total of dated features only; % = % of number of pits with special deposits in each phase

Further work is necessary before the details of the correlation between bird bones and special deposits can be fully understood, but there is strong evidence that the finds of bird bones are more than just random occurrences in pits.

Summary

Table 92 summarizes the distribution of special deposits in the pits, and details of the deposits are given in microfiche 17, frames E3–8.

One factor that makes analysis of any change in the distribution of animal deposits over time difficult to interpret is the very different distribution of bones in the pits of the four phases of occupation. This has already been discussed (p 536, Fig 9.14) but should be stressed again here. When looking at the coincidence of different categories of deposits in the late (b) period, it is difficult to disassociate apparent increases in such coincidences from the fact that many pits in this period contained a large amount of material which may have been deposited over a longer period than was represented by the filling of the pits of the earlier phases.

Some changes over time are indicated, but few can be given any statistical validity at present. Animal burials seem to be more common in the middle phase than in any other period of occupation, pig burials being particularly common in this phase. Comparatively few animal burials were found in the late (b) phase, but deposits of skulls, horse mandibles, and articulated legs were fairly common. Cattle burials seem to occur most frequently in the early phase of occupation. Horses and dogs seem both to have been particularly well represented among the special deposits, especially when the relatively small numbers of bones found for these species is taken into account. In the discussion of the horses and dogs, the association between horse and dog bones and special deposits was noted. In the early phase and the late (b) phase, the horse skull deposits formed a significant proportion of the total number of horse bones found in the phase.

Several pits contained more than one special deposit and several contained the skeletons or the skulls of more than one species. Inevitably, many of these pits were dated to the late (b) period, but several pits of even the early period contained more than one burial or skull. A small number of pits were notable because they contained particularly large numbers of special deposits of different categories. These were pits 674 and 1028 dated to the early phase, pit 1149 in the middle phase, pit 321 (Fig 9.30) in the late (a) phase, and pits 23, 120, 923, 935, and 1078 in the late (b) phase. However, each of them contained a larger than average amount of bone material, even if the bones involved in the special burials are excluded from the count. Thus, it is clear that these pits were by no means exclusively used for special deposits. However, this does not exclude the possibility that these pits did have some special significance.

The interpretation of the rectangular buildings in the centre of the fort as perhaps religious buildings suggests the possibility that a particular part of the site may have been reserved for ritual use. However, preliminary examination of the distribution of pits containing special deposits has shown that in all phases the special deposits were found in pits widely distributed over the excavated area of the site, and no areas seem to have particular concentrations of special deposits in them.

Discussion and interpretation

Calling these animal bone deposits found at Danebury 'special' has to some extent already given them a particular significance, which must now be justified.

It can of course be argued that these deposits are merely natural deaths and butchery waste, and it is certainly difficult to disprove this in any individual instance. In only exceptional circumstances can the manner of death of an animal be detected. Thus, natural deaths can rarely be distinguished *per se* from deliberate killings. Some of the few exceptions were the pole-axed cattle skulls found at Portchester Castle (Grant 1975a, 386). If a society chose not to eat animals that died of natural causes, one might expect to find complete animal skeletons. However, many of the neonatal animals, which are very likely to have died of natural causes, are found widely distributed amongst the bone refuse. Those that were not and were found as complete, or relatively complete, burials were the exceptions. Although natural mortality cannot be ruled out as the cause of death for many of the animal burials at Danebury, several phenomena suggest that animal burials cannot be simply explained away in this manner. Firstly, there is the deliberate positioning of two or more animals together. The likelihood of two animals dying of natural causes at the same time, particularly when they are of different species and not new-born animals, seems low. Examples of such multiple burials are the dog and the horse in pit 321, the two sheep and the cat in pit 365, and the pig and two calves in pit 809.

Secondly, there is the manner of deposition of some of the burials, discussed above. Some animals were associated with sling stones or chalk blocks and others were

placed on the bottom of what appear to have been at the time empty pits. Such ceremony implies more than a haphazard disposal of animals who died of natural causes, although it is of course possible that a special burial might have been given to an animal which died a natural death.

Thirdly, the incidence of burials of each species at Danebury does not reflect the percentage contribution of each species to the total sample of animal bones, although examples of all the domestic animals represented at Danebury were found as burials. Amongst the neonatal and very young animals, there are fewer sheep and more cattle and pigs than would be expected, although the presence of particularly large numbers of very young sheep was indicated by the tooth wear evidence for the site as a whole. The small number of burials involved makes it difficult to assess the significance of the differences between the proportion of the burials of young animals and the proportion of the remains of very young animals found incorporated in the domestic refuse. However, the ratio of the numbers of mandibles at MWS 1-5 for sheep, cattle, and pigs for the site overall is 4.5:1:1.2, while the ratio of the numbers of sheep, cattle, and pig burials with MWS 1-5 is 1.5:1:1.3, suggesting that far fewer sheep burials were found than would be expected if the burials of young animals were merely a reflection of naturally occurring mortalities.

Amongst the older animals burials of sheep and pigs are the most common, but horses and dogs are more common than would be expected from the percentages of their bones in the whole bone sample.

If one turns to the largest category of special deposits, namely skulls, one sees a similar situation, with skulls of sheep in the majority, but a smaller proportion than might be expected, together with a much higher incidence of dog and especially horse skulls than would be expected.

Explanation of skull deposits as butchery waste does not stand up to closer examination on another count. From the evidence of butchery marks found on the broken skull fragments from the site as a whole, it is clear that skull meat was commonly eaten. Sheep skulls particularly were frequently chopped in half along the line of the frontal suture, suggesting removal of the brain. Therefore, a deposit of an animal skull would seem to represent the deliberate foregoing of food resources normally utilized. This certainly seems to be the case for sheep, cattle, and pigs, but the situation is not so clear for horses and dogs. Although butchery marks on the bones of dogs and horses strongly suggest that the meat of these animals was eaten, butchery marks were rare on the skulls of these two species. In fact, very little skull bone of horse was found, apart from that found as special deposits. This raises the possibilities either that horse and dog skull meat was avoided for some reason of taste or that horse and dog skulls were considered as important ritual offerings and were usually reserved as such. The finds of articulated limbs were most frequently the limbs of horses, but in this case there is evidence that these are deposits of bones bearing meat that was in other circumstances eaten.

Danebury is not alone amongst Iron Age sites in having evidence for special deposits. Although no published excavations have described as many deposits as were found at Danebury, all categories of special deposits from Danebury have been found at other domestic sites. A full discussion of Danebury in its Iron Age context will be given in the second part of this report, but some examples of parallels to Danebury special deposits may be cited here. Animal burials were found at Twywell (Harcourt 1975) including two pigs and a dog in a single pit associated with large glacial pebbles and lumps of blue clay. A pit at Swallowcliffe Down (Jackson 1927) contained the skulls of four cows, two horses, one sheep, and one dog. A horse hind leg was found at Ashville (Wilson 1978) and at Tollard Royal (Bird 1968) a complete horse skeleton was found.

The evidence does suggest that the label of 'special' for the deposits under discussion is not unmerited. If these are, then, special deposits, their possible significance must be assessed. The burial of an entire animal or a part of an animal bearing meat that was normally eaten represents a sacrifice or loss to the community. There are many examples in the anthropological as well as historical literature of sacrifices being made to ensure good fortune in the future. The Romans, for example, are known to have made a common practice of animal sacrifice (Toynbee 1973). Some form of ritual and magic have always been part of man's interrelation with the environment in which he finds himself, and in a situation where survival is dependent on factors beyond his control — good weather to ensure good harvests, high fertility, absence of disease in animals — it would not be surprising if, associated with the practices of agriculture and animal husbandry, there were some magico-religious beliefs. We may thus suggest that the Danebury special deposits represent sacrifices or propitiation offerings, although to what gods or for what precise purposes we can never know. The deposits that were clearly laid on the bottom of pits may have been dedicatory offerings.

If we accept that sacrifices were being made by the Danebury inhabitants for possible magico-religious purposes, it is interesting to note that when we examine the animals involved, there is some evidence to suggest that many of the animals being sacrificed were not those of most importance to the community. The general discussion of the animal husbandry at Danebury suggests clearly that sheep were the most important animals, providing wool, milk, manure, and meat, and formed approximately two-thirds of the animals kept. Although many of the apparently sacrificed animals were sheep, other animals, particularly horses and dogs, are more often involved in special deposits than would be expected simply from the proportions of their bones in the animal bone sample as a whole. The ambiguous status of horse as a domestic animal has already been discussed (pp 521–2). It is possible that horses were chosen as sacrificial animals both because they were special and set apart from the other domestic animals but also because their loss to the community may not in reality have been as devastating as the loss of the animals which provided the essentials of wool for clothing, manure for the fields, milk, and meat. On the other hand, if they had special status, the sacrifice of a horse would have been a very grand gesture.

Dogs too, although perhaps important as guard dogs or for herding sheep, were less central to the community than sheep, cattle, and pigs. The tradition of dog burial at Danebury seems to have been a long one. The disarticulated remains of three dogs were found in one of the four large pits outside the Iron Age defences and dated to the pre-hillfort occupation (Vol 1, p 12).

If the incidence of animal burials at other Iron Age domestic sites is examined, it is clear that at these sites too dogs and horses are the species most frequently reported as special deposits.

The goat burial and goat skull included among the special deposits are interesting in relation to the evidence from Uley (Ellison 1980). Excavation at this site, an Iron Age and Roman religious site, has uncovered approximately 250,000 animal bones, of which 80% were identified as goat, mature male goats predominating. The goat may have had a special status as a sacrificial animal, again perhaps because it was not an animal that played a vital role in the economy. Toynbee (1973), discussing the Roman period in Italy, says that goats served as cheap, easily obtainable sacrificial victims, offered particularly to the rustic gods such as Faunus and Silvanus. The Uley sacrifices were interpreted as part of a cult involving the worship of Mercury.

Ritual deposits of parts of animals, skulls or whole legs, would be another way of minimizing the real loss to the community of an apparent sacrifice. Whether the animals were deliberately killed for sacrifice, or were animals that had died of natural causes or were to be killed for economic reasons — animals reaching the end of their useful life and uneconomical to feed, or growing animals of the 'wrong' sex — if only the head or a single leg was the ritual deposit, the rest of the animal could be eaten and utilized for raw materials. And, although in the case of skulls, some meat was being sacrificed, the skull is not one of the major meat-bearing areas of the body. The skull could thus have the double advantage of seeming to represent the whole animal, while in fact being one of the less important areas of the body in terms of food resources, and thus not constituting too much of a real loss.

It is interesting that the incidence of special deposits at Danebury, and for that matter at many other domestic sites of the Iron Age, suggests strongly that some form of ritual or religion involving animals was a significant aspect of Iron Age society, and one that was not just confined to the burial places and sacred sites more frequently discussed. Although there is evidence that some of the animal deposits may have been associated with human burials, it was clearly not mainly a funerary ritual. The nature of the deposits suggests that although sacrifices, in the economic sense, appear to have been made, in many instances the real loss to the community may have been minimized by the choice of animals or parts of animals of least economic value to the community.

9.5.12 Discussion and conclusions
Animal husbandry

There can be no doubt that the animal husbandry at Danebury was centred around the raising of sheep. This is clear both from the very high proportion of sheep bones found and from the nature of the environment at Danebury. The well-drained chalk downland is well suited to sheep, but much less suitable for cattle. However, this is not to deny the importance of the other domestic animals to the economy. Sheep have many uses and will have supplied a wide range of products including wool, manure, milk, and meat. However, cattle can provide traction, particularly important for ploughing and agriculture generally, and they produce far more meat and milk per individual animal than sheep. Pigs too have advantages over other animals — they can rapidly convert normally inedible foodstuffs to first class protein for human consumption, and, if the environment is suitable, this can be done for a minimum of effort and cost.

Thus we can assume that a balance was kept between the three main domestic animals, the controlling factors perhaps being largely environmental but also reflecting deliberate choices on the part of the Iron Age farmers. A mixed animal husbandry and farming economy has great advantages; it makes it possible to maximize the use of all available resources. Surplus milk or the byproducts of cheese and butter making can be fed to pigs, and the waste from cereal cultivation provides good animal food. Pigs can find food in the stubble fields even after they have been grazed by sheep and cattle, and all three species will thus manure the land and replenish the fertility of the soil for agriculture.

It is difficult to know how much of what has been shown in recent years to have a sound scientific basis has been known intuitively for centuries. Many modern drugs use synthetic substances which are in fact almost identical to substances that occur naturally in plants which were used by ancient herbalists. A modern farmer will graze sheep and cattle on the same land in rotation because he knows that the parasites that affect sheep are not the same as those that affect cattle. Thus, if animals are kept off land that has been grazed by the same species in the previous year, the cycle of worm infestation is broken. The Danebury farmers will not have understood the complex host-parasite relationship, but they may have been aware that animals become sickly if kept on the same pastures for several years in succession. Alternating cattle and sheep on pasture is a way of utilizing the available land to the maximum advantage.

The numbers of bones recovered give us little idea of the numbers of animals kept, nor do we know how large an area was available for grazing. Many of the problems of modern farming have resulted from too heavy a use of land, encouraged by the availability of modern fertilizers. Stocking rates for farms have generally in the past been much lower than today. Speedy (1980) suggests that stocking rates of 35 ewes per hectare cause little long-term damage to well-drained pasture, but this assumes supplementary feeding of cereals and root crops and we may suppose that much larger areas were required for the same number of animals in the Iron Age. Even larger areas are required for cattle. Nineteenth century figures suggest that one hectare is required to feed a single ox or cow, but Stamp (1964) suggests that to feed an eight ox team in Saxon times might have required as much as 80 hectares of rough pasture. Of course, this varies enormously depending on the nature of the land and the amount of supplementary food available. Whatever the precise ratio of animals to land, we can be sure that the sheep and cattle will have required access to considerable areas of land for grazing. The possible exploitation of the Test valley has already been discussed in relation to cattle keeping, and pigs are kept most effectively with access to woodland areas. Thus, the area exploited for animals may have included a variety of environments, although chalk downland will inevitably have predominated.

Sheep and cattle are normally kept in flocks and herds — it makes no sense to keep them individually on downland. Thus, the animals kept at Danebury suggest a social organization that involved considerable communal cooperation. Pigs can be kept by individual households, but it is perhaps more likely that they were kept in herds and driven for part of the year to wooded areas. Goats, which are found in only very small numbers, may well have been kept individually. Horses, and perhaps dogs too, may only have been kept by those of high status in the community.

There may have been considerable movements of animals, especially of cattle and sheep at particular times of year. The suggestion has been made that sheep, cattle, and pigs were all bred within or very close to the hillfort, but for much of the year they may have been kept at some distance from the fort — sheep on the open downland, pigs in the wooded areas, and cattle on the lowland areas. The boundary ditches and enclosures associated with the fort may have been connected with the movement and confinement of animals.

It has been suggested that the cattle may have been bred in the fort and then moved down to lower ground where the conditions were more suitable for cattle grazing. This raises the possibility that animals and animal products may have been part of the trade network system, for which we have other evidence at the site. Horses, for example, do not seem to have been bred at Danebury and, although they may have been rounded up from wild herds, this could have been done by other communities who then traded the horses. Other domestic animals could have been a part of trade exchanges, and such movements of animals would have had great benefits to the animal population. If an animal population is too isolated, problems are likely to arise because of inbreeding. However, if there is cross-breeding with animals from other populations, there is frequently an improvement in the offspring. This is known to geneticists as 'hybrid vigour'. Although this will not have been understood in the Iron Age, any movement of animals would have had a generally beneficial effect on health and performance.

It seems likely that most movement of animals will have been of live animals. Sheep and cattle are easy to drive and can be moved over large distances, whilst meat, unless salted or otherwise preserved, decays very rapidly. Although the pig cannot be driven so easily, the meat of the pig can be more readily preserved than that of sheep and cattle, since it has a higher fat content. However, there is no suggestion from the bone evidence of any trade in deadstock.

Animal products may have been traded, with wool and woollen goods perhaps being among the most likely to have had value to other communities. If large numbers of sheep were kept, there may have been a considerable surplus of wool. Communities living in environments less suitable for sheep farming may have provided the market. Other animal byproducts, such as bone tools, seem less likely to have been trade items. Bone is available to any community that keeps animals and the skill required for much boneworking is of a relatively low level compared to the skill involved in weaving, potting, and metalworking.

Animal husbandry and agriculture

It is generally accepted that the growing of cereals and other foodstuffs was more important in supplying the food needs of prehistoric populations than the rearing of animals for meat. Certainly, in developing countries today, the majority of food consumed is vegetable in origin and little meat is eaten. Eating vegetable products makes sound economic sense. At each successive level in the food chain, there is a considerable loss in energy, so that eating foodstuffs at low trophic levels is more energy-efficient.

Although we have no way of knowing the relationship between vegetable matter and animal protein in the diet at Danebury, we may assume that the diet was mainly a vegetarian one. The evidence obtained from the age at death of the sheep and cattle found at the site suggests that these animals were not reared specifically for meat, although production of meat was clearly one of the main reasons for keeping pigs. The relationship between the number of individuals represented in each phase and the calculated storage capacity for cereals may give some clue

Table 93 Relative proportions of sheep, cattle, and pigs

Species	Early %	Middle %	Late (a) %	Late (b) %
Sheep	75	80	79	80
Cattle	25	20	21	20
Sheep	80	74	79	89
Pig	20	26	21	11
Cattle	57	42	50	66
Pig	43	58	50	34
Sheep	63	63	65	72
Cattle and pig	37	37	35	28

Percentages calculated from 'epiphyses only' figures (Table 62)

as to changes in the relationship between vegetable and animal food in different phases of occupation, but there are too many unknown factors for a very realistic impression of this relationship to be formed.

Whatever the importance of meat to the human diet in a primitive system, the efficiency of the agriculture must be vitally linked to the animal husbandry. Cultivation of the same area of land for more than a few years will lead to a considerable loss of fertility, unless the essential nutrients for plant growth are returned to the soil. This can be done very effectively by the use of animal manure. Animals, grazed on the stubble, will, while utilizing food that is of no value to humans, manure the soil for the next crop. Thus, there is likely to have been a close relationship between the agriculture and the animal husbandry, each supplying essential requirements for the other. Agriculture will have supplied supplementary foodstuffs for the animals, while the animals supplied fertilizer to promote growth of plant food. Animals may also have had a more active part in the agricultural system. Cattle were almost certainly used to pull the ploughs, and even pigs may have had a practical value, in that the effectiveness with which they turn over the soil while grubbing for roots may well have been exploited for agricultural purposes.

There will have been a balance between the animal husbandry and the agricultural systems to ensure that the support given to the agricultural system by the animals was not exceeded by their demands for food from that system. While the animals could be fed mainly on grass and other foodstuffs, such as leaves and pannage that could not be utilized as food by humans, the relationship would be mutually beneficial. If environmental or social changes reduced the available natural animal foodstuffs so that the animals started to compete with the humans for food, the system would fall out of balance.

Changes over time

The discussion so far has assumed a consistency in the animal husbandry over the 500 years of occupation at the site. The evidence suggests that there was indeed a remarkable consistency, with little evidence for change in many of the aspects of the animal husbandry that have been investigated. Throughout the period of occupation sheep raising predominated, and examination of the age structure for sheep suggests that even the management practices in relation to these animals remained largely unchanged. There even seems to have been a continuity

in the ritual practices. All types of special deposits identified were found in all four phases, although their relative proportions and frequencies changed over time. The middle phase particularly seems to have been one of increased ritual activity.

However, other evidence of variation in the four phases of occupation was noted. Over the whole period of occupation there were slight fluctuations in the proportions of the three main domestic animals. These changes are summarized in Table 93, which takes each combination of two of the three animals and shows how their proportions varied over time. Both pig and cattle bone numbers seem to have declined relative to sheep from the early to the late (b) phase, but the relationship between cattle and pigs seems to have fluctuated in a less consistent manner. Cattle bones were more common than pig bones in the early and late (b) phases, but in the middle phase pig bones were rather more common than cattle bones, and were also more plentiful in relation to sheep bones than at any other period of occupation.

A particularly high percentage of pig burials and of animal burials generally was found in the middle phase (Table 88). If the number of sheep bones is compared to the numbers of cattle and pig bones together, it is clear that the proportion of sheep bones remains very constant in relation to the bones of these two animals until the late (b) period, when a higher proportion of sheep bones is found. This seems to be due mainly to a decrease in the proportion of pig bones, since the relation between sheep and cattle bones remains stable from the middle to the late (b) period.

When the hillfort was first occupied at the beginning of the 6th century BC, the type of farming and animal husbandry chosen must have been to a considerable extent dictated by the environment. However, over a long period of occupation, that environment will itself have been changed by the nature of the occupation. We can in some sense equate the situation with that of dynamic equilibrium in chemical reactions. Any external change will upset the equilibrium and result in an internal readjustment until equilibrium is again reached. In this way, the farming and the animal husbandry practices will have reacted to changes in the environment and made adjustments accordingly. It is in fact remarkable that so little seems to have changed over the first 250 years of the settlement.

Some differences in particular aspects of the animals have already been noted in the discussion of the individual species. However, many dramatic events may have occurred that have left no trace. Plagues of animal disease, droughts, severe winters, all will have had effects on the animals and their management, but we are only able to look at gross changes from this distance.

There is some evidence from a general analysis of the animal bones to suggest that in the late (b) phase, the situation that had existed for the first 250 years had begun to change, and that the animal husbandry system was being put under some pressure.

Firstly, there was a decline in the numbers of pigs kept. The considerable use of wood for the construction of defences, homes, and other structures within the hillfort may have caused a reduction in the amount of available woodland in the area. The pigs themselves, by eating the nuts and acorns and rooting up the tree seedlings, will, unless carefully managed, have had an effect on the natural regeneration of the forest, thus contributing to a decline in the food available. Once there was not enough natural food available in the local environment and the pigs started to need food that might otherwise have been

**Table 94   Minimum numbers of individuals found
per ten years of occupation**

Phase	Approx date BC	Sheep	Cattle	Pigs	Dogs	Horses	All species
Early	550–450	13.0	3.0	3.3	0.5	0.8	20.6
Middle	450–400	16.8	3.6	4	0.6	1.2	27.6
Late(a)	400–300	11.1	1.7	2.4	0.7	0.5	16.4
Late(b)	300–50	18.0	2.9	2.8	0.4	0.6	26.2
All phases	550–50	16.3	2.7	3.1	0.4	0.7	23.3

used for human consumption, pigs would no longer have been an economic proposition. The smaller number of older pigs represented in the MWS distribution for the late (b) phase (Fig 9.25) may be further evidence of an inability to provide enough food to fatten up pigs to the same stage as had been done in earlier periods.

The reduction in the number of pigs kept would not in itself have constituted an economic crisis but if, as we have postulated, the animal husbandry and agricultural systems were kept in balance, the change in any part of the relationship might have had effects on the whole. The reduction in the proportion of pigs may, for example, have reduced the amount of manure available to fertilize the soil.

There are other indications of change in this period. The slightly higher incidence of periodontal disease in sheep may have resulted from overgrazing the land. Although the figures calculated in Table 94 for the number of animals represented for each ten years of occupation may be biased by many factors, particularly any changes in the manner and location of rubbish disposal, they are the only evidence available for speculating on relative animal numbers in different phases of occupation.

They suggest an increase in the number of animals kept in the late (b) phase, at least in relation to the early and late (a) phases. The figures for the middle phase represent a very short lifespan and may be distorted by the large number of animal burials found in this phase.

Any increase in the numbers of animals kept or decrease in the amount of land available might have disastrous effects on the health of the animals. Reduced food supplies and increased exposure to infection and parasite infestation could make an animal population very vulnerable.

The evidence for special deposits in the late (b) phase suggests that, although deposits or sacrifices were still being made as in the early phase, there is an increased incidence of what can be termed tokenism. Relatively fewer special deposits were found in this phase than in any other phase of occupation, and a smaller percentage of those that were found were whole animal burials. This could indicate that the loss of a whole animal could not as easily be supported as in earlier phases.

In the early phase, horses were represented mainly by skulls and relatively little post-cranial material was found. In the late (b) phase, all parts of the skeleton were well represented and the bones included those of immature animals. This has been interpreted as possible evidence for horse breeding, but it may also suggest a greater exploitation of horse as a food source.

Taking all these trends together, we can suggest that by the latest period of occupation, the animal husbandry system that seems to have supported a settled community at Danebury for several centuries was showing signs of stress. Cultivation of the same areas of land for many centuries may, even with animal fertilizer, have resulted in a gradual depletion of the soil and a reduction in the cropping capacity of the land.

The critical factor could have been human population expansion with greater demands for food without a larger available area of land. Once the system was stretched to capacity, any natural disasters could have had catastrophic results. However, it is interesting to note that there does not seem to be any evidence of increased exploitation of wild animals during this final phase of occupation. It has been suggested for other sites that increased percentages of deer bones are indicative of a disruption to an established agricultural system (Grant 1981).

It has been possible to discuss changes over time because, by and large, the finds have come from the same type of context in each phase, and can thus be seen to be directly comparable. However, there are differences in the bone material which may have biased or affected the interpretation of the results.

The figures calculated for the minimum percentage loss for each species summarized in Fig 9.29 show that for sheep, cattle, and pigs there was a greater discrepancy between the number of the best represented elements and all the other bone elements in the late (b) phase, compared to the early phase. This was not explained by any obvious change in the kind of material disposed of in the two periods, since almost all bone elements seem to have been affected in a similar way. In all phases, the bones seem to be representative of whole animals and not of butchery waste or food debris. Until a full analysis of the bone distribution is completed, the reasons for this change remain unclear, particularly when, for dogs and horses, a pattern the reverse of that for other animals is found, with the percentage loss being greater in the early period than in the late (b) period. The other notable difference between the four phases of occupation is seen in the average number of bones found in each pit (Fig 9.14), which shows a considerable rise from a relatively small number in the early phase to much higher numbers in the late (b) phase. It is possible that these two changes in the pattern of bone deposition may in some way be related, and this possibility is being examined.

Table 94 shows how many individuals of each species are represented for each ten years of occupation. Only 23.3 individuals of all of the five most important species were found for each ten years of occupation. This is little more than two animals per year. We must, therefore, have only a *very* partial record of the animals which were kept at Danebury, and we do not know how those whose bones have survived related to the original animal populations. This is, of course, true for any animal bone assemblage, but it has been stressed here because the very large number of animal bones found at Danebury may give the impression that we have a fair representation of the animals associated with the site in the Iron Age.

The role of wild animals

It is clear from the scarcity of the remains of all wild animals that hunting cannot have played any significant part in the provision of food eaten within the settlement. The vast majority of all meat consumed must have been obtained from the domestic animals raised and tended by the fort's inhabitants.

One conclusion that might be drawn from this is that wild animals were not present in any significant numbers in the region around Danebury in the Iron Age. We know from environmental studies that the forest cover of the lighter soils, including the chalk downland, had begun to be cleared from the Neolithic period onwards (Evans 1975), but very extensive areas of forest must have remained, which would have provided a suitable habitat for deer. The density of human occupation is unlikely to have been such that a large variety of wild animals could not have existed within a short distance of the hillfort. The absence or scarcity of mammals such as badgers and foxes is not surprising, since these animals seem never to have been exploited for food. The few fox remains found at Danebury may be from animals killed as pests.

Deer bones are rare, not only at Danebury but at the majority of sites of Iron Age date. In fact, the evidence for hunting in this period is extremely slender.

There was, however, one relatively important role that wild animals played, and that was in the supply of a raw material, antler. Since deer shed their antlers every year, there would have been no need to kill the animals in order to obtain them. The best time to collect the antlers would be shortly after they were shed and before they were exposed to the elements, gnawed by the deer themselves (as a source of minerals), or eaten by insects such as ants. Thus the presence of antler on a site may suggest a seasonal activity. Expeditions could have been made to forest areas known to have been inhabited by deer in order to collect supplies of antler. Alternatively, antler may have been obtained by trading with communities that lived in more forested areas, although there is little evidence to support such a hypothesis.

The bird bones found in the pits and occupation layers represent only a very narrow range of species. Some of these birds were creatures that could have been eaten, although butchery marks on the bones were rare; thus, a very limited exploitation of the local species of birds is suggested.

The remains of fish too were extremely uncommon, although, as has been stressed previously, survival and recovery factors are likely to have particularly affected the representation of fish species.

The scarcity of the bones of all wild animals at Danebury and at the majority of occupation sites of the Iron Age shows that these settled agricultural communities had a very restricted meat diet. It has already been suggested that meat may have formed only a small proportion of the diet, but even so the scarcity of the remains of wild creatures on sites of this period must testify to the efficiency of the agriculture and animal husbandry. The only exceptions to this general picture for the Iron Age are to be seen at sites in marginal areas where farming may have been much more difficult and more subject to environmental and climatic extremes (Grant 1981). It is interesting to compare the very restricted meat diet of sites like Danebury in the Iron Age with the diets of communities in rural areas in the medieval period. These communities typically chose to exploit a much greater range of wild food resources. This could suggest that by the medieval period, the pressure of expanding population and the cultivation of the same land for many centuries was demanding more of the farming system than it could meet. Danebury, however, seems to have been abandoned before, or possibly when, this crisis point had been reached.

This analysis and discussion represent only the first stage of the work on the animal bones from Danebury. Many more bones from the recent seasons of excavation have yet to be identified and further work remains to be completed on the bones that have been examined and

that form the evidence for this discussion. Many of the ideas are speculative; it is hoped that future analysis will clarify some of the issues raised.

Acknowledgements

I should particularly like to thank Gary Lock for his patient and efficient work on the bone computing. Many other people have helped and supported me in a variety of ways and I should like to thank Philip Armitage, Don Brothwell, Jennie Coy, Barry Cunliffe, Gena Davies, Marcus Grant, Maggie Johnson, Clive Orton, and John Watson.

Bibliography

Armitage, P, & Clutton Brock, J, 1976   A system for the classification and description of the horn cores of cattle from archaeological sites, *J Archaeol Sci*, **3**, 329–48

Ashdown, R, 1979   The avian bones from Station Road, Puckeridge, in *Excavations at Puckeridge and Braughing 1975–79* (C Partridge), *Hertfordshire Archaeol*, **7**, 92–7

Bird, P F, 1968   Animal bones from Tollard Royal, in The excavation of a Durotrigian farmstead near Tollard Royal in Cranborne Chase, southern England (G J Wainwright), *Proc Prehist Soc*, **34**, 146–7

Boessneck, J, von den Driesch, A, Meyer-Lemppenau, V, & Wechsler von Ohlen, E, 1971   Die Tierknochenfunde aus dem Oppidum von Manching, *Die Ausgrabungen in Manching*, **6**, Wiesbaden

Bogucki, P I, 1980   Neolithic bird remains from Brześć, Kujawski, Poland, *Ossa*, **7**, 33–40

Boyd, J M, & Jewell, P A, 1974   The Soay sheep and their environment: a synthesis, in *Island survivors: the ecology of the Soay sheep of St Kilda* (eds P A Jewell, C Milner, & J M Boyd), 360–73

Bradley, R, & Ellison, A, 1975   *Rams Hill*

Clapham, A R, Tutin, T G, & Warburg, E F, 1962   *Flora of the British Isles*

Cohen, E, & Taverner, J, 1972   *A revised list of Hampshire and Isle of Wight birds*

Corbett, G B, & Southern, H M, 1977   *The handbook of British mammals*

Cunliffe, B W, 1971   Danebury, Hampshire: first interim report on the excavations 1969–70, *Antiq J*, **51**, 240–52

Dennel, R W, 1974   Botanical evidence for prehistoric crop-processing activities, *J Archaeol Sci*, **1**, 275–84

Ellison, A, 1980   Natives, Romans and Christians on West Hill, Uley: an interim report on the excavation of a ritual complex of the first millennium AD, in *Temples, churches and religion: recent research in Roman Britain* (ed W Rodwell), 305–20

Evans, J G, 1975   *The environment of early man in the British Isles*

Foch, J, 1966   *Metrische Untersuchungen an Metapodien einiger europäischen Rinderrassen*, Dissertation, Munich

Godwin, Sir H, 1975   *History of the British flora*

Grant, A, 1971   The animal bones, in *Excavations at Fishbourne 1961–1969* (B W Cunliffe), 377–88

———, 1975a   The animal bones, in *Excavations at Portchester Castle*, **1**, *Roman* (B W Cunliffe), 378–408

———, 1975b   The animal bones, in *ibid*, **2**, *Saxon* (B W Cunliffe), 262–87

———, 1978a   Variation in dental attrition in mammals and its revelance to age estimation, in *Research problems in zooarchaeology* (eds D R Brothwell, K D Thomas, & J Clutton-Brock), 103–6

———, 1978b   The animal bones, in *Excavations at Portchester Castle*, **3**, *Medieval, the Outer Bailey and its defences* (B W Cunliffe), 213–38

———, 1981   The significance of deer remains at occupation sites of the Iron Age to the Anglo-Saxon period, in *The environment of man: the Iron Age to the Anglo-Saxon period* (eds M K Jones & G W Dimbleby), 205–13

———, 1983a   The animal bones, in Excavations at Harrold Pit, Odell, Bedfordshire, 1974–1978 (B Dix), *Bedfordshire Archaeol J*, **17**

———, 1983b   The use of toothwear as a guide to the age of domestic ungulates, in *Ageing and sexing animal bones from archaeological sites*, (eds D Wilson, C Grigson, & S Payne), 91–108

———, forthcoming   The animal bones, in *Excavations at Portchester Castle*, **4**, *Medieval, the Inner Bailey* (B W Cunliffe)

Grubb, P, 1974   Population dynamics of the Soay sheep, in *Island survivors: the ecology of the Soay Sheep at St Kilda* (eds P A Jewell, C Milner, & J M Boyd), 242–72

Harcourt, R A, 1974   The dog in prehistoric and early historic Britain, *J Archaeol Sci*, **1**, 2, 151–76

———, 1975   The animal bones, in An Iron Age site at Twywell, Northamptonshire (D A Jackson), *Northamptonshire Archaeol*, **10**, 31–93

———, 1979   The animal bones, in *Gussage All Saints. An Iron Age settlement in Dorset* (G J Wainwright), 150–60

Helbaek, H, 1952 Early crops in Southern Britain, *Proc Prehist Soc*, **18**, 194–233

Hillman, G, 1981 Reconstructing crop husbandry practices from charred remains of crops, in *Farming practice in British prehistory* (ed R Mercer), 123–62

Howard, M, 1963 The metrical determination of the metapodials and skulls of cattle, *Roy Anthrop Inst Occas Pap*

Hubbard, R N L B, 1975 Assessing the botanical component of human palaeoeconomies, *Bull Inst Archaeol Univ London*, **12**, 197–205

Jackson, J W, 1927 Report on the animal remains, in An inhabited site of La Tène I date on Swallowcliffe Down (R C C Clay), *Wiltshire Archaeol Mag*, **43**, 90–3

Jarman, H N, Legge, A T, & Charles, J A, 1972 Retrieval of plant remains from archaeological sites by froth flotation, in *Papers in economic prehistory* (ed E S Higgs), 39–46

Jewell, P, 1958 Buzzards and barrows, *The Listener*, 13 Feb 1958, 278–82

Jones, E C, 1960 Eighteenth century changes in Hampshire chalkland farming, *Agric Hist Rev*, **8**, 5–19

Jones, M K, 1978a The plant remains, in *The excavation of an Iron Age settlement, Bronze Age ring-ditches and Roman features at Ashville Trading Estate, Abingdon, Oxon* (M Parrington), 93–110

————, 1978b Sampling in a rescue context: a case study in Oxfordshire, in *Sampling in contemporary British archaeology* (eds J F Cherry, C Gamble, & S Shennan), 191–206

————, 1981 The development of crop husbandry, in *The environment of man: the Iron Age to the Anglo-Saxon period* (eds M K Jones & G W Dimbleby), 95–128

————, in press Archaeobotany beyond subsistence reconstruction, in *Beyond domestication: subsistence archaeology and social complexity in prehistoric Europe* (eds G Barker & C Gamble)

Keepax, C, 1977 Contamination of archaeological deposits by seeds of modern origin with particular reference to flotation machines, *J Archaeol Sci*, **4**, 3, 221–9

Kiesewalter, L, 1888 *Skelettmessungen an Pferden als Beitrag zur theoretischen Beurteilungslehre des Pferdes*, Dissertation, Leipzig

Knörzer, K H, 1971 Urgeschichtliche Unkrauter im Rheinland. Ein Beitrag zur Entstehungsgeschichte der Segetalgesellschaften, *Vegetatio*, **23**, 89–111

Lambrick, G, & Robinson, M, 1979 *Iron Age and Roman riverside settlements at Farmoor, Oxfordshire*

Liddell, D M, 1935 Report of the Hampshire Field Club's excavations at Meon Hill. Second season, 1933, *Proc Hampshire Fld Club Archaeol Soc*, **13**, 7–54

Maltby, J M, 1981 Iron Age, Romano-British, and Anglo-Saxon animal husbandry: a review of the faunal evidence, in *The environment of man: the Iron Age to the Anglo-Saxon period* (eds M K Jones & G W Dimbleby), 155–203

McCance, R A, Owens, P D A, & Tonge, G M, 1968 Severe under-nutrition in growing and adult animals: 18, The effects of rehabilitation on the teeth and jaws of pigs, *Brit J Nutrition*, **22**, 357–68

Monk, M, & Fasham, P, 1980 Carbonised plant remains from two Iron Age sites in central Hampshire, *Proc Prehist Soc*, **46**, 321–44

Murphy, P J, 1977 *Early agriculture and environment on the Hampshire chalklands circa 800 BC–400 AD*, M Phil thesis, Univ Southampton

Nicholson, E M (ed), 1929 *The Natural History of Selborne by Gilbert White*

Ordnance Survey 1944 *Type of farming maps of England and Wales*

Payne, S, 1972 On the interpretation of bone samples from archaeological sites, in *Papers in economic prehistory* (ed E S Higgs), 65–81

————, 1973 Kill off patterns of sheep and goats: the mandibles from Asvan Kale, *Anatolian Stud*, **23**, 281–303

Percival, J, 1921 *The wheat plant*

Platt, M I, 1948 Report on the animal remains, in Report on the excavation of a broch at Skitten, in the Kilmster District of Caithness (C Calder), *Proc Soc Antiq Scot*, **82**, 124–45

Rackham, O, 1980 *Ancient woodland*

Redman, C L, 1975 *Archaeological sampling strategies*, Addison-Wesley module in anthropology, **55**, Massachusetts

Reynolds, P J, 1967 Experiments in Iron Age agriculture, *Trans Bristol Gloucestershire Archaeol Soc*, **36**, 60–73

————, 1974 Experimental Iron Age storage pits. An interim report, *Proc Prehist Soc*, **40**, 118–31

Riddell, W H, 1943 The domestic goose, *Antiquity*, **17**, 148–55

Ryder, M L, 1981a Fleece changes in sheep, in *The environment of man: the Iron Age to the Anglo-Saxon period* (eds M K Jones & G W Dimbleby), 215–30

————, 1981b Livestock, in *The agrarian history of England and Wales*, **1**, 1, Prehistory (ed S Piggott), 301–410

Schiffer, M B, 1976 *Behavioural archaeology*

Silver, I A, 1969 The ageing of domestic animals, in *Science in archaeology* (eds D Brothwell & E S Higgs), 283–302

Speedy, A, 1980 *Sheep production: science into practice*

Stamp, L D, 1964 *Man and the land*

Teichert, M, 1969 Osteometrische Untersuchungen zur Berechnung der Widerristhöhe bei vor- und fruhgeschichtlichen Schweinen, *Kühn-Archiv*, **83**, 237–92

Thesing, R, 1977 *Die Grössenentwicklung des Haushuhns in vor- und frühgeschichtlicher Zeit*, Dissertation, Veterinary Faculty, Munich

Townshend, F, 1904 *Flora of Hampshire, including the Isle of Wight*, 2 edn

Toynbee, J, 1973 *Animals in Roman life and art*

Trow-Smith, R, 1957 *A history of British livestock husbandry to 1700*

Turk, F A, 1968 Report on the animal remains from Nor'nour, *J Roy Inst Cornwall*, **5**, 250–65

Van Zeist, W, 1974 Palaeobotanical studies of settlement sites in the coastal area of the Netherlands, *Palaeohistoria*, **16**, 223–371

Waldén, M W, 1976 A nomenclatural list of the land mollusca of the British Isles, *J Conchology*, **29**, 21–5

Watson, A, 1938 *The farming year*

Watson, J P N, 1978 The interpretation of epiphyseal fusion data, in *Research problems in zooarchaeology* (eds D R Brothwell, K D Thomas, & J Clutton-Brock), 97–102

Westley, B, 1970 Animal bones from Budbury, in An Iron Age promontory fort at Budbury, Bradford-on-Avon, Wiltshire (G J Wainwright), *Wiltshire Archaeol Mag*, **65**, 152–4

Wild, J-P, 1970 *Textile manufacture in the northern Roman provinces*

Williams, D, 1973 Flotation at Siraf, *Antiquity*, **47**, 288–92

Wilson, B, 1978 The animal bones, in *The excavation of an Iron Age settlement, Bronze Age ring-ditch and Roman features at Ashville Trading Estate, Abingdon (Oxfordshire) 1974–6* (M Parrington), 110–39

10 Community, continuity, and change

The function of this final section is threefold: to offer a summary of the data detailed in the foregoing pages; to present the social, economic, and political development of Danebury against the background of contemporary society in Wessex; and, by raising questions, to outline directions which further research might take.

10.1 Site development

A necessary preliminary to any discussion is the establishment of a sound chronological sequence and to this much time and effort has been devoted. We may summarize the data presented above in this way:

Pre-hillfort occupation: Neolithic and Bronze Age
Sporadic use of the hilltop in the Neolithic and early Bronze Age is represented by a scatter of flints and sherds of Beaker pottery. While it is possible that some of the unassigned postholes belong to this phase, the only contemporary structure so far recognized is a single crouched inhumation accompanied by a Beaker. What may be an isolated barrow lies on the east slope of the hill outside the later defences of the fort.

The earliest organized occupation
The earliest occupation of an organized kind can be assigned to the first half of the 1st millennium BC. It was probably during this time that a series of large pits ('ritual pits' A-E) were dug, roughly on a contour, outside the first defensive earthwork. Some of the pits supported upright timbers of considerable proportion. Little is known of the precise date of these structures and nothing of their function. One plausible explanation is that they may have defined a precinct wherein certain social functions were performed, somewhat in the tradition of the earlier henge monuments, but such a suggestion is purely speculative.

No other structures or material can definitely be said to be of this phase but a single small pit (in what later became the courtyard of the east entrance) and another small pit containing a hoard of bronze scrap of Hallstatt C type could, in theory, pre-date the first defences. The hoard is most likely to have been deposited in the 7th century BC but may possibly have been buried a little later; the best date for the construction of the first rampart is in the early to mid 6th century. Thus the hoard *could* have been deposited very soon after the defences were built and not before.

The early Iron Age fort (Periods 1a–2c)
The earliest defensive circuit consisted of a timber-faced rampart, fronted by a ditch, in which were set two gates sited at opposite sides of the fort. Two main periods can be defined. In the first the east gate underwent modifications allowing three phases to be recognized (1a, 1b, and 1c). The second period was marked by additions to the back of the rampart and a remodelling of the gate which was later repaired (2a and 2b). The east gate was destroyed by fire in period 2c.

During this early period (1a–2c) the principal types of pottery in use are designated *ceramic phases 1–3* for which the best-fit dates, based on calibrated radiocarbon estimates, are 550–450 BC.

Throughout ceramic phases 1–3 the fort was densely occupied and a road ran between the gates dividing the interior into northern and southern halves. In the northern half storage pits were densely packed, while in

the southern half were houses and their associated pits. Houses and domestic refuse were also found to be concentrated in the lee of the ramparts. Throughout the century or so of occupation there were changes, the most evident being the replacement of rows of small four-post 'granaries' in the northern zone by pits. While this could represent little more than a minor shift in function in one part of the fort, it could reflect a more significant change from a communal storage function to a more domestic form of resident activity. For this reason we might tentatively refer to the 'earliest' and the 'early' period.

The middle period (Periods 2d–3b)
Following the burning of the east gate in period 2c there was a time when the entrance was gateless (2d). Then followed a rebuilding of the entrance and a subsequent repair (3a and 3b). It seems possible that during this time accumulations of soil and silt formed behind the ramparts suggesting a certain lack of activity in these areas.

Relating the gate sequence to the internal activity is difficult but broadly speaking the middle period can be correlated with *ceramic phases 4–5* for which a date of 450 to 400 BC is indicated. A number of storage pits containing this type of pottery were found scattered throughout the interior. There is however a distinct possibility that some of those producing cp 4 assemblages belong more appropriately to the early period — in other words that the gate fire of period 2c came during the currency of cp 4. The question cannot be answered on present evidence.

Another problem is whether or not there was a break in occupation at any time during the middle period. Following the gate fire there was a time when there seems to have been no gate structure, but close by, evidence of contemporary occupation was noted. If there was a period of abandonment it is more likely to have been between the middle and late periods (ie between 3b and 4) but it should be stressed that nothing in the archaeological record *requires* there to have been a cultural or occupational hiatus. The question is an interesting one and further light may be thrown on it when the south-west gate is examined in the coming years.

The date of the Middle Earthwork, which creates a subsidiary enclosure against the southern side of the fort, remains unclear but it may well belong to the middle period.

The late Iron Age fort (Periods 4-6c)
The late Iron Age period at Danebury opens with the extensive reconstruction of the defensive circuit. The rampart was heightened (a process which, on the north and east, required the digging of an internal quarry to provide sufficient material), the ditch was recut to a deep V-shaped profile, and the east entrance was partially rebuilt (period 4). Some time later, work was begun on a redesigned gate (period 5) which was to have been protected by external hornworks but the project appears to have been left unfinished. Finally in period 6 the gate and hornworks were completed.

It was probably at the beginning of the late period that the Outer Earthwork was built to provide corral space around the fort. Some time later the south-west entrance was blocked. Period 6 came to an end when the east gate was destroyed by fire.

The reconstruction of the defensive circuit, signalling the beginning of the late period, took place at (or just before) the time when pottery of *ceramic phase 6* came into use, and occupation spanned the duration of *ceramic phases 6 and 7*. In terms of the calibrated radiocarbon sequence the period lasted from 400 to 100 BC, though the opening date may have to be revised to *c* 350 BC in the light of further radiocarbon assessments.

Throughout the late period the interior of the fort was densely inhabited. The southern part of the site was divided by lateral roads into areas lined with large 4- and 6-post 'granaries' while houses and ancillary domestic structures clustered in the protected zone just behind the ramparts.

The destruction of the gate by fire in period 6c was, in all probability, a significant historical event. There is some evidence to show that houses inside the fort were burnt or abandoned at this time, while two pits, not far from the main entrance, were used as charnel pits. The bodies of *c* 25 men, women, and children were thrown in without ceremony, the open holes being left to silt naturally at a time when no occupation debris was being created. It is tempting to regard these observations as evidence of an attack and massacre followed by abandonment.

The latest occupation (Periods 7-8)
The abandonment of the fort as a strongly defended settlement probably happened about 100 BC or soon after, and although occupation of some kind continued, the gate was never again rebuilt. That the fort remained in use is shown by the considerable wear on the roadway through the entrance passage and a scatter of occupation debris of the 1st century BC found particularly in the centre of the fort in the area of the rectangular buildings which may have had religious functions. Occupation was, however, of limited extent and may have been associated with the use of the old enclosure for corraling stock — a suggestion based on an assessment of the silting patterns in the old quarry hollows and the associated molluscan fauna. By the mid 1st century AD the occupation zone (still limited in size) had shifted to the southern side of the fort to the area excavated in 1979–80.

Late refortification and subsequent use
There is clear evidence of late refortification. The ditch of the outer hornwork of the east gate was partially redug together with at least part of the fort ditch, the hornworks were heightened as was the main rampart sectioned in 1969, and the outer gate was rebuilt. If these works are part of the same programme of redefence the activity must be dated to after the middle decades of the 1st century AD on the basis of pottery in the hornwork ditch. While redefence at the time of the Roman conquest is just possible on the evidence, a late Roman or sub-Roman date would seem marginally more likely. Scraps of late Roman pottery and sub-Roman grass-tempered wares have been found unstratified in the fort.

Later use of the old fort was limited to a short-lived annual fair in the reign of Henry VII, the maintenance of a rabbit warren in the 16th and 17th centuries, sheep grazing through the late 17th to 18th century, and various amenity uses following the planting of the beech clump in the middle of the 19th century.

10.2 Hierarchy in the regional settlement pattern

The Hampshire downland of the 4th to 2nd millennia BC, unlike that of Dorset, Wiltshire, and Sussex, appears to be devoid of causewayed camps and henge monuments, but to what extent the lack of known sites results from accidents of discovery it is difficult yet to say. If, however, a concentration of funerary monuments is taken to represent foci of politico-religious significance (Renfrew 1973), then the cluster of long barrows around Danebury (seven) and Figsbury (seven) might indicate the importance of these dominant hills in the 3rd millennium. Both sites also lie within dense distributions of Bronze Age barrows, one cemetery, 1 km south of Danebury on Chattis Hill, reaching considerable proportions. There is, however, little about the archaeology of either Figsbury or Danebury to draw particular attention to the hilltops themselves as important early prehistoric foci, though both have produced artefacts of the period and it is not impossible that the 'ritual pits' at Danebury date to the 2nd millennium rather than the 1st.

Within the Danebury region the earliest known site of hillfort proportions is the 18.8 ha enclosure of Balksbury which was probably constructed in the 8th or 7th century BC and in this early phase appears to have contained only a few round houses and a number of four-post granaries sparsely distributed about the interior (Wainwright 1969 and pers comm). Much the same pattern is to be seen in the earliest phase of Winklebury in northern Hampshire (Smith 1977). Here, the first phase occupation consisted of six circular houses, 42 four-post 'granaries', and three pits in an excavated area of 1.9 ha. Winklebury is considerably smaller than Balksbury (7.6 ha compared with 18.8 ha) and may be marginally later (7th–6th century). Its defences also differ in form. At Balksbury (Wainwright 1969) the rampart was of simple dump construction while at Winklebury (Robertson-Mackay 1977), a close-set timber palisade with rear anchor posts was backed by a slight bank 1 m or so high. This was much the same kind of defence structure that Wheeler proposed for the broadly contemporary enclosure at Lulworth (Dorset) (Wheeler 1953). Another fort relevant to the discussion is Harting Beacon (Sussex) for which a date in the 8th–6th century seems reasonable. The enclosed area of 10 ha was defended by a slight timber-faced rampart, and excavation (Bedwin 1978; 1979) showed it to have been sparsely occupied with four-post 'granaries'. Further afield the early enclosures of Ivinghoe Beacon (Bucks) (Cotton & Frere 1968) and Grimethorpe (Yorks) (Stead 1968) display many of the characteristics of the sites just mentioned.

While it would be unwise to generalize from so small an excavated sample, the early enclosures of the 8th–6th centuries, though varying in size and structure, do seem to have significant features in common: their defensive circuits imply a considerable expenditure of communal effort; circular buildings, presumably houses, occur but are few in number; four-post structures (? granaries) are comparatively numerous; there is much open space within the defences; and occupation debris is very sparse in quantity. At the very best we can assume that these enclosures are likely to have been built by a social group considerably larger than an extended family and may have served a communal purpose, perhaps as a safe store for surplus grain or livestock. If this is so it is possible that they were used only seasonally but these are all questions for further research.

Early enclosures of this kind seem to be quite numerous in southern Britain. On typological grounds we might include Walbury (Hants) (33 ha), Vespasian's Camp (Wilts) (16 ha), Bathampton Down (Avon) (32 ha), Martinsell Hill (Wilts) (13 ha), and, possibly, Scratchbury (Wilts) (15 ha) and the earliest phase of Hod Hill (Dorset) (22 ha), among the more likely candidates of a potentially long list.

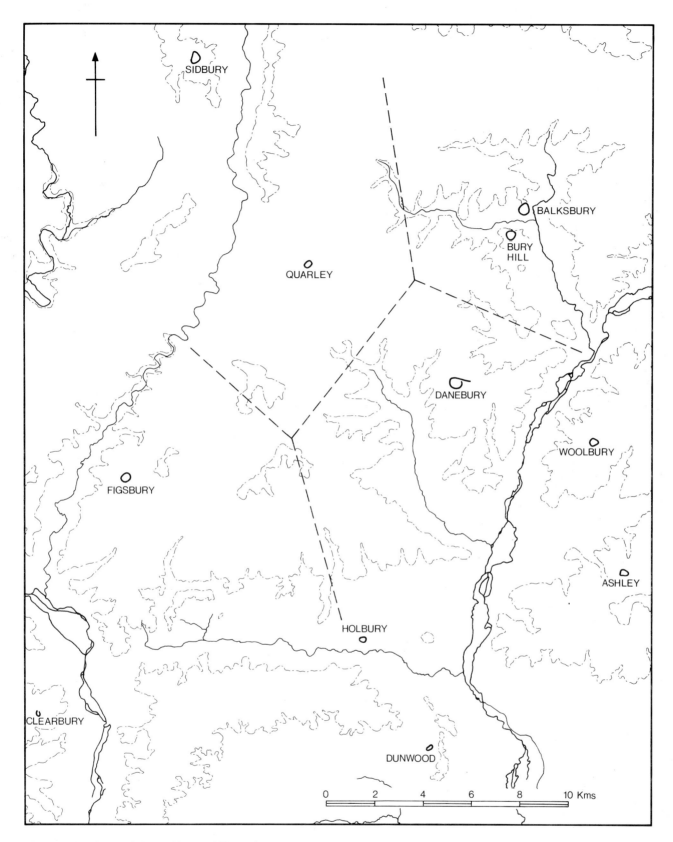

Fig 10.1 Danebury and the neighbouring hillforts showing hypothetical territories

Large enclosures of this kind seem to have gone out of vogue in the 6th–5th centuries when smaller and more strongly defended forts were being built. Of these, the earliest defence of Danebury is a good example, with its complex box-structured rampart and ditch enclosing 5.3 ha. Comparable sites in the neighbourhood are Quarley Hill (3.6 ha) (Hawkes 1939), Figsbury (6.3 ha) (Cunnington 1925), and possibly Bury Hill I (9 ha) (Hawkes 1940). Further afield Yarnbury I, Wilts (10.5 ha) (Cunnington 1933), Maiden Castle I, Dorset (7.5 ha) (Wheeler 1943), Chalbury, Dorset (4 ha) (Whitley 1943), and Blewburton, Berks (4.3 ha) (Harding 1976) provide tolerably well-dated examples. Danebury, Yarnbury I, Maiden Castle I, and Blewburton all have timber-structured ramparts, while Chalbury was walled with vertical dry stone work. At the other sites excavation has been on too small a scale to provide reliable evidence of rampart structure.

The close spacing of these early forts in central Wessex is striking. In the Danebury region, between the Rivers Test and Bourne, the four largely contemporary forts of Quarley, Figsbury, Bury, and Danebury are between 6 and 14 km apart (Fig 10.1). Each will have involved considerable expenditure of labour. At Danebury alone the rampart required 1700 timbers 5 m long for the principal verticals of the box structure, an equivalent quantity of cross-bracing, and the digging, carting, and dumping of over 20,000 cu m of chalk rubble.

Very little is known of the interior arrangements of these early forts since, apart from Danebury, only at Maiden Castle and Chalbury has an interior been sampled on a reasonable scale. At both sites sufficient was dug to show that the pattern was similar to that found at Danebury where occupation was clearly intense and included numerous circular houses, ample storage capacity both below and above ground, and domestic debris suggestive of a resident population. Without further programmes of excavation we cannot say how widespread was the intense use of these early forts. It remains a possibility that not all were as densely occupied.

After the 4th century BC some of the early forts went out of use while others continued to be inhabited undergoing a refurbishment of their defences and sometimes considerable enlargement. Yarnbury, Maiden Castle, and probably Hambledon Hill are examples of enlarged forts, while Danebury is typical of those whose defences were simply strengthened. In Wessex few new forts seem to have been built but in Surrey and west Kent, where early forts appear to be very rare, there is evidence to suggest that a number of new enclosures were built on virgin sites (Cunliffe 1982a).

The rise to dominance of selected sites at the expense of others is very well demonstrated in the Danebury region where Danebury itself was extensively remodelled and strengthened some time around 400 BC, while Figsbury, Quarley, and Bury Hill appear to have been abandoned. This pattern seems to be widespread in Wessex and Sussex (Cunliffe 1978a, 275–8) and implies an increasing degree of centralization. But the picture is evidently more complex and within the group of successful — or developed — hillforts we must anticipate a range of status from 'paramount' to 'vassal'. It is an intriguing possibility that status may have been demonstrated by such outward and visible signs as multiple earthworks and complex entrance features. If so sites like Danebury, Sidbury, and Yarnbury, in central Wessex, and Castle Ditches, Badbury, Hambledon, Maiden Castle, Cadbury Castle, Ham Hill, etc, further to the south and west, could be seen as paramount centres with the broadly

contemporary forts like Winklebury II, Beacon Hill, St Catherine's Hill, and possibly Woolbury serving as centres of lesser importance. The idea is of course purely speculative but Celtic societies are known to have been governed by rigid rules relating social status to form of habitation. There is, as yet, little archaeological data with which to test the hypothesis but the very considerable pit storage capacity at Danebury, Yarnbury, and Maiden Castle, three potential 'paramounts', contrasts dramatically with that at Winklebury and also, apparently, St Catherine's Hill (see below p 555). The question could further be explored by magnetic prospection. If the hypothesis is correct, Danebury would provide a model for a 'paramount' developed hillfort.

Before considering contemporary farmsteads, mention must be made of smaller fortified enclosures, 2 to 3 ha in extent, which lie on or close to the Tertiary soils of the Hampshire Basin, to the south of the Danebury region. If they are indeed Iron Age (and the point has not been demonstrated) then they are likely to represent another level in the social hierarchy. It remains a possibility that the socio-political organization of the predominantly sand and clay soils of the Tertiary deposits was quite differently arranged to that of the chalklands.

Below the defended hillforts, in the hierarchy of settlement, come the enclosed homesteads of Little Woodbury type which in Wessex are numerous. These fenced or ditched enclosures usually average 1-2 ha in extent and such excavation as there has been suggests that occupation was often continuous over much of the later 1st millennium BC (Table 95).

The survey of the Danebury region (published as Volume 3 in this series) gives some indication of the distribution of settlement of this kind. Fig 10.2 has been prepared, based on the survey evidence, to show those sites which, on air photographic or archaeological evidence, conform broadly to the Little Woodbury type. The data are necessarily very incomplete but in three areas, to the south of Danebury, east of Quarley, and west of Figsbury, the density of recognizable settlements is such that we may well be seeing a near total settlement pattern. Chronological and spatial uncertainties must warn against using these distributions to argue too tightly but certain generalizations are worth making.

South of Danebury, in the Wallop Brook area, the settlements all occupy like situations and are evenly spaced in relation to each other. They are all situated at about 1 km from the river and at a similar distance from each other on sloping ground between 50 and 100 m above sea level. If all are contemporary units, each would command about 200 ha of land, including well-watered river valley, good light arable soils, and unwatered higher downland — a more than adequate range to support an extended family unit.

The Quarley settlements are spaced at similar distances apart but lack permanent water supply and water meadows, which would have been a serious limitation to their farming requirements. It is, however, possible that their real territories included direct access to the valley of the River Bourne 4-5 km to the west. Since the distance would have been far too great to drive cattle on a daily basis, either the homesteads had the use of dispersed territories or cattle grazing was communal.

The settlement pattern on the west side of the Bourne, west of Figsbury, is similar to that south of Danebury but appears to include a rather greater range of enclosures, many of them sited on the higher chalkland away from the water. It may be that here we are seeing a dispersal of the farming functions to various foci within a single farming unit.

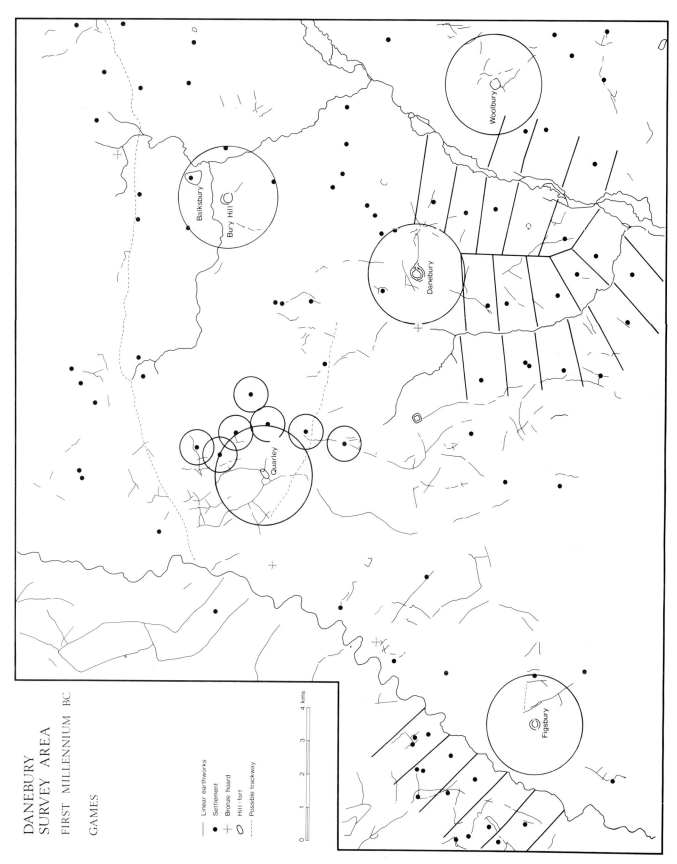

DANEBURY
SURVEY AREA
FIRST MILLENNIUM BC

GAMES

Linear earthworks
Settlement
Bronze hoard
Hill-fort
Possible trackway

0   1   2   3   4 kms

Woolbury

Balksbury
Bury Hill

Danebury

Quarley

Figsbury

Fig 10.2 The Danebury region settlement pattern

Table 95

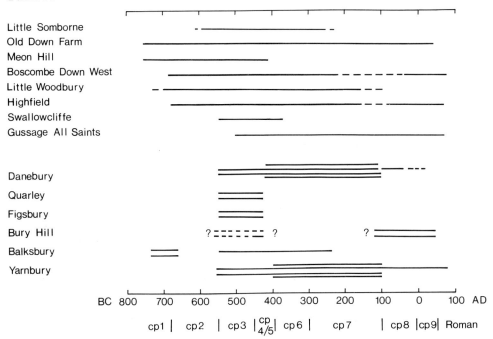

This brief consideration of the Danebury region's settlement pattern has raised more questions than it has answered, but in doing so it has shown how comparatively complex and varied the picture is and how difficult it is to make firm generalizations even in an area for which the data can be regarded as being of high quality. Problems raised here will be returned to again below. Another well-known settlement type — the banjo enclosure — has been recognized in the Danebury region. These enclosures, usually less than 1 ha in extent, seem to be small settlements, possibly single family units. Excavations at Hurstbourne Tarrant (Stead 1970), Bramdean (Perry 1974), and Micheldever Wood (Monk & Fasham 1980) show that they were in use during the later part of the Iron Age (our cps 7–9). Many of them continued into the Roman period, some being replaced by small villas. A cursory examination of their siting, in relation to Little Woodbury type settlements, suggests that they may occupy rather less favoured positions. If this is so, taken together with their late date, it is possible that they represent a late colonization of more marginal land. At any event they are likely to reflect a different socio-economic basis to the larger Little Woodbury type.

The end of intense occupation at Danebury, about 100 BC, seems to represent a fairly widespread phenomenon in southern Britain. A majority of the developed hillforts were abandoned at, or about, this time though some, like Danebury and probably Yarnbury, were used later on a much reduced scale. A few forts in the west either continued in use (eg Maiden Castle) or were refurbished after apparently being left abandoned (eg Cadbury Castle). That there was a major political, economic, and social dislocation in the early 1st century BC is clear. The reasons are complex but the change may well have been occasioned, in part, by the development of overseas trade in the wake of the Roman takeover of Gaul (Cunliffe 1982b, 49–51).

The situation in central Wessex at this time is still far from clear. With the developed hillforts no longer functioning as centres of power the most impressive settlements seem to have been the new multiple banked or ditched enclosures which were built at this time. One was inserted into the old hillfort at Bury Hill, others were built on hitherto undefended sites at Boscombe Down West (Richardson 1951) and Chisbury (Cunnington 1932). Virtually nothing is known of their socio-economic significance though they are likely to have been constructed for the emerging elite. It seems reasonable to suppose that old religious centres like the 'temple complex' in Danebury continued to be revered.

Changes can also be seen at the homestead level of settlement. Few of the Little Woodbury type farms survived but those that did seem to have been drastically modified. At Old Down Farm (Davies 1981) a much smaller, rectangular ditched enclosure, with small ancillary enclosures was built in the corner of the old settlement; similar reconstruction took place at Gussage All Saints (Wainwright 1979) while at Winnall Down conjoined rectangular enclosures were arranged along a road replacing the earlier settlement (Monk & Fasham 1980). Air photographic evidence suggests that this general pattern is quite widespread in Wessex. On the other hand the banjo enclosures continued in use largely unchanged. The implication, therefore, would seem to be that the old socio-economic system, manifest in the large Little Woodbury type settlement complexes, was replaced by one in which substantially smaller settlement units became the norm. Explanation of this change must await more extensive programmes of excavation.

Comparatively little is known of the Roman occupation of the Danebury region but three major roads cross the area and judging by the number of recorded villas it would seem that the landscape continued to be densely farmed. The coincidence of villas and Iron Age settlements strongly argues for a degree of land-holding continuity.

10.3 Subsistence economy

At the simplest level the archaeological record from Danebury shows the principal crops to have been spelt wheat and hulled six-row barley, with sporadic occurrences of emmer and bread/club wheat. Sheep/goat, cattle, pig, horse, dog, cat, and fowl are recorded. The landscape in the immediate vicinity of the fort, and in what may fairly be regarded as its territory between the rivers Bourne and Test, was thoroughly conducive to the efficient maintenance of this range. The river valleys provided ample water meadow for cattle, the upland chalk downs were suitable for flocks of sheep, while adequate pannage for pigs could have been obtained on the steeper hangers, the clay-capped hilltops, and the areas of denser forest supported by the tertiary clays to the south. The varieties of chalkland soils were well-suited to the crops produced, the wheat preferring the richer soils while the rather thinner soils of the chalk hilltops would have been quite adequate for barley growing. The analysis of the weeds of cultivation brought in with the crop (pp 488–9) show that the clay-capped hilltops and the river valleys were also cultivated.

The air photographic survey of the immediate environs of the fort shows the landscape to have been densely cultivated in the prehistoric period with fields coming right up to the Outer Earthwork. While it is impossible to demonstrate that the entire pattern is of Iron Age date, many of the blocks of fields seem to have been laid out in relation to linear boundaries, some of which were roads, which converge on the col 1 km east of Danebury. The linear earthwork, continuous with the outer earthwork of the fort, becomes part of this system (Vol 1, Fig 1.3). The col itself seems to have been a meeting point for tracks associated with an open, unploughed area. It is tempting to see this arrangement as one designed for the easy movement and collection of livestock.

The hillfort itself was provided with two enclosures: the earliest occupied the south side and was defined by the Middle Earthwork; the later encircled the fort and was delineated by the Outer Earthwork. In effect it enclosed an area of 5.3 ha all of which was within the protective range of defensive fire organized from the main rampart crest. The successive enclosures were thus admirably suited for the collection and protection of animals and were linked to the trackway network by the main linear earthwork, itself a double-ditched track for part of its length. Midway between the fort and the valley of the Test an almost continuous trackway passes an area occupied by small rectangular enclosures several of which appear to be contemporary with the track. The enclosures are about 1.5 km from the valley and from the fort and are therefore optimally sited to provide temporary corrals for cattle, being down between the fort and the water meadow.

Without an extensive programme of fieldwork and sample excavation any analysis of the land utilization pattern around Danebury must necessarily be on a very general level since contemporaneity of its various elements is almost impossible to demonstrate, but sufficient will have been said to indicate that the immediate environs of the fort seem to have been organized to facilitate the management of arable and pastoral farming direct from the fort.

An analysis of the plant remains has shown that the agricultural regime was based on the growing of spelt wheat and hulled six-row barley. The crop was brought to the site, already freed from the stalk, for threshing, storage, milling, and baking — all processes which can be attested in the archaeological record. It seems possible

Table 96   Pit: area ratios (no of pits per m²)

Danebury	1 : 11
Maiden Castle	1 : 14
Yarnbury	1 : 46 (depressed)
Winklebury	1 : 156
Gussage	1 : 20
Little Woodbury	1 : 39
Old Down Farm	1 : 78
Little Sombourne	1 : 93

that waste products from threshing and winnowing were mixed with barley to produce animal feed. This is an interesting reminder of the need to offer special care, at certain times during the year, for the flocks and herds. Indeed it has been argued, on the basis of the faunal remains, that the sheep and cattle were driven to the fort for lambing and calving. The corral space would have been well fitted to the purpose but it would have been necessary to have sufficient animal feed in store. Specially prepared barley and chaff mix, stored leaf fodder, and crusts of grain cleared out of storage pits, once they had been emptied of their useable contents, would all have provided a nourishing diet for beasts at this crucial time of the year.

An attempt to quantify the grain storage capacity of the fort will be offered below (pp 557–8). Here it is sufficient to draw attention to the fact that the density of storage pits in Danebury is considerable. In Table 96 we have prepared comparative pit:area ratios (PAR) for a number of sites. The figures have been arrived at simply by dividing the total area of the site excavated by the number of pits found in that area. Two assumptions are made: (a) that the duration of occupation is about the same for each site; (b) that the excavated area is typical of the settlement as a whole. To approximate more closely to (a) all pits earlier or later than the date range of Danebury cps 3–7 have been omitted. As far as can be judged assumption (b) is likely to hold good except in the case of Yarnbury where the excavation concentrated on the line of the silted earlier defences which would have been the least attractive area for the later pit diggers. The PAR for Yarnbury is therefore likely to be depressed.

It is evident that the 'paramount' developed hillforts of Danebury, Maiden Castle, and probably Yarnbury have a low PAR while the settlement sites are significantly higher. Winklebury appears to be an anomaly but until we know more of hillforts of this type it would be unwise to attempt an explanation. If the ratios for the settlements are averaged, then Danebury emerges with about five times the pit storage capacity per unit area when compared with contemporary settlements, and since the fort is about four times the area of the average settlement then its gross pit storage capacity is in the order of twenty times that of a contemporary farmstead. Without prejudice to the more detailed discussion to follow (pp 558–9) we can already see that the potential exists for Danebury to have stored surplus grain. Whether it did depends, among other factors, on the size of its resident population.

Among the other surpluses which may have been produced is wool. Throughout the life of the fort sheep greatly outnumbered all other domestic animals and there are sufficient faunal data to show that wool-production is likely to have been an important facet of sheep rearing. The considerable number of loom weights from the excavation, as well as the so-called 'weaving combs', are sufficient to show that cloth production was carried out on a large scale. Spindle whorls are not as frequent as might be expected (pp 438–9), an observation which, if substantiated, might suggest that a percentage of the yarn had been spun elsewhere and brought to the fort for weaving. A surplus of woollen fabric would have provided an eminently suitable commodity for exchange.

The question may reasonably be asked to what extent the large flocks were kept for their meat and wool yield or for the part they played in a more integrated agricultural regime. Sheep are enormously valuable as a means of manuring upland arable, unsuitable for pasturing cattle and inconveniently distant from settlements for the hand-carting of manure. With the spread of arable farming into upland regions, accompanied by rapid impoverishment through overuse of these thin soils, the need for adequate manuring must have become acute. It is a distinct possibility that the large flocks of sheep were developed to alleviate this problem and that surplus wool was a byproduct.

The study of both the animal and plant assemblages emphasizes the stability of the food producing regimes throughout the 500 years or so of the fort's existence. There appears to have been little recognizable change in crops and crop treatment, or in animal populations and their age structures. One observation however deserves note: whereas in the early and middle periods the only horse bones recorded are of mature individuals, in the later period immature beasts are well represented. The implication would seem to be that horses were being bred away from the fort in the early period but close by in the later. It is tempting to wonder whether the extensive linear ditch system which dominated the eastern half of the Danebury region, and was probably laid out in the late 2nd or early 1st millennium, may have been associated with large-scale horse ranching. Its gradual abandonment throughout the 1st millennium and the development of corrals around the fort could be related to a change in the methods of horse rearing; the speculation is, of course, entirely beyond proof. At Gussage All Saints and Longbridge Deverill only mature horses were found (Wainwright 1979, 189) and a similar picture seems to have been true of Old Down Farm (Davies 1981). Since all three sites span the early and late periods it would seem as though the evidence for horse breeding at Danebury in the late period sets the hillfort apart from the contemporary farmsteads.

Many of the interesting suggestions to emerge from an analysis of the faunal and floral remains from Danebury can only be expanded and tested in the light of comparisons with data of similar quality from other sites. The acquisition and publication of such data should be a priority.

10.4 Production, distribution, and exchange

Like essential foodstuffs, by far the greatest bulk of the raw materials used at Danebury would have been derived from the immediate vicinity of the fort. Timber for the construction of buildings and defences, together with wattles for walling and hurdle making, was cut from well-managed woodland, while straw and reeds for roofing (as well as basketry and matting) would have been readily available in the fields and water meadows. Clay was brought to the site in quantity and mixed in specially constructed conical pits to make daub for walls, ovens, and hearths. The same clay could also have been used for the manufacture of small objects like loom

Table 97   Quantities of bronze and iron by weight (gm) for each ceramic phase

	cp 1-3	cp 4-5	cp 6	cp 7-8
Bronze	30.0	1.4	14.0	348.4
Iron	4.6	91.2	103.1	898.9

weights and spindle whorls and, perhaps, also pottery. Animal carcasses, once stripped of meat, would have provided bone, horn, and sinew for tools and ornaments, as well as leather for a variety of uses. The expertise necessary for all these crafts was readily available in every Iron Age community and the acquisition of the necessary raw materials could have been organized on a family or even an individual basis.

Certain necessary raw materials had to be imported from much further afield through more complex but unknown mechanisms of exchange. A wide range of stone was needed, mainly for whetstones and quern stones. Analysis suggests that the great bulk of it (78%) was Upper and Lower Greensand, probably from the vicinity of Shaftesbury or Westbury 30–50 km to the north-west of Danebury. Tertiary sandstones from the Hampshire Basin, 10–40 km to the south, were the next most common (9.4%). Smaller quantities of gritstone (2.7%) were brought in from the Mendips, up to 80 km away, while small amounts of other stone, such as quartz conglomerates, limestones, and red sandstones also came from the west, from the Bristol region and possibly Devon. Since querns wear out there would have been a constant need for replacement.

Both iron and bronze must also have been imported (though the possibility of the limited local production of iron from pyrites should not be overlooked). In the later period (cp 7), iron was brought in in the form of currency bars which were cut up in the fort and forged into tools and weapons. A hoard of scrap iron found in 1979 shows that recycling was practised. How the iron was imported in the early period is less clear but in the absence of firm evidence for smelting (as opposed to forging) we must suppose that the metal arrived as ingots or finished items. Table 97 shows how little iron was being discarded or lost in the early period. The low figure does not necessarily represent the paucity of iron in use but simply implies that little was being abandoned. The greater loss in the later periods may in part reflect a decline in value brought about by more readily available supplies. The source of the raw iron has not yet been defined with precision but the Weald is thought to be a possibility.

That forging was taking place on site is suggested by the chopping up of currency bars and is demonstrated by the presence of slag and tuyère fragments. Analysis of the tools shows that some of the smiths were sufficiently skilled to select and treat metal to suit specific tool types.

Little is known of bronzeworking at Danebury. If one excludes the Hallstatt C hoard, the quantity discarded and lost is very small and consists largely of sheet fragments from vessels, bindings, and decorative fittings or ornaments (Table 97). Crucible fragments and tuyères indicate that casting was undertaken on site, presumably reusing local scrap. Analysis however, points to a distinctive alloy being employed for sheet bronzework.

The only other commodity which can be shown to have been imported on a large scale is salt. It was brought to the site, from the Hampshire and Dorset (?) coasts, in containers of briquetage, the quantity of which seems to increase significantly with time.

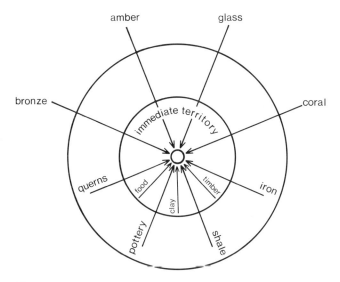

Fig 10.3 Diagram to illustrate imports to Danebury

a evidence of a storage capacity greater than that provided at normal homesteads and in excess of the potential needs of the dependent population
b signs of careful measurement
c evidence of the division of raw materials
d the presence of large-scale manufacturing activities
e a stable economy in which easily transportable surpluses could be produced

The question of storage capacity has already been raised and we have shown that, simply by pit counting, Danebury had about twenty times the pit storage capacity of the average contemporary homestead. It is worth examining the figures in more detail. Certain parameters have been considered above (Vol 1, pp 132–7) including average pit capacity in each phase, and in Table 98 potential capacity per year is estimated on the (unproven) assumption that pit life averaged ten years. Although we cannot be sure that all or even most of the pits were used for grain storage, or that the same percentage were used for grain storage in each phase, we have no means of examining the problem further. At best we may accept the figures as reflecting the maximum grain storage capacity of the pits, bearing in mind the effects on the totals of using a different estimate for pit life.

Even more uncertainties emerge when the potential storage capacity of the post structures is considered, not least because the precise dating of the types is uncertain; but assuming that we can divide them roughly into an early-middle period group (cps 1–3/4–5) and a late period group (cps 6 and 7), and allowing useable storage height to be 2 m, then certain estimates for total storage capacity can be offered (Table 99).

On the untestable assumption that the useable life of a post structure was twenty years, some comparison can be offered between the two sets of figures (Table 100).

Given all the provisos and uncertainties the figures allow the possibility that the potential (maximum) grain storage capacity remained much the same throughout the life of the fort, the only significant difference being a change in emphasis towards above-ground storage in the later period. Taken at its face value this could simply mean a change in storage technology, but if the assumption is made that seed corn was stored below ground and consumption corn above then more complex explanations are demanded. It could, for example, be argued that in the early and middle periods the fort was used primarily to store the seed corn of the surrounding rural community while in the later period surplus grain for exchange was collected in quantity. Attractive though this type of speculation is, when it is remembered that we cannot even be sure that the post structures were granaries, let alone what the preferred storage conditions for each type of grain were, then the weakness of

Of the manufactured goods brought in from outside the territory we may list fine haematite-coated pottery imported from the Salisbury region in ceramic phase 3, a range of vessels from the Nadder Valley in Wiltshire dating to ceramic phase 7, and a very few pots from the West Country. Later, in the 1st century BC (cp 8), Italian amphorae and vessels made in the vicinity of Poole harbour found their way to the fort. Exotic ornaments are understandably rare but include a few items of Kimmeridge shale, and beads of glass, amber, and coral.

The commodities brought into Danebury can therefore be divided into three groups: those from the immediate territory; those from adjacent territories up to *c* 80 km from the site; and exotic materials from further afield (Fig 10.3). It is only to be expected that the quantity imported diminishes as the distance of the source increases.

One model for explaining the function of developed hillforts like Danebury is to suppose that they served as redistribution centres for their territories, places where, by means of a variety of social mechanisms, local products in surplus were accumulated and exchanged for raw materials brought in from outside the territory, and for manufactured goods which would not otherwise have been accessible. Something will be said later of the possible social systems within which such exchange could have taken place; here we must consider what evidence there is to support the hypothesis.

If Danebury had served as a redistribution centre we would expect to find:

Table 98 Pit storage capacities assuming ten-year pit life

a Phase	b duration (yrs)	c no of pits excavated	d estimated total no of pits (= c × 4.7)	e no of pits per yr	f total capacity (cu m)	g total annual capacity (cu m)
cp 1-3	100	605	2844	284	6213	621
cp 4-5	50	162	761	76	1852	370
cp 6	100	114	536	54	1495	150
cp 7	200	181	851	86	3699	185

Table 99 Granary capacity

a phase	b duration (yrs)	c types	d nos excavated	e estimated total (= d × 4.7)	f av floor area (sq m)	g volume (= f × 2m)	h total annual capacity (cu m)
cp 1-3/4-5	150	CEF	47	221	6.25	12.5	368
cp 6-7	300	ABGHJ	90	423	21.8	10.89	615
		D	2	9	20.25	40.5	24

whatever tissue of compossibilities we may construct becomes evident.

What is relevant to the present argument is that the potential grain storage capacity of Danebury is very considerable. Even allowing one-twentieth to be seed corn, 860 cu m per year would feed 1600 people (at 12–14 bushels per person: 1 cu m =27.5 bushels), a figure far in excess of the estimated resident population (below, p 560). Moreover, if yield is asessed at one cu m per acre (0.42 ha), and allowing for only two-thirds of the arable to be under cultivation at any one time, then the total arable would be about 540 ha which would suggest a territory covering three or four times that area. Remembering that the maximum total territory of the average farmstead was 200 ha, something of the order of magnitude can be perceived. A productive territory of 2,000 ha (20 sq km) around Danebury would necessarily include a number of contemporary farms. In other words the maximum storage capacity at Danebury could not have been filled unless a tithe of the produce of neighbouring farms was included. Given all the imperfections and dangers inherent in arguments of this kind, it would seem fair to conclude that grain storage at Danebury is likely to have been considerably in excess of the needs of the resident community and probably represents provision for the accumulated surplus of neighbouring farms.

The argument above has been conducted on the unlikely assumption that all the storage capacity of the site was devoted to grain. What else was stored, and in what quantity, remains unclear, but bearing in mind the unusually large number of loom weights found and the dominance of sheep among the faunal remains, there could well have been an accumulated surplus of woollen goods. The corral space around the fort would also have allowed livestock to be assembled for slaughter or redistribution. All of these aspects of the archaeological record — massive storage capacity, intense production of woollen fabrics, and extensive corraling facilities — serve to distinguish the fort from other contemporary sites.

The question of careful measurement is difficult to approach with any assurance but the collection of finely finished stone weights, which broadly conform to multiples of a Celtic pound standard, demonstrate that weight measurement was practised at Danebury. Similar weights have been found at the hillfort of Winklebury

(Smith 1977, 108) but are otherwise unknown from the published farmsteads of Wessex.

The currency bar hoard is evidence for the standardization of raw iron in ingots of roughly uniform weight. It may be relevant to recall that, of the bars listed by Allen (1968), about half the locations are in hillforts. Given the number, area, and range of Iron Age sites examined this reflects a distinct bias towards fortified sites. A final observation which may be relevant here is that there appears to be a degree of standardization among pit volumes. This suggestion is based on a clumping of base diameter measurements. A more thorough analysis, accompanied by statistical testing, is now underway. If the suggestion is substantiated, then it would imply that the volume of stored commodities might have been standardized thus making the contents of each pit of comparable value. This line of approach is clearly one of considerable interest and may prove to be of relevance on a more general level.

From this brief survey it can be seen that there is some evidence to suggest that careful measurement may well have been understood and practised at Danebury. The fact that, on present showing, stone weights and currency bars seem to be concentrated at hillforts may be thought to emphasize the special functions centred on these sites.

If exchange was practised on a large scale at Danebury one might expect to find evidence that raw materials and other commodities were being divided into smaller portions within the fort. That currency bars were being cut up need not be interpreted in this way but the presence of comparatively large quantities of briquetage salt containers is of some relevance. Salt was imported to the site from the Hampshire/Dorset coast packed in containers most of which were of cylindrical type, cut vertically so that the two halves would come apart exposing the compacted salt cake. This somewhat elaborate arrangement may have been designed to allow the contents of a single container to be halved. While fragments of briquetage have been found on farmstead sites (though mainly in unrecorded quantities) the sheer volume from Danebury strongly suggests that the fort was in direct receipt of quantities of salt and may therefore have been a centre from which the commodity was distributed. The hypothesis can only be tested quantitatively and at present comparative data are not available.

The last two criteria listed above (p 557)—the presence of large-scale manufacturing activities and the existence of a constant supply of easily transportable surplus goods — are both satisfied by the evidence from Danebury. The manufacture of iron tools and weapons and bronze items is well attested; the tool kit shows that elaborate carpentry was practised; there is ample evidence of weaving on a large scale and of spinning, and it is possible that some pottery was also being made in the fort. The extent to which other activities, such as

Table 100 Potential grain storage capacity

	Pits annual capacity (cu m)	Post structures annual capacity (cu m)	Total (cu m)
cp 1-3/4-5	538	368	906
cp 6/7	173	639	812

leatherwork, basketery, dyeing, and craft work of a similar kind, were being undertaken is beyond recovery. Surplus in the form of woollen fabrics, leather goods, corn, and animals could easily have been produced and stored for subsequent exchange.

In summary, of the criteria one would expect to be met if Danebury had served as a redistribution centre, all can be satisfied by the archaeological evidence. This does not, of course, prove that Danebury functioned in this way; it merely allows the hypothesis to be put forward with some assurance. The only feasible way to test the matter further is quantitatively in relation to the archaeological record of sites that may be supposed to occupy a different socio-economic level in the settlement hierarchy. Data of adequate quality are not yet available; their acquisition and publication should be a research priority.

The mechanisms by which exchange was effected, and the manner in which the processes were embedded in the social system of the larger community, are beyond recovery but some speculations will be indulged in below. Here it is sufficient to emphasize that the bulk of necessities which could not be produced in the immediate territory of the fort, ie querns, fine pottery, salt, and iron, could have been obtained directly from neighbouring 'paramount' developed hillforts in whose domains supplies were available. In other words, a simple system of reciprocal exchange between 'paramounts' would have been sufficient to account for the products reaching Danebury for redistribution into its own social network. Small quantities of luxuries, such as bronze, rare materials for ornaments, and the contents of the 'Glastonbury' type pots, could have reached the fort through gift exchange mechanisms. There is no need to suppose that complex systems of long distance trade were in operation at this time.

10.5 Society and ranking

The occupation of Danebury shows no definite break between c 550 and c 100 BC, and as the analyses of the animal bones and seed remains indicate, the subsistence economy changed little throughout four or five centuries, apart from a shift in the type of storage provisions in use. There were, however, other areas of significant change. Sometime about 400 BC the defences were considerably improved and strengthened after which the main (east) gate continued to be modified on an increasingly grandiose scale, while, in parallel, there was a marked upsurge in activity reflected in a greatly increased quantity of detritus of all kinds. Taken together the evidence suggests that the status of the fort became enhanced as its productive capacity increased. As we have seen, these processes, compared to the evidence from other forts in the area, suggest that Danebury rose to dominance in its natural geographical territory, between the Test and the Bourne, and may have held a position of prominence within an even larger region (Fig 10.4).

We might reasonably ask what tangible evidence of status there is at Danebury. The collection of artefacts is not particularly revealing but building CS8 yielded a fine collection of bronze fittings for horse gear, building CS20 produced a pair of linch pins, building CS22 contained a hoard of currency bars, while, in a house excavated nearby in 1979, another collection of ironwork, including a pair of iron cauldron hooks, was found. Add to this the scraps of bronze from small vessels and cauldrons and the fine La Tène I fibula, and the principal elements of wealth and status are assembled. There is little in the

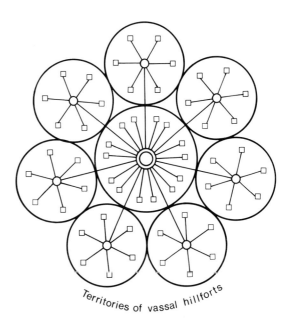

Fig 10.4 *Model for the relationship of Danebury to neighbouring settlements*

collection to indicate a significant difference between Danebury and neighbouring settlements. Old Down Farm produced a decorated bronze strap junction and two linch pins while another strap junction came from Bury Hill. Further afield, at Gussage All Saints, an accumulation of founder's debris must have represented the large-scale production of a range of bronze horse and chariot fittings. It is not an unreasonable assumption, therefore, that elaborately adorned horses and chariots were owned by the social class residing in both farmsteads of Little Woodbury type and hillforts. The trappings of the feast, the bronze cauldrons and iron cauldron hooks, are much less frequently found but it seems unlikely that they were insignia of status any more exclusive than the chariot and chariot team, nor are the personal ornaments of bronze, glass, shale, and amber necessarily an indication of exceptional prowess. In short, there is nothing among the surviving material culture of Danebury to indicate the presence of an individual or family of pre-eminent status. The absence of evidence need not, of course, mean that such a person was not present.

Among the circular buildings revealed in the excavated area there are two distinct size groups: 6–7 m in diameter and 8–9 m in diameter. The large buildings are usually found singly, though sometimes in association with other structures, while the smaller buildings have been found in rows. The contrast between the two arrangements is particularly striking when the last structural phases, exposed in the 1973–5 and the 1977–8 areas, are compared. The implication must surely be that we are dealing with two different kinds of social manifestation, the larger, isolated houses of 1977–8 representing the residence of people whose status was greater than that of those occupying the smaller houses in the row excavated in 1973–5. Another possibility worth considering is that all the buildings in the lee of the rampart (an area liable to flood during storms) were subsidiary in status and/or function to houses built on the shoulder of the hill, like buildings CS23 and CS24. Both were delineated by gullies which might be considered to be a mark of rank. Clearly the complexity of the development in the two sample areas, and the fact that the total sample is only a small part of the sheltered circumference of the fort, is a warning against constructing over-ambitious social models, however attractive such a pastime might be.

Mention of houses raises the vexed question of population. There is a considerable literature, some of it quite useful, reflecting upon the problems of reconstructing settlement population from archaeological evidence (a critical summary is to be found in Hassan 1981). Two formulae are currently in vogue. The first, using data derived from rural settlement in south-west Asia, suggests that

$$\text{population} = 146\sqrt{A}$$

where A is the total area of the settlement. Using this approach the total population of Danebury at any period would be 335.

The second formula, derived from comparative data from a wide range of non-industrialized societies, uses house area. It claims that

$$\text{population} = \frac{A}{10\text{m}^2}$$

where A is the total area of all houses expressed in metres. Now if it is assumed that all houses at Danebury lie in the circumference zone, 18.9% of which has been excavated, and that within the excavated area there were ten houses in use in the late period, the total number of houses in the fort at that time would be 53, assuming that the excavated sample is representative of the overall situation. Given that the average diameter of a house is 7 m (area 38.5 m^2) the total population would be 204. Since this assumes that there were no houses in the centre of the fort, which is unlikely, the figure must be regarded as a minimum estimate.

The calculations are, of course, based on a multitude of assumptions but that the two totally different methods (using different preconceptions) arrive at comparable figures is reassuring.

Another way to approach the problem is in terms of the grain storage capacity of the site. An average figure for the potential annual grain storage capacity is 860 cu m. Allowing one-twentieth to be seed corn and estimating that one cu m could feed two people per year, the absolute maximum population which could have been supported would be just over 1600. Now since many of the pits and 'granaries' would have been used for a variety of purposes other than grain storage, and since it is likely that a percentage of the stored grain represented surplus for exchange, the actual grain available for consumption by the residents would have been very considerably less than the estimated maximum, and the number of occupants would have been well below 1600. Playing with parameters in this way would point to a figure of 300–400 as being a reasonable guess — but it is only a guess. It is difficult to see how a more reliable figure could ever be arrived at.

The excavation has so far yielded skeletal remains representing about 70 individuals, most of which were discovered in pits. Comparatively few were complete burials. The analysis of the burial data makes explicit two points of prime interest: burial within the fort (less than one body per year) reflects only a small percentage of the total population; and the frequent occurrence of parts of bodies and isolated bones strongly suggests that deposition in pits was often the last stage of a complex ritual which in all probability involved a period of excarnation. If the exposure of the body was the normal method of disposing of the dead it would explain why cemeteries are unknown in central southern Britain throughout the latter part of the 1st millennium. The human remains discovered in pits must represent a range of behaviour including the clearing away of skeletal remains after the symbolic process of excarnation was complete, the disposal of bodies deprived of normal burial honours, and the deposition of whole or part bodies for ritual reasons such as the propitiation of the gods. The archaeological record has yielded examples which can be interpreted as the products of all these activities. How, if at all, the pattern of burial at Danebury differs from that found on other settlements it is difficult to say in the absence of comparative recorded data, but the fact that adult females are under-represented in the Danebury sample (only 17.2%), as are children under the age of 8, while quite the reverse is true of the burial record from Gussage All Saints, at least hints that burial patterns may relate to the social status of the site.

There is no archaeological evidence from Danebury to suggest that the hill possessed any unusual significance as a place of burial, but towards the centre of the site were four rectangular structures which may have been temples or shrines. The buildings were prominently sited, facing the entrance, on what would have appeared to be the crest of the hill when viewed from the gate. Although dating evidence is sparse, the buildings were erected at different times and there seems always to have been at least one in use throughout much of the period of occupation, the last possibly continuing after intensive settlement had ceased c 100 BC. Similar shrines are known in the hillforts of Maiden Castle and Cadbury and the phenomenon may prove to be widespread on sites of this kind. The continuation of religious observance at Maiden Castle, where a masonry temple was built in the Roman period, is a reminder that the sanctity of old rural shrines may well have lived on to be revived in Roman times. Shrines in hillforts reflect another aspect of the complex social functions which many of these sites performed.

The very construction of the fort implies the wielding of a high degree of coercive power, though we remain totally ignorant of the manner in which the population was manipulated. The communal will of the people, a theocracy, or a dominant aristocracy are all possible mechanisms of direction. What is clear is that, once constructed, the fort was maintained and improved, while the interior was organized into functionally discrete zones which remained in similar use for decades. In the southern part of the site the creation of parallel roads fronted by rows of granaries, themselves often rebuilt, is a striking indication of the control which society exercised over its space.

There is no direct internal evidence to demonstrate the nature of the social organization within the fort or between the fort dwellers and the neighbouring homesteads, but the documentary evidence reflecting on Celtic social structure is potentially revealing if only on the level of model building. The most complete evidence we have of a Celtic society refers to the situation in Ireland in the early 1st millennium AD. The principal unit of both territory and administration was the *tuath*, best translated as 'tribe', but also applied to the land the tribe inhabited. The *tuath* was ruled by a king (*rí*) who was bound by ties of personal allegiance to a higher king (*ruiri*) who in turn owed allegiance to a paramount king (*rí ruirech*). Below the king in status were the noble warriors (*flaithi*) and the skilled men (*oes dána*). These were craftsmen, poets, lawyers, teachers, and keepers of the tribal histories, all of whom enjoyed the patronage of the *flaithi* and the *rí*. Lower down the social hierarchy were the ordinary freemen (*grád féne*) who worked the land and paid a tithe of their produce to the king. Most of the freemen were *céle* who placed themselves in a state of voluntary clientship to the nobles.

Clientship (*célsine*) provided the system of production and exchange by which society was articulated. In its simplest form the noble provided cattle for the use of his client in return for a rent made up of an agreed tithe of products and of service: the client in return also enjoyed the protection of his lord. The Irish law tracts provide considerable detail of the different kinds of clientship and lay down precise details of the rent a lord would be eligible to receive. For example, in one kind of clientship agreement, for the use of 24 cows, the client would have to pay annually a fat cow, a salt pig, eight sacks of malt, a sack of wheat, and three handfuls of rush candles. Such a system, therefore, divided the nobility from the freeman farmers who formed the productive class of society.

Land was owned not by an individual but by the extended family (*derbfine*) — a family of four generations constituting the descendents of a common great-grandfather. A number of families of this kind made up the tribe.

The situation in Wales is rather less certain because the surviving documents refer to a later period but there appears to have been much in common with Irish society. The family group (*cenedl*) was a four generation kin group, a number of which constituted a tribe (*cantref*) which was ruled by a king (*brenin*). One significant difference was that the king was responsible for the maintenance of a considerable court performing a range of judicial and administrative functions.

It is only to be expected that Celtic social structure will have differed considerably from place to place and time to time, and to apply any one historical model to the archaeological evidence of another place is a dangerous exercise. Nonetheless, it may be thought to be marginally more relevant then considering African or Asian analogies.

The Irish model provides an interesting yardstick against which to compare the archaeological evidence for central southern Britain. Settlement sites of Little Woodbury type have a storage capacity adequate to support an extended family group of 40–80 individuals, which is a reasonable estimate for the size of a *derbfine*, although one might doubt whether a community of that size could be accomodated in an enclosure of 1–2 ha. There is, however, no need to suppose that all nuclear families of the kin resided together — indeed the variety in the settlement pattern suggests otherwise — but the 'home farm' may have been the social and residential centre of the kin group where surplus food was gathered and stored.

Now, if all farmsteads of Little Woodbury type were agricultural centres worked by freemen of the *grád féne* class, where did the nobility reside? One possibility is that they, together with the king, occupied the hillfort. The estimated population of 300–400 would be in keeping with such a suggestion while the excessive grain storage capacity and provision for corraling animals would be appropriate to receiving a tithe of grain and redistributing cattle. In such a model the hillfort community would be totally divorced from day-to-day agricultural activities. Not all of the nobility need have lived within the fort; some may have occupied lesser forts such as Lockleys and Dunwood or lived within the ramparts of earlier hillforts like Balksbury and Winklebury, the defences representing a mark of status.

The hypothesis has certain attractions. The analysis of the floral data has shown that the corn coming into the enclosure was grown in a variety of environments distant from the fort and had already been partially processed by

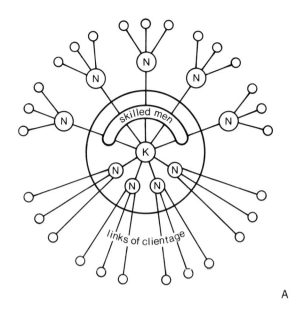

A

K king
N noble
O freemen farmers

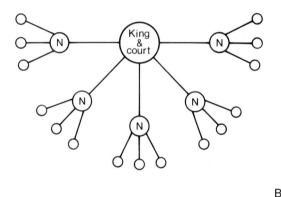

B

Fig 10.5 Models for the possible social structures relating to Danebury

being removed from the stalk. We have also seen that there is evidence of weighing, a necessary facility if tithes were to be collected. A wide range of craft skills was also being practised, while the existence of shrines would indicate the presence of a religious elite. In other words the archaeological evidence is consistent with the view that Danebury was occupied by the king, the nobility, and the skilled men (*oes dána*).

The alternative view, that strongly defended developed hillforts like Danebury were the residences only of kings and their immediate entourage, with the nobility living in other less pretentious hillforts, is a possibility. It would require the tribe to be a much larger group, which is not impossible, but would imply that the nobility were few in number, which seems unlikely. Another alternative is that the nobility lived in some or all of the settlements of Little Woodbury type with their freemen clients occupying less imposing settlements. Against this it might be argued that Little Woodbury settlements seem to be too numerous for them all to have been the seats of nobility. They are also closely related to agricultural production, and, if only some were nobles' households, one might expect an obvious mark of distinction which on present evidence is not now apparent. If, then, the social

561

organization dependent upon Danebury was comparable to that described in the Irish literature, the likely structure can be summed up as in Fig 10.5a.

Too close an adherence to the Irish pattern may be unwise. It would, on the archaeological evidence available, be possible to produce a simpler social model which would see the hillfort as the residence of a king and his followers, including the skilled men appropriate to his status, the nobility living in the surrounding farms of Little Woodbury type working the land with the aid of their families and such slaves as they may have owned. Below them would have come freemen farmers of lower social status who may have been bound to the noble farmers by ties of clientage in much the same way as they were in the Irish system. These farmers might have lived in close proximity to the noble or in separate establishments like the banjo enclosures. Fig 10.5b represents such an arrangement. A scheme of this kind would allow skilled specialist craftsmen to practise at the farms of the nobility and would thus accomodate the evidence for specialist bronze casting found at Gussage All Saints.

If the agricultural base was universal to all freemen classes then the distinction between noble and non-noble may well be less evident in the archaeological record, though it might, of course, be manifest in the greater storage capacity of a noble farmer's establishment.

It is worth mentioning a third possibility — that the king lived in an establishment outside the fort, while the inhabitants of the fort provided specialist functions for the community at large, attending to the gods, overseeing the processes of production and exchange, and guarding the society's surplus. While theoretically possible such an arrangement would be in conflict with what is known of Celtic society and need not be seriously entertained.

The two preferred models put forward above are the best that can be offered on the available evidence. Neither need be a close approximation to the real situation, which may, anyway, have changed significantly throughout the life of the fort. Whether it is within the scope of the archaeological evidence to allow us to go further it is difficult to say; much will depend upon the results of current and future excavations.

10.6   The dynamics of change

Danebury was in active occupation for about four and a half centuries during which time there were significant changes. In this section we will examine some of the possible causes of change and consider the way in which society developed.

The first question to raise is the degree to which the inhabitants of the fort, and their dependents, considered themselves to belong to a larger ethnic group. One of the ways to approach the problem is by considering the symbols which the group displayed in relation to those of adjacent groups. In reality few symbols survive in the archaeological record except in the form of preferred decoration on pottery, and there can be no assurance that pottery decoration always, or even sometimes, reflected on ethnicity. It is, nonetheless, interesting to speculate that it may have done and to explore the potential implications of such a hypothesis to Danebury. In the early period of occupation (550–450 BC) Danebury and the contemporary sites of Figsbury, Quarley, and Meon Hill were in receipt of high-quality decorated ware, covered with a haematite slip, of a kind thought to have been produced in the Salisbury region. The quantities found in these sites, all of which lie between the Rivers Bourne and Test, is considerable, but east of the Test quantities are negligible. Although this may be an accident of discovery, taken at face value it suggests that the Test may have formed a boundary beyond which the pottery was not distributed. If so then at this time Danebury would have been firmly within a Wiltshire-centred territory.

By the time that decorated saucepan pottery was coming into vogue (300–100 BC) it is evident that a major reorientation had taken place. Although a small quantity of Wiltshire-made vessels was reaching the site, the vast bulk of the pottery was locally made, adopting decorative motifs common in the zone spreading from the Bourne to the Adur and from the sea north to the Kennet-Thames Valley. In other words, if decorated pottery is symbolic of ethnicity, then Danebury had changed its allegiance some time in the 4th century from the west to the east.

It may possibly be significant that it was at about this time that Danebury seems to have become dominant in its immediate territory, with the demise of Figsbury, Quarley, and possibly Bury Hill, and to have undergone considerable refurbishment of its defences. A single major socio-political upheaval about 400 BC could explain all these phenomena.

A hillfort incorporates two concepts: that of enclosure and that of defence. Enclosure may have symbolic connotations or may reflect status but the need for defence must imply that society was in a state of stress. The evolution of the hillfort phenomenon in central southern Britain strongly suggests that the stress conditions intensified with time, the developed hillforts becoming increasingly more massively defended with complex entrance earthworks and multivallation. Danebury provides a good example of these processes at work. Moreover, the east entrance in its final stage seems to have been designed to be held by men, armed with slings, against frontal attack. The quantity of sling stones in the entrance passage and stored in pits just inside the gate shows that the defenders had ample supplies of ammunition at the ready.

Other signs of aggression are not plentiful. A few spears, a sword hilt guard, a chape, and fragments of scabbard binding are all that survives of the arms and armour of the defenders (other than sling stones), but several of the skeletons buried within the fort bear signs of sword blows and spear thrusts. Nor should the two charnel pits be overlooked as potential evidence of conflict.

Against this archaeological background must be viewed the copious literature, classical, Welsh, and Irish, which together makes clear that raiding was a normal facet of the Celtic social system. It would be fair to say that in much of the Celtic world warfare was endemic. In central southern Britain the evidence suggests that warfare intensified as the 1st millennium progressed.

A likely cause for aggression in primitive society is stress brought about by a population reaching the holding capacity of its territory. The evidence from several parts of Britain is strongly suggestive of a significant population increase in the Iron Age (Cunliffe 1978b) while in the Danebury region, as we have seen, the landscape is densely packed with settlement. The data are, therefore, consistent with the hypothesis of a rapidly increasing population and the view that in some areas the holding capacity may have been reached. Supporting evidence is difficult to obtain but the suggestion has been put forward above (p 506) that the animal population was also showing symptoms of stress which could be explained if the agricultural regime was coming under pressure from over-production or soil fatigue resulting from long-term mismanagement. A closer analysis of animal pathology may provide further insights.

The picture emerges of a potentially unstable society in a state of stress. At Danebury the burning of the main gate, the two charnel pits, and the abandonment of the site as an intensively occupied settlement, all happening at about 100 BC, are clear evidence that, even if the events were not exactly contemporary, stress had reached such a point that at least one long-established socio-political centre collapsed and with it the systems dependent upon it. A general survey of the evidence from other parts of southern Britain suggests that a similar collapse may have been widely experienced.

The causes of the breakdown of the old system are no doubt complex. They may well lie solely within the tensions and instabilities within the society but there may have been some external stimulus to act as a catalyst. The immigration of settlers from the Belgic area of Gaul into the lower Thames valley and the opening up of long distance trade contacts with the Roman world through ports like Hengistbury Head are likely to have had far-reaching effects on central southern Britain. It may be that the new social and economic systems that were introduced into eastern Britain caused sufficient disruption for the ripples to topple the unstable Wessex system. Alternatively the creation of new foreign markets eager for products like slaves may have led to a spate of slave raiding sufficient to destroy the tenuous constraints that, hitherto, had maintained the equilibrium. At any event the old order passed, the social system readjusted, and as a consequence hillforts like Danebury passed gently into oblivion.

The writer is well aware that much in this section is purely speculative and that alternative explanations have not been fully explored, but the intention has been to parade some of the broader implications of the Danebury evidence. Rather than serve as a conclusion let it be the opening salvo of a continuing debate.

Bibliography

Allen, D F, 1968 Iron currency bars in Britain, *Proc Prehist Soc*, **33**, 307–35

Bedwin, O, 1978 Excavations inside Harting Beacon hill-fort 1976, *Sussex Archaeol Collect*, **116**, 225–40

————, 1979 Excavations at Harting Beacon, West Sussex, second season, 1977, *ibid*, **117**, 21–36

Cotton, M A, & Frere, S S, 1968 Ivinghoe Beacon excavations 1963–5, *Rec Buckinghamshire*, **18**, 187–260

Cunliffe, B W, 1978a *Iron Age communities in Britain*, 2 edn

————, 1978b Settlement and population in the British Iron Age. Some facts, figures and fantasies, in *Lowland Iron Age communities in Europe* (eds B W Cunliffe & R T Rowley), 3–24

————, 1982a Social and economic development in Kent in the pre-Roman Iron Age, in *Archaeology in Kent to AD 1500* (ed P E Leach), 40–50

————, 1982b Settlement hierarchy and social change in southern Britain in the Iron Age, *Analecta Praeh Leidensia*, forthcoming

Cunnington, M E, 1925 Figsbury Rings: an account of excavations in 1924, *Wiltshire Archaeol Mag*, **43**, 48–58

————, 1932 Chisbury Camp, *ibid*, **46**, 4–7

————, 1933 Excavations in Yarnbury Castle Camp 1932, *ibid*, **46**, 198–213

Davies, S M, 1981 Excavations at Old Down Farm, Andover. Part 2: prehistoric and Roman, *Proc Hampshire Fld Club Archaeol Soc*, **37**, 81–164

Harding, D W, 1976 Blewburton Hill, Berkshire, in *Hillforts. Later prehistoric earthworks in Britain and Ireland* (ed D W Harding), 133–46

Hassan, F A, 1981 *Prehistoric demography*

Hawkes, C F C, 1939 The excavations at Quarley Hill, 1938, *Proc Hampshire Fld Club Archaeol Soc*, **14**, 136–94

————, 1940 The excavations at Bury Hill, 1939, *ibid*, **14**, 291–337

Monk, M A, & Fasham, P J, 1980 Carbonized plant remains from two Iron Age sites in Central Hampshire, *Proc Prehist Soc*, **46**, 321–44

Perry, B T, 1974 Excavations at Bramdean, Hampshire, 1965 and 1966, and a discussion of similar sites in southern England, *Proc Hampshire Fld Club Archaeol Soc*, **29**, 41–77

Renfrew, C, 1973 Monuments, mobilisation and social organisation in Neolithic Wessex, in *The explanation of culture change* (ed C Renfrew), 539–58

Richardson, K M, 1951 The excavation of Iron Age villages on Boscombe Down West, *Wiltshire Archaeol Mag*, **54**, 123–68

Robertson-Mackay, R, 1977 The defences of the Iron Age hill-fort at Winklebury, Basingstoke, Hampshire, *Proc Prehist Soc*, **43**, 131–54

Smith, K, 1977 The excavation of Winklebury Camp, Basingstoke, Hampshire, *ibid*, **43**, 31–129

Stead, I M, 1968 An Iron Age hill-fort at Grimthorpe, Yorkshire, England, *ibid*, **34**, 148–90

————, 1970 Excavation in Blagden Copse, Hurstbourne Tarrant, Hampshire, 1967, *Proc Hampshire Fld Club Archaeol Soc*, **23**, 81–9

Wainwright, G J, 1969 The excavations at Balksbury Camp, Andover, Hants, *ibid*, **26**, 21–55

————, 1979 *Gussage All Saints. An Iron Age settlement in Dorset*

Wheeler, R E M, 1943 *Maiden Castle, Dorset*

————, 1953 An Early Iron Age 'beach-head' at Lulworth, Dorset, *Antiq J*, **33**, 1–13

Whitley, M, 1943 Excavations at Chalbury Camp, Dorset, 1939, *ibid*, **23**, 98–121

phases 237, 238, 549–50; social hierarchy 552, 561–2; soils 1, 3, 14; stratified sequences 43–5, 157, 167, 172; structural elements see buildings, houses, post–built structures; survey of region 8, 550–4, 551, 553; territory 259, 475, 550–5, 551, 562; trackways 4, 21–2, 26; trade 544, 556; trenching of 5, 14, 49

daub 41, 56, 62, 63, 65, 74, 76, 110–15, 111, 112, 118, 146, 148, 438, M3:D1–G9; baked clay 70, 110; with burials 450, 541; fabrics 110, M3:D2–5, D6–7; miscellaneous M3:F5; tempering with chalk/flint 110, 113; wall 110, 111, 113–15, 121, 130, 483, M3:E1–8; see also hearths, ovens

deer 525–6, 547; antler 525–6; red 12, 498, 525; roe 12, 498, 525

discs, chalk marl 419, 419, M12:B6–8; chalk perforated 422–5, 424, M12:D1–14; iron 346, 367, 370, M9:E2–3; pottery 401

disease 450, 464; dental caries 473; dental pathology 473; head injuries 471; leprosy not proven 467–8, 469; osteoarthritis 465–7, 466; osteomata 469; osteomyelitis 468; osteoporosis 468–9; pathology 465–73; spina bifida 469; spondylolysis 469; torn muscles 469–71; see also bone, human, burials

ditches 1, 15, 16, 18, 19, 21, 22, 23–4, 25, 28, 38–9, 43; boundary 544; filling 18, 19, 21, 22, 28, 30; linear system 556; recutting 28, 39, 43, 44, 46

dog 12, 451, 453, 454, 461, 463, 498, 522–5, 543, 544; age 523–4; burial 534, 536, 540, 541–2, 543; butchery 524; gnaw marks 524, 525; measurements M16:A3 (key), 17:D13 (measurements taken), 17:D14–E2 (data); in pits 522–3; pre-hillfort 12, 543; size 524–5; skull 538, 542; special burial 541, 452, 523, 525, 537

door frames/posts 54, 58, 62, 63, 65, 68, 69, 71, 72, 74, 76, 77, 79, 80; sills 58, 62, 68, 69, 81

duck 530

earthworks 1–4, 5, 15–22, 15; inner 1, 15–18, 17, 19, 20, 21, 47, 549; linear 4, 555; middle 1, 21–2, 37, 39, 549, 555; outer 1, 16, 22, 23, 549, 555; pottery from ditch of inner M1:E7; pottery from middle and outer M1:E8

elm 45, 481, 482

entrances 1, 5, 15; blocked 1, 15, 21, 22, 23–4, 24; development sequences 23, 24, 25, 30–6, 43, 43–5, 549; destruction by fire 29, 33, 36, 42, 44, 45, 173, 549, 550, 563; eastern 1, 4, 6, 12, 21–2, 25–42, 26, 27, 28, 30, 30–6; eastern courtyard pottery M1:E11, 14; east gates 26, 27, 29, 30–6, 37, 173, M1:E3; eastern postholes and palisade slots M1:C1–D1, D2–3; eastern postholes and pottery M1:F1, F7–10; hornworks 1, 12, 21, 22, 23, 24, 25, 26, 28–9, 30, 37–41, 42, 43, 44; outer E gate 41–2, 44; pottery from hornworks M1:E2, E8–10, F2–3, F6; south-eastern 22; south-western 22, 23–5, 23, 24, 25; walkway over E gate 34, 35, 36, 43, 44; wheeled traffic 36

enclosures 544; stock 4, 21, 44, 137, 189, 549, 550, 555

features 52, and see buildings, houses,pits, postholes, post–built structures

fences 58, 482; see also gullies

ferrules, iron 346, 353, 354, M9:C5

fields 475, 488, 555

Figsbury, Wilts 245, 258, 550, 552

files, iron 346, 353, 354, 435, M9:C6

finds, baked clay 398–407, M9:E9–F14; beads 396–8; briquetage 426–30; bone 371–95; bronze 335–46, M9:A9–B4, B5–8; chalk 419–25; coins 332–5; Kimmeridge shale 396; iron 346–71, M9:B9–E8, E9–F14; stone 407–18, 425–6

fish 498, 531, 547

flint 63, 70, 74, 76, 110, 115, 127, 244, 450, 549; building 18, 19, 26, 27, 28–9, 30, 36, 62, 66, 171; burnt 41, 63, 69, 70, 115, 146, 148, 153, 453; cobbles 36, 44; implements 11–12; Neolithic and Early Bronze Age M1:A6–10

food 249–50, 495, 508, 518, 522, 530, 531, 546–7; see also agricultural practices, cereals, etc

fowl, domestic 529, 555

forgery 332, 334

fox 498, 508, 526

frog 12, 526

furnace, crucible see under crucibles

gang chain 371

geese 529

glass see beads

Glastonbury, Somerset 113, 115, 246, 259, 349, 351, 354, 357, 361, 375, 377, 380, 382, 385, 387, 389, 392, 398, 401, 406, 407, 439

goat 498, 509, 544; burial 536, 537, 543; special deposit 509

gouges, bone 371, 382–7, 383–4, 386, 438, M10:B12–C5; iron, socketed 346, 351, 352, M9:C4

graffiti, on chalk blocks 424, 425

grain 136–7; carbonized 452, 483, 489, 490, 493; rcd 190–3; storage see pits, post–built structures; type exported 494; yield 137, 555, 558, 560

gullies 41, 51, 58, 69–70, 71, 74, 78, 79, 86, 96, 97, 109, 146, 148, 149, 157, 162, 166, 168, 169, 185, 187; complexes 55, 82, 99, 122, 123–7; complex 1 122, 123–4; complex 2 123, 124; complex 3 82, 124–6, 184, 187; complex 4 82, 124, 126, 187; complex 5 125, 126–7; complex 6 126, 127; defining enclosures 162, 166, 169; drainage 89, 96, 98, 99, 123, 157, 166, 169, 189; linear boundary 85, 123, 187, 189; wall- 60–2, 63, 81

Gussage All Saints, Dorset 93, 118, 121, 345, 357, 380, 398, 401, 407, 415, 418, 439, 454, 460–1, 463, 514, 521, 525, 530, 554, 556, 559, 562

Hallstatt C 12, 149, 335–49, 549

Hampshire 5, 429; Basin 1, 552; County Council 4, 6; Downland 550

handles, antler 344, 351, 352, 371, 392, 393, M10:D2–3; wood 354

hare 526

harness, horse, bronze 341, 342, 345, 559

hawthorn 481, 482

hazel 96, 114, 481, 481–2

hearths 60, 110, 115, 148, 153, 438; daub 115, M3:E8–9; distribution M3:F6; inside structures 60, 62, 65, 73, 76, 153, 166; plans M3:G10–11

Heathrow, Middx 86–7, 187

Hengistbury Head, Dorset 232, 233, 248, 259, 563

hillforts 137, 398, 550, 551, 552, 554, 555, 558, 560

hilt-guard, iron 346, 362, 366, M9:D2

hoards, analyses of LBA 430–1, M13:A3–4, 9–10; bronze, Hallstatt C, LBA 12, 149, 335–40, 549, M9:A6–8; iron, currency bars 357

Hod Hill, Dorset 349, 354, 357, 361, 425, 550

hollow–way 41, 42, 44, 49, 128

homesteads (Little Woodbury type) 552, 553, 554, 561

hooks, iron 368, 370, M9:D14

horse 498, 518–22, 543, 544, 555, 556; age 520; bone for tools 522, 531–3; burial 534, 540, 541–2; butchery 521, 522; measurements M16:A3(key), M17:C12(measurements taken), M17:C13–D12(data); pits 518–19, 522; size 520–1; skull 450, 452, 519–20, 538, 542; special deposits 450, 452, 522, 537, 539; use of wild 521–2

horseshoes, iron 346, 356, 357, M9:C9; nails, iron 346, 356, 357, M9:C10, F2–3

houses 6, 179, 549, 559–60; Circular Structure 1 60–2, 61, 122, 153, 185; CS2 62, 63, 153, 185; CS3/4 62–5, 64, 121, 122, 153, 185; CS5 65–6, 65, 122, 157, 185, 419, 422; CS6 66–7, 66, 157, 185; CS7/8 67, 67–70, 122, 157, 185, 186, 345, 419; 438, 555; CS9 68, 70–1, 158, 176, 177, 443, 462; CS10/11 69, 71–2, 97, 121, 122, 166–7; CS12 70, 72, 166–7; CS13 71, 72–3, 166–7; CS14 72, 73–4, 76, 98, 122, 166–7; CS15 73, 76, 98, 121, 122,

166–7; CS16 74, 76–7, 166–7; CS17 75, 77–8, 98, 121, 162, 189; CS18 76, 78, 98, 166–7; CS19 77, 78–9, 166–7; CS20 79, 79–80, 121, 122, 166–7, 189, 366, 422, 559; CS21 80, 80, 99, 122, 170–1; CS22 80–1, 81, 171, 184, 559; CS23 81, 82, 197; comparative plans of plank-built 56; comparative plans of stake-built 57; excavated examples of ring-groove 56; excavated examples of stake-built 60; flooring 62, 63–5, 66, 67, 71; internal features 60; occupation layers/debris 62, 63, 68, 69, 70, 72, 77, 78, 79, 80, 81, 158, 166, 171; ring-groove 54–6, 60–2, 61, 62–5, 65, 153, 185; roofing 58; stake-built 51, 60, 62–5, 64, 67–8, 153, 157, 158; wattle and daub 51, 56–8, and see daub, wattle; wigwam-type 58–60, 72–3

Hunsbury, Northants 349, 351, 354, 357, 361, 380

hurdles 113, 439, 482

hut 19, 60

Iron Age 1, 6, 430; mortuary traditions 442

iron 8, 346–71, 556; analyses results 430–6, 556, M13:B1–12, C1–3; attachments on leather-backed body armour 366, M9:D3–4; bloom 370, 371, 437, M9:E8; miscellaneous 346, 368–9, 370–1, 426, M9:E5–6, E9–F14; sheet-fittings 346, 363–4, 366, 426, M9:D4–11; slag 437, 443, M13:D6–E6; tools see individual entries; working 437, and see metalworking

kittiwake 530

knife blades, bronze 339, 340; cuts 466, 472–3; iron 346, 349–52, 350, 435, M9:B14–C3

latch-lifter, iron 346, 356, 357, M9:C10

leather, leatherworking 345, 346, 354, 366, 387, 439

linch pin, bronzed iron 369, 371, M9:E8; iron 346, 362, 366, 559, M9:D3

looms 377–8, 406, 422; weights 443, 508, 556; see also weights, clay and stone

lynchets 22, 482

Maiden Castle, Dorset 115, 118, 256, 351, 361, 375, 377, 380, 382, 387, 392, 398, 401, 406, 425, 439, 552, 560

Malchair, J B 5

maple 481, 482

Meare, Somerset 113, 375, 377, 398, 439

Meon Hill, Hants 245, 253, 258, 259

metallurgical analyses 430–6, 556; bronzes, Iron Age 431–3, M13:A3–4, 5–6; iron 433–6, M13:B1–C7; LBA hoard 430–1, M13:A3–4; methods 433; sources of metal 436

metalworking 351, 354, 435–6, 436–7, 556; clay accessories 406–7

mouse 526–7

nails, bronze 186, M9:B2; iron 346, 368, 370, M9:E3–4

nave hoop, iron 369, 371, M9:E8

needles, bone 371, 380–2, 381, 443, M10:B5–12; function 382; iron 354, 355, M9:C8; netting 395, 439, M10:D3; wear patterns 382

Neolithic 11

Nether Wallop, Hants 5

oak 45, 96, 107, 426, 481, 482

ores 8, 556

ovens 41, 60, 65, 69, 70, 74, 110, 115–21, 166, 438, M3:E9–F1; bases 110, 115, M3:E9–F1; covers 120–1; daub 41, 115–21, 116, M3:E9–F1 (type 1), M3:F2–4 (type 2); decorated daub 120, 121; plans M3:G10–11; plates 110, 115–21, 117, 119, M3:E9–F4

paddle see shovel

palisade slots 32, 33, 34, 36, 148; east entrance M1:D2–3; pottery from east entrance M1:F10

phallus, carved chalk 424, 425, M12:E2

picks, iron socketed 346, 351–4, 353, M9:C5

pig 12, 498, 514–18, 543–4, 545, 555; age 515–17; burial 536, 540, 541, 542, 545;

butchery 517; manure 518; measurements M16:A3(key), M17:B8(measurements taken), M17:B9–C11(data); meat 517–18, 544; size 517; skull 538; special deposits 450, 452, 462, 463, 537

pins, bronze *338*, 339; iron, ringhead *369*, 370, M9:E7

pits 6, 7, 18, 19, 39–41, 47, 51, *53*, 128–46, *138–44*, 148, 149, 153, 158, 166, 168, 170, 171, 173, 174, 176, 179, 231, M4, M5; animal bone 497, 536, 539; basin-shaped M5:E12, F6; beehive 130–1, 132, 137, 145, 174, 176, 443, M4:B1–6, 8–10, 12–14, C2,4–5, 8–14, D2, 4–5, 8–10, 13, E1–2, 5–6, 11, 13–14, F1, 3–14, G1–6, 8, 10, 12, 14, M5:A2–7, 12, B1–4, 6–8, 10–11, 13, C2–3, 7, 9–14, D1, 5–6, 8–10, E1–3, 5–10, 13–14, F1, 3, 5, 8; Bronze Age 11, 37, 549, M1:A2; burial 158, 442–3, 447, 454, 456–7, 458–9, 461; charnel 442, 451–2, 562, 563; clay puddling 137, 438, 556, M4:G7, M5:A13, M8:E2–3; computing M4:A3–4; conical 128, 131, 137, 145, 556, M4:G7, M5:A13, M8:E2–3; constructing/digging 128–9; cylindrical 131, 132, 145, M4:B11, C1, 7, D3, 12, E8, F2, G11, M5:A9, B5, 14, C1, D7, 11–12, 14, F2; decay 137; dog bones 522–3; duration of use 135–6, *136;* filling 40, 41–2, 129, 137, 146; function 132–7, 555; grain storage 132, 136–7, 176, 443, 489, 490, 491, 493, 557, 560; horse bones 518–19; intercutting 128, 129, 239–42, M8:A8–11; lack of evidence for linings/covers 129–30; other excavated examples 137; plant seeds 489–90, 491; pottery assemblages 128, *175*, 174–84, 314–26, M8:E6–G8; rcd 128, 314, 316; ritual 12, 37, 41–2, 158, 162, 340, 543, 549, 550, M1:B1–3; rubbish 137, 145, 166, 174, 179, 189; snails *478, 499*, 479–80; standing timber 12,549; storage 19, *20*, 51, 132, 134–5, 153, 157, 162, 166, 177, 185, 442–3, 456, 457, 461, 462, 463, 549; sub-rectangular 131, 132, 145, 146, 174–6, 443, M4:B7, C6, D1, 6, 11, 14, E3, 9–10, 12, G9, 13, M5:A8, 10–11, 14, B9, C4–6, 8, D3–4, 13, E4, 11, F4, 7; toolmarks M4:C3, 8, 10–13, D1–2, 5, 7–9, 11, 13–14, E1, 6, 7, 11, 14, F1–11, G4, 11–14, M5:A2, 9–12, 14, B2, 6, 11, C7, 9–14, D1, 3–6, 8–10, 14, E1, 2, 6, 8, 9, 11, 13, 14, F1–5; tools used 129; unfinished M4:C3, D7, E4, 7, M5:B12; volume 131, 132; within structures 60, 62, 65, 70, 76, 77, 79, 84–5, 132, 134, 135

planks 54–5, 56, 60–2, 63, 71, 85, 114–15, 122–3, 153, M3:E7, 8

platters, wood 250

ploughshares, iron 346, 354–7, *356*, M9:C8–9

points (Class 4–7), bone 371, 387–9, *388*, M10:C9–12

'pond' 1, 127–8, *177*, 187

population 442–6, 457–61, 463, 546, 555; ages at death 443, 463–4; determination of sex 464–5; height 465; increase 562; size 560; skeletal adaptation 465; society and ranking 559, 560

porches 54, 58, 79

post-built structures 87–110, *88, 89, 90*, 171, 174, 179, 185, M2:A2; associated with human remains 457; construction 94–5; daub from 115, 121; discussion 92–5; function 94–5; granaries 95, 549; other excavated examples 93; plans, PS16–30 M2:C1–14; PS31–55 M2:D1–14; PS56–76 M2:E1–14; PS79–92 M2:F1–14; PS93–109 M2: G1–14; PS110–23 M3:A2–14; PS 124–40 M3:B1–14; PS141–3 M3:C1–3; pottery 100, 105, 107, 108, 110, 174, 179, M3:C4–6, M3:C7(cp); rcd 96; roofing 94; sheds 95; statistical tests M2:A3, 4; storehouses for grain containers 137; tabulated data M2:A5–14, B1–9; types 87–92; A (large 6-post) 91, 98, *99*, 100, 101, *103*, 104, *104, 106, 107*, 109, 162, 179; B (large 6-post) 91, 107–8, *107, 108*, 109, *109*, 110, 185; C (small 6-post) 89, 110, *110;* D (large 6-post) 91, 104, *105;* E (small 4-post) 87–9, 100, *103*, 105–7, *106, 107*, 174, 176, 177; F (small 4-post) 89, 100, *102, 108*, 109, 174, 176, 177; G (large 4-post) 89, 101, *103*,

104, 105, *106, 107;* H (large 4-post) 89, 96, *96*, 98, 99, *100, 102, 122*, 162, 171, 179; J (large 4-post) 89, 97–8, *97, 98*, 162; K (large 5-post) 91, *95*, 96, 157; L (2-post) 92, 98–9, *101*, 162

postholes 7, 12, 18, 19, *20*, 30–7, 41, 42, 47, 49–51, *59*, 62, 65, 67, 69, 70, 76, 77, 78–9, 80, 81, 84, 123–7, 146, 148, 153, 157, 158, 169, 170, 171, 173, 176, 231, 442, 482; antler fragments/sheep horn cores 506, 509, 525, 531; charred stump M1:C6; east entrance M1:C1–D1; posts 45, 193

pottery, All Cannings Cross style 233, 234, 254, 258, 259, M8:D2–3; analysis 231–58; archive 326, 331; Atrebatic 233, 234, 256–8; associated with burials 443, 450, 453; Beaker 11, 12, 549, M1:A3, 11–14; bowls(B) 232, 233, 234, 249, 253, 254, 281–93, *287–93, 294;* ceramic phases 45, 54, 86, 92, 100, 105, 107, 108, 110, 124, 126, 127, 128, 172–3, 173–4, *175*, 179, *180–4*, 189, 193–5, 233–4, 234–40, 140–4, 249–50, 251, 258–9, 314, 316, 323, 325, 326, 345, 346, 495, 501, 549, 550, 554, M3:C4–7, M8:D5–7; cp sequence and rcd 231, 233, 234, 242, 258–9, 314, 316, 325, M8:A5–7; classificatory system 231–3, *260*, 259–307 (App 1); computerization 231, 237, 242–4, 331, M8:A3–4; cordons 233, 242–4, 248, 255–6, 308–13 (App 3); decoration 233, 242–4, 248, 255–6, 308–13 (App 3); defences and earthworks (stratified) 45–6, M1:E1–10; dishes(D) 232, 250, 293, *295–6;* distribution in fort by cp 231, 250–1, *252*, M3:C8–12; Dressel 1A amphorae 189, 247–8, 258, 259, 326, 557, M8:E4; early prehistoric 11; fabrics 8, 231, 232, 244–8, 308, M8:C1–7, D13–E1; fabrics distributed in time 237, 239, M8:D8–12; fabric change quantified 235–7, *236;* fillers 232, 244–5, 246, 248, 256, 308, M8:D8–12; firing 248; food 249–50; form and types 231, 232, 242–*4, 249, 250, 251;* function 231, 249–50; furrowing 233; Gallo-Belgic 189; geometric motifs 233, 310–13, *311–13;* glauconitic sandy wares 245–6, *246*, 247, 259, M8:E1; haematite wares 169, 233, 234, 245, 248, *253–4, 255*, 259, 309, 314, 316, 557, 562, M8:E2; handles/lugs 307; imported 231, 246, 247–8; Iron Age 46, 84–5, 86, 123, 124, 126, 127, 128, 132, 149, 171, 187; jars (J) 232, 233, 249, 253, 259–81, *260, 262–80, 282–7*, 316; later prehistoric 12, 18, 37, 42; lids 249; local 231, 244–6, M8:C1–7; manufacture 438, 558; Meon Hill style 233, 234, 254; petrological examination 308, M8:D13–E3; pits *175, 180, 181, 182*, 231, 237–8, 239–40, 314–26, *315–25, 327–30*, M8:A8–11, E6–G6; post-structures M3:C4–7; potting clays 232, 244–8, *245;* quantity 231, 251; rcd of ceramic sequence 242; retrieval 231, M8:A2; Roman 4, 12, 46, 49, 550; St Catherine's Hill-Worthy Down style 233, 234, 248, 254–6, 258, 259; Saxon 12; saucepan pots(P) 22, 45, 86, 124, 126, 232, 233, 234, 249, 254–6, *257*, 293–307, *297–307*, 316, 323, 562, M8:D4, D8–E4; scientific analysis 232; seriation *183, 184*, 237–40, 242–4, M8:B1–11; scratched-cordoned 233, 234, 245, 248, 254, *255*, 256, 259, M8:D1; stratified 231, 233, 234–5, 314–26, M8:E6–G6; styles 233, 234, 253–8; subdivisions of cp 7 M8:B1–11; surface finish 232, 242–4, 308–9; technological change 231, 248–9; wheel-turning 233, 248; Yarnbury-Highfield style 233, 234, 248, 254–6, 258, 259, M8:D4

prunus 481

punches, iron 354, *355*

Quarley, Hants 5, 245, 258, 552

quarry pits/hollows 15, *17*, 18, 19, 21, 29, 39, 43, 44, 49, 51, 54, 60, 107, 108, 127–8, 146–73, 179, 184; occupation layers 146, 148, 149, 153, 157, 158, 166, 167, 169, 170, 171, 185, 335, 442; rcd 153, 172, 193; stratified deposits 123, 146–72, 173, 189, 193, 234, M6; stratified sequences 157, 167, 172

quernstones 412–18, 443, 556; illustrations M12:B4–5; rotary *413, 414, 415*, 415–18, *416*, M12:A13–14; rubbing 412–15, 418, M12:B3; saddle 412, *417*, M12:B1–2

rabbit warrens 5, *13, 14*, 14, 550

radiocarbon dating 7, 12, 45–6, 96, 146, 172–3, 179, 190–8, 233, 234, 242, 258, 314, 316, 325, 482, 549, 550, M7

ramparts 1, 6, 15–22, 27, 37, 89, 93, 97, 148, 149, 158, 167–8, 169, 179; box-structured 16, *17*, 19, 552; building 16–18, 19–21, 29, 37, 38–9, 549; counterscarp bank 1, 6, 12, 15, 16, *17*, 18–19, 21, 25, 37, 39; defensive sequence 43–5; extension 146, 148; height 15, 18, 21, 22; periods of construction 16, 18, 19, 22, 23, 29, *43*, 43–4, 168, 169, 170, 172, 235, 549–50; pottery 18, 45, M1:E2, 4–6, 7(ditch), F1, F4–5; profiles *15, 16*, 18; quarry hollows *see* separate entry; similar excavated examples 550–2; timber 16, 552

rapier, bronze *336*, 337, 430

razor, bronze *336*, 337

reels, clay perforated 398–401, *400*, M11:A6–7

religion, animal sacrifice 543; Celtic 442, 451, 461, 462, 463; *see also* rectangular buildings, 'temples'

rings, antler and bone 371, *393*, 395, M10:D3; bronze finger *342*, 343–5, M9:A10; bronze segmented *344*, 346; iron spiral *369*, 371, M9:E7; iron various 346, *365, 366*, M9:D11–12

rivets, bronze decorative 361; bronze dome-headed *344*, 346, M9:B4; iron 346, *368*, 370, M9:E4

roads *48*, 51, 54, 92, 94, 100, 101, 104, 105, 107, *127*, 128, 174, 176, 177, 179, 184, 185, 187, 189, 550; Roman 554

rodents 526–7

rods, bronze *344*, 346, M9:B2–3; iron for tools 346, 354, *355*, M9:C6–8

Royal Commission on Historical Monuments (England) 8

salmon 531

Salmonsbury, Bourton on the Water, Glos 361

salt making 426, 429, 430, 556, 558

saw blades, iron 346, 351, *352*, 361, 436, M9:C3

scabbard bindings, iron *342*, 346

settlement types, banjo enclosures 554, 562; defended enclosures, small 550, 561; enclosed homesteads 552, 554, 561; forts 552; 'paramount' centres 552, 555, 561; villas 554

shale, Kimmeridge, bracelets 396, *396*, 439, 557, M10:E1–2

sheep 5, 12, 371, 498, 501–9, 543–4, 545, 555, 556; age 502–4, 505, 506, 507; bred for meat 508; burial *535*, 536, 542, 545; butchery 506; disease 506, 507, 508, 546; horns 505–6; long bones (for tool working) 371, 382, 389–92, 506, 509, 531–3, M10:C12–D1; manuring 508–9; measurements M16:A1, 3 (key), 4–7 (measurements taken), M16:A8–G2 (data); mortality 507–8; size 504–5, 506, 507; Soay 507; special deposits 405, 451, 452, 509, 537, 542; stocking rates 544; type of wool 507, 508

shovel (or paddle), wooden, charred 370, *426*, 426, 482

sickle *see* tools, hook-shaped cutting

skulls, human 442, 452–3, 454, 461, 463; damage/injury 452–3, 462, *470*, 471; head-hunting 442, 453, 461, 462; worship 451, 453, 461

slingshots, clay 110, 398, *399*, M11:A2–3; chalk 425, M12:E2

slingstones 425–6, 448, 450, 451, 540, 562, M12:E5, 6–7, 8–F12, G1–8

snails, land 49, 189, 550; analysis 476; environmental sequence *480*, 480–1; layers *477;* pits *478, 479*, 479–80

society 559, 560; breakdown 546, 554, 562–3; Celtic 560–1; warfare 562

Somerset Levels Project 113

South Cadbury, Somerset 56, 60, 86–7